Beginning Power Apps

The Non-Developer's Guide to Building Business Applications

Second Edition

Tim Leung

Beginning Power Apps: The Non-Developer's Guide to Building Business Applications

Tim Leung
Reading, UK

ISBN-13 (pbk): 978-1-4842-6682-3   ISBN-13 (electronic): 978-1-4842-6683-0
https://doi.org/10.1007/978-1-4842-6683-0

Copyright © 2021 by Tim Leung

Managing Director, Apress Media LLC: Welmoed Spahr
Acquisitions Editor: Joan Murray
Development Editor: Laura Berendson
Coordinating Editor: Jill Balzano

Cover image designed by Freepik (www.freepik.com)

Distributed to the book trade worldwide by Springer Science+Business Media LLC, 1 New York Plaza, Suite 4600, New York, NY 10004. Phone 1-800-SPRINGER, fax (201) 348-4505, e-mail orders-ny@springer-sbm. com, or visit www.springeronline.com. Apress Media, LLC is a California LLC and the sole member (owner) is Springer Science + Business Media Finance Inc (SSBM Finance Inc). SSBM Finance Inc is a **Delaware** corporation.

For information on translations, please e-mail booktranslations@springernature.com; for reprint, paperback, or audio rights, please e-mail bookpermissions@springernature.com.

Apress titles may be purchased in bulk for academic, corporate, or promotional use. eBook versions and licenses are also available for most titles. For more information, reference our Print and eBook Bulk Sales web page at http://www.apress.com/bulk-sales.

Any source code or other supplementary material referenced by the author in this book is available to readers on GitHub via the book's product page, located at www.apress.com/9781484266823. For more detailed information, please visit http://www.apress.com/source-code.

Printed on acid-free paper

I dedicate this book to you. I want you to achieve whatever goals you want to accomplish, and I trust that Power Apps and this book will help you on your path.

Table of Contents

About the Author

Tim Leung is a software developer with vast experience in designing and building large-scale commercial applications. He is an expert in the fields of rapid application development and the Power Platform. He has published several books on software development, including the first book on Power Apps.

Tim is a Microsoft certified developer and a chartered member of the British Computer Society and holds a degree in information technology.

About the Technical Reviewer

 **Lee Zuckett** has a double degree in astronomy and physics with a minor in mathematics from The Ohio State University. When the idea of heading off to graduate school faded, life opened a door he had not considered, and he started a career working for a small company in Columbus, OH, developing applications in FoxPro (which he still misses!). Lee shortly thereafter moved to the San Francisco Bay area in the mid-1990s, where he continued to work with a couple of small partners and then onto a "start-up" named Avanade for 8 years and Microsoft for another 8 years. Next, he carried out a stint for about a year and a half at Power Objects to run their Call Center - Center of Excellence, before returning to Microsoft.

Over these many years, Lee went from FoxPro to VB 5/6, .NET, web development, architectural design, and a bit of program management, all the while picking up a focus on the call center/customer care area. Somewhere along the line, he was pulled into Dynamics CRM/Dynamics 365 and ultimately to the Power Platform.

Personally, Lee is a big fan of "outdoor" activities, everything from biking (roads and mountains) to skiing, hiking, backpacking, rock climbing, and kayaking. His 13-year-old daughter, Hannah, has been skiing, rock climbing, and biking for quite a while; more recently, his wife and he got her into kayaking and still looking toward a family backpacking trip.

Acknowledgments

I'd like to thank everyone who has worked on this book. I appreciate your hard work and efforts. Notably, I'd like to thank Joan Murray and Jill Balzano at Apress for making this book possible. I'm also very grateful to Lee Zuckett, who has done a great job in reviewing my content and providing me with advice and feedback.

Last but not least, I want to thank Samit Saini and the hundreds of readers who have inspired and supported me. There are too many people to mention, but you know who you are. It is your success that has motivated me to write this second edition.

Foreword

Samit Saini (right) with Microsoft CEO Satya Nadella (left).

Before I became an app builder, I worked as a security officer for 13 years at London Heathrow Airport, which is the United Kingdom's largest and busiest airport, as well as being the busiest airport in Europe.

After I discovered Power Apps, the first edition of this book played an active role in transforming my life. Today, I've built a significantly better life for myself. I now have the flexibility to work from home, which means I can see my kids more. Following the recent Covid pandemic, were it not for Power Apps, I would probably not have a job.

Before this book, I had never read any book on computing. This is the first book that I have ever read cover to cover, and I know the contents very well. Because this book means so much to me, I actually own two copies. I use one copy to scribble my notes, and I've left my second copy intact. Even today, I still often refer to this book because I can find formula references more easily, compared to searching online. Although there are plenty of online blogs and content, the thing I like about this book is that it provides a structured way of learning. This is a format that works very well for me.

Before Power Apps, each mobile app that we commissioned would cost around £60k. If we wanted to make subsequent changes, it would cost even more. With Power Apps, we can now build apps in a much more cost-effective and flexible manner. Not only has it transformed the way we work at Heathrow, it has also transformed the lives and careers of many of my colleagues.

I am very grateful to the Microsoft Power Apps team and the team at Microsoft for building an application that enables someone like me, with no IT background, to build an app within minutes and to share it with my colleagues. Since building my first app, my growth mindset has improved, and I now have a renewed sense of purpose.

There's no limit to what you can create with new technology. I created a new career.

Samit Saini
(Twitter, SamitSaini01; LinkedIn, Samit Saini)

Introduction

My journey with the Power Platform began in 2015. I was an early adopter of Project Siena, the product that would eventually become Power Apps.

From the very beginning, I saw great potential in Power Apps. Through my work as a software developer, I knew firsthand how difficult it was to build mobile apps that could connect to internal systems and databases. Power Apps offered a straightforward way to achieve this task.

Although Power Apps was aimed at non-developers, I found the initial learning curve steep. Although I had clear ideas of what I wanted to achieve, the intricacies of how to build these features were difficult.

I soon became proficient and started to explore the idea of writing a book. I wanted to share my experiences and to make it easier for users to get started with Power Apps.

At the time, I struggled to secure a publishing deal. It was too much of a risk for publishers to release a book on an unknown product that was at the time still in beta. But fortunately, my editors at Apress believed in my idea, and I was able to write the first edition of this book – which coincided very closely with the initial release of Power Apps.

Today, Power Apps is completely different from the product that existed when I began. It has expanded significantly and offers features that I never would have imagined. This includes the ability to build apps on top of Microsoft Dynamics 365 through model-driven apps and the ability to build publicly accessible, data-driven websites through portal apps. The inclusion of artificial intelligence (AI) is another significant and valuable feature. I applaud all the staff at Microsoft who have contributed toward building this amazing product.

I firmly believe that this momentum will continue. While this book is being released, Microsoft Teams has become hugely popular, and Power Apps is the platform that enables us to build apps that can run in Teams. If you're a beginner, now is a great time to learn Power Apps and the Power Platform. I believe it's a smart way to invest your time, and I'm sure that a positive outcome will occur – if not now, then in the years to come.

I've seen the positive changes that Power Apps can bring to businesses and people. For me, it's given me the satisfaction of being able to help others, to make a positive contribution, and to see businesses and people succeed. Wherever you happen to be on your Power Apps journey, I wish you the best of luck.

The Structure of This Book

This book requires no prerequisite knowledge, and through the chapters, we'll progressively walk through the features in Power Apps. To support this structure, this book is organized into the following logical parts:

- **Power Apps Fundamentals** – In the first four chapters, we'll walk through how to build and publish an app. We'll cover the high-level concepts, learn about subscription plans, and build an app that can retrieve and update data from an Excel data source. We'll learn how to use data entry controls, how to build screens, and how to configure the navigation linkages between screens.

- **Working with Data** – This part focuses on data. We'll find out how to set up data sources, including SharePoint and SQL Server, and how to connect to internal data sources with the on-premises gateway. We'll discover how to search, retrieve, and access data through formulas.

- **Developing Canvas Apps** – In this part, we'll explore the topic of screen layout, including how to build responsive apps that can run on multiple form factor devices. We'll also take a deeper look at data entry controls, including lookup, gallery, and date entry controls.

- **Developing Model-Driven and Portal Apps** – This part introduces Dataverse, the cloud-based database. This provides a foundation that enables us to learn how to build model-driven apps, including how to carry out advanced customizations with JavaScript. We'll then find out how to build a portal app, and we'll cover topics that include security, data access, and code customization.

- **Enhancing Apps** – In this part, we'll examine various ways in which we can enhance our apps. This includes how to take pictures, scan barcodes, store files and images, use location services, chart data, and take advantage of AI capabilities.

- **Reusability** – This part focuses on how to build reusable components. This enables us to work more efficiently by sharing code and features between apps.

- **Offline and Integration** – In this part, we'll discover how to add offline capabilities to our apps. We'll then cover integration scenarios, including how to connect to custom data sources and how to expand the capabilities of our apps with Power Automate.

- **Administration** – the final part of this book covers techniques to transfer data and apps. This section also examines ways to secure apps, including how to apply role level security, how to audit activity, and how to administer settings with PowerShell.

To create a scenario that we can relate to, we'll base the examples in this book on a fictitious property/real estate business. This provides a context that enables us to explore all the available features in Power Apps. The appendix describes the data structures that we'll refer to throughout the book.

Versioning

Microsoft applies updates to Power Apps on a regular basis. These updates include new features and bug fixes. Over time, object names and menu item locations change. As a result, the item locations in the screenshots that appear in this book may no longer be accurate. Please don't be too alarmed by this! The core concepts and principles in this book are likely to remain the same, despite any additions and cosmetic changes that take place.

Errata

The publishing team and I have taken great care to verify the contents of this book. If we discover any mistakes post-publication, we'll publish the details on the product page of this book. You can visit this page through the following link: `www.apress.com/9781484230022`.

Finally

I hope that you find this book useful. I'm confident that you'll build some great apps and solutions with Power Apps. Let's now begin!

PART I

Power Apps Fundamentals

CHAPTER 1

Introducing Power Apps

If you're completely new to Power Apps, you've probably heard that Power Apps is a tool for building mobile apps, as well as apps that can run against Microsoft systems such as SharePoint and Dynamics. Additionally, you've understood that Power Apps offers a "low code/no code" platform that enables you to build applications very quickly. But beyond these basic concepts, you might not fully appreciate the full capabilities of Power Apps or understand how a Power Apps application looks or feels exactly.

In this chapter, we'll examine the things that we can do with Power Apps by looking at the sample apps that Microsoft provides. The purpose of this is to clarify whether Power Apps can solve a specific business problem that you might have. The basic topics that we'll explore in this first chapter will include

- What we can accomplish with Power Apps

- Examples of applications

- How to get started with building apps

What Is Power Apps?

Power Apps is a subscription-based service for building applications. It offers a "low code" development environment, therefore making it suitable for users with no programming experience. We don't need to be trained software developers to use Power Apps. Microsoft uses the phrase "citizen developer" to describe the target user of the product. This could be a manager, office worker, or someone with a primary job role outside of IT.

A typical app connects to data and includes screens to display and edit data. Power Apps is a business tool for building apps to facilitate business processes. It is not a tool for building consumer-grade applications, for example, games to sell via app stores or mobile apps that require low-level, native access to hardware devices. For these purposes, there are other tools and platforms that are more suitable.

© Tim Leung 2021
T. Leung, *Beginning Power Apps*, https://doi.org/10.1007/978-1-4842-6683-0_1

The History of Power Apps

What is the history of Power Apps? Power Apps evolved from a Microsoft project called Siena – a project that began during the Windows 8 era. Siena provided a "low code" platform for building new style "metro" apps that connected to data.

Microsoft officially launched Power Apps toward the end of 2016. The highlight of this release was the ability to build apps that could run not only on PCs but also on mobile devices that include Apple and Android phones and tablets.

It provided a visual designer very similar to the one from Microsoft Excel. The designer contains a formula bar just like Excel, and many of the functions that are available in Power Apps are identical to those in Excel. This familiar interface made the product attractive to users with Microsoft Office skills. Another highlight was the ability to access a wide range of data sources, including SharePoint, Salesforce, Dynamics 365, and hundreds more. It also provided the ability to access internal, on-premise company SQL Server and SharePoint data stores. This was a valuable feature because building traditional mobile apps that can access internal company resources is a costly and difficult task.

During this time, Microsoft also released a cloud-based database called the Common Data Service (CDS). In 2020, Microsoft renamed the CDS to Dataverse; and at the same time, it introduced a cut-down version called "Dataverse for Teams." "Dataverse for Teams" is designed to provide data storage for custom apps that run inside Microsoft Teams.

The benefit of Dataverse is that it integrates smoothly with Power Apps and other products in the Microsoft Power Platform. Dataverse is perfect for users with limited experience of using relational databases. It provides a web-based interface to manage the data that we want to store. It provides many prebuilt table definitions and saves us from having to design commonly used data structures. For example, to store user details, we can simply add the "User" table to our application. The "User" table includes the data that we typically want to store for a user, such as name, address, and email address.

Since the initial release of Power Apps in 2016, there have been several significant developments to the product. An early enhancement was tighter integration with Microsoft SharePoint. Power Apps soon became the tool that enables customization of data entry forms in SharePoint lists.

In 2018, Power Apps introduced a new and completely different method of building apps. A new application type was born – the model-driven app. The apps we built previously are now referred to as canvas apps.

The key thing that differentiates model-driven and canvas apps is that model-driven apps are tightly associated with Dataverse tables and align more closely with the Dynamics 365 platform. To build a model-driven app, we first define the structure of the records and fields that we want to store by using the Dataverse designer. We can additionally define relationships between different record types – for example, one customer can have many orders.

Based on the definition of our data structure, Power Apps creates the user interface with very little or no additional input from us. It's very similar to the way that SharePoint works. With SharePoint, we can create a SharePoint list that includes definitions of the fields that we want to store, including complex types, such as choice and lookup fields. Once we define the list, SharePoint provides users with a list view that displays list items and enables users to add or edit the items in the list. When we define a list, we don't need to perform any extra work to create the UI for data entry. A model-driven app uses this same design methodology. But it also provides the ability to add processes, workflow, and business rules into our apps. For this reason, I've heard users describe model-driven app as a "SharePoint list on steroids," which I think provides a simplistic and fair description of what a model-driven app is.

With model-driven apps, the design experience is very different from that of developing canvas apps. There isn't a designer where we can add labels, drop-downs, shapes, and buttons or fine-tune the appearance of screens. There are pros and cons to this design approach. An advantage is that it can simplify the app building experience for users who are unfamiliar with more traditional software development platforms. For example, the concept of dragging a textbox control onto a design surface and using a properties window to define attributes may seem alien for completely new users. The disadvantage, however, is that we have significantly less control over the appearance and layout of our apps.

The model-driven app designer provides a surface where we can add prebuilt components, such as sitemaps, dashboards, and lists of data, into an app. It might feel as though we're building an app with blocks of Lego, hence the name "model-driven" app.

An important limitation is that because model-driven apps are based on Dataverse tables, we cannot connect model-driven apps to other data sources, such as SQL Server or Excel. Another consequence is that it isn't possible to build model-driven apps without data. With a canvas app, we could build a calculator app, a piano app that plays musical notes, or an app that displays animations. This is not possible with a model-driven app, which must be based on data.

In 2019, Power Apps added another significant new feature – the ability to build public-facing websites using the low code techniques that characterize Power Apps. These types of apps are called portal apps, and they enable us to build websites in a graphical way, without needing to understand complex web languages such as HTML or JavaScript.

With portal apps, a powerful feature is that we can retrieve, edit, and update data in a Dataverse database. Traditionally, connecting a website with a database involves a reasonable amount of programming expertise. The ability to carry out this task without code makes it much more accessible for non-developers. The portal app builder is highly visual and looks like the typical type of tool that we would use to build a blog or website.

The introduction of portal apps was well received by app builders because it offers easy access to users outside of our organization. Model-driven and canvas apps are largely restricted to users from inside our organization. With portal apps, we can now offer unauthenticated access to all Internet users, or we can implement authenticated access using single sign-on providers like Google or Facebook.

Another innovation that Power Apps introduced in 2019 was the AI (artificial intelligence) builder. With AI Builder, we can apply "low code" methods to bring AI capabilities into our apps. For example, we can apply predictive analysis to identify customers that are likely to default on payments or to predict changes in order quantities over the next month. At present, AI Builder works only with Dataverse data sources.

For reference, the technologies behind model-driven and portal apps derive from the Microsoft Dynamics CRM and Microsoft Dynamics 365 portal products, respectively.

What Are the Key Benefits of Power Apps?

The key benefit of Power Apps is that it enables quick and rapid development of apps by non-IT professionals. This encourages the wider adoption of apps throughout an organization, which can in turn lead to cost and efficiency savings.

As an example, a Microsoft promotional video features a user from a manufacturing company. Within their organization, mobile apps were once developed only for senior managers. The high cost of development made this the case. Following the adoption of Power Apps, employees throughout their organization began using mobile apps, down to factory workers and forklift truck drivers. This streamlining of processes enabled more timely delivery of information, more accurate data entry, and a reduction in physical paperwork.

The traditional method of app design includes many difficult parts. This includes security, authentication, data loss prevention, and deployment of apps. Power Apps takes care of all of this for us, so even for experienced developers, it offers a safer, easier, and quicker way of building apps.

By using Power Apps, we can more easily integrate with other products in the Microsoft Power Platform. This can help us build some very sophisticated solutions in a low code way. With the help of Power BI, we can incorporate good-looking charts and data analysis into our apps – perfect for managers. We can use Microsoft Automate to build workflow and processes into our apps. For instance, we can build a process so that when a new order arrives, we can create work tasks for employees and send a confirmation email.

What Data Sources Can We Use?

Although model-driven and portal apps work only with Dataverse data sources, canvas apps offer the ability to connect to a wide choice of data sources. Popular data sources include Excel, SharePoint, and SQL Server.

Power Apps uses a component called a connector to connect to a data source. The list of available connectors runs into hundreds and includes connectors for Dynamics 365, Salesforce, email services, Twitter, Facebook, and many more. We can connect to web services by using custom connectors, and we can also connect to on-premise SQL Server and SharePoint servers inside internal company networks by installing a program called the "on-premises data gateway."

Sample Apps

What applications can we build with Power Apps, and what tasks can those applications carry out? To help us better understand the capabilities of Power Apps, we'll now examine some of the sample apps that Microsoft provides. We'll cover all three app types in this section – canvas, model-driven, and portal apps.

Canvas Apps

Canvas apps are the most flexible and customizable of all app types. We can design canvas apps in a pixel-perfect way, almost like painting on a canvas, hence the name canvas app. The sample apps include the Asset Checkout, Budget Tracker, Cost Estimator, and Inventory Management apps.

Asset Checkout App

The Asset Checkout app enables users to check out items. However, it's not the ecommerce tool that the "checkout" part of the name suggests. It's more like a system that enables users to borrow hardware items from a library. That said, the app demonstrates some useful features. The most noteworthy is the integration of product images into the application (Figure 1-1). The first screen contains UI features such as search, a horizontal scroll control, and a tab control. The product image strip on the home screen shows the most recently checked out items. Therefore, logic exists in the application to perform this type of query.

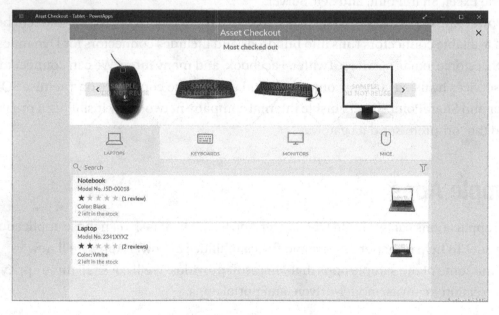

Figure 1-1. *Asset Checkout app*

Budget Tracker

The Budget Tracker app highlights the mathematical tasks that we can carry out in a Power Apps application. The home screen shows calculations that are conditionally formatted with red and green fonts. It also features a pie chart that illustrates a breakdown of expenses (Figure 1-2). With this app, users can add and delete expense records. Therefore, we can learn how to program data tasks such as adding or deleting records through this app.

A highlight of the Budget Tracker app is the ability for users to capture pictures of receipts and to assign those receipts to an expense claim. This feature demonstrates how Power Apps can integrate natively with cameras that are built into mobile devices.

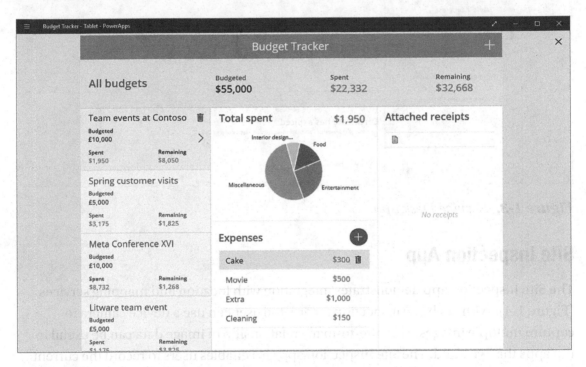

Figure 1-2. *Budget Tracker app*

Service Desk App

The Service Desk app is a nice example of a data entry application (Figure 1-3). The purpose of this app is to manage the support tickets that arise through a help desk department. I like this application because it demonstrates the data structures that developers typically expect to see in database applications. For example, the application allows users to assign a priority rating and an area (or department) to each support ticket, therefore illustrating the concept of one-to-many data structures.

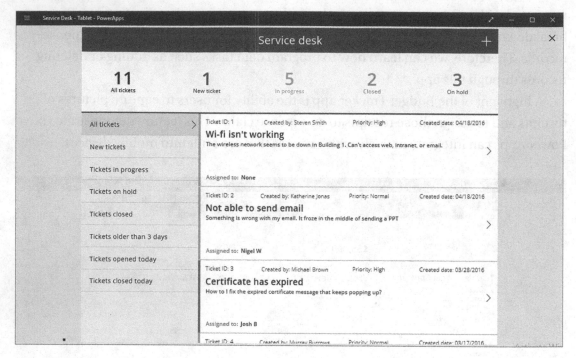

Figure 1-3. *Service Desk app*

Site Inspection App

The Site Inspection app demonstrates integration with location and mapping services (Figure 1-4). With each site inspection record, the user can use a device camera to capture multiple images. This one-to-many relationship of image data can be useful in the apps that we build. The Site Inspection app also enables users to record the current location using the GPS on the mobile device. For each record, the app can also display a map that shows the location.

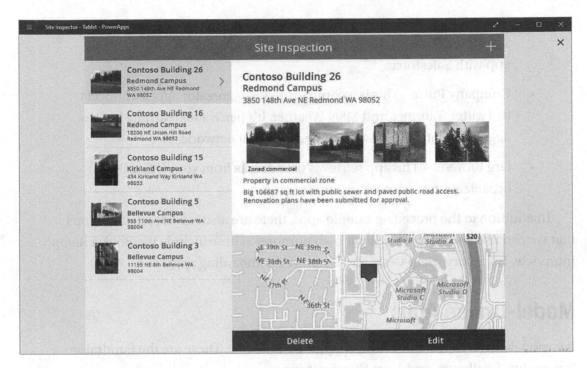

Figure 1-4. *Site Inspection app*

Other Sample Apps

The remaining sample applications are characterized by data features with a similar theme, namely, the ability to select a record from a list and to view and edit the selected record. Other notable apps include

- Power Apps Training app – This app contains 20+ exercises and teaches us how to carry out basic tasks in Power Apps. It's perfect for beginners.

- Product Showcase app – This is a well-presented app that looks great and demonstrates how to display videos in apps.

- PDF Reader app – This app allows users to view PDF documents from within the app.

- Suggestion app – This app implements some basic role maintenance. You can add users to an administrator role, and those users can carry out additional tasks in the application.

- Case Management app – A feature of this app is that it stores data in Salesforce. This app is useful if you want to learn how to integrate an app with Salesforce.

- Company Pulse – This is a company news aggregator app. It connects to Twitter, Yammer, and MSN Weather. It's perfect for learning how to aggregate data and how to connect to social networks.

- Org Browser – This app retrieves user details from your Office 365 organization.

In addition to the preceding sample apps, there are also several practical apps that we can use and adapt to suit our own purposes. These include the Book a Room, Interview, Inventory, Help Desk, and Employee Onboarding apps.

Model-Driven Apps

For model-driven apps, three sample apps are available. These are the Fundraiser, Innovation Challenge, and Asset Checkout apps:

- Fundraiser app – This app records charitable donations. Employees can start fundraisers, set goals, and track the donations received.

- Innovation Challenge – This app allows an employee to submit workplace improvement ideas. Other employees can vote and review the submitted ideas.

- Asset Checkout – This is a model-driven version of the canvas app.

Figure 1-5 shows a screenshot of the Innovation Challenge app. This image illustrates the typical look of a model-driven app, with a navigation pane down the left-hand side and blocks of components in the central section. The components on display include lists of data and colorful charts.

Figure 1-5. *Innovation Challenge app*

If we drill into one of the challenge records, we see the screen that's shown in Figure 1-6. This screen typifies how we can use model-driven apps to manage workflows and processes. In this screen, we can follow the lifecycle of a challenge from inception through to the ideas and selection review process and finally onto the selection and award process.

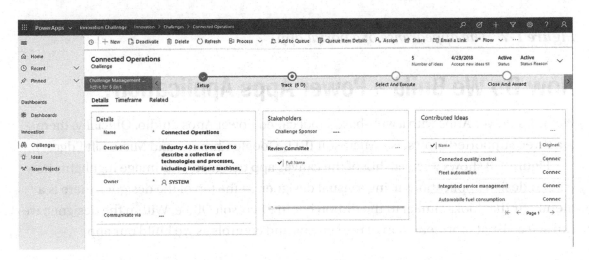

Figure 1-6. *Model-driven apps can help model workflow and processes*

Portal Apps

When we create a new portal app, Power Apps adds a set of sample pages to help us get started. This includes a login page and navigation controls. A portal app can serve the same purpose as any other website. We can use it for promotional purposes or to share company or team information. Of course, the real benefit of a portal app is that we can easily connect to company data in a Dataverse database. Figure 1-7 illustrates the standard home page of a portal app, which we can modify to suit our needs.

Figure 1-7. *The appearance of a portal app*

How Do We Build a Power Apps Application?

We build Power Apps with a web-based tool called Power Apps Studio. Officially, there are three supported browsers – Microsoft IE11, Google Chrome, and Microsoft Edge.

Figure 1-8 shows a screenshot of the canvas app designer. This image highlights how we can design applications using a visual designer. At the top of the designer, there is a menu bar that looks similar to the ribbon bar in Microsoft Office. Within the designer, we can see a visual representation of the screens and controls as we build our app.

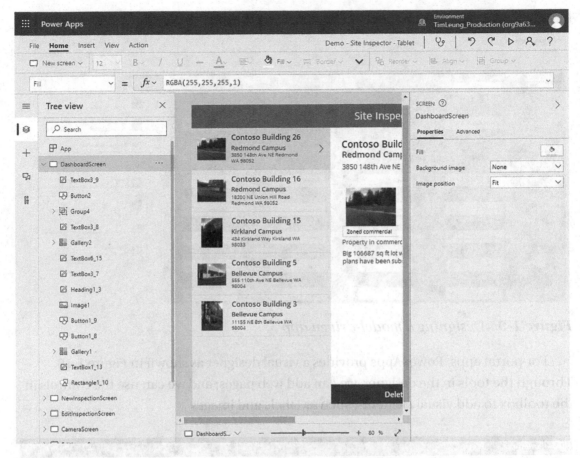

Figure 1-8. *Designing a canvas app in Power Apps Studio*

Figure 1-9 shows the design view of the Innovation Challenge app in the model-driven app designer. This screenshot highlights the component-based nature of the designer and how it is less visual, compared to the WYSIWYG (what you see is what you get) view of the canvas app designer. The designer provides a central design area to which we can add components from the right-hand side of the designer.

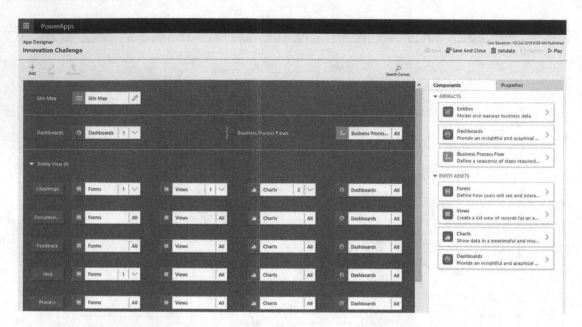

Figure 1-9. *Designing a model-driven app*

For portal apps, Power Apps provides a visual designer as shown in Figure 1-10. Through the tools in the designer, we can add web pages; and we can use the controls in the toolbox to add visual elements, such as labels and images.

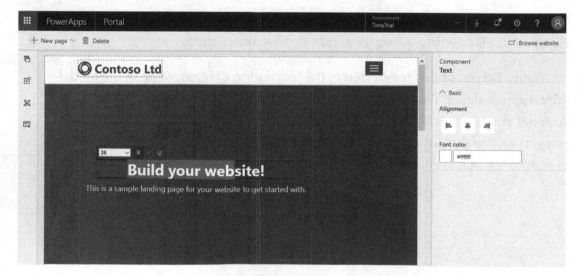

Figure 1-10. *Designing a portal app*

How Do Users Run Power Apps Applications?

Model-driven and portal apps are web based and therefore run through a web browser only. Canvas apps can also run through a web browser, but unlike model-driven and portal apps, they can also run on mobile devices through a Player app. An end user would start the Player app on their device, and through that, they can open the apps that have been shared with them. For desktop PC users running Windows 8 and above, there is a Windows Player app that is available through the Microsoft Store.

Users can download the Player app from the app store of the device. The system requirements at the time of writing are

- Android – Version 5.0 (Lollipop)

- Apple – iOS 9.3

- Windows – Windows 8.1

How Do We Write Code?

For canvas apps, Power Apps uses formulas to control logic and functionality, just like Excel. This makes it easy for Microsoft Office users to transition to Power Apps. However, traditional programmers can find it a struggle to adjust to this way of working. To illustrate, Figure 1-11 shows a typical formula.

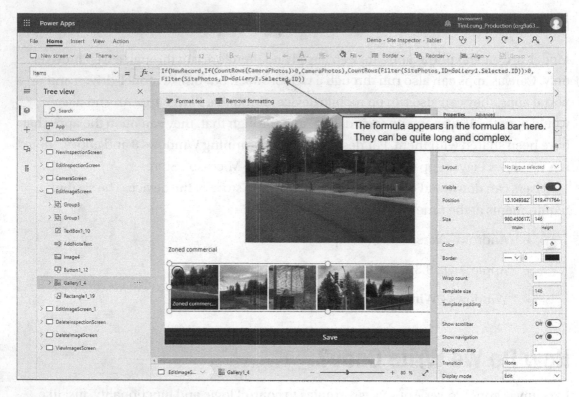

Figure 1-11. *Writing formulas*

The formula appears in the formula bar at the top of the screen, just like Excel. The purpose of the formula in the screenshot is to display a set of images. As you can see, it can take some skill to build the formula to carry out a task in Power Apps. But with the help of this book, these types of complicated formulas will soon become very simple.

With model-driven apps, there is not the option to write code with formulas. Instead, we control most of the functionality by configuring the properties of the components that we add to an app. By doing this, we can carry out tasks such as data validation. There is also the option to apply further customizations by writing JavaScript code. Note that canvas apps are not customizable with JavaScript.

Summary

Power Apps is a cloud-based platform for building business apps. Its key feature is simplicity. Using web-based graphical designers, we can build apps with minimal code. Therefore, non-IT professionals can use Power Apps with ease. Another feature is that

Power Apps provides strong support for data connectivity. Most often, apps will retrieve, create, or update data from data sources. To cater for different scenarios, there are three types of app that we can build – canvas, model-driven, and portal apps.

The traditional and most popular type of app is the canvas app. Canvas apps can connect to a magnitude of data sources, including Excel, SharePoint, SQL Server, and hundreds more. They can run on Android and iOS devices though a Power Apps Player app. Canvas apps can work offline and can access hardware such as cameras and GPS/ location services. With canvas apps, we can design apps using a WYSIWYG visual designer. Of all three app types, canvas apps offer the greatest level of control over the appearance and functionality of an app. We can program canvas apps using formulas that are very similar to the formulas in Microsoft Excel.

Model-driven apps are built around data, relationships, and processes that are defined in a Dataverse data source. Building blocks of components make a model-driven app. The model-driven app designer contains a toolbox where we can add components to an app. Due to this method of design, model-driven apps are less customizable, compared to canvas apps.

We can use a portal app to build a public-facing website. Portal apps can read and write data from Dataverse data sources. Unlike the other app types, we can configure a portal app for external access by users outside of our organization.

Power Apps is a subscription-based service, and in the next chapter, we'll cover the ways that we can license and obtain access to Power Apps.

CHAPTER 2

Subscribing to Power Apps

Now that we've covered the features and benefits of Power Apps, we'll walk through the important step of signing up to Power Apps. By the end of this chapter, we'll be ready to start building apps.

The sign-up process can be very confusing because there is a myriad of subscription options with different usage rights and price points. This chapter clarifies the subscription options and helps us choose the most cost-effective way to adopt Power Apps in any given organization. The key topics that we'll cover in this chapter include

- The methods we can use to license Power Apps, including an indication of the likely costs

- How data connections are categorized into standard and premium connectors

- An overview of the products in the Microsoft ecosystem, including Microsoft 365, Office 365, and Dynamics 365

How to Get Power Apps

To determine the best way to obtain Power Apps, the first step is to identify the data sources that we want to access. The answer to this question governs the plan that we choose. There are four ways to access Power Apps, which are

- Through a subscription to a Power Apps plan

- Through an Office 365 or Microsoft 365 subscription

- Through a Dynamics 365 subscription

- Through the free Community Plan

© Tim Leung 2021
T. Leung, *Beginning Power Apps*, https://doi.org/10.1007/978-1-4842-6683-0_2

The most powerful option is to subscribe to a Power Apps plan. This provides access to all available data sources, including the on-premises gateway and custom connectors (these enable us to connect to bespoke web services). To build portal apps or to use the AI Builder functionality, we must subscribe to a Power Apps plan.

Users with Microsoft 365, Office 365, or Dynamics 365 subscriptions can access Power Apps through a "seeded" license. This type of license offers more limited access to data and excludes access to data sources such as on-premise, SQL Server, or Dataverse data sources. The apps we build with this type of license typically feature SharePoint or Dynamics 365 as a data source.

The free "Community Plan" provides the perfect way for us to learn and to gain familiarity with Power Apps. The only limitation with this plan is we can't build apps for live production use, nor can we share apps with other users.

When we deploy an app for live use, it isn't necessary for all users to have identical plans. For example, if we build an app that uses SharePoint as a data source, we could license ten users through Office 365 subscriptions and a further five through subscriptions to Power Apps plans.

Which Plan Do I Need to Access a Data Source?

Because access to data sources plays a key role in our choice of subscription, let's look more closely at how licensing rules apply to data connections. A data connector is the component that provides access to a data source, and these are grouped into two types – standard and premium connectors. Table 2-1 summarizes the differences between these types of connector.

Table 2-1. *Differences between standard and premium connectors*

	Standard Connector	Premium Connector
Description	Standard connectors connect Power Apps with most services that Microsoft provides. For services that are available for free or based on an open protocol, a standard connector will often be available.	Premium connectors connect Power Apps with third-party and Microsoft services that require a monthly or annual charge.
Example connectors	SharePoint, OneDrive for Business, Dynamics 365, Facebook, Dropbox, Google Drive, Twitter, Gmail, Outlook, GitHub.	Dataverse, SQL Server, MySQL, Salesforce, Zendesk, SAP, on-premises gateway, custom connectors.

A subscription to a Power Apps plan provides full access to all premium and standard connectors. Seeded Microsoft 365, Office 365, and Dynamics 365 licenses provide access to standard connectors only.

Standard connectors cover most services that are offered by Microsoft and connections to social networks, such as Facebook and Twitter. Typical Microsoft services that we can access with standard connectors include SharePoint and Dynamics 365.

We can also access cloud storage providers such as OneDrive, Dropbox, and Google Drive with standard connectors. The reason why these storage providers are important is because they provide space for us to host Excel spreadsheet files. Excel files offer a simple way for Power Apps to store user data.

Any connector that is not a standard connector falls into the premium connector category. Most often, any cloud service that charges a fee requires a premium connector. Examples include SQL Server, Common Data Service, Zendesk, MySQL, and Salesforce.

Note   Access to all relational databases (including SQL Server, MySQL, and PostgreSQL) and the on-premises gateway requires a premium connector. Therefore, we can only access these data sources by subscribing to a Power Apps plan.

Subscribing to Power Apps

The best way to get started is to sign up to the Community Plan. The Community Plan is free for personal use and provides a playground for testing and learning. The registration process creates a Power Apps account that we can use with the Community Plan. Using the same user account, we can upgrade to a paid-for plan once we start using Power Apps more seriously.

When we sign up to the Community Plan, Power Apps provisions a developer environment to host our Community Plan. Environments are containers for apps and resources, and they play a key role in security and access control. When we save an app to an environment, we can control who can access our app based upon access control permissions that are defined at an environment level. Furthermore, data connections, flows, and Dataverse databases are items that are specific to a single environment. These items cannot be shared between environments.

The developer environment provides a private space where we can store our apps and set up a Dataverse database. Because we cannot share apps with other users under the Community Plan, this means that other users cannot access what we do in our environment. This therefore creates a safe place for us to experiment without fear of breaking other people's work.

To sign up to Power Apps, visit the Community Plan page (`https://PowerApps.microsoft.com/en-us/communityplan/`) and follow the link "Get started free" (Figure 2-1). Note that if we sign up using one of the sign-up links that exist in other areas of the website, the registration process signs us up to a Power Apps trial. This license expires after 60 days, so it's best to subscribe to the Community Plan, which doesn't expire.

Figure 2-1. *Signing up to the Community Plan*

One limitation with the registration process is that it accepts only corporate email addresses or addresses that end with a custom domain name. It rejects personal email addresses that are hosted by ISPs or companies like Gmail or Outlook/Hotmail.

If the domain of the email address is associated with an organization that is covered by an Office 365 or Dynamics 365 license, we may see the error that's shown in Figure 2-2. In this case, our company administrator would need to grant our user account with access to Power Apps. The administrator would do this through the Users section of the "Office 365 admin center."

Figure 2-2. Example of a registration error

Another common reason for the sign-up process to fail is if we're logged onto other Microsoft services within the same browser session. The simplest way to overcome this problem is to sign up using the "in-private" or incognito mode of our web browser.

In the case of other registration failures, the best source of help is the official help page that's devoted to troubleshooting registration failures (https://docs.microsoft. com/en-us/PowerApps/maker/signup-for-PowerApps#troubleshoot). This page translates the simple, friendly error messages that we see into technical explanations that we can act on and resolve.

Tip   Even if we access Power Apps through a Microsoft 365, Office 365, Dynamics 365, or standalone plan, we can still subscribe to the Community Plan. It's worth doing this because it provides us with a private environment where we can learn and experiment.

Obtaining a Suitable Email Address

If we want to sign up to Power Apps but don't have a suitable email address, there isn't any simple work-around to this problem. We must have a custom email address to subscribe to Power Apps.

A search on the Web reveals hundreds of companies that can sell a custom domain name. The going rate seems to be around $2 for an initial 12-month registration. Once we purchase a domain name, we can link it with a free email hosting provider such as Zoho.com to provide a low-cost method to trial Power Apps.

If we work for a large bureaucratic organization, it might be easier for us to trial Power Apps using this technique, rather than to go through any complicated internal channels.

For a short-term trial, we can sign up to a "Microsoft 365 Business" trial, which will give us time-limited access to Power Apps.

What Are the Licensing Options?

With a Power Apps plan, it's necessary to pay for a subscription if we want to build apps for live use or to share apps with other users.

We can license on a per-app or per-user basis (Table 2-2). The cost of a per-app subscription is $10/user/month. This type of subscription enables us to license up to two apps. Each end user requires a subscription, so to give an illustrative cost, let's imagine that we work on a project with one app builder and four end users. The annual license cost would be $10 x 5 users x 12 months = $600.

The per-user plan enables a user to build and run unlimited apps. The cost of this is $40/user/month. Therefore, this plan makes economic sense if we want to build four or more apps.

Table 2-2. *Power Apps plans*

	Per-App Plan	Per-User Plan
Cost	$10/user/month.	$40/user/month.
Description	Allows an individual to run up to two apps.	Allows an individual to run unlimited apps.
Portal apps	One portal.	Multiple portals.
Extra Dataverse capacity per user	Database capacity, 50 MB.File capacity, 400 MB.	Database capacity, 250 MB. File capacity, 2 GB.

Dataverse offers two types of data storage – database storage and file storage. Dataverse stores record data in database storage and file attachments (e.g., images, videos, Office and PDF documents) in file storage. Each organization receives a base, default allocation of database and file attachment storage. For example, when we first purchase a per-user plan, we receive an allocation of 10 GB database storage and 20 GB file storage. Each additional license that we purchase increases our storage allocation.

An interesting question we might ask is, why can we license up to two apps with the "per-app" plan, when the "per-app" name suggests a single app? The two-app limit provides greater flexibility in certain use case scenarios. First, it enables us to license one canvas and one model-driven app. Alternatively, we can use this two-app limit to license an app in a development environment and to license the same app in a production environment (the two-app limit applies across all environments). Outside of these use cases, we can take advantage of this allowance to license two completely separate apps.

Note   The purpose of the prices in this chapter is to the highlight the pricing structure and model. The license conditions and prices will change in time, so please check the Power Apps website before making a purchasing decision.

Licensing Portal and AI Builder Apps

To build portal apps, we must first purchase a Power Apps plan. With the per-app plan, we can create a single portal app, whereas with a per-user plan, we can create multiple portals.

With portal apps, users from inside our organization will require a subscription to a Power Apps plan or a qualifying Dynamics 365 license to access a portal. For external users (such as customers or suppliers from outside our company), there will be an additional charge. This is based on login sessions for authenticated users or page impressions for unauthenticated users.

Accessing Power Apps via Microsoft/Office 365

A common way for many users to access Power Apps is through a Microsoft 365 or Office 365 subscription. This type of subscription can provide access to many services, such as Exchange email, Office apps, SharePoint, Yammer, Stream, and Teams. It can therefore represent great value for money. However, the wide range of available plans can be confusing; so in this section, we'll examine this in more detail.

What Is Office 365?

Most people are familiar with versions of Word, Excel, Outlook, PowerPoint, and Access that run on desktop Windows PCs. In the past, many users would have purchased perpetual licenses to use these products.

In the period leading up to 2010, Microsoft faced competition from web-based products such as Google Apps. To ensure a longer-term, more consistent revenue stream, it wanted to move away from a licensing model where users paid a one-time license fee and to move toward a cloud-based subscription model where they could charge a monthly or annual fee.

As a result of this, Office 365 was born in 2011. For small businesses, Office 365 provided a subscription service that offered email hosting through hosted Exchange. The package also provided web-based collaboration services such as SharePoint and Lync (a tool for communication and conferencing) and also provided access to Office Web Apps. These are online versions of Word, Excel, PowerPoint, and OneNote that run through a web browser. At the same time, Microsoft also offered an enterprise version that included desktop licenses.

As an extension of this model, Microsoft introduced versions of Office 365 for consumers in 2013. To cater for this demographic, Microsoft sold prepaid subscriptions at shops and retail outlets, including online retailers such as Amazon.

In 2020, Microsoft rebranded the consumer and selected business editions of Office 365 to Microsoft 365. The versions of Office 365 for enterprise customers retain the same "Office 365" name.

Microsoft 365: Consumer vs. Business Plans

Although the business and consumer editions of Microsoft 365 share the same name, they are fundamentally very different. The key differences are as follows.

The consumer editions are designed for individual, home, or family use and include plans that are branded "Microsoft 365 Family" and "Microsoft 365 Personal." The business editions are designed for business or commercial use and include plans that are branded "Microsoft 365 Business Basic," "Microsoft 365 Business Standard," and "Microsoft 365 Business Premium."

The business editions of Microsoft 365 offer email hosting through Microsoft Exchange. They also provide file storage though "OneDrive for Business" and voice/video communications and instant messaging through Microsoft Teams.

In contrast to this, the consumer plans provide email hosting through Outlook.com, the name for what used to be Hotmail. The consumer plans offer file storage through OneDrive and voice/video communications through Skype.

Looking at online file storage, it's important to realize that the consumer version of OneDrive is not the same as OneDrive for Business. The consumer version of OneDrive provides cloud storage, and users typically use this service to store music and videos. On the other hand, "OneDrive for Business" is a storage system that is internally based on hosted Microsoft SharePoint and offers more administration features. Therefore, "OneDrive for Business" and the consumer edition of OneDrive are fundamentally very different.

The important thing to take away from this is that often, Microsoft services are branded with similar names, but refer to completely different services. Therefore, we cannot purchase a consumer Microsoft 365 subscription from Amazon and expect to receive the same online services as someone with a business Microsoft 365 subscription. The most important thing, however, is that none of the consumer editions of Microsoft 365 include Power Apps. Only business editions of Microsoft 365 include Power Apps.

Understanding Work Accounts and Personal Accounts

Another very important difference between the business and consumer editions of Microsoft 365 is that both services use completely separate authentication databases.

The business editions of Microsoft 365 are based on accounts that are traditionally known as Office 365 accounts. Users log on with credentials that consist of an email address and password. In general, the administrator for an organization sets up accounts for users.

The consumer editions of Microsoft 365 are based on Microsoft accounts. Like most authentication methods, a Microsoft account consists of an email address and password. These are the same credentials that we could use to log on to Windows 8 or 10 computers or the credentials we would use to log into the Hotmail or Outlook.com services.

Because each email address can be associated with two separate authentication databases at Microsoft, this can cause much confusion. For instance, if we log into a Microsoft website with a Microsoft account (e.g., Outlook.com) and then navigate to certain areas on the Power Apps portal, we might see the error message that's shown in Figure 2-3.

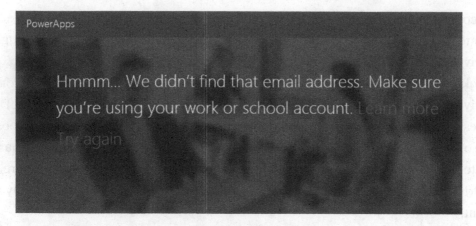

Figure 2-3. *Authentication error message*

The way to overcome this type of error is to log out from our Microsoft account or to completely close and reopen our web browser.

Figure 2-4 shows the screen that appears when we log in with an email address that is associated with both an Office 365 and a Microsoft account.

Figure 2-4. *Power Apps login screen*

To log in to Power Apps, we must choose the "Work or school account" option. One thing to highlight here is the use of the phrase "Work or school account." This is the type of account that traditional app builders call an "Office 365 account." Another name that refers to the same type of account is an "Azure Active Directory" account, often abbreviated to "AAD." We used to encounter this term mostly on technical forums and help sites, but today, the term "AAD" is much more widely understood and provides a more precise label. The main thing to understand here is that "Office 365 account," "Work or school account," and "AAD account" all refer to the same thing.

Once we begin developing apps, it's useful to relay this information to your end users, because many users may not be familiar with the differences between the Microsoft account types. Even for experienced users, it can be difficult to keep track of what account you need to log into a specific Microsoft service. For example, I use my "personal account" to log into my Azure and VisualStudio.com accounts, and this choice of account isn't perhaps the most obvious for a work-based service.

When we use Power Apps, it's useful to have this clarity about the different account types to help avoid confusion. To give a relevant example, it's not uncommon to log into Power Apps with an Office 365 account and to store application data in a personal OneDrive account.

Which Microsoft/Office 365 Plans Include Power Apps?

A common way to obtain access to Power Apps is through a Microsoft 365 Business or an Office 365 subscription. Microsoft offers business and enterprise plans. The main difference between these two types of plan is that enterprise plans support organizations with greater than 300 users and offer additional security features. Also, there are specific enterprise editions of Office 365 that target academic, government, and nonprofit organizations. These editions can include Power Apps and are priced more competitively to appeal to these target markets.

Microsoft 365 Business Plans: Features and Prices

While reviewing Microsoft 365 plans, it's useful to appreciate that most customers subscribe to Microsoft 365 for two main reasons – access to hosted Microsoft Exchange email and access to desktop versions of Office, including Word, Excel, and Outlook. The pricing structure therefore focuses around these two features.

The three available plans in the "Microsoft 365 Business" family are "Microsoft 365 Business Basic," "Microsoft 365 Business Standard," and "Microsoft 365 Business Premium" (Figure 2-5).

All three plans include Power Apps. The basic plan provides access to email and SharePoint but does not provide access to desktop versions of the Office apps. The standard plan offers everything in the basic plan and also includes access to desktop Office apps.

The premium plan offers everything in the standard plan and includes additional security features. This includes a Windows 10 Pro license (to support the additional security features), Azure Information Protection (AIP), and Microsoft Intune.

AIP enables organizations to classify, encrypt, and protect documents. We can use AIP to track who has opened a document and to prevent users from copying, printing, or forwarding documents and emails. If a user attempts to screenshot an AIP-protected document, Windows blacks out the protected area. It's also possible to revoke and destroy documents through AIP.

Microsoft Intune can restrict actions on devices such as copy and paste, save, and view, and administrators can use Intune to wipe mobile devices in the event of theft.

There is also a plan called "Microsoft 365 Apps." The main purpose of this plan is to offer access to desktop Office apps, but importantly, this plan does not provide access to Power Apps.

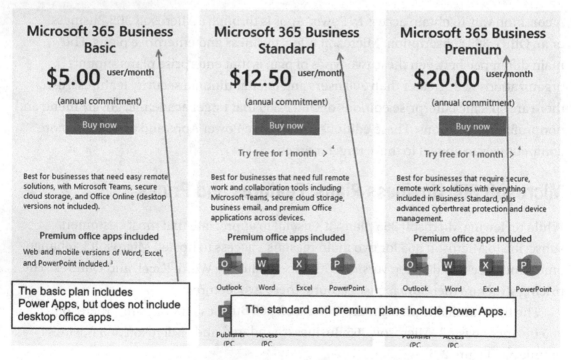

Figure 2-5. *Microsoft 365 Business plans*

Office 365 Enterprise Plans: Features and Prices

The names of the enterprise plans begin with an "E" followed by a number. Plans with a larger number include more features.

Figure 2-6 shows a screenshot of the available plans. The three Office 365 plans that include Power Apps are the E1, E3, and E5 plans.

The Office E1 plan is the most basic and does not include Office desktop apps. The Office E3 plan is popular because it provides access to email, Office desktop apps, and Power Apps. The Office E5 plan offers everything that the E3 plan offers and includes Office 365 Advanced Threat Protection (ATP), phone system integration with Microsoft Teams, and a Power BI Pro license for reporting.

ATP is a cloud-based malware and antivirus service. It can scan emails and detect phishing attempts. It can also scan the contents of email attachments and documents in Microsoft Teams, SharePoint, and OneDrive.

In addition to the Office 365 plans, there are corresponding Microsoft 365 plans that include the base Office 365 plan. For example, the Microsoft 365 E3 plan includes everything that Office 365 E3 offers and also provides the additional security features that are part of the "Microsoft 365" suite.

These features include Microsoft Intune and a Windows 10 Enterprise license. Other notable security features include Windows Hello (to support biometric face/fingerprint logins) and Windows Defender Application Control (previously called Device Guard), which is a system that controls which apps can run on a PC. Network security features include DirectAccess and Microsoft Advanced Threat Analytics. Threat Analytics is a system that monitors network traffic and detects patterns that characterize an attack.

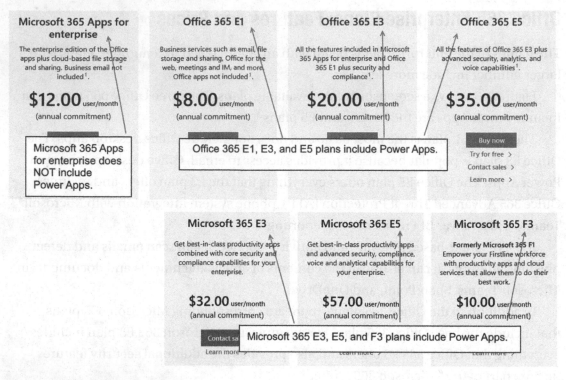

Figure 2-6. *Office 365 plans*

A notable plan is the "Microsoft 365 F3" plan. This plan is designed for first-line workers. These are users who often work away from a desk, use a shared PC, and don't need desktop versions of Office. The "Microsoft 365 F3" plan is the lowest-priced enterprise Microsoft 365 plan that provides access to Power Apps.

Does the Plan I Want to Buy Include Power Apps?

The inclusion of Power Apps doesn't usually feature prominently on the pages of the Microsoft Microsoft/Office 365 websites. Because plan details can change over time, the best way to find out if a particular edition of Microsoft/Office 365 includes Power Apps is to visit the pricing section on the official Power Apps website (`https://PowerApps.microsoft.com`). From here, we can find a licensing guide in PDF format that specifies the editions that include Power Apps. Figure 2-7 contains a screenshot from this document which highlights the plans that include Power Apps.

The PDF guide is the definitive place to check, because a web search often returns inaccurate, out-of-date results. The following link should always return the most up-to-date version:

```
https://go.microsoft.com/fwlink/?linkid=2085130
```

Qualifying Licenses	
Microsoft 365 Business Basic	Office 365 A5 for Students
Microsoft 365 Business Standard	Office 365 Education E3 for Faculty
Microsoft 365 Business Premium	Office 365 Education E3 for Students
Office 365 A1 for Faculty	Office 365 Education for Homeschool for Faculty
Office 365 A1 for Students	Office 365 Education for Homeschool for Students
Office 365 A1 Plus for Faculty	Office 365 E1
Office 365 A1 Plus for Students	Office 365 E2
Office 365 A3 for Faculty	Office 365 E3
Office 365 A3 for Students	Office 365 E3 Developer
Office 365 A3 for Student Use Benefit	Office 365 E3 without ProPlus
Office 365 A5 for Student Use Benefit	Office 365 E5
Office 365 A5	Office 365 F3
Office 365 A5 for Faculty	

Figure 2-7. Screenshot from the PDF guide (August 2020) – Microsoft/Office 365 plans that include Power Apps

Accessing Power Apps via Dynamics 365

Many larger organizations subscribe to Microsoft Dynamics 365 and can access Power Apps through a Dynamics 365 subscription. In this section, we'll look at the purpose of Dynamics 365 and the features that it offers.

What Is Dynamics 365?

Dynamics 365 is a cloud-based platform for Customer Relationship Management (CRM) and Enterprise Resource Planning (ERP). Competitors in this market include Salesforce and SAP, respectively. A selling feature of Dynamics 365 is that it provides a single platform to carry out these tasks and saves us from having to engage multiple different software vendors.

The purpose of a CRM system is to record interactions with people, such as customers, sales leads, clients, and suppliers. For example, the sales department in a company can use a CRM system to help convert prospective leads into sales.

Account managers can use the same CRM to provide customer care and to manage the relationship.

An ERP system manages the key functions of a business. This includes accounting, inventory, order management, human resources, and more. An ERP system centralizes this core data and improves business operations by allowing data to be shared between different parts of a company.

Dynamics 365 provides its functionality through a set of core apps, which are mobile friendly and can run through a web browser. Each app can run independently, as well as in connection with other apps in the Dynamics 356 suite.

Table 2-3 provides a high-level overview of the core apps with a description of how they might help us in our organization.

Table 2-3. *Dynamics 365 core apps*

App Name	Description
Dynamics 365 Finance	This app carries out finance tasks related to accounts payable, accounts receivable, budgeting, banking, asset management, and the general ledger.
Dynamics 365 Supply Chain Management	This app can record and manage processes that are related to product procurement, transportation, warehouse management, cost and inventory control, picking and packing, and delivery.
Dynamics 365 Sales	This app manages the sales pipeline process. It centralizes sales leads and details in a single place and makes these details visible to other departments in an organization. It can help identify profitable leads by scoring and qualifying opportunities. For account managers, it can collect and report data to help build relationships and to nurture opportunities.
Dynamics 365 Customer Service	This app records customer complaints and interactions and can help solve customer queries. It provides access to knowledgebase articles and can provide scripts for telephone operators.
Dynamics 365 Field Service	This app is designed for workers who work outside of the office, such as service engineers or traveling salespeople. It provides a means of communication between the field worker and office users or customers. Managers can use this app to schedule tasks or to generate work orders.

(continued)

Table 2-3. (*continued*)

App Name	Description
Dynamics 365 Project Service Automation	This app enables project managers to manage project tasks and timescales. It works well for consultancy or services that bill on a time and material basis. It can manage the quotation, time and expense recording, and billing processes. It can match employees to projects, based on role types, skill characteristics, and certifications. It can also produce financial and labor estimates for jobs based on variables such as profitability and feasibility and can provide reports that show how far through a project is.
Dynamics 365 Commerce	This app can build websites with shopping cart, checkout, and registration features. It can personalize product pages with customer rating and review features. It can build customer profiles and identify product recommendations based on previous purchases and other customer behaviors. It can also help build discount schemes, promotions, and loyalty programs.
Dynamics 365 Human Resources	This app can manage tasks that include the hiring and setting up of new employees, as well as other features such as administering organizational structures, competencies, salaries and benefits, and training courses and the monitoring of absences. It can assist employee development by providing a feedback channel, tracking performance, and supporting reward and incentivization schemes. Employees can access a portal to carry out administrative tasks such as leave requests and appraisals.
Dynamics 365 Marketing	This app can create, run, and manage events and marketing campaigns. It can create campaigns based on templates and customers' previous contact and activities. The campaign channels it can manage include email, SMS, and social media. For events and webinars, users can log into a portal to manage registrations. It can also monitor the effectiveness of campaigns and identify valuable customers based on lead scoring models. This can take into account factors such as email engagement, website visits, and event registrations.

Microsoft also offers a solution called Dynamics 365 Business Central. Business Central provides a lighter-weight and lower-cost alternative and is designed for small- to mid-size organizations. It covers a wide feature set and manages tasks that are related to finances, sales, supply chain, warehousing, customer service, and project management.

In addition to the core apps, there are a set of "insight" apps that provide reporting, analysis, data aggregation, and AI-driven predictions. These apps are called "Sales Insights," "Customer Insights," and "Customer Service Insights." These apps can identify the health of a customer relationship using red/amber/green indicators. It can also provide scores to indicate customers that are most likely to buy from us or to even identify fraud.

To help build rapport, an AI tool can scan correspondence from a given customer and identify conversational topics such as sports, holidays, and family commitments. In addition to offering communication advice, Insights can help identify cross-selling and upselling opportunities. For customer service departments, Insights can help identify actions with the biggest impact on resolving cases and improving customer satisfaction.

A great feature is that we can acquire additional apps that can run inside Dynamics 365 through an app store called AppSource. The store contains apps from Microsoft and other third-party companies, some of which are free and others paid-for. An example of an app is the Gamification app (as shown in Figure 2-8).

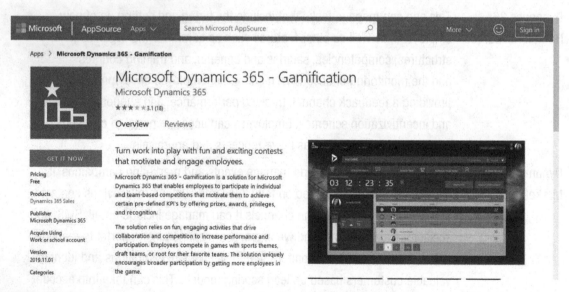

Figure 2-8. *App store*

To support the rich ecosystem of third-party apps that can work with data in Dynamics 365, there must be a common database. The common database that Dynamics 365 uses is Dataverse.

When we log onto the Dynamics 365 home page, we access all the core apps through a tile interface (Figure 2-9). We can also access any canvas or model-driven Power Apps application through this view. Model-driven apps work particularly well because they adhere to the common look and feel of Dynamics 365.

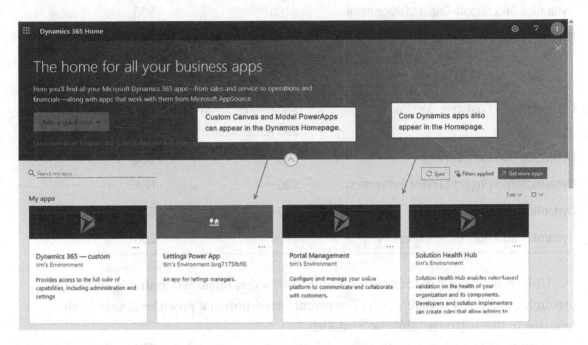

Figure 2-9. *Opening apps through the Dynamics 365 home page*

How Much Does It Cost?

Dynamics 365 pricing and licensing is a complex topic. There are many permutations of offerings that depend on whether a user can fully or partially access an app, minimum seat numbers may apply, and discount schemes might be available, based on volume or industry. Because licensing costs and conditions change frequently, the main purpose of this section is to provide ballpark figures so that we can see how Dynamics 365 prices compare with Power Apps and Microsoft 365 plans.

The high-level overview is that each user requires a separate license for each Dynamics 365 app. If a user requires access to more than one app, the "base and attach" licensing model applies. With this model, the base price of the most expensive app applies. Beyond this, there is a reduced "attach price" for each additional app. Table 2-4 provides an indication of the base and attach prices for each core app.

Table 2-4. *Dynamics 365 Pricing (per user/per month)*

App Name	Base Price	Attach Price
Dynamics 365 Finance	$180	$30
Dynamics 365 Supply Chain Management	$180	$30
Dynamics 365 Sales	$65 (Professional) $95 (Enterprise) $135 (Premium)	$20 (Premium) $20 (Enterprise) $135 (Premium)
Dynamics 365 Customer Service	$80 (Professional) $95 (Enterprise)	$20 (Premium) $20 (Enterprise)
Dynamics 365 Field Service	$95	$20
Dynamics 365 Project Service Automation	$95	N/A
Dynamics 365 Commerce	$180	$30
Dynamics 365 Human Resources	$120	$30

Unlike other apps in the main Dynamics 365 suite, Business Central is available through third-party resellers only. The premium edition that provides access to all features in the app costs $100/user/month.

With the Marketing app, the license applies at a company level. This reflects how the cost of marketing campaigns cannot be attributable to a single person, and the price of a standalone license stands at $1500/month.

A strategy that's worth mentioning is that because Dynamics licensing tends to be more expensive, it's always useful to consider the price of Power Apps plans. Take the example of a Dynamics 365 business that extends the Customer Service app with Power Apps to support a product launch. If the company wants to grant access to additional users, it can be cheaper to license these users through a Power Apps plan, because this type of plan also provides access to custom Dataverse tables and limited access to Dynamics 365 tables. With this strategy, the license cost can be $10/user/month, compared to the potential higher cost of $80/user/month for a standalone Dynamics license.

Logging On to Power Apps

Whichever way we acquire Power Apps (either through Dynamics 365, Microsoft/Office 365, or a Power Apps plan), once we have a suitable license, we can access the Power Apps Maker Portal, as shown in Figure 2-10. This portal provides the gateway to all the features that Power Apps offers.

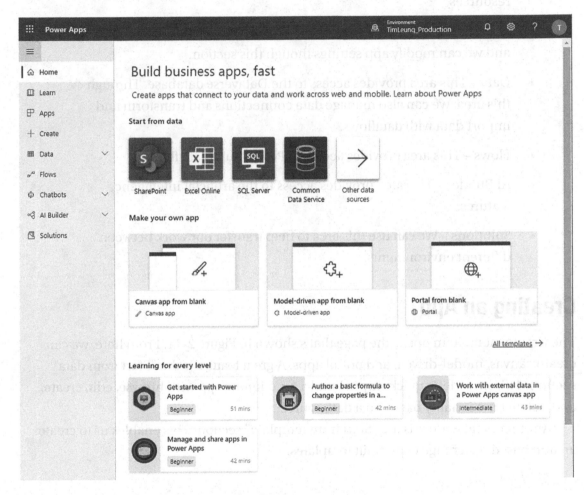

Figure 2-10. *The main Power Apps home page*

Here's a summary of the main areas that are available through the left-hand menu of the Maker Portal:

- Home – The home page provides shortcuts to the frequently used areas of the Maker Portal, including links to create and to open apps.

- Learn – This area provides help and links to guided learning resources.

- Apps – This area shows a list of apps we can edit, delete, and share; and we can modify app settings though this section.

- Data – This area provides access to the Dataverse database. Through this area, we can also manage data connections and transform and import data with dataflows.

- Flows – This area provides access to Power Automate flows.

- AI Builder – This area provides access to the artificial intelligence features.

- Solutions – We can use this area to help transfer our work between different environments.

Creating an App

The Create menu item opens the page that's shown in Figure 2-11. From here, we can create canvas, model-driven, and portal apps. A great feature is the "Start from data" section. This provides a quick way to build a functioning app with browse, edit, create, and delete functionality based on a data source.

Another great feature is the "Start from template" section. This enables us to create an app based on a range of prebuilt templates.

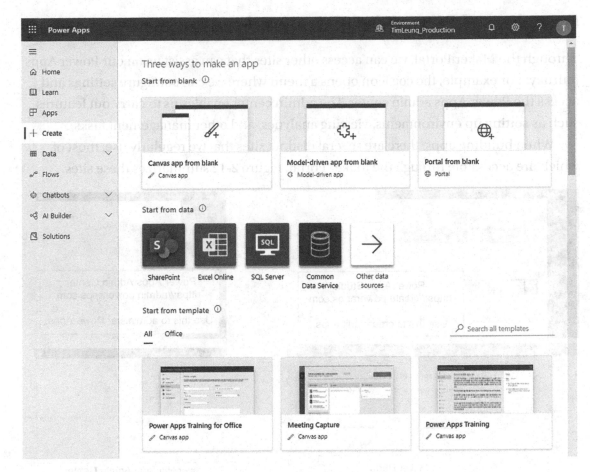

Figure 2-11. *Creating a new app*

Caution   The canvas apps that we build from a template through this area are based on static data sources. We cannot permanently save data through these apps. If instead we create an app from the "App templates" section of Power Apps Studio (by clicking the Apps menu item and choosing New ➤ Canvas app), we can base our app on an Excel file in a location that we specify.

Overview of Other Administrative Areas

Through the Maker Portal, we can access other sites that can assist us on our Power Apps journey. For example, the cog icon opens a menu where we can configure settings and access the Power Apps admin center. The admin center enables us to carry out features such as setting up environments, viewing analytics, and other management tasks.

When building apps, there are several distinct sites that we regularly use, most of which are accessible through the Maker Portal. Figure 2-12 summarizes these sites.

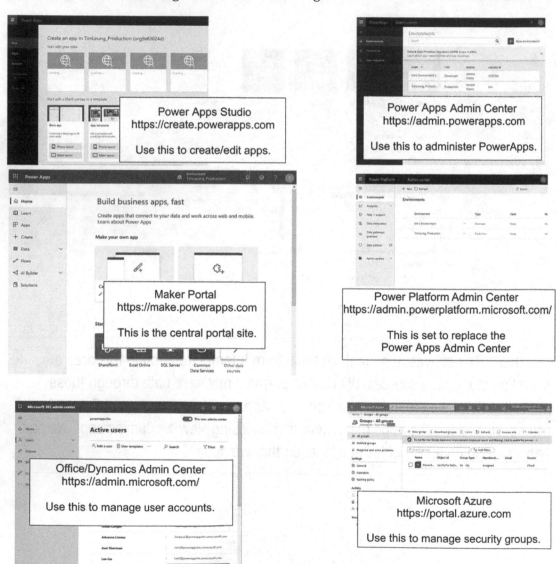

Figure 2-12. *The websites that we commonly use*

In some rare cases, often in corporate environments, the Power Apps websites may not load or work correctly. The cause of this is usually proxy or firewall settings that block connections to resources that are required by Power Apps. The online documentation contains a list of IP addresses and web addresses that must be open for Power Apps to work. Another cause is antivirus or security software, particularly those with SSL inspection functionality. This type of software can interfere with network connectivity and stop Power Apps from working.

Reviewing Our Entitlements

Through the cog menu item, we can view the plans that we are subscribed to. It may be the case that we've subscribed to the Community Plan, have a trial license, and also have access through a seeded Office 365 license. The Plan(s) section clarifies our plan entitlement, as shown in Figure 2-13.

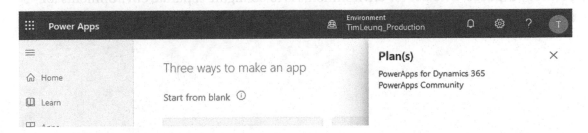

Figure 2-13. *Reviewing our entitlements*

Summary

In this chapter, we looked at how to subscribe to Power Apps. To use Power Apps, we can either subscribe to a Power Apps plan, or we can access Power Apps through a Microsoft 365/Office 365 or Dynamics 365 subscription. There is also the free Community Plan that we can use for trial or learning purposes.

To build apps that can access all data sources, including Dataverse, SQL Server, and other premium data sources, we must subscribe to a Power Apps plan. A Power Apps plan is also required if we want to build portal apps or to access AI Builder features. With this type of plan, we can license apps on a per-app or per-user basis. The lowest-cost option is to purchase a per-app license. The cost of this is $10/user/month.

A common way to access Power Apps is through a Microsoft 365/Office 365 or Dynamics 365 subscription. Typically, users with Microsoft 365/Office 365 licenses build apps that use SharePoint as a data source. The Power Apps "seeded" license that Microsoft 365/Office 365 and Dynamics 365 include provides a more limited choice of data sources.

To register for Power Apps, it's necessary to use a custom email address. The registration process rejects Gmail, Outlook/Hotmail, ISP, and government email addresses.

To log into Power Apps, we must choose the option to authenticate with a Microsoft "Work or school account." This type of account is also known as an "Office 365 account" or "an Azure Active Directory account." Once we log into the Maker Portal, we can create and edit apps and carry out tasks that are associated with Dataverse.

From the admin center section of the Power Apps portal, we can create and manage environments. Environments allow us to compartmentalize apps and users for access control purposes. One use for environments is to configure separate environments for apps that are in development and apps that are in live use.

CHAPTER 3

Creating Your First App

In this chapter, we'll walk through the steps to build a basic app that connects to data. If you've never seen a Power Apps application, this chapter provides a perfect introduction to the way that an app looks and behaves. It's simple to build this type of app because we can point Power Apps to a data source and ask it to generate an app. Because Power Apps carries out all the hard work, the challenge is to understand the app that Power Apps creates. This is important because this knowledge enables us to further enhance and develop these types of "auto-generated" apps. To demonstrate this process, we'll build an app that connects to an Excel spreadsheet. The topics that we'll cover in this chapter will include

- How to prepare an Excel spreadsheet for use in Power Apps. This step is important because Power Apps can connect only to spreadsheets that are set up in a certain way.

- How to use data forms and cards. These controls provide the ability to view and edit individual records. They are complex controls that are not easy to understand. In this chapter, we'll discover exactly how these controls work.

- How screen navigation works. We'll examine how to open an individual record when a user selects an item from a list of records and how to change the screen that is visible.

Preparing an Excel Data Source

Power Apps supports many data sources. This includes SharePoint, SQL Server, Salesforce, and many more. Of all the supported data sources, the easiest to understand is an Excel spreadsheet. Therefore, that's the data source that we'll use frequently throughout this book.

47

© Tim Leung 2021
T. Leung, *Beginning Power Apps*, https://doi.org/10.1007/978-1-4842-6683-0_3

In this chapter, we'll work step-by-step toward building a simple app. The purpose of this app is to store names and addresses. So to begin, the first step is to create the spreadsheet that's shown in Figure 3-1.

Figure 3-1. *Sample spreadsheet*

For Power Apps to recognize a spreadsheet, the first row must contain column headings, and the data must be defined as a table. To do this, select the data and click the Insert ➤ Table button from the menu in Excel.

The next step is to name our table by using the "Table Tools" menu in Excel. Figure 3-2 outlines the steps to rename our table to *User*.

If we choose not to name our table, it inherits the default name of "Table1." If we retain the default name of "Table1," it makes it difficult to identify our data from within the Power Apps designer.

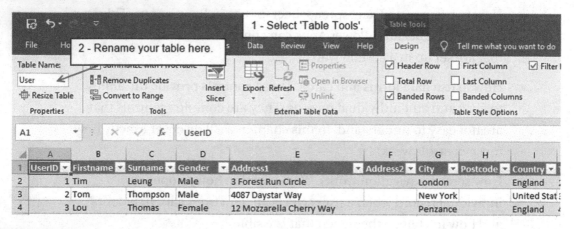

Figure 3-2. *Use the "Table Tools" ribbon option to name your table*

It's possible to add multiple tables to each Excel spreadsheet. If we decide to do this, it's a good idea to add each table to a separate worksheet. When Power Apps connects to an Excel spreadsheet, it stores working data in the cells that are adjacent to the table. By adding each table to a separate worksheet, we prevent the possibility for any data corruption to occur.

Once we complete our spreadsheet, the final step is to upload it to a cloud storage location. Two popular services that Power Apps supports are Microsoft OneDrive and Dropbox. For the purposes of this chapter, we'll upload our data to Microsoft OneDrive.

Note   Important! We must define our data as a table for Power Apps to recognize the data in our spreadsheet.

Creating an App

Once we upload our spreadsheet to the cloud, we can log onto the Maker Portal with our Microsoft work account and start to build our app. To create an app, we click the Apps menu item. The "New app" drop-down offers the choice to create a new canvas, model-driven, or portal app. We select the canvas option which opens Power Apps Studio, as shown in Figure 3-3. An effective way to build an app is to choose the "Start with your data" option. This option builds an app with screens to display, create, update, and delete records. Throughout the remainder of this book, I'll refer to these apps as "auto-generated apps."

Alternatively, we can create an app from a template. Microsoft provides some excellent templates, and I recommend that you explore these. We can learn a great deal by examining the apps that we can build from templates.

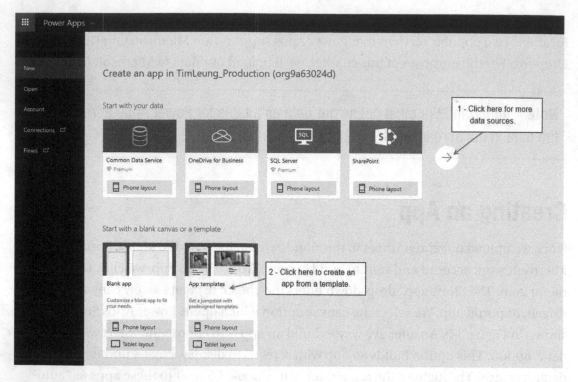

Figure 3-3. *Ways to create a new app*

Creating an Auto-generated App

To create our first app, we'll choose the option "Start with your data." The "Start with your data" section offers a choice of four data sources which include the Common Data Service, OneDrive for Business, SQL Server, and SharePoint. The right-pointing arrow icon opens the screen that's shown in Figure 3-4. From here, we can connect to a wider range of data sources.

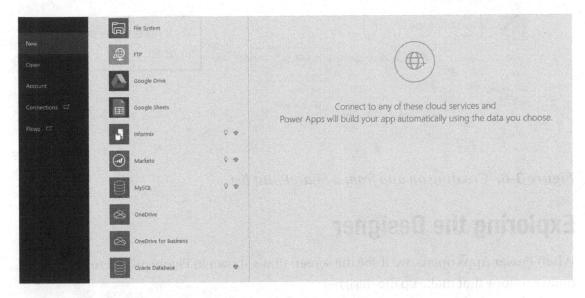

Figure 3-4. *Creating a new connection*

From the screen that's shown in Figure 3-4, add a connection to the cloud storage provider (in our example, OneDrive), and navigate to the spreadsheet location. This process requires us to sign into OneDrive (or the cloud storage provider of our choice) and to accept the Power Platform permissions.

Select the spreadsheet to show a list of available tables, as highlighted in Figure 3-5. Once we select a table from this list, Power Apps will create an app. Note that we can only select a single table from this list. It isn't possible to select more than one table as a basis for an auto-generated app.

Figure 3-5. *Choose a table from the spreadsheet*

Creating Apps from SharePoint

If we were to build an app from a SharePoint online data source, there's another method to quickly build auto-generated apps. From a SharePoint list, select the menu item to create a new app, as shown in Figure 3-6.

51

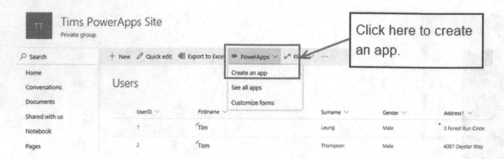

Figure 3-6. *Creating an app from a SharePoint list*

Exploring the Designer

When Power Apps opens, we'll see the screen that's shown in Figure 3-7. Here are the main sections that make up the designer:

- The top part of the designer contains a menu bar. The "File" menu enables us to perform tasks that include opening and saving apps. The remaining menu items carry out design tasks, such as inserting controls on screens.

- The tree view shows all the screens and objects in our app. We can edit a screen by selecting it from this part of the designer.

- The App node enables us to define the OnStart formula. This is code that runs when our app loads.

- The central section of the screen houses the screen designer. From here, we can edit and position the controls on a screen. Furthermore, we can also delete controls or add additional controls through the menu items in the Insert section of the ribbon menu bar.

- The right-hand side of the designer allows us to apply settings for the currently selected control.

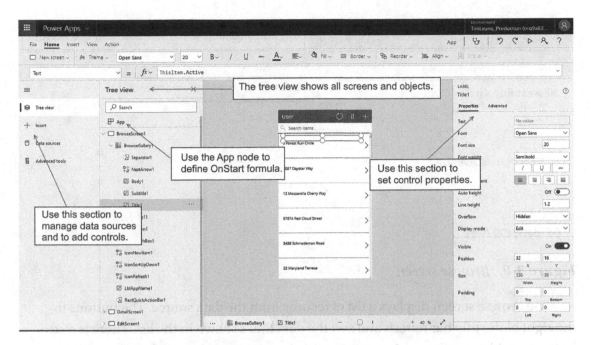

Figure 3-7. Power Apps designer

Running Your App

Without having to make any additional modifications to our project, we can run our app by selecting the first screen in the left pane (BrowseScreen1) and clicking the "play" button in the top-right part of the menu bar. We can also run our app by pressing the F5 button on our keyboard.

It's possible to run any screen in our project by selecting it through the left pane and clicking the play button. For example, to run the edit screen, we can simply select it and click the play button. There's no need to start the app from the initial start-up screen and to navigate to the screen that we want to see. To return to the designer from play mode, the simplest way is to press the Escape key on the keyboard.

Without playing our app, we can test our app in design view by holding down the Alt key to activate buttons and controls.

Examining the Screens at Runtime

Let's now examine the screens in our auto-generated app. The first screen that appears when we run the app is the browse screen, as shown in Figure 3-8. The name of this screen is BrowseScreen1.

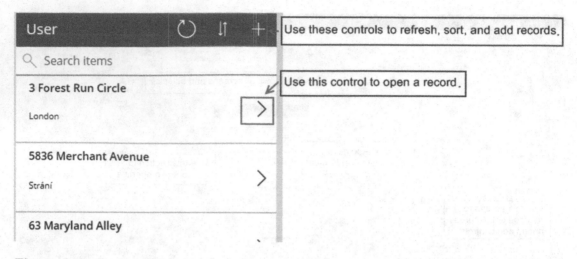

Figure 3-8. Browse screen

The browse screen displays a list of records from the data source. The buttons to the right of the title bar refresh and sort the data that's shown in the list. There is also a button to add a new record. Beneath the title bar, the "Search items" textbox enables us to filter the results. Against each record, we can click the "right arrow" icon to open the selected record in the details screen (Figure 3-9).

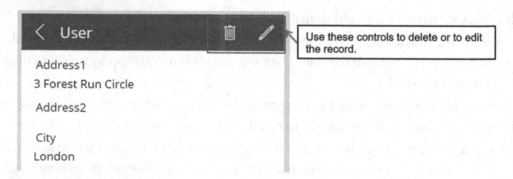

Figure 3-9. Details screen

The name of the details screen in our project is DetailScreen1. The main body of this screen shows the value of each field in the selected record. To the right of the screen title are two buttons. The first button deletes the record, and the second button opens the edit screen as shown in Figure 3-10.

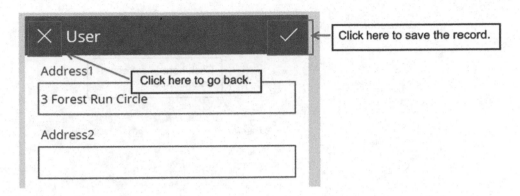

Figure 3-10. *Edit screen*

The name of the edit screen in our project is EditScreen1. From this screen, users can modify the selected record. The "tick" icon to the right of the screen title saves the record, while the cross icon on the left returns the user to the details screen.

The initial browse screen includes a button to add a new record. This button opens the same edit screen, but places the screen into "add mode," rather than "edit mode."

Understanding the Auto-generated App

Now that we've seen what an auto-generated app looks like, let's look at how it works technically.

Adding and Removing Data Sources

The data source for our app is an Excel spreadsheet. We can examine the data sources in a project by clicking the Data sources button beneath the context menu. When we click this button, the list of data sources in our project appears in the data sources pane (Figure 3-11). Here, we can see the data source in our app which is called User.

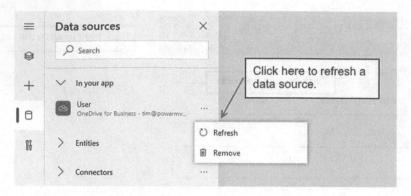

Figure 3-11. *Managing data sources*

As Figure 3-11 shows, each data source includes a context menu that we can access through the button with three dots like an ellipsis. Through this context menu, we can refresh or delete a data source.

The purpose of the refresh function is to update an app when a data source changes. For example, if we were to add additional columns to our Excel spreadsheet table, Power Apps would recognize the new columns only after we click the refresh button.

Frustratingly, there's no simple way to view the details of an Excel data source. In this example, there's no way to tell the exact location on OneDrive where our Excel file exists. To make it easier to remember the location of your Excel file, some app builders make a note of the OneDrive file path in the description setting of the app.

Let's suppose that we want to move our data source. For example, we might want to relocate our Excel file to a different location on OneDrive or to move our file from OneDrive to Dropbox. To move a data source, the best way is to delete our data source and to re-add it. The good news is that when we delete a data source, Power Apps doesn't make any breaking changes to our project. For example, it won't automatically remove screens, controls, or objects that are associated with the data source.

Tip   We can set the app description through the File ➤ Settings menu. Although the primary use of this is to describe the purpose of the app to users, we can also use it to store useful notes such as the OneDrive file location.

Adding, Deleting, and Rearranging Screens

The left part of the screen designer enables us to manage the screens in our app. When a user runs an app, the first screen that opens is the screen at the top of this list. Therefore, the way to configure an app to show a different start-up screen is to move the desired screen to the top of the list. We can move a screen by dragging it with the mouse or by using the context menu, as shown in Figure 3-12.

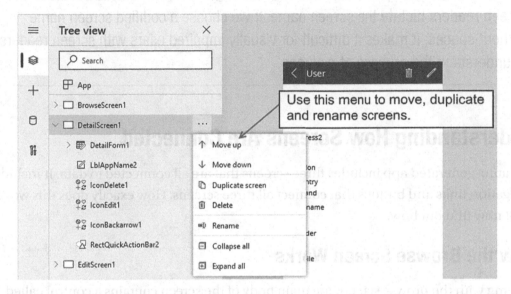

Figure 3-12. Use the context menu to manage screens

Through the context menu, we can add, delete, and duplicate screens. Each application must include at least one screen. Therefore, if only one screen exists in an application, the "delete screen" item will not appear in the menu. To rename a screen, we can use the context menu or use the screen name textbox in the properties pane, as shown in Figure 3-13.

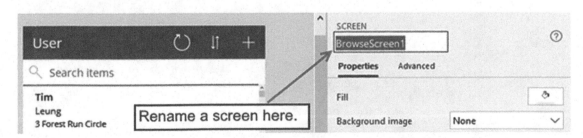

Figure 3-13. Use the screen name textbox to rename a screen

The good news is that when we rename a screen, the designer will change all formula references to use the new name. This makes it simple to rename screens because we don't need to worry about manually changing other parts of the app that refer to the screen.

Tip   The preferred naming convention is to always give screens meaningful names that include spaces and end with the word "Screen." This is because screen readers dictate the screen name. If we choose a codified screen name without spaces, it makes it difficult for visually impaired users with screen readers to understand the purpose of a screen.

Understanding How Screens Are Connected

The auto-generated app includes three screens that are all connected to data. It includes navigation links and buttons that connect all three screens. How exactly does this work? We'll now find out how.

How the Browse Screen Works

Starting with the browse screen, the main body of the screen contains a control called a gallery control. The purpose of this control is to show a list of records. It includes a property called Items. This property specifies the data the control displays.

The gallery control in the browse screen is called BrowseGallery1, and the screenshot in Figure 3-14 shows the value of the Items property. This contains the formula that implements the search and sort features of the screen. But ultimately, BrowseGallery1 connects to the User data source, which was shown in Figure 3-11.

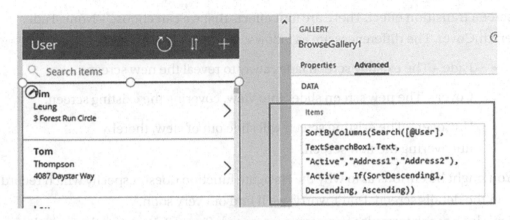

Figure 3-14. *The data source for the gallery control*

From the browse screen, the user can open an existing record or create a new record. Let's look at the formula that opens an existing record.

From `BrowseGallery1`, select the first item in the control (Figure 3-15). Because the gallery control shows multiple records, the first item acts as a template for the repeating items in the gallery.

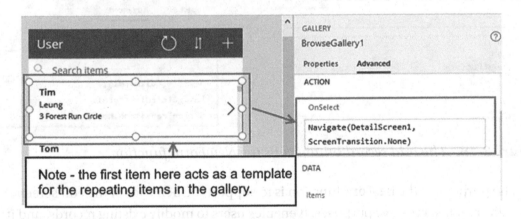

Figure 3-15. *Formula to open an existing record*

The properties pane shows a property called `OnSelect`. This defines the action that occurs when a user clicks the control.

The `OnSelect` formula calls a function called `Navigate`. This function changes the screen that is currently visible, and it accepts two arguments. The first argument specifies the screen that we want to show, and the second (optional) argument specifies the screen transition effect. There are four effects that we can choose – None, Fade, Cover, UnCover. The differences are as follows:

- Fade – The existing screen fades away to reveal the new screen.

- Cover – The new screen slides into view, covering the existing screen.

- UnCover – The existing screen will slide out of view, thereby uncovering the new screen.

You might be curious as to why the Navigate function doesn't specify which record to open in the details screen. Don't worry; we'll find out very soon.

Let's look at the formula to create a new record. Figure 3-16 shows the formula attached to the add icon at the top of the screen. This formula calls the Navigate function to open the edit screen (EditScreen1), but before it does so, it calls a function called NewForm.

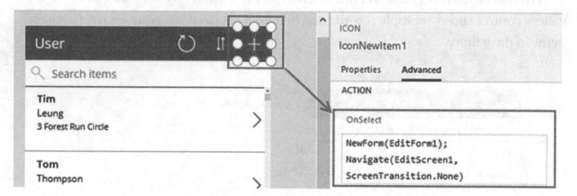

Figure 3-16. *The add record button calls the NewForm function*

The purpose of the NewForm function is to support the behavior of the edit screen. The edit screen serves two purposes. It enables users to modify existing records, and it also enables users to add new records. The NewForm function prepares the form on the edit screen to receive the entry of a new record. A form is a control that houses data entry controls; and, in this example, the name of the form on the edit screen is EditForm1.

After the call to NewForm, the next command in the formula calls the Navigate function to open the edit screen.

How the Details Screen Works

The screen that displays a single record is called DetailScreen1. The main body of this screen contains a form object called DetailForm1 (Figure 3-17).

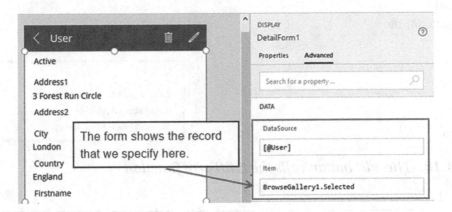

Figure 3-17. *The data source for the details form*

Forms provide the framework to display a single record on a screen. The data source of DetailForm1 is set to [@User]. A form shows a single record, and the Item property defines the record to display. In our case, the Item property is set to BrowseGallery1. Selected. This refers to the browse gallery control in BrowseScreen1. The browse gallery control keeps track of the selected item. When a user clicks an item in the gallery, we can access the selected record through the Selected property.

Because the Item property in DetailForm1 refers to BrowseGallery1, this explains why we don't need to provide a record when we open this screen with a call to the Navigate function. DetailForm1 is connected to BrowseGallery1 through the Item property of DetailForm1.

Let's now look at the formula that opens the selected record in the edit screen. Figure 3-18 shows the formula that is attached to the edit icon. The first command calls a function called EditForm. This function prepares the form on the edit screen by loading the record into the form. The next command in the formula calls the Navigate function to open the edit screen.

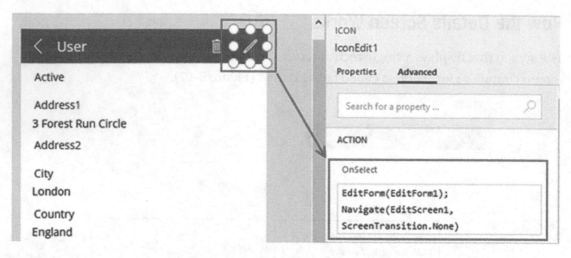

Figure 3-18. *The edit button calls the EditForm function*

Note   You may be curious as to why the data source of our details form is [@User]. Why is it not User, so that it matches the name of our Excel table? The reason is because User is the name of a built-in function (it returns the logged-on user). In instances where a data source conflicts with a reserved word, we use the syntax [@ObjectName] to fully qualify (or disambiguate) the data source.

Searching for Controls

At this stage, it's useful to clarify that control names are unique at an application level. For instance, we can only have one control named DisplayForm1 within an app. This can be a surprise because there are many other development platforms where controls are unique at a screen level, rather than an application level.

Because of the way that formulas can refer to controls on other screens, a very handy feature is the search facility. If we were looking at the application for the first time and saw a reference to BrowseGallery1, how would we know which screen to find BrowseGallery1? By using the search facility, we can search for objects throughout our project. The search facility is very useful because it makes it much easier to understand the complicated apps that we can build via the built-in templates.

To search for an item, use the search box at the top of the screen explorer. Figure 3-19 shows the result when we enter the search term edit. This returns all controls that contain this search term in the tree view. Note that this feature will not return instances of the search term that occur in formulas.

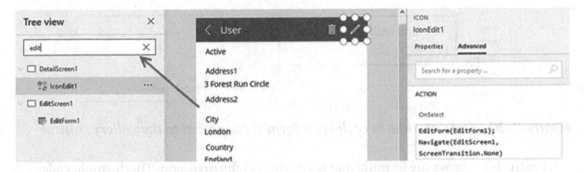

Figure 3-19. *Type into the search box to search for controls*

Caution   Control names in Power Apps are case sensitive and must be unique throughout a project.

How the Edit Screen Works

Let's now examine the last of our three screens – the screen to edit data. The name of this screen is EditScreen1, and the body of the screen contains an edit form.

The edit form provides a framework to display, update, and add records. The data source of our edit form is set to [@User]. An edit form shows a single record, and the Item property defines the record to show. Just like the form on the details screen, the Item property of the form is set to BrowseGallery1.Selected (Figure 3-20).

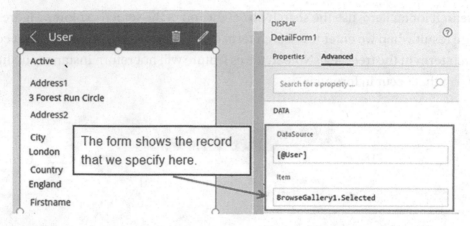

Figure 3-20. *The data source of the edit form is connected to the gallery control*

Figure 3-21 shows the formula that is attached to the save icon. This formula calls a function called SubmitForm. The SubmitForm function saves the data changes to the underlying data source. If we called the NewForm function before opening the screen, SubmitForm adds a new record to the data source. Whereas if we called the EditForm function, the SubmitForm function will update the existing record in the data source.

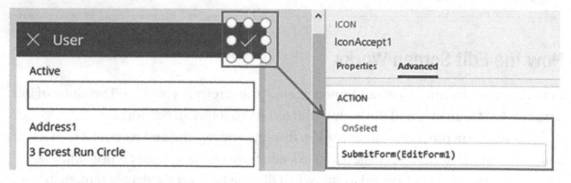

Figure 3-21. *The save button calls the SubmitForm function*

Understanding Forms and Cards

How exactly do forms retrieve and update data from a data source? In this section, we'll find out how. A form contains a series of card objects. Each card contains textboxes (or other controls) to display the field values. At the beginning, I struggled to understand the necessity of this hierarchy of controls. It's perfectly possible to add textboxes directly to a screen. So why introduce a complex structure that requires us to connect textboxes to cards and cards to forms?

The main reason is that it provides a framework to retrieve and update data. It works in a no code way, compared to the alternative method of writing a formula to perform data access. It also works in an extensible way too. If we were to add or remove fields to or from a data source, we could easily adapt our apps in the same no code way to support the changes.

The secondary reason is that through the graphical designer, we can change the control type that renders a field.

Finally, this method enables the designer to auto-generate the user interface elements to apply validation to a field. If we were not using forms, we would have to build the user interface for validation manually.

Adding Fields to a Form

To add a field to a form, select the form and click the "Edit fields" link. This opens the fields panel, as shown in Figure 3-22. This panel indicates the fields that are shown in the form. Each field in this list corresponds to a card on the form. There is a one-to-one relationship between the cards on a form and the fields in a data source.

To add a field that isn't on the form, click the Add field link. This displays a checkbox list of fields that are not yet shown, and we can check the fields that we want to add. We can click the "add" button beneath this list to add cards to the form that are linked to the selected fields.

In the common scenario where we subsequently add a field to a data source, we would need to first refresh our data source using the View ➤ Data sources menu item and then click the "Add field" link to add the field to our form.

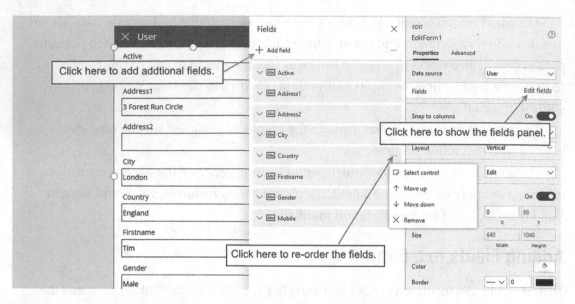

Figure 3-22. Features of cards

By default, the cards on a form appear in an alphabetical sequence. We can rearrange the sequence by dragging the cards in the "Fields" list to the desired location or by using the context menu. Through the context menu, we can also remove a card from a form.

Figure 3-23 illustrates a card on a form (taken from an app with a SharePoint data source). Inside the card are labels and text entry controls. If the underlying data source supports validation (as in the case of SharePoint), the card will include UI elements to support this, such as mandatory field indicators and validation error labels.

We can change the control type using the control type drop-down. For a text field, the control choices include "View text," "View phone," "View email," "Edit text," "Edit multi-line text," and "Allowed values."

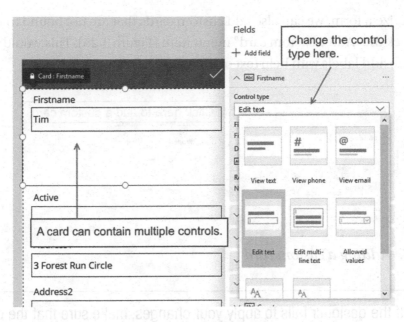

Figure 3-23. *The view of a card in the designer*

It's possible to modify the appearance of a card, but we can only do so once we unlock it. To unlock a card, select the card and click the Advanced tab, as shown in Figure 3-24. From here, click the padlock icon to unlock the card.

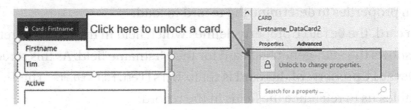

Figure 3-24. *Unlocking a card*

To customize a form, we can also add custom cards that are not bound to any field. To do this, click the "Add a custom card" menu item (Figure 3-25). This would enable us, for example, to add labels with help text or images to a form.

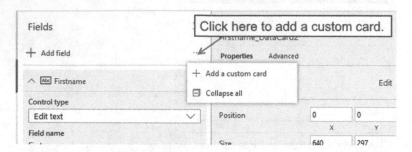

Figure 3-25. *Adding a custom card*

Caution   If the designer fails to apply your changes, make sure that the card you want to edit is unlocked.

Reading Data into a Form

Here's how a form retrieves data from its data source. The form uses the data source and selected item properties to determine the record to load.

For each card, the Default property defines which field in the record to retrieve. Figure 3-26 shows the auto-generated card for the Firstname field. As this screenshot shows, the Default property of this card is set to ThisItem.Firstname. The ThisItem keyword enables us to reference the fields in the record.

Another useful card property is DisplayName. Power Apps uses this value to set the label heading for the card.

For clarity, the similar-sounding DataField property has no impact on data retrieval. The purpose of this property (as we'll see shortly) is related to the save process.

Tip   To configure a card to read data only, the only property we need to set is the Default property. In an auto-generated card, we can clear all other property values, and the data will still load.

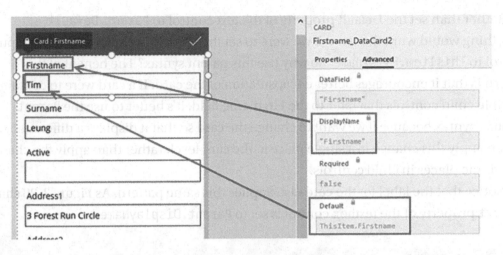

Figure 3-26. *The Default property specifies the field that the card retrieves*

How Card Controls Work

The card itself doesn't display any data directly or provide any discernible functionality to the end user. It simply acts as a container for other controls. The content of the Firstname card includes a text input control, as shown in Figure 3-27. For text input controls, the Default property specifies the text that the control displays. In this example, the value of this property is Parent.Default.

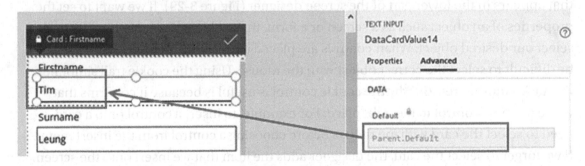

Figure 3-27. *Specifying the text that appears in the text input control*

Because the text input control belongs inside a card control, the Parent keyword enables us to refer to the properties of the parent card control. In this case, Parent. Default will resolve to the Default property of the card control, which in this case is ThisItem.Firstname.

Rather than set the Default property of the text control to `Parent.Default`, everything would work the same if we were to set the Default property of the text input control to `ThisItem.Firstname`. So why use this parent syntax? The benefit of this pattern is that it encourages better encapsulation of the card. If a card were to contain multiple child controls that refer to the Firstname field, it's better to use the `Parent. Default` syntax because if we want to change the card so that it displays a different field, we can apply this change in a single place at the card level, rather than apply the change in multiple places in child controls.

Notice that the label for the card also applies this same pattern. As Figure 3-28 shows, the `Text` property of the textbox control is set to `Parent.DisplayName`.

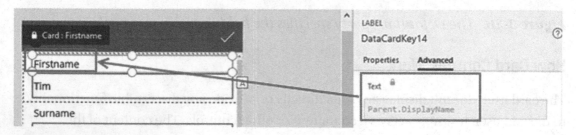

Figure 3-28. *Label control for a card*

When we work with forms and cards, a useful feature is the cookie trail control that appears in the lower part of the screen designer (Figure 3-29). If we want to set the properties of an object such as a screen or a form, the cookie trail enables us to quickly select our desired object. When controls are placed closely together on a screen, it can be difficult to select the correct object with the mouse. Using the cookie trail simplifies this task. Another reason why the cookie control is useful is because it confirms that we've added a control to the right place. For example, to insert a control onto a card, we need to select the card with the mouse before choosing a control from the insert menu. If we forget to select the card, the designer adds the item that we insert onto the screen. Therefore, the cookie trail provides confirmation when we insert child items onto a control.

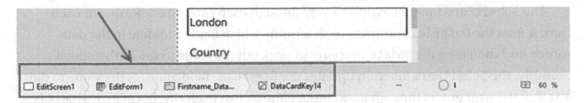

Figure 3-29. *Using the cookie control in the designer*

Tip We can also use the tree view to examine the hierarchy of controls on a screen. The tree view is especially useful because we can use this to view hidden controls.

Saving Form Data to a Data Source

How does Power Apps insert and update records? The insert or update operation begins when a user initiates a call to the SubmitForm function. The save icon in EditScreen1 calls this function and supplies the name of the edit form. The SubmitForm function retrieves the data that the user enters through the child controls on the cards and updates the data source.

Figure 3-30 shows the Firstname card on the edit form. The card properties that are pertinent to the save operation are the DataField and Update properties.

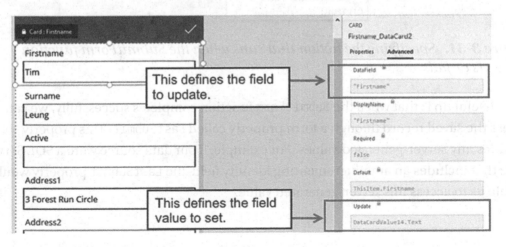

Figure 3-30. *Inserting or updating a record*

The SubmitForm function works its way through each card on the form. For each card, it uses the DataField property to determine which field to update in the data source and then uses the Update property to work out the value to set. In this specific example, the SubmitForm function updates the Firstname field and sets the value to the text that the user enters through a text input control. Just to clarify, DataCardValue14 is the name of the text input control inside the Firstname card.

The SubmitForm function can update an existing record, or it can insert a new record. This depends on the function that we called prior to opening the screen. If we called the EditForm function, SubmitForm will update an existing record in the data source. If we called the NewForm function, SubmitForm will add a new record to the data source.

If SubmitForm completes the save operation successfully, it runs the formula that's defined in the OnSuccess property. In this case, it calls the Back function (Figure 3-31). This function navigates the user back to the screen that was previously open. In the event of a failure, the formula in the OnFailure property will run instead. The default value of false here specifies that no custom action will occur in the event of a failure.

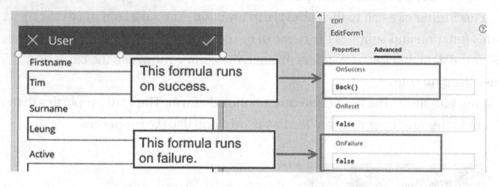

Figure 3-31. *Specifying the action that runs when the SubmitForm function succeeds or fails*

A useful tip is that when the SubmitForm function completes successfully, we can access the saved record through a form property called LastSubmit. This property includes any server-generated values. For example, if our data source were a SQL Server table that includes an auto-incrementing identity field, the LastSubmit property would enable us to access this server-generated value.

Note   In the event of a failure (e.g., a primary key violation error), Power Apps displays a banner message with the error message. Some app builders use the OnFailure property to display a friendly message by calling the Notify function. Note that this suppresses the underlying error message and can make it more difficult to identify the exact cause of an error.

Choosing Not to Use Forms and Cards

Although there are benefits to using forms and cards to read and write data, it's possible to build data entry screens without the use of these controls. We could add custom text controls to a screen and call a function named Patch to update the data source.

One reason not to use forms and cards is the ability to build data entry screens with a greater level of customization. There may also be situations where we need to update more than one table. Edit forms are associated with single tables; and in scenarios where we want to update more than one table, it can be easier to write custom formula, rather than build screens with multiple forms.

Recap of Concepts

We've covered a lot, so here's a summary to reinforce some of the concepts that we've learned. Figure 3-32 illustrates how screen navigation works in an auto-generated app.

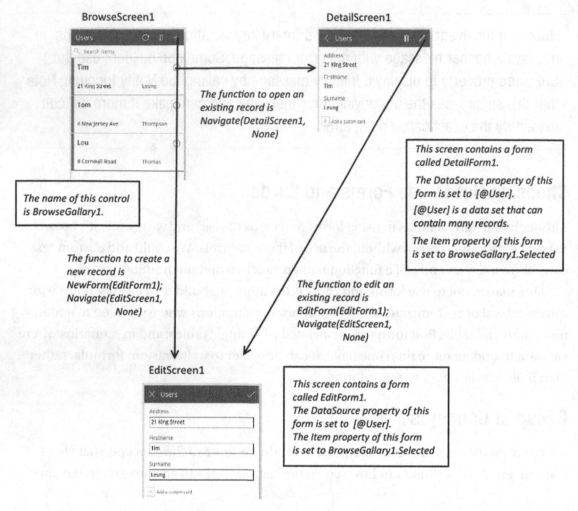

Figure 3-32. *How the screens are connected*

Figure 3-33 illustrates how the read process works in the form of a diagram, and it describes the role that forms and cards play in this process.

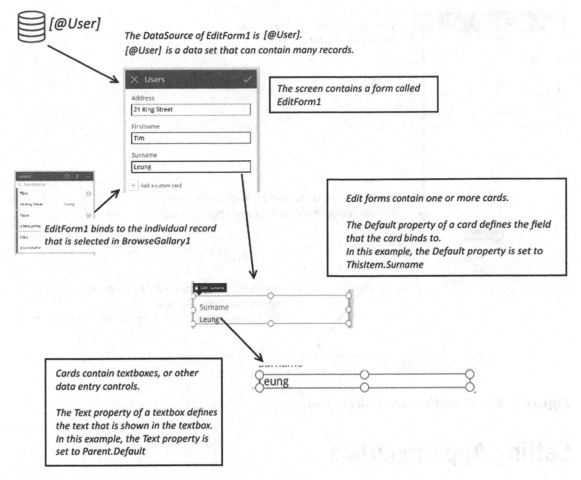

Figure 3-33. *How the data read process works*

Finally, Figure 3-34 illustrates how the save process works in the form of a diagram.

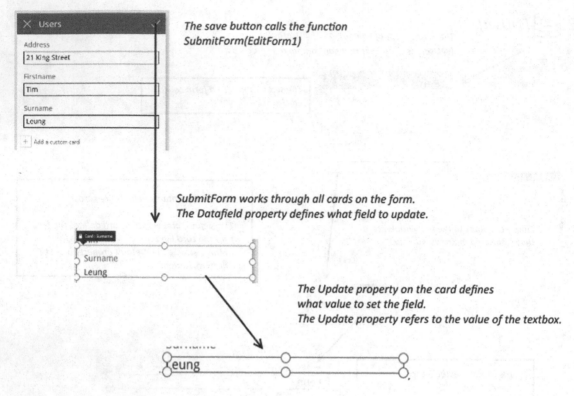

The save button calls the function SubmitForm(EditForm1)

SubmitForm works through all cards on the form. The Datafield property defines what field to update.

The Update property on the card defines what value to set the field. The Update property refers to the value of the textbox.

Figure 3-34. *How the save process works*

Setting App Properties

Through the "Settings" section of the designer, we can specify the properties of an app. These include the app name, description, background color, and icon (Figure 3-35). When we share our app with other users, the app name and description help other users to identify our app.

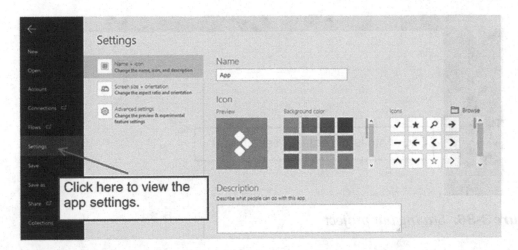

Figure 3-35. App settings

Through the "Screen size + orientation" section, we can configure the target screen size and orientation for apps that run through the mobile players.

The "Advanced settings" section provides some useful features. Here, we can enable preview features. These are upcoming features that will be enabled soon. By enabling a preview feature, we can test our apps in anticipation of the feature release. We can also enable experimental features. These are less stable features that may not be released, depending on feedback.

Caution   Occasionally, Microsoft releases preview or experimental features that might cause some part of an app to break. To diagnose such problems, it's worth checking the "Advanced settings" section to see if there are any experimental settings that might be the cause.

Saving and Opening Apps

To save our work, use the File ➤ Save as menu item, as shown in Figure 3-36. There are two places where we can save our project – to the cloud or to our local PC.

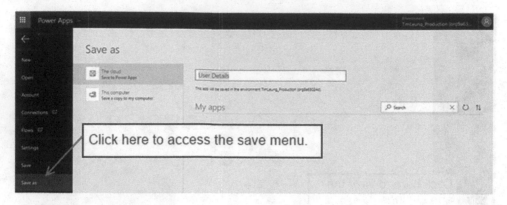

Figure 3-36.   *Saving our project*

If we choose the cloud option, Power Apps saves our work to the current environment. We can switch environments through the Account menu. However, we can't switch environments at the point at which we want to save because we'll be prompted to discard our changes.

When we choose the option to save to our local computer, Power Apps creates a file with a .msapp extension. Saving work to the local computer is a good way to make backup copies of our work. It also provides a good way to share apps with other users, for example, by emailing the msapp file as an attachment or posting it on a forum.

Tip   An msapp file is a compressed zip file. From Windows File Explorer, we can rename the .msapp extension to .zip and decompress the file. This archive contains various XML files that define our app. We can manually modify these files to carry out unsupported operations (e.g., to change a phone app to a tablet app). However, these types of hacks are not officially supported by Microsoft.

The File ➤ Open menu item enables us to open an app. From this screen, we can open apps that are saved in the cloud, and we can also open a "file browser" dialog to load .msapp files from our local machine.

Summary

In this chapter, we learned how to build an auto-generated app based on an Excel spreadsheet. To use Excel as a data source, we must define the data as a table for Power Apps to recognize the data. Once we complete our spreadsheet, we need to save it to a cloud storage provider that Power Apps supports. This includes Microsoft OneDrive, Google Drive, Dropbox, and more.

When we create an app, Power Apps offers several options. The first is to build an app from a built-in template. These provide a great way to learn more about Power Apps.

Another option is to choose the "Start with your data" option. This option builds an auto-generated app that enables users to create, update, and delete records from a data source.

Once we create an app, we can use a simple graphical designer to modify our app. The left part of the designer shows the screens in an app, and the menu options in the menu bar enable us to add content. Through the properties pane on the right, we can modify the settings of objects such as screens and controls.

Auto-generated apps contain three screens – a browse screen, a details screen, and an edit screen. The browse screen contains a gallery control. This control displays a list of data, and a user can use this control to open a specific record in the details screen. The details screen shows the full details of a record and includes a link that opens the record in the edit screen. The edit screen enables users to make modifications to a record.

To display a single record, the display and edit screens utilize a control called a form control. A form connects to a record, and typically, we would configure a form to connect to the selected item in a gallery control. Forms are containers for cards. A card is an object that connects to a specific field in a record, and the purpose of a card is to retrieve and update fields from a data source. Cards are containers for data controls, which are controls that users interact with. Examples of these controls include text input controls or drop-down boxes.

A benefit of the form system is that we can build data entry in a no code way. Through the graphical designer, we can change the control type for a field and easily adapt a form when we add or remove fields to or from a data source.

Here's a summary of some the functions that we've covered in this chapter. The function that switches the visible screen is called Navigate. A form control can modify an existing record, or it can create a new record. To prepare a form to edit an existing record, we would call a function called EditForm. To prepare a form to create a new record, we would call a function called NewForm. To save the form changes to the data source, we would call a function called SubmitForm.

To round off an app, we can use the Settings area to define the name, description, icon, and other properties of our app. Finally, we can save apps either to the cloud or to our local computer.

CHAPTER 4

Sharing Apps

Now that we've developed and tested our app, the final step is to publish and to share it with users. This chapter guides you through this exciting step, including how to set up users and how to share apps with external users.

Unfortunately, we can sometimes introduce bugs when we introduce new versions of an app. To mitigate any ongoing damage, we'll cover the topic of version control. We'll look at how to roll back apps to a previous version.

If you're a contractor or work for a software house, a typical process is to develop your app in an independent tenant and to deploy your changes to the client when the work is complete. To support this method of working, we'll find out how to export and import apps between different environments and organizations.

Other important topics that we'll cover include

- How we can more effectively organize and manage users through security groups.

- How to manage data connections. Some data sources require all users to share the same connection. We examine how this works so that you can understand what impact this has on the security of your data source and to understand what credentials a user needs to supply when an app starts.

- How apps behave in languages other than English. We'll look at how to change the language that Power Apps uses and the language of the Maker Portal.

Sharing Apps with End Users

Before we begin, let's look at the permissions structure of an app. Each app must have at least one owner. By default, the user that creates an app is the owner. Owners have full control of an app, including the ability to modify or delete the app.

81

© Tim Leung 2021
T. Leung, *Beginning Power Apps*, https://doi.org/10.1007/978-1-4842-6683-0_4

It's possible to define additional co-owners for an app. For apps in live use, it's good practice to define co-owners. This makes it simple for someone else to modify or take control of an app, if the original owner were to leave the organization.

For each app, we can also specify the users that can have access to the app. Users can run but not edit an app.

When an owner modifies and saves an app, all co-owners can see the changes. However, the changes will not be visible to users until we publish the app.

Specifying Owners and Users

The share screen that's shown in Figure 4-1 enables us to configure the owners and users of an app. We can access this through the File ➤ Share menu item in Power Apps Studio or through our list of apps in the Maker Portal.

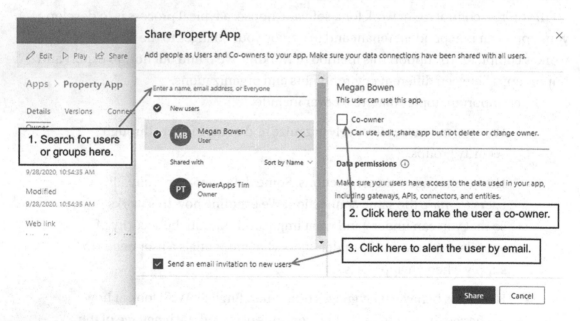

Figure 4-1. *Configuring additional users*

From this screen, we can search for users within our organization and configure those users as co-owners or standard users.

If we want to share an app with everyone in our organization, we can grant permissions to the user "Everyone."

This screen also provides the option to email the target user with a link to the app. For apps that use Dataverse as a data source, we can also use the data permissions section to grant access through security roles.

Creating Users

To share an app (as an owner or user) with a user that doesn't yet exist, the first step is to create a work account for the user. The place to do this is through the Microsoft 365 Admin Portal (Figure 4-2). All users require a license, so it's important to assign a license that includes Power Apps.

If we choose to use "per-app" licensing, it isn't necessary to assign licenses at a user level. With per-app licensing, we first purchase our licenses and assign those to an environment through the Resources ➤ Capacity section of the Power Platform admin center. We can then set up an app to use per-app licensing by enabling the "pass assignment" option through the app settings (we can access these settings through the apps list in the Maker Portal).

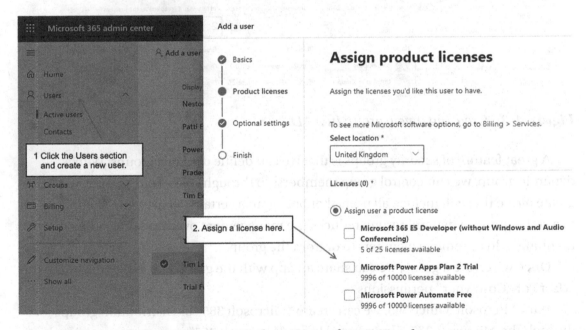

Figure 4-2. *Creating a new user in the Microsoft 365 portal*

Note that we may not have permissions to access the Admin Portal for the organization that we're working on. In this case, our Microsoft/Office 365 or Dynamics 365 administrator would need to create the users for us.

Setting Up Security Groups

Rather than share apps directly with users, we can share apps with groups of users. This works well if there are many apps that we want to share with the same set of users. By using groups, we can remove or add additional users from or to the group, which avoids the more time-consuming alternative of carrying out this task repeatedly for each app.

Power Apps works with AAD (Azure Active Directory) security groups. To set up a group and to add members, the first step is to register an Azure account through `https://portal.azure.com/`. The next step is to visit the Azure Active Directory section of the Azure Portal and to set up AAD (Figure 4-3). The easiest way is to search for "Azure Active Directory" in the search box.

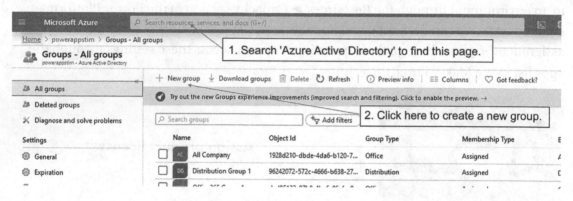

Figure 4-3. *Creating a new group in AAD*

A great feature of security groups is that we can define dynamic groups. With a dynamic group, we can control group membership through rules. For example, we can create a rule that will include all users that belong to a certain department. Compared to a static group, a dynamic group reduces the management overhead of needing to manually add or remove members to or from the group.

Once we create a group, we can share an app with the group and assign the group the "User" or "Co-owner" permissions.

With Microsoft/Office 365, we can create "Microsoft 365" or Distribution groups through the Microsoft 365 Admin Portal (note "Microsoft 365" groups were previously called "Office 365" groups). It isn't possible to share apps with Distribution groups, which are a type of group for distributing email. However, it's possible to share apps with Microsoft 365 groups.

What's the difference between a security group and a Microsoft 365 group? The benefit is that Microsoft 365 groups include additional collaboration features. For example, each Microsoft 365 group has its own Exchange mailbox and SharePoint site collection, with integration into Microsoft Teams – a great way to enable online chat between group members.

To share an app with a Microsoft 365 group, we need to "security enable" the group. This is a complex process that requires us to locate the object ID of the group and to complete the task with PowerShell. The following link contains the exact steps, including details of how to install the requisite Azure AD PowerShell components:

https://docs.microsoft.com/en-us/powerapps/maker/canvas-apps/share-app#share-an-app-with-office-365-groups

Setting Up External Users

It's possible to share apps with users that are external to our organization. This works well in scenarios where we want to share apps with customers or suppliers. Consultancy companies can also use this method to share apps with clients.

To grant access to an app to an external user, the first step is to configure the user as a guest user through the "Azure Active Directory" section of the Microsoft Azure Portal (Figure 4-4).

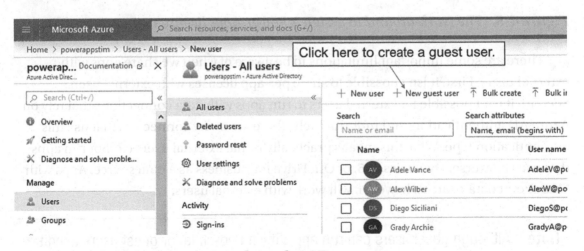

Figure 4-4. *Creating a guest user through AAD*

The external users require a Power Apps license to run any apps that we share with them. If the target user has a Power Apps user license or belongs to an organization with Microsoft/Office 365 or Dynamics 365, the existing license will suffice.

If the external user doesn't have a Power Apps license and we want to allocate one of our licenses to that user, there are some steps that we need to carry out. It isn't possible to directly allocate licenses to external users, so we need to employ a work-around. The trick is to create an AAD group, add the external user to the group, and assign the Power Apps license to the group (Figure 4-5).

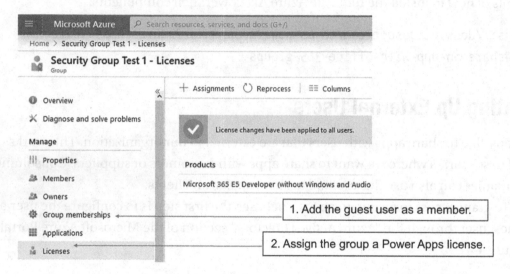

Figure 4-5. *The work-around to assign a Power Apps license to an external user*

There are some important limitations to be aware of when we share apps with external users. First, it isn't possible to share per-app licenses with external users. Second, it isn't possible for external users to run apps with data connections that rely on Azure AD authentication; and unfortunately, there are many connectors that use this authentication type. What this means practically is that external users cannot run apps that use Dataverse, Dynamics 365, or OneDrive for Business as a data source. Apps with SharePoint data sources, however, will work with external users.

Note   Although guest users can run apps, it isn't possible for guest users to edit the apps that we share with them.

Sharing App Data Sources

Once we share an app with a set of users, we must ensure that the users have permissions to access the underlying data sources for the app. Power Apps supports many data sources, and it's important to understand how an app authenticates to a data source.

Data connections are always protected in some way. For example, a username and password combination secures the data in a SQL Server database. In the case of an Excel spreadsheet, access to the underlying file storage such as OneDrive or Dropbox controls access to the data. When we publish an app, how does the end user authenticate to the underlying data source at runtime? The answer is that it depends.

With many data sources, including SharePoint and OneDrive, Power Apps displays an authentication dialog when the user starts the app. This allows the user to authenticate to the underlying data source. In this scenario, we would need to configure the SharePoint or OneDrive security settings to allow read and write access for the data source.

With some other data sources, users authenticate using the credentials that the app builder specifies at design time. One example is SQL Server. We can identify these shared data sources by viewing the Connections page, beneath the Data section of the Maker Portal (Figure 4-6). A share option will be visible against the data connections that are shared.

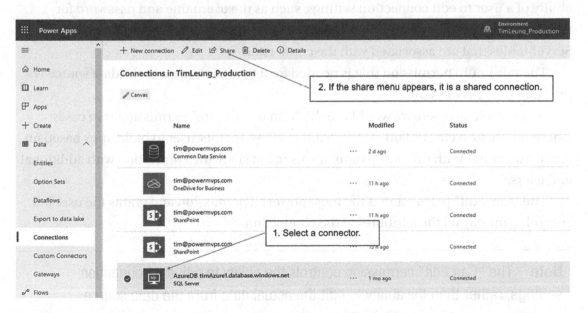

Figure 4-6. *The presence of a share menu item indicates a shared connection*

For shared connections, we must grant permissions to our intended users through the share menu item. Figure 4-7 shows the share dialog for a shared SQL Server connection. Using this dialog, we can search for users and apply one of three permissions – "Can use," "Can use + share," and "Can edit."

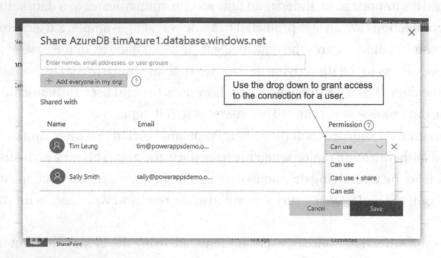

Figure 4-7. Configuring a shared connection

An important point of clarification is that the terminology here applies to the connection, rather than the data. For instance, the "Can edit" setting controls the ability of a user to edit connection settings, such as the username and password for the connection. It isn't designed to control whether a user can edit the data in the SQL Server tables that are associated with the connection.

The minimum permission that is needed for a user to connect to the data source is the "Can use" permission.

An example of where we would use the "Can use + share" permission is in cases where we create a connection and we want to allow another user to build apps based on that connection. With this permission, the user can share the connection with additional end users.

The "Can edit" permission is the most powerful permission and grants the user full control to modify all the attributes of the connection.

Note   The "Can edit" permission controls the ability to edit the connection settings, rather than the ability to edit the actual data from the data source.

Running Apps

After we share the app and data source, users can open the app by navigating to the Apps section of the Maker Portal. The app will appear in the list of available apps.

Alternatively, users can run an app by directly entering the app URL into a web browser. We can find the URL of an app through the details section of the app in the Maker Portal (Figure 4-8).

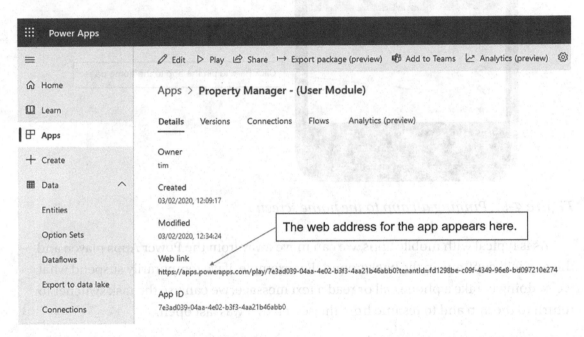

Figure 4-8. *Finding the web address for an app*

Installing the Mobile Player

Mobile users can run apps on phone or tablet devices either through a web browser or a mobile player. Mobile players are native apps that can run but not edit an app. We can install the mobile player through the app store for our device. For example, we would use the Google Play Store to install the mobile player for an Android device.

When the mobile player starts for the first time, it prompts the user to log in with the username and password for their Microsoft work account. The next screen shows a list of available apps. The mobile player caches the login credentials. This is convenient because if a user turns the device off and on again, it won't prompt for the login credentials again.

A useful feature is that we can pin an app to the home screen, as shown in Figure 4-9. When we select this option, the application creates a shortcut on the home screen of the mobile device, outside of the Power Apps player. This shortcut starts the specified app directly and bypasses the app selection screen.

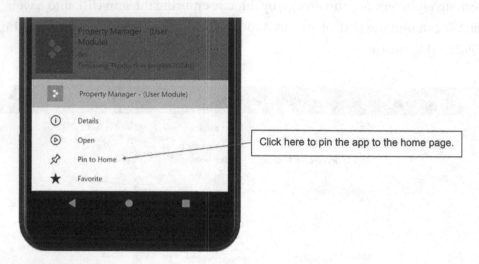

Figure 4-9. *Pinning an app to the home screen*

As is typical with mobile apps, we can move away from the Power Apps player, and the app will continue in the background. For example, if we temporarily suspend what we're doing to take a phone call or read a text message, we can use the task switcher to return to the app and to resume from the screen that was last open.

Note   Apps can always run in either a browser or the mobile player. There isn't a way to specify that an app can run only on a specific platform.

Understanding Environments

Now that we understand how to share apps with users, we'll now explore the features that are related to the organization and ongoing development of apps.

The high-level container that organizes apps and connections is an environment. An important and useful attribute of an environment is that it can host zero or up to one Dataverse database. If we want to create additional Dataverse databases, we can only do so by provisioning additional environments.

Environments are hosted in a region. This specifies the geographic location of the data center that hosts apps, connections, and the Dataverse database. Choosing a region that matches the location where most of our users are based can make a big difference to performance.

There is a default environment for each organization, and each new user in the organization will inherit permissions to create apps in the default environment.

Although it's perfectly fine to use only the default environment, a common observation in many companies is that the default environment quickly becomes cluttered with apps. To avoid this, a helpful strategy is to create environments for users before Power Apps becomes too widely adopted. This can make it easier to manage and organize all the apps in an organization.

Tip It can be a good idea to plan our environment setup before the widespread adoption of Power Apps to help better manage and organize our apps.

Creating New Environments

The Power Platform admin center enables us to manage our environments. We can access this through the cog icon at the top of the Maker Portal. The Environments section enables us to view a list of existing environments and to create a new environment (Figure 4-10).

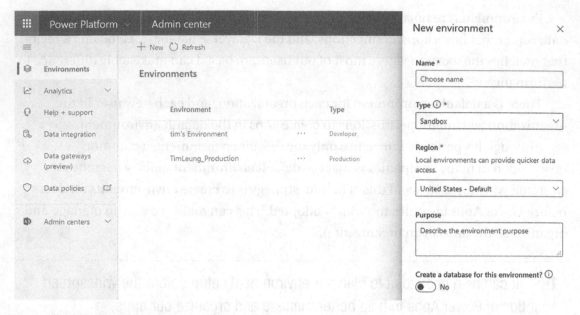

Figure 4-10. *Managing environments*

In addition to the default environment, we might also see a developer environment. Power Apps provisions this type of environment when we sign up to the Community Plan. The biggest limitation with the developer environment is that any apps that we create here cannot be shared with other users. Also, any apps that we create in the developer environment are not officially licensed for production use. Putting these limitations aside, a key benefit of the developer environment is that we can build apps that can access Dataverse and other premium data connectors, such as SQL Server. Also, developer environments do not expire after a set period.

Note that the ability to create environments is limited mostly to users with a Power Apps plan. Users with trial licenses or seeded Microsoft/Office 365 or Dynamics 365 licenses cannot create new environments.

Choosing an Environment Type

When we create a new environment, we can specify one of three environment types – sandbox, trial, and production.

Production environments are designed for live production use. This is the type of environment we would select if we wish to create a self-contained area for specific departments or teams or if we want to reprovision apps to a different region to improve performance. Each new environment requires 1 GB of Dataverse storage space, irrespective of whether we choose to provision a Dataverse database or not. This can limit the number of environments that we can create and may require us to purchase additional Dataverse storage space.

Trial environments are designed for test purposes. Unlike a developer environment, we can share apps in this type of environment with other users. The main limitation with a trial environment is that it expires after a certain time. A business that wants to trial Dataverse would be a good use case for a trial environment. With this type of environment, we can provision a Dataverse database and build an app that uses this database. We can share the app with team members and to trial the platform. If we're happy, we can purchase the required licenses and promote the trial environment to a production environment for continued use.

Sandbox environments allow us to test changes or modifications before we deploy those changes to a production environment. They are well suited for testing Dataverse apps, and there is no time limit on these types of environment. To support this task, there is an option in the settings of a production environment that copies the entire contents of a production environment onto a target sandbox environment. This provides an ideal base platform from which we can carry out our testing. The sandbox environment includes a reset function. This feature clears all apps and data and resets the environment to a clean, default state.

Another reason why sandbox environments are helpful is because Power Apps provides automated scheduled backups of environments. If we want to restore a backup, the target destination must be a sandbox environment. We can convert sandbox environments to production environments and vice versa through the settings of the environments.

Tip   The region drop-down includes a special region called "Preview (United States)." This region contains prerelease features that are scheduled to be released in the next release of Power Apps. We can use this feature to make sure that existing apps work against upcoming future releases of Power Apps.

Setting Environment Permissions

There are two security roles that are associated with each environment – the Environment Admin and Environment Maker roles.

Users that belong to the Environment Admin role have full control of the environment. They can remove or add additional users from or to the Environment Admin or Environment Maker role. They can view and manage all resources in the environment, including the ability to provision a Dataverse database. They can also configure data loss prevention policies. This is a feature that secures corporate data by preventing users from copying data between different data sources in an app.

Users that we add to the Environment Maker role can create apps in the environment. They can also share apps with other users in the organization.

When we build an app in an environment and share it with other users in the organization, those users do not need to belong to any role or to have any specific permission in the environment.

At the time of writing, Microsoft is migrating administrative functions from the old "Power Apps admin center" to the new "Power Platform admin center." The ability to add users to environment roles is available only in the older "Power Apps admin center," which we can access through `https://admin.PowerApps.com`. Figure 4-11 shows the area in the admin center where we can manage security roles.

To aide administration, we can add AAD security groups as members to the Environment Admin and Environment Maker roles.

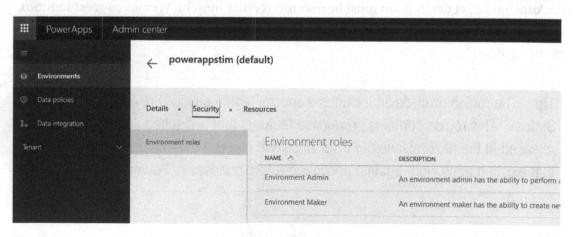

Figure 4-11. *Managing environment permissions through the Power Apps admin center*

An important point is that the Environment Admin role applies only to environments without a Dataverse database. Once we provision a Dataverse database, it's necessary to add users to a role called System Administrator.

Figure 4-12 shows the security section of the environment once we provision a Dataverse database. This screen describes how the Environment Admin role has now become the System Administrator role.

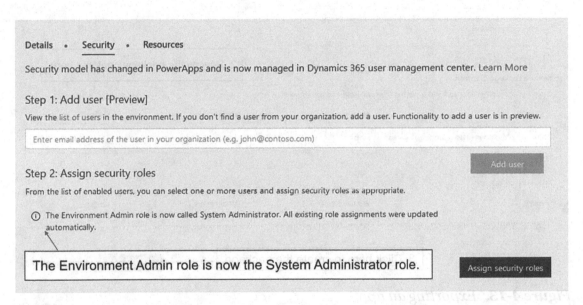

Figure 4-12. Managing security in environments with a Dataverse database

Moving Apps Between Environments and Tenants

An important part of working with environments is the ability to move apps between different environments and tenants. To help us, Power Apps provides the ability to export and import apps. We'll now look at how this feature works.

Exporting an App

Through the Maker Portal, we can choose an app and select the export menu item. Through this feature, we can package an app as a zip file and import it into a target environment or tenant. Figure 4-13 shows the export package screen.

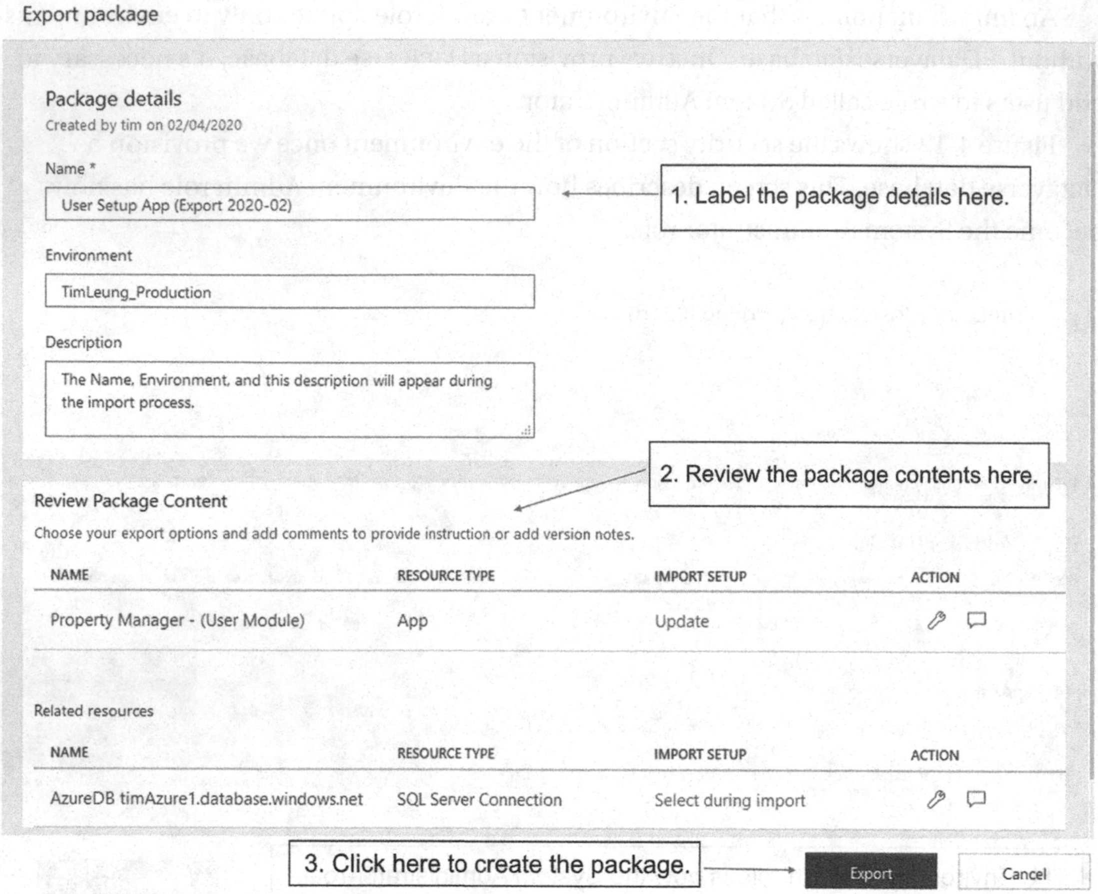

Export package

Figure 4-13. *Exporting an app*

The top part of this screen enables us to enter the Name, Environment, and Description for our export package. These details will be visible during the import process. As a point of clarification, the Name and Environment details that we enter here are for labeling purposes only. The purpose of these fields is not to specify the source name and environment of the app that we want to package.

The lower part of the screen shows a summary of the app and any related resources, such as data connections. The "Import Setup" link enables us to specify the default import behavior. We'll examine this in the next section – "Importing an App."

Once we're ready, we can click the Export button to generate and download our export package. An important note is that the export feature exports the latest published version of an app. To move an unpublished version of an app, we can save our app from Power Apps Studio onto our local machine (as an .msapp file), and we can then open this app in our target environment.

> **Caution**   The export feature exports the latest published version of an app. It does not export unpublished changes. When moving apps from one environment to another, some users have accidently lost changes by deleting the source app before realizing that the export file doesn't contain all unpublished changes. Please don't make this same mistake!

Importing an App

To import an app, the first step is switch to the target environment and to click the Import button that appears in the apps list. This opens a screen that we can use to upload our package file. When the upload process completes, we will see the screen that is shown in Figure 4-14.

The top part of this screen shows the Name, Environment, and Description details that we specified during the export process.

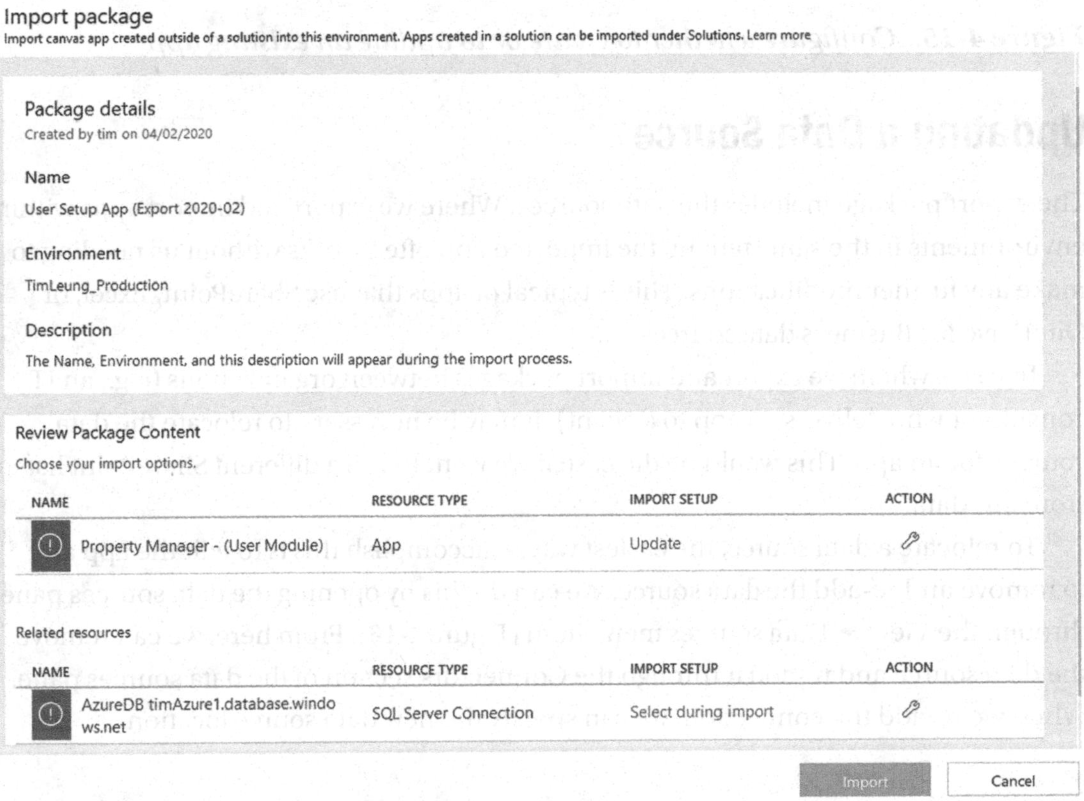

Import package

Import canvas app created outside of a solution into this environment. Apps created in a solution can be imported under Solutions. Learn more

Package details
Created by tim on 04/02/2020

Name
User Setup App (Export 2020-02)

Environment
TimLeung_Production

Description
The Name, Environment, and this description will appear during the import process.

Review Package Content
Choose your import options.

NAME	RESOURCE TYPE	IMPORT SETUP	ACTION
Property Manager - (User Module)	App	Update	🖉

Related resources

NAME	RESOURCE TYPE	IMPORT SETUP	ACTION
AzureDB timAzure1.database.windows.net	SQL Server Connection	Select during import	🖉

Import   Cancel

Figure 4-14. Importing an app

Through the "Import Setup" link, we can modify the import behavior that we specified when we created the export package. The import setup can work in two ways (Figure 4-15). Where an identical app or resource exists, we can choose to update what is already there. Alternatively, we can choose to create a new app and to recreate any associated resources in the destination environment.

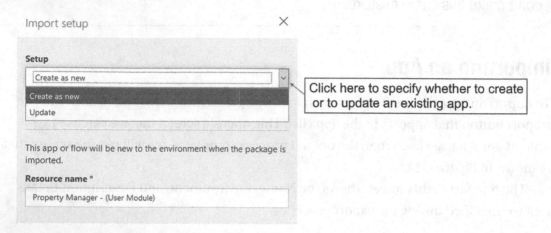

Figure 4-15. *Configure whether to create or to update an existing app*

Updating a Data Source

The export package includes the data sources. Where we export and import apps within environments in the same tenant, the imported app often works without us needing to make any further modifications. This is typical of apps that use SharePoint, Excel, or OneDrive for Business data sources.

In cases where we export and import packages between organizations (e.g., an IT consultant who delivers an app to a client), it may be necessary to relocate the data sources for an app. This would be the case if we want to use a different SharePoint list to store our data.

To relocate a data source, the easiest way to accomplish this is to edit the app and to remove and re-add the data source. We can do this by opening the data sources pane through the View ➤ Data sources menu item (Figure 4-16). From here, we can remove the data source and re-add it through the Connectors section of the data sources pane. When we re-add the connection, we can specify the new data source location.

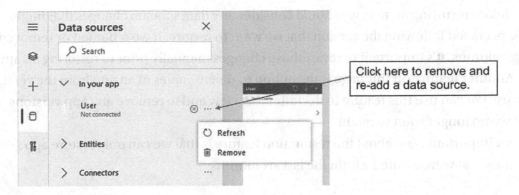

Figure 4-16. *Updating a data source to use a new connection*

Versioning Apps

Each time we save an app to the cloud, Power Apps maintains a history of our changes. We can access the version history for each app through the apps list in the Maker Portal. The details section includes a Versions tab that shows the version history for an app (Figure 4-17).

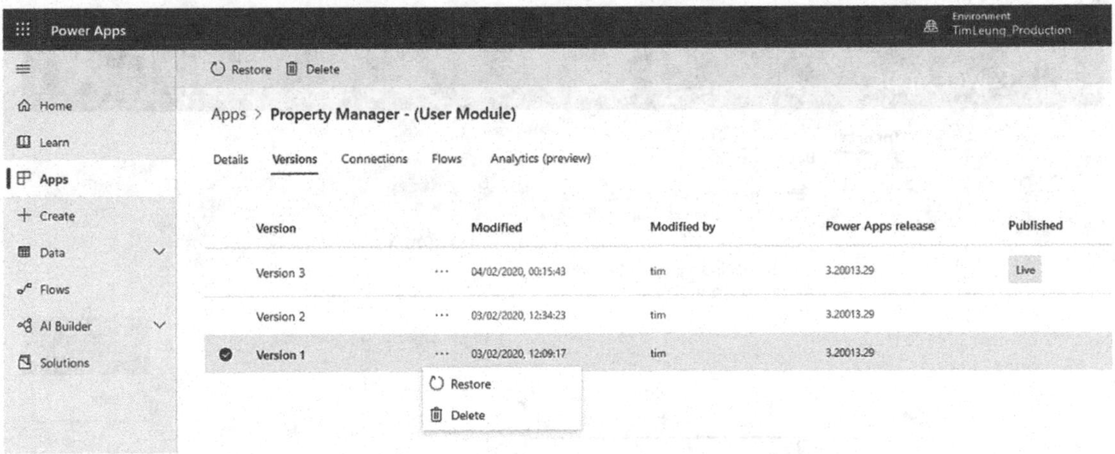

Figure 4-17. *Maintaining app versions*

Through the context menu, we can click the restore button to restore an app to a previous version. In the example shown in Figure 4-17, let's suppose we want to restore the app to version 1. When we click the restore option for version 1, the system will create version 4 of the app and restore version 1 into version 4. This enables us to restore our app back to version 2 or 3, if we later change our mind.

Before restoring an app, we should consider any data schema changes that might have occurred following the version that we want to restore. If we renamed or removed data columns, it's important to revert those changes manually prior to restoring an app.

Another feature on this page is the option to delete copies of an app from the version history. We can use this feature to declutter this view and to remove any app versions that we no longer want to retain.

An important note about the restoration feature is that we can only restore app versions that were created within the last six months.

Running with Foreign Languages

In the final part of this chapter, we'll examine how apps behave in languages other than English. This is important because it may be necessary for us to share apps with users in different countries, particularly in the case of larger global organizations.

The language that Power Apps uses in the app designer depends on the language setting of the web browser. Figure 4-18 shows the appearance of the app designer with the language of the browser set to Spanish. As we can see, all menu items and dialogs appear in Spanish.

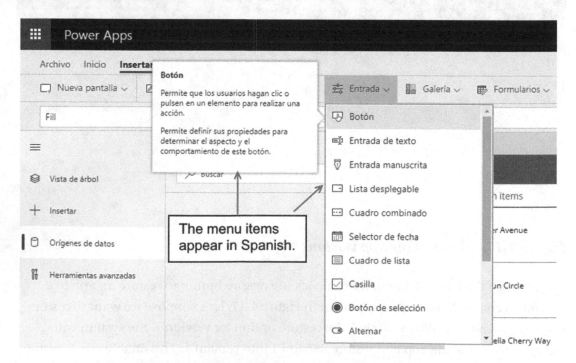

Figure 4-18. *Power Apps running in Spanish*

Many of the European languages, including French, Spanish, and German, are interesting because these locales use the comma character as a decimal point separator. To allow us to use decimal values as arguments in calls to functions, the formula syntax changes for these languages. In places where we use a comma, we would use a semicolon instead. Where we would use a semicolon in English to terminate a function, we would use a double semicolon instead.

The language of the Maker Portal depends on the language setting, which we can set through the settings menu as shown in Figure 4-19.

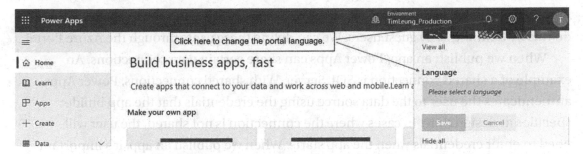

Figure 4-19. *Changing the language of the Maker Portal*

Caution   Compared to English, most other European languages use the **;** character in formulas instead of the **,** character. Where we use the ; symbol in English, the European equivalent is ;; (i.e., a double semicolon).

Summary

In this chapter, we learned how to publish and share apps with end users and how to organize apps and resources using environments.

Each app can have one or more owners. Owners have full control of an app, including the ability to modify or delete the app. Users can run an app, but not make any modifications to the app. We can specify the owners and users of an app though the File ➤ Share menu of the app designer.

To make our app changes visible to users, it's necessary to publish the app. Without publishing the app, any changes that we save will only be visible to co-owners.

If we need to share multiple apps with a set of users, we can make this process more maintainable by creating groups of users and assigning the group as an owner or a user of an app.

The Office 365 admin center is where we create new user logins. Only AAD security groups and Office 365 groups are compatible with Power Apps. The benefit of Office 365 groups is that they provide additional collaboration features, such as a group mailbox and a SharePoint site. With Office 365 groups, it's necessary to security enable the group first before we can use it with Power Apps. We do this by running a PowerShell script. With both security and Office 365 groups, we define and administer these through the Azure Portal. If we want to share an app with users outside of our organization, we can do this by defining AAD guest users. We can define these users through the Azure Portal.

When we publish an app, Power Apps can share certain data connections. An example of a shared connection is SQL Server. With shared connections, Power Apps authenticates the user to the data source using the credentials that the app builder specifies at design time. In cases where the connection is not shared, the user will need to enter credentials when the app starts. When we publish an app, it's important to visit the Data ➤ Connections section of the Maker Portal and to share any shared connections with the end users.

Power Apps maintains a version history of the changes that we make to an app. We can restore previous versions through the Maker Portal. This feature enables us to roll back mistakes or unwanted changes to an app.

By using environments, we can compartmentalize apps and resources. This is useful in cases where we want to group apps based on teams or departments. Environments are hosted in a geographic location. We can optimize performance by choosing a region that's closest to our users. A useful type of environment is the sandbox environment. We can restore environment backups into a sandbox environment, and Power Apps also provides a feature that allows us to copy a production environment into a sandbox environment. We can use this feature to test our changes before publishing them to a production environment.

To move apps between environments or organizations, Power Apps offers a packaging feature that enables us to export and import apps.

Finally, Power Apps provides support for multiple languages. The language of the app designer matches the language settings of our web browser. If we choose to use a language that uses a comma as the decimal point separator (e.g., French, German, Spanish), we will need to use the semicolon character in places where we would usually use a comma in English while writing formulas.

CHAPTER 5

Using Formulas

Power Apps is similar to Excel because it relies on formulas to carry out tasks. Formulas are the lifeblood of an app because they provide the capability to add logic, calculations, and functionality to an app.

This chapter introduces how to write formulas to help enhance the functionality of our apps. The topics include functions that operate against data types such as text, numbers, and dates. We also cover the use of variables, conditional operators, and formulas for app navigation.

This chapter provides tables of formulas that serve as a reference guide for our day-to-day use of Power Apps. This chapter also demonstrates some key techniques that we can incorporate into our apps, including

- How to use variables to make property assignments. This is important because it enables us, for example, to add a button that sets the text value of a label or textbox.

- How to work with text, number, and date values. We'll cover the use of text manipulation functions and pattern matching techniques. These techniques help us parse semi-structured input data and can help validate details such as social security numbers, postal codes, phone numbers, and more. We'll also cover mathematical tasks, including date arithmetic and trigonometric functions.

- How to develop navigation features. We'll discover how to launch screens depending on conditions and how to show a specified record at start-up. We'll find out how to launch websites, compose emails, and send SMS messages.

103

© Tim Leung 2021
T. Leung, *Beginning Power Apps*, https://doi.org/10.1007/978-1-4842-6683-0_5

Writing Formulas

We'll begin by exploring the basics of how to write formulas. Let's look at the formula that's associated with the edit icon from the details screen in an auto-generated app (Figure 5-1). This formula places the edit form on the edit screen into edit mode and navigates the user to the edit screen.

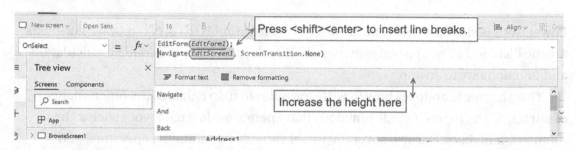

Figure 5-1. *Formula bar*

Let's use this formula to examine the basic characteristics of how formulas work. Formulas can include calls to several functions, and each function is separated by a semicolon. Each function executes synchronously. That is, Power Apps will complete the execution of a single command before it moves onto the next command.

The formula bar provides several helpful features (Figure 5-1). To make it easier to read long formulas, we can use the mouse to extend the height of the formula bar. The "Format text" button adds line breaks and indentation between calls to functions. This makes it easier to read formulas, particularly when we nest calls to functions. To manually tidy up a formula, we can also insert line breaks by typing <shift><enter>.

The formula bar also includes code coloration and offers help through IntelliSense. IntelliSense provides in-line help and auto-completion and identifies the arguments that a function expects.

The standard Windows shortcuts work in the formula bar. We can use <ctrl><c> to copy formulas into the Windows clipboard and <ctrl><v> to paste the text from the clipboard. For very long formulas, it can be more readable to use these shortcuts to copy the content into Microsoft Notepad.

A very useful feature is that the formula bar allows us to inspect the data type and data values of objects (Figure 5-2). This feature can be very useful for debugging our apps.

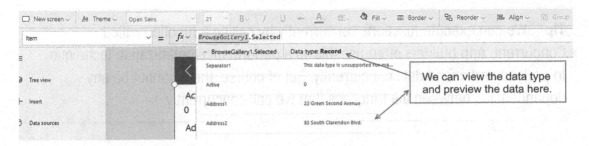

Figure 5-2. *Using the formula bar to preview data values*

To help find the function we need, we can use the function panel (Figure 5-3). This groups all the functions into areas of functionality and provides help and usage instructions for each function.

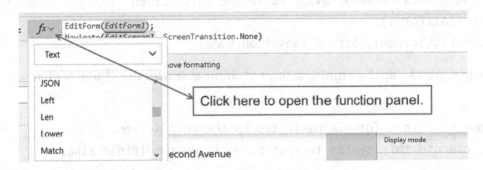

Figure 5-3. *Using the function tool*

With formulas, there are two important points to be aware of. The first is that all function names and objects are case sensitive.

The second is that certain languages use the comma symbol as the decimal point separation character. If we were to use a non-English computer that follows this convention, we would need to use a semicolon in places where we would normally use a comma. Because of this, we would need to use two semicolons to separate the commands in a formula. I'll mention this concept again in a few other places to clarify the syntax for non-English readers. Because the majority of articles and code samples on the Web are specified in English, non-English users can experience errors when they follow such examples.

Tip   We can execute functions concurrently by calling a function called Concurrent. App builders often use this as a performance optimization technique to preload and cache data concurrently. But of course, there cannot be any dependencies between the functions that we call concurrently.

Adding Comments

To make our apps more maintainable and to help other app builders, we can add comments to formulas. There are two ways to carry out this task. First, we can prefix individual lines of comments with the // character like so:

```
//Comment - this formula navigates to the edit screen
EditForm(EditForm1);
Navigate(EditScreen1, ScreenTransition.None)
```

Second, we can enclose multiple lines of comments with the /* and */ characters like so:

```
/*  Comment - this formula navigates to the edit screen.
    We can use this syntax to span comments over multiple lines.
*/
EditForm(EditForm1);
Navigate(EditScreen1, ScreenTransition.None)
```

Working with Variables

Variables are a core component of all programming languages. They help us build functionality by storing working copies of data. With Power Apps, variables are very important because they enable us to set property values. You'll understand what this means exactly by the end of this section.

Variables have a *scope*. This defines the boundary from which we can access a variable. We can create variables that are accessible from individual screens only or variables that are accessible throughout an app.

Unlike other systems, Power Apps is relaxed in the way that it deals with variables. We don't need to declare variables beforehand, nor do we need to specify the data type of a variable.

Setting Screen Variables

Screen-level variables are called *context variables*. This name derives from the fact that we can access these variables only within the context of a screen.

To give an example, here's how to add a variable that stores a screen-level user preference. This variable would control whether to show only active records in a gallery. The syntax to define a context variable looks like this:

```
UpdateContext({ ShowActiveOnly: true })
```

The function `UpdateContext` sets the value of a variable. Here, this function sets the value of a context variable called `ShowActiveOnly` to `true`. Readers with experience of using other programming languages might be tempted to use syntax that looks like this:

```
ShowActiveOnly = true
```

With Power Apps, this syntax is not valid. The `UpdateContext` function is the only way to set the value of a context variable.

When the `UpdateContext` function runs for the first time, it creates the `ShowActiveOnly` variable if it doesn't exist. A very interesting and useful characteristic is that context variables can store more than just simple numbers and strings. We can store records and tables in context variables, and this can be very powerful.

Once we run our app and call the `UpdateContext` function, the variable will appear in the variables section of the app (Figure 5-4). This screen is very helpful because it summarizes all the places that set or retrieve the variable.

From within our screen, we can now refer to the `ShowActiveOnly` variable by name in formulas. In this scenario, we can use the variable to help filter the items of a gallery control.

Figure 5-4. *Viewing the variables in an application (File ➤ Variables menu)*

> **Caution**   Variable names are case sensitive. Because there's no need to declare variables beforehand, it can be easy to introduce bugs by setting a variable that differs just by case. Therefore, it can be a good practice to define and set up our variables in a single place to help make our apps more maintainable.

If we attempt to retrieve a variable before it is set, what value will the variable return? In most cases (including string, date, and numeric variables), the variable returns a null or a blank value. With Boolean variables such as the one in this example, the variable will return false if it is not set.

Example of Context Variables

To better understand the use of context variables, let's examine the sort button on a browse screen (Figure 5-5).

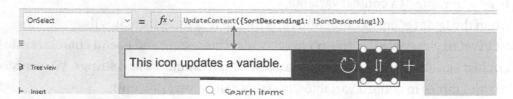

Figure 5-5.   *The sort button on a browse screen updates a variable*

The purpose of this button is to toggle the sort order of the data. The `OnSelect` action of this button calls the following function:

```
UpdateContext({SortDescending1: !SortDescending1})
```

This code sets the value of the SortDescending1 variable to the logical negative of the current value. The initial state of the SortDescending1 variable is false. The ! operator returns true if its argument is false and returns false if its argument is true. Therefore, the effect of this code is to toggle the value of the SortDescending1 variable.

Now that we see how the SortDescending1 variable is set, how exactly does the screen use this variable? The Items property of the gallery control refers to the SortDescending1 variable (Figure 5-6).

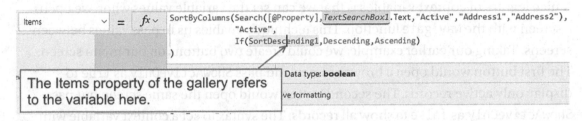

Figure 5-6. *The Items property of the gallery control*

As this screenshot shows, a function called SortByColumns populates the items of the gallery control. This function expects three arguments – a data source, the column to sort by, and the sort direction.

The data source for the SortByColumns function is the result of a function called Search. This function accepts a data source, a search term, and the columns to match against. The next argument to the SortByColumns function defines the column to sort by – address, in this example. The final argument specifies the sort direction. This can be one of two values – Descending or Ascending.

The sort direction argument refers to the function called If. This function enables us to run commands conditionally. The syntax of the If function is

```
If (logical test,
    action(s) to run if true,
    action(s) to run if false
)
```

In this example, the If function checks the value of the SortDescending1 variable. If the value is true, it returns the result Descending. Otherwise, it returns the result Ascending.

To summarize this feature, the sort icon does not change the sort order of the items in the gallery directly. Instead, it changes the value of a variable. The gallery control responds to this change as soon as it happens and updates the sort sequence of the items in the gallery. The reason for this is because the Items property of the gallery refers to the variable.

Note   Context variables and the If function are crucial building blocks. Even the simplest apps will rely heavily on these structures, and we see evidence of this in all the Microsoft sample apps.

Passing Values to Screens

A nice feature of context variables is that we can set the variable values when we open a screen with the Navigate function. This technique enables us to pass values between screens. Taking our earlier example, we could create two buttons on our menu screen. The first button would open a browse screen and pass ShowActiveOnly as true to display only active records. The second button would open the same screen but pass ShowActiveOnly as false to show all records. The syntax to set a context variable with the Navigate function looks like this:

```
Navigate(BrowseScreen1, ScreenTransition.Fade, {ShowActiveOnly:true})
```

With this example, the Navigate function opens a screen called BrowseScreen1 and sets the value of the ShowActiveOnly context variable to true.

When we build apps with screen navigation and context variables, there's an important piece of behavior to be aware of. When Power Apps switches the currently visible screen, it doesn't completely close the existing screen. Instead, the existing screen becomes invisible and remains active in the background. If a user opens other screens and returns to a screen that was previously open, the screen will retain the context variable values that were previously set. This can result in some unexpected behavior and is something to be aware of. To help mitigate these types of problems, there is a screen property called OnHidden. The formula we add here runs whenever the screen becomes invisible, and we can add a formula here to clear any relevant context variables.

Setting Property Values from Code

What we're about to cover here is a very important concept, perhaps the most important concept in this book. With Power Apps, we can't use formulas to assign property values from other objects. To explain this in more detail, let's build a simple *Hello World* program – a program that teaches programmers the very basics of a language by outputting the text "Hello World."

To build this feature, we'll create a screen and add two controls: a label called `LabelHello` and a button called `ButtonSayHello`. The aim of this program is to show the text "Hello World" in the label when a user clicks the button. Let's attempt to build this feature by setting the `OnSelect` property of the button to the following formula:

```
LabelHello.Text = "Hello World"
```

As Figure 5-7 shows, this code looks OK. The designer doesn't underline the formula with a squiggly red line, and it doesn't show a warning icon next to the control. What do you think will happen when we click the button? Will the text "Hello Word" appear in the label?

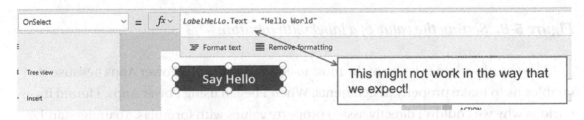

Figure 5-7. Screen with a button and label

The answer to this question is no! When we run this screen and click the button, nothing happens. The reason for this is that we cannot assign property values in this way. This syntax is not valid.

So how do we overcome this problem? The answer is to use variables. To demonstrate, we'll enhance our example slightly so that label shows "Hello World" and the current date and time when the user clicks the button. To build this feature, we add the following formula to the `OnSelect` property of the button:

```
UpdateContext({locLabelText: "Hello World " & Now()})
```

We then set the Text property of the label to the name of this variable, `locLabelText`. Figure 5-8 illustrates how this appears in the designer.

When we click the button at runtime, the label will show the current date and time. If we click the button again, the label will update to show the later time. This highlights an important principle, which is whenever a property of a control references a variable, the control will respond every time the value of the variable changes.

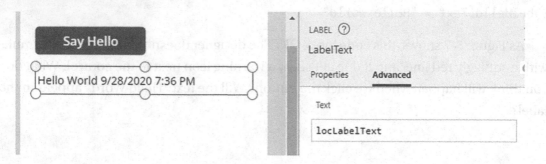

Figure 5-8. *Setting the value of a label with a button*

The use of variables is one of the most useful techniques in Power Apps because it enables us to make property assignments. When I began using Power Apps, I found it curious why we couldn't directly assign property values with formulas. To understand why Power Apps behaves like this, I realized that Excel worked in this way, and it then made sense that Power Apps should behave in the same way. To illustrate this, in Excel, we can't write a formula in the A2 cell to set the value of the A1 cell using the type of formula that's shown in Figure 5-9.

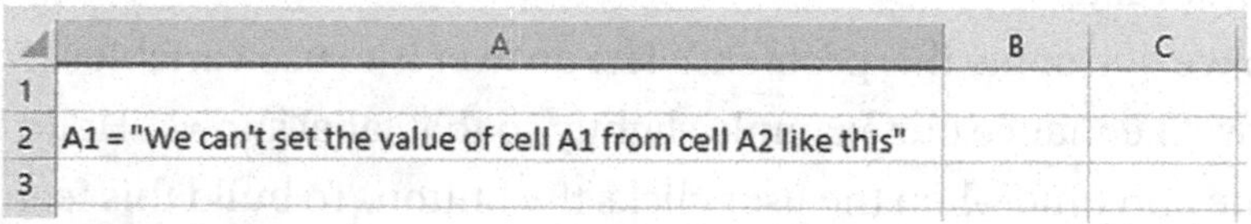

	A	B	C
1			
2	A1 = "We can't set the value of cell A1 from cell A2 like this"		
3			

Figure 5-9. *In Excel, we can't assign cell values from other cells*

Setting Global Variables

In addition to context variables, we can store values in global variables. The main difference between a global variable and a context variable is that we can access global variables throughout an app, rather than just on the screen where we define the variable. To give an example, we could add a settings screen to our app and use global variables to store user preferences.

In addition to simple strings and numbers, we can store records, tables, and object references in global variables. Compared to context variables, the syntax to set a variable value is much easier. Here's how to define a global variable called `PreferredMeasurement` and to set the value to 2:

```
Set(PreferredMeasurement, 2)
```

Unlike the `UpdateContext` function, there's no need to enclose the variable name and value within curly brackets. Once we define a global variable, we can refer to it by name in formulas.

The name of a global variable cannot match the name of an existing data source or collection. However, it can share the same name as a context variable on a screen. To clarify how to distinguish between variables that are named identically, let's suppose that we declare a context variable on the same screen using the following syntax:

```
UpdateContext({PreferredMeasurement:5})
```

In this scenario, `PreferredMeasurement` will refer to the context variable. To refer to the global variable with the same name, we would use the syntax `[@PreferredMeasurement]`.

A final point is that in cases where we set a global variable in multiple places, we must always assign values with matching data types. The designer will show a warning if we attempt to assign a value to a global variable that doesn't match the data type of a value that we assigned elsewhere.

In these cases, we can fix the problem by passing the value that we want to store through a data type conversion function such as `Value` or `Text`. This ensures that we consistently store values of the same type in the global variable. The `Value` function converts an input value to a number, whereas the `Text` function converts an input value to text.

Note   The Power Apps documentation provides a naming convention guide. It recommends that we prefix context variables with `loc` and global variables with `var`. By adopting this convention, we can avoid situations where we accidently provide the same name for a context and global variable.

Working with Basic Data Types

In this next section of the chapter, we'll examine the basic data types in Power Apps, which include text, numbers, and dates. We'll look at functions that manipulate and operate against these data types. Let's begin by exploring how to work with text values.

Tip   For further reading, the following link contains a full list of all supported data types:

`https://docs.microsoft.com/en-us/powerapps/maker/canvas-apps/`
`functions/data-types`

Working with Text

A fundamental part of building any app will involve working with text data (also known as string data). The elementary things to know about working with text are

- Defining strings – To specify a piece of text in a formula, the text must be enclosed inside double quotes. To include a double quote within a string, we would use a double set of double quotes instead.

- New lines – To introduce a new line into a string, type <Shift><Enter> into the formula bar. Alternatively, we can use the Char function. Char(10) represents a carriage return, and Char(13) represents a line feed.

- String concatenation – To combine strings, use the & operator.

- Char function – We can call this function to obtain a character by ASCII code.

- Text function – Use this to convert numbers, dates, and other data types to text.

To highlight some of these techniques, Figure 5-10 shows a formula that sets the text of a label. This formula illustrates the basic concepts that are described here.

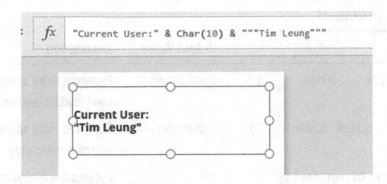

fx `"Current User:" & Char(10) & """Tim Leung"""`

Current User:
"Tim Leung"

Figure 5-10. *Using the Char function and escaping double quote characters*

Tip   To display richly formatted text on a screen, we can use the HTML text control rather than the label control.

Text Manipulation Functions

There are many useful functions that can extract parts of an input string. The examples in Table 5-1 demonstrate how to call these functions against an input string.

Table 5-1. *Text manipulation functions*

Function	Output Value	Description
Left("The quick brown fox",3)	The	Returns the first three characters from the left of the input string.
Right("The quick brown fox",3)	fox	Returns the first three characters from the right of the input string.
Mid("The quick brown fox",11,5)	brown	Returns five characters, starting from character 11 of the input string.
Mid("The quick brown fox",20,5)		Returns an empty string if the start position exceeds the length of the input string.

(*continued*)

Table 5-1. (*continued*)

Function	Output Value	Description
Trim(" quick brown ")	quick brown	Removes extra spaces from the start, middle, and end of a string.
TrimEnds(" quick brown ")	quick brown	Removes extra spaces from the end of a string only.
Len("The quick brown fox")	19	Returns the length of the input string.
Left("red2", Len("red2") -1)	red	We can combine these functions to remove the final character from a string.

The final example in Table 5-1 shows how to remove the last character from an input string. Given an input value, we can call the Left function to return the number of characters that matches the length of the input string, minus one. A practical example of where this pattern comes in useful is in situations where we want to remove trailing commas from a CSV input string.

This example highlights how powerful it can be when we chain functions together. Experienced app builders understand the patterns of chaining operators together to accomplish a task, and we'll see a few more examples as this chapter progresses.

A useful tip is that with all these functions, we can supply a single-column table, as opposed to a single input value. The ability to pass a single-column table to a function can be very powerful. When app builders face the challenge of needing to manipulate multiple rows from a table, they often discover a function called ForAll and attempt to process the rows one by one.

Because most text functions accept single-column tables, we can carry out this task in one swoop, with just a single call to a function. Later in this chapter (splitting text to rows), we'll see an example of how to use this technique.

Modifying the Casing of Sentences

To modify the case of an input string, there are three functions we can call as shown in Table 5-2.

Table 5-2. *Text casing functions*

Function	Output Value	Description
Lower("Brown FOX")	brown fox	Converts every input character to lowercase.
Upper("brown fox")	BROWN FOX	Converts every input character to uppercase.
Proper("brown fox")	Brown Fox	Converts the first character in each word to uppercase and the remaining characters to lowercase.

Why are these functions useful? One reason is that string comparisons in Power Apps are case sensitive. For instance, the following statement resolves to false:

"tim@myDomain.com" = "TIM@myDomain.com"

By applying the lower or upper function to both sides of the comparison, we can carry out case-insensitive matches.

This example illustrates a problem that typically occurs when app builders attempt to search a data source for records with matching email addresses. If there are fewer results than we expect, one of the first steps is to check the casing of our data.

The Proper function is useful because it offers a great way to clean up the names and addresses from data input screens. On mobile devices, users often enter details all in lowercase because of the awkwardness of using a soft keyboard.

Again, these functions can operate against a single-column table, in addition to operating against a single input value.

Replacing Text

Power Apps provides two basic functions to carry out text substitutions – the Replace and the Substitute functions.

The Replace function carries out a single text replacement, based on a start position and length. The Substitute function replaces every instance of an "old text" value with a "new text" value. The examples in Table 5-3 demonstrate how to call these functions.

Table 5-3. *Text substitution functions*

Function	Output Value	Description
Replace("The quick brown fox", 11, 5, "red")	The quick red fox	Starting from character 11 of the input string, replace the next five characters with the replacement string, red.
Replace("The quick brown fox", 30, 5, "red")	The quick brown fox red	If the start character (30) exceeds the length of the input string, the Replace function appends the replacement string to the end of the input string.
Substitute("The fox and the dog", "the", "a")	The fox and a dog	This substitutes each instance of the word "the" from the input string with the substitution word "a." Note that this function is case sensitive.
Substitute("A fox, the dog, and the cat", "the", "a", 2)	A fox, the dog, and a cat	If there are multiple instances of the search text, we can specify which instance to replace.

I often see app builders use these functions to strip HTML tags for the purpose of screen display. It can be painful to watch users build formulas that consist of multiple nested replace statements to account for every possible start tag and end tag character.

In practice, there are two simple ways to simplify this task. The first is to call the PlainText function, as shown in Table 5-4. This function converts HTML or XML to plain text. The second is to use an HTML text control rather than a label control. This control handles HTML without needing to carry out any substitutions.

Another scenario where I see app builders call the Substitute function unnecessarily is while working with decimal values. If we choose to store decimal values in a SharePoint or database text column, this can result in the situation where some of the records use the period character as the decimal point separator and other records use the comma symbol. This happens when apps are used across international boundaries, with some users using a language that uses a period as the decimal point separator and others a comma. In these situations, it's necessary to call the Substitute function to help normalize the decimal point character. We can avoid this by always choosing to store decimal values in fields that are designed for decimal values.

Table 5-4. Web-related functions

Function	Return Value
`PlainText("<div><b>Hello</b></div>")`	Hello
`EncodeURL("AT&T store")`	AT%26T%20store

Another useful function is the `EncodeURL` function. This function enables us to escape any special characters from strings that we want to convert for use in a hyperlink. In the preceding example, we can use `EncodeURL` to help build a hyperlink that searches Google Maps for AT&T stores. The URL would look like this:

`https://www.google.com/maps/search/AT%26T%20Store`

In this example, it's necessary to encode the search term because the & symbol is a special character that separates the request parameters in a web address.

Searching Within Strings

We can identify the existence of words or phrases from an input string using the functions shown in Table 5-5. The `Find` function identifies the character position of a search phrase. This is useful because we can use the result in conjunction with other functions to extract specific parts of an input string, as shown in the last example in Table 5-5.

Table 5-5. Search functions

Function	Return Value	Description
`Find("the", "The fox, the cat, the rat")`	10	Returns the character position of the first occurrence of the search text. Find is case sensitive. It returns an empty string if the search text is not found.
`Find("the", "The fox, the cat, the rat", 12)`	19	Returns the character position of the first occurrence of the search text, starting from character 12 (inclusive).
`StartsWith("Mr Fox", "mr")`	true	This returns true if the input string starts with the search string. It is case insensitive.

(continued)

Table 5-5. (*continued*)

Function	Return Value	Description
EndsWith("sales.pdf", ".PDF")	true	EndsWith returns true if the input string ends with the search string. It is case insensitive.
Mid("sales.pdf" Find(".", "sales.pdf"), 3)	pdf	This combines the Mid and Find functions to extract the three characters that immediately follow the period character.

Matching String Patterns

Power Apps provides functions that can test whether an input string matches a defined pattern. There are many business scenarios that require pattern matching, but one of the most useful is input validation. We can call these functions to verify if the user entered an email address, telephone number, or other pieces of data in the correct format.

The basic function is called IsMatch. This function accepts two arguments – an input value and a pattern. The function returns true if the input value matches the pattern and false if it doesn't.

To define the pattern, Power Apps provides building blocks of match characters which are shown here:

Any, Comma, Digit, Email, Hyphen, LeftParen, Letter, MultipleDigits, MultipleLetters, MultipleNonSpaces, MultipleSpaces, NonSpace, OptionalDigits, OptionalLetters, OptionalNonSpaces, OptionalSpaces, Period, RightParen, Space

We can combine these with the & symbol (the string concatenation character) to build a complete pattern. Table 5-6 shows some examples of how to call the IsMatch function.

Table 5-6. *IsMatch function*

Function	Description
IsMatch("tim@domain.com", Email)	This returns true if the input value matches the inbuilt email pattern.

IsMatch("123-45-7890",
      Digit & Digit & Digit & Hyphen &
      Digit & Digit & Hyphen &
      Digit & Digit & Digit & Digit)
	This pattern matches a US social security number. We construct our pattern by combining the digit and hyphen match characters.

IsMatch("Pls contact client urgently.",
      "urgent",
      Contains & IgnoreCase)
	We can supply a third argument to specify the match option. This example demonstrates how to return a case-insensitive "contains" search. This example returns true.

The final example demonstrates how the `IsMatch` function accepts an optional third argument that defines which section of the input text we want to match against. We can provide one of the options listed in the following, or we can combine multiple options with the & symbol:

`BeginsWith, Complete, Contains, EndsWith, IgnoreCase, Multiline`

Although this feature provides us with powerful search capabilities, it's useful not to overlook the simple functions that carry out the same tasks, such as the `StartsWith` or the `EndsWith` function.

Also, I occasionally see app builders use pattern matching techniques to validate decimal input values. They test the existence of a period symbol to validate the entry of decimal places. It's useful to remember that certain cultures use the comma symbol to denote a decimal place. To build a formula that is compatible across multiple regions, we can call the `IsNumeric` function to check numeric input.

Caution   If we use string matching techniques to validate decimal values, it's useful to remember that depending on the region, the decimal point separator can be a comma, rather than a period.

Matching with Regular Expressions

To match input values against more sophisticated patterns, we can build custom regular expressions. A regular expression is an industry standard way to define a search pattern. Through regular expressions, we can carry out wildcard-type searches, but in a much more powerful way.

The regular expression language isn't easy to comprehend. Fortunately, there are plenty of websites on this topic, and there are many websites that contain listings and libraries of expressions (e.g., `www.regexlib.com`). Through these websites, we can find expressions to cater for most imaginable scenarios – for example, patterns to match HTML color codes, credit card numbers, vehicle registration numbers, and more. When faced with a pattern matching task, the technique I recommend is to look up a pattern on the Web and to then adapt and test it to suit our needs.

To demonstrate this technique, let's imagine that we want to validate postal codes. The first step is to find an expression, and Figure 5-11 shows one of the search results from `www.regexlib.com`.

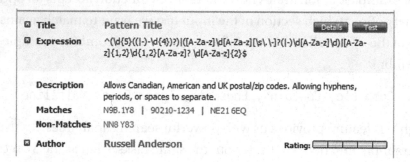

Figure 5-11. *Use the Web to find regular expressions*

Next, we can copy the expression and pass it to the `IsMatch` function (Figure 5-12). This example contains a label with the text "Warning – Postcode not in correct format!" The formula in the Visible property of this label calls the `IsMatch` function to return whether the postcode in the text input control matches the format.

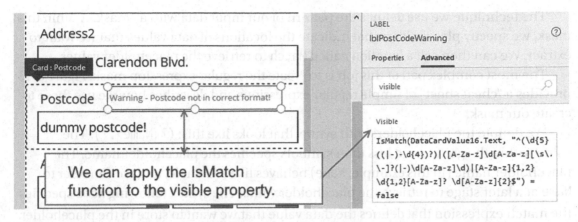

Figure 5-12. *Using the IsMatch function to control the visibility of a validation warning label*

An interesting piece of behavior is that the match characters that we applied earlier with the IsMatch function are regular expressions. To see the regular expression, we can type the match character (e.g., Match.Email) into the Text property of a label to reveal the expression.

Extracting Text with Regular Expressions

Regular expressions are very powerful. We can use them not only to check if an input value matches a pattern, but we can also use regular expressions to extract sections from an input string.

In business situations, we sometimes need to process data where we have no control over the layout or formatting. This type of data could come from web services, suppliers, or other third parties and could include information such as stock quotes, weather data, or product details.

To give an example, let's suppose we receive the details of a room from a web service in the following format:

```
Bedroom 4.27m (14'0) x 3m (9'10)
```

Our task is to extract the width and length values (i.e., 4.27 and 3) so that we can calculate the floor area, which would enable us to provide a valuation.

We could solve this problem by building a formula that includes nested calls to the Mid and Find functions. This type of logic can be complex, so an alternative is to use a regular expression.

The technique we use defines the pattern of our input data with a "mask." Within this mask, we specify placeholders that indicate the locations of data values that we want to extract. We can then call a function called Match to retrieve the placeholder values.

The most complex part of this job is to create the regular expression mask. Figure 5-13 provides a "cheat sheet" of simple regular expressions and describes how we use these to create our mask.

We denote the placeholders with syntax that looks like this: (?<Name>.*). The value within the greater and less than symbols specifies the placeholder name. The placeholder name (in this example, Name) behaves like a variable, and we can refer to Name at a later stage to retrieve the placeholder value. The syntax following Name specifies the match expression that defines the data value that we want to store in the placeholder.

Regular Expression Cheat Sheet.

Match exact characters (abc)	abc	Any Whitespace	\s	Zero or more repetitions	*
Match exact characters (123)	123	Any Non-whitespace character	\S	One or more repetitions	+
Any Digit	\d	Any Alphanumeric character	\w	Optional character	?
Any Non-digit character	\D	Any Non-alphanumeric character	\W		
Any Character	.	Period	\.		
Only a, b, or c	[abc]	Matches abc or def	(abc|def)		
Not a, b, nor c	[^abc]	m Repetitions	{m}		
Characters a to z	[a-z]	m to n Repetitions	{m,n}		
Numbers 0 to 9	[0-9]				

1. Building a 'mask expression':

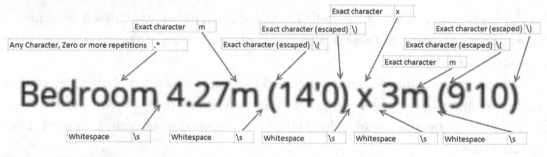

2. Building a 'capture group' expression:

Capture group start (?
Capture group name <widthM>
Any Character, Zero or more repetitions .*
Capture group end)

4.27

3. The complete expression:

.*\s(?<widthM>.*)m\s\((?<widthF>.*)\)\sx\s(?<lengthM>.*)m\s\((?<lengthF>.*)\)

Figure 5-13. *How to build our mask expression*

Once we've worked out our "mask" expression, we can use it with the Match function. This function accepts two arguments – the input data value and the expression. As shown in Figure 5-14, we can now access our placeholder values in code.

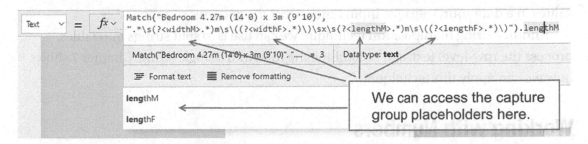

Figure 5-14. How to access placeholder values in code

Stripping Characters with Regular Expressions

By calling the Match function, we can strip certain characters from an input string. This technique can be useful when we want to extract parts of codes, such as order numbers or batch codes. Another use case scenario is if we want to capture data that might be used to create a file or folder name and we want to strip all invalid file characters. The examples in Table 5-7 demonstrate the use of this technique.

Table 5-7. Using regular expressions to strip characters

Function	Result	Description
Match ("INV 0989873", "[^0-9]+").FullMatch	INV	This removes all numbers by matching characters that fall outside of the range 0–9.
Match ("INV 0989873", "[0-9]+").FullMatch	0989873	This removes all non-numeric characters by matching characters that fall inside of the range 0–9.
Match ("INV\098~9873", "^[a-zA-Z0-9]+").FullMatch	INV 0989873	This removes all punctuation symbols by substituting all characters outside the ranges of a–z, A–Z, and 0–9 with an empty string.

A limitation with the Match function is that the regular expression patterns must be statically defined. This means that we can't generate match patterns based on a variable or an input value that the user supplies. To give a practical example, this limitation would prevent us from using the Match function to build a search feature that matches values in a data source against input criteria that the end user supplies.

Another string manipulation technique we can use is to split strings into tables, process the row-level text, and recombine the rows into a single string. Chapter 7 shows how we can apply this technique.

Working with Numbers

Power Apps provides a wide range of mathematical functions, and in this section, we'll look at how to work with numbers. Starting with the basics, Power Apps provides basic arithmetic operators that include add (+), subtract (-), multiply (*), and divide (/).

To demonstrate a simple mathematical task, here's a simple screen that converts square meters to square feet. This screen contains a text input control that accepts a value in square meters. When the user enters a value, the result in square feet will appear instantly in a label. Figure 5-15 illustrates this screen. The name of the text input control is TextInputMeters, and the name of the label that displays the result is LabelResult.

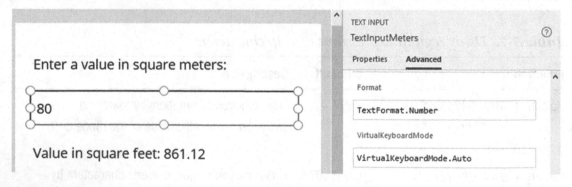

Figure 5-15. *An example screen to convert square meters to square feet*

To implement this functionality, set the Text property of LabelResult to the following formula:

```
"Value in square feet: " & Value(TextInputMeters.Text) * 10.764
```

This formula calculates the value in square feet by multiplying the input value by 10.764. The formula prefixes this result with the text "Value in square feet:"

This example highlights two useful points about using user input for calculations. The first is the use of the Value function. The data we retrieve from the text input control is of type text. It's not possible to perform mathematical operations on text data, so we must convert the input data to the numeric representation. This is what the Value function does.

The second point is that with the text input control, we can set the Format property to TextFormat.Number. This prevents users from entering non-numeric figures by setting the control to accept only numbers.

Formatting Numbers

A common requirement is to format numbers in a certain way. We can accomplish this by calling the Text function. This function accepts two arguments – a numeric input value and a format string. Table 5-8 provides some examples of how to call this function. Notice how the text formatting implicitly rounds numbers depending on the format string.

Table 5-8. Formatting numbers (using English formatting characters)

Function	Output Value
Text(60934.2, "#,#.000")	60,934.200
Text(60934.2, "#,#.###")	60,934.2
Text(22934.23624, "#.00")	22934.24
Text(22934.83324, "#")	22935
Text(60934.2, "#,#.###")	60,934.2
Text(60934.2, "$#,#.00")	$60,934.20
Text(Value("85934.20000"), "#,#.00")	85934.20
Text(60934.20, "[$-en-US]#,#.00", "fr-FR")	60 934,20

To build a format string, there are two principal placeholder characters that we use: # and 0. The # character denotes an optional placeholder. If the input value contains a number that maps to the position where the # character appears, the output will include the value. If not, nothing will appear.

The 0 character denotes a static placeholder and enables us to display preceding or trailing zeros. The output will display the value in the position where the 0 character appears or display 0 if nothing maps to the position where the 0 character appears. Notice that we can also use the comma symbol to display thousand value separators.

In situations where we want a number to always display in a certain format, irrespective of the locale of the end user, we can pass an optional third argument to the Text function that specifies the display region. Here's the example of this syntax:

```
Text(60934.20, "[$-en-US]#,#.00", "fr-FR")
```

To clarify how this works, the second argument specifies a region for the format specification, and the third argument defines the output region. In this example, we are asking the Text function to return the French equivalent of the US format string "#,#.00." As the result shows, the function produces a result with a space character as the thousand separator and a comma as the decimal point separator.

At first, this syntax can seem confusing. It's easy to mix up the language specifiers for the second and third arguments, and it might not be clear why we need to specify the source language. The reason why it's necessary to specify the source language is to facilitate the ability for users in multiple regions to open and to run apps. Figure 5-16 illustrates what happens when a user opens an app that was authored in a different locale. It shows how the language codes help to provide a common output format across different locales.

Step 1 – Creating an App

- Tim works in France.
- His app performs a common pricing calculation: Unit price * Quantity * Tax.
- This result won't be very readable so he wants to format the output to 2 decimal places, with 1000-unit separation characters.
- To cater for US users, he wants the output to be in US format.

The input values are in French format, with commas as decimal separators.

The formula is expressed in French format, with semi-colons as parameter separators.

The format string is expressed in French dialect.

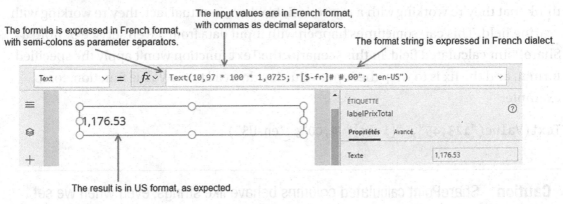

The result is in US format, as expected.

Step 2 – Second user edits App

- Sally works in the US.
- She opens and runs Tim's app.

The designer converts the Input into English format, with periods as decimal separators.

The designer converts the formula to English format, with commas as parameter separators.

The original format string remains the same.

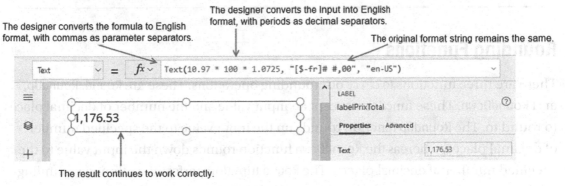

The result continues to work correctly.

This display works globally because the source format includes the language code.

Figure 5-16. *The purpose of language codes*

One final tip is that on occasions, app builders attempt to format a number and find that it doesn't work. What could be the cause of this? A typical cause is when app builders apply this technique against a text input value. An important point is that this technique works only with numeric input values. Sometimes, app builders mistakenly think that they're working with a numeric field when, in actual fact, they're working with a string field. This can sometimes happen with input data from a web service or from a SharePoint calculated field. In this scenario, the Text function won't apply the specified format, and the fix is to wrap the input value inside a call to the Value function, for example:

```
Text(Value("123,45", "[$-fr]# #,00", "en-US")
```

Caution   SharePoint calculated columns behave like strings, even when we set the data type of the column to "Number" in SharePoint. We must call the Value function to convert the value to a number before we can format it with the Text function.

Rounding Functions

There are three functions to carry out rounding operations. These are Round, RoundUp, and RoundDown. These functions accept an input value and the number of decimal places to round to. The RoundUp function rounds up the input value to the specified number of decimal places, whereas the RoundDown function rounds down the input value to the specified number of decimal places. The Round function performs arithmetic rounding on the input value. Here's an example:

```
Round(85.665,2)
```

This example rounds the value 85.665 to two decimal places. The result of this function is 85.67. One thing to be aware of is that unlike rounding functions that we might find in other systems, the Round function performs arithmetic rounding rather than bankers rounding. Bankers rounding prevents the upward bias that occurs when rounding up as soon the minor fractional unit reaches 5. It does this by rounding to the nearest even number.

Trigonometric Functions

Power Apps provides the standard trigonometric functions Cos, Cot, Sin, and Tan. These functions accept an input angle in radians and return the result of the trigonometric operation.

We can also call the inverse trigonometric functions which are Acos, Acot, Asin, Atan. With these functions, we can calculate arccosine, arccotangent, arcsine, and arctangent values. These functions accept an input value and return the result of the operation in radians. With all these trigonometric functions, we can supply a single value, or we can supply a single-column table.

There are two functions to convert values between degrees and radians. The Degrees function converts an angle in radians to degrees, and the Radians function converts an angle in degrees to radians. Finally, the Pi function returns the value of π – the number that begins with 3.14159.

While these functions are useful for mathematical tasks, they also play a role in building animations. For example, we could add controls to a screen and use a timer to change the x and y coordinates. By incorporating a sine calculation on the timer, we can produce a wavelike effect and animate, for example, the appearance of a snowflake falling from the sky.

Other Mathematical Functions

Table 5-9 provides a list of other mathematical functions and a description of how to call these functions.

Table 5-9. Mathematical functions

Example Function Call	Function Description	Example Output Value
Abs(-80)	Absolute positive value	80
Exp (5)	e raised to the power of 5	148.41315910
Ln(50)	Natural logarithm (base e) of 50	3.91202301
Power(8, 3)	8 raised to the power of 3 (8*8*8)	512
Sqrt(3)	Square root of 3	1.73205081

As a brief comment, we'll cover Power Automate later in this book. Power Automate is a large, separate product in the Power Platform that carries out automation tasks. Power Automate lacks these higher-level mathematical and trigonometric functions. Therefore, when we build systems that encompass the wider Power Platform, it's helpful to understand that Power Apps is the place where we can carry out more complex mathematical tasks.

Working with Dates

Power Apps provides functions that work with dates and times. Here are the functions that retrieve the current date and time:

- Now – This function returns the current date and time.

- Today – This function returns the current date with the time set to midnight.

To create a date, we call the Date function. This function accepts year, month, and day arguments and returns a date with the time set to midnight. Here's how to create a date set to the value of July 12, 2017:

```
Date(2017,7,12)
```

To create a time object, we call the Time function. This function accepts hour, minute, second, and millisecond arguments. Here's how to create a time object, set to the value of 2:15 PM:

```
Time(14,15,0,0)
```

Notice how we can't specify a time element with the Date function. This function always creates a date with a time of midnight. To create a date object with a specific date and time, we can call the DateTimeValue function. This function accepts a string argument and returns a date object. Here's how to create a date object with the value set to July 12, 2017, 12:15 PM:

```
DateTimeValue ("12/07/2017 12:15 PM", "en-GB")
```

In this example, we provide a language code to specify that the input date is in British format (i.e., day/month/year). This language code argument is optional. If we don't specify a language code, the function uses the locale of the current user.

Two other useful conversion functions are DateValue and TimeValue. The DateValue function accepts an input string and returns a date object. The TimeValue function accepts an input string and returns a time object.

Once reason why these strings to date and time functions are useful is because Power Apps doesn't include a standalone time picker control. Therefore, these functions help us convert the text representation of dates and times that users enter into objects that we can use to perform date arithmetic or to save into a database.

Caution   When building screens, it's important to understand the behavior of the date picker controls. If we incorrectly configure a date control, this can result in apps storing dates that are one day out. Chapter 10 contains more details.

Formatting Dates and Times

To format dates and times, we call the Text function. We can format dates using predefined formats, or we can specify our own custom format.

Starting with the predefined formats, Power Apps offers a choice of date and time formats, in long and short formats. A long date format includes the full month name, whereas the short format includes an abbreviation of the month name. Table 5-10 shows a list of the predefined formats that we can use.

Table 5-10. Predefined date and time formats

Function Call	Example Output Value
Text(Now(), DateTimeFormat.LongDate)	17 December 2017
Text(Now(), DateTimeFormat.LongDateTime)	17 December 2017 02:00:00
Text(Now(), DateTimeFormat.LongDateTime24)	17 December 2017 14:00:00
Text(Now(), DateTimeFormat.LongTime)	02:00:00
Text(Now(), DateTimeFormat.LongTime24)	14:00:00
Text(Now(), DateTimeFormat.ShortDate)	12/17/2017
Text(Now(), DateTimeFormat.ShortDateTime)	12/17/2017 02:00:00

(continued)

Table 5-10. (*continued*)

Function Call	Example Output Value
Text(Now(), DateTimeFormat.ShortDateTime24)	12/17/2017 14:00:00
Text(Now(), DateTimeFormat.ShortTime)	02:00
Text(Now(), DateTimeFormat.ShortTime24)	14:00
Text(Now(), DateTimeFormat.UTC)	2017-12-17T14:00:00.000Z

With these predefined formats, we can optionally provide a language code like so:

```
Text( Now(), DateTimeFormat.ShortDate, "en-GB" )
```

This function formats the date in British format (day/month/year) and produces the output "17/07/2017." If the predefined formats are too rigid and we want to customize our output further, we can provide a custom format string. Here's an example:

```
Text( Now(), "dddd dd-mmmm-yyyy mm:hh ss f ", "es-ES")
```

This example specifies a Spanish language code, and this formula would produce output in the format "domingo 17-diciembre-2017 14:00 00 0."

Looking more closely at this format string, the initial four characters "dddd" denote the day of the week in long format. The format "ddd" returns the day of the week in short format, that is, "dom" in Spanish or "Sun" in English. The "mmmm" section of the string returns the full month name, whereas "mmm" would return a three-character representation of the month (e.g., "dic" in Spanish or "Dec" in English). The format string "mm" returns a two-digit numeric representation of the month.

One important point about custom formats is that the "mm" placeholder can represent the month number or the minute component of the time. When we specify a custom format that includes the "mm" placeholder, the first instance of "mm" will always output the month component. Therefore, it isn't possible to construct a custom format that shows the minute component of the time prior to the month. To do this, we would need to format the times and dates separately and concatenate the results.

Caution   The mm placeholder can represent the month or minute component of a date and time value. The first instance of the mm placeholder will always return the month component.

Performing Date Arithmetic

The two main functions to carry out date arithmetic are called `DateAdd` and `DateDiff`. The `DateAdd` function adds or subtracts durations to or from a date. The `DateDiff` function returns the number of days, months, quarters, or years between two dates.

To demonstrate the `DateAdd` function, here's how to retrieve yesterday's date:

```
DateAdd(Today(), -1, Days)
```

The first argument specifies the input date. The second argument defines the number of units to add. This can be a positive or a negative value. The third argument defines the units, and the possible options include days, months, quarters, or years. The third argument is optional. If we don't specify the units, the `DateAdd` function uses days as the unit for calculation.

To demonstrate the use of the `DateDiff` function, the following formula returns the number of days between January 1, 2017, and January 14, 2017:

```
DateDiff(Date(2017, 01, 01),Date(2017, 01, 14), Days)
```

The return value from this formula is 14. The first argument specifies the start date, the second argument specifies the end date, and the third argument specifies the type of unit.

Although `DateDiff` appears simple to use, we shouldn't be fooled into thinking that calculating date differences is a trivial task. A challenging task for developers is to calculate a person's age (or any time duration) expressed in years, months, and days. Part of the challenge is that it's not possible to carry out the base calculation by taking the difference in days and dividing by 365. The reason for this is because the time span can include leap years. Another challenge is that date difference functions can often return ambiguous results. As an illustration, the following formula calculates the difference in months between December 30, 2016, and January 2, 2017:

```
DateDiff(Date(2016, 12, 30),Date(2017, 01, 02), Months)
```

What do you think this call to `DateDiff` returns, given these dates? In this example, `DateDiff` reports a one-month difference for a time span of three days. In fact, it would even return a time difference of 1 year if we were to specify the unit as years. The point of this is that it's important to be aware of this behavior, especially if, for example, we were building apps for billing purposes.

Caution   When we calculate date differences with `DateDiff`, the result may be greater than we expect.

Importing Static Dates

In business scenarios, there is often the need to calculate and produce lists of specific dates – for example, the first Monday for each quarter, the second Tuesday for each month, and all Mondays for the year.

If we search the Web for solutions, we can often find complex formulas that other app builders have shared. But when faced with these complex logic problems, a great cheat is to generate our data in Excel and import it into our app as static data, through the Insert ➤ Data sources menu item.

If, for example, we needed to generate a list of all Mondays, we could enter a date for a Monday in cell A1 of our spreadsheet and, in cell B1, enter a date 7 days after the date in cell A1. We can then select cells A1 and B1 and use the "fill down" feature to populate several hundred rows of Mondays (Figure 5-17).

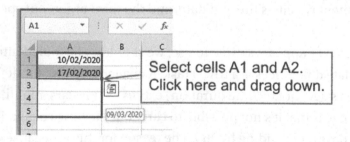

Figure 5-17. *Using Excel's fill down option to generate static data*

While this doesn't offer a pure formulaic solution, in practice, it provides a very quick and easy way to solve these types of problems.

Calendar Functions

Power Apps provides functions to retrieve a list of month names or weekday names in the language of the logged-in user. The results from these functions are ideal for use in drop-down boxes or for date selection scenarios.

The Calendar.MonthsLong and Calendar.MonthsShort functions return a table that contains month names. The MonthsLong function returns a table that begins with "January," "February," "March," and so on, whereas the MonthsShort function returns a table that begins with "Jan," "Feb," "Mar," and so on.

The Calendar.WeekdaysLong and Calendar.WeekdayShort functions return a table that contains weekday names. The WeekdaysLong function returns a table that begins with "Sunday," "Monday," "Tuesday," and so on, whereas the MonthsShort function returns a table that begins with "Sun," "Mon," "Tue," and so on.

As an example, Figure 5-18 demonstrates how to provide a feature that enables a user to select a month. Here, we add a radio control to a screen, and we set the Items property to Calendar.MonthsLong.

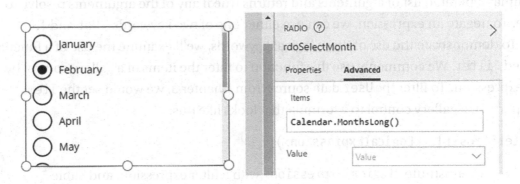

Figure 5-18. Using the calendar functions

Conditional Statements and Logical Operations

So far, we've already seen how to use the If function. This is one of the most useful and widely used functions in Power Apps. Here's a reminder of how to use this function:

```
If( logical test, functions to run if true, functions to run if false)
```

In addition to the If function, there are other conditional functions which include CountIf, RemoveIf, and UpdateIf.

> **Note**   Because the If function is so widely used, here's a quick reminder that in
> French and other languages that use commas as a decimal point character, we
> should use semicolons to separate the arguments inside the If statement.

To build the conditional tests for use with the If function, Power Apps provides all
the logical operators that we would expect to find. These operators include the obvious
operators such as equals (=), greater than (>), less than (<), greater than or equal to (>=),
and less than or equal to (<=).

There are two keywords we can use to carry out a logical and operation. These are
And and &&. We can use the And and && operators to combine sets of conditions. Another
way to carry out this task is to pass a comma-separated list of arguments to the And
function. This will return true if all the arguments are also true.

Likewise, there are two keywords that we can use to carry out a logical or operation –
Or and ||. The Or and || operators enable us to supply sets of conditions, and the return
value will be true if any of the conditions resolve to true. The Or function accepts a
comma-separated list of arguments and returns true if any of the arguments resolve to
true. To negate an expression, we can use either one of two keywords – Not and !.

To demonstrate the use of these logical keywords, we'll examine the use of a function
called Filter. We commonly use this function to filter the items of a gallery control by
an expression. To filter the User data source from Chapter 3, we would set the Items
property of a gallery control to a formula that looks like this:

```
Filter([@User], <LogicalExpression>)
```

We can substitute <LogicalExpression> with a filter expression, and Table 5-11
illustrates how we can incorporate the logical operators into the expression.

Table 5-11. *Logical operators*

Logical Expression	Description
StartsWith(Surname, "A") && Country="US"	Returns records where the surname starts with A and the country matches US. This uses the && keyword.
And(StartsWith(Surname, "A"), Country="US")	Returns records where the surname starts with A and the country matches US. This uses the And keyword.
StartsWith(Surname, "A") And Country="US"	Returns records where the surname starts with A and the country matches US. This uses the And keyword.
Country="US" || Country="UK"	Returns records where the country matches US or UK. This uses the || keyword.
Or(Country="US", Country="UK")	Returns records where the country matches US or UK. This uses the Or keyword.
Country="US" Or Country="UK"	Returns records where the country matches US or UK. This uses the Or keyword.

Calling the Switch Function

To test a single condition against multiple outcomes, we can call a function called Switch. This function provides a more concise way to express this type of evaluation, compared to nesting multiple If statements. Here's an example of how to call this function:

```
Switch(ThisItem.PropertyTypeID,
        1, "House",
        2, "Apartment",
        3, "Bungalow"
        )
```

This illustrates the typical syntax that we could use on a label within a gallery control to display the description that corresponds to a numeric code.

The first argument expresses an input value – in this example, a numeric ID. We can then specify one or more match value and result pairs.

Color Functions

There are a set of functions that can help us work with colors. Let's say we want to set the foreground color of a piece of text to red. The functions that can return a color value are shown in Table 5-12.

Table 5-12. *Obtaining a color value*

Method	Example Call
Use predefined color	Color.Red
Obtain color from hex code	ColorValue("#ff0000")
Obtain color from red/green/blue/alpha values	RGBA(255, 0, 0, 1)
Obtain a lighter/darker shade of color	ColorFade(Color.Red, -0.2)

The simplest way to set a color is to assign one of the built-in colors through the `Color` enumeration. Through this method, we can access all of the common colors.

We can call the `ColorValue` function to return a color value from a hex code. This is perfect if you're familiar with the color codes that HTML and CSS (Cascading Style Sheets) use.

The `ColorFade` function returns a brighter or darker version of a color. This function requires us to provide two arguments – a base color and a fade value that ranges from -1 to 1. A fade value of -1 fully darkens the color to black, whereas a fade value of 1 fully lightens a color to white. By using this function, we can improve the appearance of an app by applying subtle offsets of colors to borders or adjacent controls.

Navigation Functions

We've seen how the `Navigate` and `Back` functions work in the auto-generated and sample apps. We'll now examine these functions in more detail.

The `Navigate` function changes the visible screen, and we can pass values to the target screen by providing context variables in the call to the `Navigate` function.

The Back function returns the user to the previous screen. Both of these functions will return true or false, depending on the outcome. Here's a formula that demonstrates how to use the return value:

```
If(Back(), true, Navigate(BrowseScreen1,ScreenTransition.Cover))
```

This formula calls the Back function. If the call to the function fails, the code navigates the user to a screen called BrowseScreen1 instead. A call to the Back function could fail if we run a specific screen in the designer and there isn't a screen that we can return to.

Similarly, the Navigate function will return false if the navigation operation fails. This could occur when we attempt to navigate to a screen that we've stored in a variable using the Set function.

To make it easier to write the navigate code, we can select a control and use the Navigate item in the toolbar. This feature inserts the correct formula and saves us from typing the formula manually (Figure 5-19).

Figure 5-19. *Setting the navigate action with the designer*

When building apps, we might want to open screens conditionally or to add gallery or drop-down controls to navigate the user to a different screen. As an example, we may want to open different screens or remove the ability to open a screen depending on the logged-on user.

The challenge with building this type of feature is that the Navigate function expects us to pass a screen object, rather than the string representation of the screen name. We can work around this limitation by storing the screen references in a table.

As an example, let's imagine that we want to add a gallery control that shows a list of browse screens in our application. When a user selects an item from the control, the app should navigate to the selected screen. To build this function, we would add a gallery control to a screen. We would then set the Items property of the control to the following formula:

```
Table({Desc:"View Users", ScreenObject: BrowseUsers},
     {Desc:"View Properties", ScreenObject: BrowseProperties}
)
```

This code is based on the assumption that we have two screens in our app – one called BrowseUsers and the other BrowseProperties.

We can now add an icon to our gallery template and set the OnAction property to this:

```
Navigate(GalleryControl1.Selected.ScreenObject)
```

Figure 5-20 illustrates how this feature appears in the screen designer.

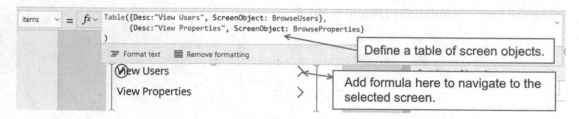

Figure 5-20. *Using a gallery control to provide screen navigation*

Note   The Table function creates a table from a list of records, and we can use it to set the items of a gallery to a set of hardcoded values. Chapter 7 covers this function in greater detail.

Launching Websites and Apps

From within our apps, we can launch websites in a browser by calling the Launch function. To demonstrate, here's how to add a button that opens the currency conversion page from Google.

The first step is to determine the web address that we would use. If we were to open the currency conversion web page in Google and convert 50 US dollars to euros, the address of the page would look like this:

```
https://www.google.com/finance/converter?a=50&from=USD&to=EUR
```

The a parameter specifies the amount to convert. The from parameter specifies the source currency type, and the to parameter specifies the target currency type.

To open this web page from a screen, we can add a button and set the OnSelect property to the following formula:

```
Launch("https://www.google.com/finance/converter",
       "a","50","from","USD","to","EUR")
```

The first argument that we pass to the Launch function defines the address of the web page to open. We can optionally provide a list of parameters, and in this example, we provide the a, to, and from arguments to specify our search terms.

To add additional functionality to our apps, we can exploit this technique and call the Launch function to open the telephone dialer, email client, SMS, or message apps. Table 5-13 demonstrates the syntax we can use.

Table 5-13. *Launching apps*

Description	Launch Function Syntax
Send an email	Launch("mailto:recipient@emailaddress.com")
Open the telephone dialer	Launch("tel:07876987656")
Send SMS	Launch("sms:07876987656", "body", "Our SMS message")
Initiate Skype call	Launch("skype:skypeRecipient?call")
Send WhatsApp message	Launch("whatsapp://send/07876987656", "text", "our message")

Retrieving Start-Up Parameters

We can use the Param function to retrieve web address arguments that were used to open an app. This feature is very useful because it enables us to configure what happens when an app starts. For example, we could open a specific screen that shows a specific record based on a parameter value. This feature can be useful for workflow-type apps.

143

If the status of a record changes, for example, we could send an email with a link that directly opens the specified record in Power Apps.

To demonstrate this technique, we'll adapt an auto-generated app to optionally open a record on start-up. Our auto-generated app will be based on a table of issues, and the URL parameter that prompts the app to open an issue record is called IssueID.

We can find the web address for an app through the details page for the app in the Maker Portal. The address will look something like this:

```
https://apps.PowerApps.com/play/c4c89866-5b53-4668-9a67-
bd9e06ee56a0?tenantId=fd1298be-c09f-4349-96e8-bd097210e274
```

To help build this feature, we'll utilize a property called OnStart. This property specifies the formula that runs when an app starts. It provides a perfect place to carry out initialization tasks. An example of the type of functionality we could perform here includes a formula that caches records into local collections, to help improve application performance.

To build this feature, the first step is to build an auto-generated app. The data source for our example app is called Issue. In the browse screen, we set the OnStart property to the following value:

```
If(Not(IsBlank(Param("IssueID"))),
        Navigate(DetailScreen1,ScreenTransition.Fade),
        Set(RecordSeen, true))
```

On DetailScreen1, we then set the Item property of DetailForm1 to this:

```
If(RecordSeen=true,
        BrowseGallery1.Selected,
        LookUp(Issue, IssueID= Param("IssueID")))
```

We can now test our app by opening a browser and appending an issue ID argument to the end of the address, like so:

```
https://apps.PowerApps.com/play/c4c89866-5b53-4668-9a67-bd9e06ee56a0?
IssueID=12
```

This link opens the app and shows the record that matches issue ID 12 in the details screen. From this screen, the user can click the back icon to navigate to the browse screen.

Exiting an App

Power Apps provides a function to close an app called Exit. This function accepts a single argument that controls whether to log the user out of Power Apps.

In the mobile versions of Power Apps, the Exit function closes the app, and the user will remain in the Power Apps app. If we were to call the Exit function while previewing our app in the Power Apps Studio designer, the function would not exit our session.

Managing Errors

Power Apps deals with errors in a relaxed way. In most cases, the apps continue to run when they encounter errors and won't crash or grind to a halt.

Here's a screen that demonstrates how Power Apps copes with errors. This screen contains a button that calls the formula that's shown in Figure 5-21. The screen contains a label, and the Text property of this is set to a context variable called LabelText.

This formula contains two errors. The second line in the formula contains the nonsense text BlahBlah. A subsequent command in this formula divides the number 80 by zero. This is a classic type of error that often crashes other types of application.

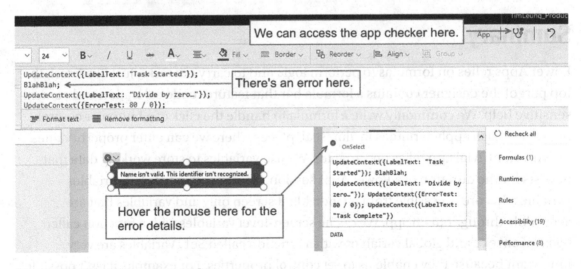

Figure 5-21. Formulas with errors

How do you think Power Apps behaves when this formula runs? Will it execute the commands that are syntactically correct? The answer is that the whole block of code fails to run due to the unknown expression BlahBlah. If we were to remove this offending line, the code would run, despite the divide by zero error, and the label would display the text "Task Complete."

Another place where errors can occur is during data operations. Errors can occur when an app tries to read or to save data to a data source. When such errors occur, we can retrieve a list of error messages by calling a function called `Errors`. This function accepts the name of a data source, and here's the syntax we would use to call this function:

```
Errors(Properties)
```

This function returns a table. Therefore, we can set the `Items` property of a gallery control to this function to view a list of errors that have been generated for a specific data source.

To help avoid errors and to build higher-quality code, we can run the "App Checker" tool. This shows an overview of all formula errors in an app. To help speed up an app, it highlights the formulas that are candidates for optimization. Finally, it indicates controls where we haven't set the "accessible label" property. For visually impaired users who use a screen reader, the "accessible label" property defines the text that the screen reader reads out.

Summary

Power Apps relies on formulas to perform logic and to carry out tasks. Just like Excel, the top part of the designer contains a formula bar that features code coloration and context-sensitive help. We commonly write a formula to handle the click of a button or control, but we can also apply formulas in almost all places where we can enter property values.

Any nontrivial app relies on variables. We use variables to store working data that persists for the duration of a Power Apps session. There are two types of variables – variables that are accessible from an individual screen only and variables that are accessible throughout an app. We define screen-level variables with a function called `UpdateContext` and global variables with a function called `Set`. Variables are very important because they enable us to set control properties. For example, it isn't possible to write a formula that directly sets the Text property of a label. The work-around is to set the Text property of the label to a variable. We can then modify the text on the label by modifying the variable value. The variable acts as the conduit that enables us to set property values, and this is the reason why they are so important. We can store all types of data in variables, including simple numeric and text values, as well as rows and tables.

Text processing and manipulation often plays a key role in app development. If we need to process unstructured data from third parties or to validate input data from end users, there are many functions that can help us. There are functions that can find and extract parts of a larger string and functions to carry out text replacements and substitutions. We can chain these functions together to carry out more sophisticated text processing tasks, and we looked at various patterns that we can apply. A key feature is that many text processing functions can operate against an input table of data. This enables us to work efficiently by avoiding the need to loop through records and to process on a row-by-row basis.

A very powerful feature is the ability to match text patterns through the use of regular expressions. This enables us to easily validate input data such as email address, telephone number, or social security numbers. If an input string matches a predefined pattern, we can use regular expressions to extract specific parts of the string. We can also extract specific elements of an input string into a table structure, and we learned how to build regular expressions to carry out this task.

There are many mathematical functions that we can call to process numbers. These include arithmetic operators, rounding operators, trigonometric functions, and many more. Many functions also exist to carry out date arithmetic and to display dates in the format of our choice. Notable functions that app builders use commonly are Text and Value. The Text function converts other data types to text and can apply formatting. The Value function converts a text value to a number.

Finally, we learned how to implement screen navigation and how to launch processes such as the telephone dialer or SMS composition app. We also found out how to customize an app's start-up behavior by passing user-supplied arguments.

PART II

Working with Data

CHAPTER 6

Setting Up SharePoint, SQL, and More

So far, we've seen how to use Microsoft Excel as a data source. Although Excel is simple to use and understand, Power Apps supports many other data sources. For data storage, two common data sources that outperform Excel are SharePoint and SQL Server. These data sources are capable of storing greater amounts of data and provide several additional features, which we'll find out more about in this chapter.

We'll also cover the on-premises data gateway. This enables us to connect to SQL Server and SharePoint servers that are hosted inside internal company networks. It provides a great data storage option for companies with existing on-premises data or companies that wish to retain data inside private networks for security reasons. Other key topics that we'll cover in this chapter include

- How to get started with SharePoint. This chapter provides a basic guide on how to set up a list and to take advantage of SharePoint features such as choice lists, row versioning, and conflict detection.

- Getting started with SQL Server. We'll cover the high-level steps that are needed to set up a SQL Server database, including the tools that are needed to manage the database and to create tables. We'll look at how to optimize data retrieval with views.

- How to extend an app with other data sources. We'll look at other helpful and useful data sources. This includes how to add static read-only data to an app, how to send push notifications to mobile devices, how to translate text, and how to retrieve the current weather.

What's the Best Data Source?

When starting out, a common question for many app builders is, what's the best data storage platform for my app? Here's a quick summary of the pros and cons of the common data sources.

Starting with Excel, Excel spreadsheets provide a simple way to work with data. Through Excel, we can easily visualize all our data, it's simple to add new fields by defining additional columns, and we can easily modify and bulk enter records using Windows and Office features such as copy and paste. We can use the file system to back up, copy, and distribute the Excel files, which provides safety and versatility.

For anything more complex however, Excel doesn't work well. There are two main limitations. The first is that due to data retrieval limits, it's not possible to retrieve more than 2,000 rows of data. We'll cover this topic in greater detail in Chapter 8. The second issue is that the Excel connector cannot connect to Excel files that are greater than 2 MB in size. We can partly overcome this issue by splitting our data over multiple Excel files.

An additional problem with Excel is that the spreadsheet files must be hosted through a cloud storage provider such as OneDrive. Let's suppose that a user creates an app that's based on an Excel file in OneDrive for Business. The user then shares the app with several team members. If the user leaves the company at a later point in time, the business will want to delete all the Microsoft accounts associated with this ex-employee. Because OneDrive accounts are associated with an individual and it isn't possible to reassign the ownership of a file in OneDrive to another user, it becomes necessary to relocate the Excel file elsewhere, update our application to reference the new location, share the new connection, and republish our app. We can avoid this headache by choosing to use SharePoint, SQL Server, or Dataverse.

To support greater numbers of users and greater amounts of data, SharePoint is a better option. It provides better support for querying data that exceeds 2000 rows, and there are far larger limits to the amount of data that we can store (30 million rows in a list). It supports many more data types, including lookup lists, people lookup fields, and file attachments. For multiuser apps, SharePoint provides row versioning and can prevent conflicting changes. In terms of pricing, SharePoint is cost-effective because it is included in almost all Microsoft/Office 365 subscription plans, so those users will have a license to use SharePoint as part of that subscription.

Moving beyond SharePoint, the two premium options for data storage are SQL Server and Dataverse. SQL Server offers excellent performance and much better support for working with very large amounts of data.

We can fine-tune many parts of SQL Server to help optimize performance. Two key features include views and stored procedures. A SQL view enables us to query data that joins multiple tables or to generate aggregated results that can include the sum or the count of a group of records. With stored procedures, we can bulk update data or perform data operations in a more precise way. Views and stored procedures can address many of the performance issues that SharePoint struggles with. With SQL Server, there is also a rich ecosystem of tools that can support backup, data import and export, performance optimization, and more. SQL Server is perfect for organizations with preexisting data in SQL Server databases.

Another premium data store is Dataverse. This is a requirement for model-driven or portal apps, so for these types of app, we have no choice but to use Dataverse. Dataverse is the native database for Dynamics 365. If we want to build apps to enhance the functionality of Dynamics 365, Dataverse is a natural choice.

Dataverse provides great performance and is simple to use. It provides prebuilt data models for common business scenarios, and we can manage the database through a web front end. Unlike SQL Server, there's no need to learn how to use additional tools or to learn how to write SQL. We can secure access to records in a more granular way, and because each Dataverse database is associated with an environment, the apps in an environment can connect to Dataverse without us needing to specify specific data source settings. Dataverse is a large topic, and therefore, Chapter 12 is devoted to this topic.

For apps that use SQL Server or Dataverse as a data source, all users will require a per-user or per-app license. Therefore, these data sources are more expensive, compared to SharePoint or Excel.

Using a SharePoint Data Source

SharePoint is a very popular source because it provides some excellent features and is included in almost all Microsoft/Office 365 plans. This section introduces the basic features of SharePoint, including how to create lists and how to connect to SharePoint from Power Apps.

Creating a SharePoint List

Assuming that we have sufficient permissions, the menu in a SharePoint site includes the option to create a new list. A SharePoint list contains columns, and Figure 6-1 shows the screen for creating new columns. This screenshot illustrates the type of information that we can store in a SharePoint list.

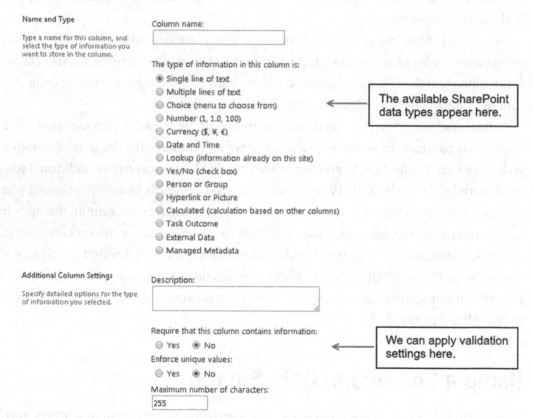

Figure 6-1. *Creating a SharePoint column (also showing validation rules)*

SharePoint can apply validation rules to columns, such as whether the data is mandatory and the maximum number of characters that the field can store. From within an app, Power Apps will apply the validation rules that are defined in SharePoint.

Apps work well with all the standard data types, including calculated columns. For text data, SharePoint provides single-line and multiline text types. With the multiline text type, we can set the text type to rich text, and Power Apps provides a rich text editor for data entry purposes (Figure 6-2).

154

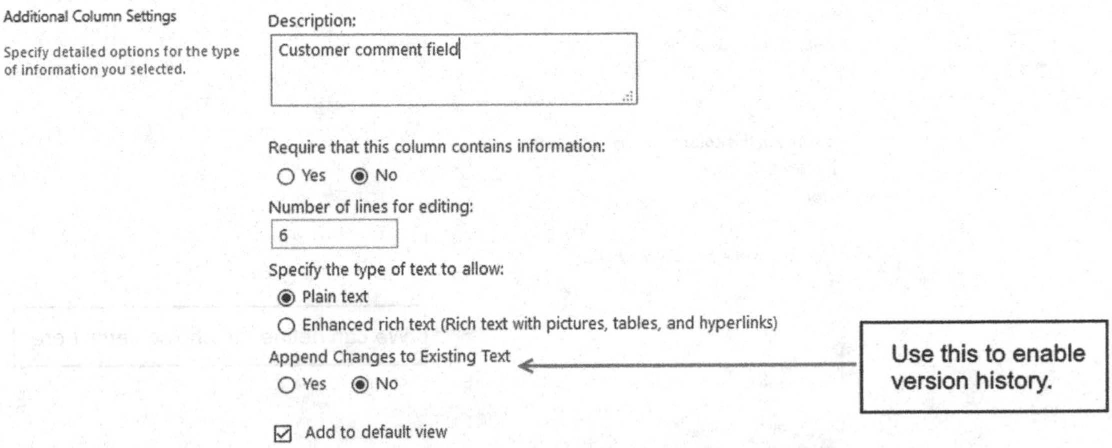

Additional Column Settings

Specify detailed options for the type of information you selected.

Description:

Customer comment field

Require that this column contains information:
○ Yes ◉ No

Number of lines for editing:
6

Specify the type of text to allow:
◉ Plain text
○ Enhanced rich text (Rich text with pictures, tables, and hyperlinks)

Append Changes to Existing Text ◀───────────────────── Use this to enable version history.
○ Yes ◉ No

☑ Add to default view

Figure 6-2. *Configuring a SharePoint multiline column*

A useful feature is that SharePoint can store version histories of list items. For a multiline field, we can enable this feature by enabling the "Append Changes to Existing Text" option. After we enable this, we can view historical values through the SharePoint list. However, note that from within Power Apps, we can only retrieve the very latest version of a record. If there's a requirement to view historical versions from within an app, a work-around is to add a hyperlink that opens the SharePoint record in a new browser window.

Another notable data type is "Person or Group." We can configure this type of column to store a single person or multiple persons. In the apps that we build, SharePoint and Power Apps provide the ability to populate a field of this type with the names of the users in our organization.

Choice Items

We can limit the data that users can enter by defining choice or lookup columns. When we create an app that connects to one of these columns, Power Apps can populate drop-down boxes with the choice values to limit the values that a user can enter. We can also define multiple selection choice columns, like the setup that's shown in Figure 6-3. For these types of field, Power Apps provides a multi-select drop-down control for data entry.

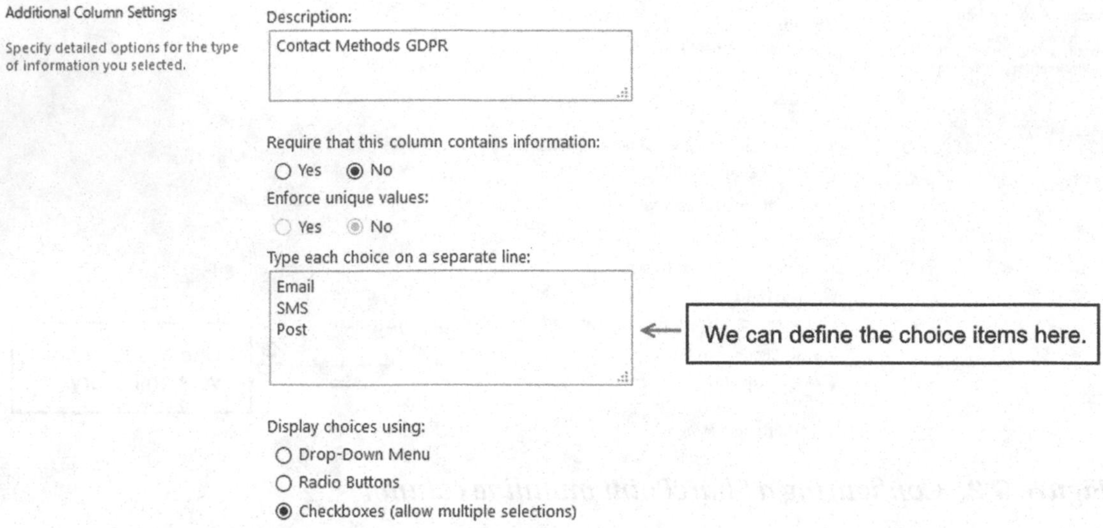

Additional Column Settings

Specify detailed options for the type of information you selected.

Description:

Contact Methods GDPR

Require that this column contains information:

○ Yes   ◉ No

Enforce unique values:

○ Yes   ◉ No

Type each choice on a separate line:

Email
SMS
Post

← We can define the choice items here.

Display choices using:

○ Drop-Down Menu
○ Radio Buttons
◉ Checkboxes (allow multiple selections)

Figure 6-3. *SharePoint multi-selection choice columns*

SharePoint also provides a Boolean "Yes/No (check box)" data type. To store Boolean values, another possibility is to use a choice column with the values "yes" and "no." This can provide greater flexibility when we build the user interface, and it also enables us to store an empty value, which is something that we cannot do with a "Yes/No (check box)" column.

Note   To display an editable list of choice items using radio or checkbox controls, we can use the list box or radio controls. We would set the Items property of these controls to the following formula: `Choices(SharePointListName.ChoiceColumnName)`

Understanding SharePoint Special Columns

By default, all SharePoint lists include special, built-in columns. These include columns that store the name of the user who created a record, the user who last modified a record, and the date and time that those actions took place. Another notable column is the ID column. The ID column contains a unique numeric value that SharePoint automatically generates whenever a user adds a row to a list.

Here are two important things that can catch out app makers. The first is that although the ID column stores unique numeric values, the data type of this column is textural. Why is this a problem? The problem arises when an app builder tries to use this field to retrieve records. For example, an app builder may attempt to retrieve a batch of SharePoint records by filtering a SharePoint list using criteria that utilize the ID value and the greater and less than operators. This is the type of operation that we would carry out when we attempt to preload and cache records to improve performance or to overcome row retrieval limitations. Because we cannot apply numeric query operators to text columns, it limits our capability to query SharePoint lists based on the ID field.

The second important attribute that can catch us out is that SharePoint columns have both an internal and an external name. When we rename a column, the external name changes, but the internal name remains the same. Figure 6-4 illustrates a typical example. In the settings area of SharePoint where we edit a column, the internal name appears as an argument called field in the web address.

Here, we have a SharePoint list called Furnishings. By default, SharePoint lists include a column called Title. In this example, the Title column was renamed to Furnishing.

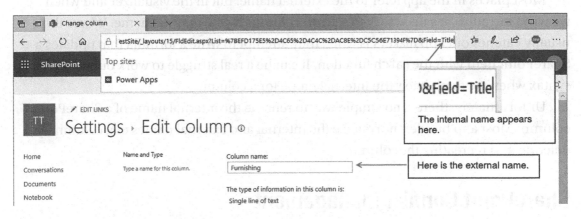

Figure 6-4. *Finding the internal name of a SharePoint column*

Why would the existence of an internal and an external name cause us a problem? The reason is because there are some places in Power Apps that refer to the internal name, whereas others refer to the external name. This can be very confusing for app makers who have inherited lists that were created by other users, particularly if there is a significant difference between the internal and the external names.

To illustrate, Figure 6-5 shows a screenshot of two different places in an app.

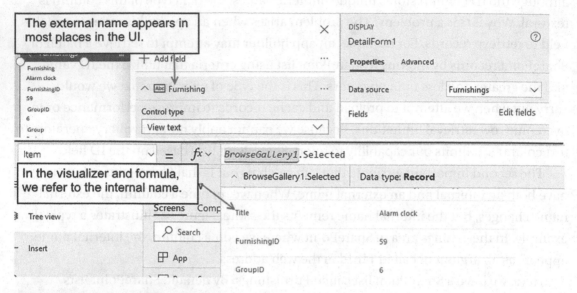

Figure 6-5. *Internal and external SharePoint names*

Most places in the app refer to the external name. But in the visualizer and when we write formulas, it's necessary to refer to columns by the internal name. Where this usually catches out app makers is when they attempt to write a formula that updates a SharePoint item with the Patch function. It can be a real struggle to work out the correct syntax when we don't know the internal name for a column.

Unfortunately, there is no simple way to rename the internal name of a SharePoint column. Most app builders normalize the internal and external names of a column by deleting and recreating the column.

SharePoint Conflict Management

One reason why SharePoint is more robust than other data sources is because it provides built-in conflict management. Let's suppose that two users attempt to modify the same record at the same time. When the second user attempts to save the record, Power Apps detects the conflict and prevents the save operation from succeeding. It displays the error that's shown in Figure 6-6.

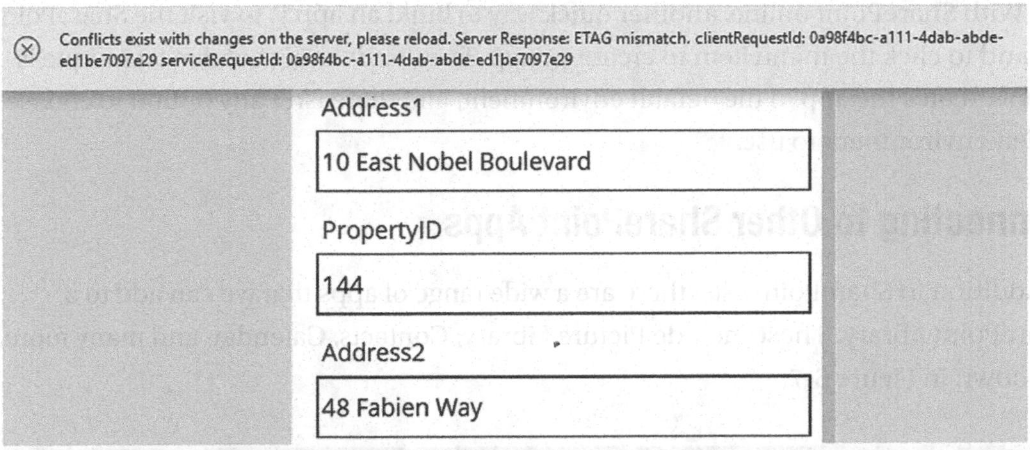

⊗ Conflicts exist with changes on the server, please reload. Server Response: ETAG mismatch. clientRequestId: 0a98f4bc-a111-4dab-abde-ed1be7097e29 serviceRequestId: 0a98f4bc-a111-4dab-abde-ed1be7097e29

Address1

10 East Nobel Boulevard

PropertyID

144

Address2

48 Fabien Way

Figure 6-6. *Error that occurs when a conflict occurs in SharePoint*

When this type of error occurs, Power Apps reloads the record and discards the changes that the user attempted to make.

Although this feature provides additional safety for our data, it can also be a source of much frustration for app builders. If these ETAG mismatch errors are too obtrusive, we can create our apps so that in the case of a conflict, the last user always wins. The way to do this is to call the Refresh function to refresh the SharePoint list before we attempt the save operation. In the case of a form, we would call the Refresh function before we call the SubmitForm function; and if we were writing code to perform the save operation, we would call the Refresh function before calling the Patch or other data modification functions.

Connecting to a SharePoint Data Source

There are several ways to connect to SharePoint from Power Apps. The first is to create an app from data or to add a new data source from an existing app. The new data source option enables us to choose a SharePoint online data source or on-premises installation of SharePoint. The next screen prompts us to enter the address of our SharePoint site, and we should enter this in the format

```
http://mysharepointserver.com/MySharePointSite
```

Once we enter the address, the following screen will display the SharePoint lists that we can connect to. We can create a connection by selecting one of the available items.

With SharePoint online, another quick way to build an app is to visit the SharePoint list and to click the menu item to create an app. The disadvantage of this technique is that it creates the app in the default environment, and there isn't any option to choose which environment to use.

Connecting to Other SharePoint Apps

In addition to SharePoint lists, there are a wide range of apps that we can add to a SharePoint library. These include Picture Library, Contacts, Calendar, and many more, as shown in Figure 6-7.

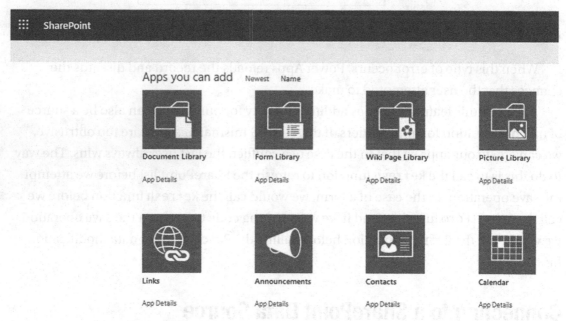

Figure 6-7. *SharePoint apps that we can add to a library*

A feature that many app builders overlook is that it's possible to connect to most of these SharePoint apps. It isn't obvious how we connect to these items, so this is a great tip to understand.

Let's suppose we add a calendar to our SharePoint library and name it "Property Viewings." To connect to this calendar from Power Apps, we would start to create a connection as we normally would. When we reach the stage where we choose a SharePoint list, we discover that the calendar doesn't appear in the list of available items. The trick is to scroll to the end of the list and to manually type "Property Viewings" into the textbox that appears at the end (Figure 6-8). This then enables us to connect to our calendar.

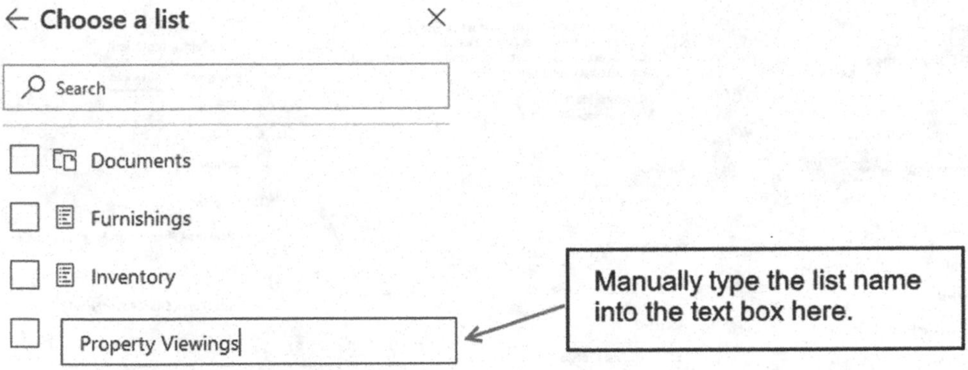

← **Choose a list**   ✕

🔍 Search

☐ 🗐 Documents

☐ 🗐 Furnishings

☐ 🗐 Inventory

☐ Property Viewings|

Manually type the list name
into the text box here.

Figure 6-8. *Connecting to SharePoint from an app*

Tip   We can connect to SharePoint items that don't appear in the list by typing the name into the textbox that appears in the "Choose a list" panel.

Building SharePoint Forms

Each SharePoint list includes a built-in editor that enables users to create and edit list items. We can modify the built-in data entry forms with Power Apps by selecting the "Customize forms" menu item from the list. This opens the Power Apps designer, and we can customize the SharePoint form in the same way that we would edit a canvas app.

A key difference is the presence of a SharePoint Integration item (Figure 6-9). We can use this to write a formula that defines what happens when a user opens the form in new, edit, and view modes. We can also modify the formula that runs when a user clicks the built-in save or cancel button.

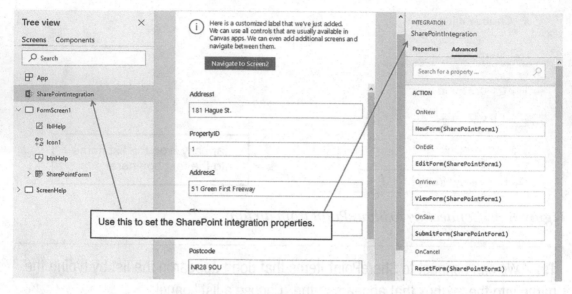

Figure 6-9. *SharePoint Integration item*

When we complete our modifications and publish our form, the changes will be visible in SharePoint when a user creates or modifies a record (Figure 6-10).

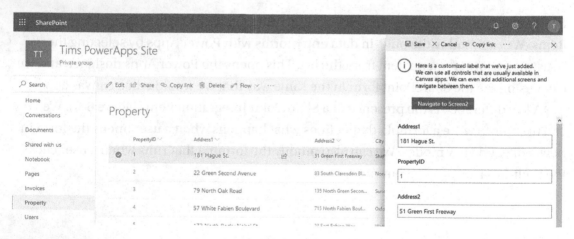

Figure 6-10. *A customized SharePoint form*

There are a couple of key things to be aware of when we customize a SharePoint form. First, it isn't possible to modify, hide, or disable the save and cancel buttons on the form. Second, it isn't possible to export an app or to move a customized form between SharePoint lists. This can be quite limiting because it makes it difficult for us to move changes between SharePoint lists and difficult to reuse changes and modifications.

SQL Server

We'll now move on and look at SQL Server. There are two types of SQL Server that are compatible with Power Apps. We can use the cloud-based SQL Server Azure, or we can use the on-premises data gateway to connect to an on-premise instance of SQL Server.

The benefit of SQL Server Azure is that we don't have to understand or manage the installation and maintenance of a database server. The service is subscription based and scalable, meaning that if demand for our app increases, we can provision additional SQL Server resources to meet that demand.

On-premises SQL Server is perfect for organizations that already use SQL Server or companies that wish to protect their data by keeping it on-premise. For those new to SQL Server, the SQL Server Express edition provides a great place to start. We can download and use this in commercial applications for free. The main limitation of this edition is that it imposes a maximum database size of 10 GB and it applies a memory usage limit of 1 GB.

On a security point, an important thing about the SQL Server connector is that it is a shared connector. This means that if an app builder were to create an app and share it with another user, that user could create a new app based on that connector. The second user could then use the connector to access tables that the initial app builder did not intend to share.

This can be quite a serious security weakness. To overcome this problem, there's an option with SQL Server Azure to connect using AAD (Azure Active Directory) authentication. This type of authentication relies not on a shared connection but on the connection that is dependent on the user. This type of connection can offer us better protection for our data.

SQL Server Limitations

With SQL Server, there are a few limitations to be aware of. First, Power Apps does not support some of the more advanced data types, such as XML, geometry, and geography. If a table includes one of these data types, Power Apps will refuse to create or update rows in that table.

Another problem with SQL Server is that it doesn't support tables with triggers. Triggers are pieces of SQL Server code that run each time we insert or update a record in a table. SQL developers often use triggers to create audit records or to initiate other workflow processes. Power Apps will return an error if we attempt to update a table with a trigger.

A previous limitation was that there was no support for temporal tables. These are tables that maintain a history of record changes. The good news is that Power Apps now works with temporal tables.

Setting Up SQL Azure

The easiest way to start learning SQL Server is to use SQL Server Azure; therefore, here's an overview of the main steps to get started. The first step is to create a Microsoft Azure account through the Azure website (`https://azure.microsoft.com/`).

New users can receive 12 months of free services, which include the use of SQL Server Azure. With an Azure subscription, we can also create Azure functions. We can use these to implement functionality beyond the capabilities of the functions that are native to Power Apps. To call an Azure function, we would need to use Power Automate or to create a custom connector. These two topics are covered later in this book.

After we subscribe to Microsoft Azure, we can navigate to the SQL Server section in the Azure Portal and configure a new server and database (Figure 6-11). The most important settings that we need to define are the server name, the server admin login and password, and the database name.

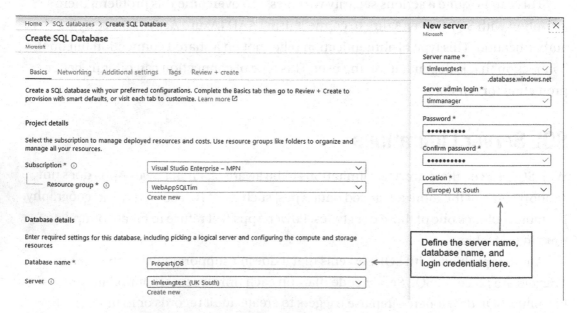

Figure 6-11. *Creating a SQL Azure database*

The next step is to grant permissions to both us and Power Apps to access our database server. The place to do this is the "Firewalls and virtual networks" page. We can access this through the overview page for the database server.

In the Firewalls page, we can click a button to create a firewall exception for our current IP address. To enable access to our database through Power Apps, it's necessary to add the IP addresses of Power Apps users to the firewall exception list. We can find a list of IP addresses in Power Apps Help (`https://docs.microsoft.com/en-us/Power Apps/maker/canvas-apps/limits-and-config#ip-addresses`).

There are separate IP address ranges that correspond to the region, and it's necessary to choose the IP address range that matches the region of our host environment.

In terms of cost, the most basic SQL Azure plan starts at around $5 per month. This is for a 2 GB, 5 DTU (Database Transaction Units) plan. A DTU is a measurement of compute power. The higher the DTU rating, the more powerful and expensive the server.

Managing a SQL Database

After we set up an Azure server and database, the next step is to create tables to store our data. The tool that we use to do this is called SQL Server Management Studio, and we can download this from the Microsoft website.

When we first start SQL Server Management Studio, it will prompt us to enter the server name, username, and password that we specified when we created our database server (Figure 6-12). Set the authentication type to SQL Server Authentication.

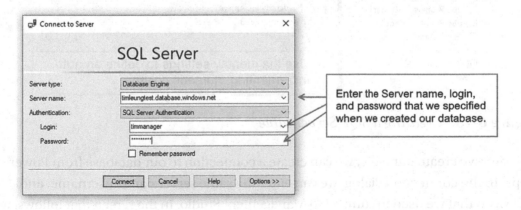

Figure 6-12. *Connecting to SQL Server from Management Studio*

When we successfully connect, our database will appear in the left-hand pane. We can then expand the node and choose the option to create a new table. A very important point is that any new table we create must have a primary key field. The purpose of a primary key value is to uniquely identify a record, and therefore, all primary key values in a table must be unique. Power Apps cannot add or update rows in tables without a primary key field.

A typical way to set up a table is to create an int column as the primary key field and to enable the "is identity" property (Figure 6-13). By doing this, SQL Server automatically generates a sequential unique primary key value for each row in the table.

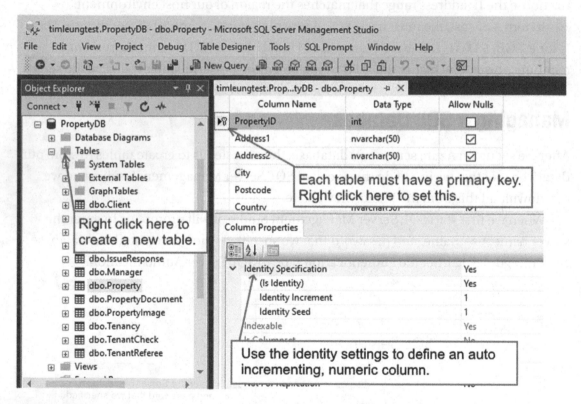

Figure 6-13. *Creating a SQL Server table*

After we create our table, we can create a connection to our database from Power Apps. In the connection dialog, we can enter the same server name, username, and password that we used to connect to Management Studio. In the screen that follows, we will see all tables and views in the database that we can connect to.

SQL Database Views

One feature that sets SQL Server above other data sources is the ability to create database views. We can use these to query data in a much more optimal way, and they provide a perfect way for us to calculate aggregated values, such as counts or sums or averages of a group of records.

As an example, let's imagine we have a table in our database that stores property details. The fields in this table include the price and a property type ID that indicates the type property. With the help of a view, we can calculate the average price grouped by property type ID and return this as a table to Power Apps. Figure 6-14 shows how we can use the graphical designer to build a view in Management Studio.

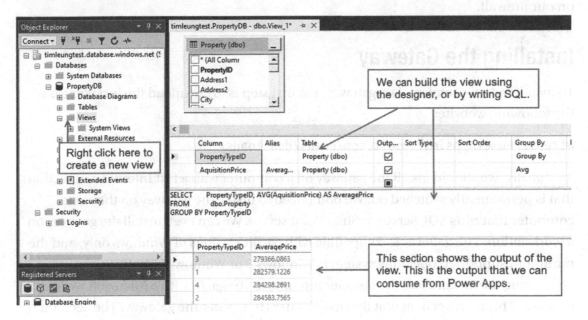

Figure 6-14. *Creating a SQL Server view*

With other data sources including SharePoint, this type of calculation can sometimes be impossible to perform, especially if the data source contains a large number of records.

On-Premises Data Gateway

One of the most attractive features of Power Apps is the ability to build apps that can connect to SQL Server databases or SharePoint servers that are inside our internal network. The tool that enables us to do this is the on-premises data gateway.

Technically, here's how the gateway works. When an app queries an on-premises data source, the app passes the request to a cloud service called the Azure Data Bus. The on-premises gateway polls the Azure Data Bus regularly and responds to any requests that it finds. The on-premises gateway doesn't require any incoming ports. In most cases, it doesn't require any special firewall configuration. But if we install the gateway in a more secure environment, the online help provides the specific ports we need to open on our firewall.

Installing the Gateway

To install the on-premises data gateway, the first step is to download the installer from the following website:

```
https://PowerApps.microsoft.com/en-us/downloads/
```

Ideally, we should install the gateway on a computer with a fast Internet connection that is permanently switched on. We don't need to install the gateway on the same computer that runs SQL Server or SharePoint server. We can even install the gateway on a workstation. The gateway is compatible with 64-bit versions of Windows only, and the minimum supported operating system is Windows 8 or Windows 2012 R2 Server.

During the installation, the installer prompts us to sign in with a Microsoft work account. This is an account that the installer uses to register the gateway. The account that we enter here will become the administrator of the gateway. Next, the installer prompts us to specify a gateway name and recovery key, as shown in Figure 6-15.

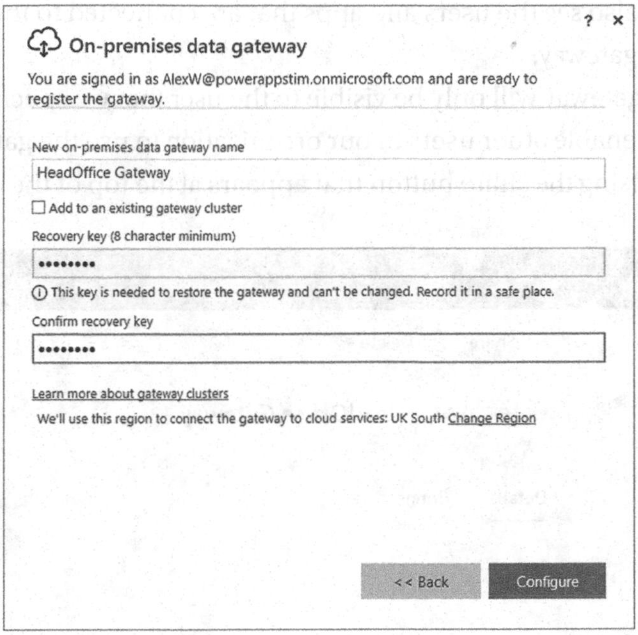

Figure 6-15. Configuring the gateway server

We can install multiple instances of the on-premises data gateway on different networks, so the gateway name enables us to identify the gateway when we make a connection from an app. The recovery key enables us to restore the gateway, and it's important to remember what we enter here. The reasons why we might need to restore the gateway service can include hardware or operating system failure on the gateway computer. Microsoft also provides occasional bug fixes and updates to the gateway service. The recovery key would enable us to reinstall the gateway in this scenario.

For resilience purposes, we can group gateway machines into a cluster. With this type of setup, if one machine in the cluster were to fail, the remaining machines could continue to provide a service. If we have an existing on-premises gateway in our network, we can create a cluster by selecting the "Add to an existing gateway cluster" checkbox.

At any point following the installation, we can return to the on-premises gateway application, and we can use this to check connectivity, view logs, and carry out diagnostic tasks. This provides an ideal way to troubleshoot any problems that we may encounter with the gateway.

Another place where we can monitor the on-premises gateway is through the Maker Portal (Figure 6-16). We can use this to check the operational status of a gateway. If the gateway were to lose Internet connectivity, we could detect this from the status page.

From here, we can also see the users and apps that are connected to the gateway, and we can also delete the gateway.

By default, the gateway will only be visible to the user that we specified at the time of the installation. To enable other users in our organization to use the gateway, we need to share the gateway using the share button that appears at the top of the page.

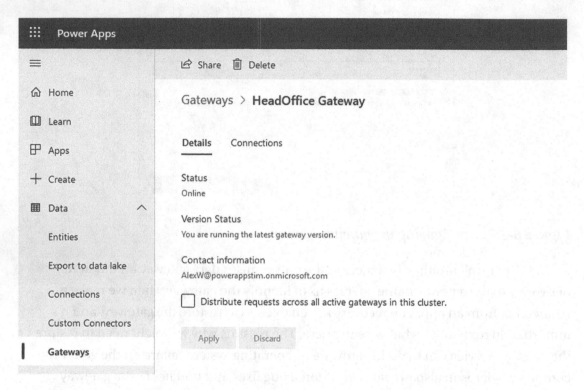

Figure 6-16. *Monitoring the gateway server*

Previously, we could only use the on-premises gateway with the default environment. The good news is that improvements to Power Apps now make it possible to access the gateway through any production environment.

Starting the Gateway Service

The gateway runs as a Windows service, and therefore, the Services snap-in that we can find through the Windows Control Panel is the place that we would check in the event of the gateway not working. The exact name of the service is the "On-premises data gateway service," as shown in Figure 6-17.

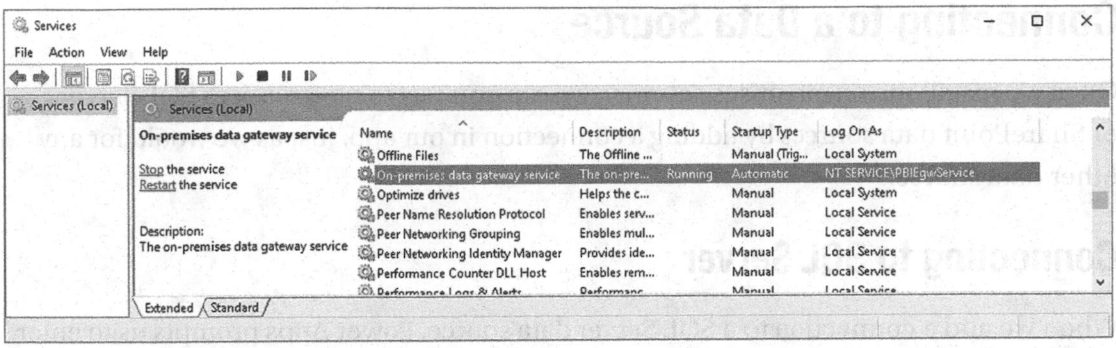

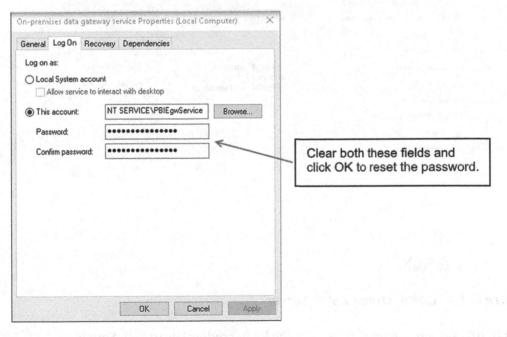

Figure 6-17. *Configuring the gateway service via Control Panel ➤ Administrative Tools ➤ Services*

If the gateway fails to work, the first thing to check is if the service is running. By default, this service runs under an account called NT SERVICE\PBIEgwService. If the service fails to start with a logon failure, we can reset the service account password by clearing the password fields and applying the change (Figure 6-18). Alternatively, we can change the log-on option to use a different account.

Figure 6-18. *Resetting the service account*

Connecting to a Data Source

Once we install the on-premises gateway, we can connect to on-premises SQL Server or SharePoint data sources by adding a connection in our app, just as we would for any other data source.

Connecting to SQL Server

When we add a connection to a SQL Server data source, Power Apps prompts us to enter the name of our SQL Server, as shown in Figure 6-19.

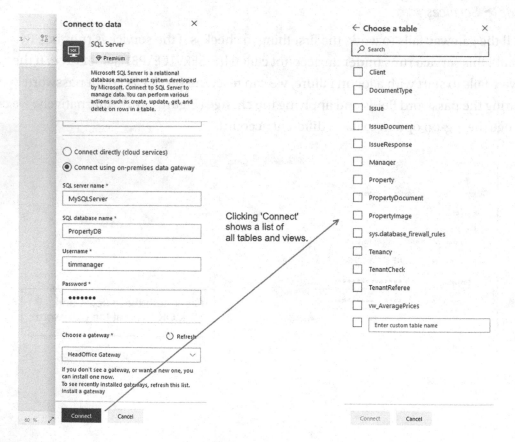

Figure 6-19. *Connecting to SQL Server*

On this screen, we need to specify the login credentials to SQL Server. Depending on how our target SQL Server is set up, we can connect either using Windows authentication or SQL Server authentication (which is labeled Basic in the authentication type drop-down). Note that the credentials we enter here are encrypted and stored in the Power Apps gateway cloud service. The credentials are decrypted on the local computer that runs the gateway service.

Provided that all goes well, we should see a list of tables and views that we can connect to. If we want to call a stored procedure, we can do this with a Power Automate flow (Chapter 25).

Sometimes, it can be difficult to determine the correct server connection details. This is because we need to enter all the details through textboxes, and these need to be precisely correct.

The typical value that we enter for a server name looks like this: "MyServerServer\SQLInstanceName." In SQL Server terms, an instance refers to an installation of SQL Server. On a given server, for example, we could install the free SQL Server Express edition, plus the full version of SQL Server 2019. The instance name enables us to differentiate between these two side-by-side installations. An interesting thing is that the server name setting works relative to where we install the gateway. Supposing that we installed SQL Server Express on the gateway machine, we can use the name localhost to refer to the host machine.

If the connection fails, some of the things to check are firewall and antivirus settings, and in the case of named instances, it's also important to confirm that the SQL Server Browser service is running. We can also try to use a different authentication type. If we used Windows authentication, we can try using SQL authentication instead. We can also try to use the IP address of the server, rather than the server name. If this fails, the next thing to do is to examine the gateway log files and the Windows event log. Figure 6-20 summarizes the main troubleshooting tips to diagnose gateway problems.

Setup 1: Gateway and SQL Server on same machine	**Setup 2**: Gateway and SQL Server on different machines
• **Gateway Name and IP address:** GatewaySrv: 192.168.0.10 • **SQL Server Name and IP address:** GatewaySrv: 192.168.0.10	• **Gateway Name and IP address:** GatewaySrv: 192.168.0.10 • **SQL Server Name and IP address:** SQLSrv: 192.168.0.11
The 'server name' values that we can enter in the connection dialog for the different instances that are installed on the machine:	
Instance 1: SQLExpress • GatewaySrv\SQLExpress • 192.168.0.10\SQLExpress • localhost\SQLExpress • 192.168.0.10,1234 *(assuming 1234 is the port number for the instance)* **Instance 2: SQL2019** • GatewaySrv\SQL2019 • 192.168.0.10\SQL2019 • localhost\SQL2019 • 192.168.0.10,5678 *(assuming 5678 is the port number for the instance)* **Instance 3: Default instance** • GatwaySrv • 192.168.0.10 • localhost	**Instance 1: SQLExpress** • SQLSrv\SQLExpress • 192.168.0.11\SQLExpress • 192.168.0.11,1234 *(assuming 1234 is the port number for the instance)* **Instance 2: SQL2019** • SQLSrv\SQL2019 • 192.168.0.11\SQL2019 • 192.168.0.11,5678 *(assuming 5678 is the port number for the instance)* **Instance 3: Default instance** • GatwaySrv • 192.168.0.11
Troubleshooting	
• Are there firewall, or proxy servers that are blocking the ports or network connections that on-premise gateway requires? • Use the network ports test in the on-premises gateway application to diagnose.	• Is there a firewall exception for the SQL Server process? • Is there antivirus software that is blocking the SQL Server ports? • For named instances, is the SQL Server browser service running (this returns the port number for the instance)? • The SQL Server browser service listens on port 1444. Is this open? If we choose not to use the browser service, we can specify the port name in the server name.

Figure 6-20. *Identifying the SQL Server name and diagnosing gateway problems*

Uninstalling a Gateway

To uninstall the gateway, choose the uninstall option from the Programs and Features section of the Control Panel on the machine where the gateway is installed. When we uninstall the gateway service, the gateway will still appear in the Gateways section of the Power Apps web portal. This provides us with the option to install the gateway service on a new computer.

If we want to completely delete the gateway registration, we can do this from the Power Platform admin center. Deleting a gateway won't delete any connections that use the gateway.

Other Data Sources

Moving forward from SharePoint and SQL Server, we'll now take a brief look at other interesting and novel data sources that we can use in this final section of the chapter. The main focus of this section is to demonstrate ways to connect to non-database sources of data.

Static Excel Data

In cases where we want to access static read-only data, we can import Excel data directly into our app. To import an Excel file, the first step is to define the data as a table and to give it a meaningful name, just as we would for any other Excel data source.

The next step is to click the "Add static data to your app" item from the data sources list, as shown in Figure 6-21. This opens a file dialog that we can use to select our Excel file. Once the import process completes, we can access the data just like any other Excel data source. The only difference of course is that we cannot update or add rows in this data – it is strictly read-only.

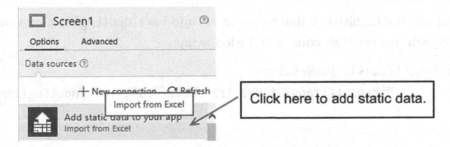

Figure 6-21. *Select the "Add static data to your app" option*

Microsoft Translator Data Source

The Microsoft Translator service provides a method for us to build multilingual support into our apps. With this service, we can translate the data in our apps, as well as the static user interface elements that make up our screens. Here's a basic demonstration of how to translate the contents of a text input control from English to Spanish.

To use the Microsoft Translator service, the first step is to add a connection (Figure 6-22). In the data sources dialog, we will see two connectors – the original version and a V2 connector. As Microsoft improves and develops the connectors, we will find that many of the original connectors are replaced with V2 connectors. The original connectors remain for backward compatibility purposes. In many cases, the method names and parameters may have changed in the newer version.

For this example, we'll choose the newer V2 connector. When we add this data source, the connection dialog will prompt us for a subscription key. If we leave this blank, the connector uses a built-in key that is limited to translating 55,000 characters per day.

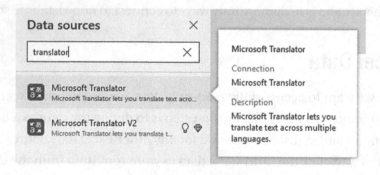

Figure 6-22. *Adding a connection to the Microsoft Translator service*

After we add this data source, we can build the screen that's shown in Figure 6-23. This screen contains two text input controls called TextInputEnglish and TextInputSpanish.

To translate the English text that a user enters into TextInputEnglish, we would set the OnChange property of this control to the following:

```
UpdateContext({TranslationResult:
        MicrosoftTranslatorV2.Translate("es", TextInputEnglish.Text)
        }
)
```

This stores the result of the translation into a variable called `TranslationResult`. We can then display this value in the `TextInputSpanish` control by setting the Default property of this control to `TranslationResult`.

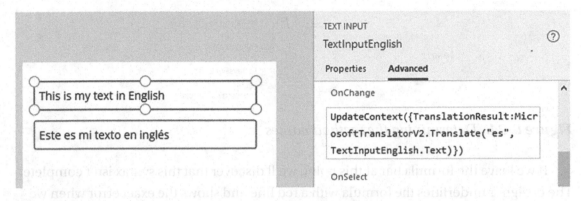

Figure 6-23. *Translating text from English to Spanish*

The `Translate` method accepts two arguments – the target language and the text to translate. In this example, "es" denotes the language code for Spanish.

Note   The connectors that we use throughout our apps appear in the Data ➤ Connections section of the Maker Portal. We can use this section to update credentials, such as subscription keys.

Microsoft MSN Weather Services

Another interesting data source is the MSN Weather service. Here's how to add a label that shows the current weather in London.

Many of the more unusual data sources are not well documented. A key lesson here is to highlight the importance of using IntelliSense to determine the capabilities of the service and the correct syntax to use. When we type the name of a data source into the formula bar followed by the period symbol, the formula bar will show a list of methods and provide a description of the arguments that we need to supply.

To illustrate this technique using the MSN Weather service as an example, let's add a connection to this service and add a label to a screen. Next, select the `Text` property and type the name of the data source `MSNWeather` into the formula bar. At this point, IntelliSense reveals a method called `CurrentWeather` (Figure 6-24), in addition to methods to obtain forecasts for today and tomorrow. If we choose the `CurrentWeather` method, IntelliSense prompts us to provide a location and to specify the measurement units for our results. We can choose either metric or imperial.

Figure 6-24. *Determining the method names*

If we leave the formula bar at this point, we'll discover that this syntax isn't complete. The designer underlines the formula with a red line and shows the exact error when we hover the mouse over the red cross icon, as shown in Figure 6-25.

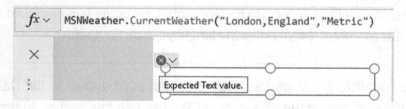

Figure 6-25. *Hover the mouse over the red cross icon to see the exact error*

To resolve these problems, the trick is to add a full stop character to the end of the formula to see what IntelliSense suggests (Figure 6-26). As we build up a formula, we can use the formula bar to interrogate the response of any given property.

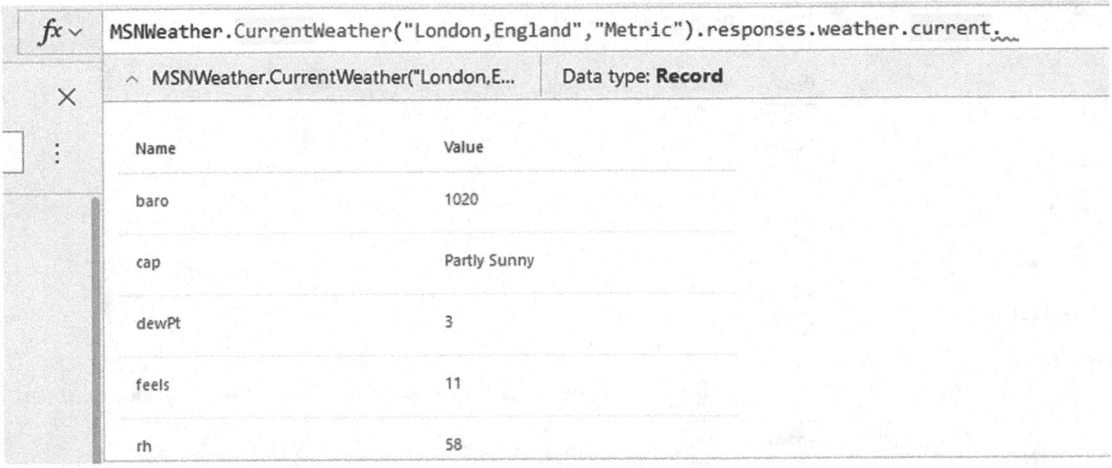

Name	Value
baro	1020
cap	Partly Sunny
dewPt	3
feels	11
rh	58

Figure 6-26. Use IntelliSense to determine the correct syntax

By using this technique, we can discover that we can retrieve the current temperature by using the following syntax:

```
MSNWeather.CurrentWeather("London, England",
                    "Metric").responses.weather.current.temp
```

When we enter the correct formula, Power Apps immediately calls the weather service and displays the temperature in the design view of the screen.

Sending Push Notifications

For Android and iOS users, we can alert users through the notification area of the mobile operating system. When a user receives an alert, the user can click the message to open the specific app that's associated with the message.

We can send notifications from any app or from a Microsoft Automate Flow. To send a notification from an app, we would add a data connection to the "Power Apps Notification" provider and use this to send our notifications. The notifications must be targeted at specific users which are identified by email address.

To demonstrate this feature, here's how to modify an auto-generated app of issues so that it sends a notification to a manager whenever a user creates a new record.

Because the notifications must be associated with an app, the first step is to find the unique identifier of the app. To do this, find the app in the Maker Portal and navigate to the details section (Figure 6-27). A quick way to go to the approximate place in the portal is to click the share menu item in Power Apps Studio.

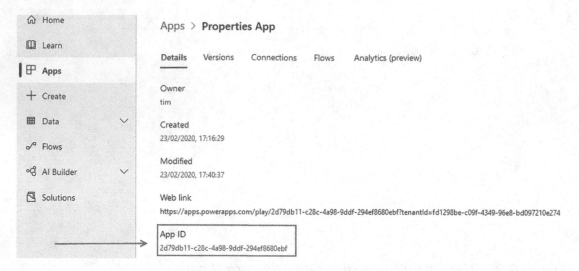

Figure 6-27. *Determining the ID of an app*

Tip   When working with an app in Power Apps Studio, a quick way to navigate to the app settings section of the Maker Portal is to click the share menu item.

The next step is to add a data source to the Power Apps Notification provider. When we add the data source, the designer prompts us to enter the app ID or web link.

To avoid any confusion, note that there is a similar data connector called Notifications. The purpose of this connector is to send email notifications, rather than mobile device alerts (Figure 6-28).

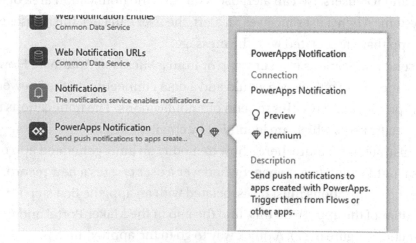

Figure 6-28. *Adding a data source to the Power Apps Notification provider*

The next step is to open the edit form and to modify the formula for the save icon. Modify the OnSelect property as shown in the following:

```
If(EditForm1.Mode=FormMode.New,
    SubmitForm(EditForm1);
        PowerAppsNotification.SendPushNotification(
            {recipients:["tim@timleung.co.uk"],
            message:"A new issue record was created",
            openApp:true}
        ),
    SubmitForm(EditForm1)
)
```

This formula uses the value of EditForm1.Mode to test if the user is entering a new record. If this is true, the formula calls the SubmitForm function to save the record and then calls the function to send the notification. If the user is not entering a new record, the code calls the SubmitForm function only.

One thing that can catch us out is that when a user enters a new record, the value of EditForm1.Mode changes to edit mode immediately after the call to SubmitForm succeeds. Therefore, if we want to use the value of EditForm1.Mode to test that a user is entering a new record, we need to carry out this test before we call SubmitForm.

At this point, we can run our app. When we add a new record, the app will send a notification to the mobile device of the recipient, as shown in Figure 6-29.

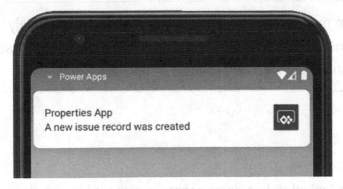

Figure 6-29. *How the push notification appears in an actual device*

There are two useful features about the SendPushNotification function that are worth mentioning. The first is that we can specify multiple recipients by providing a comma-separated list. The second is that we can specify a table of parameters. When the user starts the app by clicking the notification message, the parameter values will be available to the target app. Here's an example formula to illustrate these concepts:

```
PowerAppsNotification.SendPushNotification({
    recipients:["tim@timleung.co.uk","administrator@timleung.co.uk"],
    message:"A new issue record was created",
         openApp:true,
    params:Table({key:"IssueID",
                      value: EditForm1.LastSubmit.IssueID }
                      )
}
)
```

This formula shows how to retrieve the IssueID of the newly created record. On the assumption that the data source is a SQL Server table and that the IssueID field refers to an identity value that the server generates, we can use the LastSubmit property of the form to retrieve any values that have been generated by the server.

In our app, we could then call Param("IssueID") to retrieve the parameter value. We can then apply the technique that we covered in Chapter 5 to open the specified record directly in the app.

Note   The form mode of a form changes to edit mode immediately after a call to SubmitForm succeeds. We should keep this mind, especially in cases where we include conditional logic that checks value of the form mode.

Summary

In this chapter, we looked at data sources that are compatible with Power Apps. We covered the pros and cons of the most popular data sources, and we looked at how to set up two of the most popular data sources – SharePoint and SQL Server.

Of all the data storage options, Excel is the simplest to use. However, it doesn't cope well with large quantities of data. For multiuser apps, SharePoint provides a more robust platform. Its features include a wide range of data types, conflict detection, row versioning, and data validation. Best of all, it is included with most Microsoft/Office 365 plans, so requires no additional licensing.

For the most demanding applications, SQL Server and Dataverse offer the best choice. Dataverse is the natural choice for Dynamics 365 users, because this is the database that Dynamics 365 uses natively. By using Dataverse, we can extend the capabilities of Dynamics 365. Dataverse is a requirement for model-driven and portal apps; therefore, this would be the data source of choice if we were building those types of app.

SQL Server copes very well with large amounts of data and provides excellent query capabilities. It provides many ways to optimize performance. For example, we can create views to retrieve data in ways that wouldn't be possible with other data sources. We can also build stored procedures to carry out data tasks that are slow or impossible to accomplish with other data sources.

With the help of the on-premises data gateway, we can connect to SQL Server or SharePoint data sources that are hosted inside an internal company network. This provides a very powerful option, especially in cases where we have existing data that is hosted in on-premises data sources or in situations where we want to keep data inside a private network for security reasons.

The process for setting up an on-premises gateway involves installing the software and signing in with a Power Apps account. Provided there are no networking issues, we can start to use the gateway by creating a SQL Server or SharePoint connection in our app and choosing the option to use on-premises data.

In the final part of this chapter, we looked at other data sources that we can utilize in our apps. The first is the ability to add static Excel data to an app. This solution is ideal if we want to incorporate read-only data that rarely changes into an app. We also looked at the Microsoft Translator and MSN Weather data sources. With these two data sources, we can translate data and obtain the current weather. Because many of the less used data connectors are not well documented, we covered the method of using IntelliSense to determine the correct methods and syntax to use.

Finally, we looked at how to send push notifications to mobile devices using the notifications connector. Using this connector, we can send notifications based on email address. We can set the notification message, and we can also configure the message to open Power Apps and to navigate the user to a specific record on a screen.

CHAPTER 7

Working with Tables, Rows, and Collections

Tables and rows play a crucial role in the vast majority of apps. Most apps require us to build functionality that can process and manipulate data in tables.

In the first part of this chapter, we'll cover the syntax to define records, and we'll explore the functions that enable us to work with tables and rows. For practical guidance, we will build an inventory screen. This will enable us to see the ways in which we can combine table-level functions in a real-life situation.

Later in this chapter, we'll learn how to manipulate strings with the help of these functions. This includes how to generate HTML output, how to split comma-separated values, and how to extract subsections of an input string.

Other useful topics that we'll cover in this chapter include

- How to work with collections. Collections play a key role in app development because they enable us to store in-memory, working copies of table data.

- How to save data. We'll find out how to write formulas to create, update, and delete single or multiple rows from a data source, including how to work with SharePoint lookup fields (which can be very tricky). We'll also learn how to create sets of parent and child records in one go.

- How to aggregate data. We'll find out how to work with groups of data, including how to calculate counts, sums, and averages and to determine minimum and maximum values.

© Tim Leung 2021
T. Leung, *Beginning Power Apps*, https://doi.org/10.1007/978-1-4842-6683-0_7

Basic Syntax

Let's begin by looking at the basic syntax to define rows, columns, and tables. To demonstrate, we'll use the data structure that's shown in Figure 7-1.

PropertyTypeID ▼	PropertyTypeDesc ▼
1	House
2	Apartment
3	Bungalow

Figure 7-1. *Example data structure*

The syntax that defines a record (a row-level item) looks like this:

```
{'PropertyTypeID': 1, 'PropertyTypeDesc': "House" }
```

Curley start and end brackets define a record. Within these brackets, field name and value pairs are separated by the colon character. To support field names or values with spaces, the field names are delimited with single quote characters, whereas the field values are delimited by double quote characters.

The simple way to define a list of items is to enclose comma-separated values within square brackets. Figure 7-2 illustrates this technique, as applied to the Items property of a drop-down box that displays hour values.

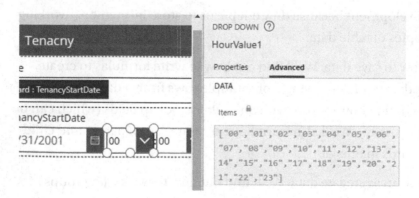

Figure 7-2. *Setting the data source of an item*

This technique works well for simple, single-value items. To define a list of records, in other words, a table, we can use the same method of enclosing the records inside square brackets like so:

```
[
  {'PropertyTypeID': 1, 'PropertyTypeDesc': "House"},
  {'PropertyTypeID': 2, 'PropertyTypeDesc': "Apartment"},
  {'PropertyTypeID': 3, 'PropertyTypeDesc': "Bungalow"}
]
```

Another way to define a group of records is to call the Table function. The input to this function accepts one or more records, like so:

```
Table(
      {'PropertyTypeID': 1, 'PropertyTypeDesc': "House"},
      {'PropertyTypeID': 2, 'PropertyTypeDesc': "Apartment"},
      {'PropertyTypeID': 3, 'PropertyTypeDesc': "Bungalow"}
)
```

Overview of Collections and Functions

One topic that all app builders should understand well is how to use collections. These play a crucial role in developing almost every app. A collection is simply an application-scoped variable that stores table data. We can access collection data from any screen in an app. They exist in memory and exist only for the duration of a session. The data in collections are destroyed when the user closes the app.

Collections are very important because they enable us to store working copies of our data. Suppose that we want to transpose or to aggregate data. We can carry out a series of steps to shape our data and to use collections to store our workings during the interim steps.

Another important use for collections is to cache data. If we were to perform a time-consuming data operation, we could store the results in a collection for later use. Because collections are held in memory, we can load frequently used data in collections to help speed up our apps. App builders often cache data in collections using the OnStart property of an app. If we want to preload multiple tables, we can speed up the process through the help of the Concurrent function. This improves performance by carrying out data operations in parallel.

Power Apps provides a series of functions to define and work with collections. It also provides functions that shape the columns in a collection. Table 7-1 shows the functions to create and add rows and to clear data in a collection.

Table 7-1. *Collection functions*

Function	Description
Collect(colFurnishings, FurnishingsList)	This function appends rows to a specified collection. It creates the collection if it doesn't exist. This example copies rows from the FurnishingsList data source to a collection called colFurnishings.
Clear(colFurnishings)	This removes all rows in a specified collection (colFurnishings, in this example).
ClearCollect(colFurnishings, FurnishingsSP)	This combines both the Collect and Clear functions. It creates the collection if it doesn't exist and clears any existing data prior to adding rows from the specified data source.

Table 7-2 shows the functions that can carry out column-related tasks. We can call these functions to return tables with additional columns, excluded columns, renamed columns, or only selected columns from a data source.

Table 7-2. *Column functions*

Function	Description
AddColumns(Property, "AcquisitionPriceUSD", AcquisitionPrice * .129)	This returns a table with the additional columns that we specify. This formula adds a column called AcquisitionPriceUSD to the Property data source and sets the field value to AcquisitionPrice multiplied by an exchange rate.
DropColumns(colFurnishings, "FurnishingID")	This returns a table that excludes the columns that we specify. This example returns the colFurnishings collection with the FurnishingID column excluded.
RenameColumns(Property, "AquisitionPrice", "AquisitionPriceGBP")	This returns a table with the specified columns renamed. This example renames the AcquisitionPrice column to AquisitionPriceGBP.
ShowColumns(Property, "PropertyID", "AquisitionPrice")	This returns a table that includes only the columns that we specify. In this example, we return only the PropertyID and AquisitionPrice columns from the Property data source.

With all these column-level functions, an important thing to understand is that they return a copy of a table. They do not change or modify the input data. For example, if we were to call the DropColumns function against a SharePoint list, this would not remove the actual column from the SharePoint list.

The examples in Table 7-2 show how to work with a single column. However, all these functions are capable of accepting multiple columns in a single call. With the AddColumns function, for example, we could provide additional comma-separated column name and value pairs, if there were a need to add more than one column.

A great use of the AddColumns function is to populate the items of a gallery or table control. Where we need to display the result of a calculation that affects many rows, we can perform this more efficiently by calling the AddColumns function.

As an example, let's take a table that stores property details and acquisition prices in pounds sterling. We can calculate the US dollar equivalent for all records in this table by making a single call to AddColumns. We can wrap this inside a call to RenameColumns to adjust the column header names. We can directly set the Items property of a data table to this formula, as shown in Figure 7-3. This illustration also summarises the data structure following each individual function call.

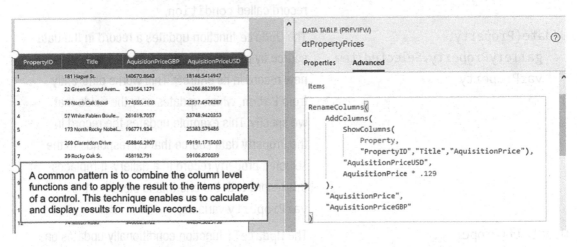

Figure 7-3. *Combining column-level functions*

Finally, Power Apps provides functions to add, update, delete rows in a collection or data source. These are illustrated in Table 7-3.

Table 7-3. *Row-level functions*

Function	Description

`Patch(Property,`
`    galleryProperty.SelectedItem,`
`    {AcquisitionPrice: 100000}`
`)`
	This updates the selected item of the gallery control in the Property data source and sets the AcquisitionPrice field to 100,000.

`Patch(Property,`
`    Defaults(Property),`
`    {Address1: "10 High St",`
`    AcquisitionPrice: 50000}`
`)`
	This adds a new record to the Property data source. To indicate that we want to add a new record, we provide a new record as the second argument to the Patch function. The `Defaults` function accepts a data source name and returns a new record that corresponds to the specified data source.

`Patch(varProperty,`
`    {condition: "Good"}`
`)`
	We can call `Patch` to add additional fields to a record in a collection. In this example, varProperty is a variable that stores a property record. This formula adds an additional field to the record called `condition`.

`Update(Property,`
`    galleryProperty.SelectedItem,`
`    varProperty`
`)`
	The Update function updates a record in the data source by replacing the target record with the new record in its entirety. This works differently from `Patch`, which updates only the fields that we specify. This example updates the record in the Property data source that corresponds to the selected property record in a gallery. It replaces this record with the one that is stored in the varProperty variable.

`UpdateIf(Property,`
`    AcquisitionDate <`
`        DateValue("01/01/2010"),`
`    {Active=false}`
`)`
	The UpdateIf function conditionally updates one or more records in a collection or data source. This example updates the Active field to false for all records in the Property data source where the acquisition date is before January 1, 2010.

(continued)

Table 7-3. (*continued*)

Function	Description

`Remove(Property,`
`    galleryProperty.SelectedItem`
`)`
	The Remove function removes a record from a data source. This example deletes the record in the Property data source that corresponds to the selected property record in a gallery.

`RemoveIf(Property,`
`    Active=false`
`)`
	The RemoveIf function conditionally removes one or more records in a collection or data source. This example deletes all records in the Property data source with an Active field value of false.

One of the most versatile functions is the `Patch` function. We can call this to create and update new records and to add additional fields to a record in a collection. Because this function is so powerful, it is one that all app builders should understand well, and we can find countless references to its usage on the Web and in forums.

The most common use of `Patch` is to create and to update records in a data source. We can also call `Patch` to add additional fields to a record. A question we might ask is - how does this use of `Patch` differ from the `AddColumns` function? The answer is that `AddColumns` operates against an input table, whereas `Patch` operates against a single record.

Tip   We can easily build a feature that enables users to delete multiple records by calling the `RemoveIf` function. To prevent accidental deletion, we can display a confirmation screen and we can see an example of how to implement this in Chapter 9.

Working with Collections

We've now covered all of the functions that we need to work with row- and table-level data. In practical situations, however, it's rare for us to call these functions in isolation. These functions work best when we chain them together and use them in conjunction with one another. It's important to understand the common patterns for combining table-level functions, and this is an area that may not be completely clear for beginners.

To provide some practical guidance, we will therefore build a feature that takes advantage of many of these table-level functions. The feature that we will build will enable a property manager to build an inventory of items in a property. The left side of the screen shows a list of furnishings from a SharePoint list. The user can add furnishings to an inventory and append comments and valuations. When the process is complete, the user can save the data to SharePoint and can generate a neatly formatted HTML report. This feature will enable us to explore the use of collections; it demonstrates the methods to save data into a SharePoint list (in practice, these techniques will work similarly for any other data source). Figure 7-4 illustrates the screen that we will build and highlights the technical learning points that we will cover in this section.

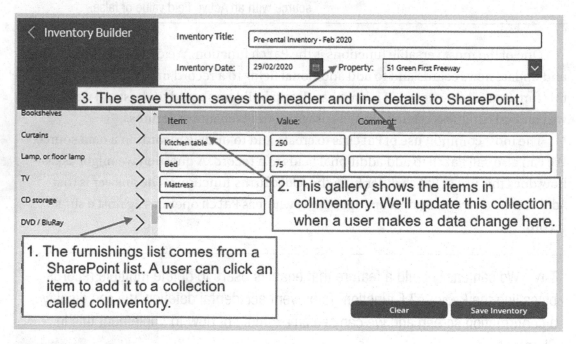

Figure 7-4. *Using collections to build features in an app*

Setting Up Our Demo App

Our example relies on four SharePoint lists – a furnishings list, a property list, an inventory list, and an inventory items list. Figure 7-5 illustrates this setup.

Inventory	
Title	Single line of text
InventoryDate	Date and Time
Property	Lookup
Comment	Single line of text
NextInspectionDate	Date and Time

Inventory Items	
Title	Single line of text
Inventory	Lookup
Description	Single line of text
ItemValue	Currency

Property	
Address1	Single line of text
Address2	Single line of text
City	Single line of text
Postcode	Single line of text
Country	Single line of text
Telephone	Single line of text
AquisitionPrice	Currency
AquisitionDate	Date and Time

Furnishings	
Title	Single line of text

Figure 7-5.   The SharePoint list definitions in our example app

This setup includes several lookup lists. In particular, the setup includes the inventory list that stores the inventory title and date. In addition to this, there is an inventory items list that stores the items that are related to an inventory record. This setup enables us to demonstrate how to work with the parent-child relationships that are typical in many business applications (Figure 7-6).

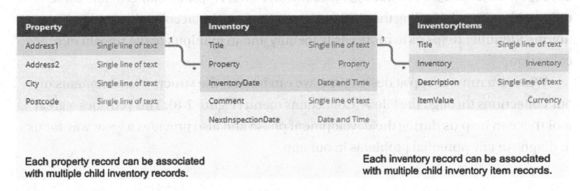

Each property record can be associated with multiple child inventory records.

Each inventory record can be associated with multiple child inventory item records.

Figure 7-6.   Data relationships

Adding a Single Row (Uniquely Identifiable)

The left part of our screen contains a gallery control that shows a list of rows from the SharePoint furnishings list (Figure 7-7). When a user clicks the icon in this gallery, the formula collects the selected item into a collection called colInventory. The item that it collects is a record that contains a single field, Title. Within the call to the Collect function, we call the Patch function to expand the record by adding three additional fields: Comment, ItemValue, and InventoryGuid.

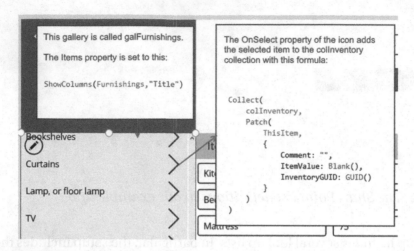

Figure 7-7. *Adding a record to a collection*

The purpose of the InventoryGuid field is to enable us to uniquely identify each record in our collection. A GUID (globally unique identifier) value looks like this: 123e4567-e89b-12d3-a456-426655440000. With Power Apps, we can generate these unique identifiers by calling the GUID function. When we build collections, adding a unique identifier helps us to more easily identify and to manipulate the rows in our collection.

When we run our app at design time, we can inspect the structure and contents of our collections through the File ➤ Collections menu (Figure 7-8). This provides a great tool that can help us during the development phase and also provides a great way for us to diagnose any potential problems in our app.

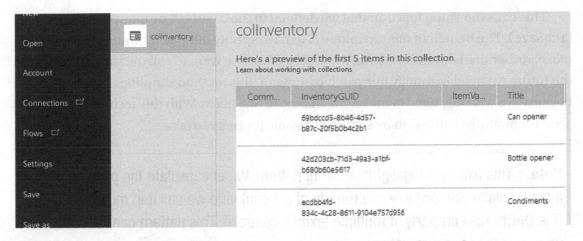

Figure 7-8. *Viewing the structure and contents of collections*

Updating a Single Row

To update a single row in a collection or data source, we call the `Patch` function.
Figure 7-9 shows the formula to update a record in a collection.

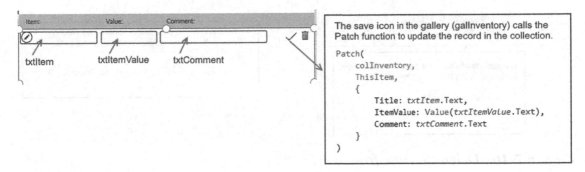

Figure 7-9. *Updating a row in a collection*

In this example, we attach the patch formula to the `OnSelect` property of an icon.
It's possible to adapt our screen to update the record in the collection as soon as a user
modifies a data item and leaves the text entry control. An effective way to do this is to add
the following function to the `OnChange` property of each text entry control:

```
Select(icoSave)
```

This calls the Patch function that we defined in the OnSelect property of our icon (icoSave). The benefit of this technique is that we specify our patch formula in a single place, rather than duplicate it in all the places where we want to call the same logic. If in the future we need to modify our patch command, this method simplifies maintenance because we will only need to make our change in one place. With this technique, we can also optionally hide the icon by setting its Visible property to false.

Note   This example highlights a useful pattern. We encapsulate the patch logic in a single place (the OnSelect property of an icon), and we call it in multiple places (the OnChange property of multiple textbox controls). This pattern can reduce unnecessary code duplication.

Deleting a Single Row

Figure 7-10 shows the formula to delete a single row from a collection or data source.

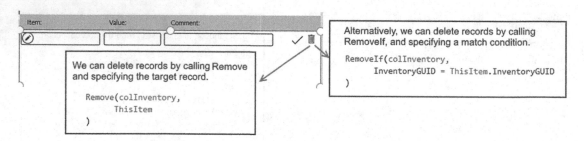

Figure 7-10. *Deleting a row from a collection*

The Remove function takes two arguments. The first specifies the data source, and the second specifies the record to delete. The second argument must be a record object. To specify multiple records, we provide a comma separated list of records.

This technique works well in this scenario because we can reference the selected record in a gallery control through the ThisItem identifier. Collections can contain multiple instances of the record. The Remove function accepts an optional third argument to specify whether to delete all instances of the record or only the first matching instance.

In situations where it's difficult to specify a record object, another method is to call the Remove If function. This method works well against databases or data sources with a unique primary key field. This function takes two arguments. The first specifies the data source, and the second specifies a match condition. The function will delete all records that satisfy the match condition. Because we added a GUID field to our collection, it provides us with the flexibility to utilize conditional functions which include RemoveIf and UpdateIf.

A known issue that can catch us out is if we attempt to delete a record by referencing the selected item of a gallery control using syntax in the following format:

```
Remove(colInventory, galleryInventory.SelectedItem)
```

Although this pattern works well with connected data sources such as SharePoint, Excel and SQL Server, it does not work with collections. With a collection, this will not delete the intended record. The reason is because the SelectedItem property of a gallery also exposes controls that exist in the template of the gallery. This mismatch in the schema of the selected item causes the Remove function to fail against a collection.

Caution   With a collection data source, it is not possible to specify the record that we want to remove by referencing the selected item of a gallery.

Working with Data Sources

Once the inventory is complete, the user can save the changes to the underlying SharePoint list. To save data, the two functions we rely on most are Patch and Collect. Figure 7-11 illustrates the formula that runs when the user clicks the button to save the inventory. In this section, we'll examine this formula in depth to explore how to carry out two common practices when saving data. The first is how to set the value of SharePoint lookup lists with Patch, and the second is how to retrieve auto-generated values from the server (e.g., SharePoint or SQL Server). This enables us to add parent and child records in a single operation, and the focus of the next set of code samples will be on this technique – how to add a parent and associated child records in one operation.

```
//Save the parent inventory record
UpdateContext(
    {
        locInventory: Patch(
            Inventory,
            Defaults(Inventory),
            {
                Property: {
                    '@odata.type': "#Microsoft.Azure.Connectors.SharePoint.SPListExpandedReference",
                    Id: drpProperty.Selected.ID,
                    Value: ""
                },
                Title: drpProperty.Selected.Address2,
                InventoryDate: Now()
            }
        )
    }
);

//Save the child inventory records
Collect(
    'Inventory Items',
    ShowColumns(
        AddColumns(
            colInventory,
            "Inventory",
            {
                '@odata.type': "#Microsoft.Azure.Connectors.SharePoint.SPListExpandedReference",
                Id: locInventory.ID,
                Value: ""
            }
        ),
        "Title",
        "ItemValue",
        "Inventory"
    )
)
```

Figure 7-11. *The formula that runs when a user clicks the save button*

Saving Records That Include SharePoint Lookup Values

Starting with the first logical step of our formula, let's look at how to save our parent record to the inventory list. To add a new record to a data source, we call the `Patch` function. The first argument defines the data source, and the second argument defines the record. To specify that we want to create a new record, we call the `Defaults` function to return an instance of a new record, and we pass this as the second argument to the `Patch` function. The third argument specifies the record values to add. Here is the precise part of the formula that adds a new record:

```
Patch(
    Inventory,
    Defaults(Inventory),
```

```
{
    Property:{
     '@odata.type':"#Microsoft.Azure.Connectors.SharePoint.
    SPListExpandedReference",
        Id:drpProperty.Selected.ID,
        Value:""
        },
        Title:txtTitle.Text,
        InventoryDate:Now()
    }
```

In our example SharePoint data source, an inventory record includes a lookup field that stores the property.

To specify this lookup value in the inventory record, we must specify a property record that corresponds to the property that the user selects in the property drop-down. If the name of the property drop-down box is drpProperty, we might imagine that we could define an inventory record that refers to the selected property of the drop-down box like so:

```
{
    Property:drpProperty.Selected, Title:txtTitle.Text, InventoryDate:Now()
}
```

Sadly, for the purposes of specifying a lookup value, this is not valid syntax. Instead, we have to use more obscure syntax that looks like this:

```
Property:{
        '@odata.type':"#Microsoft.Azure.Connectors.SharePoint.
    SPListExpandedReference",
            Id:drpProperty.Selected.ID, Value:""
}
```

The most important value that we specify in this code is the SharePoint ID value that relates to the record that we want to set. The Value property is unimportant, and we can always set this to an empty string. The lookup record will always include the '@odata. type' type property.

Patching Complex SharePoint Types

To give some background to this slightly obscure syntax, Figure 7-12 shows a screenshot from the first edition of this book.

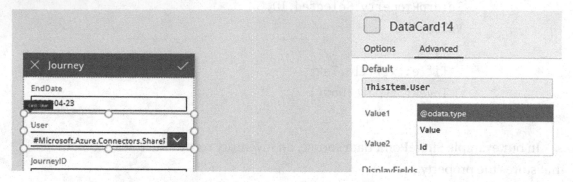

Figure 7-12. *In the first release of Power Apps, we could view the* `@odata.type` *values*

In the first release of Power Apps, integration with lookup fields was not as rounded as it is today. As this early screenshot shows, the schema of a lookup record includes `@odata.type`, `Value`, and `Id` fields. This hopefully provides some context as to the origins of the syntax that we still use today.

It can be really difficult to work out the syntax that we used to patch a SharePoint field. For example, how do we patch a choice field, or how do we set a lookup field to null? With person columns, how do we set a single person or set multiple persons? To provide a useful reference, the snippets of code in Listing 7-1 illustrate the syntax that we use to patch SharePoint fields of various data types.

Listing 7-1. Syntax for patching SharePoint fields

```
//SharePoint LookUp Column - Set the lookup value to null
{
    '@odata.type':
        "#Microsoft.Azure.Connectors.SharePoint.SPListExpandedReference",
    Id: -1,
    Value: ""
}
```

```
//SharePoint Choice Column
{
    '@odata.type':
        "#Microsoft.Azure.Connectors.SharePoint.SPListExpandedReference",
    Value: "Approved"
}

//SharePoint Person (Single Person)
{
    '@odata.type':"#Microsoft.Azure.Connectors.SharePoint.
    SPListExpandedUser",
    Claims:"i:0#.f|membership|tim@emaildomain.com",
    Email:"",
    Department:"",
    DisplayName:"",
    JobTitle:"",
    Picture:""
}

//SharePoint Person (Multiple People)
Table(
        {
            Claims:"i:0#.f|membership|tim@emaildomain.com",
            Department:"IT",
            DisplayName:" ",
            Email:"",
            JobTitle:"",
            Picture:""
        },
        {
            Claims:"i:0#.f|membership|tom@emaildomain.com",
            Department:"",
            DisplayName:" ",
            Email:"",
            JobTitle:"",
            Picture:""
        }
    )
```

Retrieving Server-Generated Values

When we call the Patch function to add a record, the return value of this function includes all server-generated data. This includes calculated fields, auto-generated numbers from databases, or SharePoint ID values. In our example, we store the return value from Patch into a variable called locInventory. By doing this, we can retrieve the newly added inventory record from SharePoint.

Adding Multiple Child Rows

To add multiple records to a data source, we call the Collect function. With this mode of usage, the first argument defines the data source, and the second argument defines a table of data to add.

The column names in the source table must match the column names of the target data source. Therefore, we can apply some of the table shaping functions such as AddColumns, RenameColumns, and DropColumns to build a source table with columns that correspond to those of the target data source:

```
Collect(
    'Inventory Items',
    ShowColumns(
        AddColumns(
            colInventory,
            "Inventory",
            {
                '@odata.type': "#Microsoft.Azure.Connectors.SharePoint.
                SPListExpandedReference",
                Id: locInventory.ID,
                Value: ""
            }
        ),
        "Title",
        "ItemValue",
        "Inventory"
    )
)
```

This code sample refers to the header, inventory record that we created in the previous step, which is stored in the variable locInventory.

To build the source table to pass to the Collect function, we take the colInventory collection as the main source and call the AddColumns function to append a lookup value that corresponds to the parent inventory record that we added. We can then call the Collect function to add the inventory items to the inventory items list.

Updating Multiple Rows

To demonstrate the next set of data-related formulas, we'll build a second screen which would enable the user to manage inventory items. Figure 7-13 illustrates this screen.

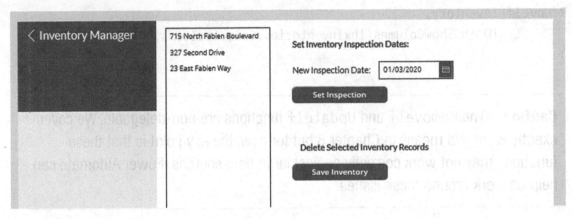

Figure 7-13. *Screen to manage inventory records*

The purpose of this screen is to update the inspection date for the selected records. The left part of the screen contains a list box control that enables the user to select one or more records. A date picker allows the user to enter a new inspection date, and the "Set Inspection" button in the central section updates all selected records with the new date.

The function that enables us to update multiple records is UpdateIf. The first argument to this function defines the source data, and the second argument defines the match condition. This function updates all records that satisfy the match condition. The third argument specifies the new values that we want to set:

```
UpdateIf(Inventory,
        ID in ShowColumns(lbxInventories.SelectedItems, "ID"),
        {NextInspectionDate: dteInspectionDate.SelectedDate}
)
```

In our example, we build a match condition using the in function. Any ID values in the SharePoint list that belong in the list of selected values in the list box will satisfy the condition.

Deleting Multiple Rows

The process to delete multiple rows works almost identically to the way that we update multiple rows. But instead of calling the UpdateIf function, we call the RemoveIf function. The first argument specifies the source data, and the second argument specifies the match condition. This function deletes all records that satisfy the match condition. Here is the formula to delete the records that the user selects in the list box:

```
RemoveIf(Inventory,
        ID in ShowColumns(lbxInventories.SelectedItems, "ID")
)
```

Caution   The RemoveIf and UpdateIf functions are non-delegable. We cover exactly what this means in Chapter 8 but for now, the key point is that these functions may not work correctly against large data sources. Power Automate can help us work around these issues.

Processing Data Row by Row

When we work with data from data sources or collections, a common requirement is to process data on a row-by-row basis. For example, we may want to loop through a data source and conditionally update or add records in a second data source. The ForAll function enables us to carry out this task. This function accepts two arguments – an input data source and the actions to carry out for each row:

```
ForAll (<InputTable>, <ActionsForEachRow>)
```

Although the ForAll function is very powerful, there are two important things to consider whenever we use this function. The first is that we cannot rely on this function to carry out actions sequentially for any given input table. This is because Power Apps can carry out actions in parallel to speed up performance. This can limit us if we want to carry out tasks such as generate row numbers or perform some other action that requires us to process data in a strict sequential manner.

Because of this parallel operation, there are restrictions on the functions that we can call inside the ForAll function. The second restriction is that we cannot refer to variables, meaning that we cannot utilize the Set, UpdateContext, or ClearCollect function.

However, two functions that we can utilize from within the ForAll function are Collect and Patch. The trick is to use these two functions to overcome the restriction of not being able to set variables from within ForAll, and this is the technique that we'll now cover.

Using ForAll to Build HTML

To demonstrate a practical use case scenario, here's how to build an HTML report. This report takes a list of inventory items and produces an HTML table with separate rows for each inventory item. Figure 7-14 shows the target HTML markup that we want to produce. This is a simple example that demonstrates the basics of this technique. In practice, we would generate markup that includes additional presentational attributes, such as font styles and colors.

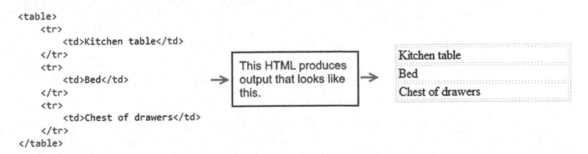

Figure 7-14. The HTML that we want to produce

The underlying logic to produce this HTML is shown here:

```
ClearCollect(colHTML, {data:"<Table>", orderNum:1});
ForAll('Inventory Items',
        Collect(colHTML, {data:"<tr><td>" & Title & "</td></tr>",
                            orderNum:2}
        )
);
Collect(colHTML, {data:"</Table>", orderNum:3})
```

Because we cannot use variables inside the ForAll loop to construct our output, we have to apply a work-around. Instead of using variables, we collect our values into an interim collection, and we process that further outside of the ForAll loop.

The first part of this formula builds the start tag for the table, and we add this to a collection called colHTML. This collection includes an order number column called orderNum. This helps us later when we build our final output.

Within the ForAll loop, we iterate through the source data, and we build the HTML markup that represents each row of our output table. After the call to ForAll, we append a final row to the colHTML collection to build the end tag for the table. Figure 7-15 illustrates how this formula transforms the source inventory items/rows into the interim colHTML collection.

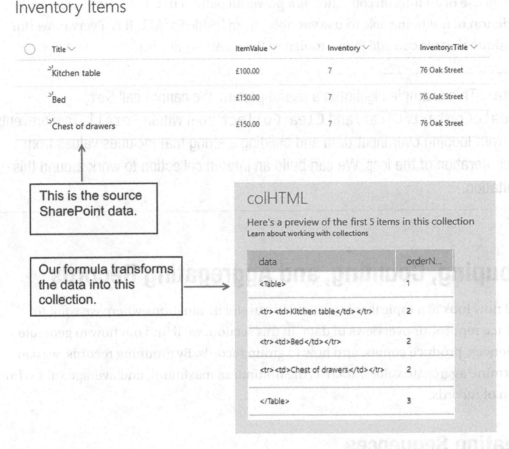

Figure 7-15. *The design view of the source data and the colHTML collection*

To produce the final HTML markup, we can combine all the rows in the colHTML collection with the Concat function. Here's the formula that we use:

```
Concat(SortByColumns(colHTML, "orderNum"), data)
```

The Concat function takes two arguments. The first is the input table data, and the second is an expression that defines the output that we want to produce for each row in our source data. For the input data, we sort the colHTML collection by the orderNum field. This ensures that we recombine our output in the correct sequence, with the table start tag at the start of the output and the table end tag at the end.

To display this output, we can add an HTML text control to a screen and set the HtmlText property to the output of the Concat function.

A useful limitation that more experienced web developers should understand is that we cannot apply CSS classes to the HTML that we want to display. The HTML text control only supports in-line HTML styles.

The use of an interim collection is a powerful pattern that helps us overcome the restriction of not being able to use variables from inside ForAll. It is a very powerful technique that we can add to our toolkit of Power Apps patterns.

Note   This example highlights a useful pattern. We cannot call Set, UpdateContext, Clear, and ClearCollect from within ForAll. This prevents us from looping over input data and building a string that includes values from each iteration of the loop. We can build an interim collection to work around this limitation.

Grouping, Counting, and Aggregating Records

We'll now look at a topic that is particularly useful in situations where we want to produce reports, or overviews of data. In this section, we'll find out how to generate sequences, produce counts, and how to group records. By grouping records, we can determine aggregate values, such as the minimum, maximum, and average values from a group of records.

Creating Sequences

In cases where we need to generate a set of sequential numbers, we can call the sequence function. This function returns a single column table of sequential numbers with the column header name Value. We can optionally specify start and step values.

The step value defines the increment for each number in the sequence. It's possible to specify a decimal step value, and we can even specify a negative value. By defining a negative step value, we can create a sequence that counts down.

The first argument specifies the number of records to create. The second optional argument specifies the start number (the default is 1), and the third argument specifies the step value (the default is 1).

Table 7-4 illustrates some example calls.

Table 7-4. *Creating tables of Sequences*

Function Call	Return Value
Sequence(5)	[1, 2, 3, 4, 5]
Sequence(5, 10)	[10, 11, 12, 13, 14]
Sequence(5, 10, -1)	[10, 9, 8, 7, 6]

A practical use of the sequence function is to incorporate it with a call to the ForAll function. This enables us to build a looping construct that carries out an action for a set number of iterations.

As another example, Figure 7-16 shows how we can limit users to entering dates that fall within the past six days only. Here, we add a radio control and we set the Items property to the following formula:

```
AddColumns(Sequence(6,0,-1),
        "Date",
        DateAdd(Today(),Value,Days)
)
```

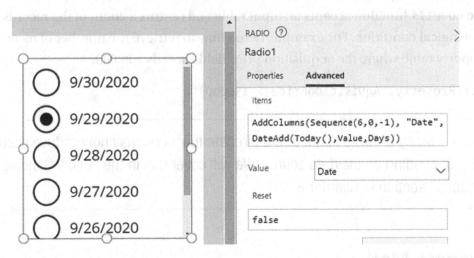

Figure 7-16. *Using sequences of numbers*

Counting Records

There are four main functions that we can use to count the number of records in a table, which are shown in Table 7-5.

Table 7-5. *Functions to count records*

Function Call	Provides a Count of...
Count(<SingleColumnTable>)	Records that contain a single number.
CountRows(<Table>)	Records in a table.
CountA(<SingleColumnTable>)	Records that are not blank, including "".
CountIf(<SingleColumnTable>)	Records that match a logical condition.

At first glance, these functions look very similar. In particular, the Count and CountRows functions appear to do the same thing, because they provide a total count of records. The main difference is that the Count function accepts a single-column table, whereas CountRows can accept a table with multiple columns.

As an example of how to use the CountRows function, we could apply the CountRows function directly against a data source and show the count of records in a label.

The CountIf function accepts an input table and returns a count of the records that match a logical condition. For example, here's how to retrieve the number of records in the property table where the acquisition price field exceeds 150,000:

```
CountIf(Property, AquisitionPrice > 150000)
```

Caution   Many of these count and aggregate functions may not produce accurate results, depending on the data source. We will cover this in the "Understanding Delegation" section in Chapter 8.

Aggregate Maths

Power Apps provides several functions to aggregate tables of data, as shown in Table 7-6.

Table 7-6. *Functions to return aggregate values*

Function	Returns the...
Average (<Table>, Expression)	Mean average
Max(<Table>, Expression)	Maximum value
Min(<Table>, Expression)	Minimum value
Sum(<Table>, Expression)	Sum of the arguments
VarP (<Table>, Expression)	Variance
StdevP (<Table>, Expression)	Standard deviation

All of these functions accept two arguments – a data source and an expression. The expression could consist of a single column or a mathematical expression. Here's an example of how to call the Sum function with an expression:

```
Sum(Property, ExpectedRental * 1.05)
```

In this example, the Sum function returns the sum of the ExpectedRental field in the property table, multiplied by 1.05, to mimic the type of forecast we would carry out to calculate income following a rise in inflation. With all these functions, we can apply the Filter function against the data source to limit the aggregation to a subset of records.

The Min and Max functions are self-explanatory. They return the minimum and maximum values from a data source.

With regard to the VarP and StdevP functions, variance is a measurement of how spread out a set of numbers are, and standard deviation is the square root of the variance.

Finally, these functions can work against a comma-separated list of expressions, instead on an input table. For example, this formula would return the result 88:

```
Max(1, 14,  5 * 0.45, 50, 88. -5)
```

Returning Min and Max Records

A common requirement is to return the record with the highest or lowest value for a given field. To carry out this task, a simple pattern we can apply is to sort the input data in either ascending or descending order and to return the first record.

As an example, here's how to return the most expensive item in the furnishings list:

```
First (SortByColumns(furnishings, price, descending))
```

To return the cheapest item, we can sort the records in price ascending order and retrieve the first item:

```
First (SortByColumns(furnishings, price, ascending))
```

Grouping and Aggregating Values

Very often, we will want to produce counts or aggregated values based on a group of records. As an example, let's suppose we want to show the maximum property price, grouped by property type. We can perform this calculation with the help of the GroupBy function. Figure 7-17 shows the formula that we can add to the Items property of a data table control.

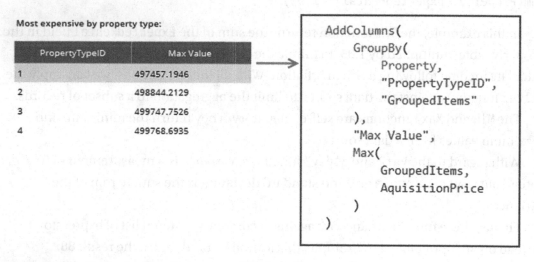

Figure 7-17. *Calculating the max value by group*

The GroupBy function returns a table with the output grouped by the columns that we specify. The first argument specifies the data source. Next, we can specify one or more columns to group by. The final argument specifies our preferred column name for the set of grouped records. Any columns outside those that we want to group by will appear in the final column (GroupedItems, in this example). Figure 7-18 illustrates the structure of the data after we apply the group by function.

PropertyTypeID	GroupedItems			
1	**PropertyID**	**Address**	**AquisitionPrice**	**More...**
	5	173 North Rocky Nobel St.	196771.934	
	9	744 South Second Freeway	482358.8201	
	...	...	...	
2	**PropertyID**	**Address**	**AquisitionPrice**	**More...**
	13	77 Cowley Blvd.	131972.4938	
	17	98 Rocky First Parkway	281134.5592	
	...	...	...	
3	**PropertyID**	**Address**	**AquisitionPrice**	**More...**
	21	66 South White First Way	114543.0604	
	25	380 Green Hague Road	299226.7943	
	...	...	...	
4	**PropertyID**	**Address**	**AquisitionPrice**	**More...**
	29	566 Oak Boulevard	299170.1484	
	33	16 White Hague Blvd.	397526.4625	
	...	...	...	

```
GroupBy(
    Property,
    "PropertyTypeID",
    "GroupedItems"
),
```

Figure 7-18. *The result of the GroupBy function*

In our main example, we call the `AddColumns` function on the grouped output to add a `Max Value` column. The `Max` function retrieves the maximum acquisition price that relates to each set of `GroupedItems`.

This example illustrates the use of the `Max` function. We could easily substitute this with one of the other aggregate functions, such as `Min`, `Sum`, or `Average`. One thing to be careful with is that due to record retrieval limits, it may not be possible to retrieve accurate results depending on the data source that we choose. At the time of writing, the count functions are not delegable, meaning that we cannot produce accurate grouped counts on data sources that exceed 2000 records.

Ungrouping Records

The `Ungroup` function carries out the reverse of the `GroupBy` function. Let's suppose we collect our previous data into a collection called `GroupedProperties`. We can call the following function to ungroup the data:

```
Ungroup(GroupedProperties, "PropertyTypeID" )
```

The `Ungroup` function takes two arguments. The first argument specifies the data source. The second argument specifies the column name by which to ungroup the data source. Figure 7-19 illustrates how this works in the form of a diagram.

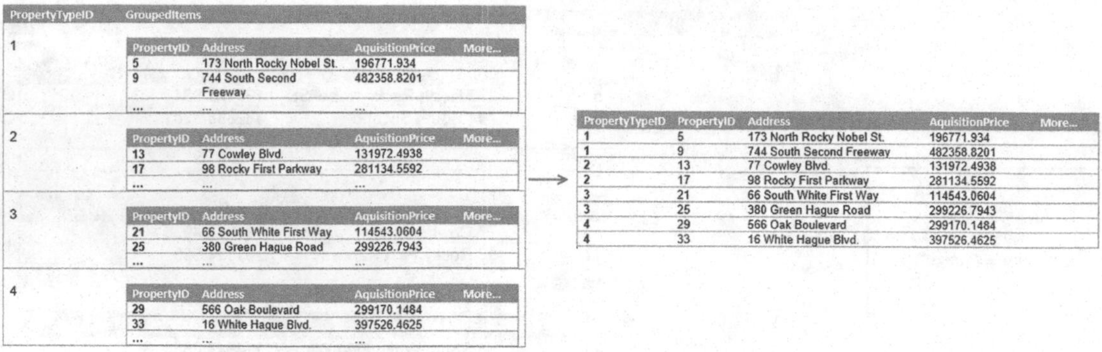

Figure 7-19. *Ungrouping data*

Combining Rows (Union Results)

Occasionally, there are cases where we want to combine rows from multiple data sources. As an example, let's suppose we have two data sources – a table of users and a table of tenants. One way to combine the rows from both of these tables is to collect the records into a collection. This works well if we can initiate the collection from an event such as the click of a button or the on visible event of the screen. The formula we would use would look like this:

```
ClearCollect(colUnion,
        ShowColumns('[dbo].[Tenant]', "Firstname", "Surname"),
        ShowColumns('[dbo].[User]', "Firstname", "Surname")
)
```

To avoid the step of needing to first collect the records into a collection, we can apply a different technique that utilizes the Ungroup and Group functions.

This technique is suitable in cases where we want to directly set the Items property of the control to a formula that combines multiple rows. Here's the formula that we would use:

```
Ungroup(
    Table({TableSet: ShowColumns('[dbo].[Tenant]', "Firstname", "Surname")},
        {TableSet: ShowColumns('[dbo].[User]', "Firstname", "Surname")}
    ),
    "TableSet"
)
```

How exactly does this technique work? In this example, the central part of this formula calls the Table function to define a two-row table called TableSet. Each row in this table contains a child table of records from the two separate data sources. The outer call to the Ungroup function combines the child tables as shown in Figure 7-20.

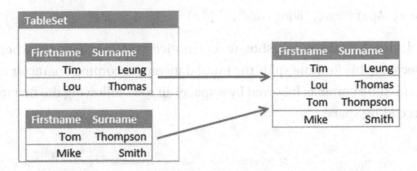

Figure 7-20. *Combining rows with the Ungroup function*

An important caveat of both these techniques is that we can retrieve only a maximum of 2000 rows from each data source. The "Data row limit for non-delegable queries" value in the advanced settings menu defines this limit.

Splitting Text into Rows

In the final part of this chapter, we'll look at some additional string manipulation techniques. In Chapter 5, we covered various techniques, including how to manipulate text with regular expressions. Although regular expressions are very powerful, one limitation is that the match patterns cannot be dynamic. They must be statically defined regular expressions, meaning that we can't generate match patterns based on a variable or an input value that the user supplies.

Now that we're familiar with how to work with table-level data, we can explore string processing techniques that rely on table processing functions. The typical method we use is to split, process, and recombine the strings that we want to work with.

Splitting CSV Strings

The key function that opens many possibilities with string manipulation is Split. This function splits an input string into a single-column table based on a delimiter character. This is useful because it enables us to parse data such as comma-delimited lists, dates that use a slash between date parts, IP addresses, and more.

The following example shows how to split a comma-separated list of property types into a single-column table with the column name result. The following screenshot (Figure 7-21) shows how we can directly set the Items property of a drop-down control to the result of the Split function:

```
Split("House, Apartment, Bungalow", "," )
```

If we look closely at this screenshot, we can notice a typical challenge when we parse CSV data. Because this formula splits the input data on the comma character and the input values include commas followed by a space, all rows following the first item will contain a preceding space.

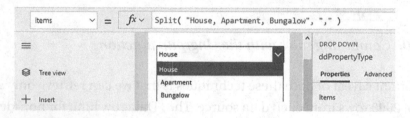

Figure 7-21. *Dealing with extra spaces*

The solution is quite simple. To remove the preceding spaces, we call the Trim function as shown in the following:

```
Trim(Split( "House, Apartment, Bungalow", "," ))
```

Here, the Split function returns a single-column table with three rows. The Trim function takes this single-column table as an input, performs the trim operation on each row, and returns a single-column table as an output.

Most of the text functions (e.g., Left, Right, Mid, Upper, Lower, Replace, Substitute) can accept a single-column table as an input and return a single-column table as an output. In terms of processing, it is quicker and more efficient to use these functions to work directly with an input table, compared to using the ForAll function to work through a table row by row.

Another characteristic of CSV data is that individual values might be escaped with double quotes, especially if the individual values include commas. Using the same methodology, we can remove these quote characters by processing the result as a table with the help of the Substitute function.

Splitting and Concatenating Rows

A powerful technique for processing text is to split an input string into rows, process the table-level result, and recombine the result with the help of the Concat function. This is a great technique to add to our collection of useful patterns, and it helps to address some of the shortcomings of other string manipulation techniques.

To demonstrate, let's suppose we take an input string that denotes a file path which looks like this:

```
C:\folder\subfolder\file.txt
```

Our challenge is to extract specific portions of this file path, including just the file name, just the parent folder, or the full path up to the parent folder name. By calling the Split function to split the file path using the backslash character, we can incorporate other row-level functions to extract parts of the string that we want. Figure 7-22 illustrates the formula to extract various parts of this input string.

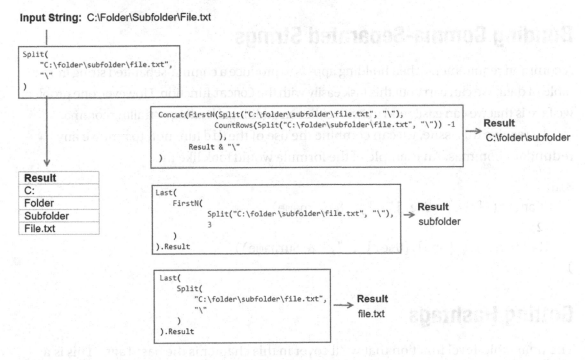

Figure 7-22. *How to extract parts of an input string*

The output from the Split function is a single-column table. Each row in this table contains an element of the file path. To return the file name (file.txt), we apply the Last function to return the last row from this table.

217

To return the folder path (C:\folder\subfolder), we can combine all rows from the result table, except the last (in this example, a total of three rows). We call the FirstN function to return the first three rows. We calculate that three rows are required by counting the number of rows in the result table and subtracting one. We can then combine the data in these three rows with the Concat function. The Concat function accepts two arguments – an input data source and an expression that defines the output to produce for each row of the input data. Because we removed the backslash character from the file name during the split process, the expression re-appends the backslash character in the result.

To return just the parent folder (subfolder), we need to retrieve the third row from the result table. The technique that we use is to call the FirstN function to return the first three rows. We then apply the Last function to this result to return the third row only.

This FirstN/Last method is a valuable technique because it provides the means for us to return a row from any table by ordinal number. There are many wide-ranging applications for this technique. For example, we can use it to separate first, middle, and last names or to separate the day, month, and year from a date string.

Building Comma-Separated Strings

A common requirement when building apps is to produce a comma-separated string from a table of data. We can carry out this task easily with the Concat function. However, one problem we face is that we can easily end up with either an additional leading or trailing comma.

To resolve this issue, we can combine the use of the Mid function to remove any redundant commas. An example of the formula would look like this:

```
Mid(
    Concat('[dbo].[User]', "," & Surname),
    2,
    Len(Concat('[dbo].[User]', "," & Surname))
)
```

Getting Hashtags

The final table-level function that we'll cover in this chapter is the HashTags. This is a niche function that is helpful in social media scenarios. It extracts the hashtags from a string and returns the result in a single-column table. This table will contain one row for each hashtag. Figure 7-23 shows the appearance of the gallery control when we set the Items property to the result of a call to the HashTags function.

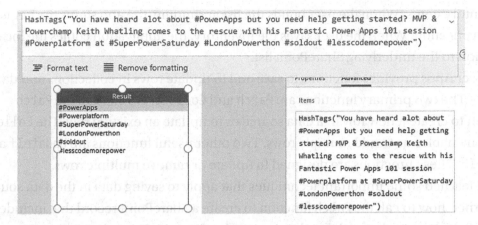

Figure 7-23. Extracting HashTags

Summary

In this chapter, we discovered many useful techniques for working with tables and rows. We began by covering the syntax to define a record. We can define a record by enclosing field/value pairs inside curly brackets.

A core feature in Power Apps is collections. These are in-memory variables that can store table data. They play a crucial role in building apps because they enable us to store working copies of data. They can help us transpose or aggregate data, and they can help improve the performance of an app by caching frequently used data. A key function is the `ClearCollect` function. This function defines a collection and populates it with row data that we specify. Collections are application scoped, meaning that we can access the collection from any screen in an app.

Power Apps provides a host of functions to help shape the columns in a collection. It provides functions to add, drop, and remove and to show only specific columns from a data source. These functions accept an input data source, and they return a copy of the data with the transformation that we specify. To give an example, if we were to call the `AddColumns` function to add an additional column using a SharePoint list as the data source, the function would return a copy of the data with the additional column. The important point is that it does not alter or add a column to the underlying SharePoint list.

These column shaping functions are most useful when we chain and combine them together. To demonstrate the use of these functions and collections, we built a screen that relies on these features. The screen that we built allows a user to build a list of inventory items. When the user builds the list at runtime, the app stores the items in a local collection. When the user saves the inventory, the application copies the local collection to the underlying SharePoint list.

Power Apps provides functions to save and to update rows in collections and data sources. The two primary functions are `Patch` and `Collect`. We can call the `Patch` function to create a new row in a data source or to update an existing row. The `Collect` function enables us to add multiple rows. Two other useful functions are `UpdateIf` and `RemoveIf`. These functions are designed to update or remove multiple rows.

We learned some important techniques that apply to saving data in the data source. We learned how to call the `Patch` function to create a SharePoint record that includes a lookup field. We also learned that the return value from the `Patch` function exposes any server-generated ID values when we add a new record. This technique enables us to create a set of parent and child records in one go.

To process records row by row, we can call the `ForAll` function. This function accepts an input data source and enables us to define expressions to carry out for each row in the input data. The biggest limitation with this function is that we cannot set variables from within a `ForAll` loop. We can work around this restriction by storing working data in an interim collection, and we worked through an example of how to use this technique to generate HTML output from an input table.

A very useful function is `CountRows`. This enables us to count the number of records from an input table. Other useful functions include `Average`, `Max`, `Min`, and `Sum`. We can use these in conjunction with the `GroupBy` function to calculate aggregated values. We can expand grouped records with the `Ungroup` function, and we saw an example of how we can apply this function to unite two sets of data.

In the final part of this chapter, we investigated how to utilize several of these table shaping functions to manipulate input strings. A very useful technique is to split an input string into rows by calling the `Split` function. We can manipulate the data in the rows and produce the end result by recombining the rows with the `Concat` function. To help process our row data, we can retrieve a specific row by ordinal number by combining the `FirstN` and `Last` functions. There are wide-ranging applications for these string techniques; and as an example, we can use them to separate first, middle, and last names or to separate the day, month, and year from a date string.

CHAPTER 8

Searching and Retrieving Data

The ability to retrieve and search data plays an important role in many apps. We've seen the basic search capabilities that the auto-generated apps offer. But what if we want to provide more sophisticated search capabilities, such as the ability to filter records by date or drop-down values? In this chapter, we'll find out how to add these features to our apps.

Another important topic is the technical implementation of data retrieval. For performance reasons, Power Apps can limit the number of rows that it retrieves, and this can prevent us from retrieving the records that we expect. As a result of this, one of the most popular topics on Power Apps forums is delegation – the term that describes this behavior. With the help of this chapter, we'll explore techniques to help minimize these limitations. Other key topics that we'll cover in this chapter will include

- How to build a typical search screen that includes the ability to enter multiple search criteria and how to initiate the search through the click of a button.

- How to join tables of data. Taking the analogy of an order processing app with two tables, customers and orders, how could we join these tables to show the customer detail that is associated with an order? How can we show customers who have not made orders or show the distinct customers who have made orders? We'll find out how in this chapter.

- The search scenarios that are most problematic, including a bug with datetime searches that can catch us out. We will also cover how we can overcome some of these issues by using features outside of Power Apps, including SQL Server views and SharePoint lists.

221

© Tim Leung 2021
T. Leung, *Beginning Power Apps*, https://doi.org/10.1007/978-1-4842-6683-0_8

Basic Behavior

Data row retrieval limits and the term "delegation" can be a headache for many app builders. They can prevent us from retrieving our desired data, particularly in cases where we want to sum or to count fields from a data source. However, these limits exist for good reason. They prevent us from building features or writing formulas that can disproportionately slow down our apps. But with proper understanding of how data retrieval works in Power Apps, we can overcome many of the typical challenges that app builders face, and we can end up building more performant systems. Let's find out more.

Understanding Delegation

Query delegation is a feature that speeds up data retrieval. Not all data sources support delegation, but SharePoint, SQL Server, and Dataverse are the popular data sources that do support delegation.

What exactly does the term delegation mean? When we search data from a delegable source, the data source performs the search and returns the result. If we carry out the same operation against a non-delegable data source, the data source returns all the data, and Power Apps then carries out the search on the local device. The non-delegable search works inefficiently because Power Apps needs to download more data than is necessary. Because the network connection is often the slowest link in any computerized system, non-delegable searches perform far more slowly. Additionally, mobile devices generally contain slower hardware compared to servers, and therefore, filtering data on a mobile device will be slower. Figure 8-1 illustrates this concept in the form of a diagram.

Without delegation, the data source returns all the data to the client. The client filters the data.

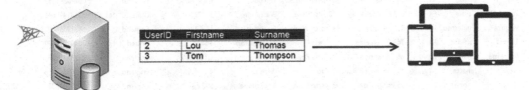

UserID	Firstname	Surname
2	Lou	Thomas
3	Tom	Thompson

With delegation, the data source returns only the records that are required.

Figure 8-1. *How delegation works*

The two core functions that we use to search for data are the Filter and LookUp functions. Both these functions accept a data source and a formula that expresses the match condition. The operator we use in the expression determines whether the query is delegable. The common delegable operators that SharePoint, SQL Server, and Dataverse support include

- Equals operator (=) – We can apply the equals operator against string, numeric, and Boolean data types.

- Comparison operators (=, <>, >=, <=, >, <) – We can apply comparison operators, such as greater than or less than, against numeric fields.

- StartsWith – We can utilize the StartsWith function to test for text fields that start with a string that we specify.

SQL Server and Dataverse provide delegation support for a wider range of operations. For example, they both support the EndsWith and the Search functions. The Search function enables us to search multiple columns for values that match an input string. With SharePoint, there is no support to carry out this type of "contains" search in a delegable way. Another benefit of SQL Server and Dataverse is that there is delegation support for aggregate functions that include Sum, Average, Min, and Max.

Because it's preferable to write a formula that is delegable, the designer shows a warning when we write data access formulas that are non-delegable. To demonstrate the type of warning we would receive, let's take the SQL Server table that's shown in Figure 8-2.

TenantID	Firstname	Surname	Gender	Address1	Address2	City	Postcode	Country	Telephone
1	Tim	Leung	M	550 South New ...	98 Clarendon St.	Toledo	BA3 7KD	England	061-0290359
2	Wendell	Cassie	F	371 First Freeway	240 First Street	Washington	60172	United States	131314-6042
3	Virginia	Guillermo	M	12 Nobel St.	34 North White ...	Anaheim	LN2 1IV	England	169-705-1005
4	Tomas	Lamont	M	763 Green Hag...	50 White Cowle...	Washington	14424	United States	204914-9299
5	Angelina	Charity	M	86 Clarendon Fr...	940 New Road	Birmingham	CT88 7DS	England	977331-0871
6	Cari	Janette	M	65 White First B...	485 North Clare...	Wichita	CV1 6WM	England	209666-9156
7	Nora	Donna	F	15 White Cowle...	99 North Rocky...	Anchorage	S92 6BS	England	5053338838
8	Victoria	Angelica	F	543 Second Blvd.	36 Old Parkway	Anchorage	BS26 5JL	England	0439223167
9	Gena	Allen	F	48 West Cowley...	74 Clarendon ...	Houston	14424	United States	175-9389635
10	Scottie	Clay	F	13 Rocky Cowle...	87 Fabien Way	Toledo	TF45 9XT	England	827-587-2870

Figure 8-2. *Table structure that we'll use in this chapter*

Let's suppose we want to show records where the country field matches the value United States or England. If we implement this search by calling the in function, the designer shows the warning in Figure 8-3.

```
fx ⌄   Filter('[dbo].[Tenant]',Country in ["England","United States"])
```
Delegation warning. The highlighted part of this formula might not work correctly on large data sets.

Figure 8-3. *Delegation warning*

Is there any way for us to avoid this problem? One way is to rewrite our formula using operators that are delegable. Here's an example of how to express the same query with the || operator:

```
Filter('[dbo].[Tenant]', Country="England" || Country="United States")
```

With this expression, the designer will not show a warning.

Increasing the Data Row Limit

By default, the data row limit for non-delegable queries is 500 rows. We can increase this to 2,000 rows through the advanced settings of an app, as shown in Figure 8-4.

In cases where it isn't possible to rewrite a query using non-delegable operators, we can retrieve more accurate results by increasing the limit to the maximum value of 2,000. Of course, this isn't a complete fix, and the problem will still exist if our source data exceeds 2,000 rows.

Figure 8-4. *Increasing the delegation limit*

It is useful to note that delegation support is a feature that Microsoft improves continually. It is likely that in the future, delegation support will extend to support a wider range of operators.

Tip   We can reduce the "Data row limit for non-delegable queries" to a low value (e.g., 1). This can help us more easily detect parts of our app that are affected by delegation limits during the development and test phases of an app.

How Do Controls Manage Large Quantities of Data?

Let's suppose we add a gallery control to our screen and we attempt to display all records with a country that matches England or United States. In total, there are 10,000 records. This is a large quantity of data. What do we think will happen when we run our screen? Will there be a delay as Power Apps loads the data, or will this amount of data be too much for Power Apps to handle?

The actual experience feels very smooth and quick. The gallery control populates almost instantly with data. The reason for this is because Power Apps optimizes this process by retrieving only the first 100 records. If we scroll to the end of the gallery control, there will be a slight delay while Power Apps retrieves the next set of 100 records and appends those to the end of the list. This method of retrieving records in bite-size pieces provides a more responsive and fluid experience for the end user.

One benefit of using SQL Server is that we can use a free tool called SQL Server Profiler to monitor how Power Apps is accessing the database. Figure 8-5 shows the output from a SQL Server trace.

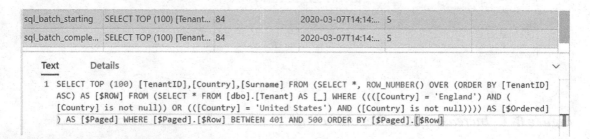

Figure 8-5. *The output from a SQL Server Profiler trace*

Although the content of this trace may look obscure, the important point is that it verifies that Power Apps retrieves data in 100 record chunks, and it also demonstrates how we can use this tool to diagnose and optimize data retrieval.

As an example, let's suppose that we attempt to collect all 10,000 records into a collection with the following function:

```
ClearCollect(colTenants,
        Filter('[dbo].[Tenant]',
            Country="England" || Country="United States"
        )
)
```

Will this function succeed in retrieving all 10,000 records? Unfortunately, the answer is no. The ClearCollect function will collect only up to the maximum number of records that is specified in the "Data row limit for non-delegable queries" setting, even if we specify a data source and query condition that supports delegation.

Searching Data

An important requirement in many apps is the ability for users to search for data. In this section, we'll look at how to build this functionality. To illustrate a typical scenario, we'll develop a custom search screen that enables users to filter data more precisely by search criteria. Figure 8-6 shows the screen that we'll build in this section. This screen enables users to search issue records by a drop-down list of tenants. The user can also filter the records by date.

Figure 8-6. *The example screen that we'll build*

Developing these types of screen isn't as easy as it first appears. There are several complexities that we need to cover. The first is to configure the search feature to not filter by date if the user leaves the date field blank. Additionally, there is also a difficulty that can arise when we attempt to apply date filters. If the underlying data field contains both date and time components and we want to filter just by the date component, we need to customize our search formula to take this into account.

The user can also choose not to filter by tenants by selecting the "Show all tenants" option from the drop-down; therefore, we need to build the formula that applies a wildcard search if the user chooses this option. The final challenge is to initiate the search operation from a search button.

To demonstrate these topics, this section uses a SQL Server table called '[dbo]. [Issue]', shown in Figure 8-7.

If you don't have access to SQL Server, you can easily substitute this with any other data source of your choice. The benefit of using SQL Server in this chapter is that it enables us to explore some of the performance optimization techniques that are available with SQL Server.

227

IssueID	TenantID	PropertyID	Description	IsEmergency	CreateDateTime	CloseDateTime
1	9	35	Noise complaint from neighbours	False	2020-02-18 00:5...	2020-05-22 14:2...
2	2	17	Damp permanenting bathroom wall	False	2020-02-07 05:4...	2020-03-31 08:2...
3	50	35	Lights in communal area not working	True	2020-05-23 01:2...	2020-03-29 13:4...
4	46	6	Vermin spotted near rubbish area	False	2020-05-16 22:1...	2020-06-24 13:2...
5	16	38	Car park being used by non-residents	False	2020-01-20 05:3...	*NULL*

Figure 8-7. *Issue table ([dbo].[Issue])*

Basic Search Functions

Let's review some of the search functions that enable us to build a search screen. The key functions that we can call include Search, Filter, and LookUp. These functions all sound very similar, so what are the differences? Here's a brief overview:

- Search – This function matches input *text* against the data in one or more columns.

- Filter – This function matches records based on a *formula* that we provide.

- LookUp – This function matches records based on a *formula* that we provide and returns the first record only.

In the sections that follow, we'll examine how to use these functions in greater detail.

Filtering by Drop-Down Values

The core parts that make up our search screen are a gallery control and a combo box. Figure 8-8 shows how our screen is set up.

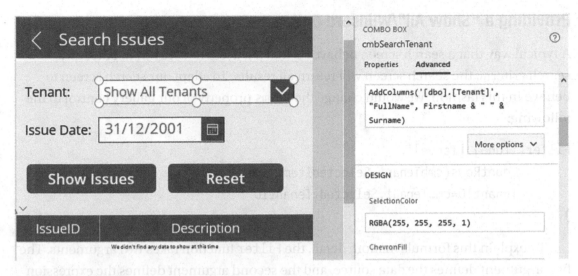

Figure 8-8. *The layout of our search screen*

There are two steps required to build our basic search screen. The first step is to add a combo box and to configure the data source for this control. The second step is to configure a gallery control so that it filters by the selected item in the combo box.

As Figure 8-8 shows, we add a combo box called cmbTenant, and we set the Items property to the following formula:

```
AddColumns('[dbo].[Tenant]', "FullName", Firstname & " " & Surname)
```

This technique sets up the combo box to show friendlier item values by combining the Firstname and Surname values. To set up our gallery control to display the filtered results, we set the Items property to the following formula:

```
Filter('[dbo].[Issue]', TenantID=cmbTenant.Selected.TenantID)
```

This formula shows how the Selected property of the combo box enables us to retrieve additional fields, in this example, the TenantID field. This example demonstrates the common practice of showing a friendly description in a combo box and the formula that we would use to retrieve the numeric key value that is associated with the selected item.

Providing a "Show All"/Wildcard Option

A typical way that a search screen behaves is that if a user chooses not to enter any search criteria, the search screen will return all results. To adapt our search screen to behave in this fashion, we would change the Items property of our gallery control to the following:

```
Filter('[dbo].[Issue]',
        CountRows(cmbTenant.SelectedItems)=0 ||
        TenantID=cmbTenant.Selected.TenantID
)
```

To explain this formula in more detail, the Filter function takes two arguments. The first argument defines the data source, and the second argument defines the expression for inclusion into the result. The Filter function evaluates this expression for each record in the data source and includes the record if the expression resolves to true.

The expression in this example evaluates the number of selected items in the combo box. If no items are selected, the expression resolves to true, and the item will appear in the result.

If the combo box contains a selected item, the second part of the "or" operator will be evaluated (the || keyword denotes the logical "or" operator). In this case, the record will be included if the tenant ID value matches the selected tenant ID in the combo box.

For this example to work correctly, we need to configure the combo box to allow only one selection by disabling the "Allow multiple selections" property. Another feature of the combo box control is that we can set the placeholder text that appears when the combo box is empty. We can use this to indicate that the search will return records for all tenants (Figure 8-9).

Just for some background, the combo box control did not exist during the first edition of this book. In the initial release, we needed to manually append a blank row to the top of the combo box control to provide a wildcard search. The combo box control provides a great improvement because it includes a blank entry by default.

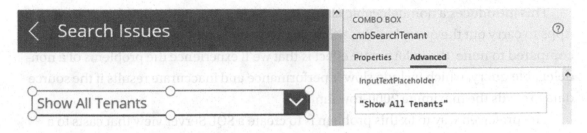

Figure 8-9. *The InputTextPlaceholder property*

Searching by Date Criteria

Let's now extend our search screen to enable users to additionally filter by create data. In doing so, we will also investigate a bug that often catches out app builders.

On our search screen, we'll add a date picker control called dteSearchIssue. To default this control so that it shows a blank value, we can do so by clearing the DefaultDate property.

To highlight a slightly nontrivial example, the create date column in our issue table stores both the date and time. Therefore, to match a single input date against date and time values, we need to filter for records that fall between midnight and 23:59 of the target date. For most data sources, the formula we would add to the Items property of the gallery control is shown in the following:

```
Filter('[dbo].[Issue]',
      CreateDateTime >= dteSearchIssue.SelectedDate &&
      CreateDateTime < DateAdd(dteSearchIssue.SelectedDate, 1, Days)
)
```

However, if we were to run this formula against our SQL Server data source, we would discover that this formula returns zero records. This highlights a bug where the Power Apps connector fails to filter date and time fields properly. We can slightly improve the behavior by amending the formula like so:

```
Filter('[dbo].[Issue]',
      CreateDateTime >= dteSearchIssue.SelectedDate &&
      CreateDateTime < DateAdd(dteSearchIssue.SelectedDate, 1, Days &&
      Day(CreateDateTime) > 0
)
```

This introduces a non-delegable clause into the filter operation that forces Power Apps to carry out the query locally. Although this amendment will return some rows compared to none, the unfortunate effect is that we'll experience the problems of a non-delegable query, which include slower performance and inaccurate results if the source data exceeds the maximum 2000-row limit.

The preferred way to fix this problem is to create a SQL Server view that casts to a DATETIMEOFFSET data type. We'll cover this technique later in this chapter.

Caution   The date filtering bug applies to SQL Server and SharePoint data sources. You can find out more about this problem here:

```
https://powerusers.microsoft.com/t5/PowerApps-Forum/
Filtering-on-prem-SQL-data-source-by-date/m-p/6151
```

Searching by Numeric Criteria

To filter a numeric column against a value that a user enters on the screen, a key step is to convert the input string to a numeric value by calling the `Value` function. Suppose we want to return issue records where the `IssueID` value matches the value that the user enters into a text input control. Here's the formula that we would use:

```
Filter('[dbo].[Issue]', IssueID = Value(txtIssueID.Text))
```

With text input controls, a useful tip is that we can set the Format property to "Number." This provides a simple way to validate numeric input.

Searching by Text Criteria

The `Search` function provides a simple way to search columns that match an input string. Here's how to return records where characters in the description and comments fields match the value that a user enters into a textbox:

```
Search('[dbo].[Issue]', txtSearchDesc.Text, "Description",  "Comments")
```

The `Search` function accepts three or more arguments. The first argument defines the data source. The second argument defines the search string, and the following arguments define the target columns to search against. As shown in this example, a nice feature of this function is that it's possible to specify multiple columns to search against.

The Search function matches records that contain the exact search phrase that we provide. That is, if the search phrase were to contain multiple words, the Search function would not return records that contain only one of the input words.

By default, the Search function carries out case-insensitive searches. With SQL Server, however, the behavior depends on the collation sequence of the database. If we search against a database with a case-sensitive collation sequence, any searches that we perform with the Search function will be case sensitive.

The main limitation of the Search function is that it works only against string column types. Also, it cannot search against SharePoint lookup fields. Although this function works fine against SQL Server data sources, a major limitation is that with SharePoint data sources, the Search function is not delegable.

Therefore, with SharePoint, the closest way that we can search text fields is to use the StartsWith operator, as shown here:

```
Filter(Issues, StartsWith(Title, txtSearchDesc.Text))
```

Adding a Search Button

The implementation of our current search screen connects the gallery control directly to the data entry controls. Because of this, the gallery control refreshes as soon as a user enters any data into any of the controls. This behavior is not ideal because the gallery control will refresh more than it needs to, particularly if the user wants to enter multiple search criteria. To address this issue, here's how to add a search button to the screen to trigger the search operation.

To build this feature, we would amend the Items property of the gallery control so that it filters the data by variables, rather than control values. We would then set the variable values on the click of the search button. Figure 8-10 illustrates the formulas we would use.

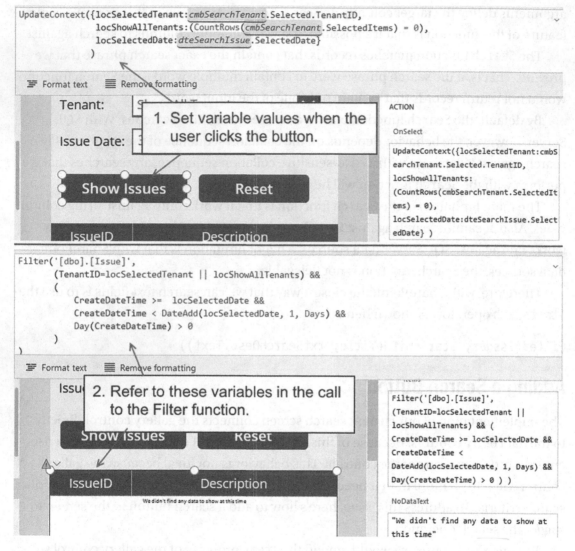

Figure 8-10. *Initiating a search through the click of a button*

Tip   To build a search screen where users can enter multiple pieces of search criteria, we can provide a better user experience by triggering the search from a button.

Sorting Data by Multiple Columns

To help users more easily find data, we can sort the items in the gallery and other data controls by multiple fields. The browse screen in an auto-generated app sorts the records by a single field, as shown in Figure 8-11.

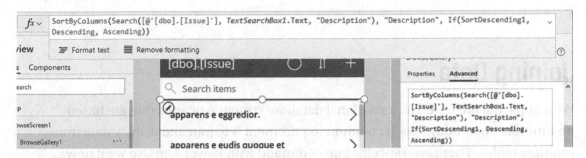

Figure 8-11. *The default sort formula in an auto-generated app*

We can sort by additional fields by providing additional sets of field names and sort sequences to the SortByColumns function. Here's the formula to sort the User table by surname, followed by first name:

```
SortByColumns(Filter('[dbo].[User]',
            StartsWith(Surname, TextSearchBox1.Text)),
         "Surname", If(SortDescending1, Descending, Ascending),
         "Firstname",If(SortDescending1, Descending, Ascending)
)
```

In addition to the SortByColumns function, there is also a function called Sort that provides similar functionality. The difference between SortByColumns and Sort is that with Sort, we provide a formula to sort by rather than a string column name. Why is this useful? One reason is to resolve a problem that some app builders encounter when they attempt to sort by numbers that are stored in a text field.

Let's suppose our table includes a text field and that there are two records. The first record contains the value 10, and the second record contains the value 1. When we sort by text, 10 occurs before 1, and this would result in a set of data that is not in strict numerical order. By calling the Sort function, we can convert the text values to numbers, and this will result in the expected sort sequence. Here's an example of how we would call this function:

```
Sort ('[dbo].[User]',
     Value(IDField),
     Ascending
)
```

Joining Data

With apps that are based on a relational database structure or apps that are based on multiple SharePoint lists, a common requirement is to join and display data from multiple tables. There is no specific join command with Power Apps, so we'll now explore some techniques that we can use to display related data.

Joining Records: Showing Related Records

One technique we can use to show related records is to apply the LookUp function. To highlight the use of this method, here's how to set up the gallery control in our app to show a list of issue records combined with the associated tenant details. To accomplish this, we would set the Items property of the gallery control to the following formula:

```
AddColumns('[dbo].[Issue]',
        "TenantRecord",
        LookUp('[dbo].[Tenant]',
              TenantID = '[dbo].[Issue]'[@TenantID]
        )
)
```

This formula calls the AddColumns function to append the associated tenant record to the issue data source. The interesting thing this demonstrates is how we can create a structure of nested tables. Figure 8-12 shows the output of this function.

IssueID	TenantID	PropertyID	Description	TenantRecord		
3	50	35	Alarm malfunction code			
				TenantD	Firstname	Surname	....
				50	Tom	Tompson
4	46	6	Lights not working			
				TenantD	Firstname	Surname	....
				46	Lou	Thomas
5	16	38	Leak			
				TenantD	Firstname	Surname	....
				16	Keith	Higgs

Figure 8-12. *Joining records to create a nested data source*

This formula also illustrates an important learning point. It demonstrates how to fully qualify field names when we nest data with functions such as AddColumns, Filter, and LookUp.

In this example, both the issue and tenant tables include a field called TenantID. In formula, how would we distinguish between these two fields? Specifically, from the inner LookUp function, we need some way to distinguish between the TenantID field in the issue table and the TenantID field in the tenant table. When we nest functions, any field name that we specify will refer to the innermost data source. In this example, therefore, when we specify TenantID from inside the LookUp function, TenantID will refer to the TenantID field in the tenant table. To refer to the TenantID field from the issue table, we need to prefix the TenantID field with the table name in the format TableName [@Fieldname]. Therefore, we would refer to the TenantID field in the issue table with the following syntax:

```
'[dbo].[Issue]'[@TenantID]
```

The name for the @ operator is the *disambiguation* operator. Another scenario where this operator applies is in situations where a variable, collection, or data source matches a field name. In this case, we would specify the variable, collection, or data source in the format [@ObjectName] to distinguish it from the field name.

Now that we've set the Items property for our gallery control, we can access all the fields in the tenant record for each issue record through the TenantRecord column, as shown in Figure 8-13.

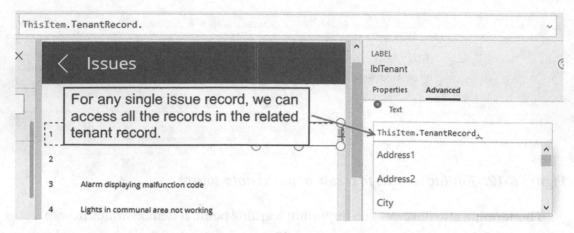

Figure 8-13. Showing related records

Aliasing Record Items

Rather than use the @ syntax, a friendlier way to resolve ambiguity is to use the As function. This function creates an alias for the current record and enables us to write a formula that is more intuitive to understand.

We can use the As function against record-scoped functions such as ForAll and Filter. We can also use it to alias expressions directly in the Items property of a gallery control.

To demonstrate, here's how we would express our previous formula using the As function instead:

```
AddColumns('[dbo].[Issue]' As IssueRecord,
        "TenantRecord",
        LookUp('[dbo].[Tenant]',
            TenantID = IssueRecord.TenantID
        )
)
```

Here, we call the As function to alias each record in the issue table with the name IssueRecord. From within the nested LookUp function, we can then refer to the TenantID field from the issue table with the identifier IssueRecord.TenantID.

Tip   The As function provides a great way to help resolve ambiguity in field names when we nest record-scoped functions.

Search Procedures That Can Cause Difficulties

Although Power Apps provides some powerful search capabilities, there are some areas where Power Apps doesn't perform so well, especially in areas where there is a lack of delegable query support.

In this section, we'll identify the areas where we need to apply caution. The purpose of this is to enable us to predetermine scenarios that can cause us difficulties at an earlier stage in the design process.

Fortunately, we can resolve many of these limitations through the use of SQL Server views. In the first release of Power Apps, there was no support for SQL Server views. We are very fortunate that Power Apps now supports views, because this enables us to query data in ways that were once impossible to accomplish in Power Apps.

Matching Against Lists of Data

The first type of query that causes difficulties is where we want to find records that match a user-supplied list. As an example, Figure 8-14 shows a screen where the user can select multiple tenants from a list box. The search feature returns all records that contain any of the selected tenants.

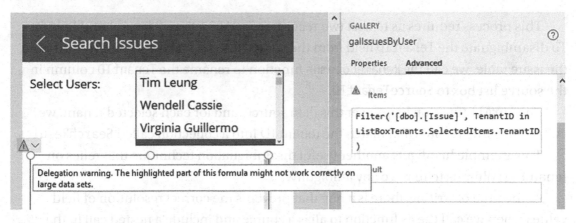

Figure 8-14. *The in function is not delegable*

The function that we use here is the in function. This function can be particularly confusing because there are two versions of this function which carry out different tasks. We can call the in function to check if a string contains an input value, or we can call it to check if a table contains one or more values that we provide as an input.

239

For the latter use, the in function is not delegable. Therefore, this type of search will never work accurately against data sources that exceed the maximum 2000-row limit:

```
Filter('[dbo].[Issue]', TenantID in ListBoxTenants.SelectedItems.TenantID)
```

If we know that our source data will never exceed 2,000 rows, this will not be a problem. But in situations where it can, we need to find an alternate way to carry out the search.

One work-around is to loop through the items in the list box with the ForAll function, search the data source for each item row by row, and collect the results in a collection. This technique enables us to retrieve up to 2,000 issue records per tenant, rather than 2,000 records in total.

Here's the formula that we can add to a button to populate a collection of the search results:

```
ForAll(RenameColumns(ListBoxTenants.SelectedItems,"TenantID","SourceTenant
ID"),
      Collect(SearchResults,
            Filter('[dbo].[Issue]', SourceTenantID=TenantID)
      )
)
```

This process requires us to nest two record-scoped functions – ForAll and Filter. To disambiguate the TenantID field from the source list box and the TenantID field from the issue table, we call the RenameColumns function to rename the TenantID column in the source list box to SourceTenantID.

The ForAll function loops over this data source, and for each selected tenant, we collect the issue records that match the tenant ID into a collection called SearchResults.

This example highlights another useful disambiguation technique that relies on renaming columns to remove any ambiguity.

At the time of writing, there is a bug that prevents the correct resolution of field values when we call the As function to alias a source and include a nested call to the Filter function to filter a SQL Server data source. Hopefully, this problem will be fixed in a future release; but until then, the rename technique provides an effective alternative.

Tip   We can rename columns to help resolve ambiguous field names when we nest record-scoped functions.

Using in to Match Substring Text

As we've just seen, the reason why the in operator can be confusing is because there are two usages for this function. Not only can it test that an input set of records belongs to a table or collection but it can also test for the existence of a string within another string. Figure 8-15 provides a simple way to illustrate this type of usage.

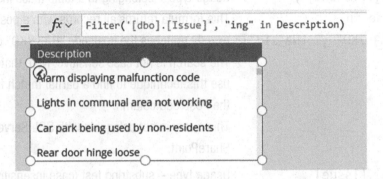

Figure 8-15. *Using the in function to match a substring*

This example returns all records where the description field includes the characters "ing." Although this formula works fine with SQL Server, a caveat is that with SharePoint, this formula is not delegable.

A closely related function is the exactin function. From a Power Apps perspective, the exactin function works the same way as the in function, except that the matches are case sensitive. Unfortunately, the usefulness of the exactin function is limited because it is not delegable for both SharePoint and SQL Server data sources.

When we call the in function with SQL Server to match a substring, Power Apps will delegate the query to SQL Server as we would expect.

The case sensitivity of queries with SQL Server depends on the collation sequence. If the collation sequence of the target database columns is set to a case-sensitive collation, any searches that we make with the in function will be case sensitive, as opposed to the standard behavior in Power Apps which is case insensitive.

Here's an interesting way that we can take advantage of this behavior. Let's take the example of an app that connects to a SQL Server instance with a case-insensitive collation sequence. If we want to carry out case-sensitive searches, we can create a SQL Server view that casts our target columns to a case-sensitive collation. Any queries that we carry out with functions such as Filter or Search will now be case sensitive. The section "SQL Server Views" later in this chapter provides the example SQL syntax that we can use.

The in and exactin functions can be difficult to comprehend, so to help summarize all the different usage types, Table 8-1 provides some example syntax.

Table 8-1. *Examples of how to call the in and exactin functions*

Function	Description

`Filter('[dbo].[Tenant]',`
`    Postcode in`
`        ["BA3 7KD" ," LN2 1IV"]`
`)`
	Usage type – belonging to a table (case insensitive). This formula returns all records with a postcode that exactly matches the postcode "BA3 7KD" or "LN2 1IV". The search is not case sensitive. Note that we cannot use this technique to find a partial match from within the Postcode column. This query is not delegable with SQL Server and SharePoint.

`Filter('[dbo].[Issue]',`
`    "smith" in Firstname`
`)`
	Usage type – substring test (case insensitive). This formula returns all records that contain the string "smith" in the Firstname column. This query is delegable with SQL Server, but not delegable with SharePoint. With SQL Server, this search might be case sensitive, depending on the database collation sequence.

`Filter('[dbo].[Tenant]',`
`    Postcode exactin`
`        ["BA3 7KD" ," LN2 1IV"]`
`)`
	Usage type – belonging to a table (case sensitive). This formula returns all records with a postcode that exactly matches "BA3 7KD" or "LN2 1IV". This search is case sensitive. This query is not delegable with SQL Server and SharePoint.

`Filter('[dbo].[Issue]',`
`    "Smith" exactin Firstname`
`).`
	Substring test (case sensitive). This formula returns all records that contain the string "Smith" in the Firstname column. This search is case sensitive and will not return records that contain the lowercase value "smith". This query is not delegable with SQL Server and SharePoint.

Checking for Nonexistence

An important task that we often need to carry out is to check for the nonexistence of a group of data within another dataset. As an example, traditional order processing systems will use this technique to find customers who have not placed any orders. To highlight this technique, here's how to show the names of tenants that are not associated with any issue records.

To show this data, add a gallery control to a screen and set the Items property to the following formula:

```
Filter('[dbo].[Tenant]',
    Not(TenantID in ShowColumns('[dbo].[Issue]', "TenantID"))
)
```

This formula filters the tenant table to show records where a matching TenantID doesn't exist in the issue table. Just like the previous example, the syntax we use here is not delegable; and therefore, the code here may not return all expected records.

Matching Blank Fields

Another common requirement is to search for records with null, empty, or blank fields. To demonstrate this topic, Figure 8-16 shows an excerpt from the issue table. We'll use this to examine how to filter by empty or null values in the Description and CloseDateTime columns.

IssueID	TenantID	PropertyID	Description	IsEmergency	CreateDateTime	CloseDateTime
1	9	35	NULL	False	2020-02-18 00:5...	2020-05-22 14:2...
2	2	17		False	2020-02-07 05:4...	2020-03-31 08:2...
3	50	35	Alarm displaying malfunction code	True	2020-05-23 01:2...	2020-03-29 13:4...
4	46	6	Lights in communal area not working	False	2020-05-16 22:1...	2020-06-24 13:2...
5	16	38	Car park being used by non-residents	False	2020-01-20 05:3...	NULL

Figure 8-16.   Example data in the issue table

With this type of data structure, a typical requirement could be to return all records with a null CloseDateTime value. This would enable users to see all records that are in an open status.

The function that tests for null or empty values is called IsBlank. This function accepts an input value and returns true if the input is empty string or null.

To apply this function, we can set the Items property of a gallery control to the formula shown in the following:

```
Filter('[dbo].[Issue]', IsBlank(CloseDateTime))
```

This function would return all records with a null or empty date. However, a big limitation is that the IsBlank function is not delegable. If there are more than 2000 records in the issue table, the results will not include all matching records.

Let's look at how the IsBlank function behaves against text fields. With SQL Server and other relational databases, text fields can store null (undefined) values or empty strings. The IsBlank function deals with these values slightly differently. Take the following example:

```
Filter('[dbo].[Issue]', IsBlank(Description))
```

This expression returns records with the IssueID values 1 and 2. In other words, the IsBlank function matches both null and empty string values.

Taking into consideration that the IsBlank function is not delegable, if our intention is to return only records where the issue field contains an empty string, an alternate approach is to use the formula shown in the following:

```
Filter('[dbo].[Issue]', Description="")
```

This formula would return the record for IssueID 2 only. Power Apps can delegate the operation of matching against an empty string, so we can use this method to help overcome delegation limitations.

The inverse operation is to return records that are not blank. To do this, we can use the delegable expression that's shown in the following. This formula returns the records that match the IssueID values 3, 4, and 5:

```
Filter('[dbo].[Issue]', Description <> "")
```

Finally, the following expression returns only the records that are null, excluding records that contain an empty string. This expression will return the record for IssueID 1 only. Note that this expression is not delegable because it includes a call to the IsBlank function:

```
Filter('[dbo].[Issue]', IsBlank(Description) && Description <>"")
```

Returning Distinct Records

Sometimes, there may be the requirement to return a list of distinct records. To give an example, let's suppose we want to return a list of distinct tenants who have raised issues.

To obtain this information, we would retrieve a list of distinct TenantID values from the issue table, and we can do this by calling the GroupBy function. The following formula returns a list of issue records grouped by TenantID:

```
GroupBy('[dbo].[Issue]', "TenantID", "IssueRecordsForUser")
```

Figure 8-17 shows how this data looks after the GroupBy operation.

TenantID	IssueRecordsForUser		
9			
	IssueID	PropertyID	Description
	3	35	Alarm displaying malfunction code
	4	6	Lights in communal area not working
2			
	IssueID	PropertyID	Description
	5	38	Car park being used by non-residents
	6	3	Moss growth on patio – slip hazard
50			
	IssueID	PropertyID	Description
	8	45	Toilet cistern leaking
	9	30	Thumping noise from heating

Figure 8-17. *Grouped data*

The TenantID column shows the distinct data. Once we apply this formula to a gallery control, we can add a label and call the LookUp function to retrieve the user details that are associated with the TenantID, as shown in Figure 8-18.

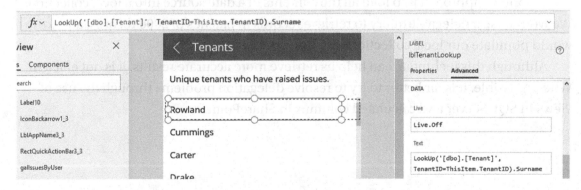

Figure 8-18. *Calling the LookUp function from a label*

A typical business requirement is to show distinct records that have been created over a defined period. As an example, let's suppose we want to show a list of distinct tenants who have raised issues in the current month. Theoretically, we could accomplish this by filtering our source data like so:

```
GroupBy(Filter('[dbo].[Issue]',
            StartDate >= Date(2017,6,1) &&
            StartDate < Date(2017,7,1)
    ),
    "TenantID",
    "IssueRecordsForUser"
)
```

However, with SQL Server and SharePoint data sources, the date filter bug prevents this formula from returning correct data. As we saw earlier in this chapter, filtering data sources by date will incorrectly return zero rows.

One way to overcome this problem is to add the criteria && Day(StartDate) >0 to force the filter operation to run on the local device. The caveat of this approach is that this expression is non-delegable and will not return accurate results with data sources that exceed 2000 records.

Resolving Delegation Issues

These delegation issues can be a headache because they prevent us from retrieving the accurate results that we want. What approaches can we use to work around these delegation issues?

A popular approach is to load all the contents of a data source into a local collection. We would use a delegable query to retrieve records in batches of 2000 records, and we would populate our local collection with the results.

Although this technique can help us retrieve more accurate results, it is not efficient. Where possible, it is far better to try to resolve delegation problems through the use of views in SQL Server and calculated columns in SharePoint.

SQL Server Views

With SQL Server, a great way to overcome delegation issues is to build a view. Because SQL Server is a large separate topic, we won't cover this in too much detail. However, the important thing to take away from this section is that there is an effective technique that we can apply to overcome query delegation problems.

To provide a brief demonstration, let's return to our earlier example. Let's say we want to return a list of distinct tenants who have raised issues in a given month. We can use the following SQL to build a view that returns distinct issues by the tenant and the close date:

```
SELECT DISTINCT TenantID,
       MONTH(CloseDateTime) AS CloseDateMonth,
       YEAR(CloseDateTime) AS CloseDateYear
FROM
       dbo.Issue
```

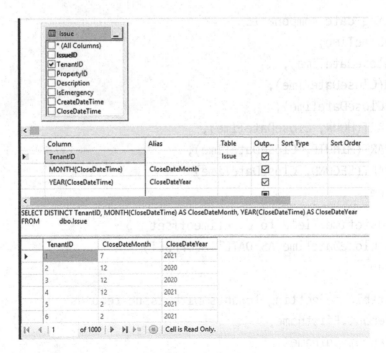

Figure 8-19. *Building a view*

Figure 8-19 shows the design of the view in Management Studio. The SQL in this view returns a numeric representation of the month and year of the CloseDateTime field by calling the SQL Month and Year functions. By converting datetime fields to integers, we can now query the data in a delegable way. From Power Apps, we can now return a distinct list of tenants who have raised issues in the current month with the following function:

```
Filter('[dbo].[viewDistinctTenants]',
 CloseDateMonth = Month(Now()) &&
        CloseDateYear = Year(Now())
)
```

This hopefully provides an overview of how we can incorporate SQL Server views into our apps. For additional reference, Listing 8-1 shows the most common snippets of SQL that we can use in views to overcome delegation issues.

Listing 8-1. Cheat sheet of SQL statements to use in views

```
-- 1 Extracting date components
SELECT CloseDateTime,
       DAY(CloseDateTime),
       MONTH(CloseDateTime),
       YEAR(CloseDateTime),
       DATEPART(HOUR, CloseDateTime),
       DATEPART(MINUTE, CloseDateTime),
       DATEPART(SECOND, CloseDateTime)
FROM dbo.Issue;

-- 2 Cast a datetime field to datetimeoffset
SELECT  CAST(CloseDateTime AS DATETIMEOFFSET)
FROM dbo.Issue

--2 Joining tables - getting tenants with issue records
SELECT dbo.Tenant.Firstname,
       dbo.Tenant.Surname
FROM dbo.Issue
    JOIN dbo.Tenant
        ON Tenant.TenantID = Issue.TenantID;
```

```
--3 Non existence - getting tenants without issue records
SELECT dbo.Tenant.Firstname,
       dbo.Tenant.Surname
FROM dbo.Tenant
WHERE TenantID NOT IN (
                    SELECT TenantID FROM dbo.Issue
             );
```

```
--4 Null check - getting issues without close dates
SELECT *
FROM dbo.Issue
WHERE CloseDateTime IS NULL;
```

```
-- 5 Change the Description column to use a case sensitive and accent
sensitive collation
SELECT
[Description] COLLATE SQL_Latin1_General_CP1_CS_AS AS [Description]
FROM dbo.Issue
```

Tip The <, <=, >, and >= operators are not delegable against date fields in SQL Server. By using a view to convert the day, month, and year components to numbers, we can filter dates from Power Apps using these comparison operators.

SharePoint Columns

With SharePoint, the options to work around delegation issues are more limited. SharePoint calculated columns do not help because these are also not delegable.

If we need to query date columns, a good approach is to add an additional numeric column and to store copies of the dates in yyyymmdd format. We would modify any data entry forms or calls to functions such as Patch to also record a numeric version of the date. Here's the formula that we would use to produce this numerical representation of a date:

```
Value(Text(dtpInputDate.SelectedDate, "yyyymmdd"))
```

By storing this date value in a number column, we can then filter the value using operators that include the greater than and less than operators.

If we were adding these new fields to an existing list, we could use a Power Automate flow to carry out the initial population.

Summary

This chapter focused on how to retrieve data and how to provide search capabilities for users. We covered one of the most challenging and widely discussed areas of Power Apps – delegation.

When we want to retrieve a filtered set of data, the ideal outcome is that the data source filters the records and returns the results to the app. This is the definition of a delegable query – Power Apps delegates the search query to the data source.

For more complex query conditions, Power Apps may not be able to delegate the search query to the data source. In this situation, the data source returns a maximum of 2000 records, and Power Apps executes the query on the local device. A non-delegable query misses records that fall outside this maximum 2000-record limit, and because of this, it may not return all results. This behavior presents a challenge for many app builders.

Data sources provide varying support for query delegation. Dataverse and SQL Server provide the best support, whereas SharePoint offers more limited support.

Areas where we are most likely to encounter problems with query delegation are queries where we use the IsBlank function to search for empty or null values, queries that call the in function to test that an input set of records belongs to a table or collection, and – by extension – queries that call the not and in functions to find records that do not match an input set of records. Another problem to be aware of is that there is a bug that prevents SQL Server and SharePoint data sources from filtering date columns using the greater than and less than operators.

With SQL Server as a data source, we can solve the majority of delegation problems by creating SQL Server views. The chapter provides a summary of the most common SQL statements that we can use to overcome delegation problems.

The three most common functions to query data are Search, Filter, and LookUp. The Search function matches input text against one or more text columns, the Filter function matches records based on a conditional formula, and the LookUp function returns the first record based on a conditional formula. The LookUp function is particularly useful because we use it to join or to show the details of a related record.

Another common user requirement is to return distinct records. We can return distinct records by grouping by the column where we want to show distinct values.

In the main part of the chapter, we walked through the process of building a custom search screen. This included the ability for users to filter records by a combo box control and a date picker. To build this type of search screen, we use the Filter function to filter our source data against the values that the user enters into the data entry controls. We also learned how to initiate a search from the click of a button by attaching a formula to the button to store the criteria values into variables and setting the Filter function to filter the data source by the variables.

PART III

Developing Canvas Apps

CHAPTER 9

Canvas App Design

In this chapter, we'll cover the cosmetic and layout features of canvas app design. This will be the first of three chapters on canvas apps. In the subsequent two chapters, we'll cover the topic of data controls.

To start this chapter, we'll look at simple features that can enhance our app building experience. We'll look at the new screen layouts that are available. This time-saving feature enables us to add screens with prebuilt layouts and features. Next, we'll look at shapes and icons, and we'll find out how we can use themes to modify the color scheme of an app.

Different users can choose to run our apps on devices that range from a phone to a desktop PC. We can design our apps responsively so that the same app renders differently, depending on the available screen space. We'll find out how to build this type of responsive app.

The main part of this chapter focuses on screen layout and the ways that we bring together the parts that make up a feature-rich app. We often encounter sophisticated-looking apps through the inbuilt templates and other samples that we can find on the Web. However, it can be difficult to work out how all the pieces fit together in a complex app; and therefore, we'll cover some of the typical app patterns that include

- How to build a list and details screen – A screen that shows a selectable list of records and a central section that shows the details of the selected record, along with summary details that could include counts of child records or totals and summaries of financial values.

- How to implement a tabbed user interface – There is no native tab control, so we'll look at how to build a tab-like interface where users can change visible sections by clicking tabbed headings.

- How to add confirmation screens – We'll find out how to display a confirmation screen when a user attempts to delete a record or to carry out some other action.

© Tim Leung 2021
T. Leung, *Beginning Power Apps*, https://doi.org/10.1007/978-1-4842-6683-0_9

Using Screen Predefined Layouts

Let's start this chapter by looking at screen templates. When we add a new screen, the menu provides a choice of ten screen templates, as shown in Figure 9-1. The simplest layout is the blank screen layout, which adds an empty screen to an app. Other basic screen templates include

- List/form – The list template creates a screen that's identical to the browse screen in an auto-generated app. The form template creates a screen that's identical to the details screen in an auto-generated app.

- Success – The success template creates a screen with a tick icon and a label with the text "This was successfully completed." We can navigate to the screen that's based on this template when an operation succeeds.

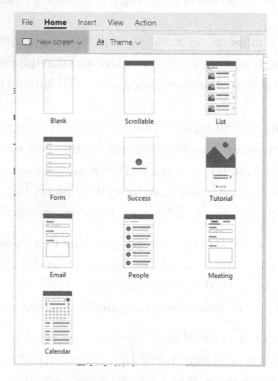

Figure 9-1. *The new screen templates*

Other interesting templates include the scrollable, tutorial, and Office 365 templates, which we'll now cover.

Scrollable Screen Template

A notable template is the scrollable template. This template enables us to build long scrollable screens. Why is the scrollable template so interesting? The reason is because a scrollable screen contains a control called a "fluid grid" control. The only way that we can add this type of control to an app is through the scrollable template. We won't find the option to add this control through any of the menus in the designer.

This fluid grid control behaves similarly to the form control. It acts as a parent for card controls. A card is a container for child controls, and we can add as many cards as we want to a fluid grid. At runtime, the cards stack next to or on top of each other. The user can scroll down the control to view the cards that are lower down in the stack.

A key feature is the Columns property. This defines the number of cards that we can fit per row of the fluid grid. The reason this is so useful is because it enables us to build a tile interface. For example, to build a screen that contains three tiles per row, we would set the Columns property to 3 and add cards for each tile that we want to display.

Within this multicolumn configuration, we can use the mouse to resize the width of a card so that it spans more than one column. The "Snap to columns" setting controls the column span behavior of a card. With this setting enabled, we can resize the width of a card so that it spans entire columns only. If we disable this setting, we can resize the width of a card to any arbitrary width up to the width of the fluid grid. For example, we could resize a card so that it fills 1.5 columns.

Figure 9-2 illustrates how the fluid grid control appears in the designer. This screenshot illustrates a fluid grid with four cards and a Columns setting of 3. The background color of each card is set differently to highlight each card. Notice how the bottom card spans two columns.

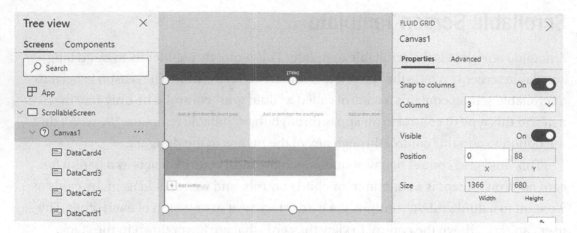

Figure 9-2. *The scrollable screen template*

From a design perspective, another reason why the fluid grid control is useful because it extends the visible design surface of the screen. Some app builders use cards to group together sets of controls in situations where they want to conditionally show or hide groups of controls. By housing the controls in cards, they can organize and design groups of controls more easily.

Are there any limitations to the fluid grid control? The main limitation is that we cannot nest a form control inside a fluid grid, which makes it slightly more difficult to incorporate data entry features. If we attempt to add a form control to a card in a fluid grid, the designer adds the form outside of the fluid grid control instead.

Tip   We can use the fluid grid control to build a tile interface.

Tutorial Screen Template

The "tutorial screen" template creates the screen that's shown in Figure 9-3. This screen contains an image control, text label, and forward and backward navigation icons. The data in the label and image control changes when a user clicks one of the navigation icons.

The reason why this template is useful is because it contains useful logic that we can reuse, particularly when we want to design screens to guide a user through a series of steps.

How precisely does this screen work? A gallery control stores the data items for the screen. When we examine the Items property of the gallery, we see that it calls the Table function. This function returns a table with the columns, step, text, and image.

The forward and backward icons increment and decrement the value of a variable, respectively. The label and image control display the data that corresponds to the variable.

Figure 9-3. *The tutorial screen template*

Office 365 Screen Templates

To help us rapidly build screens that interact with Office 365, Power Apps provides the Email, People, Meeting, and Calendar templates (Figure 9-4).

The Email template enables users to send emails using the Office 365 Outlook connector. The People template enables users to search for users in the organization using the Office 365 Users connector. The Meeting template enables users to send invites through Outlook, and the Calendar template enables users to view the schedule for any given date.

An important prerequisite is that we can only create screens based on these templates if we have an Office 365 mailbox.

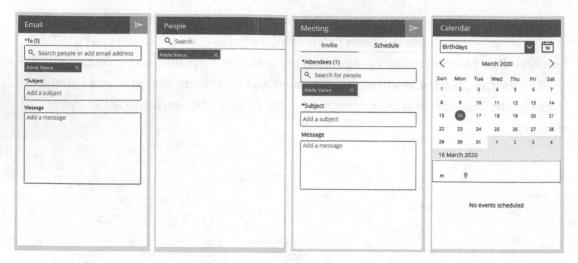

Figure 9-4. *The Office 365 screen templates*

Icons and Shapes

Power Apps provides a set of icons that we can add to our screens. Most often, we use icons to respond to user interactions and to carry out tasks. We can insert icons through the Icon button in the insert menu. Figure 9-5 shows the available icons. These are grouped into the heading actions, navigation, objects, and glyphs.

When we add an icon, the designer adds an icon control to our screen. The properties pane of this control enables us to change the icon. We can also use the Color property to change the color of the icon. This comes in useful when we add an icon to a dark background. In these cases, we can change the color of the icon to white, to help it stand out more clearly.

Figure 9-5. *Icons that we can add to a screen*

In addition to icons, we can also add geometric shapes, such circles, rectangles, and triangles. Figure 9-6 shows the shapes that are available. The option to add shapes is slightly hidden away. We can access shapes through the Insert icons menu button. They appear at the end of the list, beneath one of the icons.

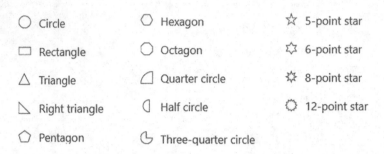

○ Circle	○ Hexagon	☆ 5-point star
□ Rectangle	○ Octagon	✩ 6-point star
△ Triangle	◁ Quarter circle	✴ 8-point star
◿ Right triangle	◖ Half circle	❂ 12-point star
⬠ Pentagon	◕ Three-quarter circle	

Figure 9-6. *Geometric shapes that we can add to a screen*

These shape controls are useful because they can serve as a background for other controls. For example, we could add a rectangle control and add child controls over the control. We could then apply background colors and borders to group controls together and to improve the appearance of a screen.

Using Icons and Shapes as Buttons

In most cases, we configure icons to respond to user taps or clicks, in the same way as a button control. The Action menu provides a no code way to carry out this task. As Figure 9-7 illustrates, the Action menu enables us to navigate to a new screen, add or remove items to or from a collection, or call a Power Automate flow.

To carry out more complex tasks, we can manually add a formula to the OnSelect property of the icon.

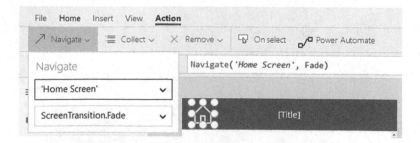

Figure 9-7. *The options that are available through the Action menu*

Using Themes

Themes provide a simple way to apply a consistent color scheme to all the screens and controls in an app. There are 12 predefined themes that we can access through the Home menu, as shown in Figure 9-8.

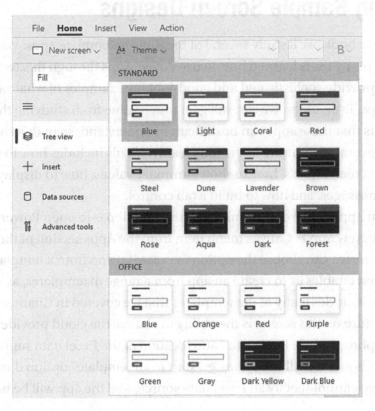

Figure 9-8. *Applying a theme*

When we apply a theme, the designer changes the control and background colors in every screen in the app. To prevent us from losing custom changes, the designer will not update any controls where we've modified the colors.

There are themes that consist of a light background and themes that consist of a dark background. A useful tip is that dark themes can help preserve the battery life of mobile devices. This is because a device requires less power to light up a screen that is predominantly dark.

> **Note**   A theme will not change any controls where we've manually modified the colors.

Examining Sample Screen Designs

In this part of the book, we'll study several of the built-in template apps. When Power Apps was new, many users learned how to use Power Apps through this technique. The template apps provide sophisticated and good-looking examples of what we can achieve with Power Apps. Even today, we can still gain much value from studying these apps. The main problem is that these apps can be difficult to understand, so in this chapter, we'll walk through several of the more interesting features. This includes how to construct list and details screen layouts, how to show summary values, how to display delete confirmation messages, and how to build a tab control.

To create an app for one of the templates, the first step is to open Power Apps Studio by selecting the New app ➤ Canvas menu item from the Apps section of the Maker Portal. From here, we can choose the option to create an app from a template. This opens a view that enables us to create an app from a range of templates, as shown in Figure 9-9. This includes many of the templates that we covered in Chapter 1.

A useful feature on this screen is the ability to change the cloud provider (e.g., OneDrive, Dropbox, Google Drive, etc.) and location of the Excel data source for the app. Note that if we choose the All templates ➤ "start from template" option directly from the Maker Portal, we cannot specify an Excel data source, and the app will be based on static read-only data.

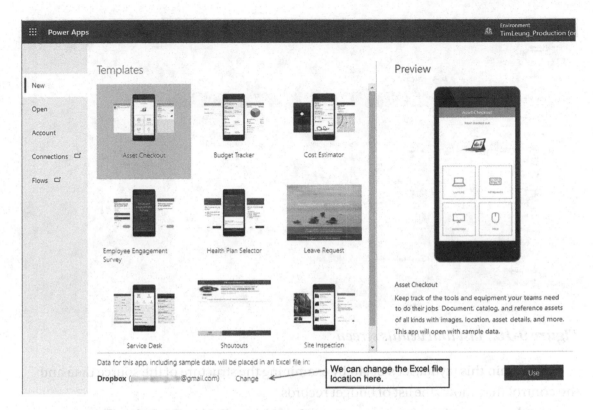

Figure 9-9. Creating an app from a template

Caution   If we create an app from a template directly from the Maker Portal, we cannot specify an Excel data source location.

Building a List and Details Screen

The first app that we'll look at is the tablet version of the Budget Tracker app. The layout of this app shows a list of budgets in the left-hand pane, as shown in Figure 9-10. When a user selects a budget item from this list, the other sections of the screen update themselves with the data that relates to the selected budget. The details section includes a pie chart that shows the total amount spent, a list of expenses, and summary values at the top of the screen that apply to the selected budget record. What ties all of this together? What is it that links the various controls on the screen with the list of budget records?

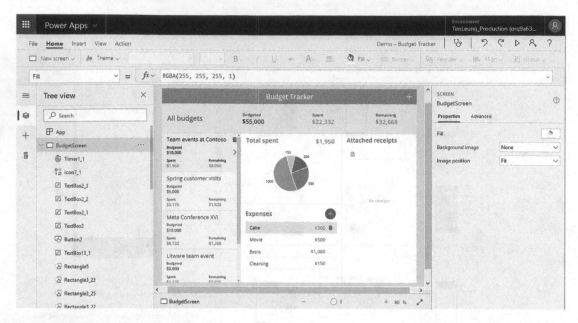

Figure 9-10. *List and details screen*

To explain this layout, let's begin by examining the structure of the source data and the control that shows the list of budget records.

The data source for this app is an Excel spreadsheet held in OneDrive. This spreadsheet contains five tables, and the details of these are shown in Table 9-1.

Table 9-1. *Data source for the Budget Tracker application*

Table Name	Table Columns
Budgets	BudgetTite, BudgetAmount, BudgetID
Expenses	Id, ExpenseName, BudgetTitle, Category, Expense, BudgetId
Categories	CategoryName
Receipts	Id, BudgetId, ExpenseId, ReceiptList[image], ReceiptName
ExpenseByCategory	Category, BudgetId, Expense

On the main screen of the app, the control that shows the list of budgets is a gallery control named Gallery1. The Items property of this control is set to the Excel table Budgets.

If we look closely at this gallery control, each row includes the budget amount, the amount of money that has been spent, and the amount of money remaining, as shown in Figure 9-11.

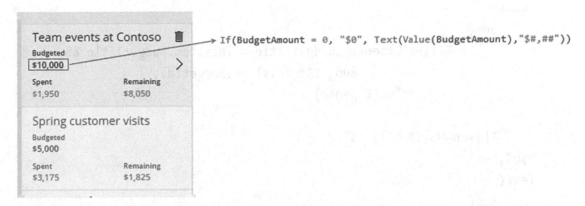

Figure 9-11. *The formula for the budgeted value*

Figure 9-11 shows the formula that displays the total budgeted amount. This formula formats the BudgetAmount value with thousand comma separators and a preceding currency symbol. You might be curious to understand why the formula includes a conditional statement to display the literal text "$0" if the BudgetAmount is 0. Could we not just apply the following formula without the If function, like so?

```
Text(Value(BudgetAmount),"$#,##")
```

The reason why the formula conditionally tests for zero is to fix a piece of behavior with the Text function. If we were to format the value zero with the format string as shown in the following, the result of this function would return an empty string:

```
Text(0,"$#,##")
```

Therefore, the purpose of the If statement is to display the value "$0" when the budgeted amount is zero, rather than an empty string.

Let's now look at the formulas that calculate the spent and remaining amounts. The amount of money that has been spent against a budget is stored in the Expenses table and not in the Budgets table. Therefore, the formulas that carry out the amount spent and the amount remaining are slightly more complex. Listing 9-1 shows the formula that carries out the spent calculation.

Listing 9-1. Formula for spent amount

```
If
(
    Text(
        Sum(
            Filter(Expenses,BudgetTitle = ThisItem.BudgetTitle &&
                            BudgetId=ThisItem.BudgetId),
                Value(Expense)
            ),
        "[$-en-US]$#,##")="$",
    "$0",
    Text(
        Sum(
            Filter(Expenses,BudgetId = ThisItem.BudgetId ),
            Value(Expense)
            ),
        "[$-en-US]$#,##"
        )
)
```

The first thing we notice is that this formula begins with an If function. Just like before, the purpose of this conditional test is to format zero values as "$0." The pertinent code that calculates the sum of the expenses resides in the true part of the If function.

This formula calls the Sum function to calculate the sum of the Expense column in the Expenses table where the BudgetId matches the selected budget ID in the gallery control.

Listing 9-2 shows the code that calculates the remaining budget amount. This code is mostly identical to the code that calculates the spent amount. The primary difference is that it subtracts the spent amount from the budget amount.

Listing 9-2. Formula to calculate the remaining amount

```
If (
        Text(ThisItem.BudgetAmount-Sum(
    Filter(
        Expenses,BudgetTitle = ThisItem.BudgetTitle &&
```

```
                BudgetId=ThisItem.BudgetId),
        Value(Expense)
      ),
            "[$-en-US]$#,##")="$"
   ,"$0",
   Text(ThisItem.BudgetAmount-Sum(
      Filter(
      Expenses,BudgetId = ThisItem.BudgetId),
      Value(Expense)
      ),
   "[$-en-US]$#,##")
)
```

In summary, this section provides a practical example of the formula we would use to calculate sums and highlights how this code might be more complex than we first expect.

Updating the Details Section of a Screen

When a user clicks a row in the gallery control, the central part of the screen shows a list of expenses that are related to the selected budget record and the total amount that has been spent from the budget. These controls work by referencing the selected budget record in the gallery control, and the formulas that these controls use are shown in Figure 9-12.

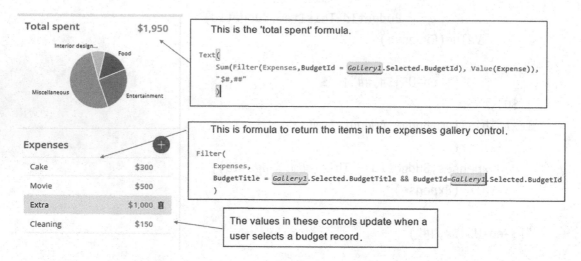

Figure 9-12. *Controls in the central part of the screen*

The control that shows the list of expenses is a gallery control. The control that shows the "total spent" is a label control. Note that the actual formula includes a call to the If statement to correctly format the zero values, but the code in Figure 9-12 omits this for brevity.

Displaying a Delete Confirmation Screen

To prevent users from accidentally deleting records, a common technique is to show a delete confirmation screen. The Budget Tracker app provides this feature, and we'll now look at how this works.

In the gallery control of budget records, each row includes a trash icon, as shown in Figure 9-13.

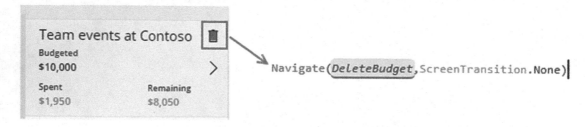

Figure 9-13. *The trash icon navigates the user to a new custom delete screen*

This icon navigates the user to a screen called `DeleteBudget`, as shown in Figure 9-14. This screen includes two buttons – a delete button and a cancel button.

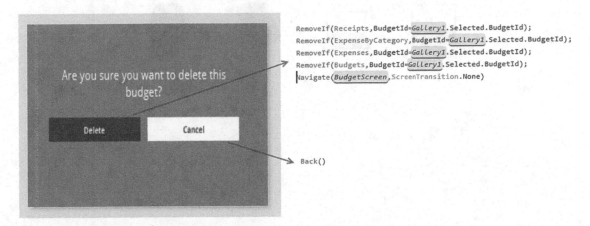

Figure 9-14. *Deleting a budget record*

As Figure 9-14 shows, the `OnSelect` property of the delete button calls the `RemoveIf` function five times. The `RemoveIf` function deletes data from a data source based on a condition. This code deletes the records in the four related tables that match the selected budget ID of the record in Gallery1 (the gallery control that shows the list of budget records). Finally, the formula navigates the user back to the main budget screen. The cancel button simply returns the user to the previous screen by calling the `Back` function.

This feature provides an ideal example of how to delete records in related child tables before deleting a record in the parent table.

Building a Tab Control Screen

To organize the layout of a screen, we can group our controls into tabs. The Asset Checkout app includes such an example, as shown in Figure 9-15. In this screen, the main screen contains four groups – laptops, keyboards, monitors, and mice. When a user selects one of these items, the background color of the selected item turns gray, and the gallery control at the bottom of the screen updates and displays the products that belong to the group.

Let's look at how this screen is constructed. The strip that shows the groups is actually a gallery control. The reason why the gallery control resembles a tab strip is because the

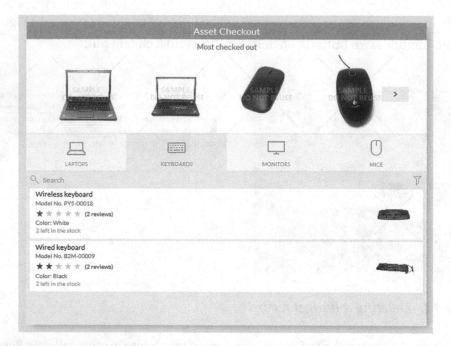

Figure 9-15. *The "Asset Checkout" app includes a tab-type control*

Layout property is set to horizontal. This configures the control so that the items sit side to side, rather than top to bottom. Additionally, the "Show navigation" setting is set to false to hide the navigation controls that would usually appear. These are the forward and backward buttons that bring into view the next batch of records in the gallery.

The background color of the gallery control is a light gray color. The Fill and TemplateFill properties of the gallery control define these colors.

The item template for the gallery control includes a darker gray color rectangle control. This rectangle control provides the canvas for the icon and text that appears in the template. The setting that makes this control behave like a tab control is the visibility setting of the rectangle control, which is set to the following formula:

```
If(ThisItem.IsSelected,true,false)
```

This formula hides the gray rectangle when the item is not selected. The final touch that rounds off the appearance of this control is the strip at the bottom of the control which is set to the same gray color. Figure 9-16 illustrates the main parts that make up this feature.

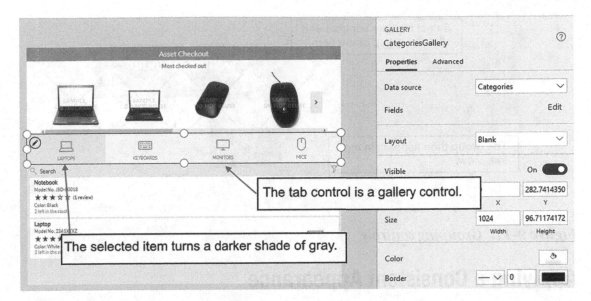

Figure 9-16. *How the tab control works*

Note   The Fill property defines the entire background color of a gallery, including the empty space that appears where there are no records. The TemplateFill property defines the background color of actual items in the gallery.

Organizing Controls

In this section, we'll look at a couple of ways in which we can work a little more effectively in the designer.

Grouping Controls

To help organize the controls on a screen, we can group a set of controls into a single container. This can make it easier to reposition groups of controls on the screen, and it makes it easier to copy sets of controls from one screen to another.

To add a set of controls into a group, we can press and hold the Ctrl key and left-click the multiple controls that we want to add to a group. With the controls selected, we can select the Group option in the context menu to add the controls to a group (Figure 9-17).

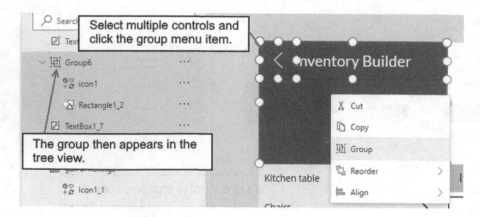

Figure 9-17. *Grouping controls*

Applying a Consistent Appearance

A limitation of the themes feature is that it isn't possible to create our own themes. To help maintain our apps, there is often the need for us to be able to control the font sizes, colors, and other presentational elements in a single place.

One way to accomplish this is to add a template screen to an app. On this screen, we would add template controls and set the size, color, or any other property to those that we want to use throughout our app.

When we add a control to a screen, we would set properties such as the font type or font size by referencing the template control (Figure 9-18). This means that if we want to change properties throughout an app, we can make the change one time in the template control.

To simplify this process further, we can reuse the template screen throughout all of our apps to help maintain a corporate style.

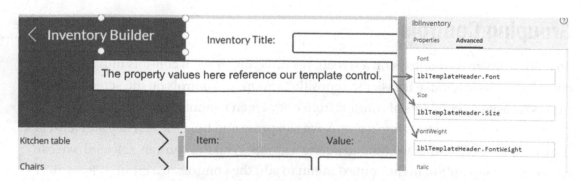

Figure 9-18. *Creating a template control*

Phone vs. Tablet Apps

When we create a new app, there are two formats that we can choose – tablet or phone layout. What exactly are the differences between these formats?

The choice we make determines the size of our design surface. A phone app has a fixed size of 640 by 1136 pixels, and it is not possible to change these dimensions. In contrast, the dimensions of a tablet app are configurable; and therefore, the tablet format is most suitable for desktop PCs and any format other than a phone.

Figure 9-19 shows the screen size options that are available through the settings menu of a tablet app. For both phone and tablet apps, we can set the orientation, and we can also choose to lock the orientation. When we lock the orientation, the app will not reorientate itself when the user rotates the device.

We can use the size section to select a preset size, or we can choose the custom option and enter a custom width and height. This size section is not available for phone apps.

The two additional advanced settings that we can set are scale to fit and lock aspect ratio. When we enable the lock aspect ratio setting, Power Apps maintains the ratio between the height and width to prevent distortion. This means that if we were to build a tablet app with the default settings of a 16:9 aspect ratio and the lock aspect ratio setting turned on, if we were to run the app on a widescreen PC monitor with a 16:10 aspect ratio, vertical black bars will appear to the left and right of the app. If we want our app to fill all the available screen space without any black bars, we would turn off the lock aspect ratio setting.

By default, the scale to fit option is enabled. With this setting enabled, Power Apps scales an app to fit the available screen space. When we turn off the scale to fit option, the designer turns off the lock aspect ratio option and prevents us from enabling this option. This is because with the scale to fit option turned off, we are no longer designing for a specific screen shape.

The scale to fit option is important because we must turn off this option if we were to build a responsive app. We will now cover this topic in the next section.

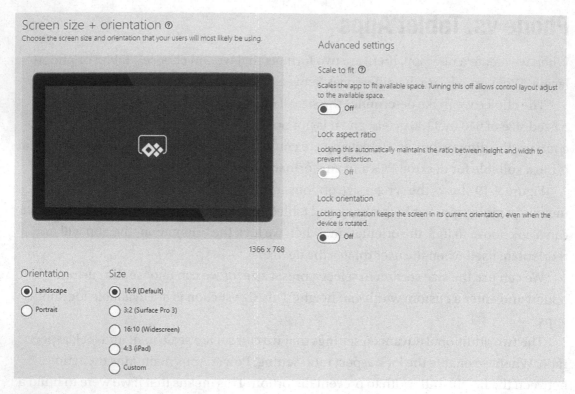

Figure 9-19. *Screen size settings (for tablet layout)*

Supporting Multiple Devices

If we want to build an app that functions well on a range of devices, from a phone to a desktop PC, what options do we have?

The first method is to build separate apps for all the devices that we want to support. Although this method is simple to implement, the big disadvantage is that it requires a duplication of effort. If we want to update an app, we need to make the same modification in several different versions of the app.

Therefore, an alternative is to build an app that renders differently depending on the target device. These types of app are known as responsive apps. They require less effort to maintain in the long term because there is just a single app and code base that we need to manage.

Unfortunately, it isn't simple to build a responsive app. The process involves identifying each control in an app and setting the x and y coordinates using a formula. The formula we write identifies the screen size and repositions the controls depending on the available space. This process can add a significant amount of development time.

How do we decide whether to create separate apps or to build a single responsive app? For apps with a simple user interface, a responsive app can provide an excellent balance between ease of development and long-term maintenance. For apps with many controls and complex layouts, the complexity and overhead of building a single app can outweigh the benefit of maintaining fewer apps. In this case, it can be easier to build and maintain separate apps.

Let's now take a closer look at the steps to build a responsive app.

Tip   If we choose to build separate apps for different devices, we can use components (Chapter 22) to implement the common features between the apps. This can provide an effective balance between ease of development, reusability, and long-term maintenance.

Designing a Responsive App

To design a responsive app, the first step is to identify the devices that we want to support. The next step is to plan how we want our screens to appear on each device. The crucial key to success lies in this planning stage.

Let's imagine an app that enables users to manage property records. The first screen will display a list of property records. On a phone, the only thing visible will be a list of properties. Through this device, the user can select a property and view the details in a separate screen.

On a desktop PC, the first screen also shows a list of properties. However, the desktop version will display the property details in a form that is adjacent to the list. This layout saves the user from having to navigate to a separate screen to view the details and makes much better use of the screen space.

A good way to plan a responsive app is to sketch the desired controls and layout on a piece of paper and to identify the rules that should apply on different devices. Figure 9-20 illustrates the high-level plan for our responsive app. Our plan here identifies five rules.

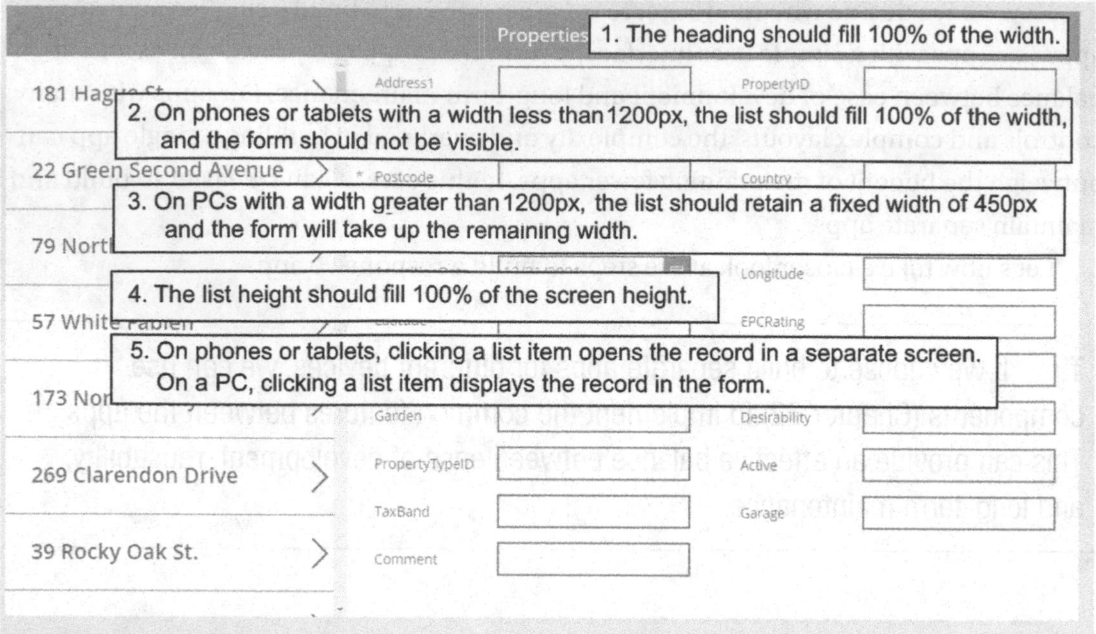

Figure 9-20. *Planning how our app behaves*

Based on the controls that we want to include on our screen, we'll decide that we need a width of 1200 px to display a list control and a form side by side. If the width of the target device is less than 1200 px, there will be insufficient space to display the form without truncation; and therefore, the list control should fill the width of the screen in this scenario.

Formulas That We Use

The crucial part to building a responsive app is to determine the amount of available screen space. There are three function types that we can use, as shown in Table 9-2.

Table 9-2. *App Sizing Functions*

Function	Description
App.Width/App.Height	These formulas return the usable/visible screen width and height.
App.DesignWidth/App.DesignHeight	These formulas return the dimensions that we specify in the app settings.
Parent.Width/Parent.Height	These formulas return the dimensions of the parent control.

The functions App.Width and App.Height return the dimensions of the device or the visible area of a web browser. If a user resizes the browser, the App.Width and App.Height values change dynamically.

The functions App.DesignWidth and App.DesignHeight return the width and height values that we specify in the settings section of an app at design time.

The Parent.Width and Parent.Height functions return the width and height of the parent control. If we were to place a control directly on the screen, Parent.Width and Parent.Height would return the width and height of the screen. For a control that we place inside a gallery control, Parent.Width and Parent.Height return the width and height of the gallery control.

To give an example as to why this Parent syntax is useful, let's suppose we build a gallery control that fills 100% the width of the screen. Within the gallery, we want to insert a navigation icon that docks to the right-hand side. By referring to the parent width, we can calculate the correct x coordinate position for the navigation icon.

Note   For a control that we place directly on the screen, Parent.Width and Parent.Height can return values greater than App.Width and App.Height. This is because Parent.Width and Parent.Height include the dimensions of any visible browser scrollbars.

Screen Sizes

Another important point to understand is, how do we know what device the user is running? Is the user using a phone, tablet, or PC?

To provide some indication, Power Apps exposes a size property that ranges from 1 to 4 and above. Size 1 is the smallest and corresponds to a phone, whereas size 4 corresponds to a PC. This is illustrated in Figure 9-21.

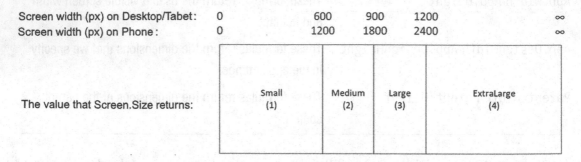

| Screen width (px) on Desktop/Tabet: | 0 | | 600 | 900 | 1200 | | ∞ |
| Screen width (px) on Phone : | 0 | | 1200 | 1800 | 2400 | | ∞ |

| | Small (1) | Medium (2) | Large (3) | ExtraLarge (4) |
| The value that Screen.Size returns: | | | | |

Figure 9-21. *The size property (with default size breakpoints)*

To return the size value, we can use the formula Screen.Size or Parent.Size. To help us more easily use these values in formulas, Power Apps provides corresponding constants (or "labels") that identify these size values. These are Small, Medium, Large, and ExtraLarge.

What exactly are the screen dimensions of a small, medium, large, or extralarge device? The place where we define this is through the SizeBreakpoints property of the app. We access this through the App node of the tree view, as shown in Figure 9-22. By default, these are [600, 900, 1200] for a tablet app and [1200, 1800, 2400] for a phone app. The higher values for a phone app reflect the higher pixel density on a phone app.

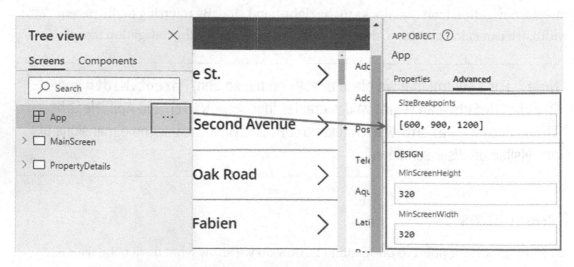

Figure 9-22. *The breakpoint size and minimum screen size settings*

Building a Responsive App

Now that we understand the basic functions to build a responsive app, we'll walk through the steps to build our app. The first step is to create a new app using the tablet layout. This is important because it provides us with the design surface that includes sufficient width to add our list and form controls. Next, we need to turn off the "scale to fit" option in the settings of our app.

Making Screens Responsive

To build the main screen that shows the list of properties, we'll use the list template so that it adds a screen with a heading section and a gallery control.

The key step to make our screen responsive is to set the Width and Height properties to the following formulas:

```
Width = App.Width
```

```
Height = App.Height
```

To configure the header so that it fills 100% of the screen width, we set the Width property to App.Width. Next, we can add a form control to our screen, as shown in Figure 9-23.

We would set the data source property of the gallery and form controls to Properties and the Item property of the form control to TemplateGalleryList1.Selected.

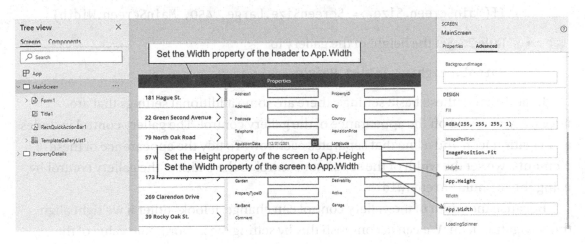

Figure 9-23. *The layout of our screen*

The next step is to add another screen using the form template. This screen will display the selected record on smaller devices, and we'll name this screen `PropertyDetails`.

We'll make this screen responsive by setting the Width and Height properties to `App.Width` and `App.Height`, respectively.

To configure the form so that it displays the correct record, we'll set the data source property to `Properties` and the Item property to `TemplateGalleryList1.Selected`.

Configuring the Gallery Control

Our next step is to configure our gallery control so that it adheres to our layout plan. The first two rules that are applicable to our gallery are

- Rule 1 – Where the width is less than 1200 px, the gallery should fill 100% the width of the screen. Where the available screen width is greater than 1200 px or more, the gallery control should be a fixed width of 450 px.

- Rule 2 – The gallery should fill 100% the height of the screen. To implement this rule, we set the height value to the height of the screen minus the height of the title bar.

Here are the settings to apply these rules:

- Rule 1 – Set the width of the gallery to

  `If(MainScreen.Size >= ScreenSize.Large, 450, MainScreen.Width)`

- Rule 2 – Set the height of the gallery to

  `Parent.Height - Title1.Height`

In addition to these basic settings, there are some additional settings that are necessary to round off the appearance of the gallery control. The gallery control includes a navigationIcon and a line that separates each row. To tidy the appearance of these elements, we set the width of the separator control to the width of the gallery control by using the formula `Parent.Width`.

Because the width of the gallery control can change, it looks tidier if we right align the navigation icon. We can accomplish this by setting the x coordinate value of the icon to `Parent.Width - 75`. This formula places the icon 75 pixels from the right of the gallery control. Figure 9-24 highlights the settings that we apply to the gallery control.

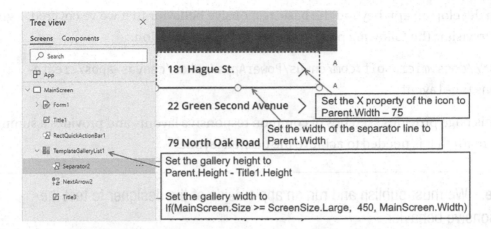

Figure 9-24. *Configuring the gallery control*

The final step is to configure the navigation icon in the gallery control to navigate the user to the details screen, only if the width of the device is less than 1200 px. To do this, we set the OnSelect property of the navigation icon to the following formula:

```
If(MainScreen.Size < ScreenSize.Large, Navigate(PropertyDetails))
```

Caution   Once we position controls with formulas, it is very important not to drag or to reposition controls in the designer. Dragging controls in the editor will overwrite our formulas with static values. It is likely that this behavior will be fixed in a future release.

Testing and Building Our App

We can now run and test our app. A very important point is that an app will not behave responsively when we run it from the designer. Therefore, it's necessary to publish and run our app outside of the designer to test the responsive behavior.

When we run our published app, we can resize our browser window to see the outcome of our responsive code. When we resize the window to a width smaller than 1200 px, the gallery control will fill the width of the screen, and clicking an item will open the selected record in our details screen.

To develop an app beyond the basic responsive behavior that we've covered, a great place to visit is the following page in the online documentation:

https://docs.microsoft.com/en-us/PowerApps/maker/canvas-apps/create-responsive-layout

This page provides sketches of common responsive layouts and provides a summary of the math that is needed to achieve the desired layout.

Note   We must publish and run an app outside of the designer to test the responsive behavior.

Using the Timer Control

The final topic that we'll cover in this chapter is the timer control. The timer control runs a formula after a predetermined time. We can configure the timer to reset itself after the elapsed time, and this enables us to repeat an action at regular intervals. The timer control can be useful for many reasons. We can use the timer control to refresh data, update caches of data, or even carry out animations. One way to do this would be to change the background color of a shape control at rapid intervals to give the appearance of an animation.

The most important properties of this control are the Duration, Repeat, Start, and AutoStart properties. The Duration property is measured in milliseconds. The Start property controls whether the timer is working and counting down. The AutoStart property defines whether the timer begins counting down immediately when the screen becomes visible. To retrieve the elapsed time, we refer to the Value property. This returns the elapsed time in milliseconds.

To demonstrate this control, here's how to build a screen that refreshes every 60 seconds and displays the details of the latest issue record in the data source.

The first step is to add a timer control to a screen. We do this through the Insert ➤ Input menu item. This adds a control that looks like a button that includes a countdown timer.

Next, set the Duration property to 60000, which is equivalent to 60 seconds. To configure the timer to start when the screen becomes visible and to restart every 60 seconds, set the AutoStart and Repeat properties to true.

To specify the behavior when the timer elapses, we add a formula to the `OnTimerEnd` property. Here's the formula to add:

```
UpdateContext(
            {LatestRecord: First(Sort(Issues, CreateDateTime, Descending))}
)
```

This formula runs each time the timer elapses, and the purpose is to retrieve the latest issue record and to store the details into a variable called `LatestRecord`. To show these details, we can add labels and populate the text with the fields from our `LatestRecord` variable. Figure 9-25 shows the appearance of this screen.

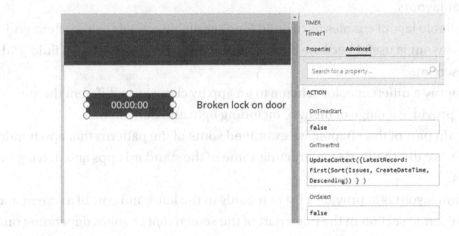

Figure 9-25. *Using the timer control*

The timer control is visible to the user, and by default, the text on the control shows the elapsed time. When the timer is visible, users can click the control to start and to pause the timer. To hide the timer control, set the `Visible` property to false.

One point to be aware of is that the timer control isn't guaranteed to be precise. If we set the duration of a timer to five minutes, the time that it takes for the timer to complete may take more than five minutes. One possible way to recreate this behavior is to use a slower device where the JavaScript in the browser may run more slowly. If we were to build a measurement app that takes readings at specified intervals, we should be cautious of the impact that this has on the accuracy of the solution.

Another useful point to be aware of is that we can configure a timer to continue running when a user navigates away from a screen. The way to enable this is to set the AutoPause property to false.

Summary

This chapter focused on topics relating to the cosmetic design and layout of a canvas app. We began by examining the layouts that we can choose when we add a screen. This time-saving feature creates screens from templates that can include standard controls such as a title bar and a data control. The available layouts include the list, form, Email, and Calendar layouts.

The scrollable layout enables us to build long scrollable screens using a fluid grid control. This layout is useful because it provides the only way for us to add a fluid grid control to a screen.

We can apply a different color scheme to an app by choosing a different theme. Power Apps provides a range of themes, including light and dark themes.

In the main part of this chapter, we examined some of the patterns that app builders regularly use. We did this by deconstructing some of the standard apps and delving into the formulas.

A common layout is to provide a list of records in the left-hand part of a screen and to create a dynamic section in the main part of the screen that changes depending on the selected record. This layout relies on a gallery control that displays the list items. To populate the central part of the screen, forms and other data controls will refer to the Selected property of the gallery control.

Another common layout is to provide a tabbed interface. We can accomplish this by adding a horizontal gallery control. We apply a conditional formula that modifies the color or appearance of the selected gallery item, and this results in an appearance that mimics the look of a tab control.

When a user attempts to delete a record, it's helpful to provide a way for the user to confirm the action. One way to implement this feature is to navigate the user to a separate screen. This screen will include a "confirm" button that contains the formula that deletes the record (or carries out some other action that requires confirmation).

Power Apps provides support for responsive design, and this enables us to build a single app that can target multiple form factors, such as phones and desktop PCs. We build a responsive app by writing formulas that position every control in an app so that it fits the available screen space. The two most important formulas that enable us to build a responsive app are `App.Width` and `App.Height`. These formulas retrieve the width and height of the browser or target device.

In the final part of this chapter, we looked at the timer control. This control executes formulas at specified intervals. It is very useful because it enables us to build animations or to schedule automatic saves or data refreshes at specific points in time.

CHAPTER 10

Using Simple Controls

Controls provide the means for users to interact with apps, and they play a crucial role in app design. This chapter focuses on controls that can edit and display a single value. These include the text input, rich text, radio, toggle, slider, rating, and date controls.

An important topic that we'll cover is how to use forms and to map data values to controls. It's common for data sources to store codified or abbreviated data values. These could include country code abbreviations or letters such as "Y" and "N" to denote true and false. It can be a challenge to configure controls such as radio or toggle controls so that they display meaningful options to the user, yet store and retrieve codified values from the data source. We'll find out exactly how to carry out this mapping task.

Another important topic that we'll cover is how to work with dates and times. Power Apps performs time zone conversions to allow users in different regions to work with times in their local time zone. The difficulty is that if we misconfigure our apps, we can store incorrect time values in our data source.

Here's the overview of what we cover in this chapter:

- The simple, single-value controls that Power Apps provides, how these controls appear, the features they offer, and how we configure these controls

- How to incorporate a variety of edit controls into a screen and how to connect those controls to forms

- How to modify the format in which we store dates and times in a data source to help avoid localization issues

Chapter Overview

To explore the controls that Power Apps offers, we'll build an app that's based on a table of property records, and we'll utilize a wide range of controls from the Power Apps toolkit. Figure 10-1 shows the end result of this exercise. The controls that we'll look

© Tim Leung 2021
T. Leung, *Beginning Power Apps*, https://doi.org/10.1007/978-1-4842-6683-0_10

at include the text input, date picker, radio, rating, and slider controls. We'll add these controls to forms and walk through the necessary modifications to support the save and update operations.

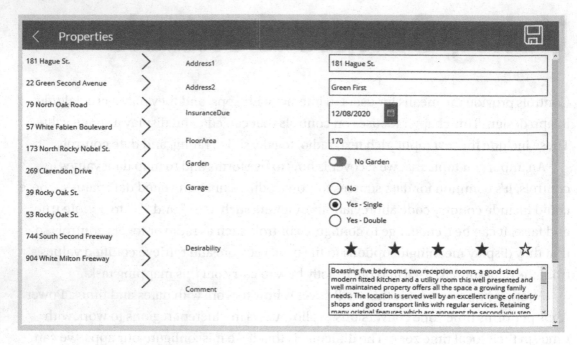

Figure 10-1. The screen that we'll build in this chapter

Building Data Structures to Support Controls

Figure 10-2 shows the Excel spreadsheet that we'll use in this chapter. This spreadsheet stores property details, with fields such as PropertyID, Address1, FloorArea, Bedrooms, Garden, Garage, Desirability, InsuranceDue, and Comment.

	A	B	C	D	E	F	G	H	I	J
1	PropertyID	Address1	Address2	FloorArea	Bedrooms	Garden	Garage	Desirability	InsuranceDue	Comment
2	1	181 Hague St.	51 Green Fir	173	7	N	N	4	2016-08-13	Boasting five bedroon
3	2	22 Green Second A	83 South Cla	81	1	N	S	5	2020-01-02	
4	3	79 North Oak Road	135 North Gr	59	6	Y	S	4	2020-03-11	
5	4	57 White Fabien Bc	715 North Fa	39	5	N	D	5	2016-03-24	
6	5	173 North Rocky Nc	23 East Fabie	29	5	N	N	5	2017-06-13	
7	6	269 Clarendon Driv	88 White Fir	47	3	Y	N	4	2017-11-23	
8	7	39 Rocky Oak St.	327 Second [	131	2	Y	N	2	2011-11-30	
9	8	53 Rocky Oak St.	35 Cowley A	149	7	N	N	4	2018-04-07	
10	9	744 South Second F	54 First Boul	102	5	N	N	5	2008-02-27	
11	10	904 White Milton F	968 Clarendc	46	3	Y	N	3	2018-08-17	

Figure 10-2. Property details spreadsheet

To demonstrate how to incorporate the controls into forms, we'll build a typical list/details screen as shown in Figure 10-3.

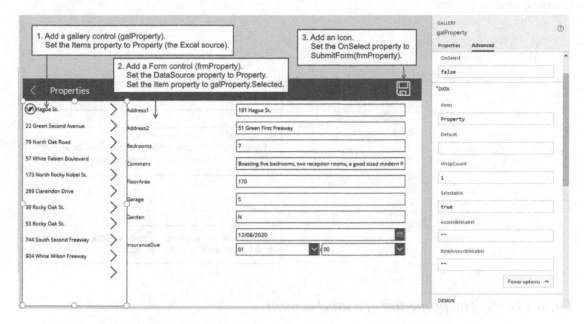

Figure 10-3. *The basic setup of our screen*

Displaying Data

To display data, Power Apps provides two controls – the label and HTML text controls. Let's take a closer look at these controls.

The Label Control

The most basic control is the label control. We can use this to show values from a data source, or we can use it to display static text. To show static text, we set the Text property to the text that we want to show. We enclose this text in double quotes, and we can display line breaks by typing <shift><enter>.

To customize the appearance of a label, there are several properties that we can set (Figure 10-4). Most of these are self-explanatory, such as the font size, font weight, style, and text alignment. The properties pane is just one place where we can set these attributes. We can also set these properties by selecting a label and using the icons that appear beneath the home section of the ribbon bar.

The fonts that we can use are limited. For example, the Wingdings font isn't available, which would enable us to enter symbols that could include checkmark, crosses, or emoticons.

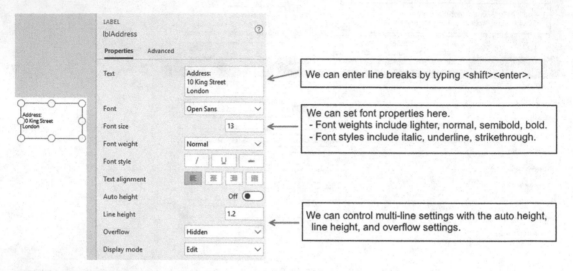

Figure 10-4. *The properties of a label control*

Although most properties are self-explanatory, there are some that warrant further explanation. First are the properties that control how a label behaves with a large amount of text. There are two properties that are relevant – the auto height and overflow properties.

With auto height turned on, the label automatically grows in height to accommodate the text in the label. If we choose to turn off auto height, we can set the overflow property to "scroll." This will display scrollbars against the label (Figure 10-5).

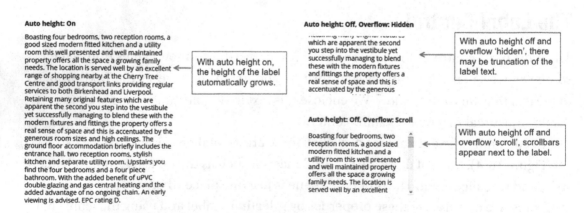

Figure 10-5. *The auto height and overflow properties of a label control*

Another interesting property is line height, which defaults to 1.2. What is this, and what is this unit of measurement? The line height property controls the space above and below the line of text. The unit of measurement defines a multiplier against the font size. With the default line height of 1.2 and the default font size of 13, this would result in a line height of 15.6 pixels (Figure 10-6).

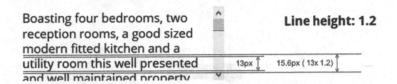

Figure 10-6. *The line height setting of a label control*

The HTML Text Control

The HTML text control is a versatile control that enables us to display richly formatted HTML content. HTML provides far greater control over the formatting of text. Unlike the label control, we can set the colors and styles of individual words in a sentence with HTML.

When we add an HTML text control, the `HtmlText` property provides example markup to help us author basic HTML, as shown in Figure 10-7. This includes how to set the text style to bold with the `<b>` tag and how to set the text color to blue with the tag `<font color=blue>`.

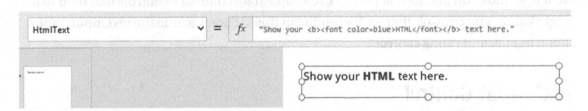

Figure 10-7. *The HTML text control provides example markup*

The HTML text control is particularly useful when we want to display characters that are unavailable with plain text. This could include the superscript characters in chemical symbols, mathematical symbols, or even musical characters. Example symbols with their corresponding HTML tags include CO^2 (CO²), ∞ (∞), and B♭ (B ♭).

Displaying Phone Numbers and Email Addresses

Another area where we see the HTML text control in action is when we change the control type of a form field to view phone or view email (Figure 10-8). These controls produce a link that opens the dialer on a phone or the default email client.

Technically, these controls are HTML text controls with markup that defines a hyperlink.

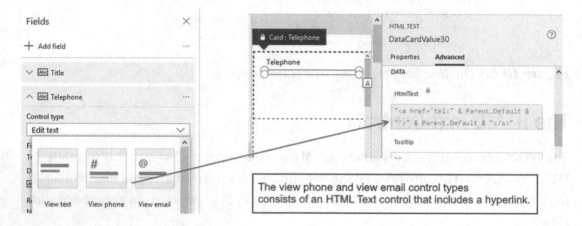

Figure 10-8. *The view phone and view email control types*

Using Simple Data Entry Controls

We'll now move on and look at how to use simple data controls – controls that bind to a single value. The controls that we'll examine in this section include the text input, radio, slider, toggle, and rating controls.

Text Input Control

The text input control is a simple control that enables users to enter text. We can customize this control in many useful ways.

To restrict the data that users can enter, this control provides a Mode property that accepts one of three values: MultiLine, SingleLine, or Password. The MultiLine and SingleLine properties control the entry of multiline text. In password mode, the control masks each character that the user enters with asterisk characters.

To limit the amount of text that a user can enter, we can set the "max length" property. The control also provides a Format property that we can set to one of two values: Text or Number. If we set the Format property to Number, the control will only accept numeric input from the user.

To provide users with additional help, there are two properties we can set – the tooltip property and the hint text property. A tooltip is a piece of help text that appears when a user hovers the mouse over the control. Since there is no concept of a mouse for mobile devices, this is where the hint property comes into play. The text input control shows the hint text when the control is empty (Figure 10-9). As soon as the user enters some text into the control, the hint text disappears, and the control shows the text that the user has entered.

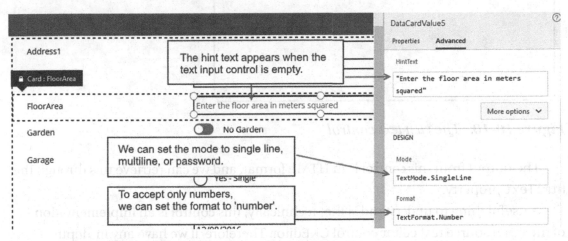

Figure 10-9. *Setting the hint text on the text input control*

The text input control also includes a property called Clear. When this is set to true, a cross icon appears in the far right of the control, and the user can click this to clear the contents of the control. On Windows, the official browsers that support this feature are IE and Edge.

Another useful property is the EnableSpellCheck property. This property enables the spell-check functionality that is built into web browsers. This includes up-to-date versions of Edge and Chrome, but not Internet Explorer.

Tip   Use the hint text property to provide help for smartphone or tablet users. Tooltips do not appear on devices without a mouse.

Rich Text Control

The rich text control enables users to enter richly formatted text (Figure 10-10). Through this control, users can set attributes such as the font size, font style, text colors, and justification. There is even the option to add web hyperlinks.

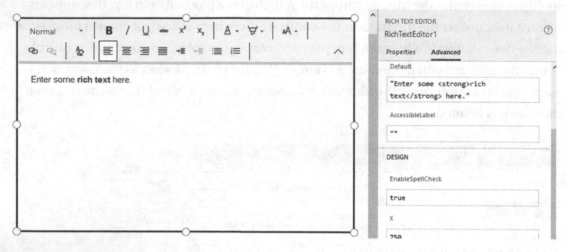

Figure 10-10. *The rich text control*

The output from this control is in HTML format, and we can retrieve this through the `HtmlText` property.

A useful thing to understand is that technically, this control is an implementation of the open source text editor control CKEditor. Therefore, if we have any in-depth questions about how this control operates, we can carry out a web search on CKEditor to help answer any queries.

Radio Control

The radio control enables a user to make a single selection from a list of choices. Although this control is simple to use, new app builders can struggle to understand how to connect the control to a codified set of data values.

To give an example, let's assume our spreadsheet contains a field called `Garage` that indicates whether a property contains a garage. There are three acceptable values for this field – N, S, or D. The value N indicates there is no garage, whereas the values S and D denote the presence of a single and a double garage, respectively.

Let's look at how to modify our form to support this data structure. To build this feature, the first step is to add a card to the form based on the Garage field. By default, the card contains a text input control. To modify the card, we must unlock the card and delete the text input control.

When we delete a text input control from a card, the designer will display two warnings. The first relates to the Update property of the card which is now invalid, and the second refers to a formula that calculates the coordinates of an error warning label. We need to change this formula so that it refers to our new control (which we'll now add), rather than the old text input control name.

The next step is to insert a radio control and to name it rdoGarage. To define the items that appear in this control, set the Items property to the following value:

```
Table({GarageId:"N", GarageDesc:"No"},
     {GarageId:"S", GarageDesc:"Yes - Single"},
     {GarageId:"D", GarageDesc:"Yes - Double"}
)
```

This formula defines a table that includes the columns GarageId and GarageDesc. The GarageId field denotes the codified value, and the GarageDesc field contains the friendly description. To configure the radio control to show the friendly description, set the Value property to GarageDesc.

The next step is to configure the card to use the selected radio item to update the Garage field when a user saves a record. To do this, select the parent card control, and set the Update property to this formula:

```
rdoGarage.Selected.GarageId
```

To complete this example, the final step is to configure the radio control to display the correct item when a user loads an existing record. The Default property defines the selected radio option; and in our example, we need to provide the friendly description, because this is what the control shows. Therefore, we need a formula that converts the values N to "No," S to "Yes - Single," and D to "Yes - Double." Here's the formula we would set for the Default property:

```
Switch(Parent.Default,
       "N", "No",
       "S", "Yes - Single",
       "D", "Yes - Double"
)
```

Figure 10-11 shows our screen in the designer and highlights the appropriate formulas. We can now run our app and set the garage type using the radio control.

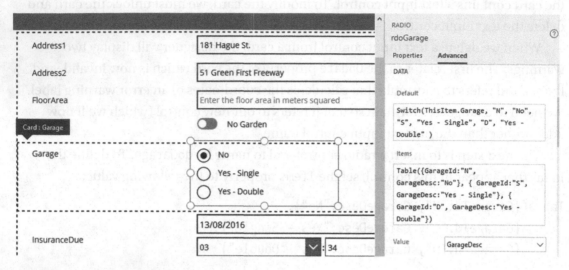

Figure 10-11. *Configuring a radio control*

A useful tip to be aware of is that we can change the orientation of the radio items. By default, the radio items always stack on top of each other. To amend the layout so that the items flow from left to right, we set the layout property to horizontal.

Storing Radio Control Options in Separate Tables or Collections

For simplicity and clarity, the preceding radio control example duplicates the definition of the ID and description values in both the Items and the Default properties of the radio control. A more maintainable solution is to store these details in a separate table or to predefine these values once in a collection.

To store these values in a collection, we can add the following formula to the OnStart property of our app:

```
ClearCollect(colGarageType,
        Table({GarageId:"N", GarageDesc:"No"},
            {GarageId:"S", GarageDesc:"Yes - Single"},
            {GarageId:"D", GarageDesc:"Yes - Double"}
        )
)
```

This stores the garage IDs and descriptions in a collection called `colGarageType` when the app starts. To modify our radio control to use this collection, we would set the `Items` property of the radio control to `colGarageType` and the `Default` property to the following formula:

```
LookUp(colGarageType,ThisItem.Garage = GarageId).GarageDesc
```

This formula calls the `LookUp` function to retrieve from the collection the description that matches the selected ID value.

Toggle and Checkbox Controls

There are two controls that can accept yes/no or true/false values from the user. These are the toggle control and the checkbox control. Both of these controls function similarly, so for brevity, we'll examine the use of the toggle control only. The toggle control is identical to the checkbox, except that the user changes the state of the control by sliding a button, rather than clicking a checkbox with a mouse.

To demonstrate this control, we'll add a toggle control to our screen to allow users to indicate whether a property contains a garden. The Garden field in our spreadsheet will contain the value Y or N (to indicate yes or no). The toggle control returns Boolean true or false values; therefore, it's necessary to add a formula that converts the toggle output to the text value Y or N.

Just like the previous example, the first step is to unlock the garden card, delete the textbox, and resolve any errors that appear. Next, insert a toggle control and name it `tglGarden`. The toggle control includes two properties called `TrueText` and `FalseText`. These define the text that appears when the slider is on or off, and the default values of these properties are "on" and "off." We can customize our control by setting these properties to "Has garden" and "No garden."

The next step is to set up the card to use the toggle control to update the Garden field when a user saves the record. To do this, select the parent card control and set the `Update` property to

```
If(tglGarden.Value, "Y","N")
```

To complete this example, the final step is to show the correct value in the toggle control when a user opens an existing record. This requires a formula that converts the value "Y" to true and "N" to false. The formula we would use to set the Default property of the toggle control is shown in the following:

```
If(Parent.Default="Y", true, false)
```

A helpful point to mention is that the equals operator is case sensitive. Therefore, Parent.Default="Y" is not the same as Parent.Default="y".

Figure 10-12 shows this control in the designer. We can now run our app and set the Garden field of a property record with the toggle control.

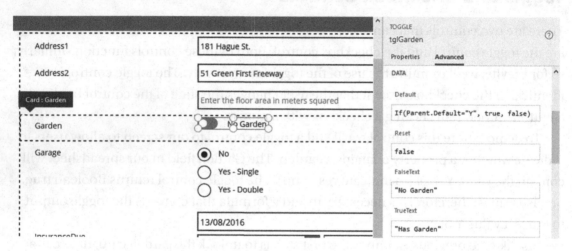

Figure 10-12. *Configuring the toggle control*

Slider Control

The slider control provides a simple way for a user to enter a numeric value between a minimum and maximum value. The fields section of the designer enables us to set the control type of a field to slider by selecting the "Edit slider" option, as shown in Figure 10-13.

Note that the "Edit slider" option appears only against numeric fields. Therefore, this option would not be available in cases where we store numeric values in a text field. To use a slider control in this scenario, we can modify a card using the same technique that we applied in the radio and toggle control examples. In the Default property of the slider control, we would call the Value function to convert the underlying text value to a number. In the Update property of the form, we would convert the value of the slider control to a text value by calling the Text function.

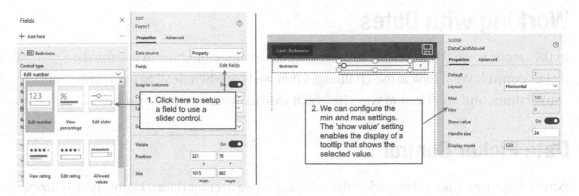

***Figure 10-13.** Setting up a slider control*

Some useful properties that we can set on the slider control are the minimum and maximum values. The minimum value can be negative, and the maximum value can be as large as the maximum number that JavaScript permits. Other cosmetic settings include the size of the slider bar and slider button.

Rating Control

The rating control works with numeric fields. It displays a series of stars, and users can assign a rating by clicking a star. To configure a field to use the rating control, we set the control type of a field to "Edit rating."

We can set the maximum value that the control can accept, as shown in Figure 10-14. Like the slider control, the maximum value can be as large as the maximum number that JavaScript permits.

Note that at present, there is no option to select a different image other than a star.

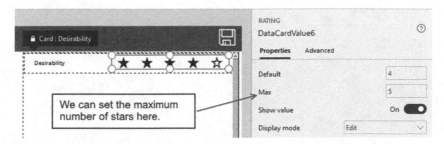

***Figure 10-14.** Configuring the rating control*

Working with Dates

In this section, we'll look at how to work with date values and how to use the date picker control. We'll look at the challenges that we face when dealing with time zone conversions, and we'll look at ways in which we can overcome these problems.

Date Picker Control

Power Apps provides a date picker that users can use to enter dates. Figure 10-15 shows the date picker control at runtime. The highlights of this control are as follows. Initially, the control appears on a single line and shows the date in short date format. The control applies the short date format that is associated with the regional settings of the device or browser, and there is no way to specify a different format. When a user clicks the control, it provides the ability to make a date selection through a calendar view.

This calendar view provides forward and backward icons to navigate through the months. Something that might not be obvious is that users can quickly change the year and month values by clicking these labels. Users who are unaware of this feature can easily become frustrated when they set a date that is significantly earlier or greater than the current date with the backward and forward navigation icons.

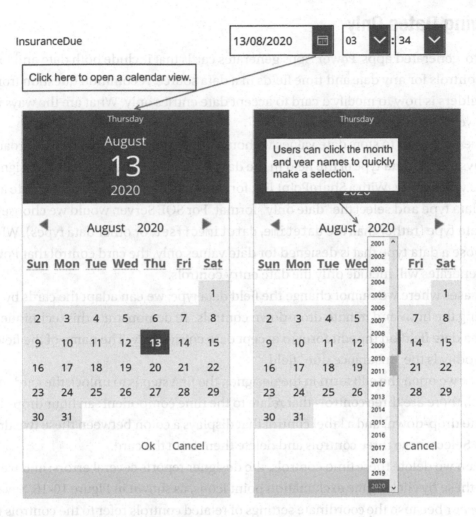

Figure 10-15. *Date picker control*

An important property to be aware of is the "start year" property. This defaults to 1970, and users cannot select a year earlier than this. It's necessary to reduce this value if we want to accept earlier dates.

Note   If we create a form based on an Excel data source, it's important to populate the spreadsheet with sample data. If the spreadsheet contains only table headings, the designer cannot identify the date fields, and any cards that we add for those fields will contain a text input, rather than a date picker control.

Showing Dates Only

For auto-generated apps, Power Apps generates cards that include both date and time entry controls for any date and time fields in a data source. A common question from app builders is how to modify a card to accept date entries only. What are the ways in which we can accomplish this?

If we only want to store date values without a time component, the best approach is to always set the data type of the field in the data source to a data type that is designed for date values only. With a SharePoint list, for example, we would select the "date and time" data type and select the "date only" format. For SQL Server, would we choose the `date` data type (rather than the `datetime`, `datetimeoffset`, or other data types). When we choose a data type that is designed for date values only, the card control that Power Apps generates will include only the date entry controls.

In cases where we cannot change the field data type, we can adapt the cards by removing the hour and minute drop-down controls. To demonstrate this technique, we'll modify a date field on the edit form to accept date entries only. The name of the field that we'll modify is the "insurance due" field.

Once we open the edit form in the designer, the first step is to unlock the card. Within the card, there are three controls that relate to the time component: an hour drop-down, a minute drop-down, and a label control that displays a colon between these two drop-downs. Select these three controls and delete them from the card.

When we delete these time controls, the designer reports several errors; and we can review these by clicking the exclamation point icons, as shown in Figure 10-16. Several of these occur because the coordinate settings of related controls refer to the controls that we deleted. For the purposes of this demonstration, we can hide these errors by setting the incorrect values to 0.

The most important setting to change is the `Update` property. One of the exclamation point icons will take us to the update formula, and we can remove the references to the time controls. At this point, we can run our app and use the date picker to save just the date value.

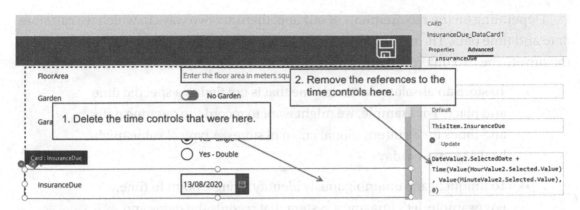

Figure 10-16. *The Update property is no longer valid when we delete the hour and minute controls*

Here's a useful tip. The designer does not provide an option to insert the time picker controls through the Insert menu. If we want to add hour and minute drop-down controls to other parts of an app, we can copy and paste these controls from an auto-generated card.

Tip   If we have a frequent need to add date and time controls to our apps, we can build a custom, reusable date and time picker component for this purpose. We cover this topic in Chapter 22.

Understanding Time Zones

One reason why working with dates and times can be so complicated is because of time zone differences. There are cases where app builders have not appreciated the nuances of time zones. They only discover the problem after they deploy an app. At this point, it becomes an enormous headache to try and repair the data that users have already entered. With the help of this section, we can avoid the common difficulties that are associated with time zones.

Depending on the requirements of our app, there are two ways in which we can store date and time data. The most important step is to be clear on what we want to store from the onset. The two different methods are

- To store an absolute date and time that is not tied to a specific time and place. For example, we might want to record the opening dates and times for an international chain of stores. A typical value might be 9 AM on weekdays.

- To uniquely and unambiguously identify a single point in time. For example, let's imagine a system that records the dates and times of online meetings. If a user in the United States creates an appointment, a user in Europe must be able to determine the meeting time in a way that aligns with the user's time zone.

Power Apps works on the premise that we always want to store points in time, rather than absolute dates and times. By default, the controls and connectors work on this basis. For everything to function correctly, the data source must also be "point in time" aware.

SharePoint is a data source that supports points in time. When we add a datetime column to SharePoint, SharePoint stores the date values in UTC (Coordinated Universal Time) format. UTC shares the same time as GMT (Greenwich Mean Time), the time zone for England, and all time zones in the world are expressed as positive or negative offsets against UTC.

There are data sources that are not "point in time" aware. Excel is one example. Another example is a SQL Server column that uses the datetime data type. These are examples of setups that we would use to store absolute dates and times.

Where we have a mismatch, that is, a scenario where Power Apps expects to work with points in time and a data source that expects to work with absolute dates and times, this is where things start to go wrong.

Excel Walk-Through

To illustrate the typical problem that app builders face with data sources that are not "point in time" aware, we'll walk through the process of configuring our Excel app to store a date.

We'll take the form that we created earlier with the "insurance due" field. Let's now assume that we're in London and that the current month is June. At this location, the current time zone is BST (British Summer Time), which equates to UTC+ 1 hour.

Let's now run our app; open a record; set the "insurance due" field to August 13, 2020; and save our record. At this stage, everything will appear to work correctly. We can reopen our record and view the insurance end date value as expected.

However, things become more interesting when we start to delve into the underlying data. Figure 10-17 shows the record that Power Apps saves to Excel, and as we can see, the date doesn't appear to be correct. It shows up as August 12, 2020, 23:00. This is because Power Apps converts the input date to UTC by subtracting one hour. When a user opens this record, Power Apps converts the value back to BST by adding one hour. Therefore, the user can enter and retrieve date values consistently because Power Apps carries out the UTC conversions during the save and retrieval operations.

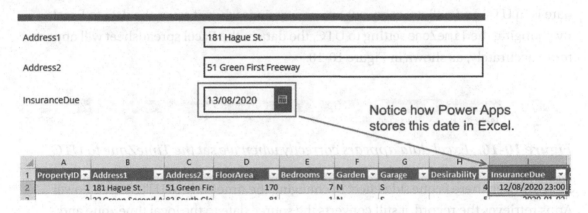

Figure 10-17. *Power Apps saves UTC times to the underlying data source*

This behavior causes a problem for other users who want to work directly with the data in Excel. The date values here will be one hour out of sync and will not be an accurate reflection of what the user intended.

We also notice that although Power Apps stores the time in UTC, the value in Excel doesn't include the offset. Let's now imagine that five months have passed and we're now in November. The clocks have now gone back by one hour, and the time zone in England is now GMT. What do you think will happen when we now reopen this same record in Power Apps? The answer is that Power Apps will convert "August 12, 2020, 23:00" to our local time, and because there is now no time difference between GMT and UTC, it will not re-add one hour. Effectively, our record is now one day off.

Storing Absolute Times

The fundamental cause of this problem is that Power Apps is set up to store "point in time" values, whereas Excel is a data source that stores absolute values. Is there a way to configure Power Apps so that it works with absolute values? The answer is yes, although with Excel, it isn't a perfect solution.

The date picker control provides a property called TimeZone. This property defines the time zone of the selected date in the control, and we can set this to one of two values: local or UTC. The default value is local, and this is the reason why in our example, Power Apps subtracts one hour when it saves the date to Excel.

If we were to change this setting to UTC, Power Apps would assume that the input date is in UTC and will not carry out any conversions when it saves the data to Excel. By changing the TimeZone setting to UTC, the data in the Excel spreadsheet will appear more accurately, as shown in Figure 10-18.

	A	B	C	D	E	F	G	H	I
1	PropertyID	Address1	Address2	FloorArea	Bedrooms	Garden	Garage	Desirability	InsuranceDue
2	1	181 Hague St.	51 Green Firs	170	7	N	S		13/08/2020

Figure 10-18. *Excel data appears correctly when we set the TimeZone to UTC*

However, there is one side effect of changing the time zone to UTC. When Power Apps retrieves the record, it still converts the source date to the local time zone and therefore adds one hour. Although dates now appear correctly in Excel, the dates that appear in an app will be one hour greater than the correct time, as shown in Figure 10-19.

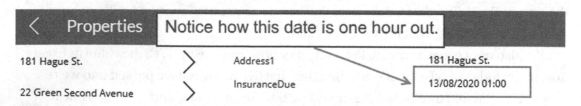

Figure 10-19. *The date that Power Apps retrieves is incorrect when we set the TimeZone to UTC*

To make sure that users can consistently save and retrieve dates, we would need to find all the places where an app displays the date and to display the UTC value like so:

```
Text(ThisItem.InsuranceDue, "UTC")
```

By default, Power Apps assumes that dates and times that it retrieves from a data source are in UTC. By using this formula to specify that we want to show the UTC value, there is effectively no conversion that Power Apps needs to carry out, and it therefore shows the exact value from the Excel spreadsheet.

By using this technique, we can now accurately save absolute dates and times in Excel. The slight disadvantage of this technique is that we now need to change all the places where the date appears and this can involve a lot of work. Also, if we've built screens to search data based on date criteria, we would need to make sure to convert the input date to UTC.

Saving Dates in Year-Month-Day Format

With SharePoint, there is less scope for problems to occur. Because SharePoint datetime columns support UTC and Power Apps expects to work against data sources that support UTC, both systems work in harmony.

Occasionally, SharePoint users may report time values that don't match those in Power Apps. Usually, the cause of this will be incorrect regional settings on the client device or browser. Alternatively, the administrator may never have set up the regional settings for the SharePoint site.

The main challenge with SharePoint are circumstances where we want to store absolute dates and times, rather than a point in time. A reliable and simple solution is not to use a date column, but instead to store the data as a number in the format yyyymmddhhmm. When we want to display a date in an app, we would format the date as required. An added benefit of this approach is that you may recall the problem where Power Apps doesn't support searches against date fields with the greater than or less than operators (i.e., filtering a SharePoint list by a date column with greater/less than operators results in a non-delegable query). This solution helps to solve that problem. Furthermore, users can still sort date values in ascending or descending order with this date format.

Here's how to amend an app to store the "insurance due" values in yyyymmddhhmm format. The first step is to add a numeric field to our data source. Let's call it InsuranceDueyyyymmddhhmm.

In the screen designer, open the form and add this field. Next, unlock the card, delete the textbox, and resolve any errors that show up. Now insert a date picker control and name it dteInsurance.

To set up the card to use the date picker control to update the field when a user saves the record, select the parent card control and set the Update property to

```
dteInsurance(DateValue1.SelectedDate, "yyyymmddhhmm")
```

Next, we need to modify the Default property of the date picker control to provide it with a valid date when a user opens an existing record. We need to call the DateTimeValue function and to provide an input string in the format "yyyy-mm-dd hh:mm," like so (Figure 10-20):

```
DateTimeValue(Left(Parent.Default, 4) & "-" &
              Mid(Parent.Default, 5,2) & "-" &
              Mid(Parent.Default, 7,2) & " " &
              Mid(Parent.Default, 9,2) & ":" &
              Mid(Parent.Default, 11,2)
)
```

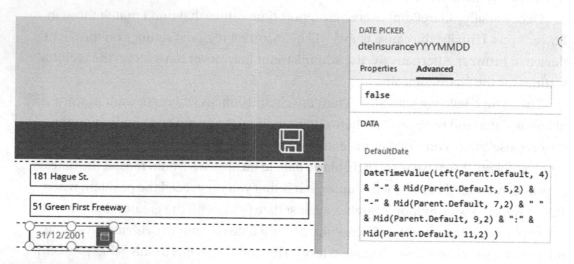

Figure 10-20. *Converting a field to yyyymmddhhmm*

The final step is to apply a more readable format to any controls that display the "insurance due" field. We can use a formula to display the date in long datetime format, like so:

```
Text(DateValue(Left(Parent.Default, 4) & "-" &
              Mid(Parent.Default, 5,2) & "-" &
              Mid(Parent.Default, 7,2) & " " &
```

```
        Mid(Parent.Default, 9,2) & ":" &
        Mid(Parent.Default, 11,2)),
    DateTimeFormat.LongDateTime
)
```

At this stage, we can run our app. The app will function as before, but the date values will be stored in yyyymmddhhmm format in the underlying data source.

Summary

This chapter covered the important topic of simple, single-value screen controls. The two controls that display text are the label and HTML text controls. The more powerful of these two controls is the HTML text control because this provides the ability to format text with different styles. Useful applications of this control include the ability to show subscript and superscript characters, mathematical symbols, and more.

The text input control receives text from the user. We can encourage users to enter valid data by specifying a maximum length, and we can also configure the control to accept numeric input only.

Other simple controls include the radio, slider, toggle, and rating controls. On the edit form of an auto-generated app, we can delete the default text input control on a card and replace it with an alternate control. To maintain the ability of the form to save and retrieve data, there are two settings we need to modify. First, it's necessary to set the Default property of the new control to show the existing data value when the form loads. In general, we would specify the Parent.Default property to retrieve the data value from the containing card, and we can also apply formulas to carry out any data transformations. For example, with a checkbox or toggle control, we can apply a formula to transform an underlying data value of "T" or "F" to the Boolean value true or false, respectively. The second step is to configure the save behavior by modifying the Update property of the containing card. We can apply formulas in the Update property to carry out any reverse transformations. For example, we could convert the Boolean value of a checkbox or toggle control to the value "T" or "F" for storage in the underlying data source.

In auto-generated apps that are based on tables with datetime fields, the card on the edit form will include date picker and time entry controls. A common requirement is to accept date entries without the time component, for example, to store birthdays. In these circumstances, the best approach is to always set the data type of the field in the data source to a data type that is designed for date values only.

Where this isn't possible, we can adapt the card by deleting the time controls and by modifying the Update property to remove any references to the time controls.

To store dates and times, we must identify whether we want to store an absolute date and time that is time zone independent or a "point in time" that should align with the time zone of the end user.

Power Apps works on the premise that we always want to store points in time, rather than absolute dates and times. For this to function correctly, the data source must also be "point in time" aware by supporting UTC. If the data source does not support UTC, we can easily end up with mismatches between the date values that we see in Power Apps and the date values that we see in the data source.

A great way to store absolute dates and times is to store in a number field, the numeric representation of the date and time in the format yyyymmddmmss. The benefit of this approach is that the date values will still be sortable. Also, this format provides better query support because we can overcome the query delegation limitations of filtering dates with the greater and less than operators.

CHAPTER 11

Using Table/Record Data Controls

This chapter focuses on how to work with controls that can bind to a single record or multiple rows. The controls that we'll cover include the drop-down, combo box, list box, form, and gallery controls.

The drop-down and combo box controls enable us to limit the data items that a user can select. We'll look at how to set up these controls, including how to customize display values and how to filter the items in the control based upon a value in a dependent control.

Next, we'll look at the ways in which we can customize the layout and appearance of the gallery control. Using this control, we'll find out how to build a feature that enables a user to amend multiple records in one go.

We'll also take a deeper look at the form control, including how to customize the layout, how to set default values, and how to validate and reset field values. Other highlights of this chapter include

- How to configure the combo box control to accept multiple selections and, importantly, how to set up data sources to support this configuration.

- How to access the items in a gallery control with a formula. We'll look at how to simplify formulas and how we can more easily identify errors by using hidden gallery controls.

- How to build data entry screens that incorporate both forms and the Patch function. By combining both methods, we can build data entry screens with more bespoke layouts while retaining the productivity that the form designer provides.

© Tim Leung 2021
T. Leung, *Beginning Power Apps*, https://doi.org/10.1007/978-1-4842-6683-0_11

Chapter Overview

To demonstrate the controls that can work against multiple records, we'll build an app that's based on a table of tenancy records. Figure 11-1 highlights the controls that we'll cover in this chapter, which include the drop-down, combo box, gallery, and table controls. We'll find out how to add these controls to forms so that we can explore some of the richer features that the form control provides.

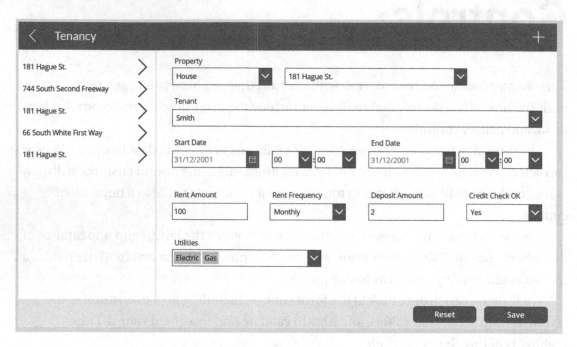

Figure 11-1. *The screen that we'll build in this chapter*

Figure 11-2 shows the data structure that we'll use. The examples in this chapter are mostly based on an Excel spreadsheet, although we'll refer to a SharePoint list with the same schema in areas where it's helpful to highlight a piece of functionality that applies only to SharePoint.

	A	B	C	D	E	F	G	H	I	J
1	TenancyID	TenantID	PropertyID	StartDate	EndDate	RentFrequency	RentAmount	DepositAmount	CreditCheckOK	Utilities
2	1	1	1	13/04/2020 12:43	27/04/2020 23:00	Monthly	£500.00	£750.00	Yes	Electric,Gas
3	2	2	9	13/04/2020 13:07	13/04/2021 13:07	Monthly	£500.00	£750.00	Yes	Electric,Gas
4	3	2	1	13/04/2020 12:42	13/04/2021 23:00	Monthly	£500.00	£750.00	Yes	Electric,Gas
5	4	2	21	13/04/2020 12:43	27/04/2020 23:00	Monthly	£500.00	£750.00	Yes	Electric,Gas
6	5	2	1	13/04/2020 13:07	13/04/2021 13:07	Monthly	£500.00	£750.00	Yes	Electric,Gas

Figure 11-2. *The data structure of the tenancy table*

Our tenancy table includes fields such as the start and end dates and payment details. It also contains lookup values that relate to the property and the tenant tables.

From the tenancy table, the `PropertyID` field stores a numeric value that corresponds to a value that's held in a property lookup table. Likewise, the `TenantID` field stores a numeric value that corresponds to a lookup value that's held in a tenant table.

These sets of tables represent the typical data structure that we would find in a relational database, and they provide an ideal way for us to look at how to work with drop-down lookup values.

Figure 11-3 summarizes the steps to build a simple list/details screen. The topics that we'll cover in this chapter will help embellish the content that appears in the main form.

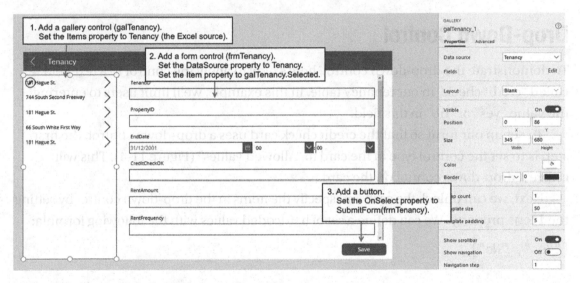

Figure 11-3. *The basic setup of our screen*

Data Entry Controls

There are two controls that display a list of selectable items – the drop-down and combo box controls. Both look very similar, so what features do these controls offer, and what are the differences between the two? We'll now find out.

Of these two controls, the most basic is the drop-down control. This control enables users to select a single item. The biggest limitation with this control is that it displays a maximum of 500 items only.

The combo box control provides many more capabilities, compared to the drop-down control. Unlike other implementations of combo box controls that we can find in other systems, it also offers a search feature. Users can type into the control, and the combo box will display all matching items that contain the search text. This feature helps us to overcome the 500-item limit that the drop-down control imposes. Another powerful feature is that the combo box control supports multiple selected items. With the drop-down control, users can select a single item only.

Note   Compared to the drop-down control, the combo box control provides many more features including search, multi-select capabilities, additional layout settings, and support for more than 500 items.

Drop-Down Control

To demonstrate the drop-down control, here's how to apply the control to a text field called "credit check" in our tenancy table. In this example, we'll limit users to entering the value "yes" or "no" in this field.

To set up our form so that the credit check card uses a drop-down control, the first step is to set the control type of the card to "Allowed values" (Figure 11-4). This will create a drop-down control on the card.

Next, we can unlock the card and specify the items in the drop-down control by setting the Items property. We can define a set of hardcoded values with the following formula:

```
["Yes", "No"]
```

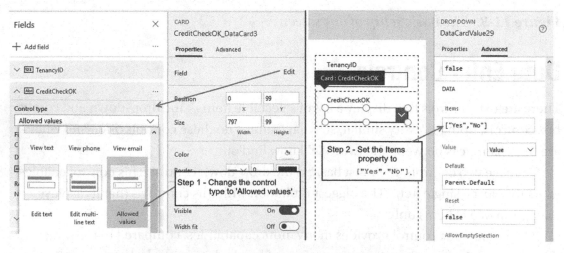

Figure 11-4.   *Changing the control type to "Allowed values"*

We can now run our app and use the drop-down control to set the "credit check" value of the record. An interesting question we might ask is this: If we open an existing record with a value that doesn't exist in the drop-down, what would happen? The answer is that the drop-down would show a blank value. In this scenario, Power Apps will not display any error messages to the user, and it will not crash or stop working entirely.

Setting Lookup Values

The simple example we've seen is not particularly future-proof because it relies on hardcoded values. To enable users to maintain the choice items that appear in a drop-down or combo box control, we can build a data structure that stores the choice items in a separate table or SharePoint list.

With SharePoint, it's very simple to develop this type of structure. In our example, we have a tenancy list that stores tenancy details. To store the property that relates to a specific tenancy record, we can define a lookup column in the tenancy list and configure this column to refer to a SharePoint list of property records.

With Dataverse, we can also easily define lookups by creating relationships between tables. With SharePoint and Dataverse data sources, the designer understands the relationships between lists or tables. This enables us to more easily build screens that use the drop-down or combo box controls.

We'll now look at how to configure a form to store lookup values, based on SharePoint and Excel data sources.

Setting Lookup Values with SharePoint and Dataverse

Starting with SharePoint, we'll base this example on a tenancy list that includes a lookup column that relates to the property list. However, what we cover here will work equally well for any list with a lookup column.

If we add a form that's based on the tenancy list and add the property lookup field, the card for this field will include a combo box control that displays items from the SharePoint property list. The great news is that it all works and there are no additional tasks we need to carry out.

How exactly does this work? If we inspect the card for the property field (Figure 11-5), we'll notice that the Items property contains the following formula:

```
Choices([@Tenancy].Property)
```

317

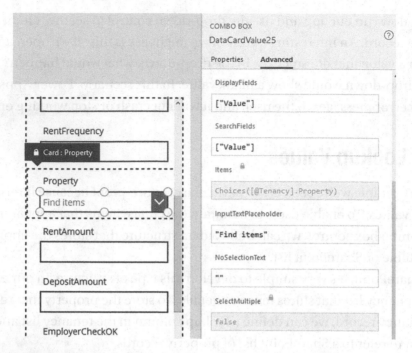

Figure 11-5. *Setting lookup values with SharePoint and Dataverse*

The Choices function accepts a field name and returns a table that contains all acceptable choice values for the input field.

Setting Lookup Values with Other Data Sources

With other data sources such as Excel or SQL Server, Power Apps cannot identify the relationships between tables; and therefore, there is more work involved to configure a combo box or drop-down control.

To demonstrate how to implement lookup columns in data sources other than SharePoint or Dataverse, Figure 11-6 illustrates the data structure that supports a lookup field. In this example, we have a property table that stores property details. This table contains a numeric PropertyID field that uniquely identifies each row in the table. In the tenancy table, the PropertyID field stores the numeric PropertyID value that corresponds to the record in the property table. Our set of tables also includes a property type table to store details of the property type.

◢	A	B	C	D	E	F	G
1	TenancyID ▼	TenantID ▼	PropertyID ▼	StartDate ▼	EndDate ▼	RentFrequency ▼	RentAmount ▼
2	1	1	1	13/04/2020 12:43	27/04/2020 23:00	Monthly	£500.00
3	2	2	9	13/04/2020 13:07	13/04/2021 13:07	Monthly	£500.00
4	3	2	1	13/04/2020 12:42	13/04/2021 23:00	Monthly	£500.00

◢	A	B	C	D	E	F
1	PropertyID ▼	PropertyTypeID ▼	Address1 ▼	Address2 ▼	City ▼	Postcode ▼
2	1	1	181 Hague St.	51 Green Fir	Sheffield	NR28 9OU
3	2	2	3 South Street	83 South Cla	Norwich	NN7 3ZK
4	3	3	79 North Oak R	135 North Gr	Sunderlan	NN7 1SE
5	4	4	57 White Fabie	715 North Fa	Oxford	BD38 7SL
6	5	1	173 North Rock	23 East Fabie	Walsall	TW51 4SG

◢	A	B
1	PropertyTypeID ▼	PropertyTypeDesc ▼
2	1	House
3	2	Apartment
4	3	Bungalow
5	4	Villa

Figure 11-6. *The data structure of the tenancy, property, and property type tables*

As a starting point, let's suppose we create a new app that includes these Excel tables. We then add a form, set the data source of the form to the tenancy table, and add the property field.

To modify the property card so that it uses a drop-down control, we change the control type to "Allowed values" and unlock the card.

Next, we set the Items property of the card to the property data source, as shown in Figure 11-7. Because the property table includes several columns, we can use the Value property to specify the field that appears in the drop-down.

The default name of the drop-down will be something like DataCardValue28. To make this control easier to identify, we'll rename it to drpProperty.

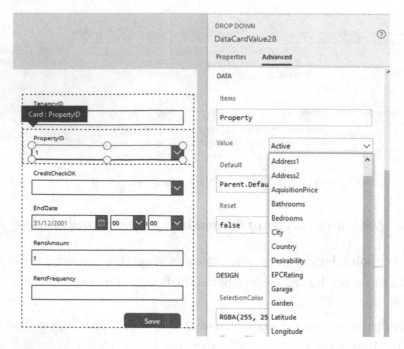

Figure 11-7. *Setting up drop-downs*

The next step is to configure the card to save the numeric property ID value when a user saves the record. To do this, select the parent card control and set the `Update` property to the following formula:

```
drpProperty.Selected.PropertyID
```

The final step is to set up the drop-down box to show the correct item when a user opens an existing record. To configure this, set the `Default` property of the drop-down to the following formula:

```
LookUp(drpProperty, PropertyID = Parent.Default).Name
```

We can now run our app and set the property value of a tenancy record using a drop-down control.

Customizing the Drop-Down Display Value

A common task is to customize and display multiple fields in each row of a drop-down. In the example that we built, the drop-down shows the first line of the address. How can we modify the drop-down to display multiple fields? The answer is to set the `Items` property of the drop-down to a formula that combines the fields that we want to display. Here's the formula we would use to display both the first line of the address and the postcode:

```
AddColumns(Property,
        "AddressDesc",
         Address1  & " (" & Postcode & ")"
)
```

The AddColumns function adds columns to a data source, collection, or table. This function accepts three arguments – a data source, the name of the column to add, and the value for each row.

Here, we add a column called AddressDesc that combines the first line of the address and the postcode in parentheses. To display this value in the drop-down, we set the Value property of the drop-down to AddressDesc.

The next step is to modify the formula for the Default property so that it selects the correct item in the drop-down for existing records. Because each row in the drop-down control now displays the first line of the address and postcode in parentheses, we need to assign a selected item value that matches this format. Here's the formula we would add to the Default property:

```
LookUp(AddColumns(Property,
             "AddressDesc",
              Address1  & " (" & Postcode & ")"),
       PropertyID = Parent.Default).AddressDesc
```

The LookUp function returns the first record from a data source that matches the formula that we provide. The data source we provide here is the formatted version of the Property table that includes the address and the postcode in parentheses. The lookup formula retrieves the record from this data source where the PropertyID value matches the PropertyID value of the tenancy record.

Figure 11-8 shows the appearance of this code in the designer. We can now run our app, and each row in the property drop-down will show the address and postcode fields.

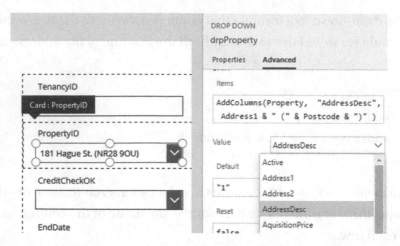

Figure 11-8. *Edit the Items, Value, and Default properties to customize the drop-down text*

Nesting Drop-Down Controls

To assist data entry, we can nest together sets of combo box or drop-down controls. There are many practical scenarios where this is useful. To give an example, an address entry screen could provide a drop-down box that displays a list of states. When a user selects a state, a corresponding drop-down box will display a list of cities that match the selected state.

To demonstrate this technique, we'll modify our example form to include a property type drop-down. This drop-down control will display a list of property types such as house, apartment, and bungalow. When a user selects an item from this drop-down, the drop-down box of properties will update to show only the property records that match the selected property type. To support this example, we'll add a table of property types to our app as shown in Figure 11-9.

⊿	A	B
1	PropertyTypeID ▾	PropertyTypeDesc ▾
2	1	House
3	2	Apartment
4	3	Bungalow

Figure 11-9. *The property type table*

Power Apps provides a simple no code method to implement nested drop-downs. This simple technique is less customizable, and there is another, more complex method that we can adopt. We'll now cover both these techniques

Setting Drop-Down Control Dependencies

Starting with the simple technique, the first step is to add an additional "property type" drop-down to the card that we adapted to include a property selection drop-down. We would set the Items property of the new "property type" drop-down to our property type table.

The properties panel of the existing property drop-down includes a link that enables us to specify a dependency. We can use this to configure the property drop-down to only show records where the property type ID matches the property type ID in the property type drop-down (Figure 11-10).

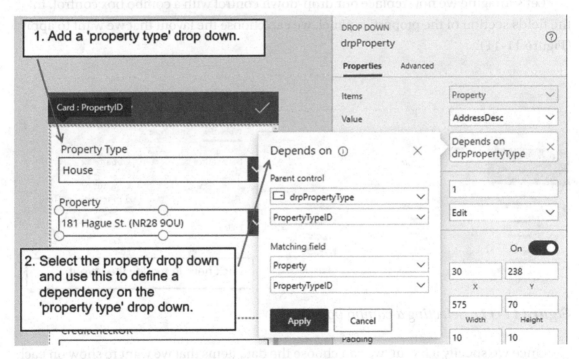

Figure 11-10. Defining a drop-down dependency

323

Although this technique is simple and involves no code, the limitation is that we must use the items drop-down to select a data source and we must use the Value property to define the text that displays in each row of the drop-down. This prevents us from customizing the text that displays in the drop-down.

Changing the Combo Box Layout

If we want to specify drop-down dependencies using a no code technique but also require more flexibility over the text that appears, another option is to use a combo box rather than a drop-down.

A useful feature of the combo box control is that it provides three row item templates. The default template displays a single data item per row. There is also a double item template that displays two data items per row and a person template that enables us to show a photo.

Let's imagine we now replace our drop-down control with a combo box control. In the fields section of the properties panel, we can choose the layout that we want to apply (Figure 11-11).

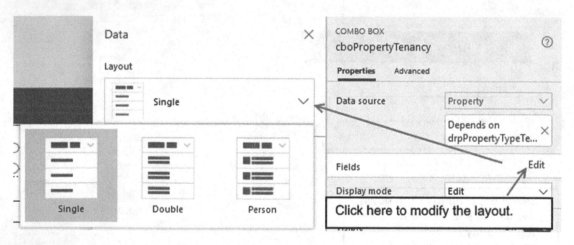

Figure 11-11. *Selecting a combo box layout*

Once we specify a layout, we can choose the data items that we want to show on each row of the combo box. In this example, we choose the double layout, and we configure the options to display the first line of the address and postcode. At runtime, the combo box will show both of these values as shown in Figure 11-12.

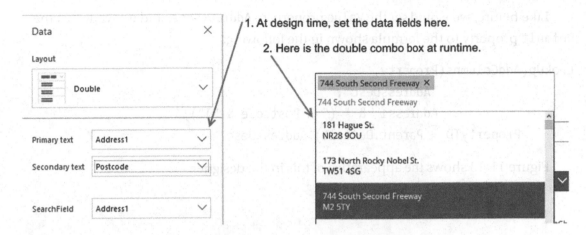

Figure 11-12. *Using the double layout to display two data values per row*

Defining Drop-Down Dependencies with Formulas

Although the combo box control provides more flexibility, it might not completely satisfy our needs. We may want to display more than two data fields per row, customize the display text, or not like the appearance of each item taking up two lines in the combo box. In these cases, we can implement drop-down dependencies by writing our own formulas.

To demonstrate this technique, we'll extend our earlier example where we customized each row of our drop-down control to display the first line of the address followed by the postcode in parentheses.

Taking the form that displays a tenancy record, the first step is to add a "property type" drop-down to the card in the form that corresponds to the property ID field. Next, set the Items property of this drop-down to the property type table and name the control drpPropertyType.

To configure the "property" drop-down to show only those records that match the selected property type, we would set the Items property of the property drop-down to the following formula:

```
Filter(AddColumns(Property,
            "AddressDesc",
            Address1  & " (" & Postcode & ")"
            ),
    PropertyTypeID=drpPropertyType.Selected.PropertyTypeID
)
```

Like before, we would set the Value property to AddressDesc, and we would set the Default property to the formula shown in the following:

```
LookUp(AddColumns(Property,
                "AddressDesc",
                Address1  & " (" & Postcode & ")"),
     PropertyID = Parent.Default).AddressDesc
```

Figure 11-13 shows the appearance of this in the designer.

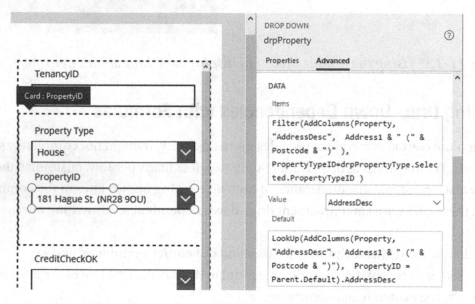

Figure 11-13. *Creating a dependency between the property and property type drop-downs*

To complete this feature, we can configure the default display of the property type drop-down. When a user loads an existing tenancy record, we can set the value of the property type drop-down to match the property type of the property that is associated with the tenancy record. To configure this, set the Default property of the property type drop-down to the following formula:

```
LookUp(PropertyType,
     LookUp(Property,
            PropertyID = ThisItem.PropertyID
     ). PropertyTypeID = PropertyTypeID
).PropertyTypeDesc
```

This formula contains a set of nested lookups. The innermost lookup retrieves the property record that relates to the tenancy record in the form. The outermost lookup retrieves the property type record that is related to the property record.

Note that we can also add the same logic to the property type drop-downs that we created with the no code method. Figure 11-14 shows the appearance of this in the designer.

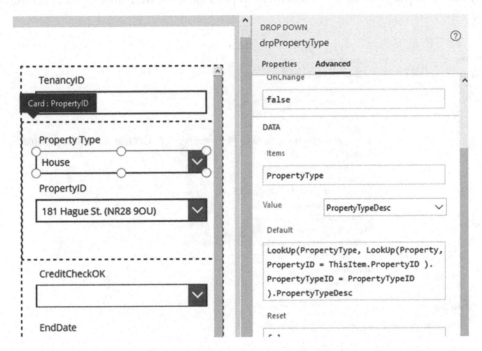

Figure 11-14. *Showing the property type that corresponds to the selected property*

When we now run our app, the items that appear in the property drop-down will display the first line of the address and postcode in parentheses, and the property type drop-down will also show the property type that correctly matches the property.

Selecting Multiple Items with a Combo Box

A powerful feature that the combo box control offers is the ability for users to select multiple items. The easiest way to set up a multi-selection combo box is to use a SharePoint data source. With a bit more work, we can also utilize multi-selection combo boxes with other data sources. In this section, we'll walk through the steps to configure a multi-selection combo box in both these scenarios.

Combo Box Multi-selection with SharePoint

With SharePoint, we can define a choice column that permits multiple selections. With this type of column, we can easily construct a data entry form without needing to write any code.

To demonstrate this feature, Figure 11-15 shows the setup of a choice column in our tenancy list. The purpose of this column is to provide a list of utilities that is related to a tenancy.

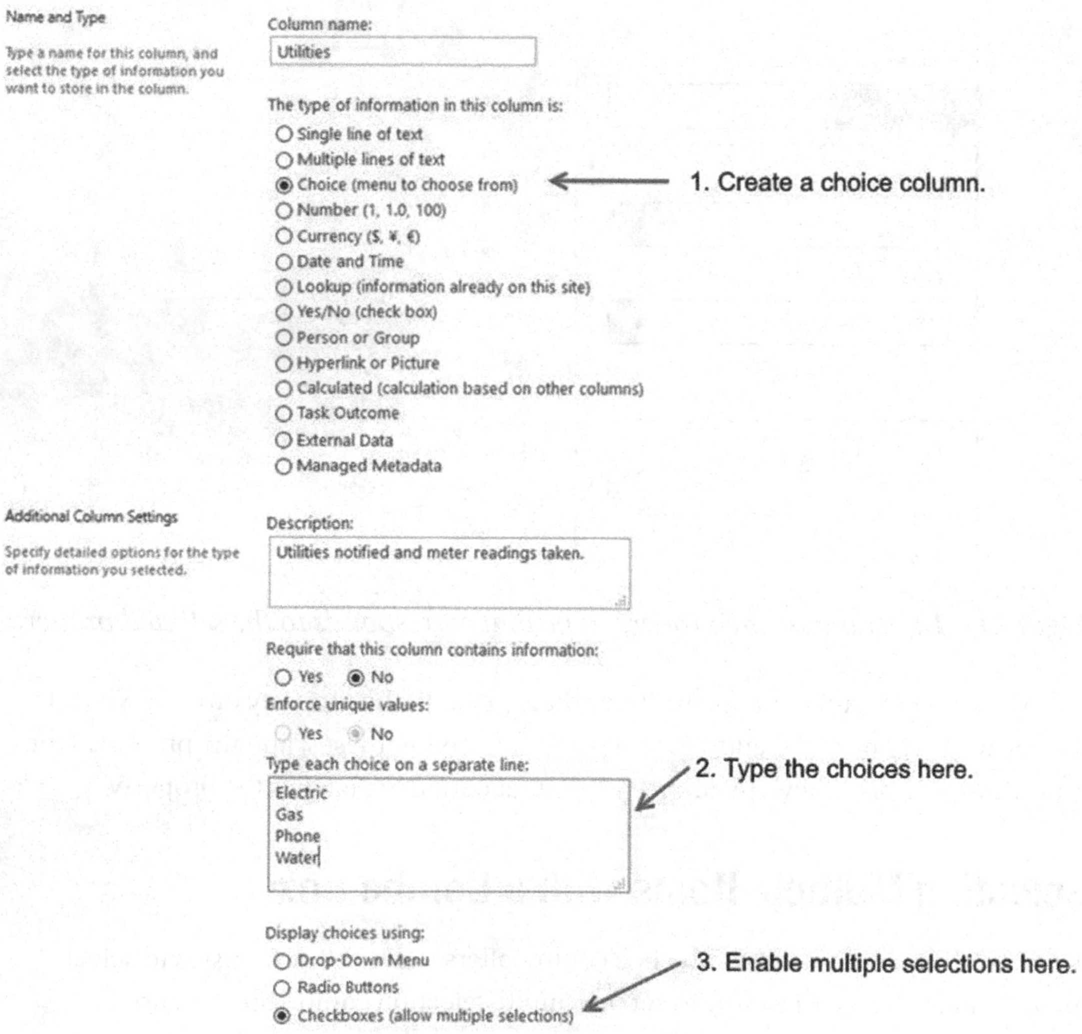

Figure 11-15.   *Creating a multi-select combo in SharePoint*

We can now add a form, set the data source to the tenancy list, and include the utilities field. The designer will create a card with a combo box control with the multi-selection feature enabled. The good news is that this now all works without us needing to perform any additional tasks.

Figure 11-16 shows the appearance of the combo box at runtime. When a user expands the combo box control, it's possible to select multiple items. The selected items appear at the top of the combo box, and it's possible to remove an item by clicking the cross icon.

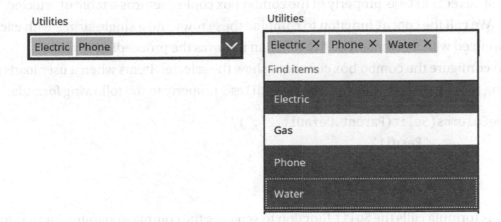

Figure 11-16. *A multi-select combo box at runtime*

Combo Box Multi-selection with Other Data Sources

With data sources other than SharePoint, we can set up a multi-selection combo box, but it involves more work and custom formulas.

To demonstrate, we'll recreate our SharePoint example with Excel. The first step is to add a column called utilities to the tenancy table in our spreadsheet. We will store comma-separated choice items in this column.

We can now add a form, set the data source to the tenancy table, and include the utilities field. By default, the utilities card will contain a textbox. We need to unlock this card, delete the textbox control, and replace it with a combo box control. We'll call this control cboUtilities.

We can define the items that we want to display in the combo box by setting the Items property to the following formula:

```
["Electric","Gas","Phone", "Water"]
```

To store the selected items in a comma-separated format, we would set the Update property of the card to the following function:

```
Mid(
    Concat(cboUtilities.SelectedItems, "," & Value),
    2,
    Len(Concat(cboUtilities.SelectedItems, "," & Value))
)
```

The SelectedItems property of the combo box control returns a table of selected items. We call the Concat function to combine these rows into a single string, with each row prefixed with a comma. The Mid function removes the proceeding comma.

To configure the combo box control to show the selected items when a user loads an existing record, we set the DefaultSelectedItems property to the following formula:

```
RenameColumns(Split(Parent.Default, ","),
              "Result",
              "Value"
)
```

This formula calls the Split function to separate the comma-separated input value into a table. The Split function creates a table with the column name Result. We call the RenameColumns function to rename this to Value. This matches the "display fields" property of our combo box control and enables it to correctly display the selected items. Figure 11-17 illustrates the appearance of our form in the designer.

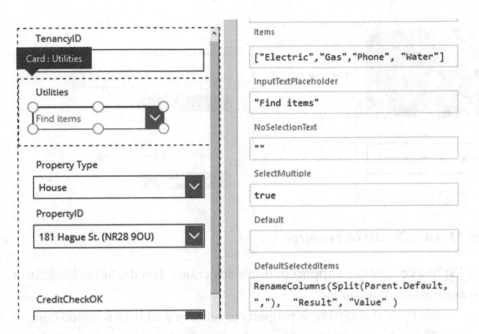

Figure 11-17. *Setting up a multi-select combo box*

Data Display Controls

In this section of the chapter, we'll look at some of the controls that we can use to display tables of data. These will include the list box, table, and gallery controls.

List Box Control

The list box control enables users to select one or more items from a list. For practical purposes, this control works almost identically to the drop-down control. In addition to the multi-select capability, the only difference is that the data items are always on display.

The Items property defines the data source, and the Value property defines the data field that is shown for each item in the control.

Just like the drop-down control, we can customize the item text by setting the Items property to a formula that utilizes the AddColumns function. We can also specify a dependency to filter the items in the control based on the value of another control.

To highlight this control, here's an example that we used earlier in this book (Figure 11-18).

Figure 11-18. *The list box control*

The list box control can support multiple selections, and the SelectMultiple property controls this feature.

We can use the SelectedItems property to retrieve a table of selected items. If we were to use this control to display a data value for an existing record, we could use the Default property to specify the selected item. However, a major limitation is that we can preselect a maximum of one item only, and this prevents us from using this control to display multiple items.

Therefore, the list box control works best for data entry purposes. A typical scenario is where we want to build a screen that accepts search criteria values.

Displaying Tables of Data

The data table control is a great control that enables us to quickly and easily display data in a tabular format. The table control is read-only and doesn't provide cell-level editing like Excel.

To specify the rows and columns to display in the data table, we can set the data source with the Items property or the data source drop-down. We can then use the fields section to define the columns that we want to display, as shown in Figure 11-19.

Figure 11-19. *Using the table control*

Through the fields section, we can define the control type. Where this comes in useful is for telephone or web address fields. With these data types, we can use the properties of the column to enable a hyperlink. This configures the cell value to display a hyperlink that opens the telephone dialer or the web address in a browser.

Through the properties of the column, we can set the header text and the column width attributes (Figure 11-20).

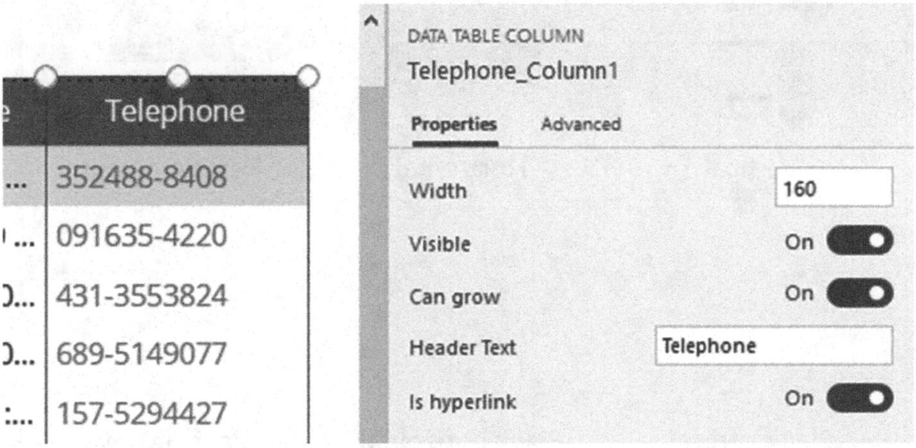

Figure 11-20. *Setting column attributes*

The data table control behaves similarly to the gallery control because it keeps track of the selected row. Therefore, we can use it for record selection purposes, or we can utilize the design pattern where we place an edit form next to the data table control and set the data source of the edit form to the selected item in the data table.

Working with Gallery Controls

The gallery control is a powerful control that is versatile and highly customizable. By now, we're familiar with the functionality that this control offers; so in this section, we'll cover some of the features that we haven't covered. This includes layout features and an example of how we can use the gallery control to help select multiple records.

Choosing a Gallery Type

There are three gallery types that we can add to a screen. These are the vertical, horizontal, and flexible height galleries (Figure 11-21).

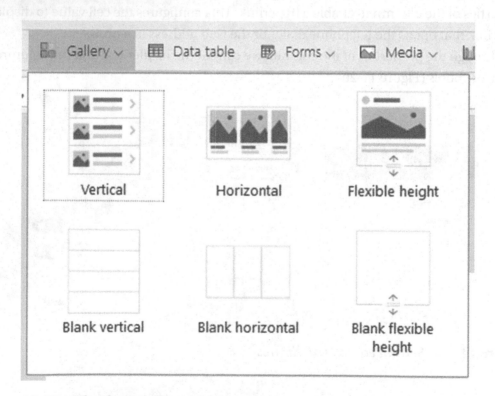

Figure 11-21. *The three gallery types*

A vertical gallery arranges items from top to bottom, whereas a horizontal gallery arranges items from left to right. A horizontal gallery works well with the landscape orientation of a tablet device.

The purpose of a flexible height gallery is to display content that could vary in length. Figure 11-22 compares the appearance of a vertical gallery with that of a flexible height gallery.

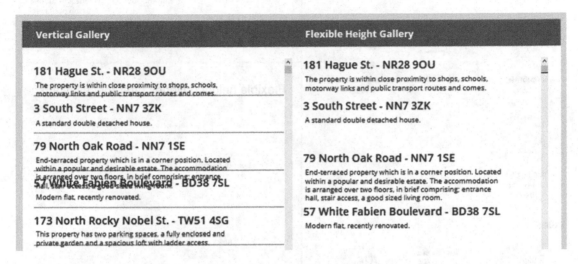

Figure 11-22. *Vertical vs. flexible height gallery*

A vertical gallery imposes a fixed row height. If the amount of data in a row exceeds the specified height, the content in the row will overlap the next row. We can avoid this problem with a flexible height gallery. With this type of gallery, the row height will grow automatically, so long as the content that we add to the item template are labels or HTML text controls with the `AutoHeight` property set to true.

Applying Layouts

To help us quickly build the item template of the gallery in a visual way, we can apply a layout. Each layout provides a templated set of placeholder controls. The choice of layout depends on the gallery type. Figure 11-23 shows the gallery layouts that are available with each gallery type. The icons in this screenshot indicate the appearance of the layout.

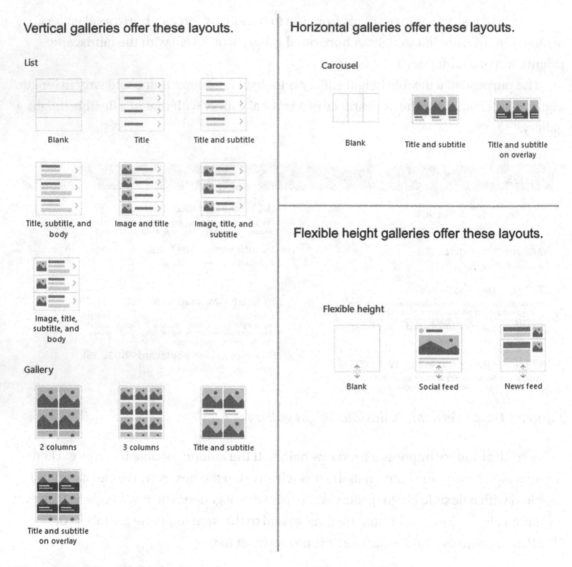

Figure 11-23. *All the layouts that we can apply to a gallery*

The vertical gallery type provides the largest choice of layouts. The horizontal and flexible height gallery types provide a choice of only three layouts each. Once we apply a layout, we can use the designer to select which fields to display in each placeholder.

Figure 11-24 demonstrates how we would apply the "title, subtitle, and body" layout to a vertical gallery and how to set the placeholder fields.

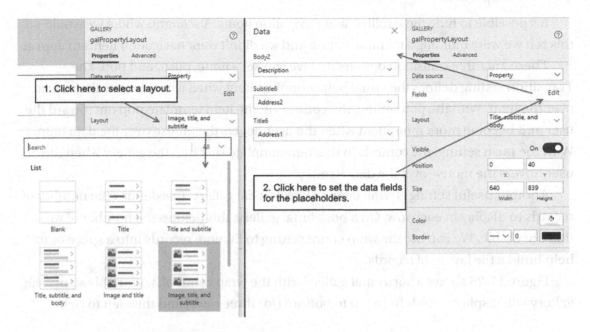

Figure 11-24. Gallery control layouts

Setting Properties

In this section, we'll explore how to modify the appearance and behavior of galleries through the gallery control settings. Figure 11-25 shows a horizontal gallery and an excerpt from the properties pane.

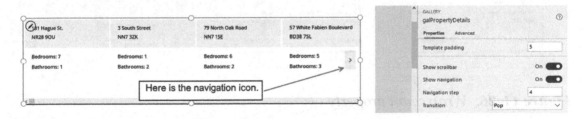

Figure 11-25. Gallery control properties

The gallery control can display forward and backward navigation buttons. The "Show navigation" setting controls the visibility of these buttons. The Navigation step setting controls how many records to move through when the user clicks the navigation button. In this example, the gallery fits four records. By setting the navigation step to 4, the user can quickly view the next or previous four records by clicking the navigation button.

337

It's possible to hide the scrollbar and navigation items. A scenario where we would do this is if we were building a menu structure and we didn't want navigation items to appear.

There are three transition options that we can set – none, push, and pop. The Transition setting defines the visual behavior of an item when a user hovers the mouse over the item. With the pop setting, the controls in the item template pop out toward the user and become more prominent when the user hovers the mouse over the data item. With the push setting, the controls in the item template sink into the gallery when the user hovers the mouse over the data item.

Another useful setting is wrap count. On a vertical gallery, this defines the number of records to display in each row. On a horizontal gallery, this defines the number of rows that are visible. We can use the wrap count setting to fit more records into a space or to help build a tile layout of records.

Figure 11-26 shows a horizontal gallery with the wrap count of 3. With this setup, the gallery will display records from top to bottom (for three rows) and then left to right.

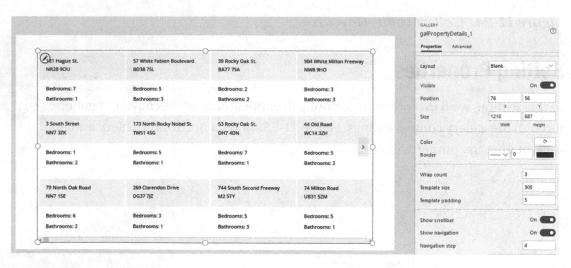

Figure 11-26. *Wrap count property*

Incorporating Data Entry Controls

The beauty of the gallery control is that we can add all sorts of controls to an item template. These include data entry controls and nested galleries. For example, we could add a checkbox control to the item template of a gallery, and this would provide a means for users to select multiple records. We could use this as an input to update or to delete multiple records.

To demonstrate how to incorporate data entry controls inside a gallery, we'll walk through the steps to build a single screen that allows a user to edit multiple records in one go. Figure 11-27 illustrates the appearance of this screen. Using this screen, the user can amend the description of multiple records and click the "Save all changes" button to save all the changes in one go.

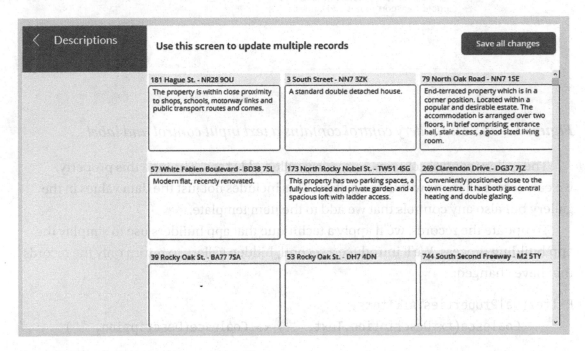

Figure 11-27. *Creating a multi-edit screen*

Let's look at the parts that make up this screen. The most crucial part is the central gallery control. The Items property of this control is set to our property data source. The item template of this gallery contains two controls – a label that displays the address and postcode fields and a text input control (Figure 11-28). The Default property of the text input control is set to the description field.

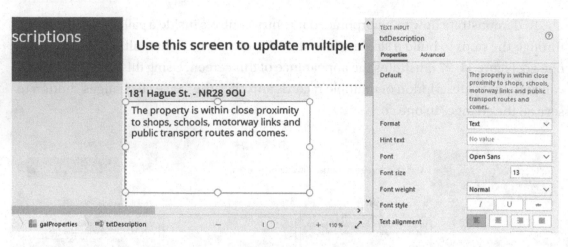

Figure 11-28. *The gallery control contains a text input control and label*

The gallery control contains a property called `AllItems`. Through this property, we can access all items within the gallery. This includes not just the data values in the gallery but also any controls that we add to the item template.

To update the records, we'll apply a technique that app builders use to simplify the app building process. We'll introduce a second, hidden gallery to return only the records that have changed:

```
Filter(galProperties.AllItems,
       Coalesce(txtDescription.Text, "") <> Coalesce(Description, "")
)
```

Within this hidden gallery, there are two controls, as shown in Figure 11-29. These include a label called `lblPropertyID` that displays the property ID and a label called `lblNewDescription` that stores the updated description.

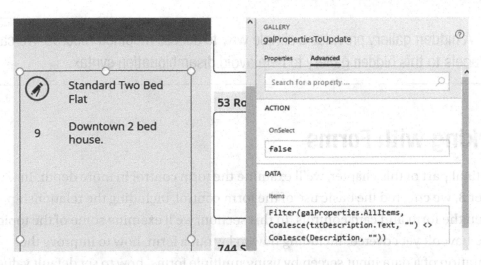

Figure 11-29. *The hidden gallery control contains two labels*

The "Save all changes" button loops through this hidden gallery and updates the data source like so:

```
ForAll(galPropertiesToUpdate.AllItems,
    UpdateIf(Property,
            PropertyID=lblPropertyID.Text,
            {Description: lblNewDescription.Text}
    )
)
```

This formula loops through the items in the hidden gallery and calls the `UpdateIf` function to update the description that corresponds to the property ID of the record. We covered the `UpdateIf` function in Chapter 7.

This example highlights the benefit of using a hidden gallery. It makes our call to the `ForAll` function easier to read because we've extracted the function that filters the source gallery for any modified records. Also, by referencing the updated values through labels, we avoid any tricky disambiguation syntax due to the data source of our updated records and the target data source sharing the same column name.

If the formula fails to update our data source, another advantage of this technique is that we can debug the problem by setting the visibility of the hidden gallery to true and inspecting the records that we want to update in more detail.

Tip   A hidden gallery provides a simple way to access modified records. We can add labels to this hidden gallery to help avoid disambiguation syntax.

Working with Forms

In the final part of this chapter, we'll examine the form control in more depth. In Chapter 3, we covered the basic use of the form control, including the relationship between the form and card controls. In this section, we'll examine some of the topics that we haven't yet covered, including how to lay out a form, how to improve the presentation of a data input screen by using multiple forms, how to set default values and reset controls, and how to validate values.

Laying Out a Form

We can use the Layout setting to define where the field labels appear in relation to the data entry controls. There are two settings we can apply – vertical and horizontal.

The default is the vertical layout. With this layout, the labels appear above the data entry controls. With the horizontal layout, the labels appear to the left of the data entry controls. Figure 11-30 illustrates a form with a vertical layout compared to a form with a horizontal layout.

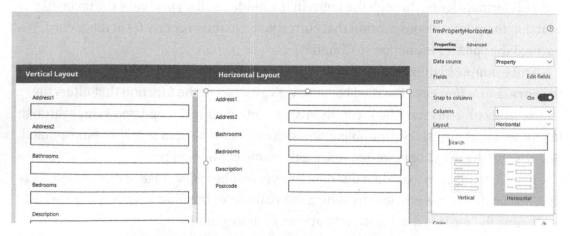

Figure 11-30.   *Selecting either the vertical or horizontal layout*

Defining Form Columns

Two other settings that control the layout of a form are the Columns and Snap to columns settings. To demonstrate how these settings work, Figure 11-31 illustrates a form with a Columns setting of 4. This example highlights a way in which we can improve the presentation of a form. For some fields such as the address fields, we would want to provide a wider text input control, whereas for some of the shorter fields, we would want to combine some of those onto the same row to help conserve screen space.

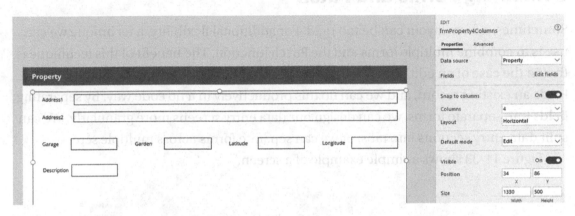

Figure 11-31. *Laying out a form with multiple columns*

With a Columns setting of 4, Power Apps applies an invisible grid beneath the form that consists of four columns. We can position cards so that they fit into a column, or we can stretch a card so that it spans multiple columns.

With the Snap to columns setting turned on, we can only stretch a card so that it fills an entire column. With Snap to columns turned off, we can stretch a card so that it partially fills a column (Figure 11-32).

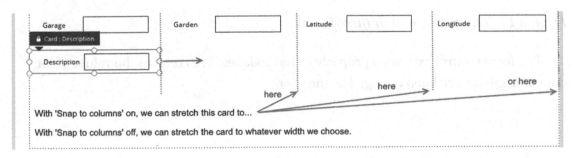

Figure 11-32. *How Snap to columns works*

Here are some additional tips. It isn't possible to rearrange the order of the cards on the form by dragging and dropping the cards in the designer. The way to rearrange the order of the cards is to click the Edit fields link and to rearrange the cards from that section of the designer.

If we want to leave an empty column, we can add a blank custom card, and we can position that into the column that we want to leave blank.

Combining Forms and Patch

Sometimes, a form layout can be too rigid. For additional flexibility, a technique we can use is to combine multiple forms and the Patch function. The benefit of this technique is that in the case of an edit screen, we can use the graphical designer to build the UI that loads an existing record, and we can do this productively in a no code way. By separating fields into separate forms, we can design our data entry screens more granularly. We can split data entry sections into tabs, or we can separate forms across multiple screens.

Figure 11-33 shows a simple example of a screen.

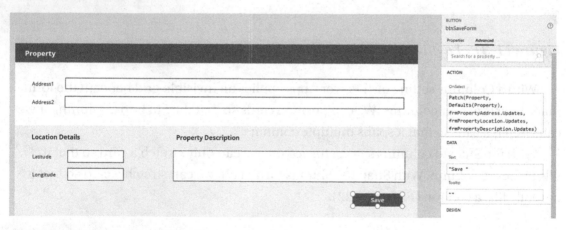

Figure 11-33. *A screen with three forms*

The form control exposes a property called Updates. This returns the values of the data fields that have been changed by the user.

On the save button for our screen, we can call the Patch function and pass the updated data fields from each form. The formula we would use to add a new record looks like this:

```
Patch(Property,
      Defaults(Property),
      frmPropertyAddress.Updates,
      frmPropertyLocation.Updates,
      frmPropertyDescription.Updates
)
```

Setting Form Default Values

To help users more easily create new records, we can set default field values for a record. With a form, we can write a formula that detects the form mode. This can be one of two modes – new or edit. If the form is in new mode, we can show a default value. If the form is in edit mode, we can show the existing field value instead. To demonstrate, here's how to modify an edit form based on our tenancy table. When a user creates a new record, we'll default the start date to today's date.

To build this example, the first step is to open the edit form and to find the card that corresponds to the start date field, as shown in Figure 11-34. We unlock the card and set the Default property of the data card to the formula shown in the following:

```
If (frmTenancy.Mode = FormMode.New, Now(), ThisItem.StartDate)
```

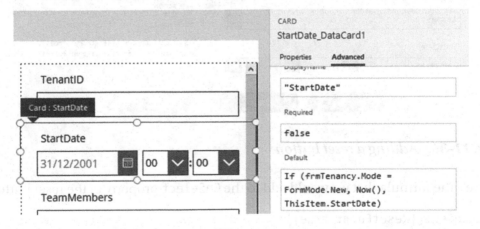

Figure 11-34. Setting default screen values

When we now run this form, the start date field will display today's date when we create a new record. When we edit an existing record, it will show the existing start date value.

Resetting Form Controls

Power Apps provides a framework to reset control values back to their default states. This feature serves a very useful purpose because we can use it to enable users to undo their changes. We'll demonstrate this feature by adding a discard button to an edit form. If a user starts to edit a record and decides not to continue, the discard button will restore the control values back to their initial state.

Every control includes a property called Reset, and all controls will respond to a change in this property. When the Reset property for a control changes to true, it triggers the control to restore its value back to its initial state. The pattern to build a discard feature is to set the Reset property of all controls to a context variable. To trigger the reset operation, we would set the value of the variable to true. Next, we would immediately set the value back to false. By setting the value to false, the user can repeat the discard operation at a later point in time.

To build this feature, the first step is to add a button that triggers the reset operation (Figure 11-35).

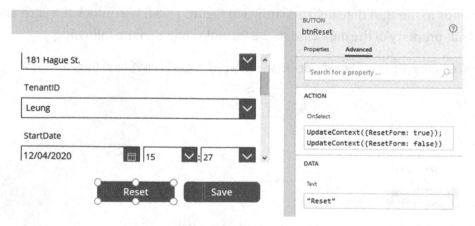

Figure 11-35. *Adding a reset button*

Here's the formula that we would add to the OnSelect property of the reset button:

```
UpdateContext({ResetForm: true});
UpdateContext({ResetForm: false})
```

We would now set the Reset property on all the data entry controls to the variable ResetForm. We can now run our screen. If we change the values on a form and click the reset button, the controls will revert to their initial values.

Validating Form Values

A great benefit of using forms with data sources such as SharePoint, SQL Server, and Dataverse is that the designer creates the controls to enforce any basic data constraints that we define at the data source. This includes mandatory field, data length, and range validation (i.e., whether an input value falls between a defined minimum and maximum range).

If we need to apply more complex validation rules, we need to build this into our application manually. To demonstrate a typical validation rule, here's how to ensure that users enter end date values that are greater than the start date.

To build this feature, the first step is to unlock the start date card. To make our formula more readable, we'll rename the start date picker and time controls to dteStart, drpHourStart, and drpMinuteStart.

Next, unlock the end date card and rename the end date picker and time controls to dteEnd, drpHourEnd, and drpMinuteEnd.

Inside the end date card, we'll add a label control and set the color to red, as shown in Figure 11-36. We then set the Text property of the label control to the formula that's shown in the following:

```
If((DteStart.SelectedDate +
      Time(Value(DrpHourStart.Selected.Value),
           Value(DrpMinuteStart.Selected.Value),
           0)
   )
    >
   (DteEnd.SelectedDate +
      Time(Value(DrpHourEnd.Selected.Value),
           Value(DrpMinuteEnd.Selected.Value),
           0)),
   "End date must be greater than start date",
   ""
)
```

This formula calls the If function to test if the end date value exceeds the start date. If a user enters valid data, the label shows an empty string. Otherwise, it shows a message that indicates the error to the user.

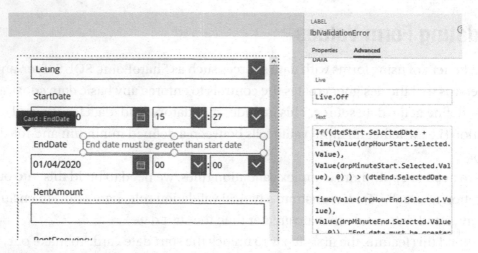

Figure 11-36. *Adding a validation message that compares two fields*

To complete this task, it's a good idea to also apply this rule to the save button. This would prevent the SubmitForm function from running when the data is invalid. The formula we would add to the OnSelect property of the save button is shown here:

```
f((dteStart.SelectedDate +
    Time(Value(drpHourStart.Selected.Value),
        Value(drpMinuteStart.Selected.Value),
        0)
   )
    >
   (dteEnd.SelectedDate +
    Time(Value(drpHourEnd.Selected.Value),
        Value(drpMinuteEnd.Selected.Value),
        0)),
    false,
    SubmitForm(frmTenancy)
)
```

Tip   A great way to validate data is to call the `IsMatch` function, as demonstrated in Chapter 5. We can call this function to check that users enter data in the correct format. For example, we can call this function to validate the format of email addresses or telephone numbers.

Retrieving Validation Rules

If we build a data entry screen without forms, we can call the `Validate` function to check if the input data adheres to the basic validation rules that we define at the data source. This technique works against data sources that support data rules, including SharePoint, Dataverse, and SQL Server.

The `Validate` function works in two modes – it can validate a single field or an entire record. Let's assume that for our SharePoint properties list, we make the postcode field mandatory and that we set the maximum length of this field to ten characters. To verify whether an input value from a text input control adheres to these rules, we can use the formula that's shown in the following:

```
Validate(Property, "Postcode" , txtPostcode.Text)
```

The output from the Validate function is a string. Therefore, we can add a label to our screen and call the `Validate` function from the Text property (Figure 11-37). If there are no errors, the `Validate` function will return an empty string.

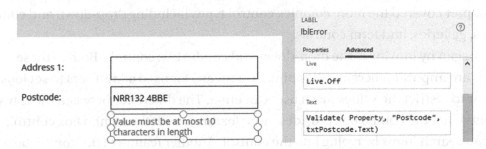

Figure 11-37. *Using the Validate function to validate a single field*

To validate an entire record rather than a single field, we can pass an existing record and the intended changes to the `Validate` function. The following formula shows how to validate a new record:

```
Validate(Property,
       Defaults(Property),
       {
             Address1: txtAddress1.Text,
             Address2: txtAddress2.Text,
             Postcode: txtPostcode.Text
       }
)
```

Because the intention here is to validate a new record, we call the `Defaults` function to return a base record that we can pass to the `Validate` function. If we were validating an existing record, we would provide the existing record to the Validate function instead.

Tip   A good way to force users to enter numeric data is to use a text input control and to set the Format property to `TextFormat.Number`. This technique can help us avoid writing specific code to validate numeric input data.

Summary

This chapter covered the more complex control types including drop-down and combo controls, galleries, and form controls.

We began by looking at the drop-down and combo box controls. Both of these controls are important because they provide a means for us to allow users to set lookup values or to restrict the values that a user can enter. The difference between these two controls is that the combo box provides more features. With the combo box control, users can search items by typing into the control. Another feature of the combo box control is that it permits users to select multiple items.

For SharePoint lists with lookup columns or Dataverse tables with relationships, the form designer can generate data entry cards that include the drop-down control. This provides a simple, no code way for us to apply the drop-down control.

With other data sources, the typical way to utilize a drop-down control is to set the data source to a lookup table that contains both a description and a corresponding code or numeric value. We would display the description in the drop-down and store the code value in the data source that references the lookup value. On the form that contains the drop-down, we would add a formula to the Update property of the card to save the selected code value of the drop-down. In the Default property of the drop-down control, we would look up the description that corresponds to the lookup ID.

We use the Value property to define the field that the drop-down control displays. The value that we enter must match one of the fields in the data source of the control. A common requirement is to customize the text in each row of the drop-down control. We can accomplish this by setting the data source of the drop-down or combo box to the result of the AddColumns function. In the call to the AddColumns function, we would construct a formula to produce the customized display text.

With both the drop-down and combo box controls, we can filter the items that these controls display by specifying a dependent control.

With a SharePoint list, we can define choice columns that permit multiple selections. If we build a form against this type of column, the data card will include a combo box control that supports the entry and retrieval of multiple selections.

Other controls that can display multiple records include the list box control and table control. The list box control works similarly to the drop-down control. But instead of the user needing to click the control to show the list of items, the data items are always visible with the list box control. For data entry purposes, the user can select one or more items from a list box. However, a limitation with this control is that when we load data into the control, we can only preselect a maximum of one item.

The table control provides a very simple and quick way for us to display data in rows and columns. The main limitation is that it is not possible for users to edit data using the control.

The gallery control is one of the most powerful and widely used controls. There are three gallery types that are available. These include the vertical, horizontal, and flexible height galleries. The vertical and flexible height galleries display data items from top to bottom, whereas the horizontal gallery displays items left to right. Each data item in the vertical gallery has a fixed height. In situations where the data that we want to show in each row can vary, the text from the previous row can overlap onto the next row. The flexible height gallery overcomes this problem by providing row heights that can vary depending on the amount of data in each row.

There are various settings that we can use to customize the appearance of a gallery. To help us quickly build the item template of the gallery, we can apply a built-in layout. When we apply a layout, the designer produces an item template that includes placeholder controls. These controls can include an image placeholder and placeholders for a title and description. Through the designer, we can choose the data field that we want to display in each placeholder using a drop-down control.

The gallery control exposes a property called AllItems. We can use this to retrieve all the data items and controls in a gallery. By utilizing the AllItems property of the gallery, we learned how to build a gallery that enables users to amend multiple records in one go. In this example, we also examined how to use hidden galleries to store working sets of data. This technique can help simplify formulas, and by temporarily showing the hidden galleries at design time, we can more easily diagnose problems.

In the final part of this chapter, we looked at how to customize the form control. We can specify where field labels appear in relation to the data entry controls by using the Layout setting. We can use this to display field labels above or to the left of the data entry controls.

The form control provides a Columns setting. We use this to apply a column structure that helps us to lay out the cards on a form. By using the designer, we can stretch a card so that it spans multiple columns. We can use this feature to produce a form that contains a wide text input control in one row and multiple shorter text input controls on another row.

The form control exposes a property called Updates. This property returns all the field values on a form that the user has modified. To produce a screen with sets of controls that are placed in disjointed locations, we learned how to add multiple forms to a screen that bind to the same record. We can save the data from the multiple forms by calling the Patch function and referring to the Updates property of each form.

We looked at how to add custom validation to a form, and in the final section of this chapter, we looked at how to restore control values back to their initial state. Each control includes a property called Reset. When this value is true, the control will reset itself back to its initial state. A typical way to build a reset or undo feature on a screen is to set the Reset property on all target controls to a Boolean variable. We would then add a button that sets the variable to true and then back to false. This would trigger all the specified controls to revert to their initial values.

PART IV

Developing Model-Driven and Portal Apps

CHAPTER 12

Building a Dataverse Database

Microsoft Dataverse is a premium, cloud-based database. As a data store, it is far superior to SharePoint, and it is Microsoft's preferred database for products in the Power Platform. Dataverse is the database that Microsoft Dynamics 365 uses, and it is the foundation on which model-driven and portal apps are based. Without a Dataverse database, we cannot create these types of apps, and this is the reason why Dataverse is so important.

In this chapter, we'll walk through the steps to set up a Dataverse database. The basic topics that we will cover include how to define tables and columns, the data types that are available, and how to define validation and data constraints with business rules. We'll also cover some of the powerful capabilities of Dataverse which include

- How to define relationships. With Dataverse, we can model complex relationship types, including many-to-many relationships and self-relationships (which enable us to build hierarchical data models).

- How to define calculated and rollup fields. With SharePoint and other data sources, query delegation limits can prevent us from aggregating data, such as summing, averaging, and counting rows. With Dataverse, we can overcome these limitations with rollup fields.

- How to create views and forms. A unique feature of Dataverse is that we can define data forms and filtered views of data. The benefit of this is that it enables us to define these objects once in a single place and to reuse these objects multiple times in multiple apps.

© Tim Leung 2021
T. Leung, *Beginning Power Apps*, https://doi.org/10.1007/978-1-4842-6683-0_12

Why Use Dataverse?

What are the benefits of Dataverse? The first benefit is that Dataverse is very simple to use. A Dataverse database is linked to the host environment. This means that when we build an app, we can connect directly to the environment's Dataverse database without needing to enter any additional credentials. Unlike SharePoint, there's no need to enter a SharePoint web address; and in the case of SQL Server, there's no need to enter a server name, username, and password.

It's very simple to manage a Dataverse database and to build a data model because we can accomplish this entirely through a web-based designer. Compared to SQL Server, there's no need to learn SQL (Structured Query Language) or to learn how to use the tools to manage the database.

Dataverse provides common data models that we can utilize. By using these models, we can save time by not having to set up and design our data models.

Other features of Dataverse include excellent security, great performance, and the ability to share data easily with other products from the Power Platform (e.g., Power BI or Power Automate). The Dataverse security model can restrict access to rows and columns of data by user. There is far greater support for delegable queries compared to SharePoint, making it possible to retrieve more accurate data more quickly.

Finally, we can easily transfer Dataverse-based apps between tenants, environments, and organizations using solutions. This is something that is not possible with other data sources. As an example, let's suppose we work for a software consultancy and that we build a Dataverse database and a model-driven app for a client. We can deliver this project by building a solution that contains both a Dataverse database and the app. The client can install all the components by deploying a single solution. If we were using a SharePoint solution, the client would need to carry out the additional manual steps to create and configure the SharePoint lists as a prerequisite.

Are there any disadvantages to using Dataverse? One issue is licensing. App builders with Microsoft 365 subscriptions require a per-user or per-app plan to use Dataverse. This additional cost can be a barrier to entry.

Another issue is that it can be difficult to access data outside of the Power Platform and Dynamics 365. The ability to edit and to create records in Dataverse is mostly limited to a Web API that provides read and write access to data. For read-only access, there is a basic feature that we can use to export Dataverse data to Excel, and there is a preview feature that exposes read-only data through a TDS (Tabular Data Stream) end point. This enables us to access Dataverse using client tools that we generally use to access SQL Server.

In comparison, SQL Server provides far better connectivity with many platforms and programming languages, and there is a rich ecosystem of native and third-party tools for backup, data transformation, and data import/export. SQL Server also provides the flexibility to manually fine-tune settings that relate to performance (such as indexes), and we can utilize features such as views and stored procedures to improve the performance of retrieving joined data and for bulk updating records.

A final issue relates to privacy. By using Dataverse, we agree to share table and column names with Microsoft to help improve the Common Data Model. Organizations that wish to protect intellectual property relating to data schemas should apply some caution before choosing to use Dataverse.

What Are the Terms That Are Used?

Dataverse uses several terms that might sound unfamiliar. Here's an overview of the features and names that we will encounter.

The main objects in a Dataverse database are tables. A table defines a structure of data. It is the equivalent of a list in SharePoint or tables in Excel or SQL Server. For each table, we define columns of data that we want to store.

Other objects that we can define in Dataverse include

- Views – These define column and filter conditions for a list of records.
- Forms – These define data entry columns, controls, and layout for a single record.
- Business rules – These define data constraints and validation rules.
- Charts – These define a visual representation of data.
- Dashboards – These define a summary of data using lists, charts, and other objects.

The ability to define all these objects at the data source is a positive feature that supports the good practice of reusability. For example, if we were to define a view or a form in Dataverse, we could reuse these objects in several other model-driven or portal apps.

An important note is that Dataverse was previously called the "Common Data Service." Microsoft renamed the "Common Data Service" to Dataverse in late 2020. With the original "Common Data Service," tables were called entities. The reason this is important is because these terms still appear frequently in technical articles and we can still find the occasional reference to the word entity in some parts of Power Apps.

Caution   Dataverse was previously called the "Common Data Service," and the previous name for a table was entity.

The Common Data Model

The Common Data Model (CDM) is a great feature of Dataverse. It provides a set of common data structures and saves us from having to build these from scratch. Let's imagine that we want to build a client messaging system. Instead of building a data model that includes the required tables, fields, and relationships, we can simply use those that the CDM provides.

App builders who are unfamiliar with database theory can struggle with normalization. This is the practice of splitting data across multiple tables to minimize data repetition and to optimize performance. For these users, the CDM delivers high-quality data models that are efficient and ready for use.

The data model is also fine-tuned to support data import and export operations. The CDM designers researched the data structures of other business systems such as SAP and Salesforce and designed the model to ease the mapping of fields between it and other popular third-party systems.

Another benefit of the CDM is data unification. If users throughout all departments in an organization use the CDM, we can more easily build a central repository of data. This can promote the sharing of data, avoid duplication, and simplify the organizational effort of managing personal data. A big benefit of centralized data is that it becomes much easier to extract insights and business intelligence.

The CDM is an open source data model, and we can view the model through the GitHub page:

```
https://github.com/microsoft/CDM
```

Figure 12-1 shows a screenshot from the project site that illustrates the data model. The CDM schema provides a set of core tables which include account, activity, and contact. These are important because they link to many of the other tables in the CDM.

The remaining tables are grouped into organizational business areas, such as sales, service, and finance. These tables support the features that are provided by the corresponding Dynamics 365 apps.

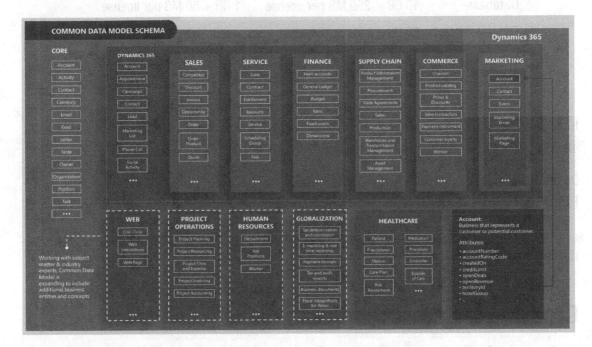

Figure 12-1.   The data schema of the Common Data Model

How Much Can We Store?

For planning and budgeting purposes, it's important to understand the cost and storage capacity of Dataverse. Dataverse provides three storage types – database, file, and log. Database storage refers to the data that we store in tables.

We can store attachments, such as documents, PDF files, images, and videos. These usage types fall into the file category. The log category accounts for data that Dataverse stores for logging, analysis, and reporting purposes.

Our storage quota depends on the licenses that we acquire. There are two plans that we can subscribe to – a per-app plan at $10 per user per month and a per-user plan at $40 per user per month. We receive a base allocation of up to 10 GB, and each additional license will increase our quota, as shown in Table 12-1.

Table 12-1. *Dataverse storage allowances*

Storage Type	Per-User Licensing	Per-App Licensing
Database	10 GB + 250 MB per license	1 GB + 50 MB per license
File	20 GB+ 2 GB per license	2 GB+ 400 MB per license
Log	2 GB	200 MB

As an illustration, let's suppose that we purchase 10 per-user licenses and 20 per-app licenses. Our database storage quota will be 13.5 GB, and the file storage quota will be 48 GB. Here's a summary of the calculation:

```
Database storage:  10GB + (0.25GB * 10) + (0.05GB * 20) = 13.GB
File storage:  20GB + (2GB * 10) + (0.4GB * 20) = 48.GB
```

In cases where we exceed our quota or require more storage, Microsoft will bill us for the additional usage.

Creating a Dataverse Database

We'll now look at how to provision a database. Databases are associated with environments, and we can create a maximum of one database per environment. To create a database, we select the *Tables* item from the Data section of the Maker Portal. This opens the screen that's shown in Figure 12-2.

When we create a database, we can tick the option to include sample apps and data. This populates the CDM tables with example data and provides a great way to learn and to familiarize ourselves with the CDM and model-driven apps.

An important point is that once we create a database, there is no way to delete it. The only way to delete a database is to delete the environment. Also, there is no way to change the currency or language settings of a database after creation.

Caution   There is no simple way to delete a Dataverse database or to change the currency or language settings.

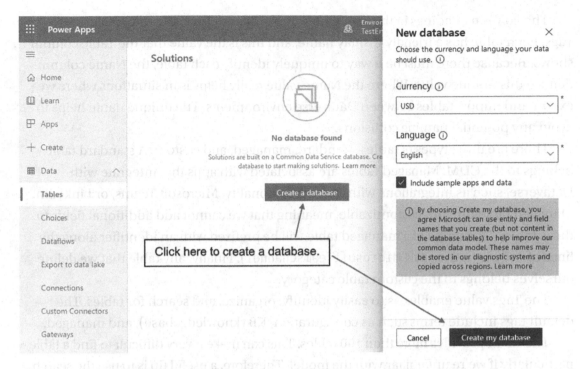

Figure 12-2. *Creating a database*

Listing Tables

After we provision a database, the Tables menu item will display all the tables in our
database (Figure 12-3).

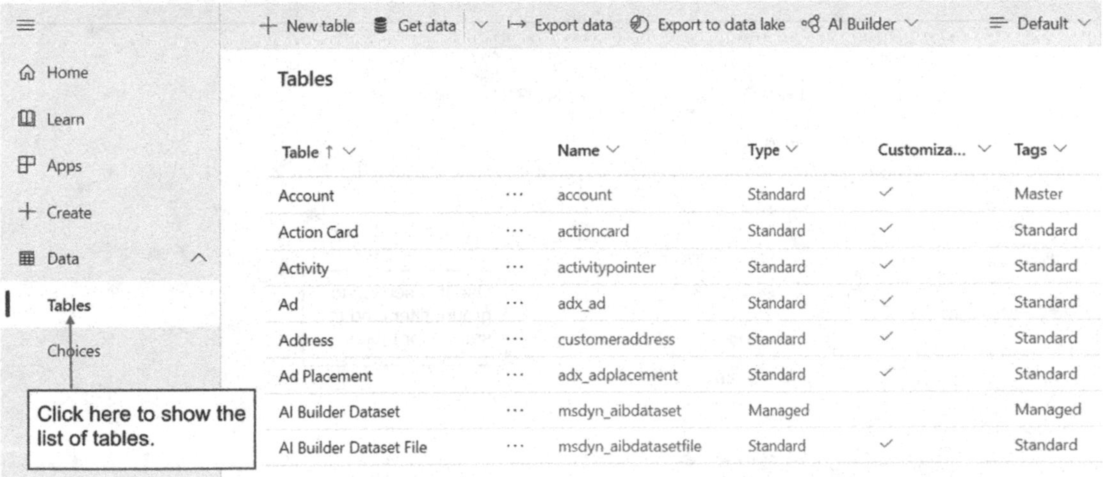

Figure 12-3. *Managing tables*

The column headings in the list include Table, Name, Type, Customizable, and Tags. Each table has a friendly display name, and this is the value that the Table column shows. Because there must be a way to uniquely identify each table, the Name column defines this unique value. Where the Name value really helps is in situations where we export and import tables between Dataverse environments. The unique name helps to avoid any potential naming collisions.

There are three types of table – standard, managed, and custom. A standard table belongs to the CDM. Managed tables are associated with apps that integrate with Dataverse, such as integrations with the AI functionality, Microsoft Teams, or LinkedIn. Managed tables are not customizable, meaning that we cannot add additional fields to these tables. The name of a managed table will be prefixed with an identifier along the lines of msdyn_ (e.g., msdyn_MicrosoftTeamsChannel). Finally, any table that we define ourselves belongs to the custom table category.

The Tags value enables us to easily identify, organize, and search for tables. The default tags include terms such as configuration, KB (knowledgebase), and managed.

The CDM provides more than 100 tables. This can make it very difficult to find a table, particularly if we're unfamiliar with the model. Therefore, a useful tip is to use the search and filter options at the top of the list. To show only the tables that we've created ourselves, we can filter the list to "Custom." Another useful tip is to group the tables by tag (Figure 12-4). This provides a simple way to navigate and to explore the tables in our database.

Note   Before we create a table, it's worth spending a few moments to check if an existing table already exists in the CDM that can cater for our needs.

Figure 12-4. *Searching and organizing tables*

Editing Tables

From the list of tables, we can click a table to open the definition of the table. Here's the definition of the standard Account table (Figure 12-5).

Home	Tables > **Account**									
Learn	Columns	Relationships	Business rules	Views	Forms	Dashboards	Charts	Keys	Data	
Apps										
+ Create	**Display name ↑ ∨**			**Name ∨**			**Data type ∨**		**Type ∨**	
Data ∧	Account	⋯		accountid			⊞ Unique Identifier		Standard	
Tables	Account Name Primary Field	⋯		name			▦ Text		Managed	
Choices	Account Number	⋯		accountnumber			▦ Text		Managed	
Dataflows	Account Rating	⋯		accountratingcode			≣ Option Set		Managed	
Export to data lake	Address 1	⋯		address1_composite			▦ Multiline Text		Managed	
Connections	Address 1: Address Type	⋯		address1_addresstypecode			≣ Option Set		Managed	
	Address 1: City	⋯		address1_city			▦ Text		Managed	
	Address 1: Country/Region	⋯		address1_country			▦ Text		Managed	

Figure 12-5. *Illustration of the Account table*

The central part of the screen shows the columns. Those in the Account table include the typical columns that are associated with an account, such as organization name and full name.

Each column stores data that matches a specific data type. The data types we can assign include numeric and text types, as well as specialized types such as email addresses and phone numbers. We can also specify option sets to constrain the values that a user can enter.

A great feature about standard tables from the CDM is that we can add additional fields. If we want to add a column called "Account manager" to the standard Account table, that's entirely possible. To do this, we would click the "Add column" button.

It's worth noting that some app builders prefer not to add columns to standard tables. The reason is to keep the standard tables "clean" and to self-contain custom changes in custom tables. A great way to support this method of working is to build custom tables that include a lookup to a standard table.

Through the remaining tabs in the table designer, we can manage relationships, business rules, views, forms, dashboards, charts, keys, and data records in the table.

Creating a Custom Table

To create a new table, we click the "New table" button to open the panel that's shown in Figure 12-6.

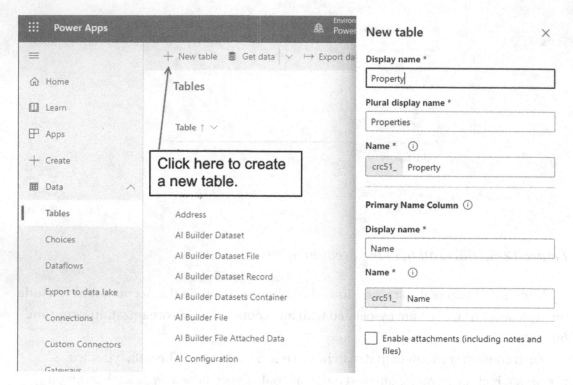

Figure 12-6. *Creating a new table*

The mandatory items that we need to enter include the display name, the plural display name, and the name. The display name is the friendly name that Power Apps uses most frequently in the designers to identify the table.

The name is a unique identifier, and no two tables in a database can share the same name. Dataverse prefixes the name that we enter with an environment-specific code. The purpose of this prefix is to build a name that is unique across multiple environments. This makes it possible to export and import tables into a new environment. We can define a custom prefix by creating a table through a solution and defining a publisher (we cover this topic in Chapter 26). App builders often refer to this combination of a prefix and name as the "logical name."

We cannot change the name after we create the table, although it is possible to change the display name and the plural display name at any time.

The "primary name column" defines the main column for a table. This is equivalent to the Title field in a SharePoint list. We use this primary column to store a text description that identifies a row in the table. Power Apps uses the primary column value in lookup fields. If we were to display a list of records in a drop-down box, the description that appears against each row would be the primary column value.

A useful option we can check is the "Enable attachments" checkbox. This activates the ability for users to store multiple file attachments against each record. An important point is that we cannot enable attachments after we create a table. To enable file attachments, we must select this option when we create the table.

Another important point is that it is currently not possible to access file attachments from a canvas app. Only model-driven apps support the attachments feature. However, it is possible for canvas apps to integrate with table fields that are of type "file." We will cover this topic in Chapter 16.

Tip   Another way to create a table is to click the "Get data" button and to import a table of data from Excel. This can provide a faster way to build a table, compared to using the designer.

Table Settings

For each table, there are a wide range of supporting properties and additional settings that we can set. These include settings that relate to the table type, ownership, and collaboration and record create and update settings. To access the settings, we would open a table and click the settings button. This opens the pane that is shown in Figure 12-7.

Many of these settings relate to Dynamics 365 integration, and we can click the information icon to display further details about the purpose of the setting.

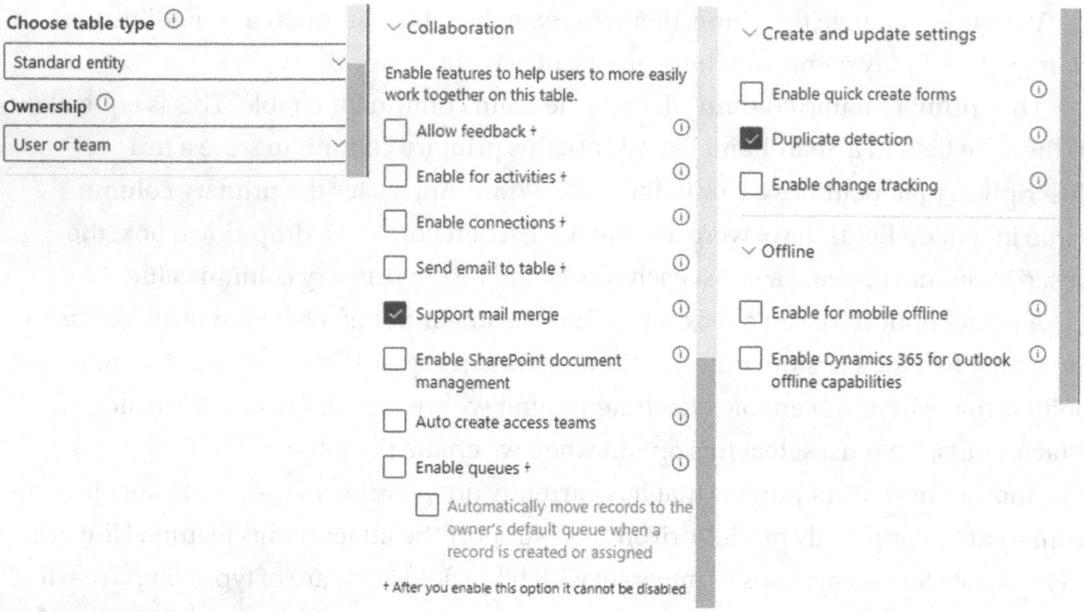

Figure 12-7. *Additional table settings*

The table that we create can be one of two types – a standard table or an activity table. The default type is a standard table. An activity represents an action that a user carries out. In the majority of cases, an activity table stores details which include a start time, end time, and duration. An activity typically tracks an action between a user and a customer, and the built-in activity tables in the CDM include phone call, task, email, and letter. By default, an activity table includes a lookup field called "regarding." This lookup can refer to the accounts, contacts, and other tables. If we want to create a table of this nature, we should select the activity table type.

There are two ownership types that we can choose – organization or "user or team." A table that is owned by an organization works well in situations where we want to store reference data that is visible to everyone in the organization. If we're uncertain, it is safest to choose the "user or team" option. With this ownership type, Dataverse adds ownership fields to the table, and we can use these to secure or to restrict access to records.

Caution   Once we create a table, there are a range of settings that we cannot modify. This includes the logical table name, the ownership type setting, and most of the collaboration settings.

Adding a New Column

After we create a new table, the designer shows the columns that belong to the table. By default, this includes many standard columns, including columns that store the create and last modified time and user, the status, and the owner.

The "Add column" button opens a panel to the right of the screen (Figure 12-8). The mandatory items that we need to specify include the display name, name, and data type.

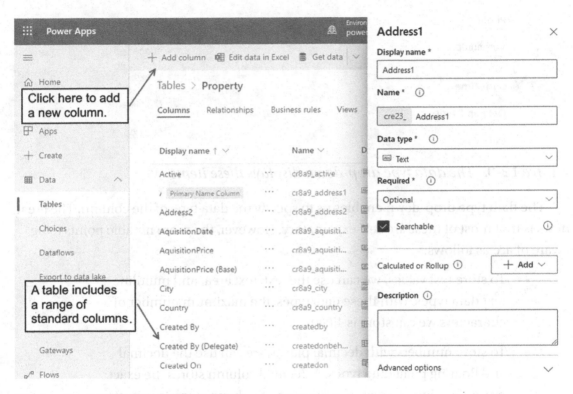

Figure 12-8. *Adding a new column*

Just like tables, the display name defines the value that Power Apps uses commonly to identify the column. The name is a unique identifier, and Dataverse prefixes the name with the code that is specific to the environment (or the publisher/solution).

Dataverse supports all the common data types, which are illustrated in Figure 12-9.

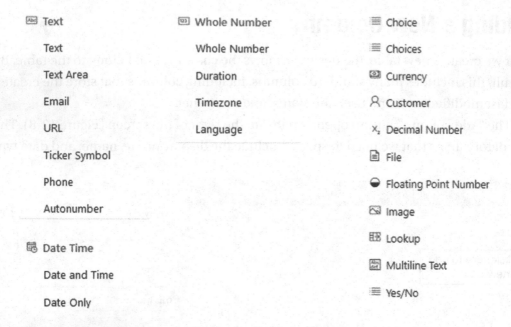

Text	Whole Number	Choice
Text	Whole Number	Choices
Text Area	Duration	Currency
Email	Timezone	Customer
URL	Language	Decimal Number
Ticker Symbol		File
Phone		Floating Point Number
Autonumber		Image
		Lookup
Date Time		Multiline Text
Date and Time		Yes/No
Date Only		

Figure 12-9. *The data type drop-down displays these items*

The data type drop-down enables us to specify the data type of the column. The great news is that most of these are self-explanatory. However, the more notable points to be aware of are as follows:

- To store text values, we can use the text, text area, and multiline text data types. With these data types, the maximum number of characters we can store is 4,000.

- To store numbers with decimal places, we can use the decimal and floating point data types. A decimal column stores the exact numeric value, whereas a floating point column stores a very close approximation. The benefit of the floating point data type is that it provides better performance. We should use the decimal data type when we want precision or if we want to use the value in a query that searches for values that are equal or not equal to another value.

- Once we save a column, we cannot change the data type. There is however one exception – it is possible to change a text column to an autonumber column.

To store Boolean values, we can use the "Yes/No" data type. In the settings for the column, we can enter the label text that represents the true or false value (e.g., yes/no or true/false). An alternative way to store Boolean values is to use the choice data type. Dataverse provides a standard choice called "a yes or no Boolean." The benefit of the choice data type is that if a future requirement arises where we need to expand the range of permissible values beyond two, the choice data type can support the addition of extra choice items.

There are several special data types that are based on text data. These include email, phone, URL, and ticker symbol. The benefit of these data types is that Power Apps provides controls that are specially designed for these data types.

Another special data type is the customer data type. A customer column provides a lookup that can refer to records in either the standard Account or Contact table. This type of lookup is unique because typically, lookup columns can refer to records from a single parent table only. The technical name for this type of lookup column is a "polymorphic lookup" column. Another place where we see a polymorphic lookup column is through the standard owner column that exists in every table. The purpose of this column is to store the owner of a record. The owner lookup column can refer to records in the standard User or Team table.

Finally, it's useful to know that following Microsoft's renaming exercise in late 2020, what were "Two Option" fields are now "Yes/No" columns, and what were previously "option sets" are now "choices." This can be helpful when we refer to older technical articles.

Storing Currencies

To store currency values, the currency data type offers several helpful features. It is optimized for global organizations that work with multiple currencies. To illustrate what this data type offers, Figure 12-10 shows what happens when we add a column called "acquisition price" to our property table. When we add a currency column, Dataverse adds several supporting columns, which include currency and exchange rate columns.

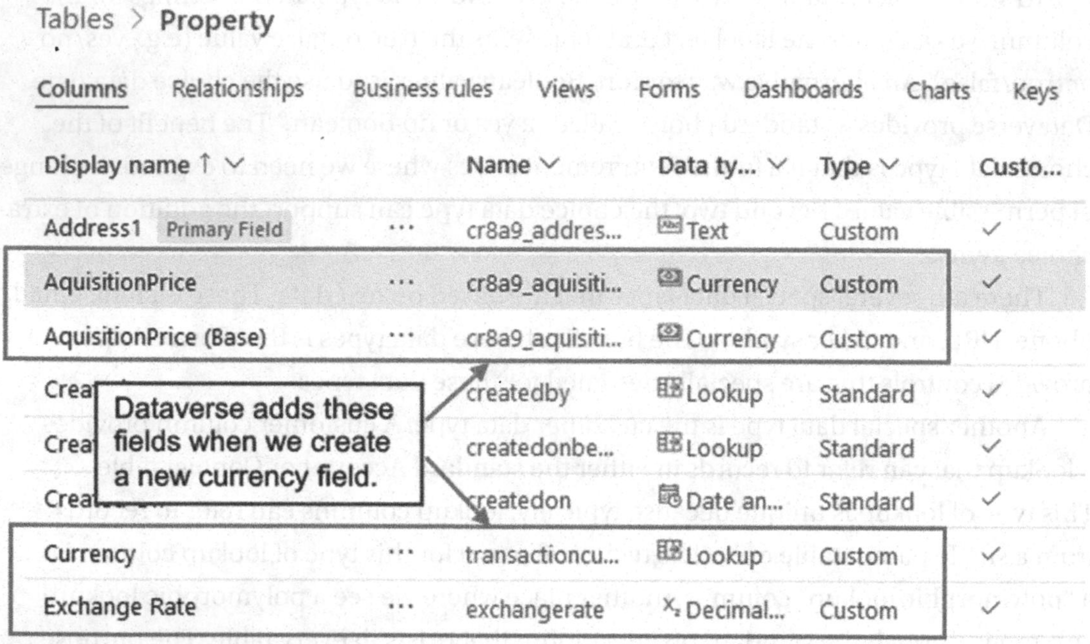

Tables > **Property**

| Columns | Relationships | Business rules | Views | Forms | Dashboards | Charts | Keys |

Display name ↑ ∨	Name ∨	Data ty... ∨	Type ∨	Custo...
Address1 Primary Field ···	cr8a9_addres...	⬛ Text	Custom	✓
AquisitionPrice ···	cr8a9_aquisiti...	🔲 Currency	Custom	✓
AquisitionPrice (Base) ···	cr8a9_aquisiti...	🔲 Currency	Custom	✓
Crea	createdby	⬛ Lookup	Standard	✓
Crea	createdonbe...	⬛ Lookup	Standard	✓
Crea	createdon	🔲 Date an...	Standard	✓
Currency ···	transactioncu...	⬛ Lookup	Custom	✓
Exchange Rate ···	exchangerate	✕ₐ Decimal...	Custom	✓

> Dataverse adds these fields when we create a new currency field.

Figure 12-10. *The currency data type*

To explain this data type, let's take the case of a global US organization with operations in Europe and Asia. For accounting purposes, the organization chooses to record all financial values in US dollars. The currency data type facilitates this mode of operation by adding two supporting columns – a lookup column called currency and an additional currency column that matches the name of our column, but includes the suffix (base).

The currency lookup references values in the settings of Dynamics 365. This is the area where an organization stores exchange rates. Figure 12-11 illustrates how to access this area through the Power Platform admin center.

If we were to create a property record and enter an acquisition price of €100,000, Dataverse stores 100,000 in the acquisition price column and euros in the currency lookup column. It calculates the value of €100,000 in the base currency (e.g., US dollars), and stores this in the acquisition price base column. It also stores a read-only copy of the exchange rate that was used in the exchange rate column.

Although the currency type can be invaluable in global financial situations, this data type can be difficult to work with. Due to all these associated columns, it is impossible to bulk update currency values from multiple rows without some assistance from another process, such as a Power Automate flow.

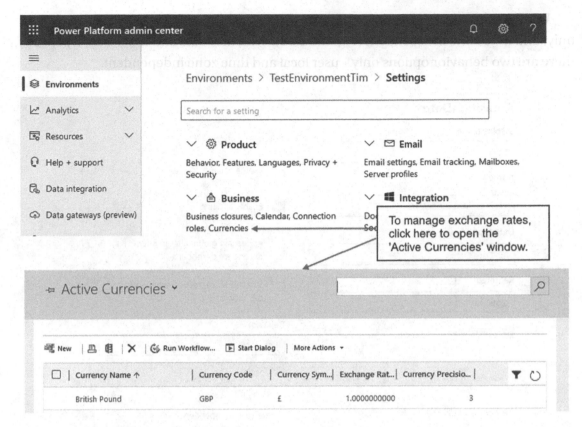

Figure 12-11. *Setting currency exchange rates*

Storing Dates

With the "date only" or "date and time" data type, a very important setting to consider is the behavior setting.

In Chapter 10, we covered two different ways in which we can represent dates and times. We can store a static date and time which will be identical throughout all time zones, or we can store a time zone–aware "point in time." An example of where we need to store a "point in time" is to store the date and time of an online meeting with participants across the world.

As an example of where to use a static date and time, let's imagine a global retail company that uses a table to store branch opening hours during public holidays. These opening hours apply to multiple branches throughout different regions. Because these opening hours (e.g., 9 AM–6 PM) apply to each branch in the local time zone, we can store these as static dates and times.

With the "date only" data type, there are three behavior options – user local, date only, and time zone independent (Figure 12-12). With the "date and time" data type, there are two behavior options only – user local and time zone independent.

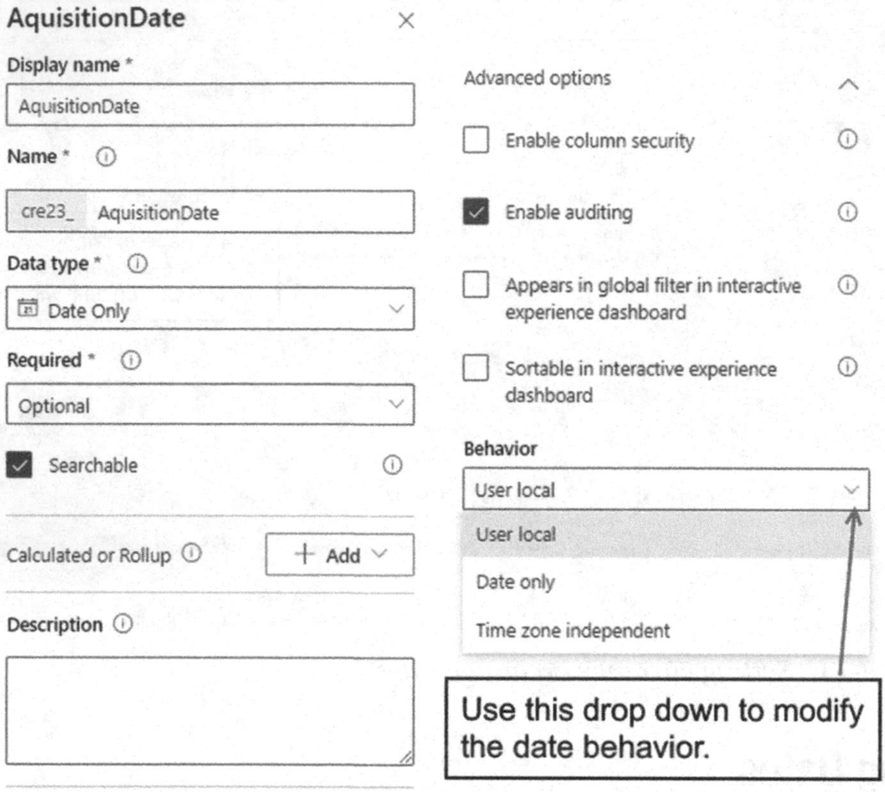

Figure 12-12. *Configuring a date column*

To store a static date, we would choose the time zone–independent option. To store a point in time that is time zone aware, we would choose the user local option.

With the date only data type, there is also a date only behavior type. This option is time zone aware and behaves the same as the user local option. The difference between user local and date only is that the user local setting returns the date with a time of 00:00, whereas the date only option returns the date without a time component. When we build apps with Power Apps, there is very little practical difference between these two behavior types. This setting is mostly useful in scenarios where programmers want to extract data through Dataverse web services.

Storing Autonumbers

A great feature of Dataverse is the autonumber data type. This enables us to generate sequential numbers for each row in a table. This task is often very difficult to carry out with other data sources. Not only can the autonumber data type create sequential numbers but it can also prefix numbers according to rules that we specify.

Three autonumber types are available – string-prefixed number, date-prefixed number, and custom. Figure 12-13 shows the settings that are available with each type.

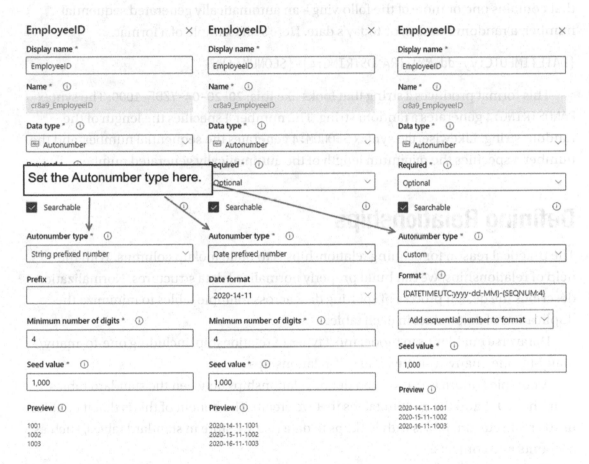

Figure 12-13. *The three available autonumber types*

The simplest autonumber type is the string-prefixed number type. This option prefixes the automatically generated number with string characters of our choice. We can choose to leave the prefix empty if we want to generate a sequential number only.

There are two settings that relate to the automatically generated number. These are the minimum number of digits and the seed value settings.

The "minimum number of digits" setting defines the format of the number. Let's imagine that Dataverse generates an autonumber of 50. With a default minimum number of digits value of 4, the number that Dataverse generates is 0050. The seed value defines the start number for the sequence. The default value of this is 1000, meaning that Dataverse starts numbering records from 1000.

The custom autonumber type is the most configurable. We can build an autonumber that contains one or more of the following – an automatically generated sequential number, a random number, or today's date. Here's an example of a format:

```
{DATETIMEUTC:yy-dd-MM}-{RANDSTRING:4}-{SEQNUM:4}
```

This format produces a string that looks like this: 20-20-04-YZDF-1000. The syntax RANDSTRING:4 generates a random string. The number 4 specifies the length of the random string. Likewise, the syntax SEQNUM:4 generates the sequential number, and the number 4 specifies the minimum length of the automatically generated number.

Defining Relationships

The practical reason for defining relationships is to build lookup columns. With the help of relationships, we can build properly normalized data structures. Normalization describes the design process of splitting data across multiple tables to minimize the duplication of data values in each table.

Dataverse enables us to model most types of relationship, including one-to-many/many-to-one, many-to-many, and self-relationships.

A notable feature is that we can define relationships between the standard tables from the CDM and the custom tables that we create. The benefit of this is that it enables us to create custom tables with lookups to data that we store in standard tables, such as accounts and contacts.

The most common type of relationship is a one-to-many relationship. To illustrate this relationship type, let's consider the following two tables – a property type table and a property table. The property type table stores a list of property types, such as house, apartment, and bungalow. The property table stores the address details of a property and includes a lookup column that specifies the associated property type. Here, we have a one-to-many relationship because for each property type, there can be many related property records.

To implement this type of relationship, we would open the property type table and click the relationship section. From here, we can click the "Add relationship" button to reveal the choices that are shown in Figure 12-14.

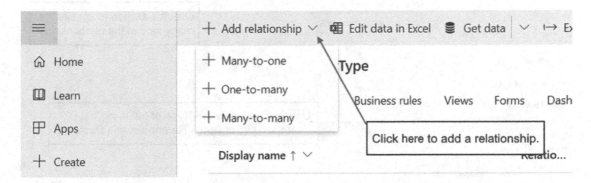

Figure 12-14. Add relationship menu

When we choose the one-to-many option, the designer opens a screen that we use to define our relationship (Figure 12-15). The designer defaults the "Current (One)" side value to the "property type" table.

On the "Related (Many)" side, we would select the property table. This relationship adds a lookup column to the property table that enables the user to select a property type.

The "Lookup column display name" specifies the display name of the lookup column in the property table, and the "Lookup column name" specifies the internal, unique name of the lookup column.

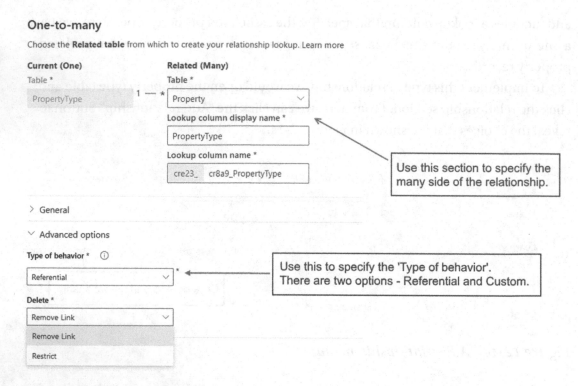

Figure 12-15. *Specifying the relationship settings*

To maintain the referential integrity of our data, we can define the relationship behavior through the "Type of behavior" drop-down. This drop-down provides two options – referential and custom.

The default behavior type is referential. With this option, we can specify the behavior when a user deletes a "property type" record. There are two options that we can set – "Remove Link" or Restrict.

The "Remove Link" means that if a user were to delete a property type record, Dataverse would set the property type lookup column on all associated property records to blank, before deleting the property type record.

With the delete behavior option set to Restrict, Dataverse would prevent a user from deleting a property type record if there are associated property records that refer to the property type.

We can customize the relationship behavior further by setting the behavior type to custom. The custom option enables many other collaboration actions, which are shown in Figure 12-16.

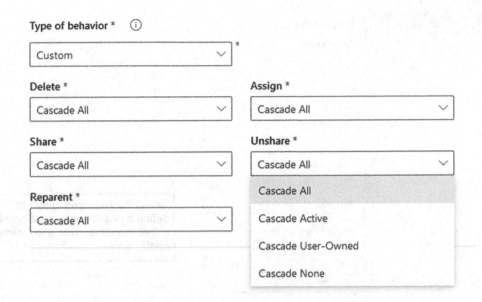

Figure 12-16. *The options that are available with "Type of behavior" set to custom*

When a user performs an action, we can cascade the action throughout all associated child records. Let's take the delete action. With the delete behavior set to "cascade all," when a user deletes a property type record, Dataverse will delete all associated property records before deleting the property type record.

Setting Up a One-to-Many Relationship

Technically, the relationship that we created between the property type and property tables was a (zero or one)-to-many relationship. The reason for this is because users can choose not to enter a property type when they add or edit a property record.

To configure this relationship so that it actually is a one-to-many relationship, we need to edit the property table. From the property type lookup column, we would choose the required option from the Required drop-down to mandate the entry of a property type for each property record, as shown in Figure 12-17.

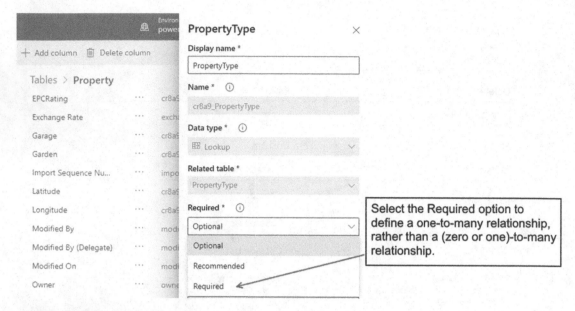

Figure 12-17. *Creating a one-to-many relationship*

Setting Up a Many-to-Many Relationship

Dataverse supports many-to-many relationships. An example of this would be the relationship between a property table and a table that stores the details of property managers. The many-to-many relationship defines a model where a property can be managed by several property managers and, conversely, a property manager can manage many properties.

To define this type of relationship, we would go to the relationship section of the property table, click the "Add relationship" button, and choose the many-to-many option. This opens the screen that is shown in Figure 12-18. In this screen, we use the drop-down on the "Related (Many)" side to select the table that stores the property managers (Employees, in this example).

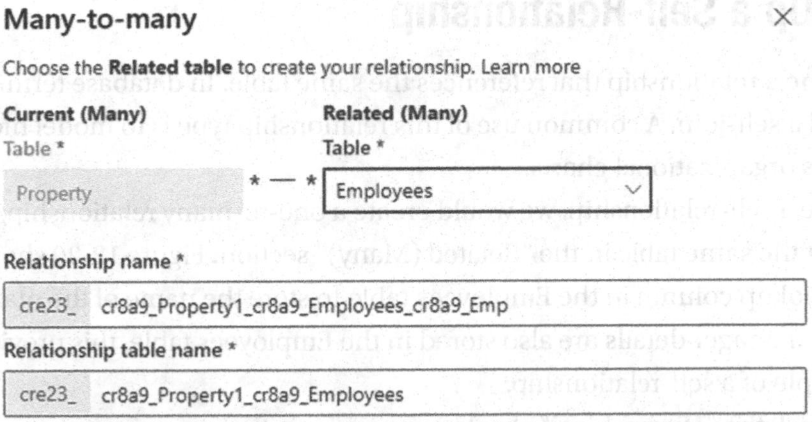

Figure 12-18. *Defining a many-to-many relationship*

To implement a many-to-many relationship, Dataverse needs to create an additional table. In database terms, this would be called an intermediate or a junction table. Each record in this table stores a lookup to a property record and a lookup to an employee record.

The "Relationship table name" specifies the name of this intermediate table. The "Relationship name" identifies this relationship and appears in the relationships view as shown in Figure 12-19.

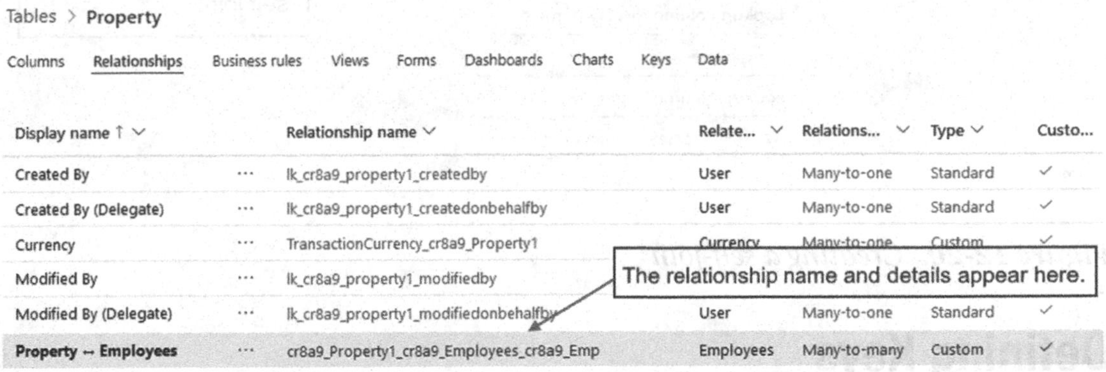

Figure 12-19. *The relationship name*

Setting Up a Self-Relationship

We can define a relationship that references the same table. In database terminology, this is called a self-join. A common use of this relationship type is to model hierarchical data, such as organizational charts.

To create a self-relationship, we would create a one-to-many relationship, and we would select the same table in the "Related (Many)" section. Figure 12-20 shows how to create a lookup column in the Employees table to store the name of the manager. Because the manager details are also stored in the Employees table, this provides a prime example of a self-relationship.

We can tick the "Hierarchical" checkbox to indicate that we are creating a self-join. This option enables additional features such as visualizations and additional query operators. For example, if we were to use the advanced search feature in a model-driven app, we could filter records using the "under" and "not under" operators. This enables users to search for records that are children of/or not children of a given record.

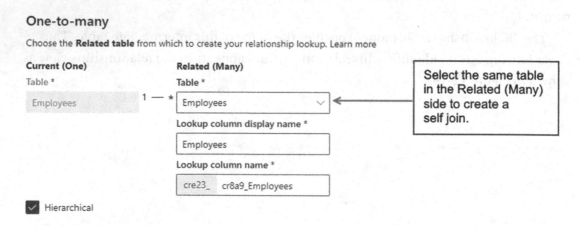

Figure 12-20. *Creating a self-join*

Defining Keys

Keys allow us to enforce unique values for a column or a set of columns. Figure 12-21 shows how to create a key on the Employees table that includes the `EmployeeID` column. Once we create this key, Dataverse will disallow duplicate values in the `EmployeeID` column.

A key can include one or more columns. It's possible to select multiple columns to create a composite key. The columns we can add to a key can include text columns (excluding multiline text columns) and numeric columns. A limitation is that it's not possible to add date columns, calculated columns, or lookup columns to a key.

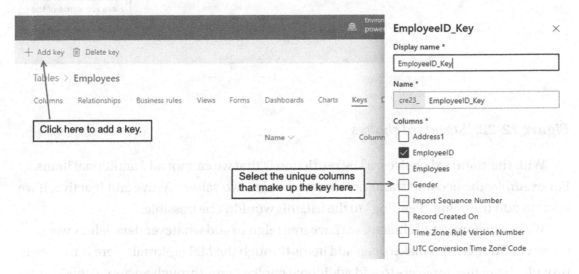

Figure 12-21. *Creating a key*

What happens if we attempt to create a key on a column that contains existing duplicate values? The answer is that Dataverse creates the key, but it won't enforce unique values. This can be very confusing because users can continue to enter duplicate data, and there is no indication in the designer that shows that the key is not active.

Caution   If we create a key on a column that contains existing duplicate values, Dataverse will not enforce unique values in the column.

Choices

Choices (which were previously called option sets) are static lists of data that limit the values that a user can enter into a column. Choices are ideal for generic lists of data that can apply to multiple tables, such as lists of colors, currency codes, or titles.

We can create our own custom choices, or we can use one of the predefined choices that Dataverse offers (Figure 12-22).

Figure 12-22. *Standard choices*

With the standard choices, a key restriction is that we cannot add additional items. For example, the account status option set includes two values: Active and Inactive. If we want to add the value "Pending" to the list, this wouldn't be possible.

With a custom set of choices, we have free reign to add whatever data values we choose. Although app makers can add items through the Maker Portal, there is no way to provide the ability for users to add additional choice items through an app. Therefore, we should only use choices to store static lists of data that are unlikely to change.

It is also not possible to sort the items that appear in a set of choices (e.g., through a drop-down control). Therefore, if we want users to be able to add and sort list items, we should create custom tables for lookup values, rather than use choices.

Creating Sets of Choices

To create a set of choices, we click the "New choice" button to open the pane that's shown in Figure 12-23.

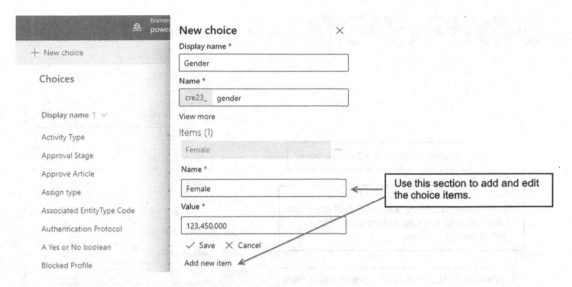

Figure 12-23. *Creating a set of choices*

The top part of this pane enables us to enter a "display name" and name. Beneath the name details, we can enter the items that make up the set of choices. Each choice item consists of a name and value pair.

The name is the value that users see when Power Apps renders a list of choices in a drop-down control. The name value does not need to be unique.

The value is a number that uniquely identifies the item. The designer automatically generates a value for each choice item. It is possible to modify the value if this is necessary, for example, for data integration purposes.

Once we create a set of choices, we can create a table column that is based on those choices (Figure 12-24). From the data type drop-down of the column, we can select the choice or choices data type. The difference between the two is that the choice data type defines a single-value lookup, whereas the choices data type defines a multi-value lookup.

A notable feature is that the choice drop-down from this panel provides the ability to create a new choice. If we choose to create a new set of choices from this section, we create a set of "local choices." Local choices apply only to the associated table and cannot be reused across multiple tables. We should only create local choices if we're certain that the choice items will apply only to a single place.

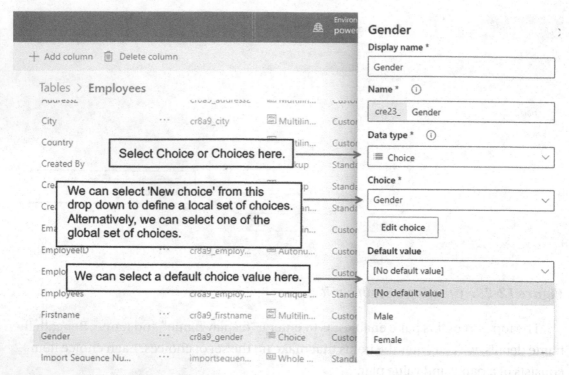

Figure 12-24. *Applying choices to a column*

What happens if we create a record, set a choice value, and subsequently delete the choice item from the set of choices? The answer is that Dataverse does not prevent us from deleting choice items that have been used. In this case, the column that relates to the deleted choice item will display the numeric ID of the deleted item, rather than the item text.

Defining Calculated and Rollup Columns

A powerful feature of Dataverse is the ability to create calculated and rollup columns. Let's find out more about these features.

Creating Calculated Columns

A calculated column is a special column that we add to a table. Unlike a normal column, a calculated column is read-only, and the value of the column derives from a calculation. The calculation can include mathematical, string, or date operators. We can also include conditional operations, such as if-else, greater than/less than, and many more. The calculation can refer to columns from the current table or related parent tables.

Dataverse performs the calculation on the server. This means that if we were to create or edit a record, the calculated value would appear only after we save the record. Some examples of where we could use a calculated column include the following:

- We can create a "full name" column that combines the title, first name, and last name columns in a record. The benefit of building this logic in a calculated column is that it avoids the repetitive job of having to write the same code to do this in all of our apps.

- We can build a calculated column to return a specific value from a lookup column. Again, this promotes the idea of reusability by saving us the task of writing lookup code multiple times in our apps.

- For invoicing apps, we can calculate a total price by multiplying the unit price and quantity columns.

- We can calculate the number of days remaining until some target date.

- Our calculations can include conditions. For an exam table, we can create a calculated column called grade that returns A if the score is greater than 70%, B if the score is between 60 and 70%, and so on.

- We can create a calculated column that converts null numbers to 0. This type of calculated column can be very useful when used in conjunction with rollup columns or when calculating aggregate results. For example, if we calculate the average of a group of records where one record contains a null, the result of this calculation would be null.

To demonstrate how to create a calculated column, let's suppose we have a table of issues. Each issue record includes a create date and a close date value. Here's how to create a calculated column to return the duration of the issue in days.

The first step is to open the issue table and to click the button to add a new column. In the new column panel, the important step is to click the add calculation option (Figure 12-25)

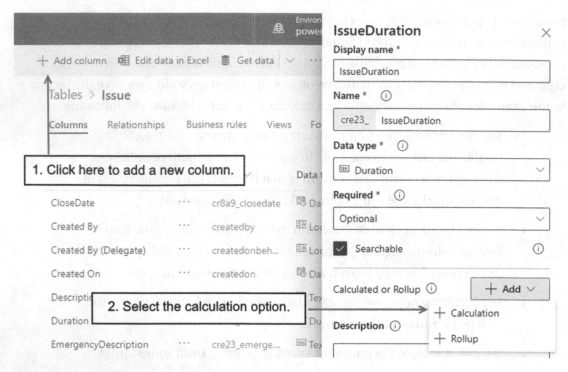

Figure 12-25. Adding a calculated column

This opens the calculated field editor, as shown in Figure 12-26. The top part of this editor enables us to specify an if condition. We can build a condition by selecting a field (i.e., another column in the table) and comparing it with another field or a static value using one of the comparison operators. The supported operators include

```
<, <=, =, >, >=, contains data, does not contain data
```

In the action part of the editor, we can specify the formula that performs our calculation. In this example, the formula would look like this:

```
DIFFINDAYS(cr8a9_closeddate, createdon)
```

To help build our formula, the editor provides IntelliSense that displays all available fields and functions. We can refer to fields in the same table, and we can also refer to lookup fields in the same table.

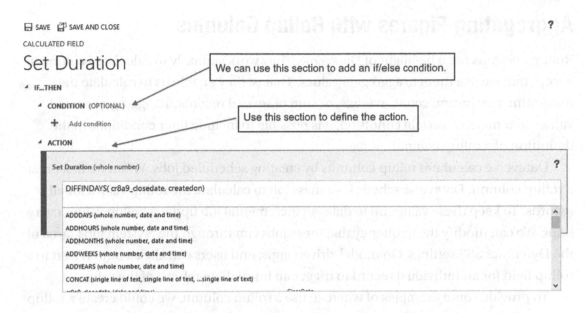

Figure 12-26. *Defining the calculation for a calculated column*

For mathematical calculations, we can apply the standard arithmetic operators such as add, subtract, multiply, and divide (these are +, -, *, /).

For date calculations, we can apply the following date-related functions:

ADDHOURS, ADDDAYS, ADDWEEKS, ADDMONTHS, ADDYEARS, SUBTRACTHOURS, SUBTRACTDAYS, SUBTRACTWEEKS, SUBTRACTMONTHS, SUBTRACTYEARS, DIFFINDAYS, DIFFINHOURS, DIFFINMINUTES, DIFFINMONTHS, DIFFINWEEKS, DIFFINYEARS

For string calculations, the following functions are available:

CONCAT, TRIMLEFT, TRIMRIGHT

Despite the wide range of available functions, there are some calculations that we cannot perform. For example, there is no function to extract parts of a date. There are also no functions to manipulate and to extract parts of a string, nor are there any operators to carry out a "contains"-type check when building an if condition.

Aggregating Figures with Rollup Columns

Rollup columns are a highlight of Dataverse. They work similarly to calculated columns, except that we use them to aggregate values. That is, they enable us to calculate the minimum, maximum, count, average, or sum of several records. To aggregate record values that match a certain condition, it is possible to include filter conditions in the definition of a rollup column.

Dataverse calculates rollup columns by creating scheduled jobs. When we first create a rollup column, Dataverse schedules a mass job to calculate the rollup values for all records. To keep these values up to date, an incremental job updates rollup values every hour. We can modify the frequency that these jobs run through the "system jobs" area of the Dynamics 365 settings. On model-driven apps, end users can click a button next to a rollup field for an individual record to trigger an immediate refresh of the value.

To provide some examples of where to use a rollup column, we could create a rollup column that calculates the total revenue by group, a rollup column to count the number of emails received, or a rollup column to count the total number of open cases.

Rollup columns provide an ideal way to show aggregated values in model-driven and portal apps. This is because these app types lack the formulas that we can use in canvas apps to carry out aggregate calculations.

One reason why rollup columns are powerful is because we can build apps that filter by a rollup column. This allows us to query, for example, records where an average or a sum exceeds some threshold criteria value.

A useful comment about canvas apps is that the Sum, Min, Max, and Avg functions are delegable against Dataverse data sources. This means that we can directly calculate up-to-date aggregate values without resorting to rollup columns.

To demonstrate how to create a rollup column, we'll walk through how to add a rollup column to our property type table. Our column will provide a count of records that match the property type.

The first step is to open our property type table and to click the button to add a new column. In the new column panel, we would click the add rollup option. Once we add our column, we can open the rollup field editor, as shown in Figure 12-27.

Note that at the time of writing, this part of the designer is still being updated to use the new terminology. Therefore, we see the word entity here, rather than table.

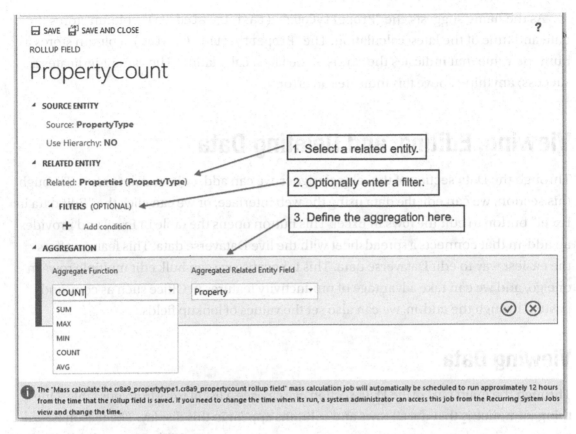

Figure 12-27. Creating a rollup column

The top part of the editor shows the source table (labeled entity). This defaults to "property type," which is the host table on which our rollup column is based.

The next section requires us to choose a related table. Here, we would select the property table. We can also optionally filter the values from this related table.

The aggregation section is the key part that defines the aggregation. In this section, we can use the "Aggregate Function" drop-down to select a function. The available functions are Sum, Max, Min, Count, and Avg. The "Aggregated Related Entity Field" drop-down defines the field where the aggregate function applies. In our example, we would select Count and Property for these two options.

The help text at the bottom of the editor indicates that Dataverse will carry out the initial rollup field population, 12 hours from the time that we save our rollup field.

When we click the save button, Dataverse creates three columns – our "PropertyCount" rollup column, a "PropertyCount (Last Updated On)" column, and a "PropertyCount (Status)" column.

As the name suggests, the "PropertyCount (Last Updated On)" column stores the date and time of the latest calculation. The "PropertyCount (Status)" column stores a numeric value that indicates the status of the latest calculation. The value 1 indicates a success; anything above this indicates an error.

Viewing, Editing, and Deleting Data

Through the Data section of the table designer, we can add, edit, or delete rows. Through this section, we can edit the data using the web interface, or we can click the "Edit data in Excel" button to edit the rows in Excel. This button opens the table in Excel and provides an add-in that connects a spreadsheet with the live Dataverse data. This feature offers the easiest way to edit Dataverse data. This is because we can bulk edit multiple rows in one go, and we can take advantage of productivity features in Office such as copy and paste. Through the add-in, we can also set the values of lookup fields.

Viewing Data

Through the main part of the Data section, we can see a list of rows from our table. One thing we notice is that not all rows and columns appear in this display. The reason is because a view drop-down at the top of the page controls the visible rows and columns, and by default, the active view limits the rows and columns that are shown (Figure 12-28).

Through the view drop-down, we can choose the "All columns" option to display all columns. We can also select one of the other views to display a list of data that includes different visible columns and filter criteria. This is the standard way for lists of data to appear in Dynamics 365 and model-driven apps.

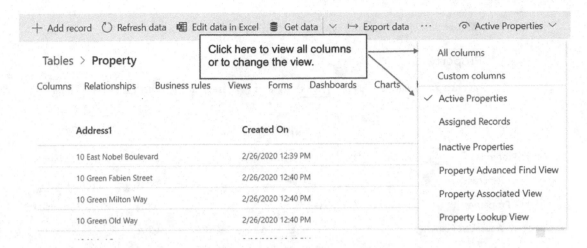

Figure 12-28. Viewing table data

To customize the visible rows and columns in this display, we would create a new view and then use the view drop-down to select the view that we've created.

Managing Views

To manage and create views, we use the Views section of the table designer. The Views section shows a list of views, which are categorized into system and public views.

As Figure 12-29 shows, each table includes views that return the active and inactive rows for a table. All Dataverse tables include an active column, and these views filter the rows based on this column.

+ Add view   ⊞ Edit data in Excel   ⊜ Get data   ⌄   ⟼ Export data   ⊘ Export to data lake   ⌄   ⋯

Tables > **Property**

Columns   Relationships   Business rules   **Views**   Forms   Dashboards   Charts   Keys   Data

Name ↑ ⌄		View type ⌄	Status ⌄	Type ⌄
Active Properties	⋯	Public View Default	Active	Custom
Assigned Records	⋯	Public View	Active	Custom
Inactive Properties	⋯	Public View	Active	Custom
Property Advanced Find View	⋯	Advanced Find View Default	Active	Custom
Property Associated View	⋯	Associated View Default	Active	Custom
Property Lookup View	⋯	Lookup View Default	Active	Custom
Quick Find Active Properties	⋯	Quick Find View Default	Active	Custom

Figure 12-29. *List of default views*

For each table, there are also four system views – the advanced find, associated, lookup, and quick find active views. What exactly are these system views, and where are they used? These system views control the visibility of data in model-driven apps. This will become more obvious when we cover this topic in Chapter 13, but here's a brief summary:

- Advanced find – With Dynamics 365 and model-driven apps, users can access an advanced find feature from the top of the page. The advanced find view controls the columns that are shown using this feature.

- Associated – Where a model-driven app displays a list of child records, the associated view controls the columns that are shown.

- Lookup – This view controls the columns that are shown in a lookup control.

- Quick find – Additional ways in which users can search for records are to use a quick find feature or to type search criteria into a lookup control. The quick find view controls the columns that are shown in these instances.

An important comment is that for canvas apps, the lookup view defines the columns that are available for display through drop-down and combo box controls. Therefore, it is important to add all the columns that we potentially want to display to the lookup view.

Creating a View

To create a new view, we would click the "Add view" button from the Views section of the table designer. This opens the view editor, as shown in Figure 12-30.

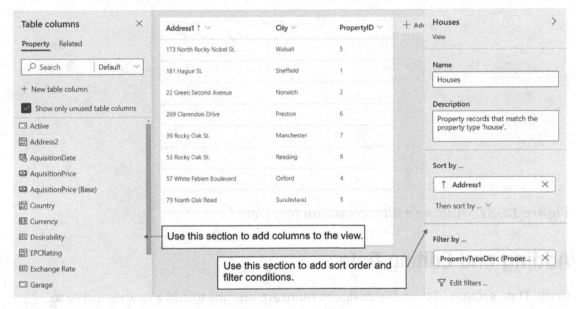

Figure 12-30. *The view editor*

We can use the "Table columns" section to add columns and related lookup columns to a view. We can also set the default column widths and sort orders.

To limit the rows that are shown, we can add a filter to a view. Filters can include columns from the same table or from related lookups.

To demonstrate how to filter by a related lookup, here's how to filter property records that match the property type description "house." The "Edit filters" button opens the editor that is shown in Figure 12-31. Here, we can choose the option to "Add related table." This then provides us with the controls to define an expression to match records where the property type description equals house.

Using the filter editor, we can build powerful filter expressions. It's possible to combine groups of conditions with the "and" and "or" operators. The editor also provides operators that we can use to match fields that contain or do not contain data. This is in addition to all the standard operators that we would expect, such as equals, greater than, less than, and so on.

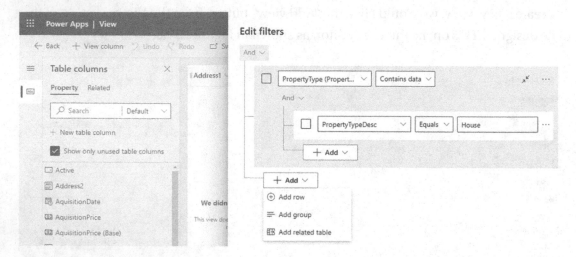

Figure 12-31. *Adding a filter condition to a view*

Adding and Editing Data

In the Data section of the table designer, there are buttons to add a new record or to edit an existing record. These buttons open a data entry form. However, the form that appears will not include all the columns in our table. This is because the data entry screens rely on forms, and the default forms will not include all columns. To enable the entry of specific field values, we will need to modify the main data entry form.

To do this, we would switch to the Forms section of the table designer. In this section, we will see three built-in forms (Figure 12-32).

Tables > **Property**

| Columns | Relationships | Business rules | Views | **Forms** | Dashboards | Charts | Keys | Data |

Name ↑ ∨		Form type ∨	Type ∨
Information	⋯	Main	Custom
Information	⋯	QuickViewForm	Custom
Information	⋯	Card	Custom

Figure 12-32. *The default forms*

Each form is associated with a form type, and there are three types that are available – main, quick view, and card.

The form type that we generally use for data entry is the main form type. With this type of form, we would generally include most of the fields from a table. In comparison, we would configure a card form to display more pertinent fields. A card form is designed for mobile devices, where we want to present a more compact data entry form. The quick view form type provides a template for viewing the details of a lookup field from a child lookup field.

Adding and Modifying Forms

To be able to fully add and edit records from the Data section of a table, we need to modify the main form to include all the columns we want to make available. From the Forms section of the table, we would select the option to edit the main form. This opens the form in the form editor, as shown in Figure 12-33.

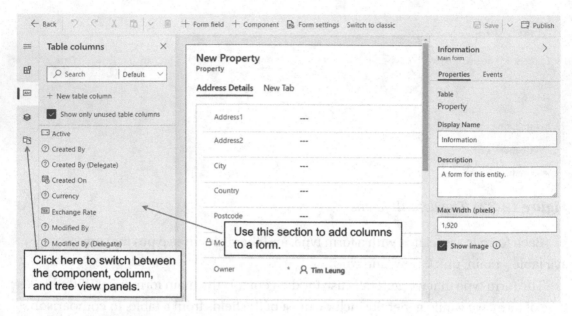

Figure 12-33. *The form designer*

The editor provides a graphical way to build a form. The icons on the leftmost part of the designer toggle the visibility of the components, table columns, and tree view sections.

Through the components section, we can adjust the layout of a form by adding tabs and columns. We can also add controls to enter numbers such as slider and gauge controls. There is also the option to add a subgrid from this section.

The table columns section displays a list of all columns in the table. We use this section to add columns to our form. Finally, the tree view section displays the overall layout of the form. Using the tree view, we can visualize the structural layout of our form. We can select components from the tree view and use the properties pane to configure component-level settings.

These settings make more sense in the context of a model-driven app. Therefore, we'll cover the topic of the form designer in greater detail in Chapter 13.

Summary

Dataverse is a sophisticated cloud-based database and forms a key part of the Power Platform. Dataverse supports canvas apps, and it is mandatory for model-driven and portal apps.

Dataverse databases are connected to environments, and each environment can have a maximum of one database. Of all the data sources, Dataverse is the easiest to connect to because it forms an integral part of the environment. Therefore, there's no need to specify database names or to provide additional authentication details to connect to a Dataverse data source. We can easily connect to a Dataverse database from Power BI or Power Automate, and there is also an API (application programming interface) that programmers can use to access Dataverse data. For business resilience, there is also a native backup mechanism that is built into Dataverse.

The number of licenses defines the amount of storage space, and therefore, it is important to consider the amount of data that we potentially want to store when we choose to use Dataverse.

A feature of Dataverse is that it provides prebuilt data models that we can utilize. As an example, if we want to build a sales or customer service app, the data structures to support those types of app are already there.

With Dataverse, we define tables to store our data. For each table, we can add columns to define the pieces of data to store for each row of data, and Dataverse supports all the common data types that we would expect. In situations where we want each row to include a unique sequential number, Dataverse provides an autonumber data type. We can configure an autonumber field to prefix a date or a set of other characters to the number.

We can define lookup columns by defining relationships between tables or by defining and using choices. Dataverse supports all the common relationship types, including one-to-many, many-to-many, and self-relationships. We can also specify data integrity rules to define what happens we delete or modify the permissions of a parent record. We can choose to cascade deletions or permission changes to all child rows. To maintain data integrity, we can also create keys to define the unique columns in a table.

Rollup columns are extremely powerful because they enable us to aggregate values and to calculate counts, averages, sums, and the minimum and maximum values from sets of rows. These calculations are difficult to carry out with other data sources, due to query delegation limits. A limitation of rollup columns, however, is that they recalculate on a schedule and will not contain up-to-date data.

From Dataverse, we can also define views and data entry forms. A view defines the filters and sort order conditions applied to a list of data. By defining views and forms in Dataverse, we can reuse these objects in multiple apps. This is a great productivity feature because it removes the need to recreate similar items in each app that we create.

Other reusable objects that we can define in Dataverse include dashboards, charts, and business rules. Because these items make more sense in the context of an application, we will cover these topics in subsequent chapters.

CHAPTER 13

Developing Model-Driven Apps

This chapter introduces model-driven apps. These apps are completely different from the canvas apps that we've seen so far. They look and behave completely differently, and they rely on a separate designer that caters specifically for model-driven apps.

The advantage of a model-driven app is that we can quickly build apps that carry out CRUD (Create, Read, Update, Delete) operations against a Dataverse database. The definition of an app lies predominantly in Dataverse. Once we set up a database, it is possible to spend minimal time in the model-driven app designer, because we've already carried out most of the work in the database. These apps rely on Dataverse views to show lists of data and Dataverse forms for data entry. This component-based way of building apps provides far greater reusability, because we can reuse Dataverse objects in multiple apps.

Model-driven apps also offer a wide range of unique and powerful features. In this chapter, we'll find out what we can accomplish using a model-driven app, and we'll walk through the steps to build a simple model-driven app. In addition to covering the basic features, we'll also learn how to take advantage of the more sophisticated features. This includes

- How to use dashboards to display summaries of data

- How to apply validation and how to implement business rules and processes

- How to customize an app through JavaScript and by embedding a canvas app

© Tim Leung 2021
T. Leung, *Beginning Power Apps*, https://doi.org/10.1007/978-1-4842-6683-0_13

Introducing Model-Driven Apps

When app builders begin to investigate model-driven apps, the initial questions can include What does a model-driven app looks like? How do the menus appear? What can we accomplish with these apps, and are there any limitations that we need to take into account? To answer these questions, we'll start by exploring how a model-driven app looks and feels from an end user perspective. This provides the context that enables us to delve into how to build these features.

Demonstration of a Basic App

We'll begin by walking through a basic model-driven app. There are several ways to start a model-driven app. Users can start an app from the Power Apps web portal, from Dynamics 365, or from the mobile app. Model-driven apps are compatible with the mobile Power Apps players on iOS and Android devices.

Each model-driven app has a title, description, and icon. These details appear in the area where a user can start an app. An app can optionally display a welcome or splash screen on start-up (Figure 13-1).

Figure 13-1. *A model-driven app can display a welcome screen*

When a model-driven app loads, the user is presented with the layout that resembles the screenshot in Figure 13-2. This demonstrates the typical appearance of a model-driven app.

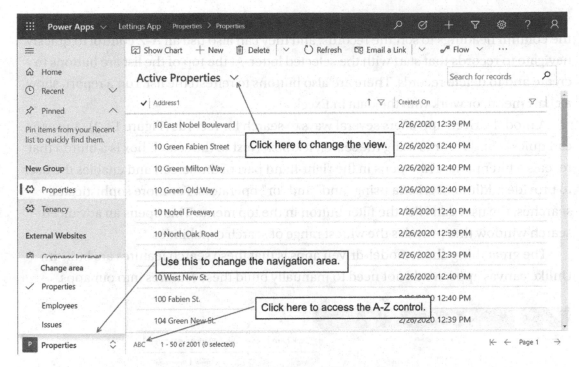

Figure 13-2. *The layout of a typical model-driven app*

The navigation area appears on the left-hand side of the screen. The top of the navigation area contains the built-in menu items Home, Recent, and Pinned. The Home item returns the user to the default start page for the app. In the same way that Microsoft Office keeps track of recently opened documents, model-driven apps keep track of recently opened records. We can access these records through the Recent menu item. For any records that appear in the Recent section, users can pin these records for easy access. Pinned records will appear within the Pinned menu section.

Beneath the built-in menu items, the navigation pane displays app-specific menu items. Most often, these will be links to lists of entities, but they can also include links to dashboards, external websites, and other resources. App builders can organize these menu items by grouping them into areas. The navigation section displays only one area at a time, and users can switch areas using a control at the bottom of the screen.

In typical use, a user will click a link to open a list of records. The list of records will appear in the center section of the screen, and the title of the list will provide a drop-down that enables the user to switch views. As we recall from Chapter 12, a view defines a set of columns and optional filter conditions for a list of entities.

There are several helpful features that are built into the list control. Users can click the column headings to sort the records, and they can also use an A–Z control to quickly navigate to records that start with the selected letter. At the top of the list are buttons to create and to delete records. There are also buttons to refresh the list, run a report, show a chart menu, or work with the data in Excel.

A model-driven app offers several ways to search for records (Figure 13-3). A user can quickly find records using the search textbox. Next to the search box is a button that reveals a filter pane. This opens in the right-hand part of the screen and enables the user to provide additional criteria using "and" and "or" operators. For more sophisticated searches, the user can click the filter button in the top menu. This opens an advanced search window that provides the widest range of search capabilities.

The great thing about model-driven apps is that these search features are built-in. Unlike canvas apps, we do not need to manually build these features into our apps.

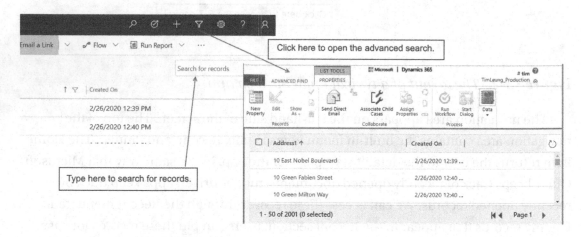

Figure 13-3. *How to search for a record*

Users can open a record from the record list. The record screen enables users to perform a series of actions (Figure 13-4). There is a button to activate or to deactivate a record. Each record includes an active status, and each table includes a built-in view that returns active or inactive records. By marking a record as inactive, we can easily filter out records that are no longer of interest.

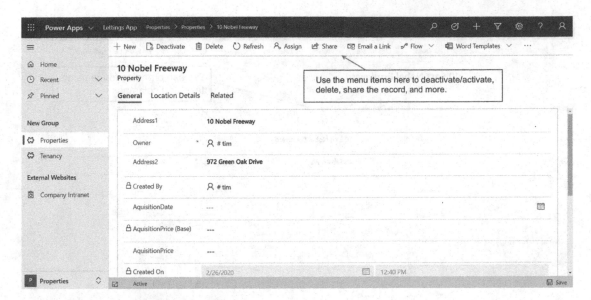

Figure 13-4. *Working with a record*

For collaboration purposes, we can assign records to users. This provides a great way to allocate tasks to users.

A feature of Dataverse is that we can tightly secure records. The share button enables us to configure the access rights of a record.

The "New" button opens a form for data entry (Figure 13-5). We can customize data entry forms with columns, tabs, and custom controls. We'll find out later in this chapter how to do this.

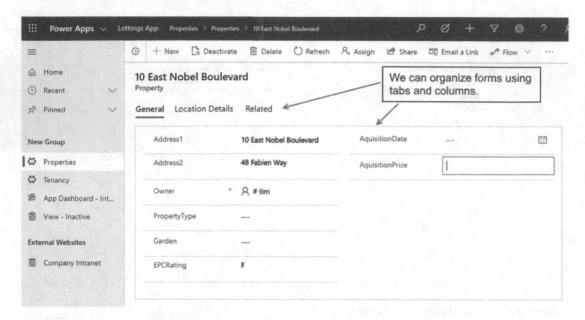

Figure 13-5. Creating or editing a record

A great feature of model-driven apps is that they provide workflow and business process capabilities. There are some situations where a record can have an implied lifecycle, from inception to conclusion. As Figure 13-6 shows, we can use a business process flow to build the UI that separates data entry into multiple steps and to keep track of the duration of each step.

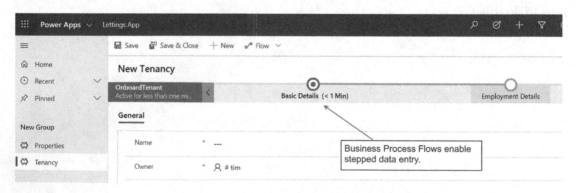

Figure 13-6. Editing a record that is associated with a business process flow

Terminology

As we delve deeper into model-driven apps, we soon discover many new terms and features with generic-sounding names such as flow, business rules, and process. All of this can be very confusing, so here's a high-level summary of these features:

- Business process flow – A business process flow provides the UI that separates data entry and business processes into separate steps. During each step, we can define conditional validation rules.

- Power Automate flow – Power Automate is a separate product in the Power Platform that automates tasks through flows. We can call a flow to access data connections other than Dataverse. We can access resources such as email, send SMS messages via Trello, access local resources through the on-premises gateway, and more.

- Business rules – We create business rules in the Dataverse database. We use these to enforce data constraints and validation. For example, if the status on a record is closed, the close date must be entered. Power Apps applies these rules on the client with JavaScript. This means that they run immediately without requiring a round-trip to the server.

Model-driven apps also expose the powerful workflow capabilities that are available through Dynamics 365. Some of the terms that we will encounter include task flow, workflow, and actions. What exactly are these?

In the context of a business process flow, a task flow defines a smaller task that contributes toward the process.

As an example, let's suppose we create a table that stores the details of sales leads. We can then build a business process flow to structure the data entry of a record, by breaking the main entry form into steps that correlate to milestones. For example, the first step would include initial data gathering such as names and addresses. The final step would be the issuance of a quotation. In this example, a task flow can relate to the entry of record that defines a phone call or a meeting request. Multiple users can run task flows at the same time. This differs from a business process flow, because the stages of a business process flow are common to all users. With a task flow, we can also edit fields from multiple entities, whereas a business process flow relates to a single table.

One reason why task flows are useful is because they appear in the Task Flows section of the header (Figure 13-7). This enables a user to quickly start a task flow, irrespective of which part of a model-driven app they are currently in.

405

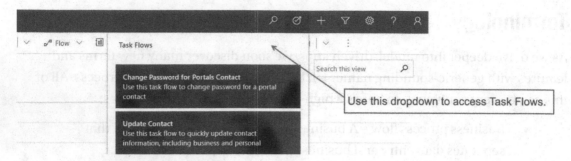

Figure 13-7. *Starting the task flow from the header of a model-driven app*

Another term we should be familiar with is workflow. This is a Dynamics 365 feature that carries out actions such as setting field values or sending emails. Microsoft is set to deprecate workflows, and they recommend that we use Power Automate instead.

The reason it is useful to understand workflows is because many organizations use this feature widely. Workflows can be simpler to set up, and they can be more cost-effective to implement compared to using Power Automate, which charges on a per–flow run basis.

As a final note, it's also useful to point out that Microsoft Flow was the old name for Power Automate. Where this is useful is if we research this topic on the Web and come across some older articles that refer to "Flow."

Creating an App

Now that we understand the basic features of a model-driven app, let's walk through the steps to build a simple app. In this section, we'll identify the parts of the designer that correspond to the features that we've just covered.

To create an app, we navigate to the Apps section in the Maker Portal. From here, we click the "New app" drop-down and select the "Model-driven" option. This opens the screen that's shown in Figure 13-8.

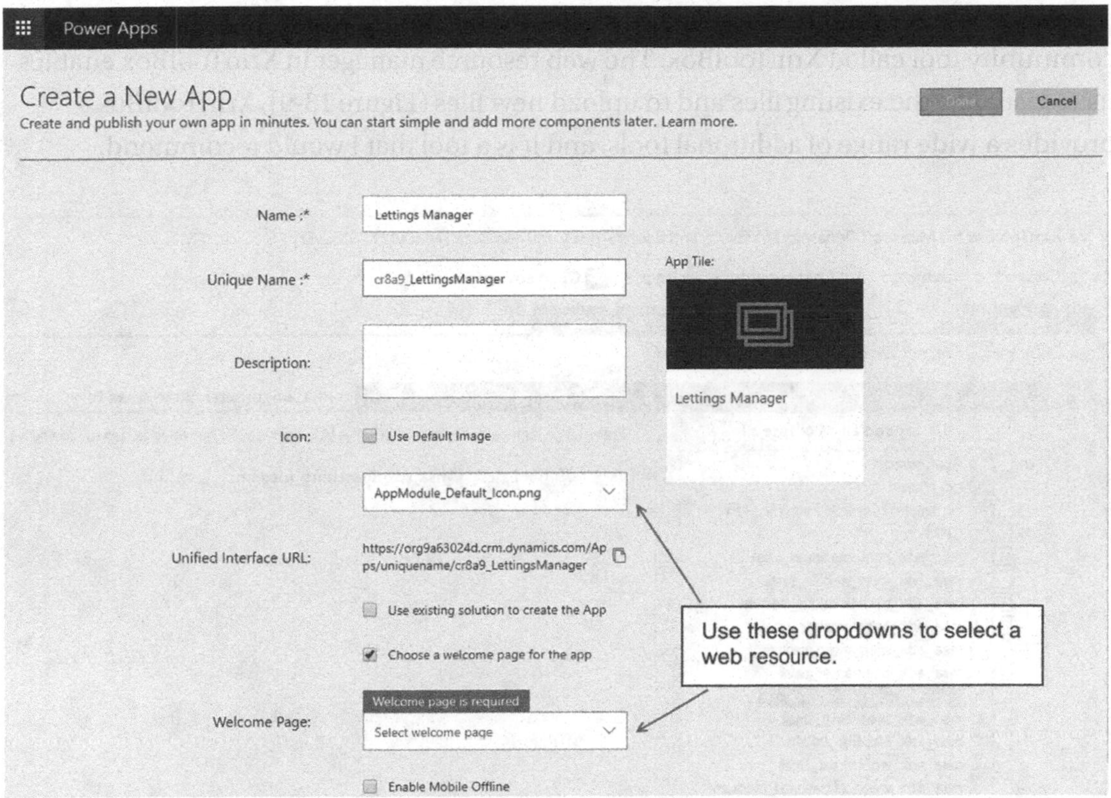

Figure 13-8. *Creating a new model-driven app*

This screen requires us to enter an app name and description. We can also select an icon and choose the option to display a welcome page at the start-up of an app. Unfortunately, it is not a straightforward task to specify an icon or a welcome page.

To set a custom icon or welcome page, the designer provides a drop-down that displays a list of web resources. Web resources are HTML, CSS, JavaScript, and other static files that we can store in the Dataverse database. A unique characteristic of a web resource is that we can retrieve it through a web address.

Uploading Web Resources

If we want to apply a custom icon or welcome page to an app, we must import these files first as web resources. We can then select them for use in our model-driven app.

There are several ways to upload web resources. A simple way is to use a third-party community tool called XrmToolBox. The web resource manager in XrmToolBox enables us to visualize the existing files and to upload new files (Figure 13-9). XrmToolBox provides a wide range of additional tools, and it is a tool that I would recommend.

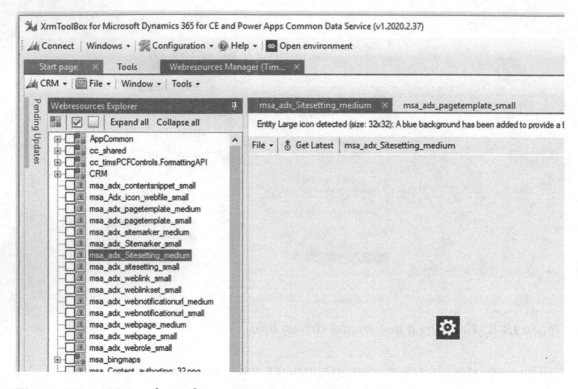

Figure 13-9. *Using the web resource manager*

We can download XrmToolBox from the following website:

www.xrmtoolbox.com/

Exploring the Designer

Once we create an app, the new app will open in the model-driven app designer. Unlike a canvas app, there is not a WYSIWYG designer. Therefore, the initial learning curve can be high. Figure 13-10 shows the appearance of the model-driven app designer.

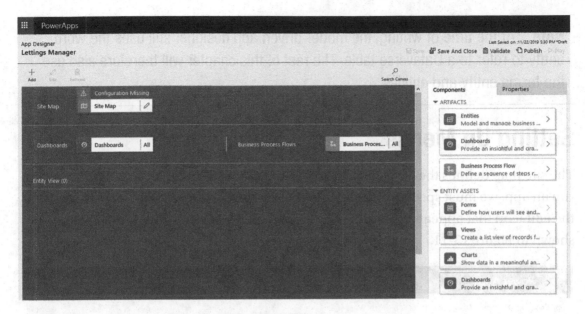

Figure 13-10. *The model-driven app designer*

The central part of the designer is called the canvas. Here's a summary of what appears here:

- Site Map – Each app contains a single site map. This defines the menu items and the entities (i.e., Dataverse tables) for an app.

- Dashboards/Business Process Flows – This section enables us to define and to add dashboards and business process flows to an app.

- Entity View(s) – When we add an entity through the site map, the entity will appear in this section. Here, we can control the views, forms, dashboards, and charts that we want to make available through the app.

The right-hand side of the designer includes two tabs – Components and Properties. The Components pane provides another way to access the objects that appear in the canvas.

The Properties pane enables us to configure our app properties. This mostly includes the settings that we provided when we created our app.

At the top of the designer, there are buttons to save, validate, run, and publish the changes to our app.

Note   At the time of writing, the model-driven app designer still uses the word entity to refer to a Dataverse table. The rest of this chapter will therefore also use the terms entity and entities.

Setting Up Menus

The site map defines the navigation structure and menu items for an app. Before we can run an app, we must specify some items in the site map. To edit the site map, we click the edit icon that appears against the Site Map node. This opens the site map editor as shown in Figure 13-11.

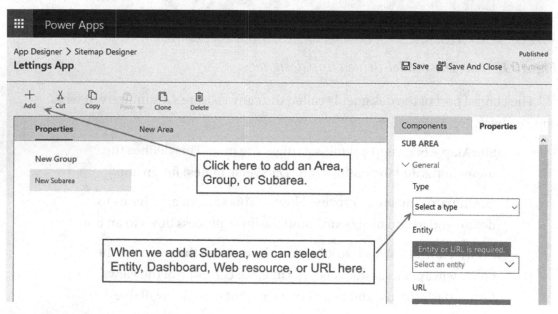

Figure 13-11.   *The site map editor*

There are three components we can add – areas, groups, and subareas. An area defines a top-level grouping. Users can access and switch areas through the Area control in the navigation area. Groups are children of areas, and each area can contain multiple groups. The purpose of a group is to organize and group together subareas. A subarea defines a link in the navigation area, and there are four types we can add – entity, dashboard, web resource, or URL.

To create a link that opens a list of records, we select the entity type and choose the entity that we want to display.

To create a link that opens a web address, we would select the URL type and enter the web address in the URL textbox.

Once we modify the site map, it's important to click the publish button from the site map designer to make our changes live. If we were to click the publish button from the main model-driven app designer, our published app would not include any saved changes that exist in the site map designer.

To change the icon that appears in the navigation panel for an entity, the process is slightly hidden away. From the main part of the designer, we would select the entity from the Artifacts section of the Components panel. This provides an edit link that opens the entity in the "classic" designer (Figure 13-12). From here, we can click the Update icons button to change the icon for the entity.

The "classic" designer enables us to modify settings that are not accessible through the table designer in the Maker Portal. Therefore, the "classic" designer is very useful because it enables us to apply more sophisticated customizations.

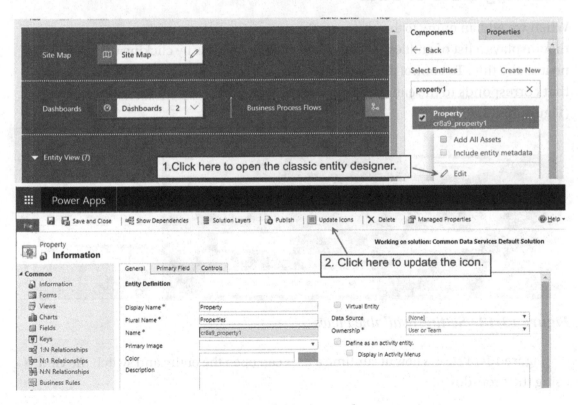

Figure 13-12. *Using the classic entity designer to change an icon*

> **Tip**   We can add links to open a specific view or a form by creating a new subarea and choosing the URL type. We'll find out the exact URL to use later in this chapter.

Working with Data

The great news is that once we add our entity to our site map, we have a working app that enables users to list, search, add, and edit records. As we can see, it takes very little effort to build a functioning app. However, in most cases, we will want to apply further customizations, so we now take a closer look at how to do this.

Showing Lists of Data

When we add an entity to the site map, the navigation link at runtime opens a view that displays a list of entities. The user can change the view by clicking the drop-down next to the title. To control the views that the user can see, we click the views group that corresponds to the entity and choose the views that we want to make visible (Figure 13-13).

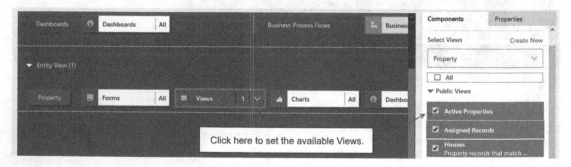

Figure 13-13.   *Setting available views*

Figure 13-14 shows how at runtime a user can open the entity and switch the view using the drop-down.

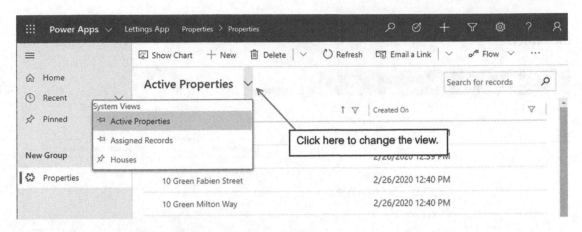

Figure 13-14. *Changing the view at runtime*

Let's look more closely at what happens when a user changes the view. As soon as a user selects a different view, the page refreshes to show the new view. If we examine the address bar of the browser, we notice that the web address includes a query string parameter that specifies the unique view ID.

This is very useful because it provides us with the web address that opens the specific view. If we want to add a navigation link to the site map that opens a view, we can add a subarea to the site map, set the type to URL, and set the address to the relative address that we've discovered here.

Showing Records Assigned to the Current User Only

A common requirement is to show only those records that were created by the current user. To build this feature, we would return to the Dataverse table designer, create a new view, and add a filter condition that filters the "Created By" field by the current user (Figure 13-15). The view designer enables us to filter a field using the "equals current user" and "not equals current user" operators.

We can then save our view and enable this view only in the list of available views for the entity.

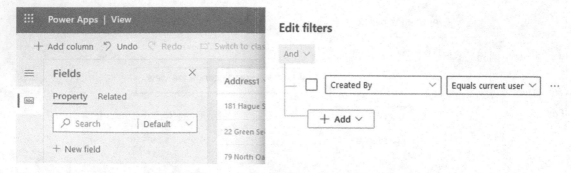

Figure 13-15. *Filtering records by current user*

Creating and Editing Records

To build data entry and edit screens, we define a form in Dataverse and assign it to our app. Chapter 12 introduced the topic of forms, and in this section, we'll cover this topic in more detail. First, we'll look at how to lay out a form. Next, we'll find out how to use and to customize data entry controls. These include controls that enable users to enter text, numbers, and dates.

Laying Out a Form

To examine the form layout options, let's return to the Dataverse designer and open a main form in the editor. The editor provides a tree view that displays the hierarchical view of a form (Figure 13-16). We can use this to select a part of a form, and we can use the "Add Components" button to add sections and tabs.

A section defines an area with a specified number of columns that can house controls. By increasing the number of columns, we can maximize the available screen space by spreading controls across the width of the page.

The fields pane enables us to add fields to a section. Within a section, we can rearrange fields by dragging and dropping the fields in the designer.

A great feature of model-driven apps is that they behave responsively. If we were to run a model-driven app on a phone, the controls would reflow to fit the smaller dimensions of the device. We can test this behavior by using the device selector at the bottom of the designer. If we define a two-column section, we can see that if we change the device to a phone, the design surface will render a single column to better fit the dimensions of the smaller screen.

At the top of the designer are save and publish buttons. To make our form changes visible to all users, it's necessary to click the publish button.

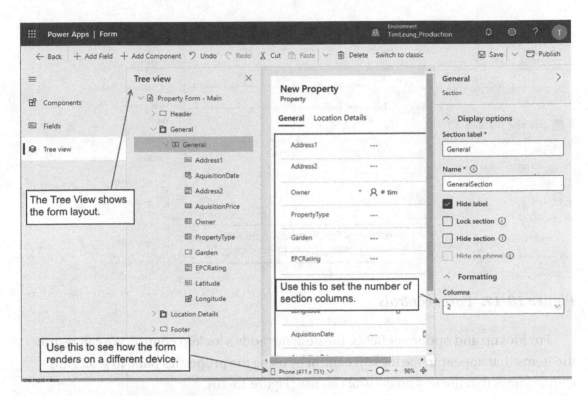

Figure 13-16. Laying out a form

Adding Fields and Components

To add a field, we click the "Add field" button to show the available fields in the fields panel. From here, we can drag a field onto the design canvas. When we add a field, the designer chooses the most appropriate control for the field. For example, it adds a text input control for text fields and a date picker control for date fields.

To make a field read-only, we check the Read-only field checkbox. With this option checked, the form displays the field value in a label instead of an editable control, such as a text input control (Figure 13-17).

Notice how there is a "Lock field" checkbox, in addition to a "Read-only field" checkbox. What is the difference between these two settings? The "Read-only field" setting applies at runtime to make a field non-editable. The "Lock field" setting applies to the designer. With this setting enabled, we cannot delete the field from the design canvas until we unlock the field. To prevent accidental deletions, we can also lock entire sections of a form.

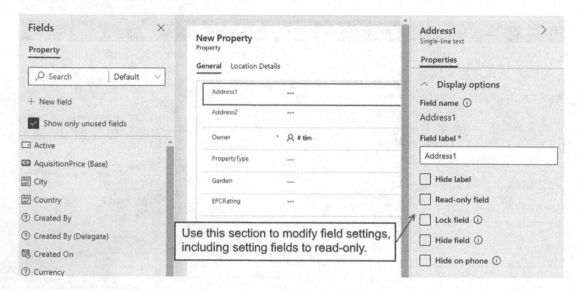

Figure 13-17. *Form controls*

For lookup and option set fields, the designer adds a lookup control. We can restrict the items that appear in the lookup control by using the properties pane to select the source views that the lookup control can use (Figure 13-18).

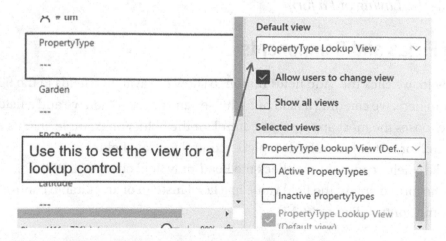

Figure 13-18. *Configuring the views for a lookup control*

A great way to improve the presentation of an app is to display numeric fields using the graphical controls that are available. From the Components pane, we can select a wide range of controls including gauge, slider, and knob-type controls (Figure 13-19). All these controls are compatible with the whole number, currency, floating point, and decimal data types. The one exception is the flip switch control. This control works only with the "Yes/No" data type.

When we drag one of these graphical controls onto the canvas, a panel opens which prompts us to select the field that we want to bind. We can also specify additional properties, such as the minimum and maximum permissible values.

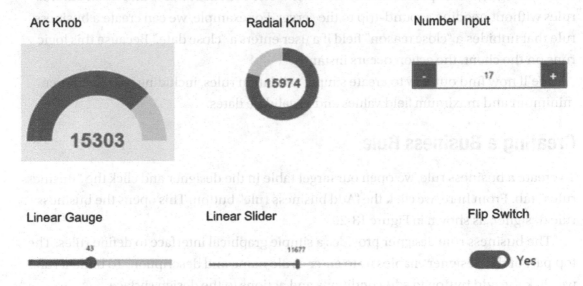

Figure 13-19. Other available components

Another visual control we can add is the website preview control. This works against URL data fields and renders a thumbnail, visual preview of a website.

To display related data, there are two controls we can use – a quick view control and a subgrid control. The quick view control displays a summary of a lookup field, and the subgrid control displays a list of related child records.

Validating Data

To prevent users from filling our databases with nonsense data, validation plays a key role in app design. The preferred way to define validation rules is through business rules. These are objects that enforce data constraints and validation rules. In keeping with good practice, business rules belong in the Dataverse database. This allows us to define rules in a single place, which can be reused by multiple apps.

Business rules are very powerful. In addition to enforcing simple validation rules, they also provide the capability to lock or to hide fields. Power Apps applies business rules through JavaScript that runs on the client. The benefit of this is that it can enforce rules without needing a round-trip to the server. For example, we can create a business rule that unhides a "close reason" field if a user enters a "close date." Because this logic runs on the client, the action occurs instantly.

We'll now find out how to create simple validation rules, including how to enforce minimum and maximum field values and to validate dates.

Creating a Business Rule

To create a business rule, we open our target table in the designer and click the "Business rules" tab. From here, we click the "Add business rule" button. This opens the business rule designer, as shown in Figure 13-20.

The business rule designer provides a simple graphical interface to define rules. The top part of the designer enables us to enter a rule name and description. To build a rule, we click the add button to add conditions and actions to the design surface.

A feature of a business rule is that it can apply to all records in an entity or only the records that the user enters on a specific form. We can use the scope drop-down from the top toolbar to define where we want the rule to apply. The lower section of the designer provides a text view that summarizes the conditions and actions that make up a rule.

Once we finish defining a business rule, the rule will not apply until we click the Activate button at the top of the designer.

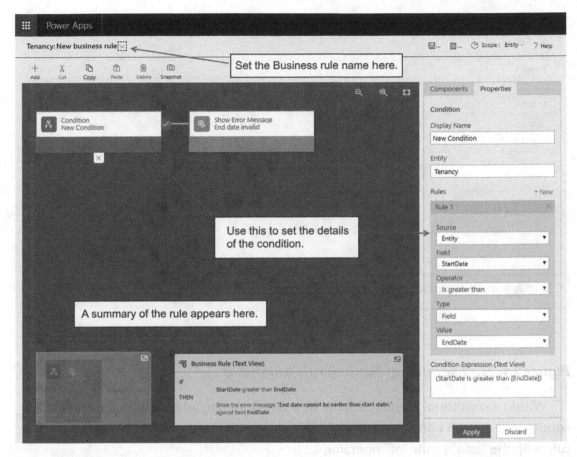

Figure 13-20. Creating a business rule

To illustrate a simple business rule, here's to create a rule that prevents the user from entering an "end date" that is earlier than the "start date." The first step is to add a condition to the design surface. The condition component enables us to select an entity and a field.

The designer presents a choice of operators which include all the common string and arithmetical operators that we would expect.

The type drop-down enables us to select the target of our condition. There are three available options – field, value, or formula. Figure 13-21 shows example conditions using these three different types. In our example, we can build the condition "EndDate is greater than or equal to StartDate."

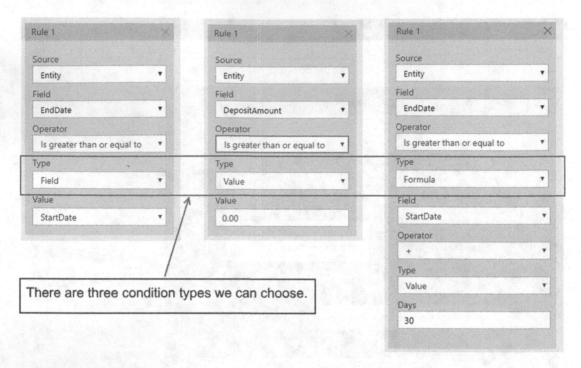

Figure 13-21. Examples of business rule conditions

Within a condition, we can click the New rule button to add additional rules to the condition. For each additional rule, a "rule logic" setting controls whether to append the rule with the "and" or the "or" operator.

Once we define a condition, we can attach an action or an additional condition to the success or failure of the condition.

To attach an action to the success of a condition, we click the "tick" symbol next to the condition and click the add button to add an action. The add menu will provide a choice of seven action types that we can add. This includes

- Recommendation – This displays a message to the user.

- Lock/unlock – This makes a field read-only or editable (for the avoidance of any doubt, this term differs from the form designer, where locking a field prevents the deletion of the field at design time).

- Show error message – This displays an error message and blocks the user from saving a record.

- Set field value – This sets the value of a field to a static value. We can set the value to an empty string if we want to clear the value of a field.

- Set default value – This specifies the value that appears when a record loads. A common application of this action is to specify the default value of a lookup field.

- Set business required – This sets a field as mandatory or optional.

- Set visibility – This shows or hides a field.

Figure 13-22 illustrates these action types and highlights how we can use the properties pane to configure the settings that are associated with an action.

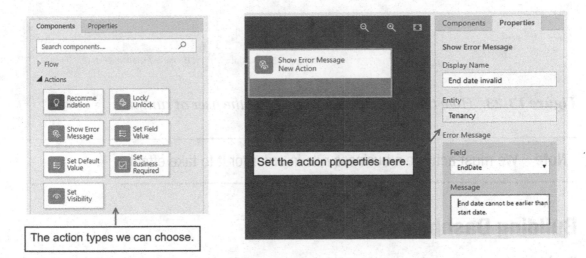

Figure 13-22. *Defining a business rule action*

With the show error message action in this example, an error message will appear if a user attempts to set an end date that is earlier than the start date.

To apply our business rule, we need to save and to activate our rule. Figure 13-23 shows the effect of this rule at runtime when we enter an end date that is earlier than the start date.

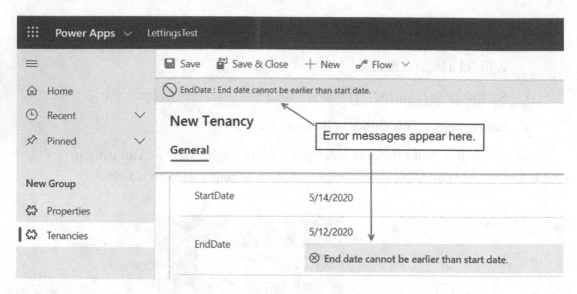

Figure 13-23. *How the error message appears to the user at runtime*

Note   We must activate a business rule in order for it to take effect.

Building Dashboards

Dashboards are a great feature of model-driven apps. They provide an attractive and graphical way to present overviews and summaries of data. A dashboard can include lists of data, charts, and snapshots of data that are pertinent to a user.

There are two types of dashboard that we can create – an application-level or an entity-level dashboard. An application-level dashboard can summarize data from multiple entities, whereas an entity-level dashboard can display only data that is associated with the entity.

Power Apps stores both types of dashboard in Dataverse, which makes it possible to reuse dashboards across multiple model-driven apps.

Creating a Dashboard

To create an application-level dashboard, we can select the dashboard item from the design surface of the model-driven app designer or select dashboards from the Artifacts section of the Components pane. From the Components pane, we can click the "Create New" link. This opens a flyout with the option to create one of two dashboard types – a classic dashboard or an interactive dashboard (Figure 13-24).

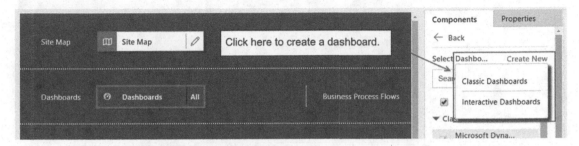

Figure 13-24. *Creating a dashboard*

The difference between these two dashboard types is that a classic dashboard displays one or more components, such as a chart or a list.

As the name implies, an interactive dashboard offers an interactive experience and provides more than a static snapshot of data. A typical interactive dashboard shows a primary list of data that is filtered by date or status. For example, this might be the number of open cases that were created this week. A user can click an item to update charts and other lists on the dashboard, thereby creating an interactive experience.

Creating a Classic Dashboard

When we choose the option to create a classic dashboard, the initial dialog prompts us to select a layout. Here, we can specify the structure of the rows and columns that make up the dashboard. Figure 13-25 shows the appearance of the designer when we select the default three-column regular dashboard layout.

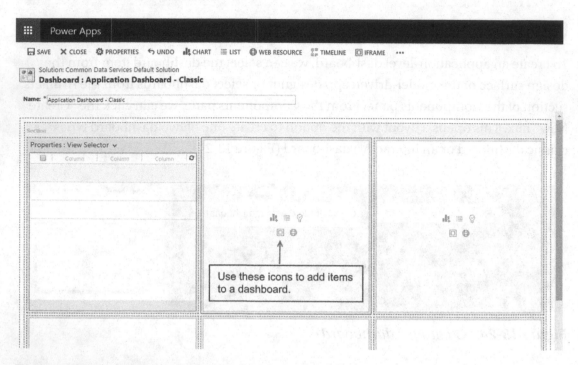

Figure 13-25. *Creating a classic dashboard*

For each cell in a layout, we can click an icon to add a chart, a list, an assistant, an iframe, or a web resource.

The list component displays a list of entities based on a view. The assistant component integrates with Dynamics 365 data and displays notifications such as accounts that are becoming inactive, messages that await a reply, or opportunities nearing a close date. The iframe component enables us to embed links to web pages.

Creating an Interactive Dashboard

When we choose the option to create an interactive dashboard, the designer also prompts us to choose a layout. In addition to specifying the number of columns, we can select one of two layout types – a multi-stream layout or single-stream layout (Figure 13-26). A stream is another word that defines a list of data.

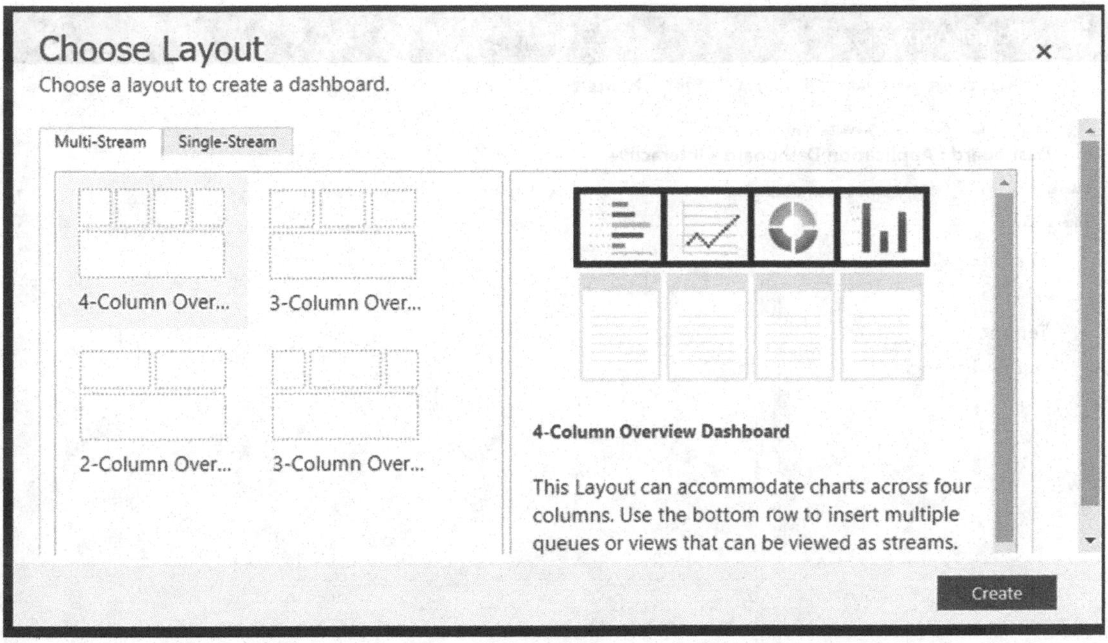

Figure 13-26. *Creating a multi-stream or single-stream dashboard*

A multi-stream dashboard usually includes multiple views from one or more entities. A typical layout is to show charts across the top row of the dashboard and to include cells in the bottom row that display the details of the selected item in the top row.

A single-stream dashboard provides a more focused view of data. This type of dashboard displays a stream of data along the left-hand side and visual charts and tiles on the right-hand side.

Figure 13-27 shows the appearance of the interactive dashboard designer for single-stream layout. The top section prompts us to enter an entity, a date field to filter by, and the time frame. This highlights how dashboards are appropriate for displaying data with a date and time dimension. The entity that we choose will appear as a stream on the left-hand side. To the right of the stream, we can select charts and tiles.

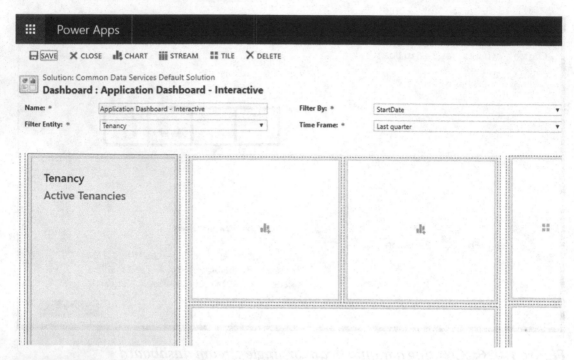

Figure 13-27. *The interactive dashboard designer*

Once we define a dashboard, we need to add a subarea in the site map to enable the user to view the dashboard. At this stage, we can publish our app and view our dashboard.

Creating an Entity Dashboard

To create an entity-specific dashboard, we would open the entity in the designer and click the "Add Dashboard" button from the Dashboard tab.

Entity-specific dashboards behave just like a multi-stream dashboard, except that the data source for a stream can derive only from the single entity. The design process for an entity-specific dashboard follows the same process as we've just covered.

Building Business Process Flows

Business process flows separate data entry into a series of steps, each of which corresponds to a milestone. The data entry screen shows the stages in the business process flow, which provides an indication as to how far through the record is in the process. A feature of a business process flow is that it keeps track of the duration of each stage. This can be very useful for monitoring purposes.

To demonstrate a business process flow, let's imagine we create an entity to store tenancy details. The information we store in this entity includes the property, tenant details, rental amounts, and tenancy dates. To onboard a tenant, we can build a business process flow that separates the process into the following steps:

- Basic details – At this stage, we collect the property, tenant, and rental details.

- Employment details – At this stage, we collect employment details and references.

- Financial – At this stage, we collect income and credit referencing details.

- Onboarding – At this stage, we collect contractual and inventory details.

To build this business process flow, we would click the "Create New" link from the business process flow area of the Components pane in the model-driven app designer. This opens the business process flow editor. This editor provides a graphical way to define a business process flow, and we can start by adding stages to the design surface, as shown in Figure 13-28.

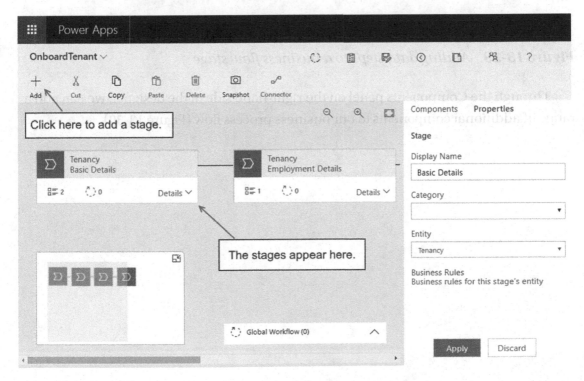

Figure 13-28. *The business process flow editor*

Looking at the first stage of this business process flow, the steps to complete this stage are to collect the tenant, property, and rental figures. To build this step, we would select the Components panel on the right-hand side of the designer and use this to add three data steps to the first stage. A data step defines a field that we want to enable. We can make a field mandatory by checking the required checkbox (Figure 13-29).

At each stage, we can optionally attach business rules. This allows us to apply more complex validation and data rules.

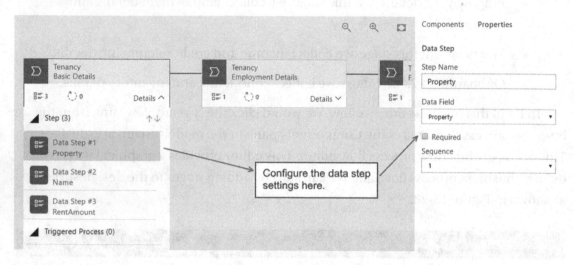

Figure 13-29. *Adding data steps to a business flow stage*

Through the Components panel on the right-hand side of the designer, we can add a range of additional components to our business process flow (Figure 13-30).

Figure 13-30. *Adding components to a business flow*

A notable item is the condition component. This component enables us to implement branching logic, and it operates in the same way as the condition component in the business rule editor. We can compare a field against another field, a static value, or a formula.

We can also attach a workflow, action step, or flow step to a stage. Because workflows will be deprecated, a flow step is the most appropriate out of these options. With a flow step, we can send emails and carry out other steps outside of the model-driven app.

Figure 13-31 shows the appearance of the first step at runtime. A notable feature is the process drop-down in the toolbar. This enables the end user to abandon the business process flow or to switch to a different business process flow. For example, we may have another business process flow on the tenancy entity called "terminate tenancy." The Switch Process option enables the user to switch to a different process.

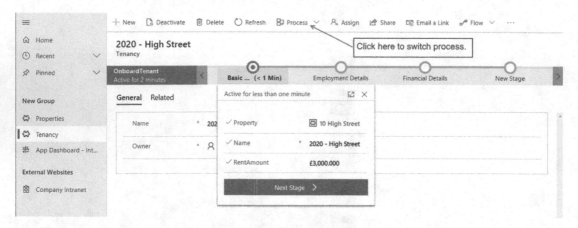

Figure 13-31. *The business process flow at runtime*

Customizing a Model-Driven App

By this point, the limitations of what we can achieve using the graphical designers are apparent. The forms in a model-driven app impose a rigid layout that is difficult to customize. There is no support for data sources other than Dataverse, and there is no programming language that we can use to carry out mathematical calculations or more complex logic. These limitations can prevent us from adding crucial features to an app. Is there some way to overcome these limitations? In answer to this question, there are two broad approaches to customize a model-driven app.

The first method is to embed a canvas app. This provides a simple way to customize a form with minimal code. The second method is to write custom JavaScript. This offers a more powerful approach; however, the complexity is far greater, and it requires basic skills in JavaScript and web design. We'll now cover both of these techniques.

Embedded Canvas Apps: Overview

The simplest way to customize a model-driven app is to embed a canvas app. We can do this entirely though the graphical designers without needing to write any code. What exactly can we accomplish with this technique?

Starting with simple features, we can add static text labels and format sections with different colors and font styles. This can be very helpful because with a model-driven app, even the simple task of displaying additional labels and help text is difficult.

Using this method, we can embellish our apps with the wide range of canvas controls, including the image, barcode, audio, and video controls.

An embedded canvas app provides access to formulas. We can use these to perform mathematical calculations, manipulate strings, or help enforce more complex validation constructs, such as matching the format of input values with regular expressions.

An embedded canvas app provides a simple way to display non-Dataverse data. We can use this technique to display SharePoint data, data from internal databases using the on-premises gateway, or data from any of the 300 or so connectors that are available.

Through an integration control, an embedded canvas app can communicate with a host model-driven app to provide a tighter, more joined-up experience.

Despite these benefits, a small disadvantage of this technique is that presentation of the embedded app doesn't look entirely seamless. The canvas app takes slightly more time to load, and the spinning wait icon will appear as this happens.

In the following section, we'll find out how to embed a canvas app onto a model-driven form. We'll embed a canvas app that displays the longitude and latitude values from a property record. This can act as a starting point for further extensibility. For example, we can later extend this canvas app to display a map using techniques that we'll cover in Chapter 18.

Unfortunately, embedding a canvas app isn't a simple case of dragging a canvas app component onto a form and providing the ID of a canvas app. It's a slightly more involved process.

If we think back to how the model-driven app form designer works, we build a form by dragging fields from the fields panel onto the design surface. Therefore, we must first associate a canvas control with an entity field in order to fit this design paradigm. Once we do this, we can drag an entity field onto a form and use the canvas app control to display our embedded canvas app. We'll now walk through the steps to carry out this task, which are as follows:

- 1 – Open the form with the classic designer.

- 2 – Choose a field to associate with a canvas control.

- 3 – Create a canvas app and associate it with the canvas control.

- 4 – Develop and integrate the canvas app with the host model-driven app form.

Designing a Form with the Classic Designer

The first step is to open our model-driven app form in the classic designer. This is necessary because the standard form designer lacks many of the advanced settings. To open the classic designer, we open our property table, switch to the Forms tab, and open our main form. In the header of the form designer, we can click the button to switch to classic view (Figure 13-32).

Figure 13-32. *Opening a form in the classic designer*

The classic form designer is very useful because it enables us to perform advanced form customizations. We will revisit the classic form designer in several other areas of this book.

Associating a Form Field with a Canvas App Control

The next step is to associate a form field with a canvas app control. It's important to choose a field that always contains data. If we choose a field that can optionally contain data, the canvas app will not refresh properly when a user changes data values on the host form. In our example, the PropertyID field provides a good candidate because it is a key field that always contains data.

The Field properties dialog is the place where we make advanced customizations to a form field. This dialog enables us to modify display, formatting, and business rule settings. It is also the place where we associate control events with custom JavaScript, which we will cover in the next section. We open this dialog by selecting a field (PropertyID, in this example) and by clicking the "Change Properties" button in the ribbon bar (Figure 13-33).

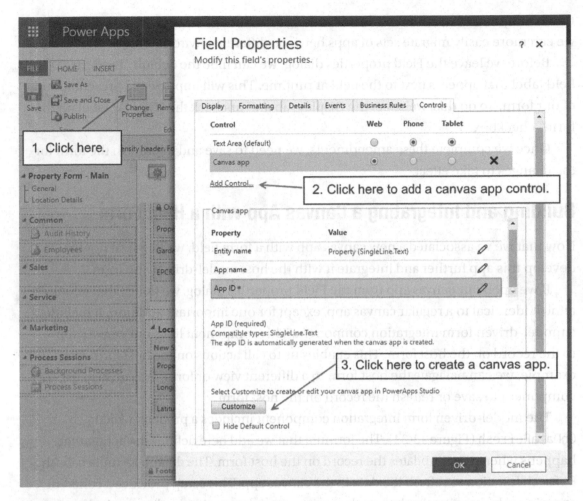

Figure 13-33. *Customizing a form field*

To associate a canvas app control with a field, we select the Controls tab and click the "Add Control" button to add a canvas app control.

Once we add a canvas app control, we can associate it with a canvas app by clicking the "Customize" button. This button creates a new canvas app and links it to the canvas app control, using the app name and app ID values as the identifier.

Let's take a closer look at how this linkage works. At runtime, the canvas app control first attempts to embed a canvas app that matches the app name setting. If it fails to find an app with a matching name, it then attempts to find an app that matches the app ID.

This behavior caters for situations where we build a set of model-driven and canvas apps in a development environment. When we move these apps to a live environment, the app ID of the new canvas app will not match the app ID of the canvas original app in the development environment. By associating a canvas app control with an app name, we can more easily migrate sets of apps between different environments.

Before we leave the Field properties dialog, we can hide the default "Property ID" field label that appears next to the field at runtime. This will improve the presentation of our form. To do this, we select the Display tab and uncheck the "Display label on the form" checkbox.

Once we complete these amendments, we need to save and to publish the form for the changes to take effect.

Building and Integrating a Canvas App with a Host Form

Now that we've associated a new canvas app with a form field, we'll look at how to develop this app further and integrate it with the host model-driven app form.

If we open our canvas app from the Field properties dialog, we notice that it looks almost identical to a regular canvas app, except for one important addition. It includes a model-driven form integration component. This component links our canvas app to the record on the host form. This enables us to call actions on the host form. For example, we can navigate the host form to a different view or form. We can also use this component to save or refresh the record on the host form.

The model-driven form integration component includes a property called OnDataRefresh (Figure 13-34). The formula that we add here defines the action that happens when a user updates the record on the host form. The default formula calls the Refresh function to refresh the data in the canvas app. This setup provides a coherent experience by keeping the data on the canvas app in sync with the data on the host form.

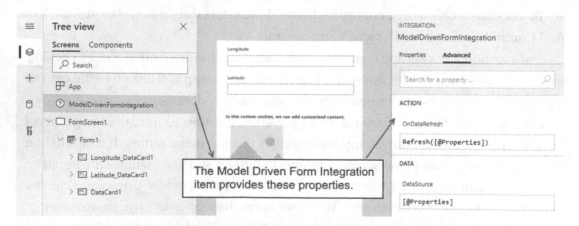

Figure 13-34. *The model-driven form integration control*

The canvas app includes a screen with a form control. A notable thing about this form is that the value of the Item property is set to ModelDrivenFormIntegration.Item. This configures the record on the form to match the record on the host model-driven app form (Figure 13-35).

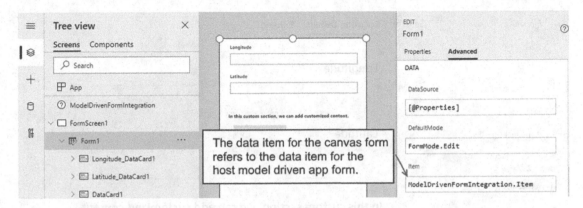

Figure 13-35. *Linking a canvas form to the current record on the host form*

In this example, we'll add the longitude and latitude fields to the form, and we'll add some additional static labels and content. Once we complete our changes, we can save our canvas app and run our model-driven app. Figure 13-36 shows the appearance of our embedded canvas app at runtime.

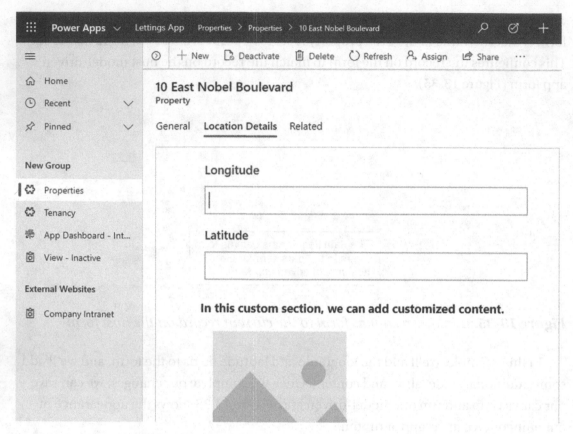

Figure 13-36. *The embedded app at runtime*

Performing Actions on the Host Form

When we run our app, the data in the canvas app keeps in sync with any data changes in the host form. The formula in the OnDataRefresh property of the "model-driven form integration component" refreshes the canvas app whenever a data change occurs in the host form.

This integration, however, does not work in the opposite direction. To configure our host form to recognize data changes that we make in the canvas app, we can add a formula to save the record and to refresh the host form. We can attach this formula to a button or to the OnChange property of a data entry control, as shown in Figure 13-37.

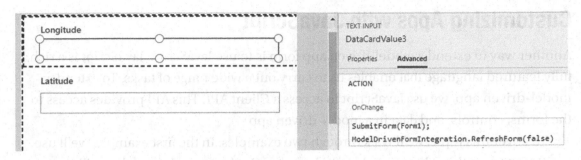

Figure 13-37. *Saving and refreshing the host form*

This formula calls the SubmitForm function to save the record and calls the RefreshForm method on the "model-driven form integration component" to refresh the host form.

The "model-driven form integration component" enables us to perform a range of actions on the host form. Table 13-1 shows some example usage of the methods that we can call on the ModelDrivenFormIntegration object.

Table 13-1. *Performing actions on the host form*

Method	Description

NavigateToMainForm(
  "cr8a9_property",
  "Property - Main",
  "94ad780a-9558-ea11-
  a811-000d3a31ed8d"
)
	This navigates the host form to a main form and displays a record that matches the specified record ID. This method requires us to pass the logical entity name, a form name, and a record ID.

NavigateToView(
  "cr8a9_property",
  "Assigned Records"
)
	This navigates the host form to the specified view. This method requires us to pass a logical entity name and the view name.

OpenQuickCreateForm("cr8a9_property")	This opens the quick create form for the specified entity.
SaveForm()	This saves the record on the host form.
RefreshForm(false)	This refreshes the host form. The argument we pass to this method specifies whether to display a confirmation prompt to the user before saving any unsaved data on the host form.

Customizing Apps with JavaScript

Another way to extend a model-driven app form is to use JavaScript. JavaScript is a rich, fully featured language that enables us to carry out a wide range of tasks. To extend a model-driven app, we use JavaScript to access a Client API. This API provides access to the forms, controls, and data in a model-driven app.

To cover this topic, we'll walk through two examples. In the first example, we'll use JavaScript to set the value of a field to today's date. In the second example, we'll use JavaScript to apply a validation rule that prevents a user from entering an input date that is greater than today's date.

Before we use JavaScript, the best practice is to always try to use business rules, business process flows, or some other no code processes in the first instance.

With the examples that we cover, the business rule and business process flow designers cannot fulfil these tasks. This is because they lack a programming language and lack the ability to call a function that returns today's date. Therefore, JavaScript is an ideal candidate for this task and for any requirement that requires computational logic of any complexity.

Custom JavaScript applies to forms, and here is a summary of the steps to customize a form with code:

- 1 – We write JavaScript functions to carry out the task. Our code can call the Client API to retrieve data values and to access the objects on the host form.

- 2 – We upload our JavaScript functions into our app as a web resource.

- 3 – We use the form designer to attach our JavaScript functions to form events, such as the load event of a form or the change event of a control.

Client API: Overview

Before we delve into our example, it's important to first cover the Client API. The Client API is essential because it enables us to reference the host form and to retrieve data. Therefore, the purpose of this initial section is to provide a reference to properties and methods that we'll use later.

From JavaScript, we can access the following top-level objects of the Client API:

- executionContext – This represents the JavaScript "environment" of the running app.

- formContext – This provides a reference to a form.

- gridContext – This provides a reference to a grid or a subgrid component.

- Xrm – This provides access to other operations that are not related to a form, grid, or data item.

The executionContext object provides access to the environment where our code runs. This object is most useful because it enables us to retrieve a formContext object with the following code:

```
executionContext.getFormContext()
```

The formContext object is a core object that facilitates JavaScript customization. Figure 13-38 shows a screenshot from the online documentation. The purpose of this is to illustrate the far-reaching scope and capabilities of this object. It enables us to access data, UI, business process flows, navigation items, tabs, and much more.

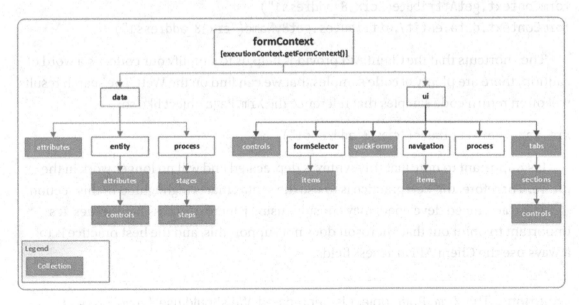

Figure 13-38. *The formContext object*

Because the Client API covers so much, we'll focus exclusively on how to work with data fields and forms. This covers the functional area that app builders tend to focus on most.

Retrieving Field Values

The Client API enables us to retrieve form field values. Here's the code to retrieve the value of a field called `address1`:

```
var formContext = executionContext.getFormContext();
var address1 = formContext.getAttribute("crx38_address1").getValue();
```

In context of the Client API, the word attribute describes a data field. Therefore, the method `getAttribute` returns an object that represents a field. This method requires us to pass the logical name which includes the organizational prefix (`"crx38_address1"`, in this example).

Once we retrieve an attribute object, we can call the `getValue()` method to return the field value.

Note that if we compare the syntax that we use here with the diagram in Figure 13-38, we see that the Client API provides shortcuts to save us from fully qualifying long method names. Therefore, the following two lines are equivalent:

```
formContext.getAttribute("crx38_address1")
formContext.data.entity.attributes.getByName("crx38_address1")
```

The shortcuts that the Client API provides help us to simplify our code. As a word of caution, there are plenty of code samples that we can find on the Web. The search results will often return code samples that reference the `Xrm.Page` object like so:

```
Xrm.Page.getAttribute("crx38_address1")
```

It's important to note that this syntax is deprecated and will no longer work in the future. Therefore, the best practice is to use the syntax that is highlighted in this section.

More advanced developers may consider using jQuery to access field values. It's important to point out that Microsoft does not support this, and the best practice is to always use the Client API to access fields.

Caution   The `Xrm.Page` object is deprecated. We should use `formContext` instead.

Accessing Field Attributes

In addition to the getValue() method, the attribute object also provides many other useful methods. These enable us to set a field value and to determine whether a field value is valid or contains unsaved changes. Table 13-2 highlights the most useful methods.

Table 13-2. *Attribute methods*

Function	Description
getIsDirty	This returns true if the field has unsaved changes.
getRequiredLevel	This returns whether the field is not required, required, or recommended.
getValue	This returns the value of a field.
setSubmitMode	This sets whether the field value is submitted when the record is saved. The available options are always, never, and dirty.
isValid	This returns true if the field value is valid.
setValid	This marks a field as valid or invalid. If we mark a field as invalid, we can provide a message that describes why.
setValue	This sets the data value for the field.

Accessing Form Attributes

The Client API also provides access to the host form. This part of the API comes in useful when we want to determine the state of the record (i.e., whether the user is creating a new record or updating an existing record) and when we want to display notifications to the user.

There are cases where we want to perform an action that depends on the state of the record. For example, we may want to set default values for a new record or to display additional details for an existing record. To help carry out this task, we can retrieve the state of the record with the following code:

```
formContext.ui.getFormType()
```

The getFormType method returns 1 when the form is in create mode, 2 when it's in update mode, 3 when the form is read-only, and 4 when the form is disabled.

In a model-driven app, there are two places where we can display notifications to the user – next to a field or in the notification area at the top of the app. The following samples of code show how to set notification messages:

```
//Form Level Notifications - Set Notification
formContext.ui.setFormNotification("Error Message", "ERROR", "uniqueId");
formContext.ui.setFormNotification("Warning Message", "WARNING",
"uniqueId");
formContext.ui.setFormNotification("Info Message", "INFO", "uniqueId");

//Form Level Notifications - Clear Notification
formContext.ui.clearFormNotification("uniqueId");

//Field Specific Notifications - Set Notification
formContext.getControl("crx38_address1").setNotification("Field Message",
"uniqueId");
```

The setFormNotification method displays a message in the notification area. We can provide the notification type "ERROR", "WARNING", or "INFO" to display an icon against the message (Figure 13-39). We can also provide a unique identifier. The reason this is important is because it enables us to clear the message from the notification area by calling the clearFormNotification method.

The setNotification method enables us to display a message against a control. This is particularly useful in scenarios where we want to show validation error messages.

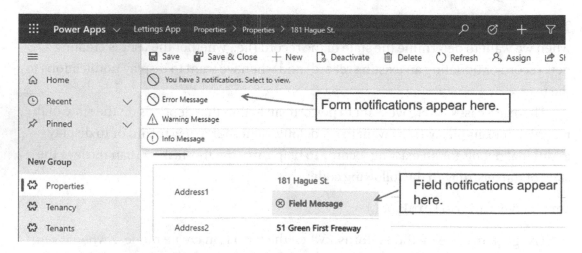

Figure 13-39. *Notifications*

Example 1: Defaulting to Today's Date

Now that we understand the Client API, we can put together what we've learned and write a JavaScript function that sets a field value to today's date. Our function looks like this:

```
var Sdk = window.Sdk || {};     //❶

function setToday(executionContext, inputField)
{
    var formContext = executionContext.getFormContext();
    var field = formContext.getAttribute(inputField);    //❷
    var fieldExists = (field == null);

    if (formContext.ui.getFormType() == 1)  //❸ Check that this is a new
                                                        Record
    {
        field.setValue(new Date());       //❹ Set the Date field to today
        field.setSubmitMode("always");    //❺ Save Disabled Fields
    }
}
```

The first line of code defines a namespace ❶. This is important because the web page for a model-driven app can combine multiple scripts. The presence of a namespace avoids any errors that can occur due to identical function names.

Our code defines a function called setToday. This function defines two parameters – the execution context and the name of the input field where we want to apply today's date. By parametrizing this function, we can easily reuse it against multiple fields and entities.

The next section of code retrieves an attribute object that corresponds to the target field ❷. We use an if statement to check that the form is in "new record" mode ❸. If this is true, the next block of code calls the setValue method to set the value of the field to today's date ❹.

By default, a form does not save values that are associated with disabled fields. The call to setSubmitMode configures the form to save the value, even if the state of the field is disabled ❺.

Note   The API reference documentation provides a list of the form type
identifiers – for example, 1=create, 2=update, 3=read-only, and so on:

`https://docs.microsoft.com/en-us/powerapps/developer/model-`
`driven-apps/clientapi/reference/formcontext-ui/getformtype`

Uploading the Script

Now that we've created our `setToday` function, we can now upload it as a web resource.
Earlier in this chapter, we used the web resource manager in XrmToolBox to upload web
resources. Another way to upload a web resource is to use the classic form designer. We'll
now walk through how to use this technique.

From the entity designer, we open the main form that corresponds to our property
entity and click the "Switch to classic" button.

From the classic form designer, we click the Form Properties button to open the
Form Properties dialog. The first tab that appears is the Events tab. From here, we click
the "add" button beneath the Form Libraries section. In the "Lookup Record" window
that opens, we can click the "add" button to create a new web resource (Figure 13-40).

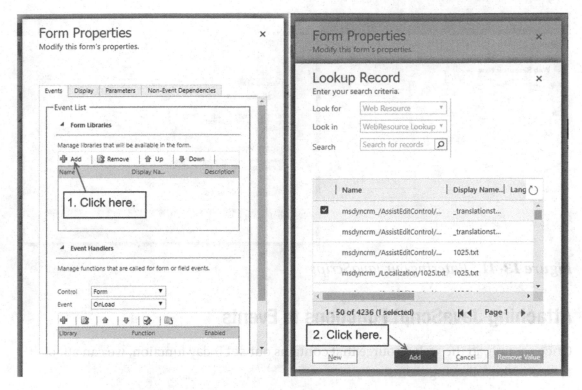

Figure 13-40. *Adding a form library*

This opens the new web resource window (Figure 13-41). From this window, we need to provide a name for our web resource. In the content section, we select the "Script (JScript)" option from the type drop-down. We can then click the "Text Editor" button to open the Edit Content window. In this window, we can enter the source code for our setToday JavaScript function.

445

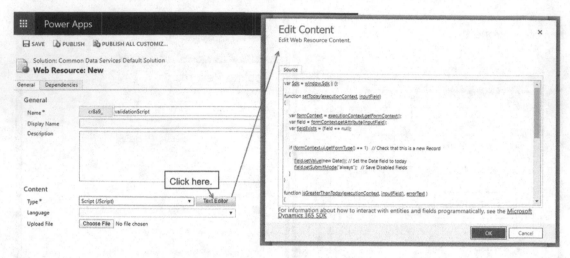

Figure 13-41. *Entering our JavaScript*

Attaching JavaScript Functions to Events

Once we upload the web resource that contains our setToday function, we can attach it to one of the following events:

- When a form loads

- When a user changes the value of a field or switches between tabs

- When a user saves a form

Because we want to set the value of the acquisition date field to today's date when the form loads, we would attach our setToday function to the OnLoad event of the form. The place where we define this is through the Form Properties window in the classic designer.

In the Events tab of the Form Properties window, there is an Event Handlers section (Figure 13-42). From here, we select "Form" from the control drop-down and OnLoad from the event drop-down. Next, we click the add button to add our event handler.

In the "Handler Properties" dialog that opens, we select the form library that contains our JavaScript function. Next, we type setToday into the function name textbox.

Our setToday function accepts two arguments – the execution context and the name of the field where we want to set the date. To pass the execution context, we check the "Pass execution context as first parameter" checkbox. In the text box beneath, we can enter a comma-separated list of additional parameter values. Here, we would enter the logical name of our acquisition date field.

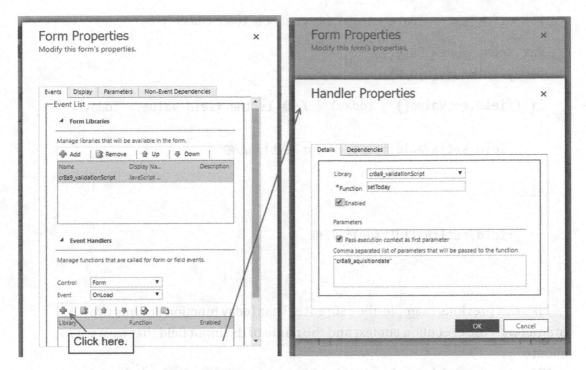

Figure 13-42. *Applying the function*

At this point, we can save and publish our form. When we now run our app and create a new property record, the acquisition date field will default to today's date.

Example 2: Validating Field values

To provide another practical example of how to use JavaScript, we'll now look at how to apply custom validation. We'll follow closely the same process as our previous example. Our example will prevent users from entering an acquisition date that is greater than today.

The first step is to write a JavaScript function to carry out the validation task. Our code will look like this:

```
var Sdk = window.Sdk || {};

function isGreaterThanToday(executionContext, inputField)
{
    var formContext = executionContext.getFormContext();
    var field = formContext.getAttribute(inputField);
```

```
    var errorText = "Date cannot be greater than today";

    var today = new Date();
    today.setHours(0,0,0);

    if (field.getValue() > today)   //❶ Is the field value > today?
    {
        field.setIsValid(false, errorText); //❷
    }
    else
    {
        field.setIsValid(true); //❸
    }
}
```

Like our previous example, the isGreaterThanToday function accepts two parameters – the execution context and the name of the input field that we want to validate.

The main part of this code calls the if function to check whether the input date is greater than today's date ❶. If true, we mark the field as invalid by calling the setIsValid method ❷. The first argument specifies that the field is invalid, and the second argument specifies the error message that appears. When we set a field as invalid, the form will prevent a user from saving the record.

If the user enters a valid date, we mark the field as valid by calling the setIsValid function and passing true as the first argument ❸. This is important because it clears the validation error if a user were to enter an invalid date and to subsequently fix the problem by entering a valid date.

The next step is to add the isGreaterThanToday function to a form library. Next, we add an event handler to handle the OnChange event of the acquisition date control. In the Handler Properties dialog, we set the function to isGreaterThanToday, check the "Pass execution context as first parameter" checkbox, and enter the logical name of our acquisition date field in the parameter textbox (Figure 13-43).

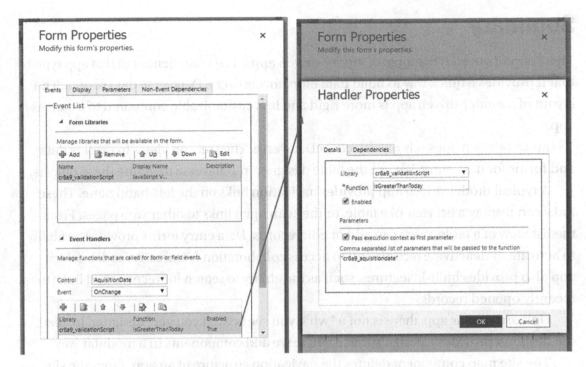

Figure 13-43. *Creating the event handler*

At this point, we can save and publish our form. When we now run our app and create a new property record, an error will appear if we attempt to set an acquisition date that is greater than today (Figure 13-44).

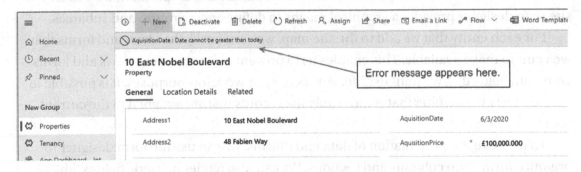

Figure 13-44. *The error message*

Summary

This chapter covered the topic of model-driven apps. The main benefit of this app type is that it provides a quick way to build data entry forms over a Dataverse data source. The layout of a model-driven app is more rigid and less customizable compared to a canvas app.

Model-driven apps rely on objects in Dataverse. They rely on views to display data and forms for data entry. We use the table designer in Dataverse to define these objects.

A typical model-driven app provides navigation links on the left-hand pane. These links can display a list view of a table, or they can open links to other web pages. From the list view of a table, users can add or edit records. Data entry forms provide the ability to activate or deactivate records and to access collaboration features. A model-driven app also provides built-in features, such as the ability to search for records and links to recently opened records.

Unlike a canvas app, there is not a "what you see is what you get" designer. Instead, the designer provides a design surface where we add components in a modular way.

The site map component defines the navigation structure of an app. From the site map, we can define the tables/entities that we want to show on our model-driven app. The navigation panel is organized by areas and groups. It can display one area at a time, and the end user can switch area using a control. A group defines a named section within an area. Each area can contain multiple groups. A group contains subareas, which are clickable links that can open a view of data, a dashboard, or an external website. The site map designer provides a graphical means to define areas, groups, and subareas.

For each entity that we add to the site map, we can specify the views and forms that we want to make available. This enables us to prevent users accessing views and forms with data fields that we want to hide. For security or workflow purposes, it is possible to create a view with a filter that returns only the records that are assigned to the current user.

To improve the presentation of data entry forms, we can use the form designer to organize forms into columns and sections. We can also render numeric fields with graphical controls, such as gauge or slider controls.

We can enforce data constraints and apply input data validation through business rules. This enables us to mandate the entry of a field, enforce minimum or maximum field values, and more. Business rules are objects that we define using the table designer in Dataverse. A business rule can apply to all records or to a specific form only. We define business rules using a graphical designer. Through this designer, we can add conditions and actions. If a record matches or fails to match a condition, we can apply an action. Actions enable us to display error messages, make fields mandatory, set default values, or hide and lock fields.

Model-driven apps can display dashboards. A dashboard offers an attractive way to present charts, summaries, and overviews of data. We can build classic or interactive dashboards. A classic dashboard presents a static summary of data, whereas an interactive dashboard enables users to click charts and areas and to drill down further into the data.

A powerful feature of model-driven apps are business process flows. These enable us to separate data entry into a series of stages or milestones. A business process flow keeps track of the duration of each stage. For each stage, we can attach different business rules, and we can also specify conditional branching logic. At runtime, the form displays the progress of a record using a control beneath the title of the record. This displays the stages that are completed and those that remain. We build business process flows using a graphical designer. The designer enables us to specify the stages and the data steps that make up each stage.

There are two broad ways to customize data entry forms in a model-driven app. We can embed a canvas app, or we can extend forms with custom JavaScript.

The simple way is to embed a canvas app. This enables us to display non-Dataverse data by using all the data connectors that are available in Power Apps. It also provides access to canvas app formulas and the wider range of controls that canvas apps offer.

To embed a canvas app, we assign a canvas app control to an entity field. Next, we associate the canvas app control with a canvas app. We can then display the canvas app by adding the field to our model-driven form. To configure the entity field and the canvas app control, we use the "classic" form designer. The classic designer provides features that are missing from the regular designer.

With an embedded canvas app, we can access a model-driven form integration object. This enables us to keep our canvas app data in sync with the host form. It also enables us to perform actions on the host form, such as saving and refreshing the host form or navigating the host form to a different view or form.

The other way to customize a data entry form is to write custom JavaScript. There is a rich JavaScript Client API that enables us to perform a wide range of actions. This includes the ability to access entities, fields, forms, and almost all the objects that are available in a model-driven app.

JavaScript is very powerful because it provides an environment where we can utilize programmatic structures, such as conditions and computational logic, and it helps us to overcome the limitations of the visual designers. In this chapter, we looked at how to set a field value to today's date and how to apply custom validation based on date ranges. This illustrates a perfect use of JavaScript because the graphical designers lack the support for mathematical and date arithmetic functions.

To incorporate custom JavaScript onto a form, we write JavaScript functions to perform our task. Our JavaScript functions can call the Client API to retrieve and set field values and to carry out other data tasks. Once we create our function, we use the classic form designer to attach our JavaScript function to form events. We can trigger a function to run when a form loads, when a user changes a field value or switches between tabs, or when a user saves a form.

Finally, a model-driven app relies on web resources. These are resources in Dataverse that are accessible through a web URL. The web resources in an app include JavaScript files, custom icons, and app welcome screens. One way to manage web resources is to use a third-party community tool called XrmToolBox. This is a helpful tool that can help simplify many parts of developing a model-driven app.

CHAPTER 14

Building Portal Apps

Power Apps portals are Internet-facing websites that we build using the low code methodology of Power Apps. Both internal and external users can access a portal. They therefore provide a great way to build apps that customers, clients, and other users can access.

Compared to other website-building platforms, a key benefit of a portal is that we can easily build data retrieval and data entry screens against the records in Dataverse. We can do this in a no code way by reusing the same views and forms from our model-driven apps.

In this chapter, we'll walk through the process to create a portal. We'll find out how to use the designer, how to build navigation structures, and how to take advantage of the templating features. This chapter covers the fundamental topics, and in the next chapter, we'll find out how to build data access screens. The key topics that we'll cover in this chapter include

- How to use the designer to add and design pages. We'll cover the areas that enable us to administer a portal, including the Portal Management app.

- How to customize the HTML of web pages and how to reuse code and implement standard layouts with page templates and web templates.

- How to authenticate users using local accounts or external providers such as Microsoft, Facebook, or Google. We'll cover how to manage website registrations and how to restrict access to web pages and entities.

© Tim Leung 2021
T. Leung, *Beginning Power Apps*, https://doi.org/10.1007/978-1-4842-6683-0_14

Introduction

To begin this chapter, we'll look at the features and benefits of Power Apps portals. What is it that makes a portal so great? A number one feature is that in keeping with the products in the Power Platform, we can build Internet-facing websites without code. This is a valuable feature because building apps that interact with databases is not a simple task.

The designer features a WYSIWYG (what you see is what you get) interface that provides a visual design experience. We can get started quickly by creating a portal based on a template. A template includes images and placeholder content that we can amend and includes sets of the common pages that we typically find in websites – for example, a home page, an about page, and a login page.

Portals supports a wide range of authentication providers. This includes Microsoft, LinkedIn, Facebook accounts, and more. We can also grant public access by enabling unauthenticated access. To simplify user management, there is the option of self-service registration. Once a user registers as a portal user, there is the ability to link identities from multiple authentication providers. This improves and simplifies the authentication experience for the user.

A portal relies on a Dataverse database, and the data entry components are designed to work only with Dataverse. The benefit of this is that it provides a high level of reusability between model-driven apps and portals. We can reuse the forms or views that we built for our model-driven apps. Thanks to the visual designers, we can present data in graphical ways without code. For example, we can take a view and render it as a map or a chart.

Because Dataverse provides a security framework where we can secure records in a granular fashion, we can use this to protect access to data in portals.

For users, there is a great feature called front-side editing. Users with sufficient privileges can log in and perform in-place edits and modifications of web pages. With in-place editing, there is no need to visit a special back-end area to make content changes. These users can also add, modify, or delete web pages from the portal using these editing tools. The portal behaves like a content management system, and there is no need for content creators to install special software or to understand code.

In Europe, there is legislation called GDPR (General Data Protection Regulation) that is designed to protect user's personal data. A portal includes the ability to show terms and conditions and to collect the user consent that is needed to process their personal data. This built-in feature saves us the task of having to build this manually.

Although we can build a portal without any code, experienced app builders can customize pages by writing custom HTML, CSS, and JavaScript.

The pages in a portal are based on an open source framework called Bootstrap. Bootstrap provides a framework that produces responsive web pages. That is, the web pages we build will render on a large PC monitor and will reflow automatically to display correctly on a phone or mobile device. There are many commercial and free Bootstrap themes that have been developed by the community. We can import these Bootstrap themes into a portal and easily re-skin the look and feel of our website.

Portals also support an open source template language called Liquid. We can use Liquid to perform logical, mathematical, and string manipulation tasks. We can also use Liquid to build highly customized pages that interact with data from Dataverse.

For file storage, we can integrate with SharePoint and Azure Blob storage. The reason that this is useful is because storing binary data in Dataverse is relatively expensive, compared to SharePoint and Azure Blob storage.

To keep out spammers, we can restrict access by IP address, and we can also enable CAPTCHAs (Completely Automated Public Turing tests to tell Computers and Humans Apart) on data entry forms. A CAPTCHA prevents users from submitting data until they correctly enter the text that appears in an obscured image.

From a security perspective, a portal produces full access logs. To make the most effective use of space, it can store these in Azure Blob storage.

There are clearly many benefits to building a portal. Are there any disadvantages? One issue is cost. In situations where we want to build a simple public-facing website that doesn't require any of the advanced features a portal offers, there are more cost-effective alternatives.

Another notable issue is that unlike model-driven and canvas apps, a portal offers minimal integration support with Microsoft Automate. This makes it difficult to initiate automation and background processes from a portal.

A portal does not support the wide range of data connectors that are available in canvas apps. Therefore, it requires more advanced web development skills to connect to data sources other than Dataverse.

Pricing

Internal and external users are billed separately. Each internal user requires a seeded Dynamics 365 license or a subscription to a Power Apps per-app or per-user plan. At the time of writing, the cost for a per-app plan is $10/user/month, and the cost for a per-user plan is $40/user/month.

For external users, the pricing structure depends on whether the end user is unauthenticated or authenticated. Authenticated users are billed by the number of distinct logins. At the time of writing, the cost to enable 100 distinct user logins is $200 per month. Unauthenticated users are billed by the number of page impressions. The cost of this is $100 per month, for 100,000 page views.

Creating a Portal

To create a portal, the first step is to go to the Power Apps Maker Portal and to click the option to create a new portal (Figure 14-1).

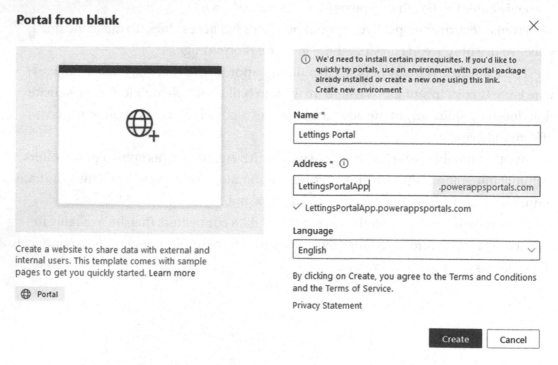

Figure 14-1. *Creating a new portal*

By default, the "Portal from blank" option provisions a portal using a starter template that includes a set of common, standard web pages. Dynamics 365 users have the additional option of creating a portal using the Customer self-service, Employee self-service, Community, and Partner templates. These templates include value-added features that integrate with Dynamics 365.

The portal creation page requires us to enter a portal name and portal web address. The portal web address must be unique. As we enter our desired web address, the form displays a label that shows whether the web address is available.

When we click the create button, Power Apps will provision a portal. This process may take some time, possibly several hours. When the provisioning process completes, Power Apps sends a notification to alert us to this. If we now return to the Maker Portal, we will see two apps – the portal that we created and a model-driven app called Portal Management (Figure 14-2).

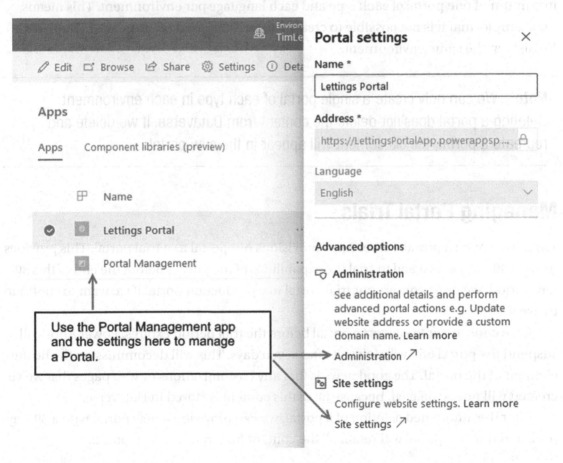

Figure 14-2. *Managing the settings of a portal app*

The model-driven app enables us to manage the metadata and the specific settings that relate to an app. For example, we can use the model-driven app to configure authentication and to create page templates.

Another place where we can find administration features is to open the settings of the portal. Here, we will find a link to open the "Power Apps Portals admin center." The admin center enables us to manage infrastructure-type settings, such as the domain name, IP filtering, and server-side logging.

An important point is that all the pages and content that we create in a portal are stored in Dataverse. This means that if we were to delete an existing portal and to create a new one from scratch, the new portal will still retain the content of the old portal because content is stored in the database.

Due to the way that portal configuration is stored in Dataverse, there is also a restriction on the number of portals that we can host per environment. We can host a maximum of one portal of each type and each language per environment. This means, for example, that it is not possible to create two portals based on the starter template in English on the same environment.

Note   We can only create a single portal of each type in each environment. Deleting a portal does not delete the content from Dataverse. If we delete and recreate a portal, the old content will appear in the new portal.

Managing Portal Trials

When we create a portal, Power Apps provisions our portal as a trial portal. This provides us with 30 days to test and to trial the capabilities of the portal. Before the end of this 30-day period, we must convert our trial portal to a production portal if we want to continue to use it.

If we choose not to convert a portal before the trial period expires, Power Apps will suspend the portal and will delete it after seven days. This will decommission the hosting element of the portal. The good news is that any customizations or web pages that we've created will not be deleted, because all of this content is stored in Dataverse.

After the automated deletion of a portal, we can provision a new portal with a 30-day trial, and the new portal will retain all the content from our previous portal.

Throughout the 30-day trial period, a banner appears at the top of the designer which shows us the number of days that are remaining in the trial. This banner contains a link that enables us to convert our portal to a production portal. To carry out this conversion, the target environment must be a production environment. Also, we should ensure that our internal users have subscriptions to a suitable Power Apps plan and that we've purchased the required licensing add-ons if we want to allow external users to access the portal.

Working with the Designer

If we open the portal that we created, we will see the view that is shown in Figure 14-3. As we can see, the portal designer enables us to design web pages in a visual way.

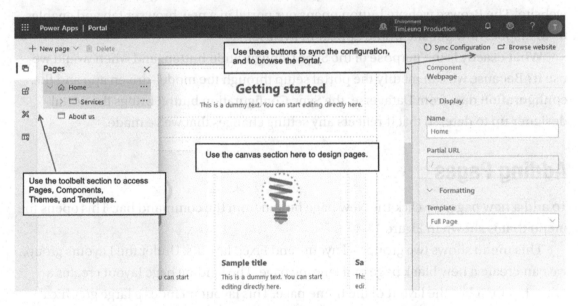

Figure 14-3. *The most important parts of the portal app designer*

The left-hand side of the designer shows a tabbed, toolbelt panel with the following four tabs – pages, components, themes, and templates. The central part of the designer (known as the canvas) shows the page that we're currently editing. The right-hand side of the designer shows a properties pane to modify item settings.

Let's take a closer look at the items in the toolbelt. The first tab shows the pages in our website. A new portal contains several default pages to help us get started. This includes a home page, an about us page, and a services page. We can quickly build a Portal by simply modifying these pages.

The second tab in the toolbelt opens the component section. We can use this to add sections, images, and text fields to a web page.

The third tab in the toolbelt opens the themes section. This section enables us to modify the overall appearance of an app by applying themes and CSS (Cascading Style Sheets).

The final tab in the toolbelt opens the templates section. Through the model-driven app, we can add frequently used content into templates. We can then add a template onto a screen, and this saves us from having to recreate content from scratch.

Along the command bar are two important icons – Sync Configuration and Browse website. The Browse website button opens our portal in a new browser tab and enables us to inspect how our site would appear in live use.

What exactly is the purpose of the Sync Configuration button, and when would we use it? Because we can modify the portal setup through the model-driven app and the configuration data from Dataverse, the Sync Configuration button brings the portal designer up to date, so that it reflects any setting changes that we've made.

Adding Pages

To add a new page, we click the New page button from the command bar. This opens the menu that is shown in Figure 14-4.

This menu shows two groups – Layouts and Fixed layouts. Under the Layouts group, we can create a new blank page or a landing page. The landing page layout creates a page that matches the layout of the home page. This layout includes a large graphical home page banner, a three-column section that contains text and images, and a two-column section. By using this layout, we can quickly construct a page by removing or editing the content to suit our needs.

The Fixed layouts group enables us to build a page based on the "Page with child links" and "Page with title" templates. The "Page with child links" template builds a page that includes a menu that shows links to child pages. The "Page with title" template builds a simple page that includes a title label and a section that we can use to add our page content.

Technically, a key characteristic of the blank and landing page layouts is that they are based on a template called the "Default studio template." This is a very simple template with minimal dependencies. The templates in the Fixed layouts group are more customized, and we'll cover these in greater detail later in this chapter.

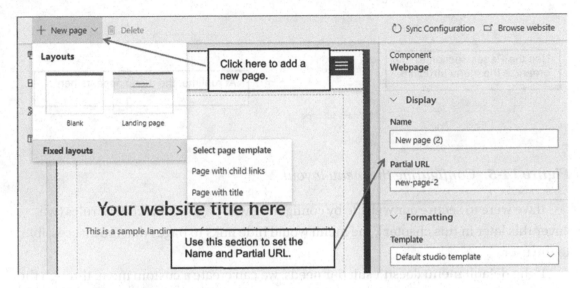

Figure 14-4. *Adding a new page*

After we add a page, we can use the properties pane to set the name and partial URL settings. The name defines the title of the page. This is the description that the portal displays in menus that link to the page. The partial URL defines the identifier that appears in the address bar. For example, if we set the partial URL of a page to properties, we can access the page through the web address

```
https://PortalAddress/properties
```

Navigation Menus

It's very straightforward to build navigation menus. A portal uses the page structure in the pages section of the toolbelt to build a menu structure. At runtime, the menu appears in the header section of the portal (Figure 14-5).

By default, each top-level page appears as a clickable link in the header of the portal. In the designer, we can organize pages so that they become child pages. The header menu will render a drop-down panel to display the child pages.

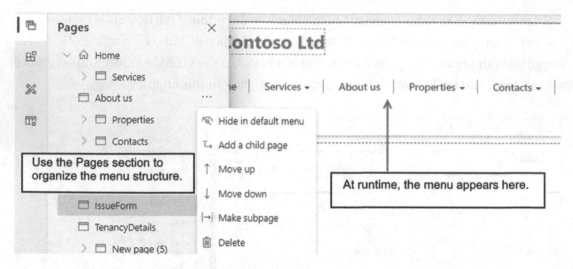

Figure 14-5. *Configuring the menu layout*

If we were to secure our website by configuring web page access control rules (we cover this later in this chapter), the menu would hide links to pages that are inaccessible to the user.

If the default menu doesn't suit our needs, we can create a custom menu through the model-driven Portal Management app.

Designing Web Pages

The page designer provides a visual and intuitive way to design a page. Most of the options are intuitive and require minimal explanation.

In the main (canvas) part of the designer, we can select the header, detail, and footer sections of the page. The components part of the toolbelt enables us to add objects to a page (Figure 14-6). We can use the section layout components to organize a page into multiple columns. For each section, we can use the properties pane to set the height, text alignment, background fill, and background image.

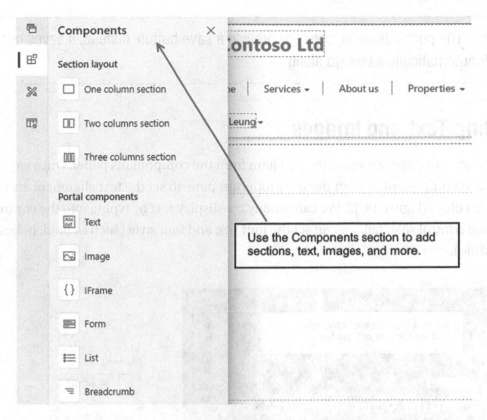

Figure 14-6. *Adding components to a page*

Other components we can add to a page include text, image, iframe, form, list, and breadcrumb. An iframe is a control that enables us to embed a separate web page into a page. The breadcrumb control is a navigation control that shows the user where they are in relation to the site hierarchy. If we were to add this control to a child page, the breadcrumb control would display horizontally aligned hyperlinks that are separated by the "greater than" symbol (>). The user can use these hyperlinks to navigate to parent pages or the root website.

One of the items that we might search for when we design a page is the save button. There is no save button in the portal designer. The designer automatically saves changes as we go along. The status bar at the bottom of the designer indicates when a same operation is in progress. Sometimes, it's possible to navigate away from a page before the save operation is complete. Therefore, a good tip is to keep an eye on the status bar and to wait for the status to change to "saved" before navigating to a different page.

Note   The portal designer does not provide a save button. Instead, it saves our work automatically as we go along.

Adding Text and Images

To add text to a page, we select the text item from the components panel. Once we add a text component, we can use the properties pane to set the text alignment and the font colors (Figure 14-7). We can modify the display text by typing into the control. With the control selected, we can set the font size and font style (such as bold, italics, or underline).

Figure 14-7. *Configuring a text component*

To display an image, we add an image component. We can upload an image or configure other attributes through the properties pane (Figure 14-8).

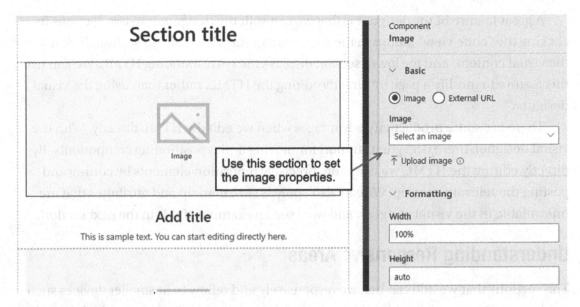

Figure 14-8. *Configuring an image control*

Adding Sections

A section enables us to organize a page into multiple columns. We can add a one-column, two-column, or three-column section through the components panel. Figure 14-9 illustrates how the page designer appears with a three-column section. Once we add a section, we can use the designer to modify and to add additional components to each column.

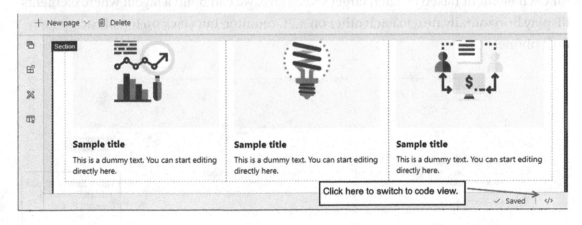

Figure 14-9. *A three-column section*

A great feature of the designer is that we can split the designer into two sections by clicking the "code view" button in the status bar. In this view, the top section displays the visual content, and the lower section displays the corresponding HTML. We can use this feature to modify a page by directly editing the HTML, rather than using the visual designer.

There are some productivity advantages when we edit the HTML directly. With the visual designer, there isn't great support for moving and repositioning components. By directly editing the HTML, we can more precisely reposition elements by cutting and pasting the relevant markup. We can also apply HTML markup and attributes that are unavailable in the visual designer, and we'll see an example of this in the next section.

Understanding Responsive Areas

The sections that we add can behave responsively and reflow to fit smaller devices such as phones. The reason for this is because portals are based on Bootstrap, which is an open source responsive framework that was developed by Twitter. This section provides an overview of Bootstrap, so that we can better understand the Bootstrap syntax that appears in the HTML.

Figure 14-10 shows the code view of a three-column section and illustrates the HTML and Bootstrap code that define this layout.

Bootstrap targets four screen sizes – phones, tablets, small laptops, and PCs. It divides the visible screen into 12 columns. Elements on a web page can span a different number of columns, depending on the target screen size. By defining the column span for each element based on each target screen size, we can build a layout where elements display horizontally next to each other on a PC monitor, but stack on top of each other on a phone.

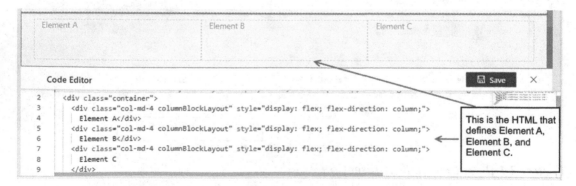

Figure 14-10. *Displaying the HTML view*

To see the syntax that defines this behavior, here's the pertinent markup for a three-column section:

```
<div class="row">
  <div class="container">
    <div class="col-md-4">Element A</div>
    <div class="col-md-4">Element B</div>
    <div class="col-md-4">Element C</div>
  </div>
</div>
```

The HTML that corresponds to elements A, B, and C is marked with the CSS class `col-md-4`.

Bootstrap uses these CSS class names to define the layout. The CSS class `col-md-4` specifies that for medium-sized devices or above, the target element should span four columns (out of the available 12). The `col` part indicates column, the `md` part indicates a medium device (e.g., a laptop), and the number 4 indicates a target column span of four. The identifiers for the four screen sizes are

- `xs` – Phones with a screen less than 768 px in width

- `sm` – Tablets with a screen equal to or greater than 768 px in width

- `md` – Laptops with a screen equal to or greater than 992 px in width

- `lg` – Laptops with a screen equal to or greater than 1200 px in width

If we want to render a section differently on a smaller device, we can append a CSS class to define the layout. Let's say that we want each element to fill the entire screen width on a phone. To do this, we can append the CSS class `col-sm-12` like so:

```
<div class="row">
  <div class="container">
    <div class="col-md-4 col-sm-12">Element A</div>
    <div class="col-md-4 col-sm-12">Element B</div>
    <div class="col-md-4 col-sm-12">Element C</div>
  </div>
</div>
```

With this syntax, elements A, B, and C will fit on a single row on laptop or PC devices. On a phone, each element will fill the width of the device and will therefore stack on top of each other.

Managing a Portal App

Now that we've covered the most important parts of the designer, the next important step is to learn how to configure the settings of a portal. The place to carry out this task is through the model-driven Portal Management app. This app enables us to manage the content, pages, and security of a portal. It also provides access to the features that the Dynamics 365 templates provide, such as forums, ads, and polls. Figure 14-11 shows a screenshot of the Portal Management app and highlights all the menu items that we can access.

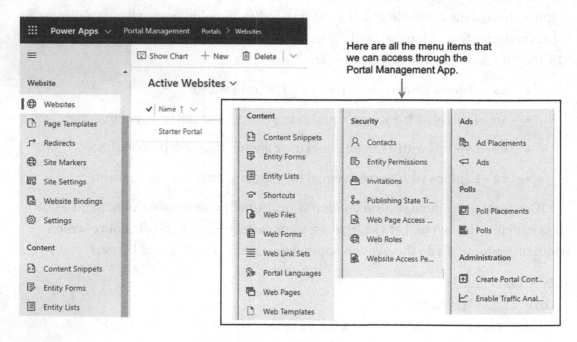

Figure 14-11. *The Portal Management app*

The Anatomy of a Web Page

When we add a new web page, the designer prompts us to choose a layout that is based on a template. Clearly, there is a templating feature that enables us to apply a consistent look and feel to all web pages in a portal.

However, the way this works can be confusing because there isn't a one-to-one relationship between a web page and a template. Instead, the place where we define the common items is through web templates. While the combination of templates and web templates provides a greater level of configurability, the concepts can be tricky to grasp.

In this section, we'll examine these in further detail; but first, here's an overview of the elements that are relevant to the construction of a web page:

- Web page – Technically, a web page is an object that corresponds to a distinct URL. It defines the page content that the user sees. Each web page must be associated with a layout.

- Layout – A layout is the term that we see in the designer to describe a page that is based on the "Default studio template" page template. A fixed layout is the term that the designer uses to describe pages that are based on other page templates.

- Page template – A page template is the object that renders a web page. There are two "rendering" options – web template and redirect. Page template is the name that we see in the Portal Management app. In the designer, page templates are simply labeled templates.

- Web template – A web template defines snippets of HTML, JavaScript, and CSS. Importantly, we can define placeholders here to inject the content of a web page or the content of other web templates.

- Headers and footers – We use web templates to define the header and footer content that applies to all pages in a portal. We use the settings of the website to specify the header and footer web templates.

Figure 14-12 illustrates these elements in the form of a diagram.

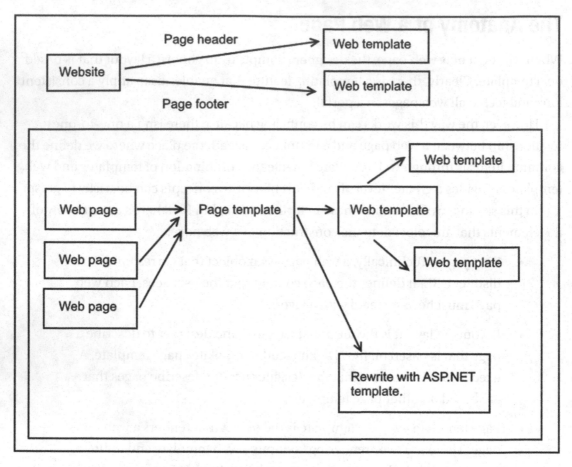

Figure 14-12. The architecture of web pages and templates

Understanding Page Templates

Conceptually, the page template object is the most difficult to grasp. It's an interim object that sits between a web page and a web template. What is the purpose of a page template, and why is it necessary? Why is it not possible to directly associate a web page with a web template?

To make sense of how this works, we can imagine that the page template behaves like a controller object. It takes the page-specific content from a web page and produces the output that the portal sends to the client. To produce this output, it can retrieve common templated content from web templates or by redirecting to an ASP.NET page.

Why are there two different rendering types – web templates and ASP.NET redirection? The answer to this question is partially historical. The technology behind Power Apps portals comes from a product called Adxstudio Portals.

Adxstudio Portals is based on the Microsoft ASP.NET Forms platform, and it provides the foundation of what Power Apps portals are today. Adxstudio Portals shares the same concept of web pages and page templates. To implement templated layouts, developers can create an ASP.NET page and link it to web pages through a page template.

When Microsoft ported the ASP.NET-based Adxstudio Portals to the cloud, it retained this setup. However, it wasn't conducive to carry forward the ability to render web pages with user-generated custom ASP.NET pages. Therefore, the alternative method of web template rendering became the designated way to build user-generated custom layouts.

With a Power Apps portal, we can only render web pages with the ASP.NET pages that Microsoft supplies with the portal. The purpose of ASP.NET redirection is to support built-in portal pages, such as the access denied, profile, and search pages. Any custom layout changes that we make will be based on page templates with web templates.

To give a practical example of how to use page templates, we could create a page template called "page template with left menu." This page template would display a menu on the left side of the page, and we could apply this template on all the pages where we want to display this menu.

Configuring Web Pages and Page Templates

To see an example of a page template in use, let's examine one of the pages from the starter portal template – the services page. Figure 14-13 shows how this page appears in the designer.

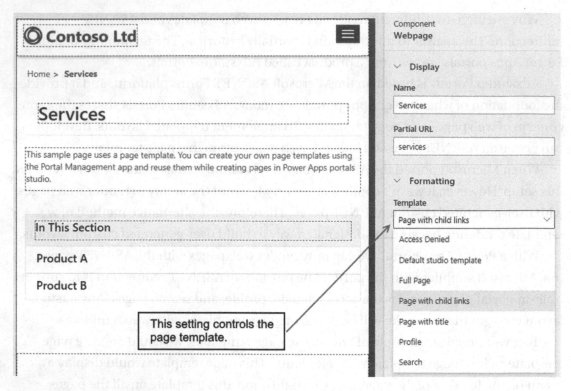

Figure 14-13. *The layout of the services Page*

If we examine the template setting in the designer, we see that this page is based on the "Page with child links" page template. This template provides a menu that shows links to child pages. The child pages are those that appear beneath the page in the tree view of the designer.

To configure this page template, we use the model-driven Portal Management app. Through the Page Templates section, we can add new page templates and modify existing templates. Figure 14-14 shows the appearance of the "Page with child links" record. The General tab includes all the important details, and the Web Pages tab is helpful because it shows all the web pages that use this template.

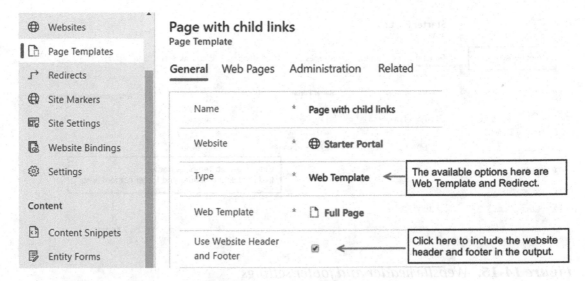

Figure 14-14. Page with child links page template

Beneath the General tab, the three most important settings are Type, Web Template, and Use Website Header and Footer.

The Type of this page template is "Web Template." The other option we can choose is "Redirect." If we choose the "Redirect" option, we would need to use a textbox to enter the path to one of the ASP.NET pages that the portal provides.

The Web Template setting shows how this page template is linked to the "Full Page" web template. This is the object we would need to edit if we want to change the aesthetic layout of the output that this page template generates.

The "Use Website Header and Footer" checkbox controls whether the page template appends the website header and footer.

Setting Website Headers and Footers

When we enable the "Use Website Header and Footer" option in a page template, the output page will include the header and footer content that we define at the website level. Figure 14-15 shows how we set this up in the website section of the Portal Management app.

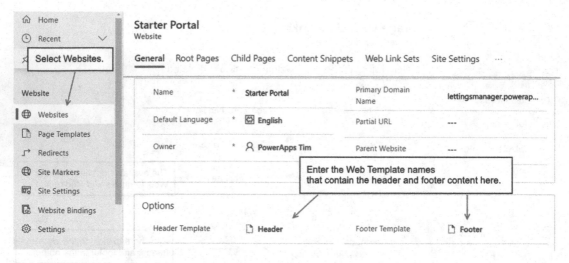

Figure 14-15. *Website header and footer settings*

Web Templates

To create and edit web templates, we use the Web Templates section of the Portal Management app (Figure 14-16).

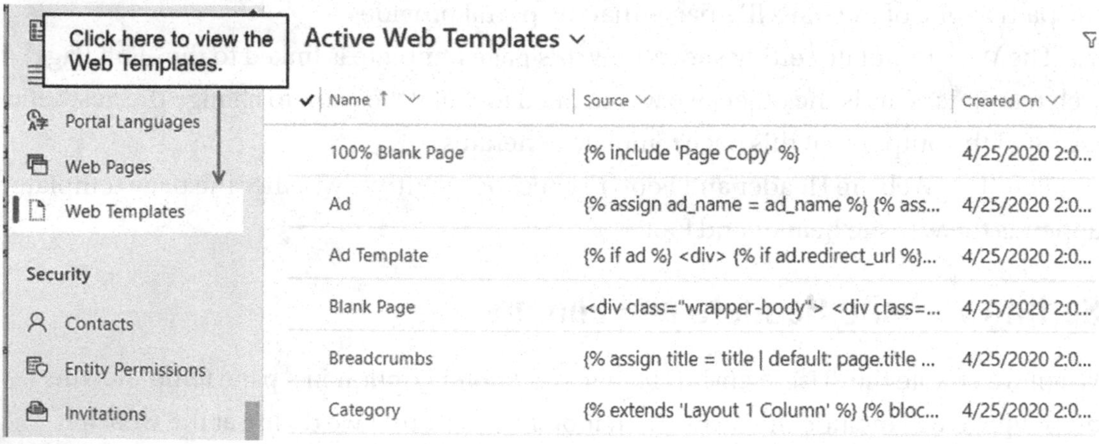

Figure 14-16. *Viewing web templates*

To highlight how a web template looks, Figure 14-17 shows the appearance when we open the "Full Page" web template. This is the web template that the "Page with child links" page template uses.

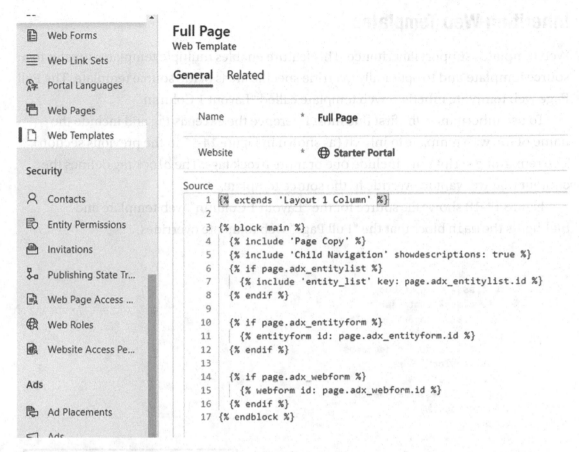

Web Forms
Web Link Sets
Portal Languages
Web Pages
Web Templates

Security

Contacts
Entity Permissions
Invitations
Publishing State Tr...
Web Page Access ...
Web Roles
Website Access Pe...

Ads

Ad Placements
Ads

Full Page
Web Template

General   Related

Name   *   **Full Page**

Website   *   ⊕ **Starter Portal**

Source
```
 1  {% extends 'Layout 1 Column' %}
 2
 3  {% block main %}
 4    {% include 'Page Copy' %}
 5    {% include 'Child Navigation' showdescriptions: true %}
 6    {% if page.adx_entitylist %}
 7      {% include 'entity_list' key: page.adx_entitylist.id %}
 8    {% endif %}
 9
10    {% if page.adx_entityform %}
11      {% entityform id: page.adx_entityform.id %}
12    {% endif %}
13
14    {% if page.adx_webform %}
15      {% webform id: page.adx_webform.id %}
16    {% endif %}
17  {% endblock %}
```

Figure 14-17. *Editing the "Full Page" web template*

The General tab shows the source code of the web template. We define the source of a web template using HTML and, optionally, Liquid script. Liquid is a templating language which we'll cover more thoroughly later in this book.

The source of this web template uses Liquid to embed the content of other web templates. The important keywords that we see in this script are extends, main, and include. The extends and main keywords support template inheritance. The include tag is what we use to add the content of another web template by name. The Liquid language supports variables, and through the include tag, we can pass values to a child web template by specifying variable names and values.

Inheriting Web Templates

Web templates support inheritance. This feature enables multiple templates to refer to a source template and to optionally override specific areas of the source template. The Full Page web template inherits a web template called "Layout 1 Column."

To use inheritance, the first line must reference the extends tag and include the name of the web template to inherit (as shown in Figure 14-17 in the previous section). The remaining script must include one or more block tags. The block tag defines the content that we want to override in the source template.

Figure 14-18 shows the source for the "Layout 1 Column" web template and highlights the main block that the "Full Page" web template overrides.

```
Source
 1  <div class="wrapper-body">
 2    <div class="container">
 3    <div class="page-heading">
 4      {% block breadcrumbs %}
 5        {% include 'Breadcrumbs' %}
 6      {% endblock %}
 7    {% block title %}
 8      {% include 'Page Header' %}
 9    {% endblock %}
10    </div>
11    <div class="row">
12      <div class="col-md-12">
13      {% block main %}
14        {% include 'Page Copy' %}
15      {% endblock %}
16      </div>
17    </div>
18  </div>
19  <div class ="push"></div>
20  </div>
```

The 'Full Page' template overrides this block in the 'Layout 1 Column' template.

Figure 14-18. *The source of the "Layout 1 Column" template*

Here, we see how the "Layout 1 Column" web template includes two other blocks – breadcrumbs and title. The "Full Page" web template does not override the breadcrumbs and title blocks. In cases where a child template does not override a block, the content that is defined in the source template will apply.

Inserting the Web Page Content

With the nested web templates that we've seen so far, where is the code that inserts the web page content?

If we examine the "Full Page" web template, we see that the `main` block uses the `include` tag to add the content of the "Page Copy" web template.

If we review the source for the "Page Copy" web template, we can find the code that retrieves the content of the web page, as shown in Figure 14-19.

```
Source
1  <div class="page-copy">
2  {% editable page 'adx_copy' type: 'html', liquid: true %}
3  </div>
```

Figure 14-19. *The source of the "Page Copy" template*

Here, we see some interesting syntax. The Liquid code references a tag called `editable`. This tag supports the front-side, in-line editing capabilities of the portal. The `editable` tag renders editable versions of portal content for users with sufficient privileges.

The first argument that we pass to `editable` defines the object. In this case, the code passes the `page` object. The second argument specifies the attribute name or key that we want to make editable. With Liquid, the `page` object provides access to the attributes of a page, including the title, the URL, the parent page, and child pages. The `adx_copy` attribute returns the content of the page, and therefore, this is the second argument that the code passes to `editable`.

The `type` argument defines the editing interface that the portal presents to the user. The valid values are `html` and `text`.

Finally, the `liquid` argument specifies whether the template should execute any Liquid code that exists in the source content of the web page.

The "Page Copy" web template provides a great way to display the content of a web page in a way that supports in-line editing. In cases where we simply want to display the content of a web page, we can use the following Liquid syntax: `{{ page.adx_copy }}`.

Securing a Portal

A very important topic is security. This is especially important because we can build web pages that can read and update data from Dataverse and we need to configure authentication, user management, and permission settings.

The high-level overview of portal security is as follows. A record in the Dataverse Contact table represents each portal user. There can be multiple authentication types associated with each contact. For example, a contact could log in with an email address and password or using an external provider such as a Microsoft, Facebook, or Google account.

To organize contacts, we group together sets of contacts with web roles.

To control access to web pages, we create a web page access control rule and associate that with web roles.

To control access to Dataverse tables, we create an entity permission record and associate that with web roles. Figure 14-20 illustrates this in the form of a diagram.

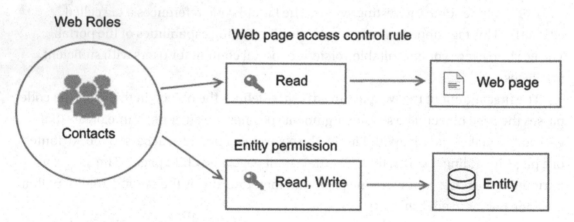

Figure 14-20.   *Contacts, web roles, web page access control rules, and entity permissions*

Setting Up Login Accounts

Portal apps can work with a wide range of authentication providers. We can configure portal apps to use local authentication, or we can delegate authentication to an external provider. The starter portal template includes basic login and registration pages. Let's look at what the portal provides out of the box. We can access the login area by clicking the login button in the header. This opens the login page, as shown in Figure 14-21.

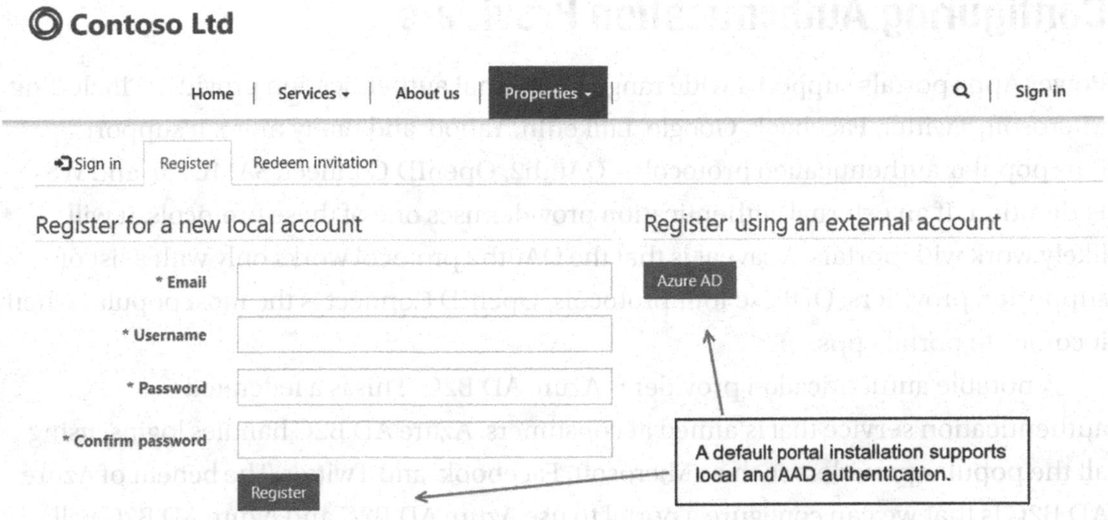

Figure 14-21. *The default login page*

A default installation enables users to authenticate using the local and AAD authentication providers. As we can see, the login screen contains two columns – the first column contains the username and password textboxes to log in locally, and the second column enables users to log in using an AAD account.

The AAD authentication option enables us to create a portal administrator. When we create a portal, it's important to use the login page to register for an account. We should use the AAD account that we used to provision the portal. When the registration process completes, our AAD account will have administrative permissions on the portal.

The local authentication provider stores usernames and passwords in Dataverse. It stores these details in the Contact table. For security reasons, Microsoft wants to phase out this practice of storing usernames and passwords in Dataverse and has therefore marked the local authentication feature for deprecation. For new projects, we should consider disabling local authentication because this would avoid the headache of needing to migrate users to an external authentication provider should local authentication be deprecated.

Tip   Local authentication is marked for deprecation. Therefore, it's a good idea to disable this authentication method for new projects.

479

Configuring Authentication Providers

Power Apps portals support a wide range of external authentication providers, including Microsoft, Twitter, Facebook, Google, LinkedIn, Yahoo, and many more. It supports four popular authentication protocols – OAuth2, OpenID Connect, SAML 2.0, and WS-Federation. If an external authentication provider uses one of these protocols, it will likely work with portals. A caveat is that the OAuth2 protocol works only with a list of supported providers. Of these four protocols, OpenID Connect is the most popular when it comes to portal apps.

A notable authentication provider is Azure AD B2C. This is a federated authentication service that is aimed at consumers. Azure AD B2C handles logins, using all the popular providers such as Microsoft, Facebook, and Twitter. The benefit of Azure AD B2C is that we can configure a portal to use Azure AD B2C and Azure AD B2C will handle the logins from other external providers. This saves us the effort of needing to configure each authentication provider that we want to support.

Another feature of Azure AD B2C is that it can handle AAD logins. The cosmetic benefit of this is that if, for example, we want to support Google, Facebook, and AAD logins, we wouldn't need to add three login buttons to a login page. We can simply a add single Azure AD B2C login button.

To configure the authentication providers that we want to support, we can use the Portal Management app. However, there is a preview feature that provides an easier way to configure authentication providers. To access this feature, we would run the preview version of the Maker Portal through the following address:

```
https://make.preview.powerapps.com/
```

From the apps list, we find our portal and click the Settings ➤ Authentication link. This opens the screen that is shown in Figure 14-22. This page shows a list of identity providers and links to configure the provider.

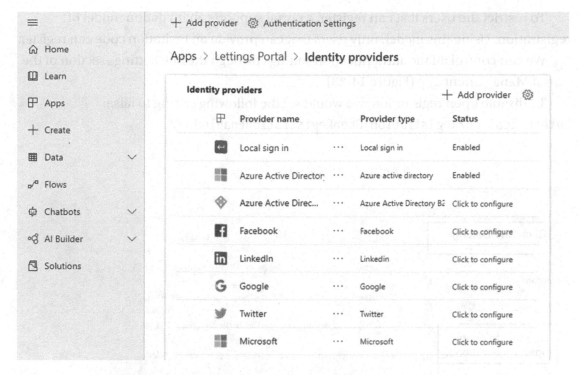

Figure 14-22. *Configuring authentication providers*

To use an external authentication provider, we need to configure the external authentication provider to support our portal.

The general process is to use the external provider (e.g., Twitter, Facebook, or Google) to create an app and to set a redirection URL. The purpose of the redirection URL is to redirect the user to our portal after the authentication succeeds. When we set up an app, the external provider also provides credentials such as a client ID and client secret. We need these credentials to complete the setup of the identity provider in our portal.

Because the process is slightly different for each external provider, the built-in help offers more specific guidance.

Controlling Registrations

The default behavior of a portal is to allow open registration. With this setting, any user that authenticates through the identity provider can register as a user on the portal. As part of the registration process, the portal will create a contact record in Dataverse.

To restrict the users that can register, a portal supports an invitation model of registration. Using this model, only users that can provide an invitation code can register.

We can control all the authentication settings through the Site Settings section of the Portal Management app (Figure 14-23).

To disable open registration, we would set the following setting to false: Authentication/Registration/OpenRegistrationEnabled.

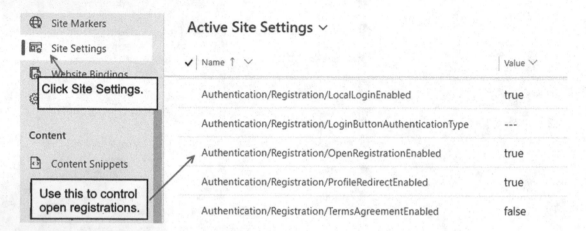

Figure 14-23. *Configuring settings*

Invitation Model

To use the invitation model, we need to generate and send an invite code to the users that want to register. The place where we generate these codes is through the Invitations section of the Portal Management app (Figure 14-24).

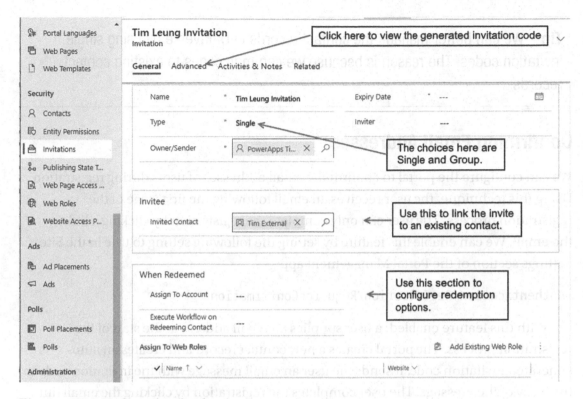

Figure 14-24. Creating invitations

Through this page, we can specify an expiry date for the invitation code. We can also specify an existing contact record. When we do this, Power Apps emails the invitation code to the contact when we save the invitation record. When the user redeems the invitation, the new registration will be associated with the contact.

If we choose not to specify a contact, the invitation code appears in the advanced section when we save the record. We can then share this code with the user that we want to invite.

There are two types of invitation – single and group. A group invitation code can be redeemed multiple times, whereas a single invitation can be redeemed one time only.

Single invitation codes can help keep a Dataverse database cleaner because the portal can map an invitation to a contact record. With a group invitation code, the registration process creates a new contact record, even if the contact record already exists.

Another feature of the invitation model is that we can use the "When Redeemed" section to assign the user to a web role when the invitation code is redeemed. Some administrators use this feature to assign existing portal users to web roles by sending out invitations.

Tip   We can better manage the contact records in Dataverse by using single invitation codes. The reason is because we can map codes to existing contact records.

Confirming Email Addresses

We can configure the portal to confirm the email addresses of users during registration. Using this technique, the user receives an email following the first stage of the registration process. The user can only complete the registration by clicking a link in the email. We can enable this feature by setting the following setting to true in the Site Settings section of the Portal Management app:

```
Authentication/Registration/RequiresConfirmation
```

With this feature enabled, a user supplies an email address at the start of the registration process. The portal creates a new contact record and creates an auto-generated invitation code. It sends the user an email message with the invitation code in the body of the message. The user completes the registration by clicking the email link and redeeming the invitation code.

Setting Up Web Roles

Web roles group together sets of users. They provide an object where we can apply access control permissions.

We create and manage web roles through the Web Roles section of the Portal Management app. Figure 14-25 highlights what we see when we open the "Administrators" web role. We can use the Related section to add users or contact records to a web role.

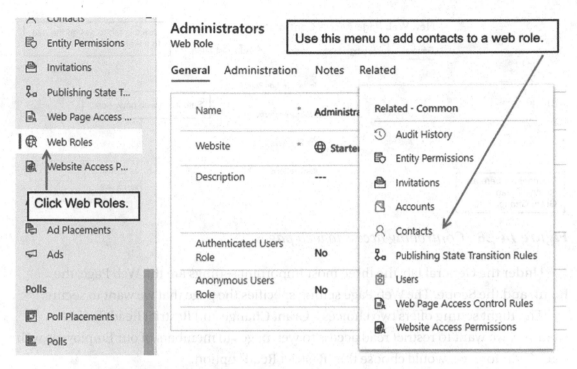

Figure 14-25. *Setting up web roles*

There are two useful built-in roles – Authenticated users and Anonymous users. Any user that successfully logs into a portal becomes a member of the Authenticated users group. The setting that enables this behavior is the "Authenticated Users Role" setting.

Likewise, all unauthenticated users are automatically members of the Anonymous users web role, and the setting that enables this behavior is the "Anonymous Users Role" setting.

Within a portal, we should only configure one web role with the "Authenticated Users Role" setting and one web role with the "Anonymous Users Role" setting.

Controlling Access to Web Pages

A common requirement is to prevent certain groups of users from accessing certain parts of a portal. To give an example, let's suppose our portal contains tenant details and we want to limit this part of the portal to employees only.

To create this rule, the first step is to create a web role and to add the employees to this role. The next step is to create a web page access control rule, as shown in Figure 14-26.

Figure 14-26. *Controlling access to web pages*

Under the General tab, the three most important settings are the Web Page, the Right, and the Scope. The Web Page setting specifies the page that we want to secure.

The Right setting offers two choices – Grant Change and Restrict Read. In this example, we want to restrict read access to web pages to members of our Employees web role. Therefore, we would choose the "Restrict Read" option.

We use the "Grant Change" right to control write access to web pages. This applies to the front-side editing capabilities of the portal.

The Scope setting controls how deep the access control rule applies. There are two values we can choose – "All Content" and "Exclude direct child web files." The default setting is "All Content," meaning that the rule will apply to the page and all child pages.

The "Exclude direct child web files" option configures the rule to apply only to the specified web page and not to any child pages.

Once we create our rule, we can use the Web Roles tab to assign the rule to our Employees web role.

A useful point to note is that the "Grant Change" right takes precedence over the "Restrict Read" right. Let's suppose we assign the "Grant Change" right to the root of a portal and that we assign this right to a user through a web role. Lower down in the portal, we secure a page with the "Restrict Read" right. A user with the "Grant Change" right can access pages where they haven't been explicitly granted the "Restrict Read" right, because "Grant Change" takes precedence over "Restrict Read."

Caution   The "Grant Change" right takes precedence over the "Restrict Read" right. Therefore, we should apply caution when applying this right to the root or top-level pages.

Controlling Access to Dataverse

To control access to Dataverse records, we define entity permission records. Figure 14-27 shows this section from the Portal Management app. Each permission applies to an entity (i.e., a table), and we can define whether to allow or to disallow read, write, create, or delete access to the entity.

| ≡ | ⟨⟩ Show Chart | + New | 🗑 Delete | ∨ | ⟳ Refresh | ✉ Email a Link | ∨ | Flow ∨ | Run Report |

📄 Web Templates	**Active Entity Permissions** ∨					
Security	✔ Name ↑ ∨	Entity Name ∨	Scope ∨	Read ∨	Write ∨	Create ∨	Delete ∨
A Contacts	Property Permission	cr8a9_property1	Global	Yes	Yes	Yes	Yes
🗐 Entity Permissions	PropertyTypePermissions	cr8a9_propertytyp...	Global	Yes	Yes	Yes	Yes
📇 Invitations							

Figure 14-27. *Controlling access to entities*

Let's say we create an entity permission record that grants write access to an entity. Which records will this rule apply to? The setting that controls this is the Scope, and there are five values that we can choose – Global, Contact, Account, Self, and Parent. The most wide-reaching is Global scope. With this setting, the permission rules apply to all records in the entity. We'll explore the remaining scope settings in the section that follows.

Once we create an entity permission record, we would need to assign it to a contact through a web role.

Restricting Access to Specific Records

Two ways to control access to specific records are through the Contact and the Account scopes. To give an example, let's suppose our Dataverse database includes a table that stores tenancy details. We want to implement a rule so that when a tenant logs into a portal, the tenant can read and update only the tenancy record that relates to their tenancy. ·

We can apply this rule using an entity permission record with Contact scope. As a prerequisite, we need to create a many-to-one relationship between the tenancy table and the Contact table. This will create a lookup field in the tenancy table that points to the Contact table.

Once we do this, we can create an entity permission record as shown in Figure 14-28. We use the Entity Name field to select our tenancy table, and we choose the Contact option in the Scope field. When we select Contact scope, the Contact Scope section appears, and we can use the "Contact Relationship" drop-down to select the relationship that links the tenancy table with the Contact table.

The final step is to set the privileges. In this example, we want to grant read and write access to the tenant. Therefore, we would check the read and write checkboxes in the Privileges section.

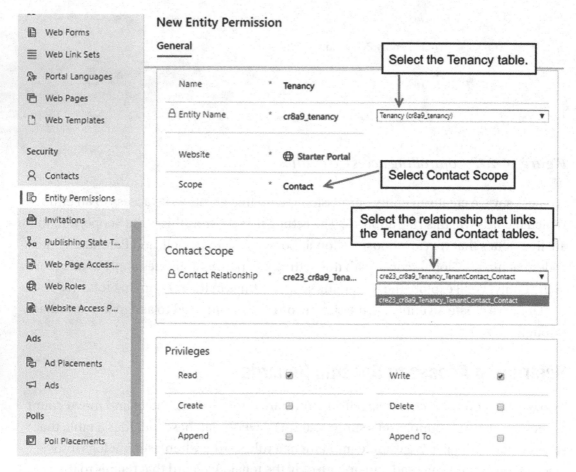

Figure 14-28. *Creating an entity permission record*

For Contact scope to work, there must be a direct relationship between the Contact table and the table that we want to control.

One way to grant access to multiple contacts is to create an entity permission record with Account scope. With Account scope, the rule will apply to the parent account of the contact. To configure this option, we need to define a relationship between the entity we want to control and the account entity.

The process to create an entity permission record with Account scope is very similar to creating an entity permission with Contact scope. We would select Account in the Scope field. This will reveal an Account Relationship drop-down which we can use to select the relationship that links the table with the Account table.

Restricting Access to Associated Records

The most complex scope type is Parent. This enables us to control permissions on records that are related to a contact through other records.

The best way to describe this scope is to give some use case examples. Parent scope caters for the requirement whereby if a user has read permissions on a parent record, that user should automatically have read permissions on related child records.

To give another example, let's imagine a system with two tables – Case and Notes. If a user has permissions to create Case records, that user should also have permissions to create related records in the Notes table.

To demonstrate how to set up this type of entity permission, we'll extend our previous example. The scenario is that a tenant can log into a portal and can read and update the tenancy record that relates to their tenancy. We'll introduce a new table to store tenancy notes. We'll create an entity permission that grants restricted access to the Tenancy Notes table. The user will only be able to read and write records that are related to a tenancy record where the user has permissions.

The starting point for this example is the entity permission that we set up for the tenancy table. This entity permission uses Contact scope to restrict record access to a specific contact.

We'll create a table called "Tenancy Notes." This table has a many-to-one relationship with the tenancy table.

Figure 14-29 shows how to create our entity permission record. For the Name field, we select the "Tenancy Notes" table. In the Scope field, we select Parent. This reveals the Parent Scope section of the form.

This Parent Scope section requires us to enter two details – the "Parent Entity Permission" and the "Parent Relationship." For the "Parent Entity Permission" field, we select the entity permission that applies to the tenancy table. For the "Parent Relationship" field, we select the relationship that links the tenancy table with the "Tenancy Notes" table.

The Privileges section defines the privileges that the user has on the "Tenancy Notes" table, so long as the user also has privileges in the parent entity.

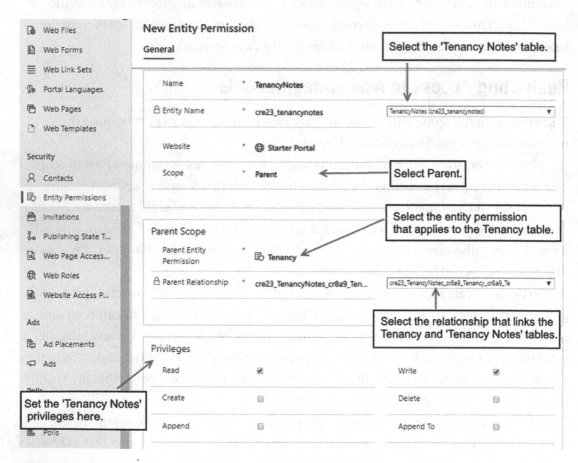

Figure 14-29. *Creating an entity permission with Parent scope*

Restricting Profile Access

The final scope type we can choose is Self. This is a specialized setting that controls the ability of a user to modify their own contact record.

To prevent a user from modifying their own contact record, we can create an entity permission record with Self scope and disable the write privilege.

It is useful to note that the portal provides a built-in profile page that enables users to modify basic contact details. This built-in page works without us needing to create a Self scope entity permission. Users can access this page through the following address:

```
https://PortalAddress/profile
```

Clearing the Cache

With all web-based systems, web servers and browsers can cache copies of web pages, images, and other documents. When a user browses a web page, the browser may return a locally cached copy to avoid a time-consuming round-trip to the server. Additionally, the server may return a cached page to minimize processing and database calls.

Although these caching features are great for maximizing performance, it can prevent us from seeing the changes we expect while we develop our portal. Therefore, it's important to understand how to clear the cache.

We can use the settings of our web browser to clear our local cache. On the server, we clear the cache by visiting a special tools page. To open this page, we log in to the portal using an account with administrative permissions and append the location _services/ about to the root address. Here's an example of how this address looks like:

```
https://lettingsmanager.powerappsportals.com/_services/about
```

Figure 14-30 shows the appearance of this page. In the tools section, there are buttons to clear the cache, to rebuild the search index, and to clear the config.

There are two types of cache in a portal. There is a page cache that caches entire web pages, and there is a config cache that caches the configuration data from Dataverse. This configuration data relates to settings that we configure through the Portal Management app, such as security settings.

The "Clear cache" button clears the entire server cache, and after we click this button, we should see more up-to-date content.

Portals 9.2.4.66 7b6d06e1-88f5-4a0e-a18e-3df0a1f6761d

Details

Geo	GBR
Org ID	70ddef99-6ae7-455a-8ccb-df7520e00b89
Portal ID	7b6d06e1-88f5-4a0e-a18e-3df0a1f6761d
Portal type	CDSStarterPortal
Tenant ID	df7b308b-854f-4f83-bb6b-bcee961c8b51
Auth key expiration date	4/25/2022 1:48:45 PM UTC

Tools

Clear cache   Warning: Clearing the cache will result in a temporary slowness in your portal as it reloads data from Dynamics 365

Rebuild search index   Warning: Rebuilding the search index will cause a temporary slowness in your portal as the search index is rebuild. This action should not be performed during peak load time.

Clear config   Warning: Clear config will clear the config data from cache and will cause a temporary slowness on first page load

Figure 14-30. *Clearing the cache*

Tip   If anything doesn't seem to work correctly, the first step is to always clear the cache. It is almost a rite of passage for all app builders to waste hours diagnosing problems that have been fixed by simply clearing the cache!

Summary

This chapter covered the topic of portals. Portals provide a simple way to build Internet-facing websites and offer many benefits. A key feature is that it offers a graphical way to build a website with data entry screens that can retrieve and update records in Dataverse. Content creators can easily edit web pages through in-place editing controls.

In terms of licensing, internal users can access a portal though a subscription to a Dynamics 365 or a Power Apps plan. External users are billed on the basis of the number of logins, or the number of page impressions.

We can create a portal from a range of templates. There are Dynamics 365 templates that can build a portal that integrates with Dynamics 365 features. When we create a portal, Power Apps creates a model-driven Portal Management app. This allows us to configure the settings of a portal, including templates and security.

The starter template creates a portal with a set of standard pages that we can customize. This includes a home page, an about us page, and other pages that commonly exist in websites. The portal designer provides a graphical design surface and enables us to add components such as text areas, images, and data entry controls. The designer also features a code view, and we can use this to more precisely build pages by writing HTML.

The standard portal layout uses the Bootstrap framework. Because of this, the default pages in the portal are responsive and render well on mobile and PC devices.

The pages in a portal can share a common layout and common components. Page templates and web templates help achieve this. All web pages are associated with a page template, and multiple web pages can be associated with the same page template. A page template provides an object that allows us to define a common layout. A page template produces the output that the portal sends to the client by combining the web page content with common elements that are defined in web templates. Each page template is associated with one web template.

A web template can contain the HTML that defines the overall layout of the page, or it can contain small snippets of HTML. To support reusability, web templates can include the content of other web templates. Through inheritance, it's possible to override elements of a source web template that we include in another web template. The content of a web template can include server-side code that we write using a templating language called Liquid. This is the language that enables us to include child web templates and to include the content that is defined on a web page.

We can use web templates to define the header and footer that appear on all pages in a portal. We assign the header and footer web templates to the website.

We can configure a portal to authenticate users through a range of authentication providers. This includes AAD, Microsoft, Facebook, and Google. The portal also supports a local authentication provider that stores usernames and passwords in Dataverse.

The registration process is configurable. The default configuration is open registration. This means that any user that authenticates successfully can register as a user. To control registrations, we can switch to an invitation-based model of registration. This requires a user to enter an invitation code to register as a user. After we create a portal, we should register onto the portal using the AAD account that we used to provision the portal. This step makes us an administrator of the portal.

A portal stores user details in the Dataverse Contact table. We can organize users by creating web roles. A web role enables us to define a group of users.

To control access to a web page, we define a web page access control rule and assign the rule to a web role.

To control access to tables in Dataverse, we define entity permission records and assign these records to web roles. An entity permission record defines permissions that include read, write, create, and delete permissions. The entity permission record can apply to all records in a table or a subset of records in a table. We can configure permissions to apply only to records that are associated with the user or records that are associated with the account of the user. We can also apply permissions based on the permissions of a parent record. We can use this to grant access to the child records that are associated with a parent record.

CHAPTER 15

Retrieving Data from Portal Apps

The chapter covers a very powerful feature in Power Apps portals – the ability to build web pages that interact with a Dataverse data source. Because this feature is so valuable, it is probably the reason why Microsoft acquired this technology from Adxstudio.

This chapter focuses on how to use data components to build data entry and data display screens. We'll also learn about the search capabilities of the portal and find out how to extend this to include data from custom tables. The topics that we'll cover in this chapter will include

- How to use the list and entity form components to display lists of records and how to build simple data entry and data modification pages. This includes how to provide record deletion capabilities.

- How to build more complex, multistep data entry forms, how to validate input data, and how to provide default values.

- How to perform data access with Liquid code. This enables us to hand-craft customized web pages that include data from Dataverse.

Working with Data

We'll start this chapter by walking through the process to build a set of data entry web pages. The pages will enable a user to list, create, update, and delete records from our property table.

The portal provides two simple controls that can connect to a Dataverse table – a list component and an entity form component.

© Tim Leung 2021
T. Leung, *Beginning Power Apps*, https://doi.org/10.1007/978-1-4842-6683-0_15

For more complex data entry scenarios, there is the web form component. This component offers multistep data entry, branching rules, and support for more complex validation rules. We'll cover the web form component later in this chapter.

Creating Data Entry Pages

To build our feature, the first step is to create a set of web pages to host the data components. To display a list of records from the property table, we'll add a web page called the `Properties` page. Beneath this page, we'll add three child pages to facilitate the creation, modification, and display of a single record. We'll call these pages `NewProperty`, `EditProperty`, and `ViewProperty`. Figure 15-1 shows the structure of these pages in the tree view.

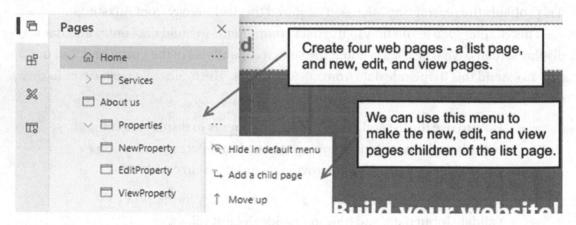

Figure 15-1. *Creating a set of data entry pages*

The next step is to set up appropriate table permissions. Without doing this, we would be unable to view or to modify records.

In this example, we'll set up a rule so that all authenticated users can create, edit, and view all records from the property entity. Chapter 14 describes this process in full detail, but to summarize, here are the two steps that we need to carry out from the Portal Management app:

- Create an entity permission record with Global scope that applies to the property table. Enable read, write, create, and delete permissions on this entity permission record.

- Assign this entity permission record to the Authenticated users web role.

At this stage, we're ready to build our data entry pages. We'll build the record entry, record modification, and record display forms first, because this enables us to link to these forms when we build our data list page.

Adding a New Record

To build our record entry page, we add a form component to our `NewProperty` web page. There are four mandatory properties that we need to set. These are the name, entity, form layout, and mode properties (Figure 15-2). Here's a summary of these four properties:

- Name – This defines the name of the form. We must provide a name that is unique throughout the portal.

- Entity – This defines the data source for the form. Here, we specify the name of a Dataverse table.

- Form layout – This defines the Dataverse form that defines the visible form fields.

- Mode – This defines the edit mode. The values we can set are Insert, Edit, and Read Only.

When we add a form component to a page, it's important to appreciate that forms are independent objects that are not wedded to a host web page. If we delete the host web page, the form will still exist in the portal. This enables us to reuse the same form on multiple web pages. The form name that we provide must therefore be unique.

The entity drop-down specifies the data source for our form. In this example, we select our property table.

The form layout defines the fields that appear on the form. The portal designer does not provide the ability to drag fields onto a form and to associate fields with data entry controls. Instead, we use the form layout drop-down to select one of the forms that we created through the table designer in Dataverse. The benefit of this architecture is that it enables us to reuse data entry forms in both model-driven and portal apps. The "Edit form" link that appears beneath the form layout drop-down opens the selected form in the Dataverse designer.

The mode property defines the behavior of our form, and there are three values that we can select – Insert, Edit, and Read Only. The Insert option configures the form to accept the entry of a new record, and this is the option that we choose for this form.

When we build our data modification and data display forms, we'll follow an identical process. The only difference is that we'll set the mode property to Edit and Read Only, respectively.

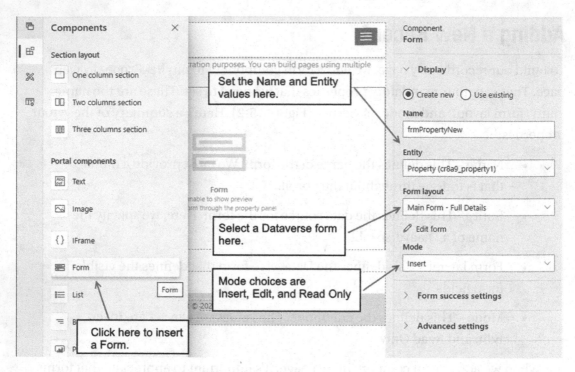

Figure 15-2. *Configuring the form designer*

We can specify the action that occurs when a user successfully saves a record. The settings in the "Form success settings" section control this behavior (Figure 15-3).

The "On success" drop-down enables us to show a success message, redirect the user to a web page, or redirect the user to a URL.

The "Advanced settings" section enables us to display a CAPTCHA on the form. A CAPTCHA prevents users from submitting a form unless they enter an obscure piece of text that appears in an image. The purpose of a CAPTCHA is to make it more difficult for spammers to submit spam messages.

An important setting that we should enable is the "Enable entity permissions" checkbox. This setting secures our form by making it honor the entity permissions on our property entity.

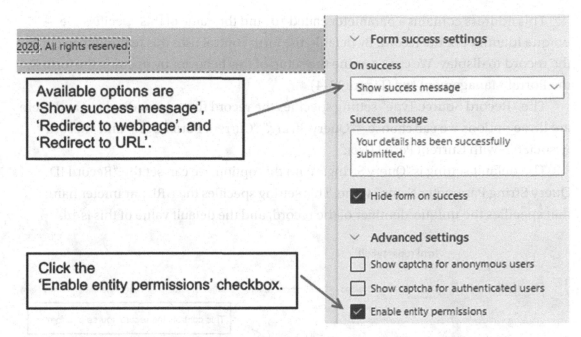

Available options are
'Show success message',
'Redirect to webpage', and
'Redirect to URL'.

Click the
'Enable entity permissions' checkbox.

Figure 15-3. *Setting what happens when a user successfully saves a record*

Tip   To secure the data entry form, remember to check the "Enable entity permissions" checkbox.

Editing a Record

To build our record modification page, we follow the same process as we carried out for our data entry page. We add a form component to our EditProperty page, and we can apply the same values for the entity and form layout properties. The only difference is that we set the mode setting to Edit.

The great news is that our page is now complete and we can now move on. However, an obvious question that arises at this stage is, how do we specify the record that appears in the form? After all, the form designer contains no property to specify the record that it shows.

The answer to this question lies in the Portal Management app. With web-based systems, the typical way to display a record is to specify a unique record ID in the web address. Here's an example of how such an address looks:

```
https://portaladdress/property/propertyEdit?id=8
```

This address contains a parameter called id, and the value of this specifies the unique identifier of the record. By default, the form control uses this technique to control the record to display. We can examine the setup of this behavior by opening the form in the Portal Management app (Figure 15-4).

The "Record Source Type" setting specifies the record that a form displays, and there are three options we can choose – "Query String," "Current Portal User," and "Record Associated with Current Portal User."

The default setting is "Query String." With this option, we can set the "Record ID Query String Parameter Name" value. This setting specifies the URL parameter name that specifies the unique identifier of the record, and the default value of this is id.

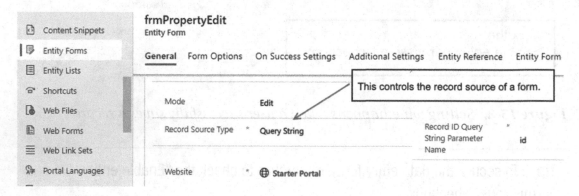

Figure 15-4. *Configuring the query string settings*

Viewing a Record

To build our record display page, we follow the same process as before. We add a form component to our ViewProperty page and set the entity and form layout properties. The difference here is that we set the mode setting to Read Only.

The record source for this form is a query string parameter with a name of id. Like our edit form, we can use the Portal Management app to configure the record source for the form.

Listing Data

Let's now build the screen that displays a list of records from our property table. To build this screen, we add a list component to our `Properties` web page.

There are two mandatory settings – the entity and views properties (Figure 15-5). The entity drop-down specifies the data source for our list. In this example, we select our property table.

The views drop-down displays a checkbox list of the views from Dataverse. We use this to specify the views that an end user can use to populate the list.

Like forms, lists are independent objects that exist outside of the host web page. If we delete the host web page, the list will still exist in the portal.

At runtime, users can select a list item and modify the selected record in the form control. The list can also provide buttons to add and to delete records.

We can control the ability to create, view, edit, or delete records through the properties of the list component. Against the create, view, and edit options, we can specify a "target type." The available options are form, web page, and URL.

The form option opens the record in a panel that floats above the list component. The web page option navigates the user to the web page that contains the form control, and the URL option navigates the user to a separate, external web page.

The settings area of the list properties contains additional useful settings. We can set the number of records to display in the list, we can check the option to "Enable search in the entity list," and we can check the option to "Enable entity permissions."

If we check the option to "Enable search in the entity list," the list component displays a search box that enables users to filter the records in the list.

To secure our list, we should check the "Enable entity permissions" checkbox.

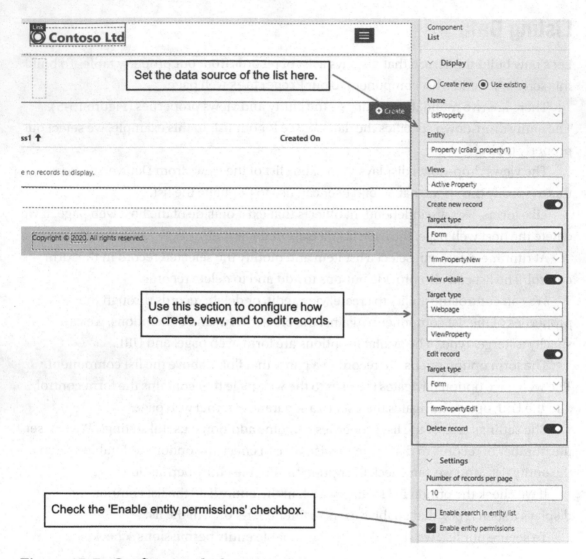

Figure 15-5. *Configuring the list control*

The Portal Management app enables us to configure the advanced settings of a list. A relevant setting is the "ID Query String Parameter Name" setting (Figure 15-6). This specifies the query string parameter name that the list control uses to call the web pages that host our form controls.

The default value here is id, which matches the "Record ID Query String Parameter Name" value for our form controls.

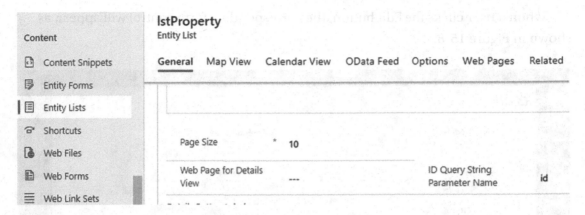

Figure 15-6. *Configuring the list control in the Portal Management app*

At this stage, we can run our portal and open our `Properties` list page. Because we secured our data by enabling entity permissions, we need to log in to our portal to be able to view and to edit the records in our property table.

Figure 15-7 shows the appearance of our list page. The property records appear in the list component; and to the right of each record, a drop-down control opens a menu that enables the user to view, edit, or delete the record.

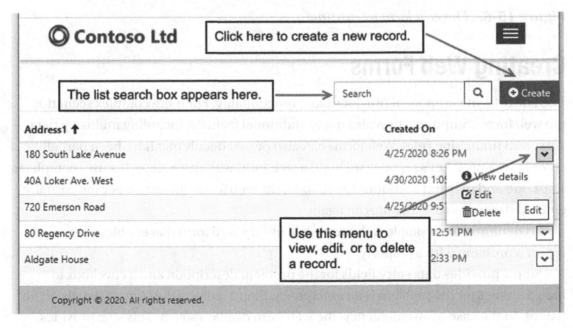

Figure 15-7. *The list page at runtime*

When a user clicks the Edit button, the corresponding form control will appear, as shown in Figure 15-8.

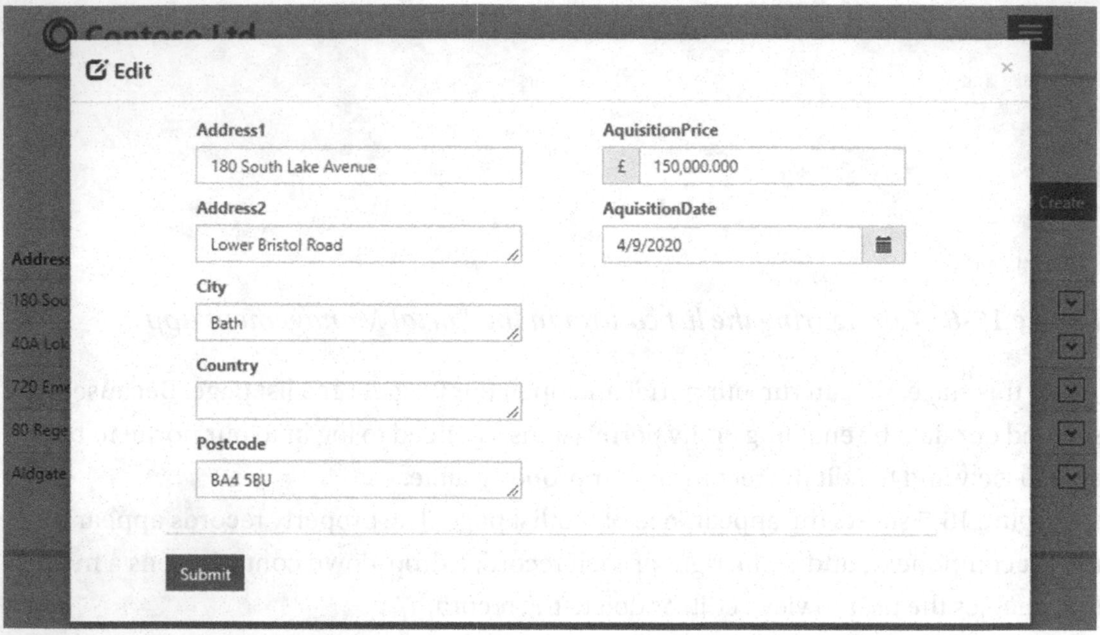

Figure 15-8. *The edit form at runtime*

Creating Web Forms

The entity form component provides basic functionality. For more complex scenarios, the web form component provides many additional features, including multistep data entry and branching rules. Web forms can also persist details that have been partially entered by a user. Let's suppose we build a web form with three steps. If a user completes steps one and two and abandons the session, the web form will remember the partially entered data when the user logs on again.

To demonstrate a simple web form, we'll build a web form that enables a tenant to report a problem with a property.

Step 1 provides data entry fields for the problem description and a checkbox to indicate whether the problem is an emergency. Step 2 collects the contact details of the tenant. In the case of an emergency, the web form displays step 3. This step provides data entry fields to establish the cause of the emergency. If the case is not an emergency, step 3 will not show.

There is no way to add a web form component through the designer. Instead, we rely on the Portal Management app to create a web form. The summary of the steps to build a web form are as follows:

- Create a web page to host the web form.

- Create a Dataverse form to define the fields and steps to include in our web form.

- Create a web form based on the Dataverse form.

- Use the web form designer to define the steps, branching rules, and web page where we want to attach the web form.

Creating a Dataverse Form

A web form is based on forms that we define in Dataverse. Therefore, the first step is to open our issue table in the Dataverse table designer and to build the form that forms the basis for our web form.

We'll create a single form and name it "Issue – Portal Form." This form will contain three tabs, with each tab representing a step in our process. Within each tab, we add the fields that we want to show for the step, as shown in Figure 15-9.

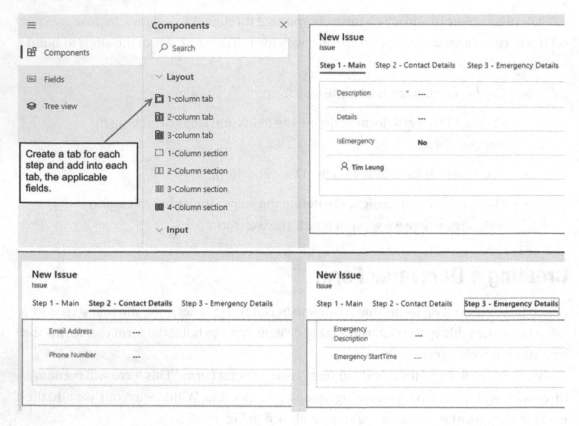

Figure 15-9.   *Creating a form in Dataverse*

Creating a Portal Web Form

The next step is to open the Portal Management app and to add a new web form through the Web Forms section. Figure 15-10 shows the view of the web form designer. Through the tabs at the top of the page, we can define the web form steps, associate the web form with web pages, and manage session details.

Beneath the General tab, there are several items that we need to set. The first is to provide a web form name – we'll name our web form "Issue Webform." We also need to specify the "Start Step" for our web form. We cannot do this right now because we haven't created any web form steps. Therefore, we'll set the "Start Step" after we create our first web form step.

A web form remembers the details that a user partially enters. The "Start New Session on Load" checkbox controls this behavior. If this is set to true, the web form creates a new session when a user loads the form, which will prevent a user from resuming previously entered data if the user abandons a session and reloads the form. The Sessions tab displays a list of all active sessions, and we can use this section to delete user sessions if necessary.

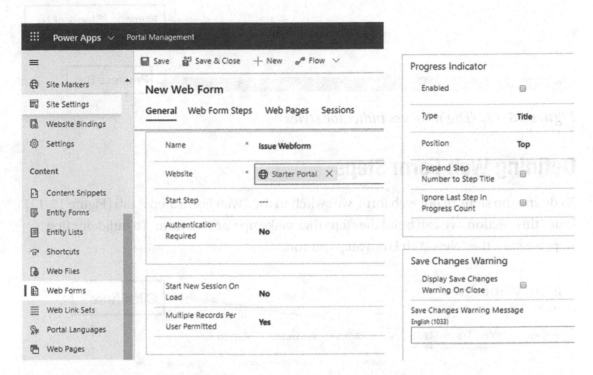

Figure 15-10. *The General options we can set when creating a web form*

Lower down in the General tab is the option to configure "Progress Indicator" settings. We can use these settings to display a progress indicator and the step number. The Type settings include Title, Numeric (Step 1 of N), and Progress Bar, which are shown in Figure 15-11.

Finally, we can use the settings in the "Save Changes Warning" section to show the warning text that appears if the user attempts to navigate away from the web form without saving their changes.

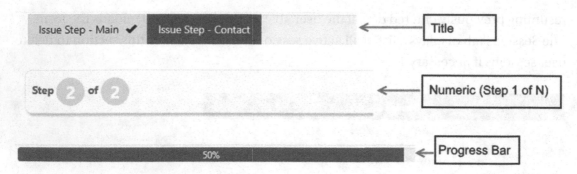

Figure 15-11. *The progress indicator styles*

Defining Web Form Steps

To define the steps of our web form, we switch to the "Web Form Steps" tab (Figure 15-12). From this section, we can build the steps that make up our web form. To build our first step, we click the "New Web Form Step" button.

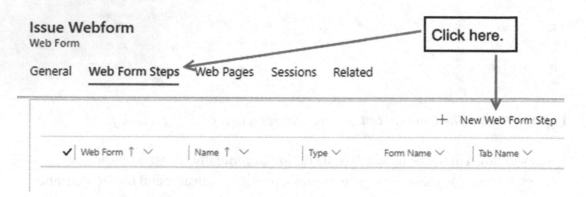

Figure 15-12. *The web form steps in a web form*

This opens the screen that's shown in Figure 15-13 that shows the settings of the web form step. Beneath the General tab, there are several settings that we need to complete. The first is the web step name. We'll name our first web step "Issue – Details Step."

The next setting is the Type, and there are five options that we can choose – Load Form, Load Tab, Redirect, Load User Control, and Condition. In this example, we want to load the contents of the first tab on our Dataverse form, so we set the Type to Load Tab.

The "Target Entity Logical Name" field defines the data source for the web step, and we set this to our issue entity.

The "Enable Entity Permissions" checkbox is important. We should check this if we want to secure this step with entity permissions.

An important setting that we need to provide is the "Next Step." However, we cannot provide this until we create step 2, so we will need to set this after we create the second step.

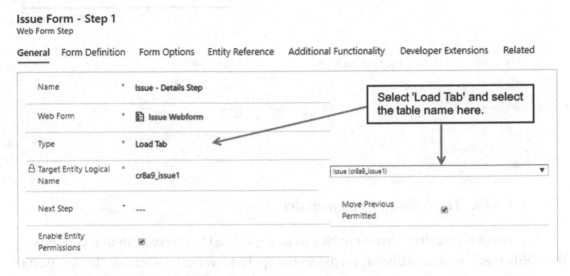

Figure 15-13. *The General details of a web step*

To define the contents of our web form step, we switch to the Form Definition tab (Figure 15-14). The mode setting provides the options "Insert," "Edit," and "Read Only." The default value is Insert, and we retain this option because we want our web form to create new records in our issue entity.

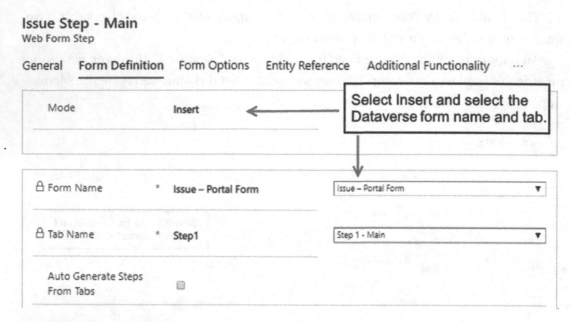

Figure 15-14. *The definition of a web step*

The Form Name drop-down enables us to select the Dataverse form that contains the fields that we want to display on the web step. Here, we can select our "Issue – Portal Form" Dataverse form; and beneath, we can select the tab on this form that contains our step 1 fields.

A really useful feature is the "Auto Generate Steps From Tabs" checkbox. We could check this checkbox to create three steps from the form we select, rather than create each step separately. In this example, we choose not to take advantage of this feature because we want to introduce a branching rule later on.

Defining Additional Steps

Once we've created and saved our first step, we can create steps 2 and 3. The process is almost identical to what we carried out for step 1. We click the "New Web Form Step" button to create a new web step. We set the Type to "Load Tab" and set the "Target Entity Logical Name" field to our issue entity.

Beneath the Form Definition tab, we specify the Dataverse form and the tab that contains the controls that we want to show on the web step.

However, the crucial difference between the first and subsequent web steps is that we must set the mode to Edit. In our example, step 1 creates the record; and therefore, the mode of all subsequent steps must be Edit.

Figure 15-15 shows the precise steps to set this up. First, we set the mode to Edit. Next, we use the Record Source drop-down to select the record source for our web step. We set this to Query String. The other Source Type options we can choose include "Current Portal User," "Result from Previous Step," and "Record Associated with Current Portal User."

By default, the web form provides the ID of the current record, so we set the "Primary Key Query String Parameter Name" value to id. The final value that we need to provide is the name of the primary key field for our entity.

For the purposes of this example, we'll name steps 2 and 3 "Issue – Contact Step" and "Issue – Emergency Step," respectively.

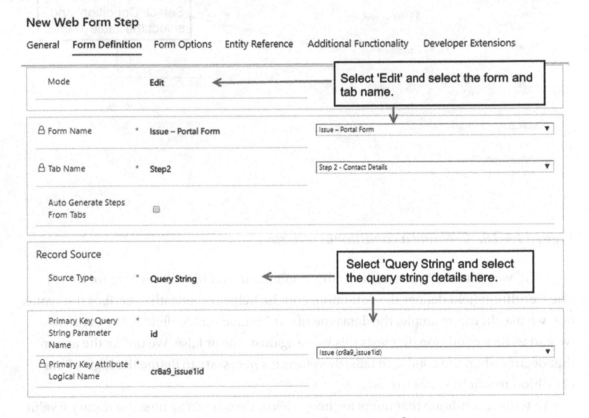

Figure 15-15. *Set the mode of subsequent web steps to Edit*

Branching Form Steps

At this point, we've created the three web steps to collect our data. Now, we can build the rule to display step 3 only if the user marks the issue as an emergency in step 1.

We use web steps to define branching rules. To do this, we create a web step and set the Type to "Condition." We also need to set the "Target Entity Logical Name" field to our issue table (Figure 15-16).

We leave the Next Step setting empty.

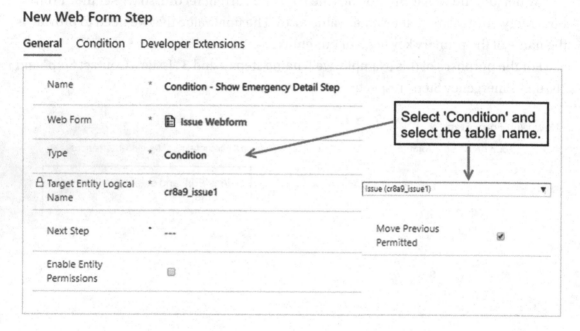

Figure 15-16. *Creating a conditional web step*

Next, we switch to the Condition tab to define our conditional rule (Figure 15-17). The Condition field defines the condition, and the help text beneath describes the syntax that we use. In this example, the data type of our "Is Emergency" field is "Yes/No," so we can write a condition that tests this value against true or false. We define the action that occurs when the condition fails; therefore, it's necessary to define the logic of our condition to suit how this works.

To write a condition that refers to choice fields, we can test against the numeric value of the choice value.

Issue Condition - Emergency
Web Form Step

General   **Condition**   Developer Extensions   Related

| Condition | * | cre23_isemergency = false |

| Next Step If Condition Fails | 🗒 Issue Step - Emerge... |

Help

Branching Logic Conditional Expression

A Web Form Step can be a 'Condition' type that indicates the step should evaluate an expression. If the expression evaluates to true then the next step is displayed. If the expression evaluates to false and if the 'Next Step If Condition Fails' has been specified, that step will be displayed. The current entity is the target used to evaluate the expression against.

The available operands and format of the expression are as follows:

Operands:

Operand(s)	Type
=, ==	Equals
!=	Not equals
>	Greater Than
<	Less Than
>=	Greater Than or Equals
<=	Less Than or Equals
&	And
|	Or
!	Not
=*, ==*, ~=	Like
!=*	Not Like

Figure 15-17. *Defining the conditional step*

Once we've defined our conditional web form step, we need to edit all the web steps that we created earlier and to set the Next Step settings as appropriate.

To summarize, we set the "First Step" setting of our web form to "Issue – Details Step." We set the Next Step setting of "Issue – Details Step" to "Issue – Contact Step." We set the Next Step setting of "Issue – Contact Step" to the conditional step that we've created.

Tip   For clarity, we built our web steps in chronological sequence. In practice, we could build our web steps in reverse order, which would enable us to set the "Next Step" settings as we go along.

Completing and Running Our Web Form

To complete our web form, the final step is to create a web page through the portal designer and to associate the page with our web form through the Web Pages tab of the web form designer.

At this stage, we can run our web page, and Figure 15-18 shows how our web form looks at runtime.

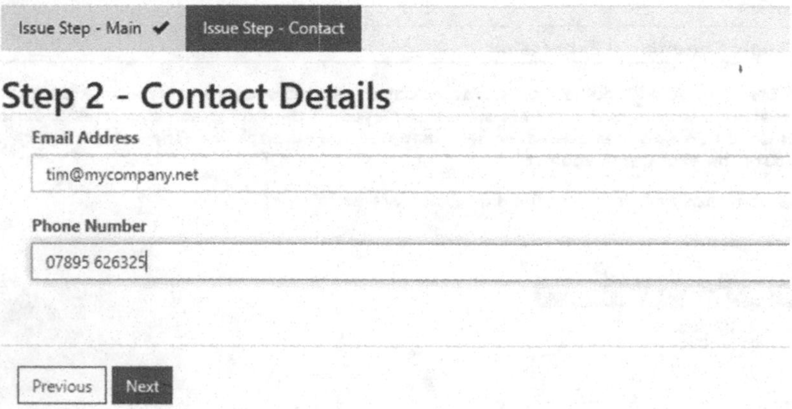

Figure 15-18. *The web form at runtime*

Configuring Form Fields

We can customize the fields on web forms and entity forms by defining metadata records. This is a powerful feature that provides the capability to carry out a wide range of field configuration tasks. This includes

- Setting the text of field labels.

- Setting field descriptions and help text that can appear above or below the field or field label.

- Setting the control type. For example, we can configure horizontal or vertical radio buttons for choice fields or configure controls that cater for the entry of geospatial data.

- Setting field values on save. When a user saves a record, we can set field values to the logged-on user or the current date and time or static values.

Two very useful tasks we can perform through metadata records are to validate form fields and to set default field values. These are the two areas that we'll focus on in this section.

To define a metadata rule through a web form step, we click the Related tab to reveal the Metadata menu. This menu shows a list of metadata records, and we can click the "New Web Form Metadata" button to create a new record (Figure 15-19).

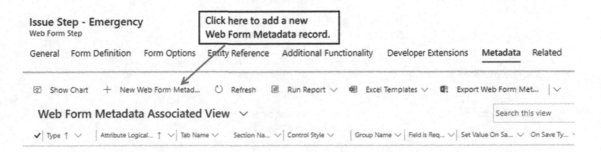

Figure 15-19. *Creating a metadata rule*

Validating Fields and Forms

We'll now find out how to apply field-level validation by using metadata rules. But before we do so, let's take a quick look at the validation settings that we can apply at a web form step level. If we open the Form Definition section of a web form, we can find the options that are shown in Figure 15-20.

We can use these settings to make all fields on the web form step mandatory. We can also make mandatory all fields that are marked as optional in Dataverse.

When a validation error occurs, the web form displays a banner at the top of the form. We can use the settings here to define the heading that appears, and we can apply a CSS class to customize the appearance of this banner.

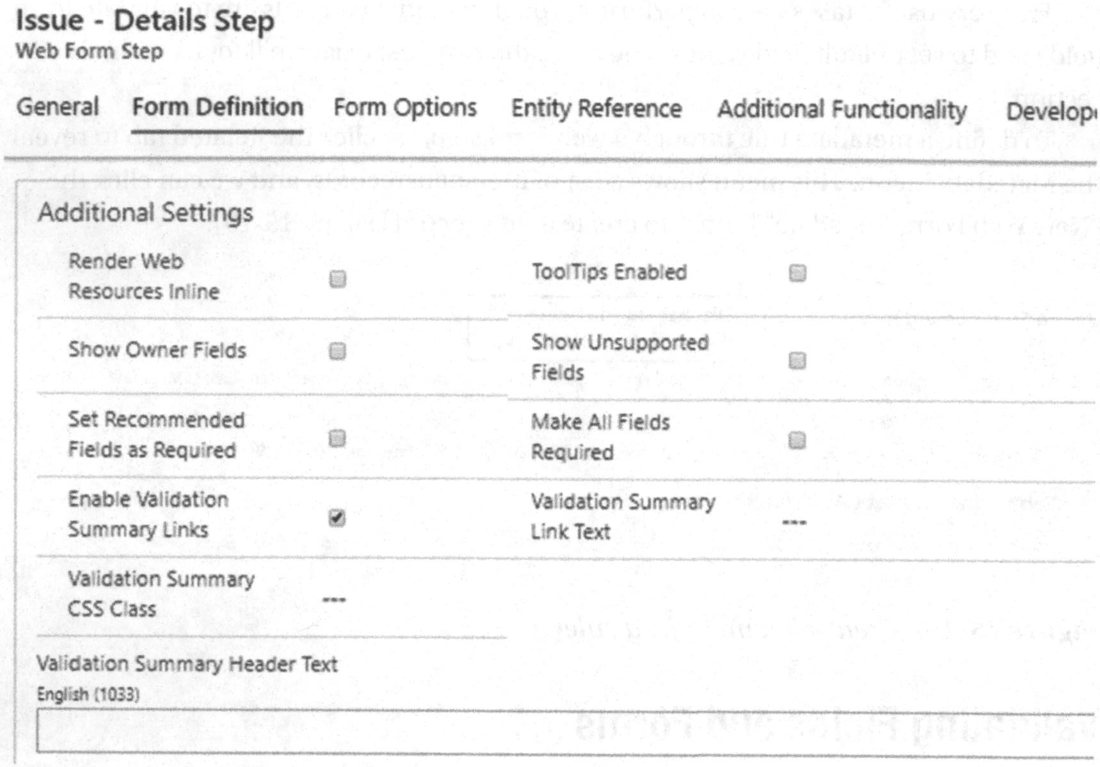

Issue - Details Step
Web Form Step

| General | **Form Definition** | Form Options | Entity Reference | Additional Functionality | Develop |

Additional Settings

Render Web Resources Inline	☐	ToolTips Enabled	☐
Show Owner Fields	☐	Show Unsupported Fields	☐
Set Recommended Fields as Required	☐	Make All Fields Required	☐
Enable Validation Summary Links	☑	Validation Summary Link Text	---
Validation Summary CSS Class	---		

Validation Summary Header Text
English (1033)

Figure 15-20. Form-level validation settings

To demonstrate how to create a field-level validation rule, we'll walk through the process to make the "Emergency Description" field mandatory. First, we create a new metadata record. The first section requires us to select a Type and an Entity. Here, we retain the default Type setting of Attribute, and we select our issue table (Figure 15-21).

Other Type values we can select here include Timeline, Notes, Purchase, Section, Subgrid, and Tab. To give an example of how to apply these different types, we can select the Tab and Section types to set the label text that appears.

New Web Form Metadata

General

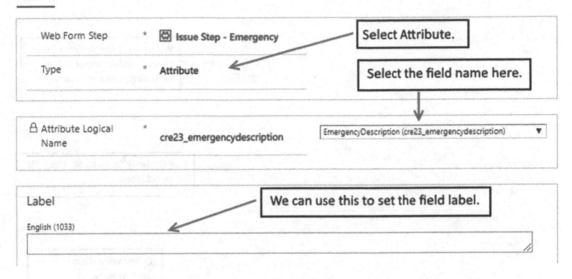

Figure 15-21. *Creating metadata for a form field*

If we now scroll down the General tab, we will find the Validation section (Figure 15-22). Through the settings here, we can define mandatory fields or apply range or regular expression validation rules.

As this screenshot shows, we can click the "Field Is Required" checkbox to make the field mandatory, and we can also provide the validation error message.

We can enforce these types of simple validation rules through metadata. For more complex scenarios, (e.g., to mandate that a date cannot be greater than today), we can write custom JavaScript to apply such rules.

Unfortunately, entity and web forms are not capable of enforcing validation logic that we define through business rules, which would be the preferred way to implement this functionality.

Caution   Entity forms and web forms do not enforce the logic that we define through business rules in Dataverse.

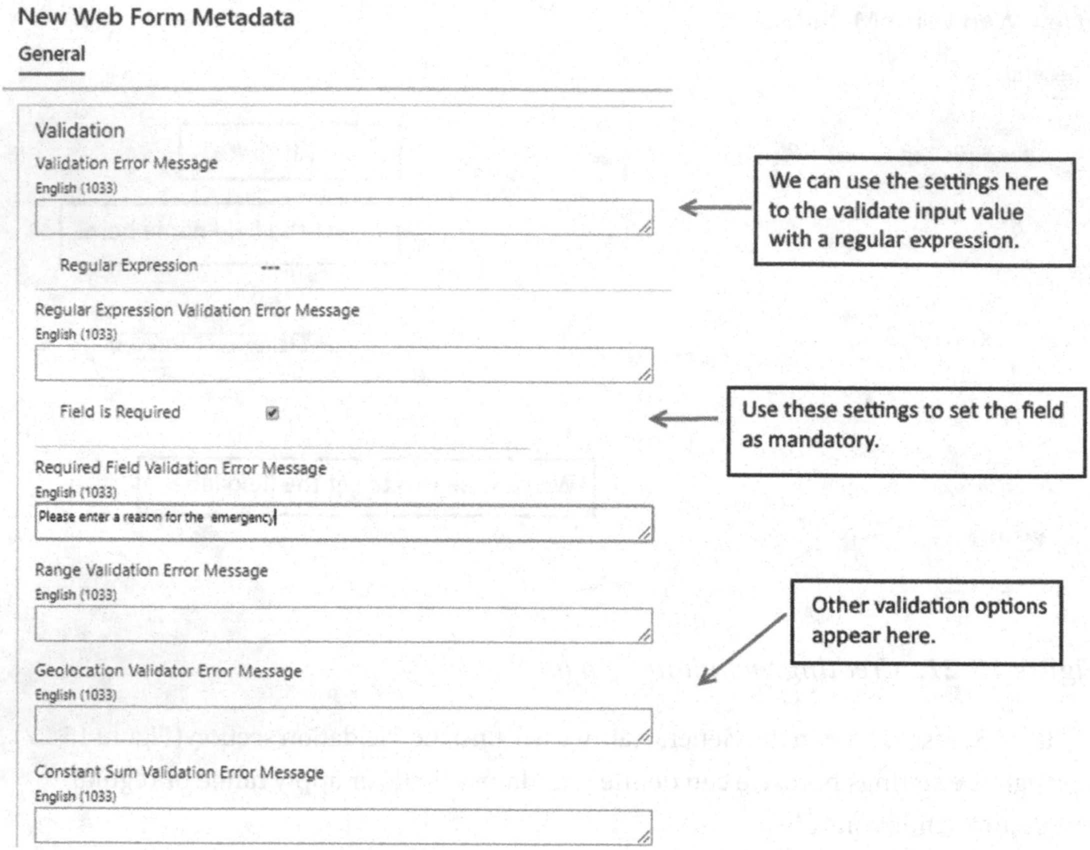

New Web Form Metadata

General

Validation

Validation Error Message

English (1033)

> We can use the settings here to the validate input value with a regular expression.

Regular Expression   ---

Regular Expression Validation Error Message

English (1033)

Field Is Required   ☑

> Use these settings to set the field as mandatory.

Required Field Validation Error Message

English (1033)

Please enter a reason for the emergency|

Range Validation Error Message

English (1033)

> Other validation options appear here.

Geolocation Validator Error Message

English (1033)

Constant Sum Validation Error Message

English (1033)

Figure 15-22. *Defining validation rules*

Setting Default Form Values

Through metadata records, we can also apply default field values. To demonstrate, here's how to set the default value of the "emergency date" to today's date.

First, we create a new metadata record. We retain the default Type value of Attribute, and we select our issue entity. Beneath the General section, we can use the Prepopulate Field section to define the default field value. In our example, we can set the Type value to Today's Date, to default our field to the current date and time (Figure 15-23).

Other Type settings include Value and Current User. With the Value type, we enter a static default value through the Value textbox.

We can use the Current User type when we want to default the value of a contact lookup field.

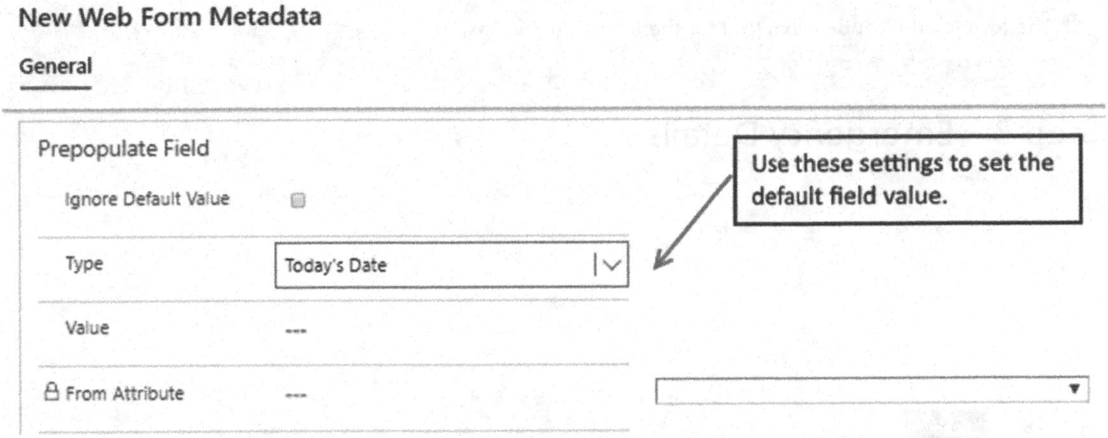

New Web Form Metadata

General

Figure 15-23. *Defaulting values using a metadata rule*

There are several other useful settings in the Prepopulate Field section. The "Ignore Default Value" checkbox is useful for Dataverse "Yes/No" fields (such as our "Is Emergency" field). The portal renders these fields using Yes/No radio buttons, and with the "Ignore Default Value" checkbox checked, no radio button is selected when our web step loads.

The From Attribute drop-down shows a list of fields from the Contact table. We can usc this option to set the default value of a field to an attribute that relates to the current user (e.g., first name, last name, or one of the address fields that relate to the current user).

Runtime Example

At this point, we can run our web form to test our metadata changes. When we reach step 3, the emergency start time field defaults to today's date, and the description field will be mandatory, as shown in Figure 15-24.

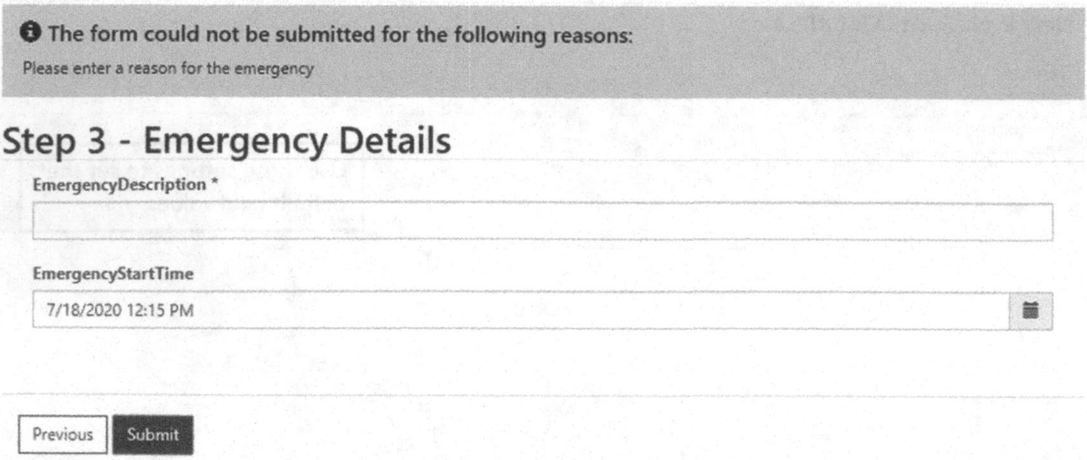

ⓘ **The form could not be submitted for the following reasons:**

Please enter a reason for the emergency

Step 3 - Emergency Details

EmergencyDescription *

EmergencyStartTime

7/18/2020 12:15 PM   📅

Previous Submit

Figure 15-24. The form at runtime

Searching Data

A portal provides built-in search capabilities. This feature adds great value because it offers integrated search across both static content on web pages and content from records in Dataverse. For portals that are based on Dynamics 365 templates, the search results include records from common entities such as knowledgebase articles, blogs, and forum posts.

To access this search page, users can click the magnifying glass icon in the header. Alternatively, users can navigate directly to the search page through the following default address:

```
https://portaladdress/search/
```

Figure 15-25 shows the appearance of the search screen. As this screenshot shows, it provides the ability to filter the search results by record type and modification date.

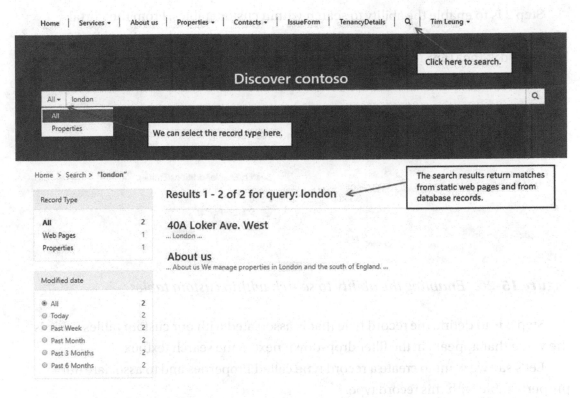

Figure 15-25. *The search page*

To include the content of custom tables in the search results, there's a little bit of work to carry out. To demonstrate, we'll walk through the steps to add the contents of our property table to the search results. There are four main steps to carry out. We need to define a view in Dataverse, enable the search feature for custom tables, define a record type group, and specify the target portal web page that opens the search result record.

The first step is to open our property table in the Dataverse designer and to create a view called "Portal Search." The purpose of this view is to define all target fields that we want the search feature to search against. It's important to name the view "Portal Search," because this is the name that the search feature expects.

Note   To include the content of custom entities in the search results, we must create a view in the target Dataverse table called "Portal Search."

Step 2 is to enable the ability to search within custom tables. From the Portal Management app, we open the Site Settings section, create a new setting called Search/EnableAdditionalEntities, and set the value of this to true (Figure 15-26).

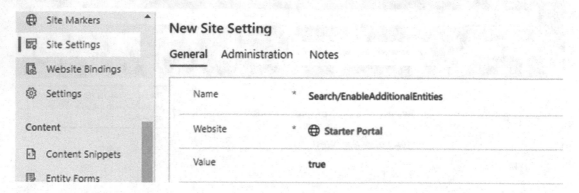

Figure 15-26. *Enabling the ability to search within custom tables*

Step 3 is to define the record type that is associated with our custom tables – this is the value that appears in the filter drop-down next to the search textbox.

Let's say we want to create a record type called Properties and to associate our property table with this record type.

To implement this, we use the Portal Management app and set the value of the search/filters setting to the following value (Figure 15-27):

Properties: cr8a9_property

The value that we set here is a comma-separated list of record types and logical entity names. For example, let's suppose we want to extend the search to include records from our issue entity and we need these results to also belong to the Properties record type. The search/filters setting that we apply would look like this:

Properties:cr8a9_property, Properties:cr8a9_issue

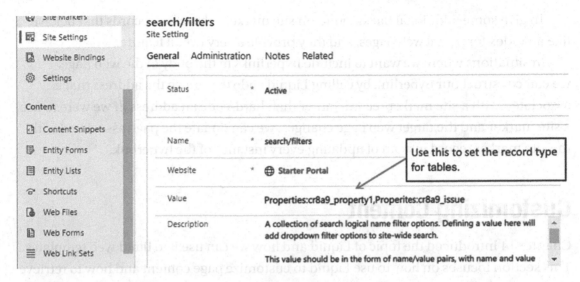

Figure 15-27. *Defining the search record type for tables*

The final stage is to define the page that displays the search result for a property record. To do this, we add a site marker record. The name that we give this record starts with the logical name of the table, followed by the suffix _SearchResultPage. We set the value of this site marker record to the name of the web page that displays the entity (Figure 15-28).

In our example, we create a record called cr8a9_property_SearchResultsPage and select the ViewProperty page that we created earlier in this chapter.

This completes all the necessary steps, and at this stage, we can clear the cache and use the search feature to search for property records.

Figure 15-28. *Defining the page that displays a search result*

To give some additional background on site markers, these are records that behave like an index for portal web pages, and they provide a very useful feature.

In situations where we want to include hyperlinks in the body of the web page, we can construct our hyperlink by calling Liquid code to retrieve the address that is associated with a site marker record, rather than hard-code an address. If we were to use a site marker and the target web page changes, we can update the page associated with the site marker record instead of updating every instance of the hyperlink.

Customizing Content

Chapter 14 introduced the topic of Liquid and how we can use it to build web templates. This section focuses on how to use Liquid to customize page content and how to retrieve records from Dataverse.

First, here's a quick revision and overview of Liquid. Liquid is a server-side templating language with constructs that include variables, if statements, and loops. A simple and common reason to use Liquid code is to build text on a page that incorporates data values from a record. We can use this to display data outside the rigid structure of an entity or web form component.

Liquid code runs on the server. Unlike JavaScript, which is a client-side language, the end user never sees the Liquid code that we write. It is a templating language, meaning that we can retrieve entity data with Liquid code, but we cannot write or modify data.

Liquid is an open source language that was developed by Shopify – a Canadian ecommerce company. The language has been ported to many platforms, and portal apps use a Microsoft implementation of Liquid. This means that if we search the Web for help on Liquid, the code that we find may not be completely compatible with the Microsoft implementation.

Liquid Language

The keywords in Liquid are categorized into three separate types – objects, tags, and filters:

- Objects help us to retrieve the content to display on a page.

- Tags define logical and control statements.

- Filters perform operations by transforming inputs into outputs.

To use Liquid, we insert in-place Liquid code into the source of a web page or web template. There are two ways to specify a block of Liquid code – we can wrap the code in either {{ }} or {% %}.

The {{ }} syntax renders an expression on a page, and we use this syntax to display object values. The {% %} syntax defines logic and control statements, and we use this to declare tags.

The objects in Liquid enable us to access entity, date, page request, and parameter values and user details. The names of the most common objects include

```
entities, now, page, params, request, settings, sitemap, sitemarkers,
snippets, user, weblinks, website
```

To support more specific portal tasks, the following tags are also available:

```
chart, powerbi, entitylist, fetchxml, entityview, searchindex, entityform,
webform
```

To define logic and control flow statements, Liquid provides the following tags:

```
if, unless, elsif/else, case/when, for, cycle, tablerow
```

Liquid supports the following logical and string operators:

```
==, !=, >, <, >=, <=, or, and, contains, startswith, endswith
```

Liquid supports a range of data types that include string, number, Boolean, array, dictionary, and datetime.

Instead of functions, Liquid relies on filters. To transform a string or to carry out a mathematical task, we pipe the input value to a filter using the pipe operator |. Here are some of the common filters that we can call:

- Array filters – `concat, size, first, last, group_by, join, order_by`

- Math filters – `plus, minus, times, divided_by, floor, round`

- String filters – `capitalize, downcase, escape, strip, concat`

Retrieving the Current User

Starting with a simple example, let's look at how to apply an if statement and how to display details that relate to the current logged-on user. At runtime, the page content will show the name of the logged-on user. If no user is logged on, the screen will display the text "Welcome to the portal."

To build out this example, we'll open a page, switch to code view, and add the following code:

```
{% if user %}
   Hello, {{ user.fullname }}!
{% else %}
   Welcome to the portal
{% endif %}
```

This code highlights the structure of an if statement. We wrap the if, else, and endif statements inside {% %} placeholders.

The user object represents the current logged-on user. If no user is logged on, the user object returns null. The user object returns the Contact record that is associated with the logged-on user. Therefore, we can access all the fields that are available through the Contact record. This includes firstname, lastname, fullname, address1_line1, emailaddress1, and more. We can see a full list by examining the logical name fields for the Contact table.

To display an object value on the screen, we wrap the value inside the {{ }} placeholders. Therefore, {{user.fullname}} outputs the value of the full name on the screen.

It is possible to test whether a user belongs to a web role. This is useful because it enables us to show or hide content depending on web role membership. Here's the syntax to test if the user belongs to the Administrators role:

```
{% if user.roles contains 'Administrators' %}
```

In code view, we can process our output further using filters. For example, we could use filters to modify the capitalization or casing of text. The best way to show this is through examples, and Listing 15-1 illustrates some common use case scenarios.

Listing 15-1. Liquid code samples

```
// Capitalizes the first character - returns Tim Leung
{{ "tim leung" | capitalize }}

// Lower case and upper case an input value
{{ "Tim Leung" | downcase }}
{{ "Tim Leung" | upcase }}

// Math functions
{{ 4 | plus: 2 }}
{{ 16 | minus: 4 }}
{{ 20 | divided_by: 7.0 }}
{{ 24 | times: 7 }}
{{ 183.357 | round: 2 }} // returns 183.38

// Format a date Sun, Jan 30, 21
{{ article.published_at | date: "%a, %b %d, %y" }}

// Return the current date and time - returns 2019-09-19 17:48
{{ "now" | date: "%Y-%m-%d %H:%M" }}

// Incorporating sitemarkers - returns the url of a sitemarker called help
{{ sitemarkers["help"].url }}
```

An interesting highlight is the syntax to perform mathematical tasks. Unlike other languages, Liquid doesn't support common keywords, such as + and -, to perform addition and subtraction. Instead, we pipe the input values to the plus and minus filters.

Another interesting highlight is the syntax to format dates. The date filter formats an input date using a string pattern. For example, the placeholder %a returns the three-character day of week name, and %b returns the short month name. These placeholder codes may seem strange because they are different from the formatting strings from other languages. For example, JavaScript and the Text function in canvas apps use the ddd format string to denote the three-character day of week.

The date format strings in Liquid are based on syntax from the Ruby programming language. They correspond to the format strings that apply to Ruby's Time.Parse method. Therefore, we can refer to the Ruby documentation to find a full list of acceptable format codes.

Retrieving a Single Record

With Liquid, we can retrieve a single Dataverse record by unique ID. As an example, here's the syntax to retrieve a specific property record by ID:

```
{% assign varProp = entities.cr8a9_property['23963eb1-2a87-ea11-99e5-
00155d26c07e'] %}
```

```
{% if varProp %}
    Address:{{ varProp.Address1}}, {{ varProp.Address2}}, {{ varProp.
    Postcode}}
{%else%}
    Property not found
{% endif %}
```

We can access tables by logical name through the `entities` object. The first line of code retrieves a property record and assigns it to a variable called `varProp`. We can then refer to this variable to output the fields.

Rather than use a hardcoded GUID, a common practice is to pass the GUID value though a URL parameter, as is the case with our ViewProperty web page. We can retrieve the request parameter value using syntax that looks like this:

```
{% assign varProp = entities.cr8a9_property[request.params[ID]] %}
```

Retrieving Multiple Records

In addition to retrieving a single record, we can also retrieve multiple records by writing queries in a language called FetchXML. FetchXML is a proprietary language that Dataverse uses, and the feature of this language is that it expresses in XML, the elements that make up a query. This includes the data source, the fields that we want to retrieve, and filter conditions. With FetchXML, we can define queries that return aggregations, such as counts, averages, and minimum/maximum values. We can also join entities and define outer joins to build "not in"-type queries.

From Liquid code, we use the `fetchxml` tag to define a FetchXML query. To demonstrate, here's how to return records from our property table that match the city London:

```
{% fetchxml my_query %}   ❶
<fetch mapping="logical">   ❷
  <entity name= name="cr8a9_property">   ❸
    <attribute name="cr8a9_ address1" />
    <attribute name="cr8a9_ address2" />
    <filter>   ❹
      <condition attribute="cr8a9_city" operator="eq" value="London" />
    </filter>
  </entity>
</fetch>
{% endfetchxml %}

<ul>
{% for result in my_query.results.entities %}   ❺
    <li>
              <a href="/Properties/PropertyView?id={{result.cr8a9_
              id}}">
            {{result.cr8a9_propertytypedesc}}
        </a>
    </li>
{% endfor %}
</ul>
```

The first block of code defines a query with the `fetchxml` tag ❶. The value that we specify after the `fetchxml` tag defines the name of the query, `my_query` in this example.

The XML between the `fetchxml` and `endfetchxml` tags defines the query. This XML begins with an opening `fetch` element ❷.

Within the outer XML `fetch` element, the `entity` element defines the logical name of the table that we want to query ❸. The child `attribute` elements define the fields to return in the query. We can also optionally define filter conditions ❹.

Following the `endfetchxml` tag, we can loop through the query results with a for loop and display the output fields on the page ❺. The code here formats the output as a list of hyperlinks. To configure a hyperlink to open a property record, we set the target `href` of the hyperlink to point to our `PropertyView` page, and we can set the `id` parameter value of this page to the unique identifier of the property record. Figure 15-29 shows the output of this code.

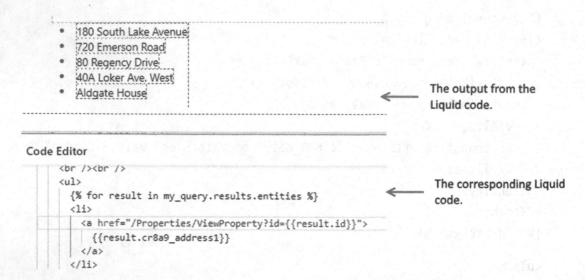

Figure 15-29. *The output of the FetchXML-based Liquid code*

To construct more complex queries that can include joins, multiple conditions, and grouping conditions, there are some simple ways to help us learn the necessary XML syntax.

A great tool is FetchXML Builder for XrmToolBox. This free tool provides the ability to construct a query using a graphical designer. This designer enables us to add the source entities and fields onto a design surface and to configure other advanced query attributes. FetchXML Builder can then construct the FetchXML code that corresponds to the query.

Other great resources are online resources that can convert queries from SQL and other query languages to FetchXML. A web search will return several sites that can carry out conversions.

Customizing Pages with JavaScript

In the final part of this chapter, we'll look at the places where we can add JavaScript to web pages. This topic requires some JavaScript knowledge, so the content here may include some unfamiliar concepts. However, the content should serve to highlight the JavaScript themes that are applicable to portal apps.

The prime purpose of JavaScript is to add client-side logic and interactivity to web pages. We can set, retrieve, and process form input values. We can also show and hide elements, carry out validation, and integrate with web services, payment processing services, and more.

The easiest way to add JavaScript to a web page is to open it in the designer, switch to code view, and enter the script directly into the source of the page.

Another place where we can add JavaScript is through web templates. To add a script that is visible to all pages in a portal, we can add it to the header template. Figure 15-30 shows how to access this through the Web Templates section of the Portal Management app, and it highlights the default script that exists in the header section.

Figure 15-30. *Adding JavaScript to the page header*

To add JavaScript to individual web pages, we can attach it using the Custom JavaScript textbox in the Advanced tab of a web page record. When we first attempt to use this method, however, we may find that the web page does not render the JavaScript that we define.

The reason for this is that a portal provides built-in localization support and the script that we add to a page can be localized to work with multiple languages. This feature is ideal when we need to build a script that contains language-specific user messages.

The default settings of a portal permit multiple active languages through the Portal Languages section of the Portal Management app. To attach JavaScript to a web page, we must add it to the localized page record, rather than the actual page record. We can find the localized pages in the Localized Content section, under the General tab. When we open the localized page record, we can enter our JavaScript using the textbox beneath the Advanced tab (Figure 15-31).

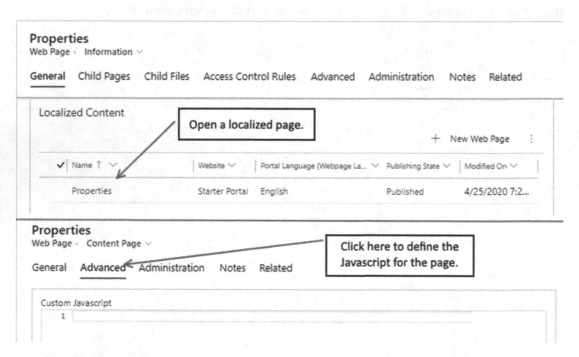

Figure 15-31. *Adding localized JavaScript to a web page*

Uploading JavaScript Files

When we develop pages that utilize JavaScript, a typical practice is to add code to separate JavaScript files and to reference those in our code. This is particularly relevant when we want to use code from JavaScript libraries.

We can host JavaScript and other static files in a portal by uploading our files through the Web Files section of the Portal Management app. To add a file, we create a new web file record. Under the General tab, we select a parent page to define the root path, and we use the Partial Uri field to the endpoint file name. In this example, we set the Parent Page to "Home" and the "Partial Uri" to moment.js. Through this configuration, the file we upload will be accessible through the following address:

https://portaladdress/moment.js

To upload our JavaScript file, we switch to the Notes tab and click the file attachment icon, as shown in Figure 15-32.

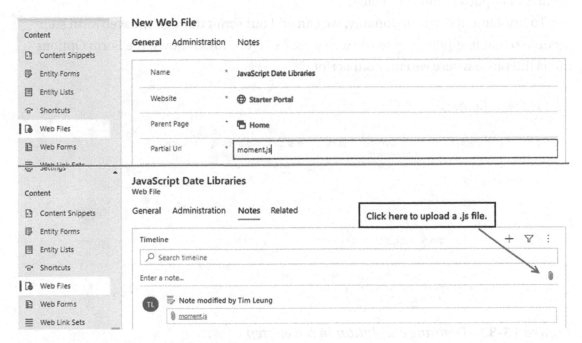

Figure 15-32. Uploading static files

Before we do this, there is one additional piece of setup to carry out. By default, the Portal Management app disallows the upload of files with a js extension. Therefore, it is necessary to remove this restriction before we can upload a JavaScript file.

Currently, we can only access these settings through the legacy Dynamics 365 settings area. We can reach this area by opening the Power Platform admin center and selecting our environment. From the settings page of our environment, we click the Resources ➤ All Legacy Settings link. This opens the Dynamics 365 settings page, and from here, we can click the System Settings link. The window that opens contains a textbox with the heading "Set blocked file extensions for attachments." We can remove the js extension from this textbox to permit the attachment of JavaScript files. After we upload our JavaScript file, it is good practice to re-add the js file extension as a blocked type.

Validating Data

A common use case for custom JavaScript is to implement custom validation. To demonstrate, here's how to add custom validation to the second step of the web form that we built earlier. This step contains two fields – email address and phone number. We'll build validation that requires the user to enter either an email address or a phone number. This is the type of validation that we cannot apply through metadata, because metadata applies to individual fields.

To implement this functionality, we can add our script through the web form step record so that it applies only to the web step. As Figure 15-33 shows, the Form Options tab is the place where we enter our script.

Issue Step - Contact
Web Form Step

General   Form Definition   **Form Options**   Entity Reference   Additional Functionality   ...

Custom JavaScript

```
1  if (window.jQuery) {
2      (function ($) {
3          $(document).ready(function () {
4              if (typeof (Page_Validators) == 'undefined') return;
5
6              // Create new validator element
7              var vldContact = document.createElement('span');
8              vldContact.style.display = "none";
9              vldContact.id = "vldContact";
```

Figure 15-33. *Defining validation in a web step*

Listing 15-2 shows the script that applies our validation logic.

Listing 15-2. JavaScript to perform custom validation

```
if (window.jQuery) {
  (function ($) {
    $(document).ready(function () {    ❶
        if (typeof (Page_Validators) == 'undefined')
          return;

        // Create new validator element
        var vldContact = document.createElement('span');    ❷
        vldContact.style.display = "none";
```

```
vldContact.id = "vldContact";
vldContact.errormessage =
    "<a href='#cre23_emergencyemail_label'>                    ❸
        Email Address or Phone Number must be entered.
    </a>";

vldContact.evaluationfunction = function () {                  ❹
    var valEmail = $("#cre23_emergencyemail").val()
    var valPhone = $("#cre23_emergencyphone").val()

    if (valEmail == "" && valPhone == "") {
        return false;
    } else {
        return true;
    }
};

// Add the validator to the page validators array:
Page_Validators.push(vldContact);

    });
}(window.jQuery));
}
```

The code in this listing contains jQuery – a JavaScript library that can help us more easily access the elements on a web page. A typical pattern is to attach a script to the jQuery ready function ❶. The code that we define here runs only when the page is ready and prevents errors that can occur if we attempt to reference values and controls before the page completely loads.

Next, we create an HTML element that contains our validation logic ❷. The error message is a hyperlink ❸ that navigates the user to the label for our email control. Note that the statement in this listing that assigns an HTML error message to vldContact.errormessage contains additional line breaks for readability. In practice, this is one line of code.

From portal pages, the HTML ID of an input field matches the logical name of the field. The HTML ID of the label matches the field name suffixed with _label. This naming convention makes it possible to easily reference controls with jQuery.

The evaluation section of this code ❹ checks that both the phone number and email fields are not blank and returns false if this is the case.

Figure 15-34 shows how at runtime the validation message appears when a user clicks the next button without entering an email address or phone number.

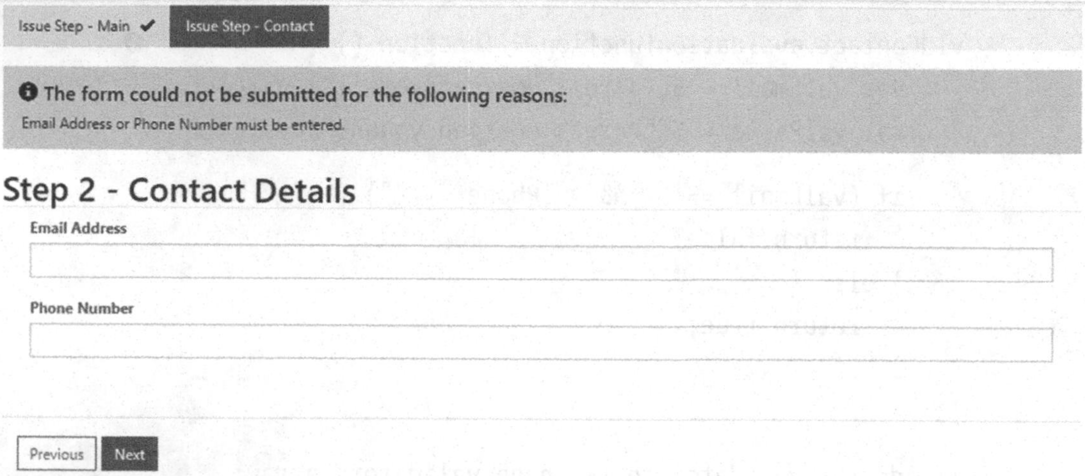

Figure 15-34. *Validation error at runtime*

Summary

The chapter covered the data processing capabilities of Power Apps portals. We learned how to retrieve, edit, delete, and create new Dataverse records using built-in components. We also learned how to retrieve data with Liquid code, and we found out how to apply custom validation with JavaScript.

To display data from Dataverse, we can use the graphical designer to add data components to a page. These components rely on forms and views from Dataverse. The data components include the list, entity form, and web form components. The list component displays a list of records, and the entity form component provides simple data entry capabilities. The web form component offers far richer capabilities, including multistep data entry, branching rules, and support for more complex validation rules.

To use the list or entity form component, we use the graphical designer to add these components to a page and use the settings in the properties pane to set the data source. The properties of the list component enable us to control the ability of users to delete records, and we can also configure the entity forms that are linked to the menu items to create and to edit records.

The graphical designer does not provide the option to add a web form to a page. Instead, we create a web form with the Portal Management app, and we can then associate the web form with one or more web pages. A web form can contain one or more steps. To define the fields on a web form, we create a Dataverse form with the fields that we want to display. We can use tabs in the form to define the fields that should appear for each step. We then create web step records based on the entity form and associate the web step records with the web form. We use the properties of the web form and web steps to configure the order in which the steps display. To implement branching conditions, we create a web step record that defines a conditional statement. We then introduce this conditional step into the steps that make up our web form.

To apply validation or default values to the fields on an entity or web form, we define metadata records. Through a metadata record, we can make a field mandatory, validate the format of input text using regular expressions, and apply range validation to numeric input. We can set the default value of a field to a static value, the current date and time, the current user, or the value of another field in the record.

A portal provides an inbuilt search feature that can search the content of a static web page and records from Dataverse. We can extend this built-in search feature to include results from custom tables. To set this up, we define an entity view that defines the target search fields. Next, we use the Portal Management app to enable custom entity search and define the result type of the entity and the name of the form that opens the result from the search screen.

To construct HTML that incorporates data from Dataverse, we can use Liquid. Liquid is a templating language, and we can use it to inject database and object values into HTML that we want to render. We can retrieve a single record by ID, or we can retrieve multiple records. To retrieve multiple records, we define a query using a language called FetchXML. This is an XML-based query language that enables us to filter and join records from multiple tables.

In the final part of this chapter, we looked at how to add custom JavaScript to web pages. To demonstrate, we used the Portal Management app to attach JavaScript to a web step record. The script that we added used jQuery to retrieve input values and to test the validity of those values.

PART V

Enhancing Apps

CHAPTER 16

Working with Images and Media

Power Apps provides rich media capabilities. We can build apps that include images and videos, and we can also integrate with the cameras that are built into smartphone and tablet devices. We can even scan barcodes and retrieve pen input. This is particularly useful because it enables us to capture signatures and to convert handwritten annotations to text.

We begin this chapter by creating an Excel-based app that can store and retrieve images. Next, we'll explore how the Site Inspection template app implements an image gallery screen that enables users to review camera photos. With this knowledge, we can apply the same technique to our apps.

In the next part of the chapter, we'll look at how to use the media controls in canvas apps to display video, audio, and image content. We'll also explore how to add image upload and display capabilities to a model-driven app. The key topics that we'll cover in this chapter include the following:

- How to configure a data store. We'll look at how to set up an Excel spreadsheet to store images and look at what options are available to store images in a SharePoint-based app.

- With a canvas app, users can upload images through an "Add picture" and a camera control. We'll examine how these controls work, including how to retrieve the binary data from these controls.

- We'll find out how to scan and retrieve barcode data, and we'll also look at the steps to configure a pen control to carry out optical image recognition.

© Tim Leung 2021
T. Leung, *Beginning Power Apps*, https://doi.org/10.1007/978-1-4842-6683-0_16

Choosing Where to Store Images

We'll begin this chapter by looking at how to add image storage capabilities to an app. The first step is to decide where to store our images. Power Apps provides first-class support for images in Excel, Dataverse, and SQL Server data sources. With these data sources, we can add a form control against the data source and develop our image storage and retrieval features in a no code fashion.

Another option is to use Azure Blob storage which is a dedicated cloud storage solution. This offers a good choice when we want to store large amounts of image data or in cases where we want to access data from web-based systems or programming languages outside of the Power Platform. It relies on a premium connector, so all users will require a per-user or per-app license. We can store a wide range of file types with Azure Blob storage, and therefore, we'll cover this topic more thoroughly in the next chapter.

Sadly, Power Apps does not integrate as well with SharePoint data sources. The camera and "Add picture" controls do not work natively against SharePoint "Hyperlink or Picture" columns. This issue impacts mostly app builders who cannot use Dataverse or SQL Server due to increased licensing costs.

In these cases, what options are available? The first option is to work around the problem by storing the base64 text representation of the image data in a text field. We'll look at how to apply this technique later in this chapter.

If we want to choose the best platform for storing images, Dataverse provides the richest functionality. We can secure images and provide access control permissions in a granular way. Dataverse can automatically generate thumbnail images. This provides a fast way for users to review images without downloading large amounts of data. Furthermore, Dataverse provides the most seamless way to integrate image capabilities into model-driven and portal apps.

Finally, for the most basic apps, we can choose Excel as a data source. Because Excel relies on user-based cloud storage such as OneDrive, it is best suited for single-user or very small systems. A benefit of using Excel is that we can easily retrieve the images in a readable format through the web-based interface of the cloud storage provider (e.g., OneDrive or Dropbox).

Setting Up a Data Source

To demonstrate the image handling capabilities of Power Apps, we'll build a simple auto-generated app. For this demonstration, we'll use an Excel data source because it is straightforward to set up.

To cover the other available data sources, however, here's a summary of the steps that are required to configure Excel, Dataverse, SQL Server, and SharePoint data sources.

Setting Up an Excel Spreadsheet

With an Excel data source, Power Apps stores the image files in a subfolder in the location where the Excel spreadsheet resides. It stores the path and name of the file in the content of the Excel file.

To set up an Excel file, we create a spreadsheet as shown in Figure 16-1. In the same way that we would set up any other Excel file, we use the Insert ➤ Table menu item in Excel to configure the data range as a table.

Figure 16-1. *Creating a spreadsheet to store image data*

In our example, we'll create a spreadsheet to store the photos and signatures of users. The PhotoData column stores the image path file name, and the Description column allows the user to provide some descriptive text.

The crucial step is to suffix our image columns with the keyword [image]. This keyword identifies the column as an image field. We'll use the UserSignature column later in this chapter to demonstrate the use of the pen control.

In this demonstration, we'll save our Excel file on OneDrive for Business.

Setting Up a Dataverse Table to Store Images

If we were to use Dataverse, it's very simple to add an image field to a table. The key step is to open the table in the table designer and to select the option to add a new field of data type image. This opens the panel that's shown in Figure 16-2, which enables us to configure the advanced features of the field. Let's look at the more notable features.

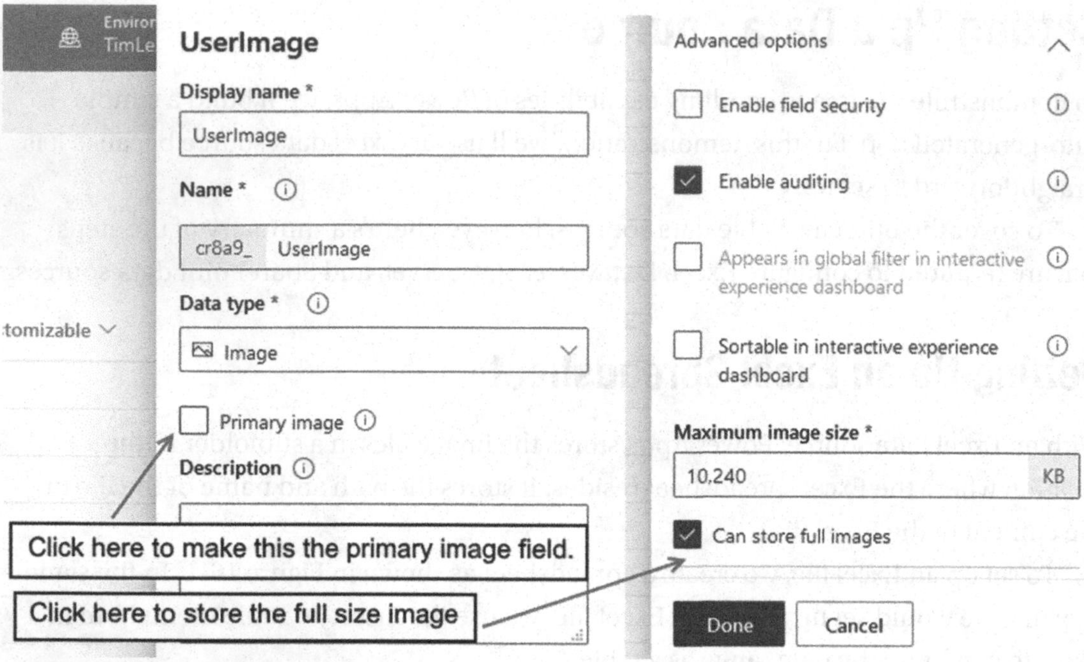

Figure 16-2. *Creating an image field for a Dataverse table*

Each record in a table has the notion of a primary image. In a model-driven app, the primary image appears in the heading of the record and helps users to identify a record. For each table, there can be one primary image field, and we can assign this by clicking the "Primary image" checkbox.

Dataverse provides efficient storage of image data by storing just a thumbnail image in the database and storing the full image in Dataverse file storage. If we only require thumbnail images, we can uncheck the "Can store full images" checkbox.

To help preserve file storage space, we can enforce a maximum image size. The default value is 10 MB, and we can increase this to a maximum of 30 MB.

Note   From a canvas app, the value of a Dataverse image field exposes a property called Full, which returns the full image.

Setting Up a SQL Server Table to Store Images

To store an image in a SQL Server table, we can add an image column to the table. Figure 16-3 shows the definition of a table in SQL Server Management Studio.

	Column Name	Data Type	Allow Nulls
🔑	UserID	int	☐
	Description	nvarchar(MAX)	☐
	PhotoData	image	☑
	UserSignature	image	☑

Figure 16-3. *Setting up a SQL field to store image data*

A valuable comment is that Microsoft recommends that we use the `varbinary` data type to store images, rather than the `image` data type. This is because Microsoft plans to deprecate the `image` data type in a future release of SQL Server.

However, there is a disadvantage of using the `varbinary` data type. If we were to add a form control to a screen and include a `varbinary` field, the designer does not provide the option to change the control type to an "add image" or "view image" control. This makes it more difficult to build a form that works with image data, and therefore, it is easier for us to work with fields that are of data type `image`.

Setting Up SharePoint

Because the camera and "Add picture" controls do not work natively against SharePoint "Hyperlink or Picture" columns, we'll cover a technique later in this chapter to store images in a text column. For this technique to work, we should specify the "multiple lines of text" data type and select the "plain text" radio option (Figure 16-4).

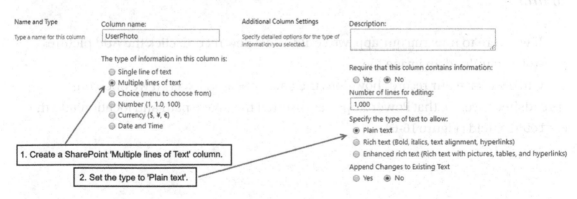

Figure 16-4. *Setting up a SharePoint column to store image data*

Creating an Image App

Assuming that we've set up an Excel data source and that we've saved it to cloud storage, we can explore the image capabilities of Power Apps by creating an auto-generated app. The edit screen from this type of app includes an "Add picture" control (Figure 16-5). This control enables a user to upload a file from the local device. The file extensions that Power Apps supports include .jpg, .jpeg, .gif, .png, .bmp, .tif, .tiff, and .svg.

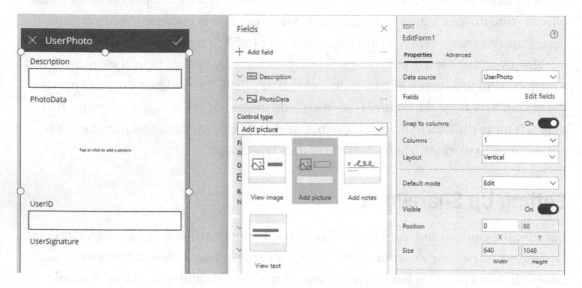

Figure 16-5. *The edit screen in an auto-generated app includes an "Add picture" control*

If we were to now run our app, we could add a new record, click the Add picture control and upload an image file.

Once we save our record, how does the data appear in Excel? If we open our spreadsheet, we see that Power Apps has inserted the image path and location into the PhotoData field (Figure 16-6).

	A	B	C	
1	UserID ▾	Description ▾	PhotoData[image]	▾
2	1	Tim Leung	.\PropertyData_images\5a7dc1425e1a4b7497e836e6e9b287b5.png	

Figure 16-6. *The Excel file contains a link to the image file*

In the location where the spreadsheet resides, Power Apps creates a subfolder to store the image files (Figure 16-7). The name of the folder matches the name of the spreadsheet with the word "_images" appended to the end.

Figure 16-7. *Folder view in OneDrive, showing the image folder*

With Excel data sources, one thing to note is that when we delete a record, Power Apps does not delete the image that is associated with the record. Therefore, it becomes necessary to carry out some additional housekeeping of image files when we choose to use an Excel data source.

Note   When we delete a record from an Excel data source, Power Apps does not delete the image that is associated with the record.

Using the Camera Control

Now that we have a basic working app, let's look at how to enhance our app by replacing the "Add picture" control with a camera control.

The key characteristic of the camera control is that it exposes a property called Photo. This returns the image from the camera at the moment when we read the property. The expected behavior on most mobile apps is to provide a method for the user to take a snapshot and to review the image before saving it. Therefore, this is the behavior that we'll build in this section.

The first step is to open the edit screen and to select the default card for our photo data field. The next step is to unlock the card and delete all the controls on the card. We can use the screen explorer view on the left-hand side of the designer to quickly delete all the controls. Next, add a camera control called CameraUserPhoto, and insert an image control called ImageUserPhoto next to the camera control, as shown in Figure 16-8.

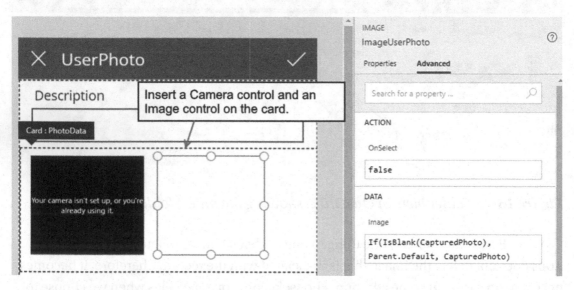

Figure 16-8. *Add a camera control and an image control*

We can now build the feature that allows the user to take a snapshot. The method we'll use is to store the photo in a variable when the user taps the camera control. To do this, we add the following code to the OnSelect property of the camera control:

```
UpdateContext({CapturedPhoto: CameraUserPhoto.Photo})
```

An important step is to clear this variable when the user navigates away from the screen. If we fail to do this, the captured image will remain when the user reopens the screen. To clear the variable, set the OnHidden property of the screen to the following formula:

```
UpdateContext({CapturedPhoto: Blank()})
```

The next step is to configure the image control so that it shows the image when a user opens an existing record or to show the image that the user captures with the camera. To do this, we set the Image property of the image control to the following formula:

`If(IsBlank(CapturedPhoto), Parent.Default, CapturedPhoto)`

Finally, we need to set up the form to save the photo to the data source. To do this, we set the Update property of the card to `ImageUserPhoto.Image`.

At this point, we can run our app and use the camera control to capture and save photos.

Switching Between Cameras

Most mobile devices provide at least two cameras – a rear camera and a front-facing camera. We can set the camera ID property to choose which camera to use. Here's how to add a control that enables the user to switch cameras.

First, add a slider control and name it `SliderCameraId`. Set the Max property to 1 and the Default value to 0. Next, set the Camera property of the camera control to `SliderCameraId.Value`, as shown in Figure 16-9. We can now run our app and use the slider control to change the camera.

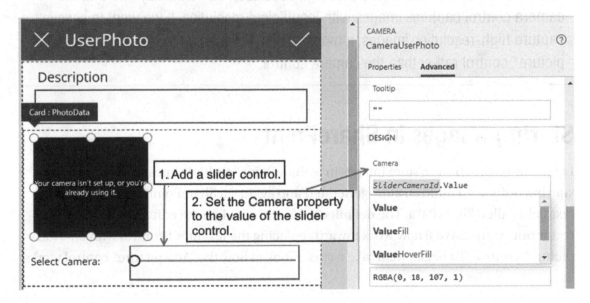

Figure 16-9. *Add a slider control to enable the user to switch cameras*

Setting Brightness, Contrast, and Zoom Levels

We can use the same technique as in the preceding text to enable users to set the brightness, contrast, and zoom levels of the camera. Simply add slider controls and set the Zoom, Brightness, or Contrast property of the camera control to the value of the slider control. Table 16-1 shows the details of these properties.

Table 16-1. *Camera control properties*

Property	Property Description
Zoom	The percentage by which an image from a camera is magnified.
Brightness	How much light the user is likely to perceive in an image.
Contrast	How easily the user can distinguish between similar colors in an image.

Note   There's no exact way to configure the resolution of the picture that the camera control captures. Users with high-resolution cameras may find that the camera control captures images with insufficient resolution. If we want to always capture high-resolution images, a more reliable way can be to use the "Add picture" control rather than the camera control.

Storing Images in SharePoint

Let's now look at how to store images in a SharePoint "multiple lines of text" field. The starting point is to build an auto-generated app against a SharePoint list with a multi-text field called PhotoData. The default card for this field on the edit form will include a text input control. We'll now work toward replacing the text input control with an "Add picture" control. To begin, we'll take a closer look at how the "Add picture" control works.

Working with the Add Picture Control

The "Add picture" control is a composite control. When we add an Add picture control to a screen, two child controls appear in the tree view – an "add media button" control and an image control (Figure 16-10). The add media button control opens the file browser dialog on the client and exposes the image file that the user selects. The image control displays the image that a user selects.

Figure 16-10. *The "Add picture" control*

The key property that enables us to access the image that the user uploads is the Media property of the add media button control. However, the syntax that we use isn't straightforward, so we'll now explore this in more detail.

When a user uploads an image, Power Apps stores the image in a locally accessible, internal location that exists for the duration of a session. We can access the image through a URI. To highlight the format of this address, we can display the Media property of the add media button control in a label. This reveals an address that begins with appres://blobmanager/.

Let's suppose we save this address to a SharePoint text field or some other external data source. If we reopen the app or if another user were to open the app, the appres:// blobmanager/ address will not retrieve the image because it is specific to a session where we originally uploaded the image.

To save an image to a data store, the important step is to retrieve the binary data from the appres://blobmanager/ URI. The technique that enables us to carry out this task relies on a function called JSON. This function returns the JavaScript Object Notation (JSON) representation of a data structure as text.

To demonstrate how to call this function, we can add the following formula to the OnSelect property of the "Add picture" control:

```
UpdateContext({locImage:
            JSON(UploadedImage1.Image, IncludeBinaryData)}
)
```

The JSON function is a behavior function, meaning that we can call it only from a button or from the OnSelect property of a control. In most cases, we capture the results of the JSON function into a variable. In this example, we call the UpdateContext function to store the results into a variable called locImage.

The JSON function accepts two arguments. The first argument specifies the data that we want to encode, and the second argument specifies a format. If our input contains binary data (as in this example), we must specify the IncludeBinaryData format to include the binary content in the output.

For this technique to work, we pass the Image property of the image control to the JSON function. This is the trick that makes this method possible. If we were to pass the Media property of the Add picture control, the JSON function would return the JSON representation of the appres://blobmanager URI, rather than the binary data that is associated with the URI.

Figure 16-11 highlights what we see when we show the contents of the locImage variable in a label.

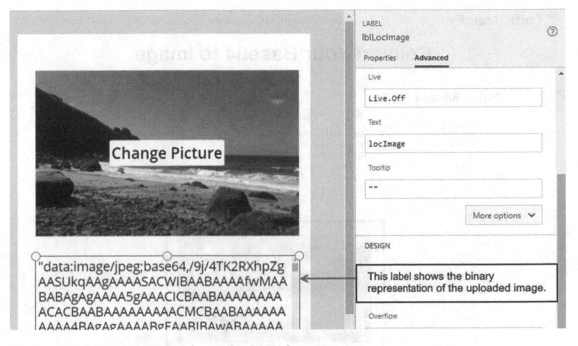

Figure 16-11. *The output from the JSON function*

The output from the JSON function is a data URI – a structure that web designers can use to embed images and other binary objects into web pages. Our example highlights a typical data URI that consists of four parts. The first part is a prefix (data:), followed by a MIME type that indicates the content type. The base64 keyword indicates that content contains binary data, and the content after the comma expresses the base64 representation of the data.

An important point is that the JSON function returns the data URI enclosed inside double quotes. When we apply this technique, it's important to remove these enclosing double quotes.

Base64 is a standard method that encodes binary data into ASCII text. Outside of Power Apps, we can find online base64 converters by searching the Web. When we process base64 encoded strings with Power Apps formulas, it's easy to make mistakes. During development, these online converters can help us validate our base64 encoded content (Figure 16-12).

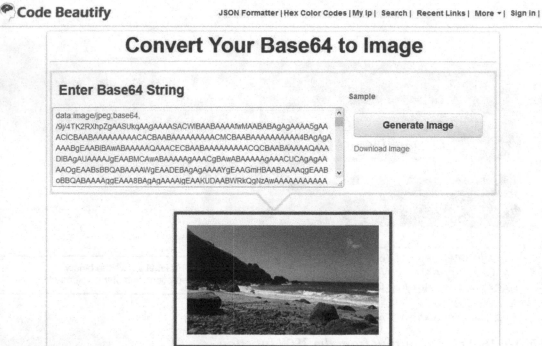

Figure 16-12. *Validating base64 encoded strings with an online converter*

Finally, it is useful to note that we can apply the same technique to the camera control. The Photo property of a camera control also returns an appres://blobmanager URI. We can set the Image property of an image control to the Photo property of a camera control, and we can then apply the JSON function to the Image property of the image control to extract the base64 encoded binary content.

Converting Images to Text

Now that we understand how to extract the base64 encoded representation of an image, we'll walk through how to adapt an auto-generated app so that it stores the image data into a SharePoint text field. We'll base this example on a SharePoint list with a multi-text field called UserPhoto.

The first step is to create an auto-generated app based on this list. On the edit form, the UserPhoto card will include a text input control. We should unlock this card and delete all the child controls.

Next, we insert an "Add picture" control to the card. In this example, we'll name this control apUploaded.

We then add the following formula to the OnSelect property of the "add media button" control:

```
UpdateContext({locImage:
            Substitute(JSON(imgUploaded.Image , IncludeBinaryData)
                """",""))
        }
)
```

This formula extracts the data URI of the uploaded image. The output from the JSON function is enclosed in double quotes. The call to the Substitute function removes these quotes. To configure the card so that it saves the binary content to the UserPhoto field, we set the Update property of the card to locImage.

The final step is to modify the Image property of the image control as follows:

```
If(apUploaded.Media <> "",  apUploaded.Media,
    Parent.Default <> "", Parent.Default,
    SampleImage
)
```

This formula displays the image that the user uploads. Where a user opens an existing record and has not uploaded a new image, it displays the existing image. In the case of a new record where the user has not uploaded an image, it displays the image SampleImage. This is a built-in placeholder image that is accessible from all apps. The appearance of this image looks like a gray, simplified depiction of a mountain and the sun.

Figure 16-13 illustrates the layout of our form.

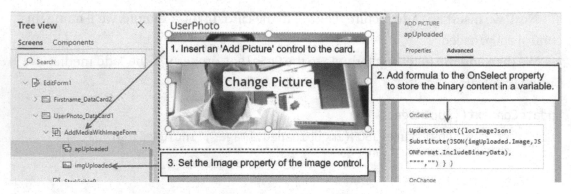

Figure 16-13. *Adapting the edit form to store images*

Note   To update a data source with a call to the Patch function (instead of using a form), we would patch the value `locImage` to our image field.

Viewing Data

To complete our example, the final step is to modify the display form so that it displays the saved image. To do this, we unlock the `UserPhoto` card and delete the label control. Next, we add an image control to the card, and we simply set the `Image` property of the control to `Parent.Default`. Figure 16-14 shows the appearance of this in the designer. This completes our app, and we can now run it and use the forms to add and view images.

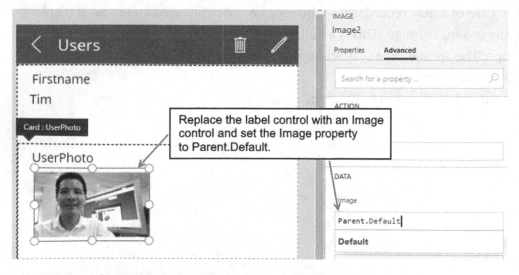

Figure 16-14. *Adapting the display form to display an image*

Building a Photo Gallery

Now that we understand how to add and view images throughout a variety of data sources, we'll explore the photo taking feature in the sample Site Inspection app. This feature provides a user-friendly way for users to take and to review photos. By understanding how this works, we can incorporate this feature into our own apps.

Figure 16-15 illustrates the screens that make up this app. From the initial Site Inspection screen, a user can edit an existing record or create a new record. If the user clicks an existing record, the Edit Inspection screen opens and displays the first image associated with the record. The user can click this image to open the Images screen. This displays the additional images that are associated with the record.

The user can click the camera icon to open the Camera screen. This screen contains a camera control that allows a user to attach up to seven photos at a time. The middle of the screen contains a gallery control that displays images that have been captured. The "done" button at the bottom part of the screen saves the images to an Excel data source. The user can also reach this Camera screen through the New Inspection screen.

To help understand how this works, let's take a closer look at the Camera screen. How exactly does this work? When the user taps the camera control (the name of this control is Camera1), the control runs the formula that's shown in the following:

```
If(CountRows(CameraPhotos) <=7,                    ❶
    Collect(CameraPhotos,
            {Note:"",
             Photo:Camera1.Photo,
             PhotoId:CountRows(CameraPhotos)       ❷
            }
    )
)
```

Figure 16-15. *The screens in the Site Inspection app*

This formula captures the images into a collection called CameraPhotos. The first part of this formula checks that there are fewer than seven items in the collection ❶. The app only collects photos when this condition is true.

Each record in the collection includes a field called PhotoId. The Collect function sets the PhotoId value of a record to the count of records when it adds a record to the collection ❷. This technique assigns a sequential PhotoId value to each record.

The "done" button calls the Patch function to save the photos to the Excel data source. An excerpt of this code is shown in Listing 16-1.

Listing 16-1. Patching the data to the data source

```
If(NewRecord,
    Navigate(NewInspectionScreen,ScreenTransition.Fade),          ❶
    If(CountRows(CameraPhotos)>=1,
        UpdateContext(
            {AddPhoto:Patch(SitePhotos,                            ❷
                            Defaults(SitePhotos),
                            {PhotoId:Max(SitePhotos,PhotoId)+1,
                             Photo:Last(FirstN(CameraPhotos,1)).Photo,
                             ID:Gallery3.Selected.ID,
                             Note:Text(Last(FirstN(CameraPhotos,1)).
                             Note)
                            })
            }
        )
    );
    If(CountRows(CameraPhotos)>=2,
      UpdateContext(
            {AddPhoto:Patch(SitePhotos,                            ❷
                            Defaults(SitePhotos),
                            {PhotoId:Max(SitePhotos,PhotoId)+1,
                             Photo:Last(FirstN(CameraPhotos,2)).Photo,
```

```
                                ID:Gallery3.Selected.ID,
                                Note:Text(Last(FirstN(CameraPhotos,2)).
                                Note)
                            })
                    }
                )
            );
```

The first part of this formula checks the value of the NewRecord variable. This value will be true if the user reached the Camera screen from the New Inspection screen. In this instance, the formula navigates the user back to the New Inspection screen ❶.

If the user is editing an existing record, the formula calls the Patch function to insert the photo records into a table called SitePhotos ❷. Figure 16-16 shows the structure of this table. The PhotoId field uniquely identifies each record, and the ID field refers to the primary key value of the parent site inspection record.

	A	B	C	D
1	**PhotoId**	**Photo[image]**	**Note**	**ID**
2	1	./data_images/1-100.jpg	Built in 1980 with signific	1
3	2	./data_images/1-101.jpg		1
4	3	./data_images/1-102.jpg		1
5	4	./data_images/1-103.jpg		1
6	5	./data_images/1-104.jpg		1
7	6	./data_images/2-100.jpg	Parking lot has two acces	2
8	7	./data_images/2-101.jpg		2
9	8	./data_images/2-102.jpg		2
10	9	./data_images/2-103.jpg		2
11	10	./data_images/3-100.jpg	Outdoor spaces have bee	3
12	11	./data_images/3-101.jpg		3
13	12	./data_images/3-102.jpg		3
14	13	./data_images/3-103.jpg		3
15	14	./data_images/3-104.jpg		3
16	15	./data_images/4-100.jpg	Smoking pavillion added	4
17	16	./data_images/4-101.jpg		4
18	17	./data_images/4-102.jpg		4
19	18	./data_images/5-100.jpg	Zoned commercial	5
20	19	./data_images/5-101.jpg		5
21	20	./data_images/5-102.jpg		5
22	21	./data_images/5-103.jpg		5
23	22	./data_images/5-104.jpg		5

Figure 16-16. SitePhotos data source

The code that patches each image follows the same pattern. Listing 16-1 illustrates the code to patch the first two images and omits the remaining code for brevity. The pertinent code that patches the first image is shown in the following:

```
Patch(SitePhotos,
    Defaults(SitePhotos),
    {PhotoId:Max(SitePhotos,PhotoId)+1,            ❶
     Photo:Last(FirstN(CameraPhotos,1)).Photo,     ❷
     ID:Gallery3.Selected.ID,
     Note:Text(Last(FirstN(CameraPhotos,1)).Note)
     }
)
```

The first interesting thing is the excerpt of code that generates the PhotoId value ❶. The formula calls the Max function to return the highest PhotoId value from the SitePhotos data source and adds one. This is the code that generates a series of sequential photo ID values. This technique is especially useful for Excel data sources where there isn't the ability to create auto-incrementing numeric fields, unlike data sources such as SQL Server and Dataverse.

Another interesting part of this formula is the logic that retrieves an individual photo from the CameraPhotos collection ❷. This utilizes the technique that we covered in Chapter 7 to retrieve a row by ordinal number. As an example, the formula to retrieve the fourth record from a collection looks like this:

```
Last(FirstN(CameraPhotos,4)).Photo
```

This formula calls the FirstN function to return the first four records from the CameraPhotos collection. The outermost call to the Last function returns the last record from the result of the FirstN function, which equates to the fourth record in the collection.

The code that we've examined so far adds photos to an existing site inspection record. In the case where a user is adding a new site inspection record, it's not possible to use this code because there isn't a parent site inspection record to relate the photos to. For new site inspection records, the logic in the app adds both the parent record and the child image records in a single operation. In this scenario, the formula returns the user to the New Inspection screen. This screen provides a form control to add a new site inspection record. When a user adds a new record, the formula in the OnSuccess property of the screen adds the photos from the `CameraPhotos` collection to the `SitePhotos` table. The `OnSuccess` formula looks almost identical to the code in the Photo Capture screen, as shown in Figure 16-17.

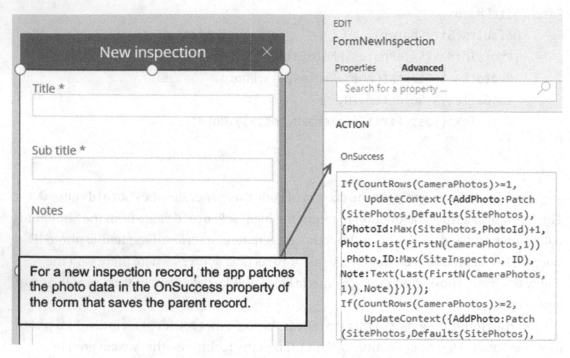

Figure 16-17. *Adding photos to a new site inspection record*

To summarize, the code in this sample app provides some excellent learning points. It shows us how to capture photos into a local collection and how to save these multiple photos at a later point in time. The formula in this app also highlights the syntax to generate a sequence of numbers and how we can retrieve a record by ordinal number (e.g., the second, third, fourth record, etc.) It is also useful to note that Power Apps now includes a built-in sequence function to simplify the generation of numeric sequences.

Note   The code in this section provides a great example on how to generate sequences of numbers and how to retrieve records by ordinal number.

Model-Driven Apps

Now that we understand how to work with images in a canvas app, we'll briefly cover how to work with images in a model-driven app. This includes how to upload images and how to view images. The great news is that it's very simple to provide image support in a model-driven app. Because of this reason, this will be a very short section.

A model-driven app works only with a Dataverse data source. Therefore, the first step is to add an image field to a table. As with all model-driven apps, the key step is to create a form for our table. From the form designer, we add our image field, as shown in Figure 16-18.

From the model-driven app designer, we need to make sure to include the table in the site map (as described in Chapter 13). At this point, we can run our app and upload and view images.

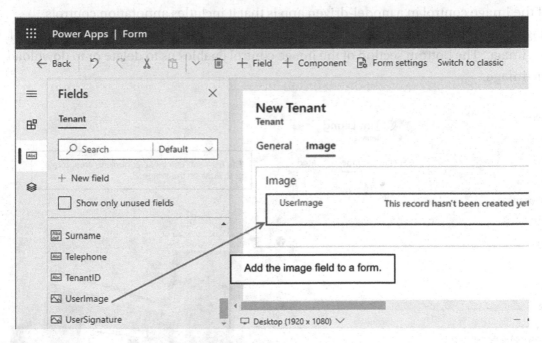

Figure 16-18. *Setting up a form with an image control*

Uploading and Viewing Images

Here's how our example app looks at runtime. When a user creates or edits a record, the form will include the option to upload an image, as shown in Figure 16-19.

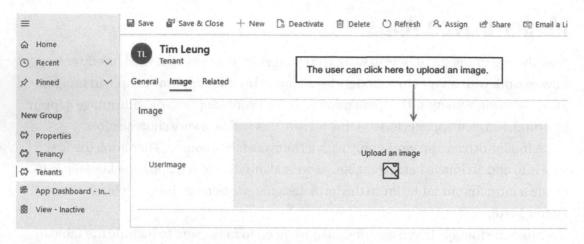

Figure 16-19. *Uploading an image at runtime*

Once a user uploads an image, the image will appear in the form. A great feature of the image control in a model-driven app is that it includes annotation controls (Figure 16-20). We can use these to draw text and highlight, rotate, and crop sections of the image. The bottom section of the image control enables us to delete or to download the image.

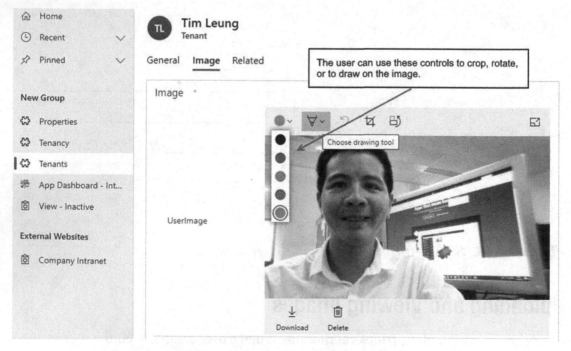

Figure 16-20. *Viewing an image in a model-driven app*

Canvas App Features

In the final section of this chapter, we'll cover a range of other features that we can add to canvas apps. This includes how to use the pen control, how to scan barcodes, and how to incorporate video and audio into our apps.

Using the Pen Control

Power Apps provides a pen control which is ideal for capturing annotations or signatures. This control generates images in png format, and we can easily assign this control to the image fields on a form. To do this, we would set the control type to "Add notes," as shown in Figure 16-21.

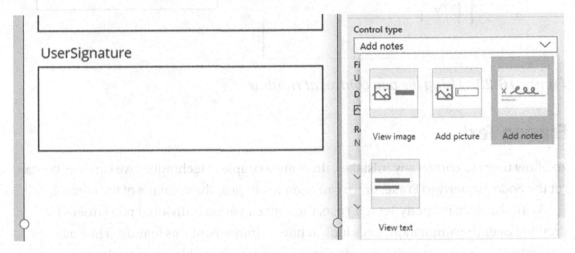

Figure 16-21. *Change the control type from Add picture to Add notes*

We can now run our app and use the pen control to enter text (Figure 16-22). With an Excel data source, the app saves the note as a PNG file in the image folder in the location where the Excel file exists. With other data sources, the app saves the binary content of the PNG file in the data field.

Just like other media controls, we can access the `appres://blobmanager` URI through the `Image` property of the pen control. We can retrieve the base64 encoded note image by using the technique that we covered earlier, by using an image control and the `JSON` function.

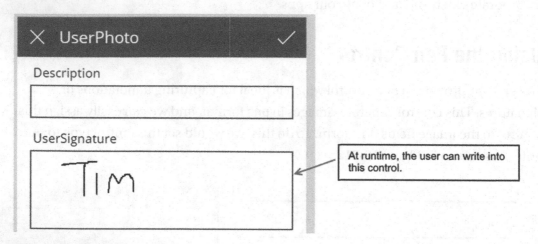

Figure 16-22. *Using the pen control at runtime*

Erasing Text

To allow users to correct any mistakes, there are a couple of techniques we can use. We can set the `Mode` property to `Erase`, or we can completely clear the contents of the control.

With the `Mode` property set to `Erase`, the user can erase individual pen strokes by drawing over the annotation. Let's look at how to implement this feature. The `Mode` property allows us to switch between the pen modes. To enable users to alter the pen mode, we can add a toggle control and apply a formula to set the `Mode` property of the pen control depending on the value of the toggle control, as shown in Figure 16-23.

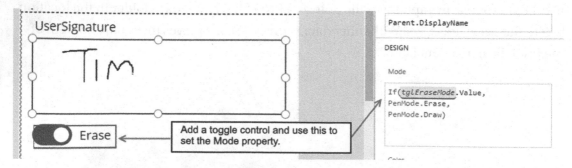

Figure 16-23. *Switching the pen mode to Erase*

Alternatively, we can use the reset property technique that we covered in Chapter 11 to completely clear the contents of the pen control. To demonstrate this technique, here's how to add a button to clear the contents of the pen control.

First, add a button and add a formula to set the value of a variable to `true` and then back to `false`. In this example, we'll name our variable `ResetPenControl`, and the formula would look like this:

```
UpdateContext({ResetPenControl: true});
UpdateContext({ResetPenControl: false})
```

Figure 16-24 shows how this looks in the designer. The next step is to set the `Reset` property of the pen control to `ResetPenControl`. We can now run our app and click the button to clear the contents of the pen control.

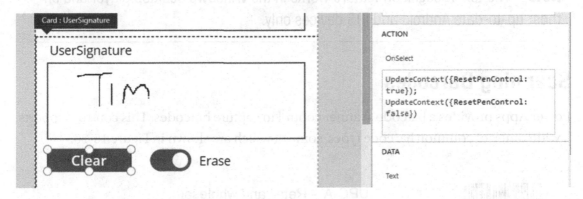

Figure 16-24. *Adding a button to clear the contents of the pen control*

Converting Annotations to Text

The pen control enables us to convert annotations to text. We can simply refer to the `RecognizedText` property of the pen control to retrieve the converted text.

A limitation of this feature is that there is limited support. It will not work in the designer or in apps that run in a web browser. In these scenarios, the `RecognizedText` property returns the message "Recognition is not supported on this platform." Text recognition works in the Windows desktop player and on most up-to-date Android and iOS devices.

To demonstrate this feature, we'll add the pen control and a label to a screen. We then set the `Text` property of the label to the `RecognizedText` property of the pen control.

At runtime, the user can use the pen control to enter words, and the label will display the recognized text following the entry of each letter. Figure 16-25 illustrates how this looks at runtime.

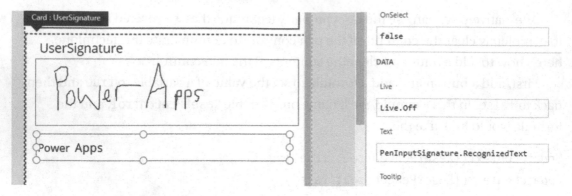

Figure 16-25. *Recognizing annotations*

> **Note**   The text recognition feature works in the Windows desktop player and on most up-to-date Android and iOS devices only.

Scanning Barcodes

Power Apps provides a barcode scanner control to capture barcodes. This control supports a wide range of common barcode types, some of which are shown in Figure 16-26.

Figure 16-26. *Supported barcode types*

The barcode scanner control also supports QR (quick response) barcode. These barcodes frequently appear in marketing materials and allow smartphone users to open web links or other web resources. To demonstrate how to use the barcode scanner, we'll create a simple screen that enables a user to scan a barcode and to extract the data. To generate a QR barcode, we can search the Web for online QR barcode generators (Figure 16-27). These enable us to generate a barcode based on an input value.

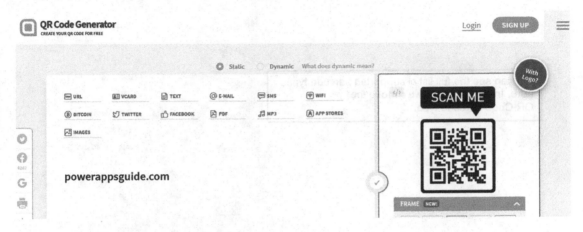

Figure 16-27. *Creating a QR barcode*

To build our app, we would insert a barcode scanner control and label control to a screen. For the barcode scanner control, we'll retain the default name of BarcodeScanner1 (Figure 16-28). To configure the control so that it scans the barcode when the user taps the control, we'll set the OnSelect property of the barcode control to the formula shown in the following:

```
UpdateContext({CapturedBarcode: BarcodeScanner1.Value})
```

Next, set the "Barcode type" property to the barcode type that we want to detect – QR code in our example.

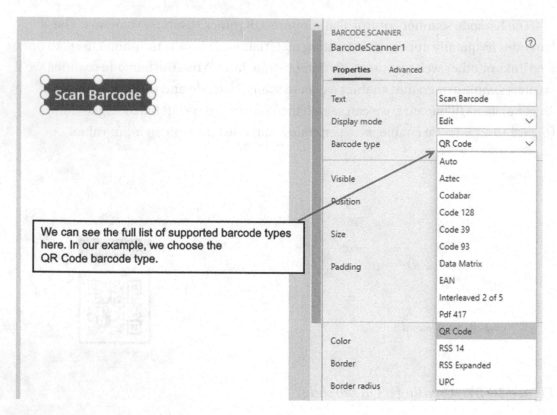

Figure 16-28. *Configuring the barcode control*

The final step is to set the Text property of the label control to the variable CapturedBarcode. At this stage, we can run our app and use the control to scan a barcode.

The barcode control renders as a button. When the user clicks the button, the app opens the device camera and enables the user to scan the barcode. When the control registers the barcode, the display returns to the screen, and the text that is associated with the barcode will appear in the label control.

Working with Media Controls

Let's now look at media controls. We can embellish our apps by incorporating sounds, images, and videos. The easiest way to add media content to an app is to use the media panel on the left-hand side of the designer, as shown in Figure 16-29. Alternatively, we can review the media in our app through the File ➤ Media menu.

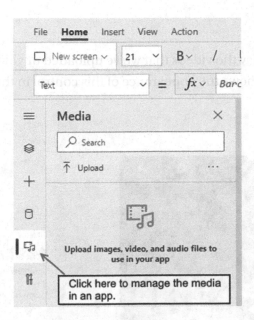

Figure 16-29. *Uploading media files into a project*

Any media we add becomes part of the app, and therefore, it's important to exercise some caution because large files can easily bloat and slow down the time that it takes to load the app. Each media file that we add cannot exceed 64 MB, and there is a limit of 200 MB for all media files in an app.

We refer to media files in formulas using the name of the file that we upload. Therefore, it makes good sense to provide files with meaningful file names before we upload them into an app. Table 16-2 shows the file types that Power Apps supports.

Table 16-2. *Supported media types*

Media	Supported File Types
Images	.jpg, .jpeg, .gif, .png, .bmp, .tif, .tiff, .svg
Videos	.mp4, .wmv
Audio	.wav, .mp3, .wma

We'll now look more closely at the controls to play back video and audio files and to display image files.

571

Playing Videos

The video control can play the videos that we've uploaded or videos from the Web or YouTube. Figure 16-30 shows the appearance of this control in the designer.

Figure 16-30. *The video control*

The Media property specifies the video to play. To specify a YouTube video, it's necessary to enclose the URL with double quotes. To specify a file that we uploaded, we set the Media property to the file name. If the file name includes spaces, we would need to enclose the file with single quotes.

There are two properties that relate to the playback of videos: Start and AutoStart. The Start property specifies whether the video plays. The AutoStart property defines whether the video plays as soon the screen becomes visible.

A typical user requirement is to provide a button that starts and stops the playback of a video. To build this feature, we would insert a button to the screen and set the OnSelect property value to the following formula:

```
UpdateContext({PlayVideo:Not(PlayVideo)})
```

This formula toggles the value of a variable called PlayVideo. The value of this when the screen first opens will be false. To link the button to the video control, we would then set the Start property of the video control to the variable PlayVideo.

Other useful properties that we can set include the AutoStart, StartTime, and Loop properties. The AutoStart property controls whether video playback starts automatically when the screen becomes visible. The StartTime property specifies the position in the video to begin playback, specified in milliseconds. Finally, the control can restart playback when the video ends when we set the Loop property to true.

Playing Audio

The audio control plays sound files. Just like the video control, the Media property specifies the file or URL to play.

With all media content, a useful feature is to provide a list of content and to play back the item that the user selects. We can accomplish this by adding a list box control to a screen and setting the Media property of the audio control to the selected item in the list box control.

For example, if we upload the audio files MusicFile1.mp3 and MusicFile2.mp3 to an app, we can set the Items property of the list box control to the following formula:

```
Table({Description:"Music File 1", AudioFile:MusicFile1},
    {Description:"Music File 2", AudioFile:MusicFile2}
)
```

Assuming that the name of the list box is ListBoxAudio, we would then set the Media property of the audio control to

```
First(ListBoxAudio.SelectedItems).AudioFile
```

Figure 16-31 illustrates this setup. This is a useful feature, and we can also apply this same technique to the video control example.

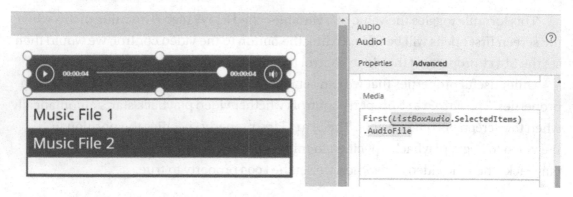

Figure 16-31. *A screen with the audio control*

Displaying Images

By now, we've encountered the image control several times in this book; and therefore, we'll be familiar with how this control works. Once we add an image control to a screen, we set the Image property of the control to define the image that displays. This value can be a data field, an image file that we upload, or an image URL. The basic use of the image control is straightforward, so we'll now examine some of the other settings that the image control provides.

Through the properties of the control, we can modify the image position. We can use this setting to display an image so that it stretches to fill all the available space in the control.

We can also set the transparency value of the control. The reason this is useful is because we can make an image semitransparent which can make it more suitable as a background for other controls.

Another useful set of properties are the radius settings. By default, the control is rectangular. By adapting the radius settings, we can make the image placeholder circular. Where we usually see this format is on screens that display a profile picture of a user (Figure 16-32).

To apply this technique, we set Height and Width of the image control to equal values. Next, there are four radius settings, and we set each of these to a value that is equal to the height. These four settings are RadiusTopLeft, RadiusTopRight, RadiusBottomLeft, and RadiusBottomRight. For each radius setting, we can reference the height of the control by using the syntax ImageControl.Height, rather than the actual numeric values.

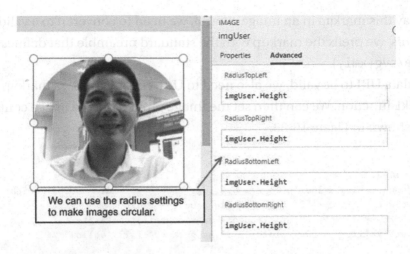

Figure 16-32. *Creating a circular image*

Displaying SVG Images

The image control can display SVG (Scalable Vector Graphics) images. An SVG image uses a text-based XML markup language to describe the content. A benefit of a vector format is that we can render an SVG image at any size without any loss of quality. However, that's not the only benefit.

Since an SVG image uses a text-based definition, it enables us to construct and conditionally modify images using the string manipulation functions in Power Apps. For example, if we want to display multiple icons that vary only by color, we can define the SVG representation of the image once and substitute the markup that defines the color. For multilingual apps, we can localize the text in images by carrying out text substitutions. Practical applications of this technique include building gauge or heat map images that include dynamic values. As we can see, this technique provides a very powerful way to add visualizations to an app.

To give a very simple example, here's the SVG markup that describes a circle, a rectangle, and a label with the text "Power Apps is great!"

```
<svg>
  <circle cx="50" cy="50" r="50" fill="blue"/>
    <text x="120" y="50" fill="red">Power Apps is great!</text>
    <rect x="110" y="60"  width="250" height="40" fill="yellow" />
</svg>
```

575

To display this markup in an image control, we need to convert it to a valid data URI. To do this, we prefix the markup with the standard preamble that defines a data URI (data:image/svg+xml,).

For the data URI to be valid, we also need to URL encode the SVG markup by calling the EncodeURL function. We can then set the Image property of the image control to this formula, as shown in Figure 16-33.

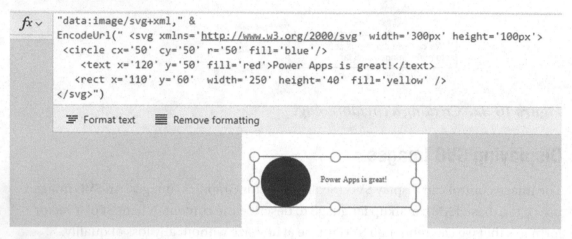

```
fx ∨     "data:image/svg+xml," &
         EncodeUrl(" <svg xmlns='http://www.w3.org/2000/svg' width='300px' height='100px'>
         <circle cx='50' cy='50' r='50' fill='blue'/>
            <text x='120' y='50' fill='red'>Power Apps is great!</text>
            <rect x='110' y='60'  width='250' height='40' fill='yellow' />
         </svg>")
```

Power Apps is great!

Figure 16-33. *Setting an SVG image*

To create an SVG file that can act as the basis of an image that we can further modify, we can use an SVG paint program. There are plenty of third-party SVG image editors that we can install, and there are online editors that are available too. A dedicated SVG editor will typically include many of the features that we often find in paint programs, including the ability to draw shapes, add layers and filters, and apply effects such as drop shadows and blur effects.

Summary

This chapter covered the media capabilities of Power Apps. The first part of the chapter focused on how to save and retrieve images, including how to use the camera control. In the later part of the chapter, we looked at how to add media capabilities to canvas apps, including how to use the pen control, how to scan barcodes, and how to use the video and audio controls.

To store images, Power Apps provides first-class support for Dataverse, SQL Server, and Excel data sources. It supports the image data types that these data sources provide. Dataverse and SQL Server provide the most robust option for storing images. With all these data sources, we can use a form control to connect to an image field. This provides a no code way for us to build data entry screens for an image field.

To store image data in an Excel spreadsheet, the key step is to define a column with a name that ends with [image]. As with all Excel data sources, we need to save the spreadsheet to a cloud storage provider. When we build an auto-generated app and save a record that includes an image, Power Apps saves the image to a subfolder of the folder that contains the Excel spreadsheet and stores the file location of the image in the spreadsheet.

There are two main controls that we can use to upload images. The first is the Add picture control. This control opens a file browser dialog that enables a user to select a file from the local file system. The second control is the camera control. This control enables users to capture photos.

The typical way to use the camera control is to configure it so that it captures a photo when a user taps the camera control. We can store this image in a variable, prior to saving it to the data source. Many mobile devices include multiple cameras, and it's possible to choose which the camera the control uses. We can also configure the brightness, contrast, and zoom properties of the camera. For apps that run through a browser on a desktop PC, the camera control can capture photos through web cams that are connected to the PC.

It is not possible to store image data natively in SharePoint. One way to work around this limitation is to convert the image to a base64 encoded string and to store this in a SharePoint multi-text field. To convert an image to a string, we call the JSON function and provide the image that we want to convert.

To help develop screens that enable users to take and to review photos, we examined the Site Inspection app. This app provides an excellent example of how to use the camera control. The app allows the user to take up to seven photos at a time. The screen collects the images to a collection and calls the Patch function to add the multiple images to an Excel data source. The app includes some useful code samples that we can reuse. This includes a formula to retrieve a record by ordinal number and code that generates numeric field sequences.

With canvas apps, there are a range of media-related controls that we can use. A very useful control is the pen control. Users can use this control to enter signatures or annotations. With auto-generated apps, we can easily apply this control against an image field by choosing this control type in the card settings of a form. The pen control provides optical character recognition capabilities, and we can easily retrieve the converted text through the `RecognizedText` property.

Another useful control is the barcode control. We can use this to scan and retrieve barcode data for a wide range of common barcode types, including QR barcodes. Finally, Power Apps provides video and audio controls that we can use to play videos and sounds.

With model-driven apps, we can easily build an app that includes image support. To do this, we first add an image field to a table. We then add a form that includes the image field and add that form to our model-driven app.

CHAPTER 17

Storing and Retrieving Files

A common requirement in many business apps is the ability to store and to retrieve files. A typical use case is to enable the storage of files that could include Word documents, Excel spreadsheets, PDF documents, images, and more.

There are several ways to integrate file handling and storage capabilities into an app. In this chapter, we'll study this topic in greater detail and find out how to store documents using all the common data sources. The topics that we'll cover will include

- How to set up a data source. We'll look at how to set up SharePoint, Dataverse, and SQL Server data sources to store files.

- How to upload, view, and download files, both in canvas and model-driven apps.

- How to integrate with the cloud-based storage provider, Azure Blob storage.

Overview

To begin this chapter, we'll review the data sources that support file storage and consider the pros and cons of each option. The options that we'll cover include SharePoint, Dataverse, SQL Server, and Azure Blob storage.

Starting with SharePoint, SharePoint offers a simple way to store file attachments. With each SharePoint list, we can enable an option to store attachments. This allows us to build an app that stores file attachments against each record. The form control recognizes attachments fields, and we can provide file handling features without needing to write any formula.

579

© Tim Leung 2021
T. Leung, *Beginning Power Apps*, https://doi.org/10.1007/978-1-4842-6683-0_17

With SharePoint, we can also connect to document libraries. This enables us to integrate with documents that are not associated with a specific record in a list. A benefit of SharePoint is that it provides a cost-effective method of file storage. Almost all Microsoft 365 plans include SharePoint, and there is no need to subscribe to a more expensive per-user or per-app plan in order to use SharePoint.

Another simple and effective way to store documents is to use Dataverse. By using Dataverse, we can take advantage of additional Dataverse features. This includes granular control of security permissions, auditing, and easy access to file content from other products in the Power Platform.

With Dataverse, we would add a file field to a table. This enables us to associate files with a specific record. Dataverse stores files in the file storage area, rather than the main Dataverse database, and it offers a maximum size limit of 30 MB per file. The benefit of the file storage area is that it offers a significantly greater storage quota, compared to the main Dataverse database.

If we were building a model-driven app, Dataverse would be the requisite choice. With canvas apps, the form control provides seamless support for Dataverse file fields.

Although SQL Server supports the storage of files and binary data, Power Apps does not integrate as well with SQL Server. The designer does not natively offer the use of the attachments control against a binary field. Therefore, we need to carry out more work to build an app that works against SQL Server. Where SQL Server works well is where we want to integrate with tables that contain existing data or where we want to store documents in a database that is easily accessible from other platforms and programming languages. If we prefer not to store our documents in the cloud, an on-premise instance of SQL Server enables us store data inside an internal network.

Finally, another file storage option is Azure Blob storage. The benefit of Azure Blob storage is that it provides low-cost, cloud-based storage for very large files (up to 2 GB). There is a connector that enables us to easily save, query, and retrieve files. The Azure Blob storage connector is a premium connector. This means that users will require a per-user or per-app license.

In the remainder of this chapter, we'll work through each of these data sources, and we'll find out how to set up an app to store documents using such data sources.

> **Caution**   From a canvas app, the primary way for users to upload files is to use the attachments control. This control supports a maximum file size of 50 MB. Therefore, the practical file size limit is 50 MB, even with an underlying data source that could support larger files.

Storing Files in SharePoint

SharePoint provides an easy way to work with files. When we add an edit form based on a SharePoint list, we can add the attachments field. The card will include an attachments control. At runtime, users can use this control to upload, retrieve, and delete file attachments (Figure 17-1).

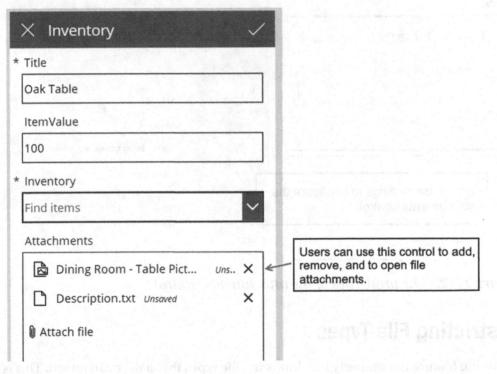

Figure 17-1.   *The attachments control at runtime*

The SharePoint attachments field supports multiple files. When we use the attachments control to display an existing record, the user can click an item in the list to download the file attachment.

581

Let's take a closer look at the properties of the attachments control. As Figure 17-2 shows, we can specify the maximum number of attachments, and we can also specify a maximum attachments size. By default, this is 10 MB. We can also specify the text that appears when there are no attachments, the text that labels the link to attach a file, and the text that appears when a user attempts to attach more than the maximum number of permitted files.

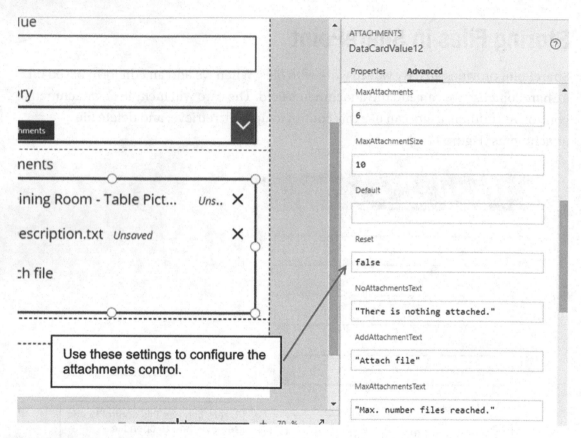

Figure 17-2. *The properties of the attachments control*

Restricting File Types

A missing feature is a property that limits the file types that a user can attach. This is a requirement that app builders often request. Let's suppose we want to restrict users to attaching only PDF files. We can apply this rule by checking for the existence of the PDF file extension in the file names of all the attached files. If not all files contain a PDF file extension, we can disable the save icon on the form. To illustrate this technique, the formula we would attach to the Display mode property of the save icon would look like this:

```
(CountRows(Filter(DataCardValue12.Attachments.Name, ".pdf" in Lower(Name)))
 = CountRows(DataCardValue12.Attachments)
)
```

This formula assumes that the name of our attachments control is `DataCardValue12`. The attachments control exposes the property `Attachments.Name`. This returns a single-column table that contains all the file names that the user has attached. We filter this table for names that include the text ".pdf," and we call the `CountRows` function to return the number of matching records. If there is a mismatch between this value and the total number of attached files, this indicates that not all attached files are of type PDF.

To alert the user to the fact that there are invalid file types, we can add a label to our form and use the same formula to control the Visible property of the label.

A final point to note is that the SharePoint option to support attachments is enabled by default. If the attachments field is missing, we can enable the support for attachments through the advanced settings area of the SharePoint list.

Connecting to Document Libraries

With SharePoint, we can also connect to document libraries. A document library is a place in SharePoint where we can store a variety of files that are not specifically associated with a list or list item. Figure 17-3 shows the standard "Documents" document library that exists in a SharePoint site. This illustration highlights how a document library can contain a range of file types, including Word, Excel, PDF, and many more.

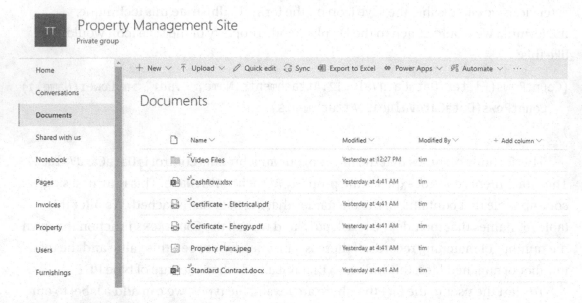

Figure 17-3. A SharePoint document library

Each file in a document library includes metadata that includes a thumbnail image, the author, and the last user to modify the file. We can retrieve all these details, including thumbnail images of the author and editor.

To connect to a document library, we use the Insert ➤ Data source menu item and choose a document library, in the same way as we would select a SharePoint list. As Figure 17-4 highlights, a different icon appears next to document library items.

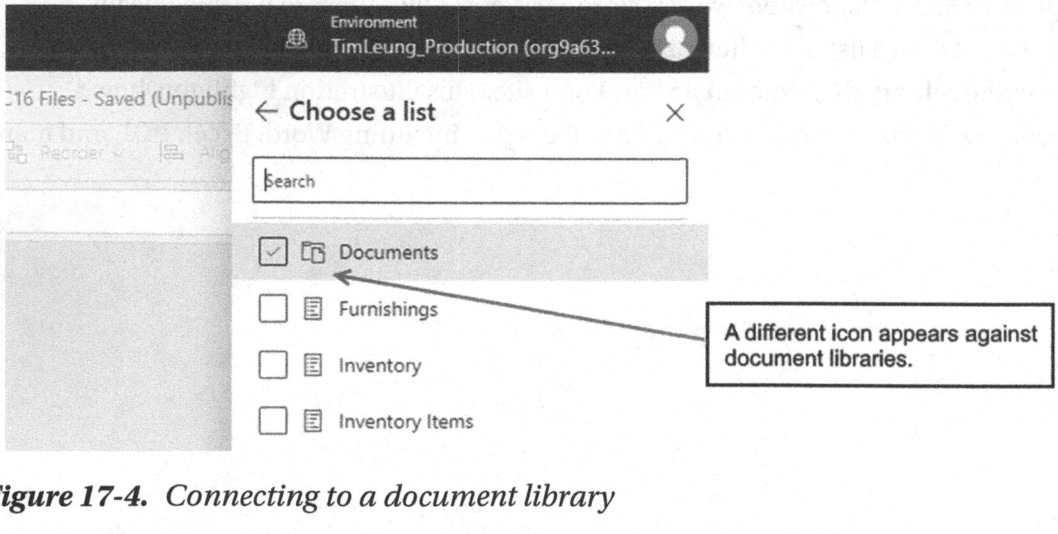

Figure 17-4. Connecting to a document library

Once we add a connection to a document library, we can display the contents of the library through data controls, and we can also write formulas to query or filter the items in the library.

Figure 17-5 shows a gallery control that is configured to show items from our document library. In this example, the name of the data source is `Documents`. If we were to set the `Items` property of this gallery control to `Documents`, the gallery would show the entire contents of the document library, including folders and files within subfolders. To only show documents, we can filter the document library by the `IsFolder` property. The formula we would use looks like this:

```
Filter(Documents, IsFolder=false)
```

An important limitation is that this query is not delegable. Therefore, it will not return accurate results against document libraries with more than 2000 items.

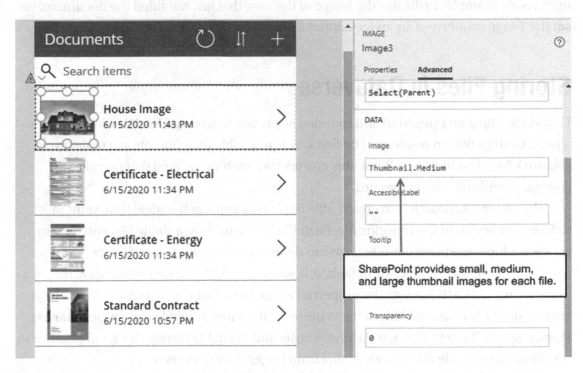

Figure 17-5. *Viewing the files in the document library*

In this example, we use the image control to display a thumbnail of the document. A great feature of SharePoint is that it generates three thumbnail images of each document. With most documents, the thumbnail images represent a preview of the document, rather than a generic image that represent the image type. We can access these thumbnails through the Thumbnail.Small, Thumbnail.Medium, and Thumbnail.Large properties.

Two other frequently used properties are the Name and the 'Link to item' properties. The Name property returns the file name, and the 'Link to item' property returns the SharePoint web address of the document. From within the gallery, we can configure an icon to open the document in a new browser tab. The formula we would add to the OnSelect property of the icon would look like this:

```
Launch('Link to item')
```

Finally, we can retrieve the details of the author and the last user to modify the file through the 'Created By' and 'Modified By' properties. These properties enable us to retrieve the DisplayName, Email, Picture, and several other attributes that relate to the user. As an example, to display the image of the user that last modified the document, we set the Image property of an image control to 'Modified By'.Picture.

Storing Files in Dataverse

Dataverse offers an integrated and rounded approach to storing files. We can configure a table to store files in two ways. The first way is to enable attachments at a table level (Figure 17-6). Just like SharePoint, this creates an attachments field that permits the storage of multiple files per record.

The second approach is to create a file field. This approach is ideal if we want to define a named field for a specific file. Each file field can store a single file, and we can create multiple file fields per table. We can define the maximum size of the files that we want to store in the file field. By default, this value is 32 MB, but we can increase this to a maximum of 128 MB through the properties of the field. Dataverse uses the file storage area to store file contents. This helps to preserve the more valuable Dataverse database storage space. To help manage Dataverse costs and available storage, it's good practice to set the maximum file size to a value that is no larger than necessary.

These two approaches are not mutually exclusive. We can enable attachments at a table level, in addition to defining one or more file fields. An important point is that once we enable attachments at a table level, it is not possible to disable this option. Also, once we define a maximum file size for a file field, we cannot subsequently change the value.

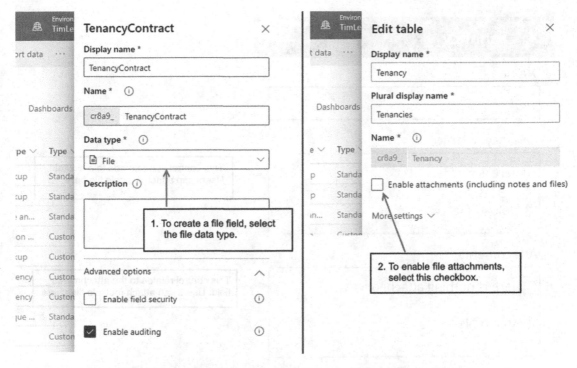

Figure 17-6. *Defining a file field and enabling attachments in Dataverse*

Figure 17-7 shows an edit form based on a tenancy table with attachments enabled and a named file field called tenancy contract. The cards for the attachments and the tenancy contract fields include an attachments control. This is the same control that we saw in the SharePoint example.

With the attachments control that is associated with the tenancy contract file field, the designer sets the maximum attachments property of the control to one. This prevents the end user from attaching multiple files.

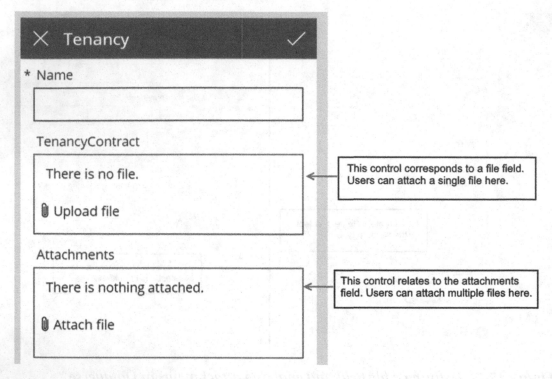

Figure 17-7.   The attachments controls at runtime

Note that the attachments control includes a MaxAttachmentSize property. This defines the maximum permissible size of an attachment. The default value of this is 10 MB, but we can increase this to a maximum of 50 MB. It is possible to enter a value higher than 50 MB, but the control will enforce a maximum of 50 MB in this instance.

Storing Files in SQL Server

As we've seen, Power Apps provides first-class support for storing files in SharePoint and Dataverse. Unfortunately, the support for SQL Server is far less rounded. There are two general issues that we face.

The first issue is that if we create an edit form based on a table with a SQL Server binary field, the designer will not generate a card with an attachments control against the field.

The second issue is that the menus in the designer provide no way to add an attachments control to a screen. The attachments control is crucial to building apps that can integrate with files. Not only does it enable users to upload files but it also enables users to download and to delete files.

To resolve this issue, the most effective work-around is to create a form that's based on a Dataverse table or a SharePoint list with attachments enabled. We then copy the attachments control and paste it onto the screens where we want to work against a SQL Server data source.

To demonstrate the file handling capabilities with a SQL Server data source, we'll walk through the process to build a screen that enables users to upload and retrieve files from a SQL Server table.

The learning points from this exercise include how to use the attachments control outside of a form by using the copy and paste technique. We'll also cover the syntax to add binary documents with the Patch function. These are techniques that we can apply to other data sources, including Azure Blob storage (which we'll cover in the next section).

Tip   For SQL Server binary fields, the designer does not generate cards with an attachments control. We can work around this by pasting an attachments control from a SharePoint-based form.

Setting Up a SQL Server Table

To set up a SQL Server table to store file content, we would first create a table with a varbinary field. This is the preferred data type for storing file data. Figure 17-8 shows the table that we'll use in this example.

	Column Name	Data Type	Allow Nulls
▶🔑	FileID	int	☐
	Filename	nvarchar(MAX)	☐
	[Document]	varbinary(MAX)	☐

Figure 17-8. *Setting up a SQL Server table*

This table includes an auto-incrementing (identity) primary key field called `FileID`. The table also contains a field to store the file name and a `varbinary(MAX)` field to store the binary document data.

Adding and Updating a Record

To build the screen that the user can use to add a record to the table, the first step is to paste an attachments control from a Dataverse- or SharePoint-based form. We'll name this control `attFiles`.

The attachments control that we copy from an existing form will include property values that are not valid on our target screen. This includes the `Items`, `BorderColour`, `Tooltip`, and `DisplayMode` properties. It's important to clear these property values to resolve the errors that appear in the designer.

To adapt the control to suit our purposes, we should set the `DisplayMode` property to `Edit` and set the maximum attachments property to 1.

Next, we can add a button to save the file attachment to the database. Here's the formula that we add to the `OnSelect` property:

```
Patch('[dbo].[Files]',
    Defaults('[dbo].[Files]'),
    {Filename:First(attFiles.Attachments).Name,
     Document:First(attFiles.Attachments).Value}
)
```

This formula calls the `Patch` function to add a record to the database. The first argument specifies the data source, and the second argument calls the `Defaults` function to specify that we want to add a record. The third argument specifies the record to add. The `Attachments` property of the attachments control returns a table object that contains the files that the user has attached. Because we configured the control to accept a maximum of one attachment, we can call the `First` function against the `Attachments` property to return the details of the file.

The `Name` property of the file attachment returns the file name, and the `Value` property returns the contents of the document.

When a user uses the attachments control to attach a file, Power Apps stores the file locally as an application resource. If we were to inspect the contents of the Value property, it would return an "app resource" URI in the following format:

```
appres://blobmanager/85936581a42c4982b9378bbb183ef86d/3
```

When we pass this URI to the Patch function, Power Apps saves the binary content that corresponds to this local address to the database. Figure 17-9 shows the layout of our screen in the designer.

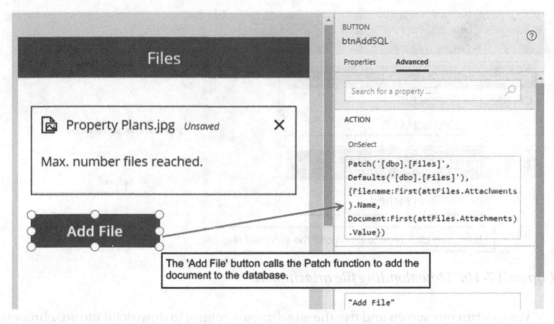

Figure 17-9.   *Adding a file to a SQL Server data source*

We can now run our screen, attach a file, and click the button to save our changes to the database.

Downloading File Attachments

To demonstrate how to enable users to download files, we'll build a screen that contains a list box. This control will enable a user to select a record from the SQL Server table. On this same screen, we'll paste an attachments control and link this to the selected record in the list box.

To configure the list box, we'll name it lbxFiles and set the Items property to our data source, '[dbo].[Files]'. To prevent users from selecting multiple items, we can set the SelectMultiple property to false.

Next, we can link our attachments control to the selected item by setting the attachments property to First(lbxFiles.SelectedItems). To configure the attachments control, it's important to set the Name and Value properties to the database fields that contain the file name and the binary file content – in our example, Filename and Document. Figure 17-10 shows the layout of our screen.

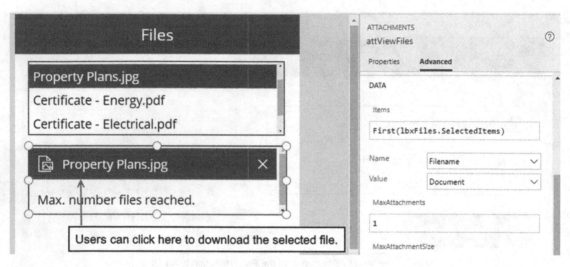

Figure 17-10. *Downloading file attachments*

We can run our screen and use the attachments control to download the attachment.

For supported file types, we can also utilize the controls in Power Apps to render the content. As an example, let's suppose we upload a PDF file. To display this content in a PDF control, we can simply add a PDF control and set the Default property to our binary data field (Figure 17-11).

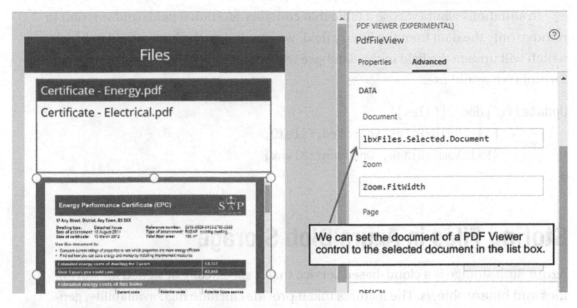

Figure 17-11. *Displaying PDF files*

Deleting a File

To delete a file, we can add a button to our screen and execute a formula to delete the selected document from the list box. We can call the RemoveIf function to delete a record, and here's the formula that we would add to the OnSelect property of our button:

```
RemoveIf('[dbo].[Files]', FileID=lbxFiles.Selected.FileID)
```

Figure 17-12 shows how this appears in the designer.

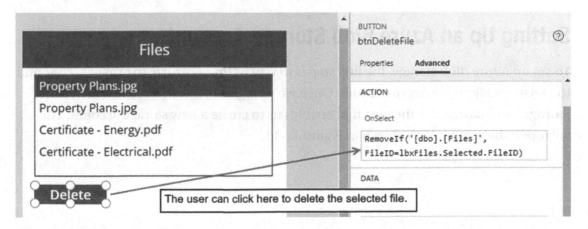

Figure 17-12. *Deleting a file*

In situations where we use a table that contains additional fields and we want to remove only the data from the binary field, we can update the binary field to Blank, which will update the field in the database with a null value. Here's an example of the formula we would use:

```
UpdateIf('[dbo].[Files]',
        FileID=lbxFiles.Selected.FileID,
        {FileName:Blank, Document:Blank}
)
```

Storing Files in Azure Blob Storage

Azure Blob storage is a cloud-based service that is specifically designed for storing files and binary objects. The features that it provides include high availability, geo-replication, security, and data encryption. Of all the available storage options, Azure Blob storage provides one of the most cost-effective solutions. Premium storage starts at US $0.15 per GB/Month. Therefore, it works very well in scenarios where we want to store large quantities of data. For data that we don't need to access frequently, we can lower our costs further by choosing a service tier that offers slower performance and a lower level of guaranteed availability.

With Power Apps, we can take advantage of the features that Azure Blob storage provides. This is possible through a connector that allows us to create and retrieve files from Azure Blob storage. In the section, we'll find out how to set up Azure Blob storage and how to create screens that users can use to create and to retrieve files.

Setting Up an Azure Blob Storage Account

To set up Azure Blob storage, the first step is to visit https://azure.microsoft.com/ and to register a Microsoft Azure account. Once we've registered, we can search for "Azure Storage" and navigate to the area that enables us to create a new storage account. This will open the screen that's shown in Figure 17-13.

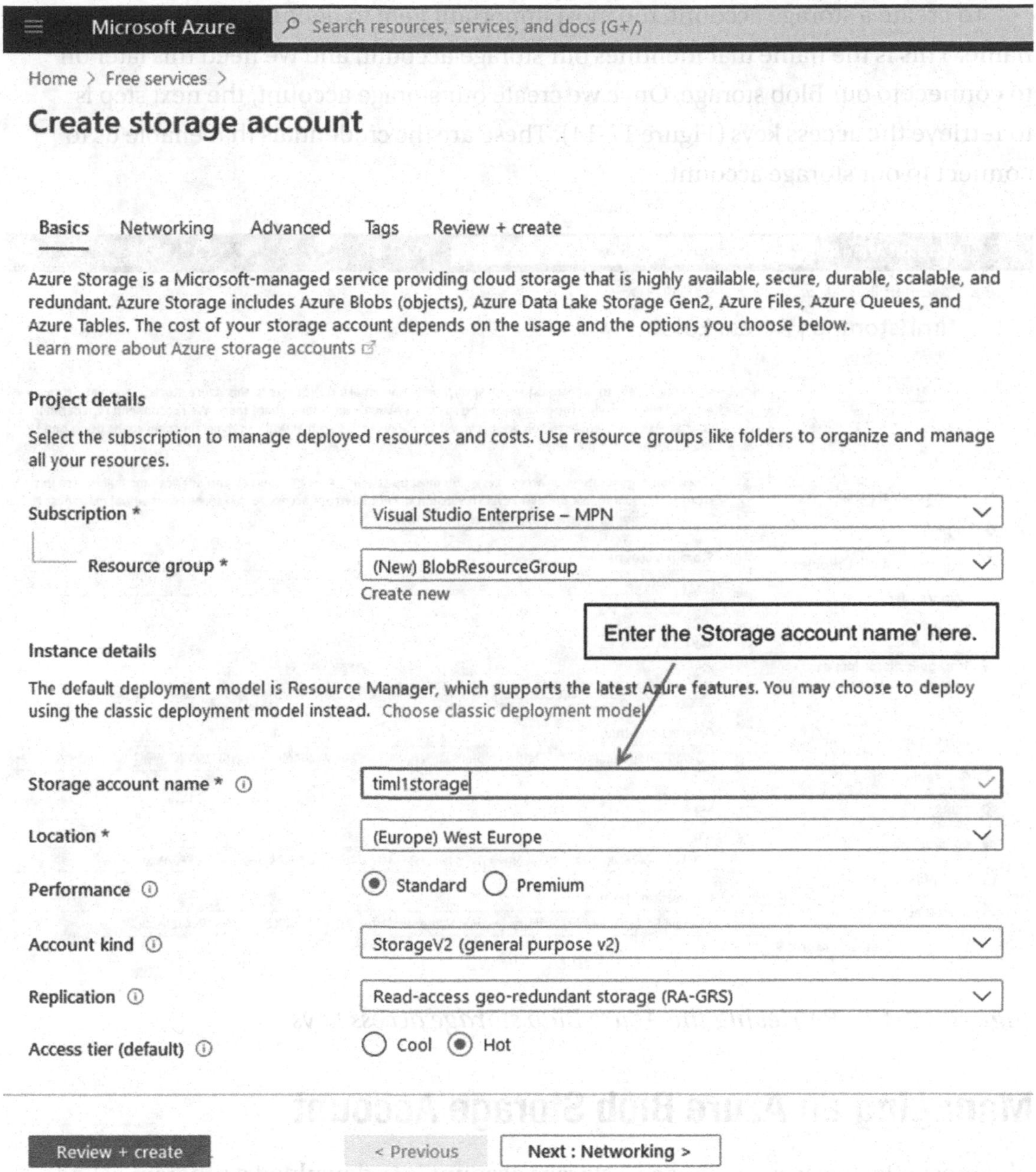

Figure 17-13. Creating an Azure Storage account

To create a storage account, the most important item to define is the storage account name. This is the name that identifies our storage account, and we need this later on to connect to our Blob storage. Once we create our storage account, the next step is to retrieve the access keys (Figure 17-14). These are the credentials that enable us to connect to our storage account.

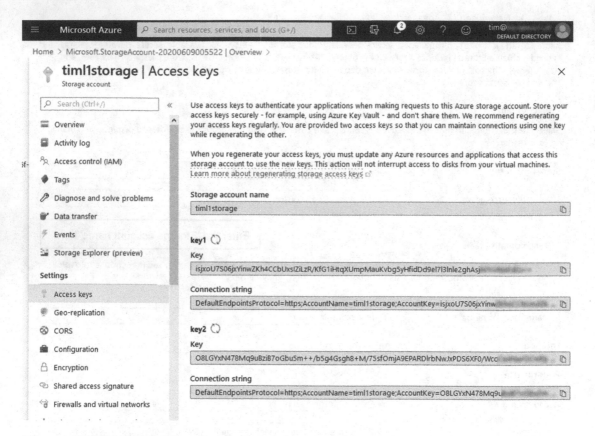

Figure 17-14. *Retrieving the Azure Blob storage access keys*

Managing an Azure Blob Storage Account

The most effective way to manage a storage account is to download a program called Azure Storage Explorer. This program enables us to upload, download, and manage files in storage accounts. We can download Azure Storage Explorer from the following address:

```
https://azure.microsoft.com/en-us/features/storage-explorer/
```

With Azure Blob storage, the key step that we need to carry out is to define a container (Figure 17-15). A container functions just like a directory on a local file system. It provides an area to store files, and it helps us to organize the files in our storage. A container provides a unit where we can apply security roles. We'll create a container called documents to illustrate the features of Azure Blob storage later on.

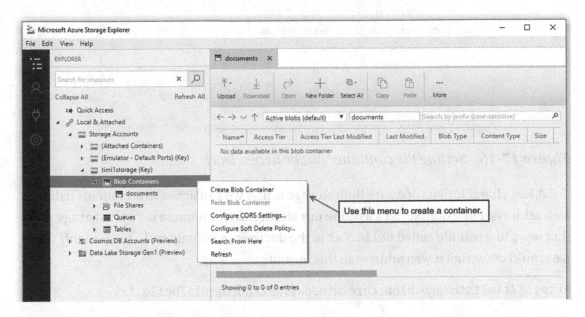

Figure 17-15. *Creating Azure Blob storage containers*

The right-click context menu on the documents container offers two settings that relate to security. The first is the "Set Container Public Access level" setting, and the second is the "Shared Access Signature" setting.

Starting with the "Set Container Public Access Level" setting, this defines whether public or anonymous users can access the items in the container. The default setting enforces security by prohibiting public access. To publicly share the contents of a container with all users, we can modify the settings as shown in Figure 17-16.

Figure 17-16. *Setting the container public access level*

A key characteristic of Azure Blob storage is that we can access the contents using a web address. For example, let's assume our storage account name is `timl1storage` and that we add a text file called `hello.txt` to the `documents` container. To retrieve this file, we would construct a web address in this format:

```
https://timl1storage.blob.core.windows.net/documents/hello.txt
```

If public read access is enabled, any user can access this file through the web address. If we retain the default "No public access" setting, the web address will return an error.

How exactly can we retrieve a file when the "No public access" setting is enabled? One way is to create a shared access signature. With this technique, we append a query string parameter value to the web address. This value authorizes access to the target resource.

To generate the shared access signature, we would right-click the container and select the "Get shared access signature" menu item (Figure 17-17). This opens a dialog that enables us to generate an access signature with an expiry time. After we create our shared access signature, the dialog will show the query string that enables us to access a file in the container. The web address that enables us to access the file will look like this:

```
https://timl1storage.blob.core.windows.net/documents/hello.txt?sv=2019-02-
02&st=2020-06-18T20%3A35%3A25Z&se=2020-06-19T20%3A35%3A25Z&sr=c&sp=rl&sig=w
2Pov5aaulJtzHji%2FM3RfW%2BjSIohM2UhpbJc8ubUP9k%3D
```

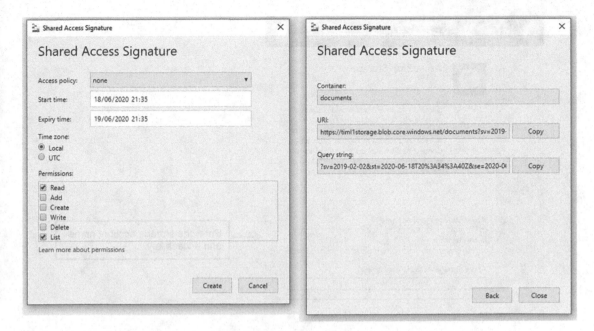

Figure 17-17. *Setting up shared access signatures*

The reason why it's important to understand these endpoint addresses is because we can call these from Power Apps to download or to open a file.

Connecting to an Azure Blob Storage Account

Once we create an Azure Blob storage account and container, we can connect to it using the Insert ➤ Data sources menu item. The connections pane requires us to provide the storage account name and the access key (Figure 17-18).

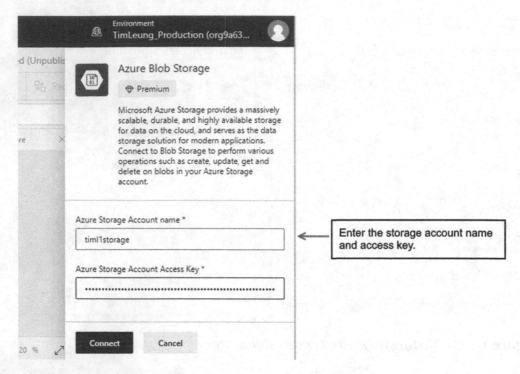

Figure 17-18. *Creating a connection to Azure Blob storage*

The Azure Blob storage connector provides a range of methods that we can call. These enable us to conduct file operations that include creating, updating, deleting, listing, and retrieving files. Table 17-1 summarizes the methods that we can call.

Table 17-1. *Azure Blob storage methods*

Action	Description
AzureBlobStorage.CopyFile	This copies a file by a source and destination path.
AzureBlobStorage.CreateFile	This creates a file. This method accepts a container, file name, and file content.
AzureBlobStorage.DeleteFile	This deletes a file by the file ID.
AzureBlobStorage.GetFileContent	This retrieves the file content by file ID.
AzureBlobStorage.GetFileContentByPath	This retrieves the file content by the file path.
AzureBlobStorage.GetFileMetadata	This retrieves the file metadata by file ID.
AzureBlobStorage.GetFileMetadataByPath	This retrieves the file metadata by the file path
AzureBlobStorage.ListFolderV2	This lists the contents of a container.
AzureBlobStorage.ListRootFolderV2	This lists the contents of the root folder.
AzureBlobStorage.UpdateFile	This updates a file by the ID.

Uploading Files to Azure Blob Storage

Let's look at how to build a screen that allows a user to add a file to Azure Blob storage. To build this feature, we'll adopt a similar approach to the one that we used to upload a file to SQL Server. We'll copy an attachments control from a Dataverse- or SharePoint-based form and call the CreateFile method to save the file attachment to Azure Blob storage.

The first step is to paste an attachments control onto a screen and clear all the invalid property references. We would set the DisplayMode property of the attachments control to Edit and set the maximum attachments property to 1.

To save the file that the user attaches, we can add a button to our screen and attach the following formula to the OnSelect property:

```
AzureBlobStorage.CreateFile("documents",
                    First(attFilesBlob.Attachments).Name,
                    First(attFilesBlob.Attachments).Value
)
```

This formula calls the AzureBlobStorage.CreateFile method to create a new file in our container. The first argument specifies the container name, and here, we provide the name of the container that we created earlier – documents. The second and third arguments specify the document name and content. Here, we refer to the attachments control to retrieve these details. Figure 17-19 shows the presentation of our screen in the designer. We can now run this screen, attach a file, and click the button to save our file into our container.

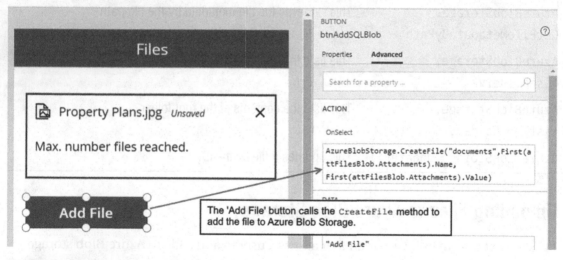

Figure 17-19. *Adding a file to Azure Blob storage*

Listing Files in a Container

To list the files in a container, we call the ListFolderV2 method. This method requires us to provide the name of the container. Figure 17-20 illustrates how to display the contents of our documents container in a list box control. Here, we set the Items property of the list box control to the following formula:

```
AzureBlobStorage.ListFolderV2("documents").value
```

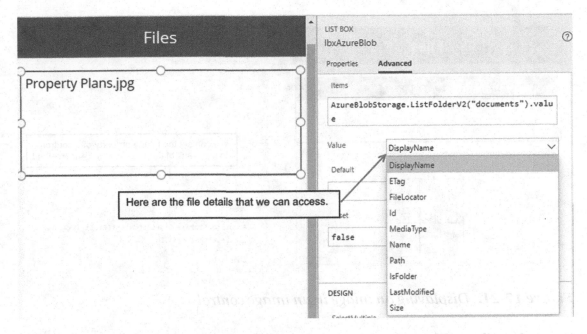

Figure 17-20. *Listing the files in a container*

As Figure 17-20 shows, the ListFolderV2 method returns a range of metadata values that we can display. This includes the display name, file size, last modified date, and many other attributes. A key attribute that we can retrieve is the Id value of a file. This value uniquely identifies a file in Azure Blob storage, and it is particularly important because most of the methods that the connector provides (e.g., DeleteFile and GetFileContent) require us to specify a file by the Id value. Here's an example of the format of an ID value:

JTJmZG9jdW1lbnRzJTJmUHJvcGVydHkrUGxhbnMuanBn

Viewing and Retrieving File Content

To retrieve a file, we can call the GetFileContent or GetFileContentByPath method. The GetFileContent method retrieves a file by Id value, whereas the GetFileContentByPath method retrieves a file by the path. An example of a path value looks like this:
/documents/Property Plans.jpg

For file types where there is a supported canvas control (e.g., PDF, image, and audio files), we can directly render the file using the control. Figure 17-21 shows how we display an image by setting the Image property of an image control to a call to the GetFileContent method.

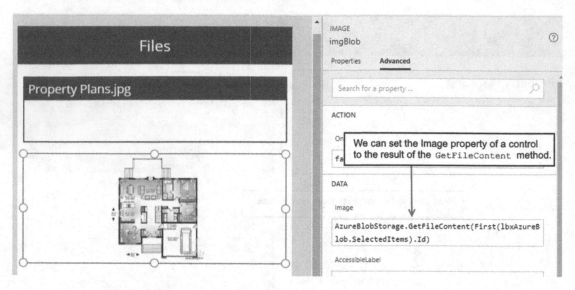

Figure 17-21. *Displaying an image in an image control*

Downloading Files

The easiest way to enable users to download a file is to provide a link to the web address of the file. We can incorporate the web address within a call to the Launch function. This function will open the file in a new browser tab.

Figure 17-22 illustrates the use of this technique. This screen contains a gallery control with the Items property set to a call to the ListFolderV2 method. This method returns a field called Path, which specifies the path to the file.

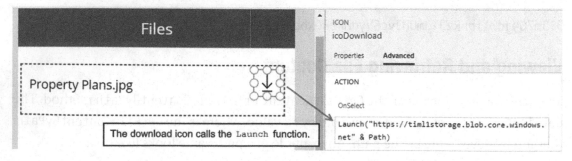

Figure 17-22. *Launching a file*

The template item of this gallery control includes a label that displays the file name and an icon. The OnSelect property of the icon contains a formula that launches the endpoint web address of the file. In this simple example, the formula we use looks like this:

```
Launch("https://timl1storage.blob.core.windows.net" & Path)
```

This address will work when public access is enabled for the container. If public access is not enabled, we can append a shared access signature query parameter to the end of the address using this format:

```
Launch("https://timl1storage.blob.core.windows.net" & Path &
"?sv=SASValue")
```

With this method, we would replace the query string parameter value (SASValue) with the value that we retrieve through the shared access signature dialog.

With public access disabled, another way to generate an authenticated file link is to call the CreateShareLinkByPath method. This method returns a link with an expiry time. The following formula would create a publicly available link that expires in 1 hour.

This technique saves us from needing to pre-generate shared access signatures and provides a great compromise between security and ease of use:

```
Launch(
    AzureBlobStorage.CreateShareLinkByPath(
                        Path,
                        {ExpiryTime:DateAdd(Now(), 1,Hours)}
                ).WebUrl
)
```

In secure situations where we don't want to expose any publicly accessible link, we can utilize the attachments control. Using the same technique as the earlier examples in this section, we would paste an attachments control onto our screen. As an example, here is the formula that we would apply to the Items property of the control to retrieve the file at the location \documents\hello.txt:

```
{
    Filename: "hello.txt",
    Document: AzureBlobStorage.GetFileContentByPath("/documents/hello.txt")
}
```

Note that in the event of an exception (e.g., if the file has been deleted or if the user doesn't have sufficient privileges), the attachments control will display a red label with the error. Therefore, there is no specific error handling that we need to carry out – the control manages this for us.

Deleting Files

Finally, we can delete files from a container by calling the DeleteFile method. This method accepts the Id value of the file that we want to delete. To demonstrate, let's assume we build a screen with a list box that displays files from a container.

To delete the selected file from the list box, we can add a button and set the OnSelect property to the following formula:

```
AzureBlobStorage.DeleteFile(First(lbxAzureBlob.SelectedItems).Id)
```

Figure 17-23 illustrates the layout of this screen.

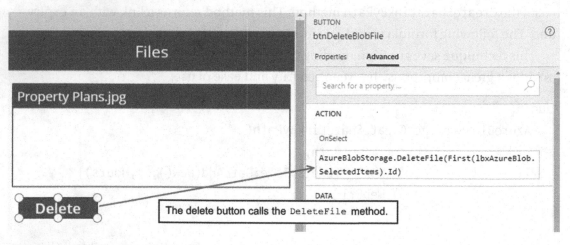

Figure 17-23. *Deleting a file*

Working with Model-Driven Apps

In the final section of this chapter, we'll briefly look at how to save and retrieve in model-driven apps. With model-driven apps, it's very simple to build this functionality. Because model-driven apps work only with Dataverse data sources, the first step is to define one or more file fields in a table. The next step is to create a form that includes the file fields.

Taking the tenancy table that we set up earlier in this chapter, Figure 17-24 shows the design view of the main form in the designer and highlights how to add the fields to the form.

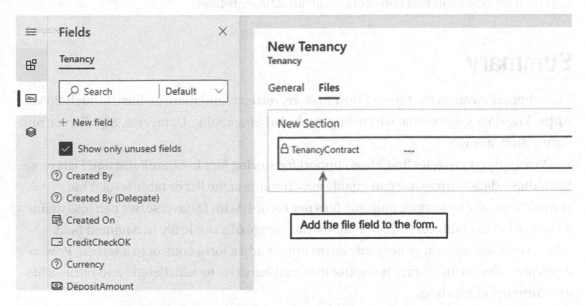

Figure 17-24. *Setting up a model-driven app form*

Once we've configured a form with the file fields, we can add the table to the site map of a model-driven app. At runtime, the app will render a file control against the file field. This enables the user to upload, download, or delete a file (Figure 17-25).

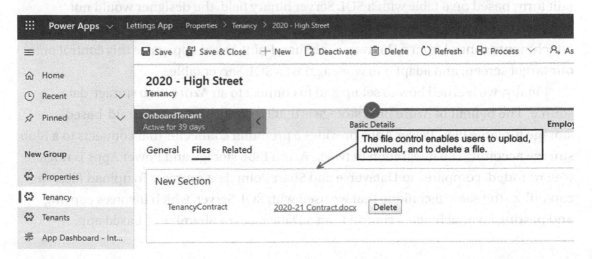

Figure 17-25. *The file control at runtime*

Unfortunately, model-driven apps do not support tables where attachments are enabled. With this type of setup, there is no built-in control to attach multiple file attachments to a record. One work-around to this problem would be to embed a canvas app with an edit form that connects to the attachments field.

Summary

This chapter covered the topic of how to store, retrieve, and manage files through Power Apps. The data sources that we covered included SharePoint, Dataverse, SQL Server, and Azure Blob storage.

Power Apps provides first-class support for storing files in SharePoint and Dataverse. With these data sources, we can enable attachments at the list or table level. This provides the ability to store multiple files per record. With Dataverse, we can also define a file field at the table level. This enables the storage of a single file in a named field. When we build an auto-generated canvas app or add a form control to a screen, Power Apps provides an attachments control that enables users to add, delete, and retrieve file attachments at runtime.

Model-driven apps support Dataverse file fields. At runtime, a model-driven app renders a control that enables users to add or to remove a file to or from the file field. However, model-driven apps do not currently support tables with attachments enabled, and it is not possible for users to attach multiple files to the attachments field.

SQL Server does not integrate as well with Power Apps. If we were to create an edit form based on a table with a SQL Server binary field, the designer would not generate a card with an attachments control. To work around this issue, we can copy the attachments control from a Dataverse- or SharePoint-based app, paste this control onto our target screen, and adapt it to work against a SQL Server table.

Finally, we learned how to set up and to connect to an Azure Blob storage data source. The benefit of Azure Blob storage is that it provides low-cost, cloud-based storage for large files. Power Apps provides a premium connector that connects to a Blob storage account. The integration between Azure Blob storage and Power Apps is not as well rounded, compared to Dataverse and SharePoint data sources. To upload files, we can utilize the same technique that we used with SQL Server, which involves copying and pasting an attachments control from a Dataverse- or SharePoint-based app.

The Azure Blob storage connector provides a range of methods which we can call to create, update, delete, or retrieve a file. The default setting of the storage container is to prohibit public access. To authorize the retrieval of the file, we can append a token to the web address that retrieves the file. We can also create a publicly accessible link to the file that expires after a short period of time.

CHAPTER 18

Integrating Maps and Location Services

With Power Apps, we can easily build canvas apps that include location-based features. Through mobile and browser-based apps, we can retrieve the location of the current user, and we can also integrate with mapping services.

Despite the relative ease with which we can retrieve location details, there are various intricacies to be aware of, especially when we want to save the results to a data source. In this chapter, we'll cover these issues, in addition to the following topics:

- How to retrieve location data. We'll discover how to retrieve values including the longitude, latitude, compass bearing, and acceleration details of the user.

- How to save location details. We'll create an auto-generated app and go through the steps to retrieve and to save location details of the user through an edit form.

- How to integrate with mapping services. We'll find out how to display maps and pinpoint locations with two of the most popular services – Google Maps and Bing Maps.

Introduction to Location Services and GPS

Mobile devices and PCs can provide the location of the current user through location services. Mobile devices rely on GPS or cellular signals to return an accurate location. On desktop PCs, the operating system and the web browser can utilize databases of Wi-Fi network names and IP addresses to determine the approximate location of a user.

611

© Tim Leung 2021
T. Leung, *Beginning Power Apps*, https://doi.org/10.1007/978-1-4842-6683-0_18

From within a canvas app, we can use formulas to determine the longitude, latitude, or compass bearing of a device. This enables us to build apps that can capture the location of the current user. A great use of this feature is to provide geo-tagging capabilities. For example, we can build an app that captures both a photograph and the location at the same time.

A question I often hear is whether we can build apps to track the location of employees or health apps that can record the route of a run. Unfortunately, Power Apps is not suitable for these use case scenarios. On a mobile device, Power Apps can only capture location data when the app runs in the foreground. When a device becomes inactive and the screen switches off, the app suspends execution and will not collect data while in this state.

Longitudes and Latitudes

For readers who are unfamiliar with longitude and latitude values, here's a brief introduction. Longitude and latitude values are measured in degrees, and we use these readings to locate a specific location on Earth. These values can be positive or negative. Locations in the Southern Hemisphere have a negative longitude, and locations in the Western Hemisphere have a negative latitude. Figure 18-1 illustrates this in the form of a diagram.

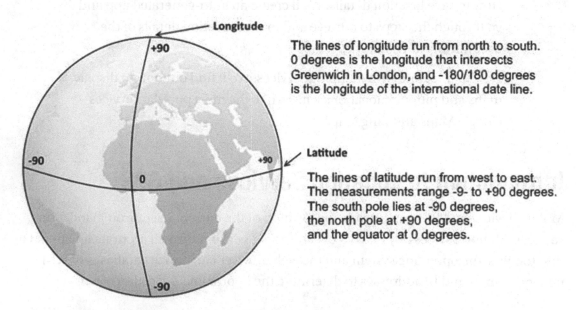

Figure 18-1. *Longitude and latitude measurements*

On a mobile device, the accuracy of the reading can vary. If the user has only just switched on location services or the GPS, there may be insufficient time for the device to retrieve an accurate reading. In this case, devices have a tendency to return the last known location. If a user starts an app with location services turned on and subsequently turns off location services at a later point, any attempt to retrieve the location will return the last known location.

When a user runs a location-enabled app through a web browser, the browser prompts the user to share their location details (Figure 18-2). The user must accept this request for us to be able to retrieve the location details from an app.

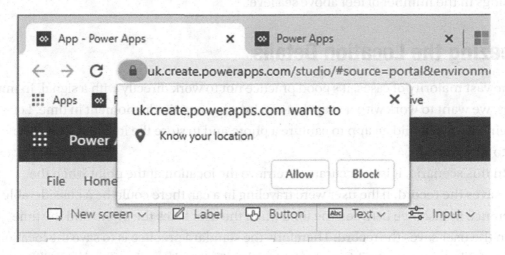

Figure 18-2. *Running an app on a browser*

Retrieving Location Details

Now that we've covered the basics, we'll walk through the process to build an app that can retrieve and store location details.

Introducing Signals

Power Apps provides objects called signals. The signals that are of most interest to us are the location, compass, and acceleration signals. The key characteristic of a signal is that its value can constantly change. We can refer to signals from formulas without any additional setup. In the case of the location signal, the value of this signal can change regularly to reflect the movement of a user.

Other signals that are available include `App.ActiveScreen` and `Connection`. The `App.ActiveScreen` signal returns the screen that is currently showing, and the `Connection` signal returns connection details, such as whether the device is connected to a network and whether the connection is metered.

We can treat signals as though they are records. In the case of the location signal, we can treat this as a record that contains three fields: longitude, latitude, and altitude. To retrieve the longitude or latitude in a formula, we would use the syntax `Location.Longitude` or `Location.Latitude`, respectively.

The location signal returns longitude and latitude readings in degrees and altitude readings in the number of feet above sea level.

Freezing the Location Details

In the vast majority of cases, it's good practice not to work directly with a signal. In many cases, we want to work with a snapshot of a location at a single moment in time. Let's imagine that we build an app to capture a photo and to store the location where the photo was taken.

In this scenario, it isn't accurate to retrieve the location at the point when the user saves the record. If the user were traveling in a car, there could be a considerable difference in distance between the time when the user takes the photo and the time when the user saves the record. Therefore, the standard practice is to save the locations to a variable and to work with the variable value. This is the technique that we'll cover in this chapter.

Obtaining Longitude and Latitude Readings

To demonstrate how to retrieve locations, we'll build a screen that retrieves and stores the location details into a variable and displays those values on screen.

To build this example, we'll add a screen and insert two labels called `lblLongitude` and `lblLatitude`.

Next, we'll add a button and set the `OnSelect` property to the following formula:

```
UpdateContext({locLocation: Location})
```

This formula stores the result of the `Location` signal to a context variable called `locLocation`.

To display the location details on screen, we set the Text properties of our longitude and latitude labels to locLocation.Longitude and locLocation.Latitude, respectively.

We can run our app to test this functionality. Provided that we allow the browser to access our location, the labels should show a location when we click the button. Figure 18-3 shows the appearance of our screen.

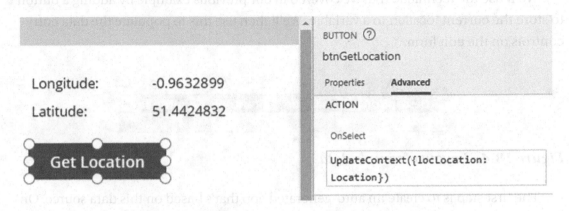

Figure 18-3. *Layout of our sample screen*

If the app fails to retrieve a location, the user may think that the app isn't working. To improve this behavior, we can show a message that indicates this condition. We can accomplish this by amending our formula so that it stores a message in a variable when location services are not available. The following formula illustrates this technique:

```
UpdateContext({locLocation: Location});
UpdateContext({LocationMessage:If(IsBlank(Location.Longitude),
                         "Location Unavailable",
                         "")
              }
)
```

When Power Apps fails to retrieve a location, it returns blank longitude and latitude readings. We can test for the presence of a blank longitude to detect that a device has failed to retrieve the location. In this example, the formula stores the message "Location Unavailable" in a variable called LocationMessage when the location details are unavailable. When location details are available, the formula sets the value of this variable to an empty string. We can then display this variable through a label on a screen.

Saving Location Details

A typical task is to store the location values to a data source. In this section, we'll walk through the steps to create an auto-generated app to store these details. Figure 18-4 shows the source data that we'll use.

We'll use the technique that we covered in our previous example by adding a button to store the current location to a variable. We'll then use this to populate the data entry controls on the edit form.

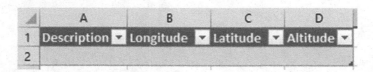

Figure 18-4. *Layout of sample data*

The first step is to create an auto-generated app that's based on this data source. On the screen that contains the edit form, we'll add a button and set the OnSelect property to the following formula:

```
UpdateContext({locLocation: Location})
```

The next step is to unlock the card for the longitude field and to change the Default property of the text input control to the following:

```
If(IsBlank(locLocation.Longitude),
    Parent.Default,
    locLocation.Longitude
)
```

This formula returns the longitude value that the user has retrieved by clicking the button. If this value is blank, the formula returns the existing longitude value for the record.

We now repeat the same process for the latitude field. We set the Default property of the latitude text input control and the Update property of the latitude card to the following formula:

```
If(IsBlank(locLocation.Latitude),
    Parent.Default,
    locLocation.Latitude
)
```

The final step is to clear the locLocation variable when the user leaves the screen. Here's the code to add to the OnHidden property of the screen:

```
UpdateContext({locLocation: Blank()})
```

Figure 18-5 shows the layout of the screen in the designer. At this stage, we can run our app and save the updated location details to the data source.

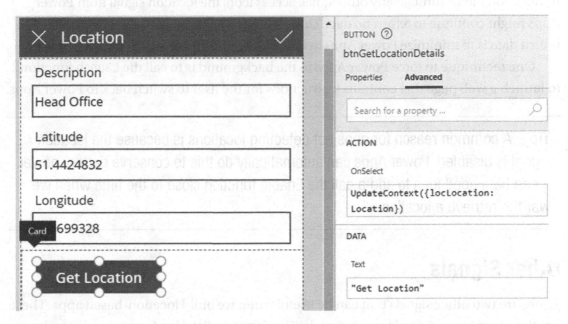

Figure 18-5. *Saving location details to a data source*

Switching the Signal On/Off

Apps that use location services can quickly drain the battery of a device. It's not just the GPS that causes the power drain. If an app includes formulas that reference the location signal, those formulas will recalculate whenever the location changes. This behavior adds additional drain on the battery.

One way to conserve battery life is to turn off the location signal when it's not needed. To turn off the location signal, we can add a button to our screen and add the following formula:

```
Disable(Location)
```

Here's the formula to turn the signal back on again:

```
Enable(Location)
```

A piece of behavior that's worth noting is that a user may start an app with the GPS of the device switched off.

In the case of an Android device, if a user turns on GPS through the icon in the notification bar or through any other quick access icon, the location signal from Power Apps might continue to return no data. One way to force the location signal to refresh and return data is to minimize Power Apps to the background and to switch back to the app.

One technique to force Power Apps to the background is to call the Launch function to launch a web page that contains instructions for the user to switch back to Power Apps.

Tip   A common reason for apps not detecting locations is because the location signal is disabled. Power Apps can automatically do this to conserve battery power. It can be a good idea to add a call the Enable function close to the time when we want to retrieve a location.

Other Signals

There are two other signals that can be useful when we build location-based apps. These are the compass and acceleration signals. The Compass.Heading function returns the heading value, measured in degrees.

The acceleration signal returns the acceleration in X, Y, and Z planes, measured in g units (g – which stands for gravity – is the standard unit of measurement of acceleration, equivalent to 9.8 meters per second squared). Figure 18-6 shows this in the form of a diagram.

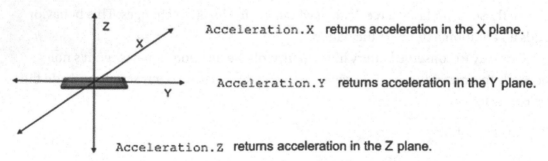

Figure 18-6. *Measuring acceleration*

The acceleration signal enables us to carry out a useful trick. Power Apps provides no way to determine whether a user is using a mobile device or a desktop PC.

Because desktop PCs rarely contain accelerometers or GPS hardware that can detect the altitude, the presence of one of these signals indicates that the target device is probably a mobile device. We can use the following formula to store the result in a variable called `varIsMobileDevice`:

```
Set(varIsMobileDevice, (Acceleration.X > 0 Or Location.Altitude > 0))
```

A good place to add this formula is to the `OnVisible` property of a screen. Due to timing issues, the signals may not return accurate results when we attach this formula to the `OnStart` property of an app.

Tip   If a device reports accelerometer and altitude readings, the device is probably a mobile device rather than a desktop.

Displaying Maps

Through maps, we can present location data in a more visual and meaningful way. In this section, we'll find out how to display maps using the two most common mapping services – Google Maps and Bing Maps.

Both these services provide a static map API that returns an image of a map based on details that we provide through the web address. To show the output, we can use an image control to display the map that the service returns.

With both Google and Bing Maps, we need to register and to obtain an API access key. The API key provides the means to authenticate to the service. Both Google and Bing provide a free monthly allowance before charges start to accrue.

The two services offer the same basic mapping features. This includes the ability to center a map based on longitude and latitude or by address or other search terms. Additional features include the ability to display markers and to switch the presentation between aerial and road map views. An added feature of Bing Maps is that it can show traffic flow and routing details between two points.

Using Google Maps

To use Google Maps, the first step is to register for an account on the Google Cloud Platform. The web address to register is `https://cloud.google.com/console/google/maps-apis/overview`.

Once we register, the next step is to create a project. Next, we use the APIs menu item to add the "Maps Static API" service. We can generate an API key through the credentials section (Figure 18-7). To activate the API key, it's necessary to enable billing on the account and to provide a credit card number. At the time of writing, Google provides $200 of free credit per month. Beyond this, the prices start at $2 per 1,000 lookups.

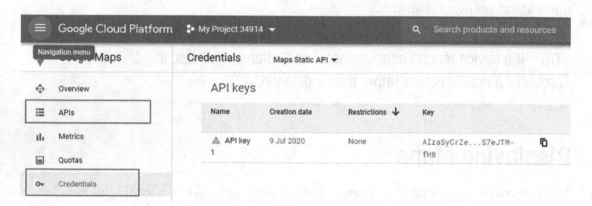

Figure 18-7.   *Creating a Google Cloud Platform account*

Once we obtain an API key, we can return an image using a web address in the following format:

```
https://maps.googleapis.com/maps/api/staticmap?center=51.51128434,
-0.11915781&zoom=12&size=400x400&key=<EnterKeyHere>
```

To specify the location, we use the `center` argument to provide the latitude and longitude values, separated by a comma. We also need to provide our API key through the key argument.

To demonstrate how to display a Google map on a screen, we'll modify the details form from the auto-generated app that we created in the previous section.

To do this, we would open the details form and add a custom card. Next, we insert an image control and set the Image property to the following value:

```
"https://maps.googleapis.com/maps/api/staticmap?center="& ThisItem.Latitude
& "," & ThisItem.Longitude & "& zoom=12&size=500x400&key=EnterYouKey"
```

For this to work, we must substitute a valid API key into the address. Figure 18-8 shows the view of the screen in the designer. We can now run our app and use the details screen to display a map that corresponds to the latitude and longitude of the current record.

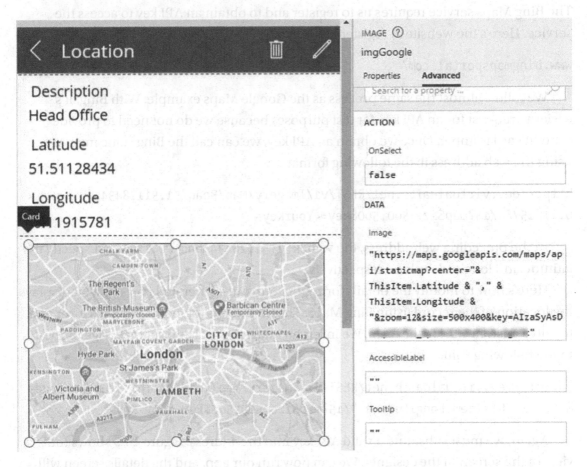

Figure 18-8. *Using Google Maps*

For more information on how to use this API, including how to change the view and how to add markers, we can visit the Google Maps Static API website through the following link:

```
https://developers.google.com/maps/documentation/static-maps/intro
```

Bing Maps

Bing Maps provides a static map API that works similarly to Google Maps. The example Site Inspection app uses this method, and we can refer to this app to find out more. The Bing Maps service requires us to register and to obtain an API key to access the service. Here's the website to register for a key:

```
www.bingmapsportal.com/
```

We follow almost the same process as the Google Maps example. With Bing, it's easier to request for an API key for test purposes because we do not need to provide a credit card number. Once we obtain an API key, we can call the Bing static map API using the web address in the following format:

```
http://dev.virtualearth.net/REST/v1/Imagery/Map/Road/51.51128434,-
0.11915781/15?mapSize=500,500&key=<YourKey>
```

In the preceding web address, the values `51.51128434` and `-0.11915781` specify the latitude and longitude values, respectively.

Here's how to modify the details form from our auto-generated app so that it displays the location of the record using Bing Maps. The first step is to open the details form and to add a custom card to the form. We insert an image control and set the `Image` property to the following value:

```
"http://dev.virtualearth.net/REST/v1/Imagery/Map/Road/"& ThisItem.Latitude
& "," & ThisItem.Longitude & "/15?mapSize=500,500&key=Your Key"
```

Again, we must substitute a valid API key into the address. Figure 18-9 shows the view of the screen in the designer. We can now run our app, and the details screen will use the Bing Maps API to display a map that corresponds to the latitude and longitude of the current record. For more information on how to use the Bing Maps API, here's the link to the help site:

```
https://msdn.microsoft.com/en-us/library/ff701724.aspx
```

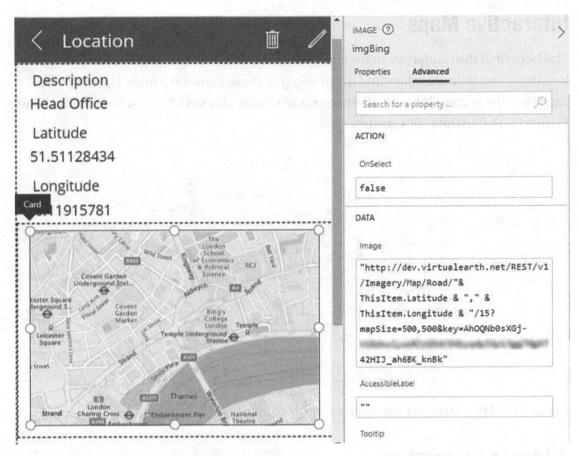

Figure 18-9. *Using the Bing Maps API*

Using Azure Maps Services

In the final part of this chapter, we'll cover two mapping features that were officially released in 2021. These are the interactive maps control and the address suggestion control.

The prerequisite to using these features is to enable geospatial features in the settings of our target environment. We can find this setting through the Power Platform admin center, under the Product ➤ Features section of the environment.

The next step is to create a canvas app and to enable geospatial features in the Settings ➤ Advanced settings menu. At this stage, the controls will be available through the insert panel.

Interactive Maps

The benefit of the interactive maps control is that it can bind to a data source with longitude and latitude values and it can also plot those items on a map. The map view can show the current location of the user, and we can also switch to road or satellite view. Figure 18-10 illustrates this control.

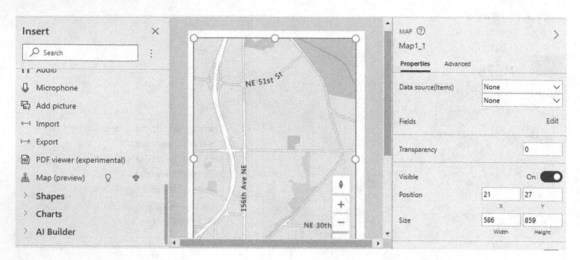

Figure 18-10. *Using the interactive maps control*

Address Suggestion

The address suggestion control makes it easier for a user to enter an address. As a user begins to type an address, the control provides matching addresses in a drop-down. An important set of properties are the latitude, longitude, and radius settings. These enable us to focus the address search on a specific geographic area.

Once a user enters an address through the control, we can call properties on the control to retrieve specific parts of the input address. For example, AddressInput1. StreetNameAndNumber will return the first line of the input address. Figure 18-11 illustrates this control.

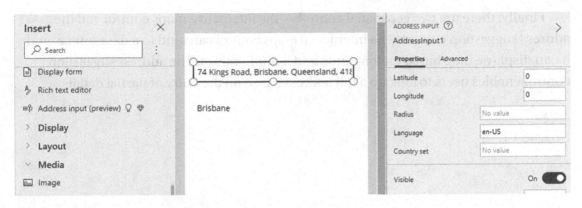

Figure 18-11. Using the address suggestion control

Summary

This chapter covered the topic of mapping and location services. We learned how to retrieve the location of the current user and how to display locations using maps.

To determine the location of the user, we can write a formula that retrieves signals. A signal is an object that returns values that can constantly change. The signals we can call include Location, Compass, and Acceleration. The location signal returns three fields: longitude, latitude, and altitude.

The Compass signal enables us to retrieve the current heading using the formula Compass.Heading. The Acceleration signal returns the acceleration of the device in the X, Y, and Z planes.

The best way to save the current location is to store the location details to a local variable and to use the variable to update the data source. This technique enables us to take a snapshot of a location and to avoid any inaccuracy that might occur if we were to retrieve the location during the time when we save the record.

Apps that use location services can quickly drain the battery of a device. We can help preserve the battery life by calling a function to disable the location signal.

To display maps and to pinpoint locations, we learned how to use Google and Bing Maps. Both these services provide an API that returns an image of a map based on longitude and latitude values that we provide through the web address. To display the map, we use an image control to display the result from the mapping service. These mapping services require us to register and to obtain an authentication key.

Finally, there are two geospatial controls – the interactive maps control and the address suggestion control. The interactive maps control can bind to a data source, and it can display a map based on longitude and latitude values. The address suggestion control enables users to look up a full address based on the entry of partial details.

CHAPTER 19

Charting Data

Power Apps provides a range of charting capabilities for both canvas and model-driven apps. With canvas apps, we can visualize data with bar, line, and pie chart types. With model-driven apps, there are even more options.

In this chapter, we'll find out how to prepare a data source and how to improve the presentation of our canvas and model-driven apps by incorporating charts. With model-driven apps, we can build dashboards that enable users to drill into data through charts. We'll find out how to build this feature.

The key topics that this chapter covers will include

- How to aggregate data. We'll look at techniques we can use to transform our data into a format that we can use with the chart controls.

- How to use charts in canvas apps. We'll learn how to add charts to a screen and how to configure settings such as legends, colors, and labels. We'll also find out how to display multiple series of data.

- How to build and use charts in model-driven apps. We'll find out how to incorporate charts in dashboards and to make advanced customizations by modifying the chart definitions outside of the editor.

Introduction

We can separate the charting capabilities of Power Apps into three distinct areas:
- Canvas chart controls
- Model-driven app chart controls
- Power BI charts

© Tim Leung 2021
T. Leung, *Beginning Power Apps*, https://doi.org/10.1007/978-1-4842-6683-0_19

For canvas apps, Power Apps offers bar, line, and pie chart controls. The properties of the chart control enable us to set the label, color, and legend settings. The controls can render multiple series. This means, for example, that we can build a line chart that displays two distinct groups of data.

A great way to learn about charting capabilities in canvas apps is to examine the Budget Tracker app, as shown in Figure 19-1. This app features a list of budget records on the left-hand pane. When a user clicks a budget record, the pie chart in the central section updates to reflect the selected record.

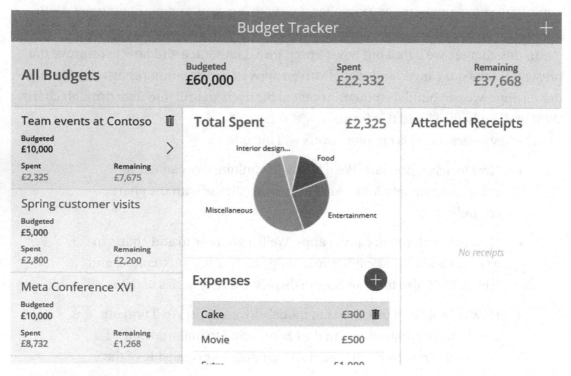

Figure 19-1. *The sample "Budget Tracker" canvas app*

Model-driven apps provide far better charting capabilities. There are eight chart types, including area, funnel, tag, and donut chart types. We can also configure the bar, column, and area charts to render stacked and 100% stacked variations of these charts. There is also ability to combine charts. For example, we can build a single chart that displays a column and a line chart.

As we saw earlier in this book, we can attach charts to interactive dashboards. This offers a way for users to use charts to drill down into lists of data. At runtime, users can select a source view and use the date filtering capabilities of a dashboard to render a chart that pertains to a specific set of data.

A useful feature is that a user can build a personal dashboard and build a chart that is visible only to the user. Due to the nature of model-driven apps, we can define charts at the table level and reuse those charts in multiple apps. This feature provides an efficiency benefit that is unavailable through canvas apps.

Behind the scenes, Power Apps defines model-driven app charts through XML. This opens a wide range of customization options because it enables us to manually modify the XML and to edit charts in ways that are not possible through the standard graphical chart designer.

A great place to find out is to study the Fundraiser Donations sample app, as shown in Figure 19-2. This app provides an interactive dashboard with pie, donut, and bar charts. This highlights how a user can click a chart section to filter the screens of data that appear in the lower section. The user can also click the date filter drop-down to modify the date range that applies to the charts.

Figure 19-2. *The sample "Fundraiser Donations" model-driven app*

The final option is not to use charting features in Power Apps, but to build charts using Power BI instead. Power BI is a separate product in the Power Platform and is designed specifically for charting and reporting. Although it provides richer charting capabilities, the key benefit of Power BI is performance. It can process large quantities of data quickly and copes well with data sources with millions of rows. We can embed Power BI charts in a canvas app through a Power BI tile control.

Given that Power BI is so much more advanced, are there any reasons not to always use Power BI? One reason is that Power BI is licensed separately and can therefore incur additional costs. Another reason is that due the richer feature set, the learning curve can be far steeper.

The Power Apps chart controls are ideal for simple charting requirements and provide an attractive and visual way to improve the presentation of an app. For anything more serious, I would recommend the use of Power BI. The first edition of this book devoted a fair amount of content on how to aggregate data and how to group data by month on the x axis. The formulas to carry out this type of task are complex and can fail to return accurate results when the number of rows exceeds the delegable row limit of 2,000.

Therefore, this chapter focuses on building simple charts, which is what works best with the inbuilt charting capabilities of Power Apps.

Canvas Apps

In this section, we'll look at how to utilize the chart controls. We'll start by exploring data transformation options that enable us to transform data into a format that can work with the chart controls. Next, we'll look at how to build some simple charts.

Transforming Data

In our demonstration, we'll build a chart that shows a count of issues by property type. To produce this chart, the chart control requires us to provide aggregated data. Figure 19-3 shows the format of our source data and the target format that the chart control requires.

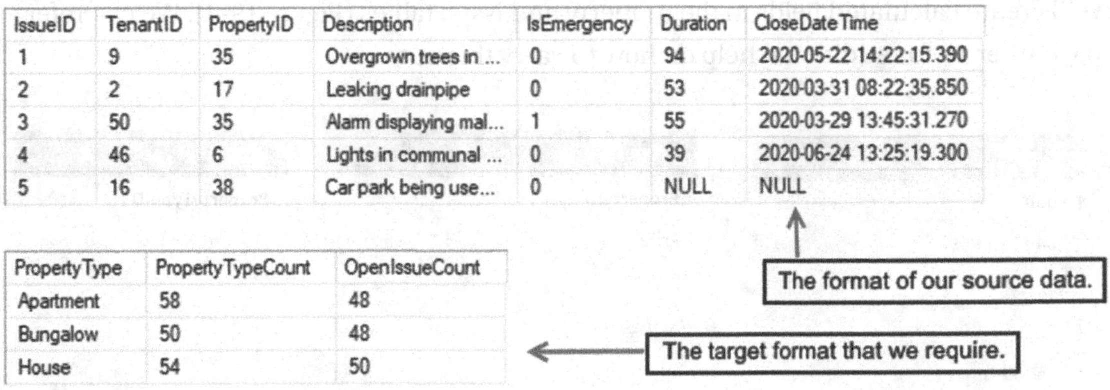

IssueID	TenantID	PropertyID	Description	IsEmergency	Duration	CloseDateTime
1	9	35	Overgrown trees in ...	0	94	2020-05-22 14:22:15.390
2	2	17	Leaking drainpipe	0	53	2020-03-31 08:22:35.850
3	50	35	Alarm displaying mal...	1	55	2020-03-29 13:45:31.270
4	46	6	Lights in communal ...	0	39	2020-06-24 13:25:19.300
5	16	38	Car park being use...	0	NULL	NULL

PropertyType	PropertyTypeCount	OpenIssueCount
Apartment	58	48
Bungalow	50	48
House	54	50

The format of our source data.

The target format that we require.

Figure 19-3. *Transforming data*

This example highlights the challenge we face when we attempt to build charts that are based on real-life, relational sets of data. Here, each issue record is associated with a property record, and each property record is associated with a property type record. To produce our target output, we need to build a query that spans three tables. How do we do this?

With SharePoint and Excel, this can be a challenging task. It is practically impossible to write a formula that aggregates data without hitting query delegation limits. This prevents us from retrieving accurate results when the source data exceeds 2000 rows. With these data sources, the easiest way to prepare a data source is to pre-aggregate the data into a separate list or spreadsheet, using Microsoft Power Automate. An alternative solution is to avoid the use of the native charting capabilities and to use Power BI instead.

SQL Server is the best data source for retrieving and aggregating data. This is because we can build a SQL Server view that joins multiple tables and produces our aggregate result. We can then use this view as the data source for our chart. SQL Server performs very quickly, especially if the source database is optimized and indexed correctly.

Dataverse doesn't provide the same low-level access to data that we can accomplish with SQL Server. However, it does provide features that can help facilitate the construction of charts. These include calculated and rollup fields. It also offers great query delegation support, including support for aggregate operators such as the Sum, Min, Max, and Average functions.

In our example, we'll use a Dataverse data source, and we'll base our chart on our issue table. Because we want to count the issue records by property type, we need to make the property type description visible through the issue table. To accomplish this, we'll create calculated fields in the property and issue tables (Figure 19-4). We can refer to Chapter 12 for additional help on how to carry this out.

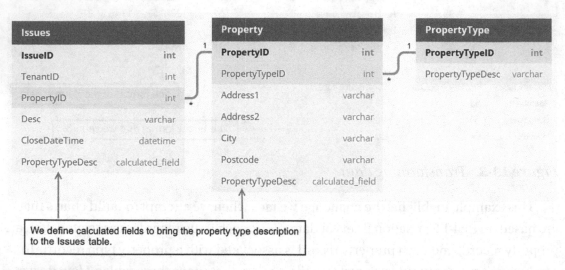

Figure 19-4.   *Using calculated columns to help build our chart*

Even with Dataverse, it can be tricky to transform data in the ways that we require. For example, calculated and rollup columns can span only one relationship. This is the reason why it's necessary to create two calculated columns (one on the property table and one on the issue table), rather than one. In a formula, the `GroupBy` function cannot group data by a lookup column; and therefore, it isn't possible to use this function to aggregate data across a relationship. In many cases, it can be much simpler or necessary to pre-aggregate data into a reporting entity for the purpose of building a chart. We can use Microsoft Automate or dataflows to carry out this task.

Building a Column Chart

To build a column chart, we use the insert menu to add a column chart control to a screen. All three chart controls (column, pie, and line) are composite controls that consist of three items: a chart, title, and legend.

In this example, we can group the records in the issue entity by property type and count the rows that belong to each group (Chapter 7 provides a full explanation of this technique). The formula that we would use to set the `Items` property of the chart control looks like this:

```
AddColumns(GroupBy(Issues,"crc51_propertytype", "GroupResult"),
          "PropertyTypeCount",
          CountRows(GroupResult)
)
```

Note that with this formula, `crc51_propertytype` refers to the name of the calculated field that contains the property type description. It's necessary to pass the logical field name to the `GroupBy` function, hence this name.

If we choose to set the data source of a chart to a collection, it's important to build the collection before we open the screen that houses the chart control. If we build the collection using a formula on the screen's `OnVisible` property, the chart control will not render the collection data due to timing issues.

Figure 19-5 shows the appearance of the chart control in the designer. Through the properties pane, we can set cosmetic attributes that include

- X label angle – By default, the labels on the x axis are slanted by 60 degrees to better accommodate charts with multiple items on the x axis. We can use this property to change the angle or to format the label text so that it appears horizontally.

- Grid style – This property controls the display of gridlines on the chart canvas. The available options include All, None, X only, and Y only.

- Markers – A column chart can display the numeric value above the bar. The markers property controls the visibility of this marker.

- Marker suffix – We can use this setting to append a label that follows the marker value.

- Items gap – This setting defines the space between columns in the chart.

- Series axis min/Series axis max – We can use this setting to define the maximum and minimum values for the y axis.

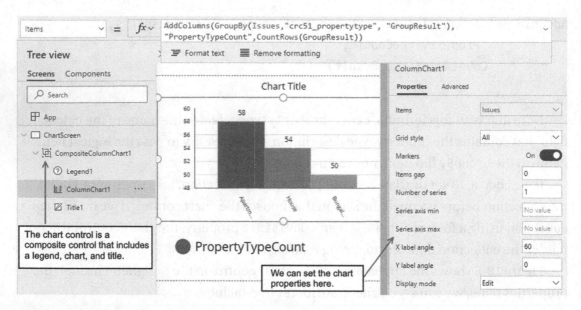

Figure 19-5.   *Configuring a column chart*

Note   If we set the data source of a chart to a collection, the chart will not display the correct data if we populate the collection using a formula on the screen's `OnVisible` property.

Setting Legends

By default, the chart label displays the name of the series. In our example, it makes more sense to display the names of the property types. To set this up, we select the legend control and set the `Items` property to the same value of the `Items` property for our chart. We then set the `Value` property to the name of the column that contains the property type description values (Figure 19-6).

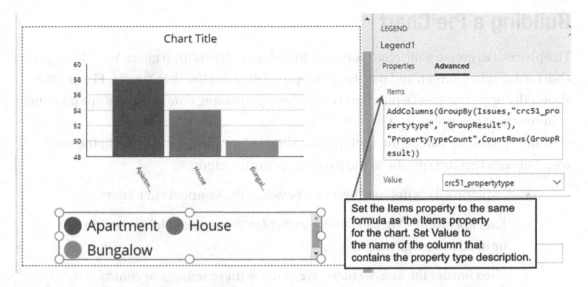

Figure 19-6. *Setting the legend text*

Applying Colors and Styles

The chart control applies a default set of colors which are defined through the
ItemColorSet property, as shown in Figure 19-7. This property contains an array of
colors, and we can modify these values to change the colors of the items in the chart.

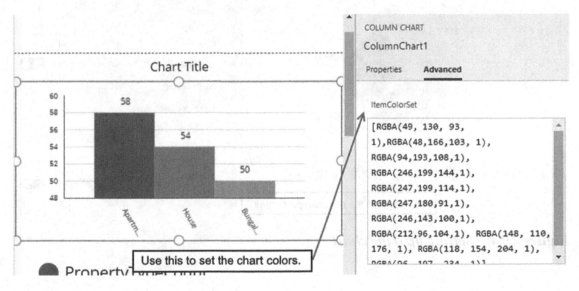

Figure 19-7. *Setting the chart colors*

Building a Pie Chart

The process to create a pie chart is mostly identical to the column chart. We add a pie chart control to a screen and use the Items property to set the data source. Figure 19-8 shows the appearance of a pie chart control, using the same data source as our previous column chart example.

Once again, we can define settings including colors and legend items in the same way. Settings that are specific to the pie chart control include

- Explode – This defines the space between the segments in a chart.

- Label position – We can choose to display the segment label outside or inside the segment.

- Slice border thickness/color – We can use these settings to control the border that surrounds each segment.

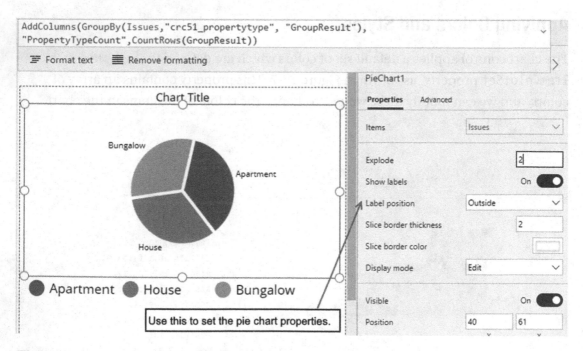

Figure 19-8. *Setting up a pie chart*

Building a Line Chart

In this section, we'll look at how to build a line chart and how to configure the chart to show multiple series.

Showing Multiple Series

The two chart types that can display multiple series are the column and line charts. Both these chart types support up to a maximum of nine series. To demonstrate this feature, we'll build a line chart that displays two series: a count of the total number of issues by property type and a count of the total number of open issues by property type.

The most difficult part of this is to build the formula that defines the data source for our chart. We can use the techniques from earlier in the book to derive the following formula:

```
AddColumns(Distinct(Issues,PropertyType),
        "PropertyTypeCount",
        CountIf(Issues,PropertyType=Result),
        "OpenIssueCount",
        CountIf(Issues,CloseDate<>Blank() And PropertyType=Result)
)
```

This formula returns the distinct property types from the issue entity. It utilizes the AddColumns function to add columns that count the issues for each property type and issues where the close date value is not blank. This produces the output format that is shown in Figure 19-9.

PropertyType	PropertyTypeCount	OpenIssueCount
Apartment	58	48
Bungalow	50	48
House	54	50

Figure 19-9. *The data source for the multi-series chart*

To build our chart, we set the Items property to our formula, set the "number of series" setting to 2, and use the settings in the advanced section to configure the series (Figure 19-10).

637

The Labels property defines the field that appears on the x axis. We set this to Result. This is the name of the field that the Distinct function returns, and the value of this field contains the distinct property type values. We then set the Series1 property to PropertyTypeCount and the Series2 property to OpenIssueCount.

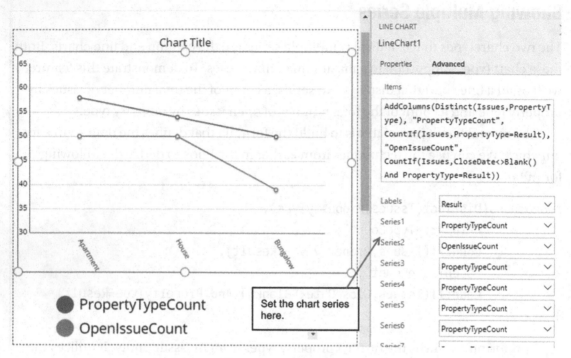

Figure 19-10.   Configuring a multi-series chart

Model-Driven Apps

We'll now explore the charting capabilities of model-driven apps. We'll walk through the steps to build a simple column chart. Once we understand how to define the series and category of a chart, changing the chart type is simply a case of simply selecting a different chart type. Therefore, this section focuses on the column chart and two features that are unique to charts in model-driven apps – the stacked chart variation and the ability to combine multiple charts.

The graphical designer provides a simple, limited set of design features. To fully customize a chart, we can manually modify the XML definition of the chart. We'll find out how to use this technique later in this section.

Using the Designer

Model-driven apps work exclusively against Dataverse data sources, and charts are defined at the table level. To build a chart, we open the table designer and select the Charts tab. From here, we can create a new chart and edit it using the chart designer as shown in Figure 19-11.

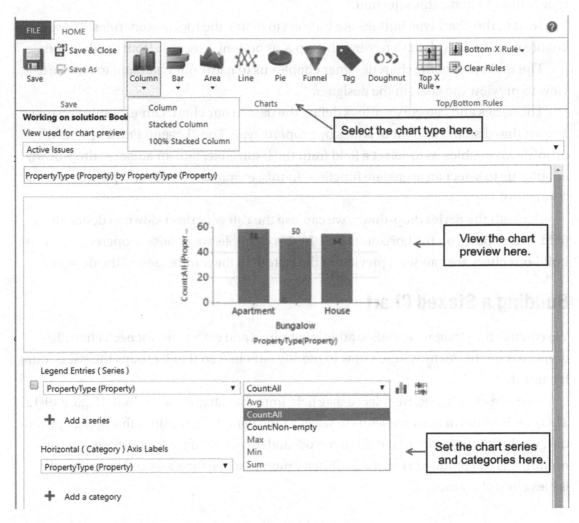

Figure 19-11. *The model-driven app chart designer*

The icons in the ribbon bar menu enable us to select one of the eight chart types. These include the column, bar, area, line, pie, funnel, tag, and doughnut chart types.

The process to create each chart type is almost identical. We configure the series and category values in the same way. The primary difference is to choose a different chart type from the ribbon bar menu. Because of the very close similarities, we will focus only on the bar chart type.

A key feature of the bar, column, and area chart types is that we can choose stacked and 100% stacked variations of the chart. We use a drop-down button beneath the chart type button to make this selection.

Next to the chart type buttons are buttons to define the top/bottom rules. These enable us to build a chart to retrieve the top X or bottom X records from the data source.

The main part of the chart designer enables us to name our chart and to choose a view to preview the chart in the designer.

The series and category settings define the data in our chart. Our example illustrates a chart that displays a count of issues by property type. The "Legend Entries (Series)" drop-down enables us to select a field from the issue table, and an adjacent drop-down enables us to select an aggregate function. In this, example we select PropertyType and "Count:All."

Beneath the Series drop-down, we can use the category drop-down to define the field that appears on the horizontal axis. In this example, we choose property type. As we build our chart, we can see a preview of the output in the middle part of the designer.

Building a Staked Chart

We can use the designer to define additional series and categories for each chart. To demonstrate this feature, here's how to modify our chart so that it groups the issue count by month.

To make this change, we select a date field from the category drop-down (Figure 19-12). This is a drop-down that enables us to select a time period. The options that appear include day, week, month, quarter, year, fiscal period, and fiscal year. If we select "close date" and month, this will produce a chart that displays months along the x axis and the count of issues along the y axis.

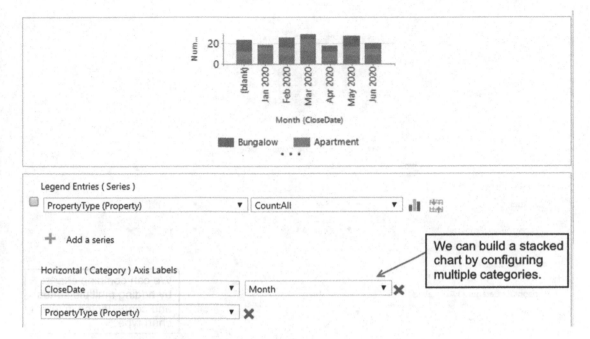

Figure 19-12. *Building a stacked chart*

We can improve our chart by further breaking down the figures for each month by property type. To do this, we add an additional category, and we select "property type" from the drop-down. We then change the chart type to a stacked column.

Combining Charts

To demonstrate how to combine charts, here's how to build a chart that shows the maximum duration of an issue and the count of issues, grouped by date.

We define our first series by selecting the duration field and choosing the Max aggregate operator. We can add another series, and we can select the property type field, and we can choose the "Count:All" aggregate operator. We can use the icons next to the aggregate drop-down to select the chart type. In this example, we choose the line chart type to show the maximum duration and column chart type to display the count of issues.

To group our results by date, we can define a category that includes close date and month (Figure 19-13).

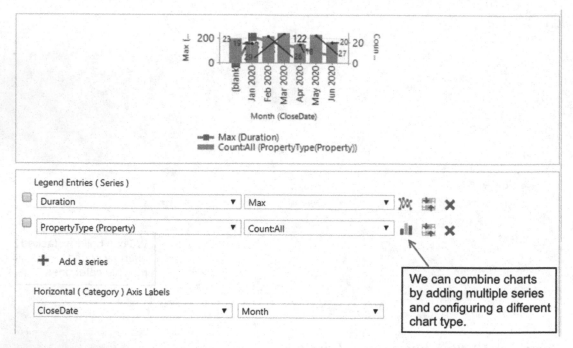

Figure 19-13. Combining chart types

Displaying Charts

There are two primary ways for a user to view a chart – through a table view or through a dashboard. Figure 19-14 shows the view of the issue table in a model-driven app.

The user can click the "Show chart" button in the header section to display the chart panel. From this area, the user can use a drop-down to display the charts that are associated with the table.

For each chart, the context menu provides the option to expand the chart, to refresh the chart, or to export and import the XML chart definitions.

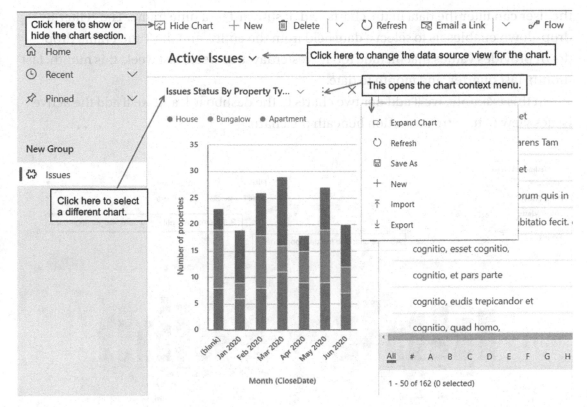

Figure 19-14. *Viewing the chart in a model-driven app*

Displaying Dashboards

A great way to utilize charts in a model-driven app is to create an interactive dashboard. Chapter 13 introduced this topic, and in this section, we'll revise the steps that we use to add a chart to a dashboard.

The two dashboard types are the classic dashboard and the interactive dashboard. The main feature of an interactive dashboard is that the user can click a chart area to filter a list (or stream) of data that appears beneath the chart area.

To create an interactive dashboard, we edit our model-driven app and select the menu option to create an interactive dashboard. In this example, we'll create a multi-stream, two-column overview dashboard. This opens the designer as shown in Figure 19-15.

In the top part of this designer, we can provide a name for the dashboard and select the source entity (a Dataverse table) and view for the dashboard. A useful pair of settings are the "Filter By" and "Time Frame" drop-downs. This configures the dashboard so that the user can filter the data in the charts and dashboard by a time frame. The "Filter By" drop-down enables us to select a date field from the entity, and the Time Frame drop-down provides values that include today, yesterday, this week, last week, this month, last month, last quarter, and month to date.

In this example, we'll add our two charts to the dashboard, and we'll add the active issues view to the stream section beneath the charts.

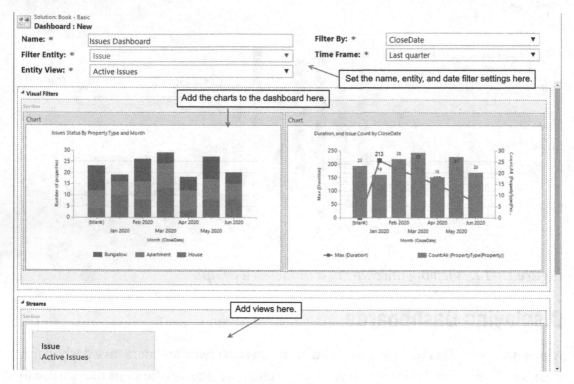

Figure 19-15. *Creating a dashboard*

After we create the dashboard, we need to add a link to the dashboard in the site map of the app. To deploy the app, it's necessary to publish the site map. It's also necessary to publish the dashboard. Without doing this, the dashboard will not appear in the list of available dashboards that the user can select.

There is currently no option to publish a dashboard from the dashboard designer, and therefore, we need to publish the dashboard from elsewhere. One way to do this is from the Default Solution (or to create a solution for our app, which we'll cover in Chapter 26).

To publish a dashboard from the Default Solution, we select the Solutions menu from the Maker Portal and open the Default Solution. From here, we can search for our dashboard and publish it using the menu item in the context menu (Figure 19-16).

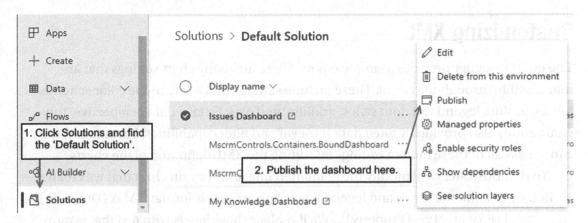

Figure 19-16. *Publishing an interactive dashboard*

Figure 19-17 shows the appearance of the dashboard at runtime. The "Show Visual Filter" and "Hide Visual Filter" buttons in the header control the visibility of the charts.

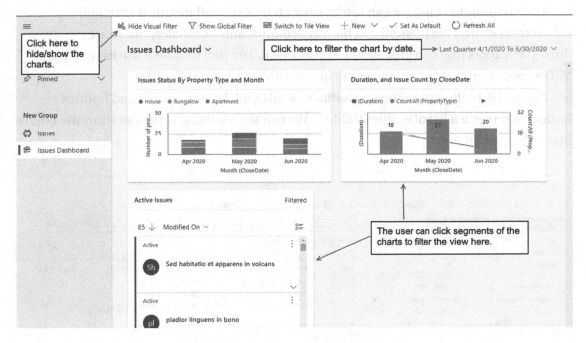

Figure 19-17. *Viewing the dashboard at runtime*

The user can use the date period drop-down to filter the records in the dashboard by date. The user can also click segments in either chart to filter the issue records in the lower part of the dashboard.

Customizing XML

The chart designer provides a simple editor. There are many chart settings that are inaccessible through the editor. These include settings that relate to the color scheme, labels, tooltip, legend text, font styles, gridline, and axis. From a data perspective, the chart editor also provides limited data retrieval and filter capabilities. Fortunately, we can access all of these hidden settings by editing the XML definition of the charts.

To demonstrate, we'll modify the combined line and column chart that we created earlier. By default, the series and legend labels appear in this format: "Max (Duration)," "Count:All (PropertyType(Property))." We'll replace these labels with text that is more user friendly.

The chart that we created earlier also appears odd because we group the issue records by "close date" and there are records without a "close date." We'll modify our chart to filter out records without a "close date."

To carry out this task, we can retrieve the chart XML and modify it manually with a text editor. This method can be very arduous, and fortunately, there are third-party tools that can greatly simplify this task. The tool that we'll use here is the "AdvancedChartEditor," which we can obtain through the XrmToolBox.

Figure 19-18 illustrates the appearance of this tool. It provides a "Load Entities" button to retrieve a list of entities (tables). We can then select an entity to show the charts that belong to an entity.

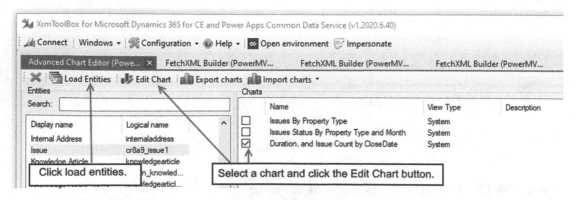

Figure 19-18. *Using the AdvancedChartEditor*

From the chart list, we can select a chart and click the "Edit Chart" button. This opens the chart editor as shown in Figure 19-19.

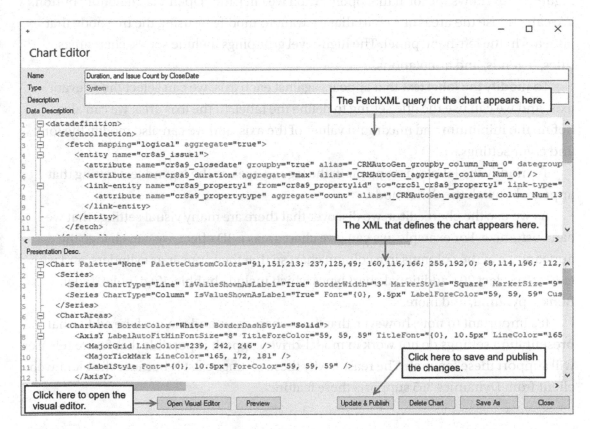

Figure 19-19. Editing the XML for a chart

There are two main parts to this chart editor. The data description textbox specifies the data source for the chart in FetchXML format. This is the same FetchXML language that we encountered when we built custom queries for a portal app (Chapter 14).

The "Presentation Desc" textbox shows the XML that defines the chart content. We can click the "Open Visual Editor" button to edit the chart definition in a form. The Preview button opens a visual preview of the chart, and it provides a useful way to verify the changes that we make. When we complete our changes, we can click the "Update & Publish" button to deploy our changes. For future enhancements and customizations, we can use this same process to amend the chart XML and to republish our changes.

Customizing the Chart

Figure 19-20 shows the form that opens when we click the "Open Visual Editor" button. We can choose the areas of a chart that we want to modify by using the tree node that appears in the left-hand panel. The high-level groupings include series, chart areas, titles, legends, and annotations.

To modify the label text that appears against each axis, we can select the relevant axis, and we can use the title setting to define the label. In the axis area, we can also define the minimum and maximum values of the axis, and we can also modify the font and color settings.

To modify the labels that appear in the legend, we use the legend text setting that appears beneath the Series node.

As we use the chart editor, we discover that there are many visual settings that we can customize. For example, we can give chart areas a 3D effect, we can change the appearance of the columns in a column chart so that they appear as cylinders, and we can even select 20+ additional chart types which include bubble, Kagi, polar, radar, Renko, pyramid, and more.

It's important to note, however, that these chart types and many of the additional presentation settings do not work in model-driven apps. It is possible that future releases will support these features. The reason why these settings exist is because the older web client from Dynamics 365 supports these features.

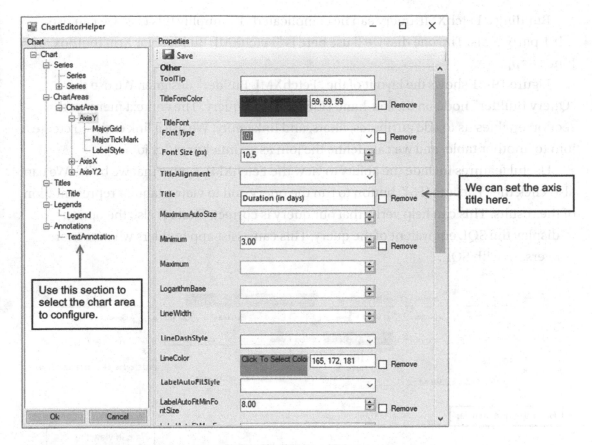

Figure 19-20. *Using the visual chart editor*

Customizing the Data Source

To customize the data source for a chart, we can modify the FetchXML query for the chart. The ability to specify a query with FetchXML provides great benefits. We can define filter, group, and sort data in ways that are not possible using the chart editor. We can also join other tables and produce aggregate results including the sum and count of a grouped set of records. We can define "outer joins" between tables to return records that do not exist (e.g., customers who have not made an order).

In this chapter, we've seen how to use computed and rollup columns to retrieve the necessary data for a chart. The disadvantage of this technique is that we can easily clutter our tables with columns that serve little purpose elsewhere. By defining the data source of a chart with FetchXML, we can keep our tables tidier.

Building a FetchXML query can be complicated. To simplify this task, we can use third-party tools. The one that we'll use here is "FetchXML Builder" for XrmToolBox, by Jonas Rapp.

Figure 19-21 shows the layout of the "FetchXML Builder" designer. We use the "Query Builder" node on the left-hand side to build a query. The context menu in this section enables us to add attributes, filters, and link entity. We use a link entity to create a join to another table, and we can define the join as an inner or outer join.

Useful features include the ability to view the FetchXML syntax that we build. We can also click the "Execute (F5)" button to run the query and to view a tabular representation of the results. This can help verify that our query is correct. There is also the option to display the SQL equivalent of the query. This can assist app builders who are more conversant with SQL.

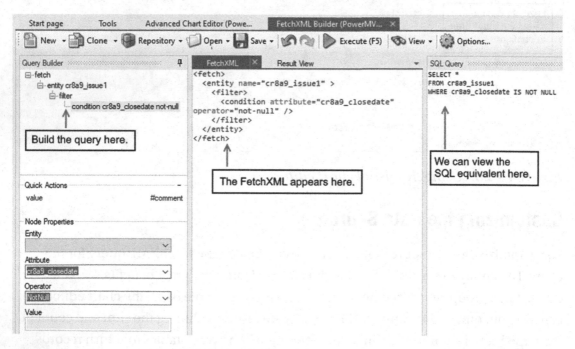

Figure 19-21. *Using FetchXML Builder*

In our example, we want to filter the source of our chart to exclude records without a close date. We can customize our query in the editor and use the result to amend the data description of our chart through the "AdvancedChartEditor."

When we finish editing our chart, we click the "Update & Publish" button to apply changes. Figure 19-22 shows the final result of our changes.

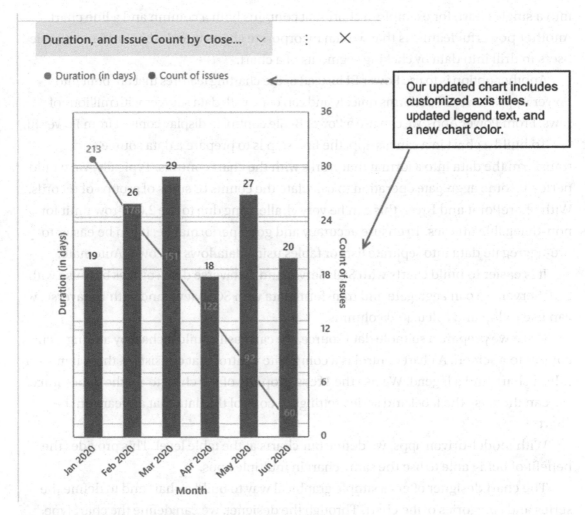

Figure 19-22. Our modified chart

Summary

This chapter covered the topic of charting. With canvas apps, we can use the chart controls to build bar, line, and pie charts. We can configure many of the visual elements on a chart, including the label, color, and legend settings. The bar and line charts also support multiple series, which enable us to display multiple groups of data on a single chart.

Model-driven apps provide better charting capabilities. There are eight chart types, in addition to staked and 100% stacked variations of the bar, column, and area chart types. A great feature with model-driven apps is that we can combine multiple charts into a single chart, for example, a chart that contains both a column and a line chart. Another powerful feature is that we can incorporate charts into dashboards and enable users to drill into data by clicking segments of a chart.

Another option is to use Power BI instead of the charting features that are built into Power Apps. Power BI performs quickly and can cope with data sources with millions of rows. From Power Apps, we can use a Power BI tile control to display content from Power BI.

To build a chart in a canvas app, the first step is to prepare a data source and to transform the data into a format that works with the chart controls. Typically, we would perform some aggregate operation to calculate the counts or sums of groups of records. With SharePoint and Excel, this can be very challenging due to the 2,000-row limit for non-delegable queries. To ensure accuracy and good performance, it can be easier to pre-aggregate data into separate lists or tables using dataflows or Power Automate.

It is easier to build charts with SQL Server and Dataverse data sources because with SQL Server, we can aggregate and transform data with SQL views and with Dataverse, we can use rollup and calculated columns.

Once we prepare a suitable data source, we can easily build a chart by adding a chart control to a screen. A chart control is a composite control that consists of three items – a title, a chart, and a legend. We use the Items property of the chart to set the data source. We can then use the label and series settings to control the data that appears on the chart.

With model-driven apps, we define our charts at the table level. This provides the benefit of being able to use the same chart in multiple apps.

The chart designer offers a simple graphical way to build a chart and to define the series and categories of the chart. Through the designer, we can define the chart type, set up charts to return the top X number of rows, and combine multiple chart types by defining multiple series and assigning a different chart type to each series.

There are many chart settings that are inaccessible through the simple chart editor, including settings that relate to the color scheme, labels, tooltips, legend text, font styles, gridline, and axis. We can access these hidden settings by editing the XML definition of the chart.

To edit the chart XML, we learned how to use a third-party tool that we can access through the XrmToolBox called "AdvancedChartEditor." This provides a form-based interface that enables us to connect to an entity (table), extract the chart XML, make changes, and republish our changes.

A FetchXML query defines the data source of a chart. We can modify the data source of a chart by manually building a FetchXML query. This enables us to implement joins and filters that are impossible to carry out through the standard editor. To help us more easily build FetchXML queries, we looked at how to use a tool called "FetchXML Builder." This enables us to build a query using a form-based designer. We can execute the query in the designer to verify the output, and we can also view the SQL equivalent of the query that we build.

CHAPTER 20

Adding Artificial Intelligence to Apps

Artificial intelligence (AI) plays a large role in modern life. Day-to-day applications of AI that are prevalent include smart assistants (e.g., Siri, Cortana, and Alexa), systems that send us targeted ads, and sophisticated developments such as driverless cars.

We can take advantage of these exciting advances through AI Builder. The biggest benefit of AI Builder is that we can develop AI features without writing code, using graphical designers that are simple and intuitive to understand. We can integrate these AI capabilities into our Power Apps applications using controls and formulas.

These AI capabilities enable us to process forms, business cards, and text. We can also use AI Builder to help us make predictions based on historical data, which in turn can help us make smarter business decisions. In this chapter, we'll start by finding out what is AI and what precisely we can accomplish with AI Builder. Next, we'll cover the features of AI Builder, grouped by the three main topic areas:

- Processing images – We'll learn how to detect objects and images and how to extract text and handwriting from images, forms, and business cards.

- Processing text – We'll learn how to conduct sentiment analysis, how to detect languages, how to categorize text, and how to extract key phrases.

- Making predictions – We'll learn how to use AI Builder to predict the likelihood of an outcome, based on historical data.

© Tim Leung 2021
T. Leung, *Beginning Power Apps*, https://doi.org/10.1007/978-1-4842-6683-0_20

Introducing Artificial Intelligence

What is AI? Artificial intelligence describes software and machines that mimic the thinking, decision-making, and problem-solving skills of humans. A key characteristic of AI-based systems is the ability to learn.

There are many companies that offer AI-based processing solutions, including big names such as Google, IBM, and Microsoft.

With Azure Cognitive Services, Microsoft plays a leading role in the field of AI. For everyday users, the learning curve associated with using AI can be steep. The Power Platform solves this problem by offering AI Builder. AI Builder is based on Azure Cognitive Services but offers a simple interface that is easy and intuitive to use. We can use AI Builder through controls and formulas in canvas apps; we can also access AI Builder through Power Automate.

Note that it is also possible to access Azure Cognitive Services through connectors in canvas apps. This can provide access to more up-to-date AI features, and it can offer a more cost-effective way to add AI features to our apps. However, this approach does not integrate as smoothly into Power Apps compared to AI Builder, and it is more complex to set up.

What Can We Do with AI Builder?

AI Builder provides a wide range of capabilities, which we can group into three categories. These are

- Vision and image processing capabilities

- Language processing capabilities

- Machine prediction capabilities

Processing Images

The first area where we can utilize AI is in the field of vision processing. Handwriting recognition is an example of vision-based AI. This requires an AI-based approach because no two people share the same handwriting; therefore, computerized writing recognition must rely on algorithms that can learn and adapt.

AI Builder also provides form processing capabilities. It can extract written and printed values from PDF and image files. The business benefit of this is that we can automate the task of data entry, which can reduce the labor cost that is associated with employing data entry clerks.

Object detection is another area where vision-based AI can provide business benefits. A typical use case scenario is on manufacturing lines. Object detection technology can process production-line images and can help identify defects, foreign bodies, or packaging faults. AI Builder enables us to train a model to recognize objects that we want to detect.

Language Processing

The second application of AI is in the field of language processing. Google Translate or other language translation systems provide an example of this type of AI. This type of processing requires intelligence because often, the source text may be grammatically incorrect or could include slang phrases.

AI Builder offers a range of language capabilities. It can extract keywords or key phrases from input text. It can categorize text and detect the language of a piece of text, and it can also perform sentiment analysis. Sentiment analysis measures how positive or negative a piece of text is. We can use this to automate the task of detecting complaints or compliments.

There are many practical ways to derive the benefits through language processing. By using text categorization techniques, we can automate the task of processing incoming messages. We can build workflow to route messages to the appropriate department.

We can also use categorization techniques to detect the category of products or services that interest a customer. We can use this to help drive sales by recommending additional products or services. It also helps us to deliver personalized content and ads to users.

With the help of sentiment analysis, we can process the conversations that we have with a customer and assess the health of the relationship. We can also automate the task of monitoring conversations on social media. This can help us intervene at an early stage if some event occurs that could cause reputational damage to our brand or organization. It can also help us to monitor our competitors and to detect positive developments in an industry field.

Making Predictions

A powerful feature that AI Builder offers is the ability to carry out predictions. It uses historical data to predict the likelihood of an outcome. We can use this information to make business decisions and to help improve the efficiency and profitability of our business.

There are numerous examples of how we can apply machine predictions to derive business benefits. In marketing, we can predict customers who are most likely to make a purchase, based on engagement with marketing campaigns and websites, customer location, and past purchases. We can make more efficient use of our marketing resources by focusing on those customers.

In finance, we can monitor transactions and other records that characterize the behavior of a customer. We can use machine predictions to identify and to prevent fraud by detecting behavior that deviates from the normal.

In manufacturing, AI can help predict events and seasons that can cause fluctuations in demand. We can use this information to increase or to decrease production and inventory as necessary.

In healthcare, we can predict patients who are more likely to not show up for appointments. We can also identify patients who are more susceptible to a disease.

Prebuilt Models vs. Custom Models

To perform a specific AI task, we use a model. A model consists of two parts – a logical part that contains the AI logic and a part that contains what the model has learned. A model describes a specific instance of AI logic that is trained against an input set of data (Figure 20-1). Therefore, it is possible to create many models using the same AI logic, even with the same training data.

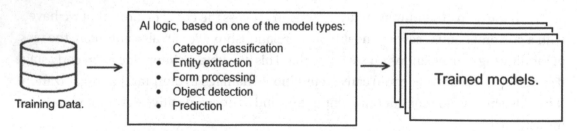

Figure 20-1. *AI models*

To use any type of AI, we can spend a significant amount of time training a model. For example, let's say we want to build a model that can detect brand logos in images. To build this model, we would need to teach the model the logos that we want to identify. To improve the detection accuracy, it is best to train the model with as many input images as possible. Therefore, training AI models can be very time-consuming.

To simplify this process, AI Builder provides prebuilt models. These are models that are pretrained and are ready for immediate use. For more bespoke cases, we can create custom models that we train ourselves. Table 20-1 summarizes the prebuilt and custom models that are available, grouped by category.

Table 20-1. *Available models*

Category	Prebuilt Models	Custom Models
Vision	Business card reader, text recognition	Object detection, form processing
Language	Category classification, entity extraction, key phrase extraction, language detection, sentiment analysis	Category classification, entity extraction
Prediction	None	Prediction

Licensing

To use AI Builder, it's necessary to purchase an AI Builder add-on. At the time of writing, the cost of this is $500 per month for one add-on unit. Each unit provides 1 million service credits, which are pooled at the tenant level.

AI Builder uses Dataverse. The canvas app controls that connect to AI Builder rely on premium connectors. Therefore, each user that uses an app with AI Builder will need to be covered by a Power Apps per-user or per-app plan.

An obvious question is – how far can we get with 1 million service credits? The best way to find out is to refer to the AI Builder calculator, which we can find here (Figure 20-2): https://powerapps.microsoft.com/en-us/ai-builder-calculator/

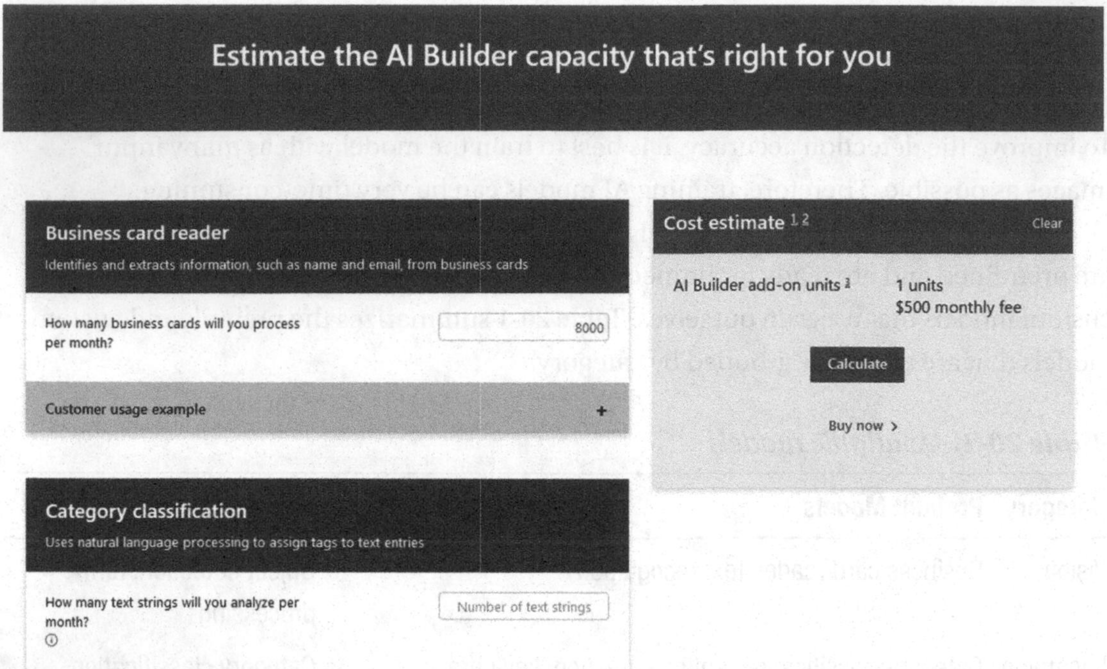

Figure 20-2. *Estimating the cost of using AI Builder*

With this calculator, we can enter how much we want to process and derive an estimate of the cost. To give a rough estimate, scanning 8,000 business cards or processing 1,600 forms will incur a price of 1 million service credits (or US $500 at the time of writing).

To get started with AI Builder, each user can subscribe to a free 30-day trial. To enable the trial, we click the AI Builder menu item in the Maker Portal. This will display a banner that enables us to start a trial (Figure 20-3).

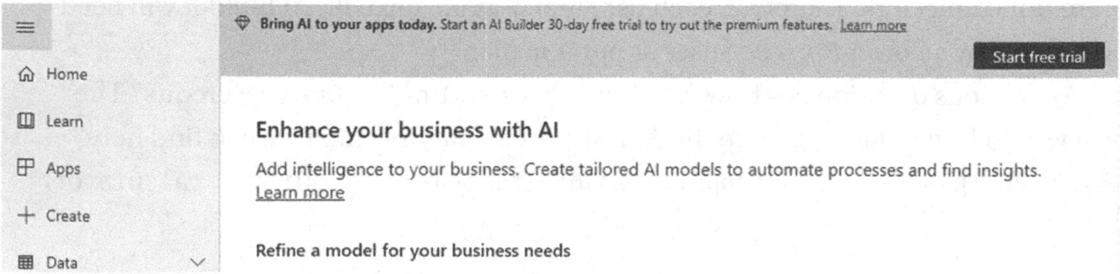

Figure 20-3. *Starting a trial*

Once we enable a 30-day trial or purchase the AI Builder add-on, we can start to use AI Builder.

Tip   Azure Cognitive Services can provide a more cost-effective way to add AI capabilities to an app. We can use the text analytics connector to connect to Cognitive Services and to carry out language detection, key phrase detection, and sentiment analysis.

Processing Images

In this section, we'll find out how to add vision processing capabilities to an app. We'll learn how to read the contents of business cards, how to recognize text, how to detect objects, and how to process forms.

Reading Business Cards

AI Builder provides a simple way to extract details from business cards. To demonstrate this feature, we'll build a screen that reads a business card and extracts those details into text input controls.

An initial question we might ask is – why does this task require artificial intelligence? How does this differ from a non-AI approach that uses optical character recognition (OCR) to extract the details from a business card? The reason this task benefits from an AI approach is because there is no common layout for a business card and the items on a business card may not be labeled. Therefore, it requires some intelligence to identify the areas on a card that correspond to the first name, last name, address, phone number, and so on.

To build this example, we use the AI Builder menu item to add a business card reader control to a screen. As Figure 20-4 shows, we can use this menu to add other AI Builder controls to a screen, such as the form processor, object detector, and text recognizer controls. We will cover all these controls as this chapter progresses.

At runtime, the user can click the business card reader control to upload an image of a business card. The acceptable file formats are JPG, PNG, and BMP. AI Builder processes the image and extracts details from the business card, including the person's name, job title, department, address, email, and more.

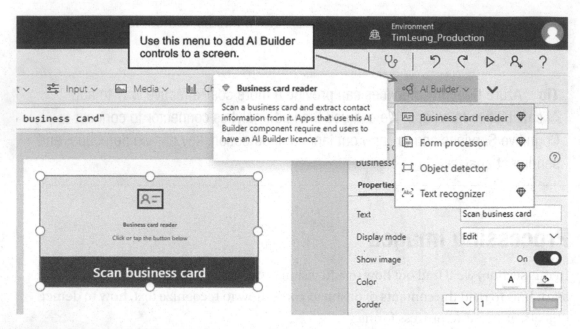

Figure 20-4. *Adding the business card reader control*

Assuming we retain the default name of BusinessCardReader1, we can access the extracted details through properties that include BusinessCardReader1.FirstName, BusinessCardReader1.LastName, BusinessCardReader1.Street, BusinessCardReader1. City, BusinessCardReader1.FullAddress, and so on. Figure 20-5 shows the design view after we play the app and upload a business card. Here, we see how we can use a formula to retrieve the full name into a text input control.

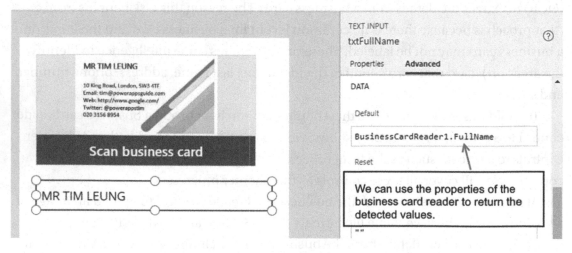

Figure 20-5. *The business card reader control*

In addition to extracting the text from the business card, we can also retrieve the original business card image and a cleaned version of the image through the `OriginalImage` and `CleanedImage` properties. These properties return a data URI, and we can apply the techniques that we learned in Chapter 16 to save these images to a data source.

It's important to note that the accuracy of the business card reader is not perfect. The business card reader can incorrectly identify fields or fail to identify the fields on the card. Because this is a prebuilt model, there is little that we can do to improve the accuracy. However, Microsoft can revise this model; and therefore, the accuracy should improve over time.

To cater for situations where the business card reader makes mistakes, it's a good idea to retrieve the detected values into text input controls. This enables the user to correct any mistakes, before we process the data further or save the details to a data source.

Recognizing Text

The text recognizer control works in a similar way to the business card reader control. It enables a user to upload a PDF or image file, and it extracts any text that it finds. The intelligent feature is that it can process handwritten text, as well as printed text.

To use this control, we use the AI Builder menu to add a text recognizer control to a screen. At runtime, the user can click the text recognizer control to upload a PDF or image file, with a maximum size of 20 MB. Once AI Builder processes the file, we can retrieve the recognized text through the `Results` property.

The `Results` property returns a table with three columns – `PageNumber`, `Text`, and `BoundingBox`. Each row in this table corresponds to a line that AI Builder recognizes in the source image. The `Text` field returns the extracted text. For multipage PDF input files, the `PageNumber` field returns the page number. The `BoundingBox` field returns the coordinates of the input text, expressed as top and left positions, along with the width and height.

Figure 20-6 shows the result when we use the text recognizer control to process the image of a sign on a commercial property.

To highlight the result that this control produces, this screenshot shows a data table with the `Items` property set to the `Results` property of the text recognizer control. Here, we see how AI Builder processes the input image and produces an output table with multiple rows.

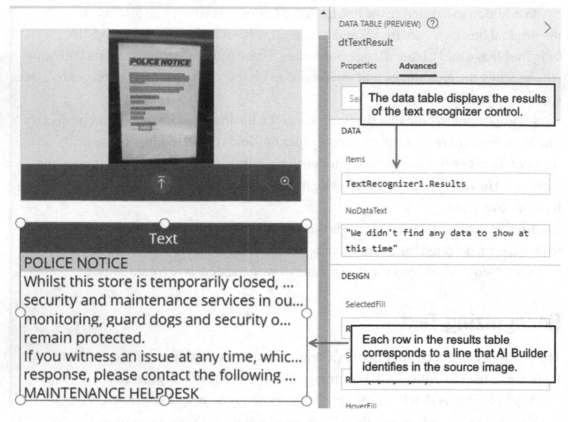

Figure 20-6. *Using the text recognizer control*

Due to this output format, the text recognizer control works best with single-column input text. If a user were to upload a newspaper or magazine article where the text spans multiple columns, the output would be more difficult to process, because each row in the output would contain content that pertains to different source columns.

Detecting Objects

We'll now look at how to perform object detection. Unlike the examples we've seen so far, object detection relies on a custom model, rather than a prebuilt model. Therefore, it is more complex because it requires us to first train a model.

To demonstrate this feature, we'll build a model to detect the presence of trees in images of properties. The example use case scenario of this could be to help identify properties that require more maintenance or properties that are more susceptible to subsidence. The prerequisite to this task is to collect several pictures of trees to enable us to train the model.

To build an object detection model, we select the AI Builder menu item from the Maker Portal and click the option to create an object detection model (Figure 20-7).

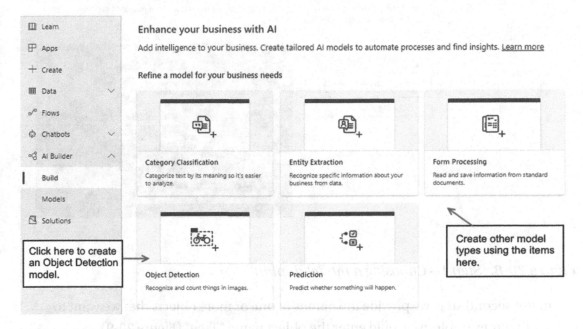

Figure 20-7. *Creating an object detection model*

This opens a window that guides us through a four-stage process. The first step is to define a model domain, the second is to define the names of the objects we want to identify, the third is to upload our training images, and the final stage is to tag the objects in our training images.

In this example, we'll manually specify our tags and manually upload our images. It's also possible to retrieve these details from a table in a Dataverse database.

Figure 20-8 illustrates the first step. Here, we define the domain of our model. The purpose of this step is to optimize the model to focus on a specific image category. There are three domain options that we can choose – retail shelves, brand logos, and common objects.

The retail shelves domain optimizes a model to detect images of products on supermarket shelves. The expected source images will depict the product, tightly packed together with other products on supermarket shelves. The brand logos domain optimizes the model to detect brand and product logos. For anything else, we choose the common objects domain. This is what we'll choose in this example.

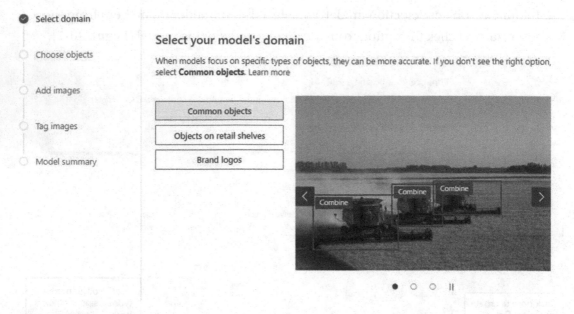

Figure 20-8. *Step 1 – Choosing a model domain*

In the second step, we provide the names of one or more objects that we want to detect. In our example, we would enter the object name "Tree" (Figure 20-9).

In step 3, we upload our training images. AI Builder requires a minimum of 15 images per object but recommends 50 or more images for best results.

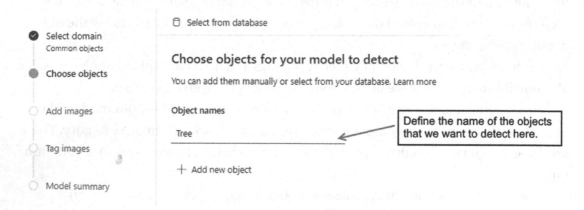

Figure 20-9. *Entering object names and uploading images*

In the final and most important step, we review each one of our uploaded images, and we tag the occurrence of each object that we want the model to recognize. To tag the objects, we use a tool to draw a rectangle around the object that we want to tag (Figure 20-10).

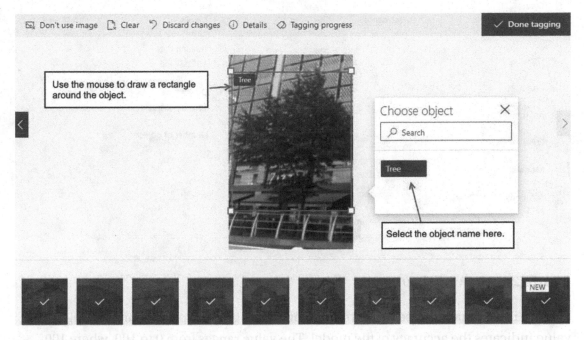

Figure 20-10. *Tagging objects*

Once we tag all our images, we can progress to the summary page. This displays an overview of the model and includes a "train" button that starts the training process. This process can take some time. When the training completes, the page will display a summary of our model as shown in Figure 20-11.

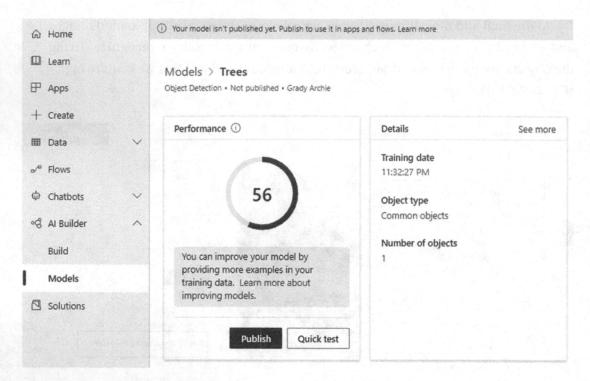

Figure 20-11. *Model summary*

The most notable piece of information on this page is the performance rating. This value indicates the accuracy of the model. The value ranges from 0 to 100, where 100 indicates the best performance.

For object detection models with low performance, we can improve the performance score by uploading and tagging additional photos. The best practice is to upload multiple images that depict different size variations of the object from different angles, with different lighting conditions and different backgrounds.

The quick test button opens a page where we can upload a test image and to test whether AI Builder can detect the object. Figure 20-12 shows the result of a test. AI Builder encloses the objects that it finds with a rectangle. A label next to the rectangle indicates the confidence rating. This example shows a confidence rating of 83, meaning that the object detection model rates the likelihood of this match at 83%.

Figure 20-12. Testing an object detection model

Detecting Objects from Canvas Apps

To incorporate object detection into a canvas app, we can utilize the object detection control. To use this control, we use the AI Builder menu to add an object recognizer control to a screen. This control requires us to select an object detection model. In this example, we would select our "Tree" model (Figure 20-13).

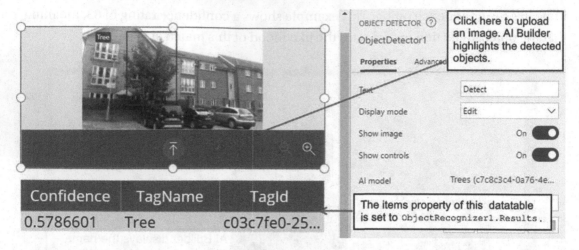

Figure 20-13. *Using the object detection control*

At runtime, the user can click the object recognizer control to upload an image. If the AI model recognizes objects in the image, it will highlight those objects and display the confidence rating next to those objects.

We can use formulas to retrieve the details of the objects that have been detected. The Results property returns a table with the object names and confidence ratings. The GroupedResults property returns a count of objects by tag name. The OriginalImage property returns the image that the user has uploaded.

Processing Forms

The form processing feature extracts field values from documents. This feature enables users to upload images in PDF, PNG, or JPG format. This feature is intelligent because it can extract handwritten as well as printed values from a form. The business benefit of automated form processing is that it can reduce the labor cost of manual data entry.

To demonstrate this feature, we'll train a model to process invoice documents and to extract values that include the invoice date, address, and line items.

A form processing model relies on a custom model, and therefore, it's necessary to obtain a set of training files. A requirement of the form processing feature is that all documents must share a common layout. The only thing that should differ between each document are the data values.

To build our example, we'll use a set of PDF invoice files from the Microsoft AI training labs. We can download these files from the following location: `https://go.microsoft.com/fwlink/?linkid=2103171`. This download also includes training files to help trial the other features in AI Builder.

The first step is to create a form detection model from the AI Builder menu item in the Maker Portal. This opens a window that consists of two main stages. The first step is to upload our training documents, and the second step is to identify the fields that we want to extract.

Each document we upload must share the same layout. The first document must contain values against all the fields that we want to detect. In subsequent documents, the values can be optionally empty.

Once we upload all our documents, AI Builder analyzes the layout and opens a designer that enables us to define the fields that we want to extract (Figure 20-14).

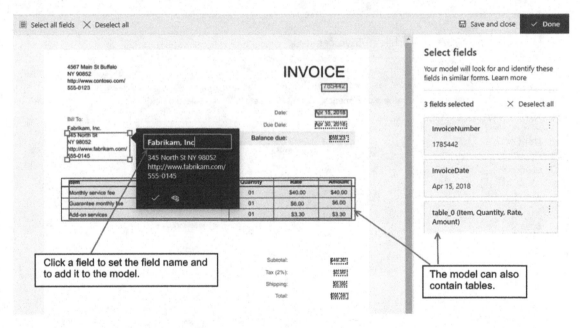

Figure 20-14. *Identifying form fields*

The designer highlights the fields that it can extract with green dotted rectangles. If we click one of these fields, the designer opens a flyout that shows an auto-generated field label and the detected field value.

671

In this example, the designer assigns the name "Fabrikam, Inc" to the field that corresponds to the invoice address. The designer derives this field name from the first line of the invoice address, and it is clearly not an appropriate identifier. To change this, we can modify the field name by typing into the label that appears in the flyout. Here, we can change the field name to something more appropriate, such as "Invoice Address."

The form processor can also process tables of data, and it detects the table that contains the invoice line items. The designer labels this field as table_0 and identifies the columns in this table. Unfortunately, it is not possible to modify the field name for a table.

Once we identify and set appropriate names for all our fields, we can progress to the summary page. This displays an overview of our model and includes a "train" button to start the training process. When this process completes, we can view the details of our model as shown in Figure 20-15.

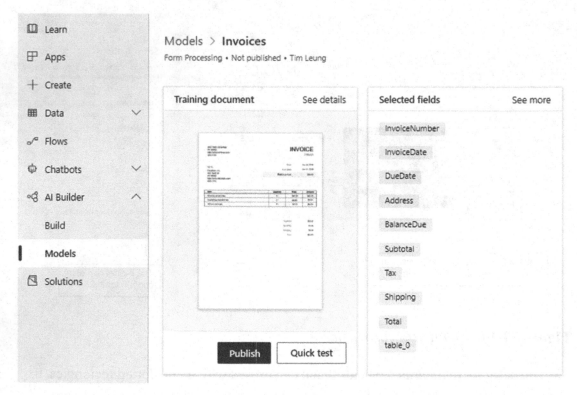

Figure 20-15. *Summary of our form processing model*

The quick test button enables us to upload a test file and to process a test document.

Processing Forms from Canvas Apps

The form processor control enables us to process forms from a canvas app. First, we add a form processor control to a screen from the AI Builder menu. This control requires us to select a form processing model; and, in our example, we would choose our "Invoices" model.

At runtime, the user clicks the form processor control to upload an image. If the AI model recognizes fields in the image, it highlights those fields with a rectangle and displays the confidence rating (Figure 20-16).

We can use a formula to retrieve the field values that have been detected. The Fields property enables us to retrieve the values. The Table property enables us to access the tables that we defined in our model. We can also access the image through the OriginalImage property. If necessary, we can save this image to a data source by calling the Patch function.

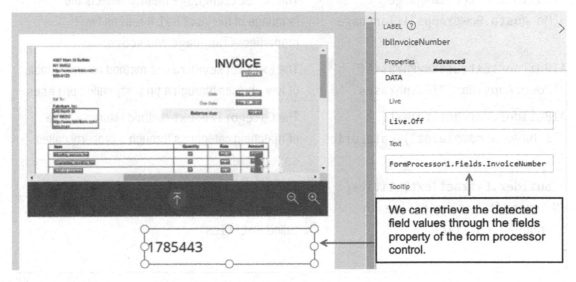

Figure 20-16. *Using the form processor control*

Processing Text

In this section, we'll cover the language processing capabilities of AI Builder. This will include features that include sentiment analysis, language detection, keyword extraction, entity extraction, and text classification.

Analyzing Text with Formulas

The difference between language processing and the vision processing features that we've seen so far is that we use formulas exclusively to carry out language processing tasks. There is not the option to use screen controls. AI Builder provides simple, straightforward functions that are intuitive to understand. Table 20-2 provides a summary of the functions that we'll cover in this section and highlights the simplicity of the syntax.

Table 20-2. *Summary of language processing functions*

Example	Description
AIBuilder.AnalyzeSentiment("PowerApps is great!").sentiment	The AnalyzeSentiment method returns the sentiment of the input text. It can return positive or negative.
AIBuilder.DetectLanguage("Me gusta PowerApps").language	The DetectLanguage method detects the language of the input text. It returns two properties – language and score.
AIBuilder.ExtractKeyPhrases("PowerApps has AI").phrases	The ExtractKeyPhrases method returns a table of key phrases through a property called phrases.
AIBuilder.CategorizeText("I have a complaint").categories	The CategorizeText method returns a table of matching categories through a property called categories.
AIBuilder.ExtractTextEntities("Microsoft has an office in London").entities	The ExtractTextEntities method returns a table of entities and values through a property called entities.

When starting out, we can be easily confused by this terminology. What's a key phrase, what's a category, and what are entities? Here's brief summary:

- Key phrase – If, for example, we process a forum post, key phrase extraction detects tags or keywords that summarize the content of the post.

- Categories – AI Builder can match input text against categories that we predefine. For instance, does an input message fall into the "billing," "complaints," or "compliments" category?

- Entity – AI Builder can extract objects (entities) and their corresponding values from input text. For example, if a sentence includes the word "London," entity extraction returns a table that contains a row with a key value of "City" and a value of "London." It's necessary to predefine the key values (or entities) that we want to detect. Note that in this context, an entity bears no relationship to an entity from Dataverse (entity was the term that described a table when Dataverse was known as the CDS).

Let's now examine these formulas in greater detail and find out how to utilize both prebuilt and custom models.

Note   The entities that an entity extraction model extracts are not the same as the entities from a CDS database.

Analyzing Sentiment

Sentiment analysis determines whether a piece of text is positive or negative. We can use this technique to prioritize customer service queries, protect our brands by monitoring conversations on social media, or monitor interesting developments in an industry.

The `AIBuilder.AnalyzeSentiment` method accepts an input string. This can be up to 5,120 characters (which is approximately the quantity of text from two pages of this book). AI Builder evaluates the input at a sentence level and derives a combined document score using these results.

A great way to explore the output from the AI Builder methods is to store the return value in a variable. We can then inspect the output using the variables section of the designer. To demonstrate, we'll call the following formula to store the output into a variable called `varSentiment`:

```
Set(varSentiment, AIBuilder.AnalyzeSentiment("PowerApps is great!"))
```

Figure 20-17 shows the result that we see in the variables section of the app designer.

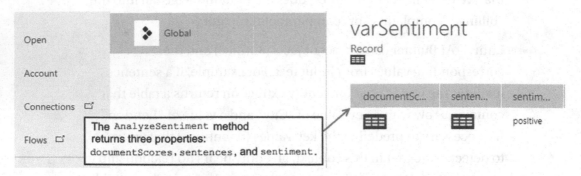

Figure 20-17. *The return value from the AIBuilder.AnalyzeSentiment method*

As this figure shows, the AnalyzeSentiment method returns three properties – documentScores, sentences, and sentiment.

The sentiment property returns a description of the overall sentiment. The values it can return are positive, negative, neutral, and mixed.

The sentences property returns a table that contains the sentiment for each sentence in the input string. This table contains two columns – sentiment and sentimentScore. The sentiment field returns the sentiment description. The sentimentScore field returns a table that shows positive, negative, and neutral ratings of the sentence.

The documentScores property returns a record that aggregates the sentiment score for all sentences. This provides a document overview of the positive, negative, and neutral ratings.

Figure 20-18 illustrates the return values that are described here.

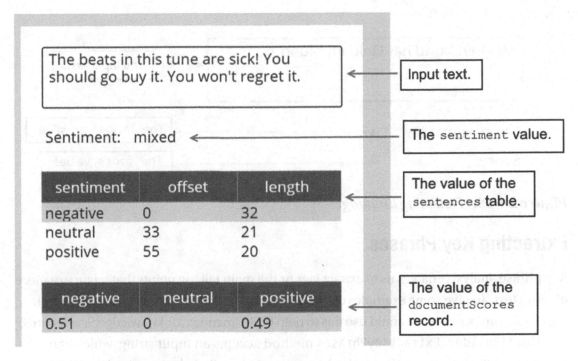

Figure 20-18. *The result of sentiment analysis*

In this example, the input contains three sentences. We can see how the sentences table returns the sentiment for each sentence. We can also see how sentiment analysis can make unintended assessments. This often occurs when the input contains slang or sarcasm. Therefore, it's important to take this into account, especially when we process social media feeds where there's a prevalence of this type of language.

Detecting Languages

To detect the language of a piece of text, we call the AIBuilder.DetectLanguage method and provide an input string which can be up to 5,120 characters.

This method returns an object with two properties – language and score. The language property returns the two-letter language code of the detected text – for example, "en", "fr", "zh_chs", or "ru". To obtain a full list of two-letter codes, we can carry out a web search for "ISO 3166 language codes."

The score property returns the confidence rating, using a scale of 0–1. 1 indicates a higher confidence. Figure 20-19 shows a demonstration of this method.

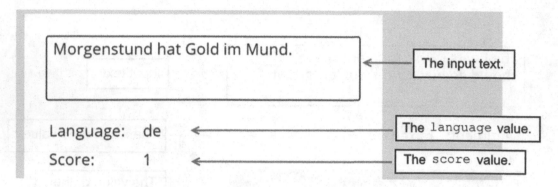

Figure 20-19. *Detecting languages*

Extracting Key Phrases

Key phrase analysis enables us to extract tags or the main talking points that relate to a piece of input text. To give some examples of how to use this feature, we could use this to build tags for forum posts, or we could use this to help build an index for knowledgebase records.

The AIBuilder.ExtractKeyPhrases method accepts an input string, which can be up to 5,120 characters. The method returns a table called phrases, as shown in Figure 20-20.

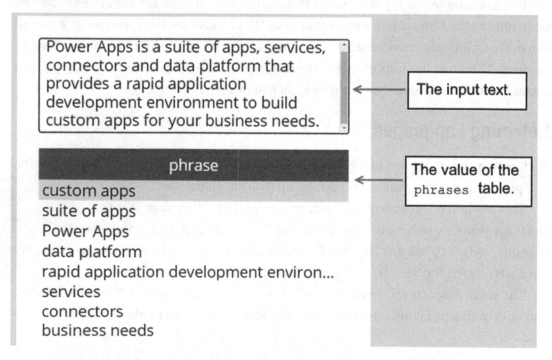

Figure 20-20. *Extracting key phrases*

Categorizing Text

With AI Builder, we can categorize text using both prebuilt and custom models. The prebuilt model caters for customer service scenarios. It enables us to use AI Builder to determine whether a message relates to billing, issues, or a range of other categories.

To extend text categorization to include other categories, we would need to create a custom model. We'll start by looking at how to use the prebuilt model.

From a canvas app, we can call the `AIBuilder.CategorizeText` method to find a list of matching categories. This method accepts an input string, which can be up to 5,000 characters. The return value includes a table called `categories`. This table returns all matching categories and includes two columns – `type` and `score`.

The `type` column returns the category name. The category types that the prebuilt model recognizes include Issues, Compliment, Customer Service, Documentation, Price & Billing, and Staff. Figure 20-21 illustrates this feature.

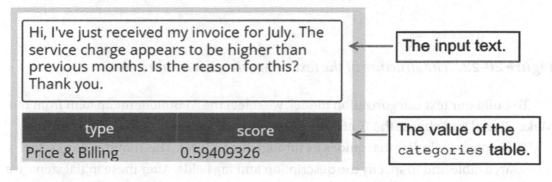

Figure 20-21. *Categorizing text*

In this example, the input text relates to billing. AI Builder detects that this message belongs to the "Price & Billing" category and assigns a confidence score of 0.59 to this match.

Building a Custom Categorization Model

To expand the number of target categories, we can build and train a custom model. To demonstrate this process, we'll build a custom model to help categorize incoming messages from customers and tenants. With the help of this model, we can detect whether a message relates to staff, cleanliness, or facilities.

To build a custom model, the first step is to build and to populate a table with training data. The table should include a list of records with example text. Against each row, a separate field should contain details of the matching categories. Where there are multiple categories, we can separate the category names with a comma, space, or tab. Figure 20-22 shows the layout of our training table.

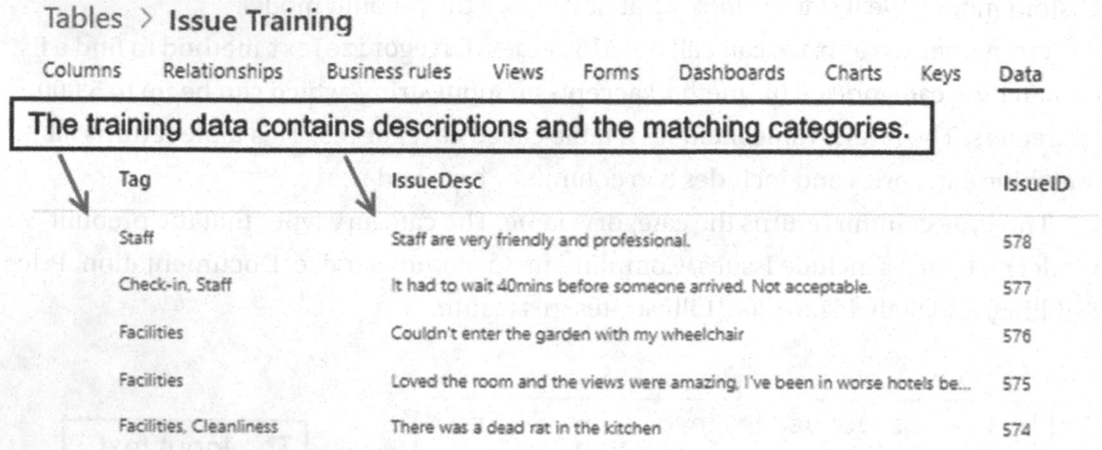

Tables > **Issue Training**

Columns	Relationships	Business rules	Views	Forms	Dashboards	Charts	Keys	Data

The training data contains descriptions and the matching categories.

Tag	IssueDesc	IssueID
Staff	Staff are very friendly and professional.	578
Check-in, Staff	It had to wait 40mins before someone arrived. Not acceptable.	577
Facilities	Couldn't enter the garden with my wheelchair	576
Facilities	Loved the room and the views were amazing, I've been in worse hotels be...	575
Facilities, Cleanliness	There was a dead rat in the kitchen	574

Figure 20-22. *The structure of the text categorization training data*

To build our text categorization model, we select the AI Builder menu item from the Maker Portal and choose the "Category Classification" option.

This opens a window that guides us through the process. This requires us to select our source table and to specify the description and tag fields. After these initial steps, we can review our data as shown in Figure 20-23.

Select text
Issue Training > IssueDesc

Select tags
Issue Training > Tag

Review tags

Select text
language

Model summary

Review your text and tags

Text	Tags
It had to wait 40mins before someone arrived. Not acceptable.	Check-in Staff
Staff are very friendly and professional.	Staff
Couldn't enter the garden with my wheelchair	Facilities
Loved the room and the views were amazing, I've been in worse hotels before.	Facilities
There was a dead rat in the kitchen	Facilities Cleanliness

Figure 20-23. *Reviewing the text and tags*

Next, we select the language and progress to the summary page. From the summary page, we can review our model and click the "train" button to start the training process. When the training completes, the details page will open, as shown in Figure 20-24. From this page, we can click the Publish button to make the model live.

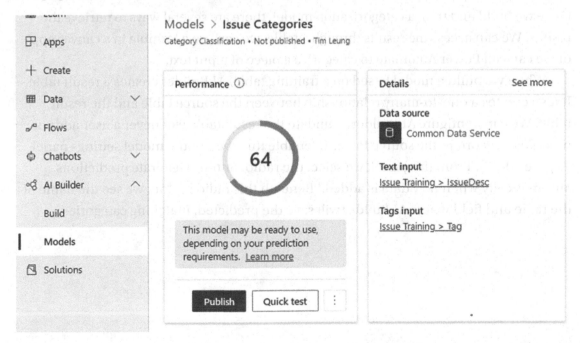

Figure 20-24. *Summary of the custom categorization model*

The details page shows the performance of our model. In cases where a category categorization model performs poorly, we can improve the model by ensuring that the training data contains an even distribution of data that pertains to each category. If, for example, our training data contained 100 records that are categorized as "Staff" and 10 records that are categorized as "Cleanliness," this will have a negative impact on performance.

The quality of the data is also important. For best results, the description should contain contextual details and, as far as possible, be grammatically correct.

Another reason for poor performance is in cases where the categories that we want to detect are very similar. For example, let's suppose we build a model that processes customer complaint descriptions. The categories we want to detect include "overseas shipping," "postage rates," "late delivery," and "failed delivery." Because the categories are very close in nature, AI Builder can struggle to differentiate between these categories, especially if there is an insufficient quantity of training data with good context.

When we build our training data, a good test is to ask another human to categorize our descriptions. If a human being fails to categorize the data in the way that we expect (due to the closeness of categories), an AI model will also struggle.

Retrieving the Results of a Categorization Model

Once we build and train a categorization model, there are several ways to retrieve the results. We can access the results through a table, we can use a formula in a canvas app, or we can call Power Automate to categorize a piece of input text.

When we build a model based on a training table, AI Builder creates a result table. It also creates a one-to-many relationship between the source table and the result table. We can configure AI Builder to update the result table whenever a user adds or modifies a record in the source table. To enable this, we use the model settings panel (Figure 20-25). From this panel, we select the radio button "Generate predictions automatically when new data is added." Beneath this radio button, we see the name of the table and field where AI Builder will save the predicted, matching categories.

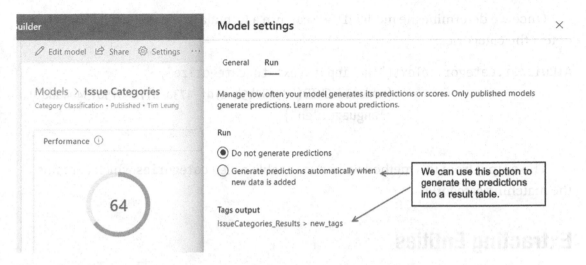

Figure 20-25. *Configuring the run settings of a custom categorization model*

This method works well in model-driven apps because the standard layout of a model-driven form enables users to view records in related tables. Therefore, it requires minimal effort to build a screen for users to view the predicted categories whenever records are added or modified.

Using a Custom Categorization Model in a Canvas App

From a canvas app, we can call the `AIBuilder.CategorizeText` method to return a table of matching categories. This works in the same way as we saw earlier. The difference is that we provide the unique identifier of our custom model in the method call.

The unique identifier for a custom model is a GUID. Unfortunately, there isn't a way to determine this through the user interface. One way to determine the unique model ID is to open the details page of a model and to examine the web address. The model ID will appear at the end, as shown in Figure 20-26.

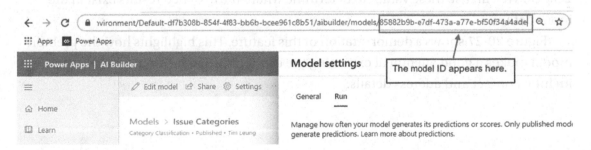

Figure 20-26. *Determining the model ID*

Once we determine the model ID, we can use a formula in the following format to detect the categories:

```
AIBuilder.CategorizeText("The input text to categorize",
                    {modelId:GUID("85882b9b-e7df-473a-a77e-bf50f34a4ade"),
                    language:"en"}
)
```

The output from this method will return a table called categories which contains the matching categories.

Extracting Entities

AI Builder provides entity extraction capabilities. In simple terms, this enables us to retrieve key and value pairs from unstructured data. AI Builder provides a prebuilt model, and we can also extend this feature by building a custom model.

The prebuilt model analyzes sentences and picks out details that pertain to the following:

```
Age, Boolean, City, Color, Continent, Country or region, Date and time,
Duration, Email, Event, Language, Money, Number, Ordinal, Organization,
Percentage, Person name, Phone number, Speed, State, Street address,
Temperature, URL, Weight, Zip code
```

From a canvas app, we call the AIBuilder.ExtractTextEntities method to return a table of key and value pairs. This method accepts an input string, which can be up to 5,000 characters. The name of the result table is called entities. This contains two columns – type and score. The type field shows the "key" entity name, and the score field shows the confidence score. The table also includes the fields startIndex and length. We can use these values to determine where the matched results exist in the input data.

Figure 20-27 shows a demonstration of this feature. This highlights how the prebuilt model makes a good attempt at extracting the elements from the input text, which include contact and address details.

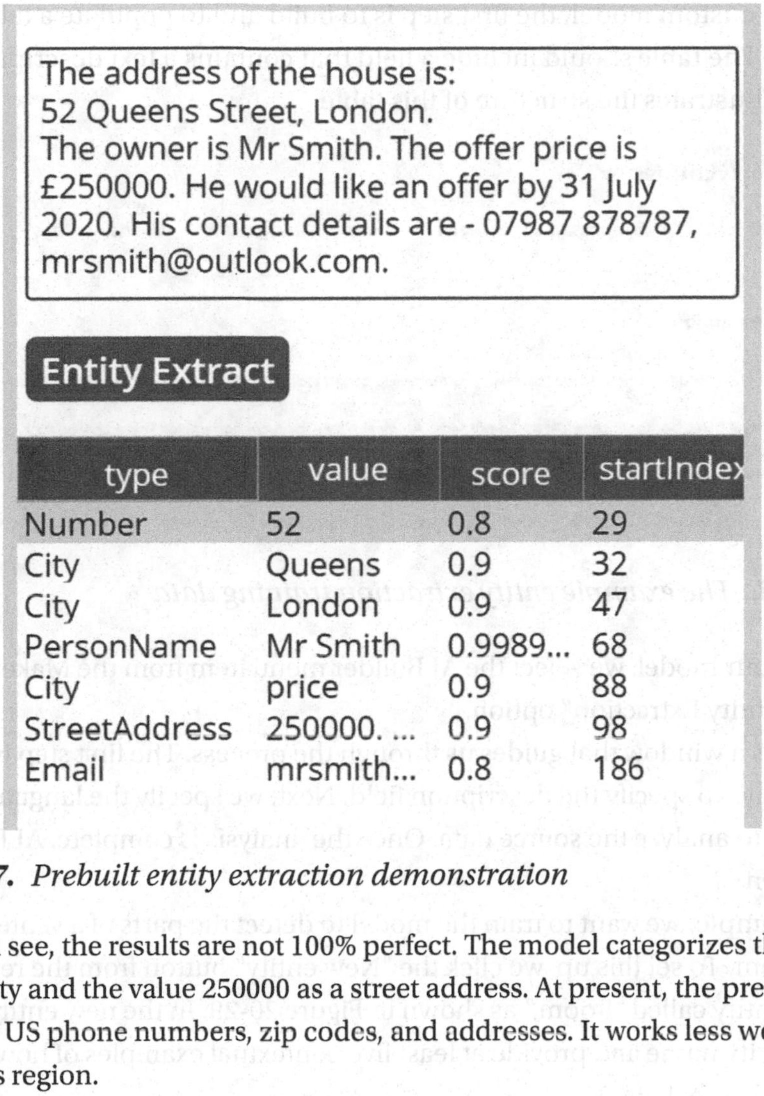

The address of the house is:
52 Queens Street, London.
The owner is Mr Smith. The offer price is
£250000. He would like an offer by 31 July
2020. His contact details are - 07987 878787,
mrsmith@outlook.com.

Entity Extract

type	value	score	startIndex
Number	52	0.8	29
City	Queens	0.9	32
City	London	0.9	47
PersonName	Mr Smith	0.9989...	68
City	price	0.9	88
StreetAddress	250000. ...	0.9	98
Email	mrsmith...	0.8	186

Figure 20-27. Prebuilt entity extraction demonstration

As we can see, the results are not 100% perfect. The model categorizes the word "price" as a city and the value 250000 as a street address. At present, the prebuilt model is optimized for US phone numbers, zip codes, and addresses. It works less well with data outside of this region.

Because this is a prebuilt model, there is not much scope for us to improve the accuracy. For best results, we should try to use high-quality input that is grammatically correct and includes contextual details.

Building a Custom Entity Extraction Model

To extend the entities that AI Builder can recognize, we can build and train a custom model. To demonstrate this process, we'll build a custom model that recognizes rooms from property descriptions, such as bedrooms or bathrooms.

To build a custom model, the first step is to build and to populate a table with training data. The table should include a field that contains a text description. Figure 20-28 illustrates the structure of this table.

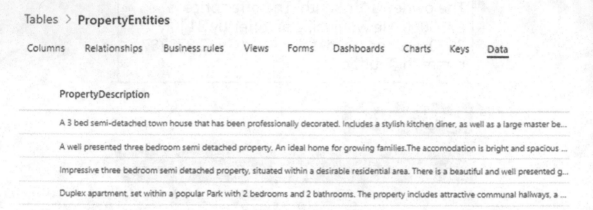

Figure 20-28. *The example entity extraction training data*

To create our model, we select the AI Builder menu item from the Maker Portal and choose the "Entity Extraction" option.

This opens a window that guides us through the process. The first step is to select the source table and to specify the description field. Next, we specify the language, and we click a button to analyze the source data. Once the analysis is complete, AI Builder opens a review screen.

In this example, we want to train the model to detect the parts of a sentence that describe a room. To set this up, we click the "New entity" button from the review screen to create an entity called "Room," as shown in Figure 20-29. In the new entity panel, we specify the entity name and provide at least five contextual examples of how the word "room" is used in real life.

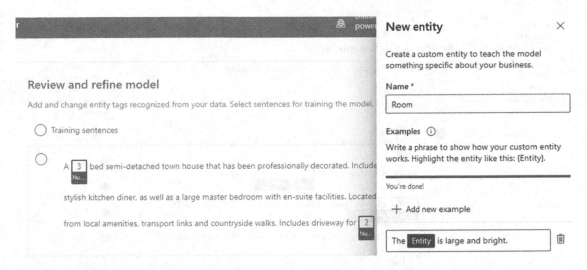

Figure 20-29. *Adding a new entity*

Once we add our entity, we return to the review screen (Figure 20-30). This screen shows the prebuilt entities that AI Builder recognizes, such as city, number, and organization.

We can use the entities panel to omit the prebuilt entities that we don't want to include in our custom model, and we can also correct instances where AI Builder incorrectly recognizes entities in our training data. We can also identify the words in our training data that are of type "Room."

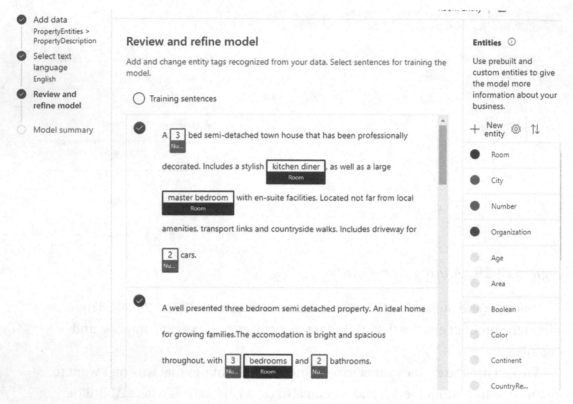

Figure 20-30. *Reviewing the text and tags*

At the next stage, we can review our model and start the training process. When the training completes, the details page will display the performance of our model. From this page, we can click the Publish button to make our model live.

Using a Custom Model in a Canvas App

In the same way that we extract entities using the prebuilt model, we can call the `AIBuilder.ExtractTextEntities` method to extract entities using a custom model.

To use a custom model, we need to provide the model ID, and we can obtain this through the same technique that we used with our custom categorization model. We open the details page for our custom model and inspect the web address.

Once we determine the model ID, we can use a formula in the following format to retrieve the detected entities and the associated values:

```
AIBuilder.ExtractTextEntities ("The input text we want to process",
                    {modelId:GUID("1e7f0e51-d0a7-4eaa-aaba-7fab1e2668ed "),
                    language:"en"}
)
```

This method returns a table called `entities` which contains our results.

Predicting Outcomes

In the final section of this chapter, we'll cover the topic of prediction models. Prediction analysis uses historical data to predict whether a business outcome will occur. We can use this to answer questions such as Which customers are most likely to place an order? Which orders will probably not arrive on time?

To build a prediction model, the key step is to obtain a source of historical data to help form the basis for our predictions. To build accurate models, we can combine a range of sources. This could include CRM, customer service, purchase histories, demographics, digital marketing, survey, web traffic, location data, and more.

To demonstrate this feature, we'll build a model that predicts the likely tenancy duration of a tenant. We'll use historical data that includes the age, income bracket, and social economic group of the tenant. Figure 20-31 illustrates our source data.

This data contains a field called `TenancyDuration`. This field indicates the duration in months for historical tenancies. Our source table also includes rows where the `TenancyDuration` field is blank. These rows represent active tenancies, and the model that we'll build will predict the values where this field is blank.

Tenancy Durations ⌄

✓ TenancyID ↓ ⌄	PropertyNumRooms ⌄	PropertyType ⌄	TenantIncomeBand ⌄	TenantAge ⌄	TenancyDuration ⌄
5,000	6	2	4	23	68
4,999	4	2	1	33	---
4,998	4	3	4	28	---
4,997	3	2	1	57	18
4,996	4	3	4	52	---
4,995	5	2	1	56	62
4,994	3	1			35
4,993	2	2	5	28	20

> Our model will predict tenancy duration values that are empty.

Figure 20-31. *The source data for our prediction analysis model*

To create our model, we select the AI Builder menu item from the Maker Portal and choose the "Prediction" option.

This opens a window that guides us through the process. The first step requires us to select our source entity (table) and to specify the field that we want to predict (Figure 20-32).

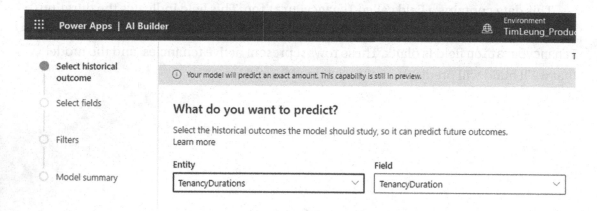

Figure 20-32. *Choosing the entity and the field to predict*

In the next step, we select the fields that factor into our prediction. In this example, we can select the TenantIncomeBand and TenantAge fields (Figure 20-33). We should uncheck all the fields that have no effect on our model, such as the create date and create user fields.

In the next stage, we can optionally filter the data. This enables us to filter out irrelevant rows in the source data, which could reduce the accuracy of our model.

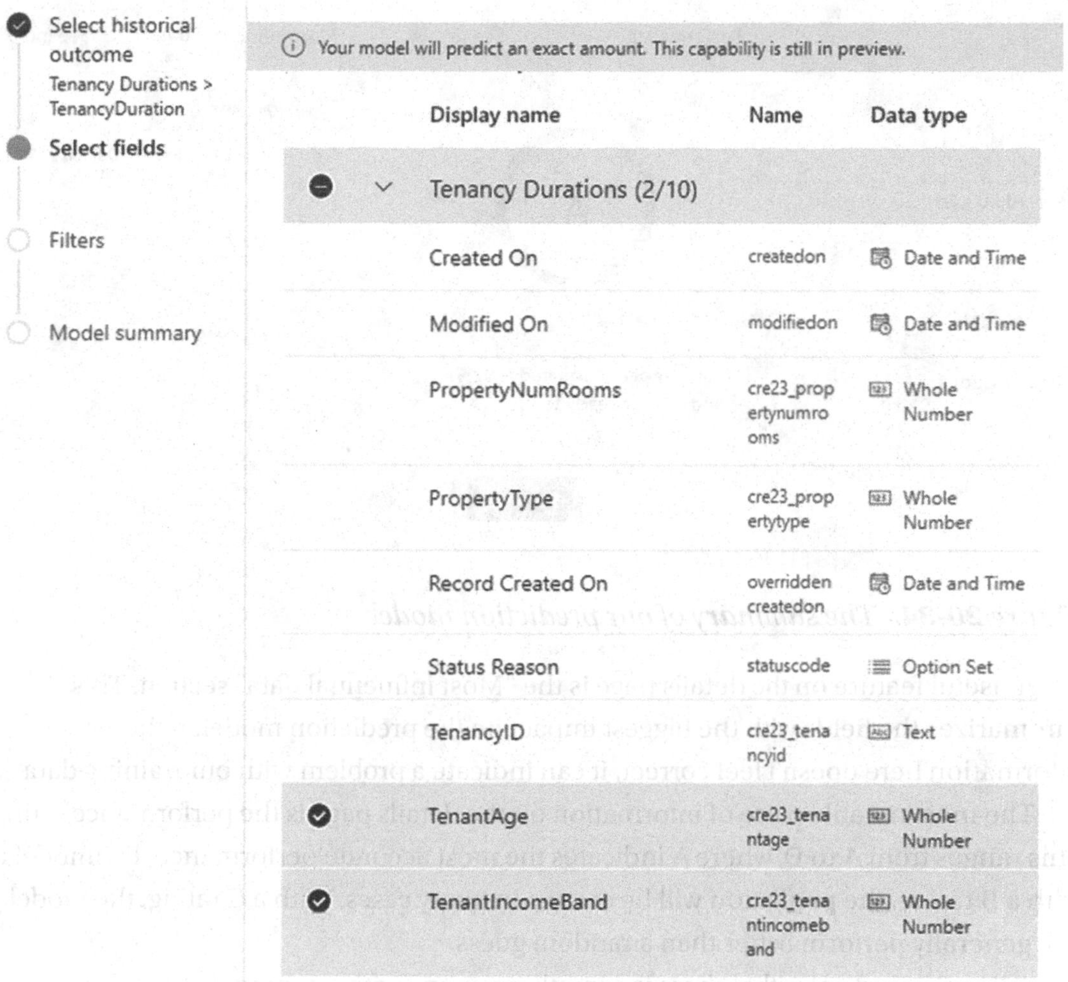

Figure 20-33. *Selecting the fields that factor into the prediction*

In the next stage, we can review our model and start the training process. When the training completes, the details page will open and display the performance of our model (Figure 20-34). From this page, we can click the Publish button to make our model live.

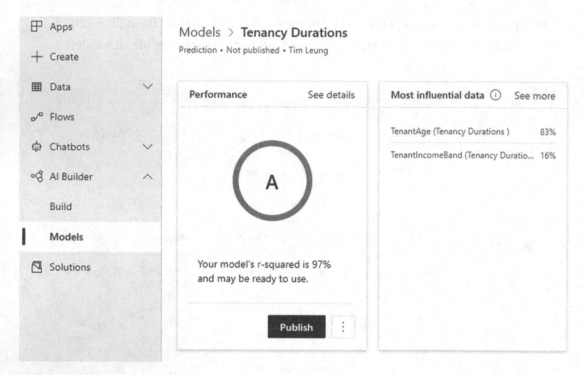

Figure 20-34. *The summary of our prediction model*

A useful feature on the details page is the "Most influential data" section. This summarizes the fields with the biggest impact on the prediction model. If the information here doesn't feel correct, it can indicate a problem with our training data.

The most notable piece of information on the details page is the performance rating. This ranges from A to D, where A indicates the most accurate performance. For models with a B rating, the prediction will be correct in many cases. With a C rating, the model will generally perform better than a random guess.

A D rating indicates that there is something wrong with our model. An underperforming model can be described as an "underfit model" or an "overfit model." An "underfit model" makes predictions with an accuracy that is worse than a random guess. On the other hand, an "overfit model" performs so well that it is almost correct 100% of the time.

The reason why an "overfit model" is problematic is because it indicates bad training data. It suggests that there may be some element that directly correlates the training data with the result, meaning that the model may perform well in training, but perform badly with live data.

Using a Prediction Model

Now that we've built a prediction model, how exactly do we use it? When we build a prediction model, AI Builder adds fields to our source table, as shown in Figure 20-35. These fields store the predicted value, the score of the prediction, and an explanation. We can use these fields to retrieve the results of the prediction model.

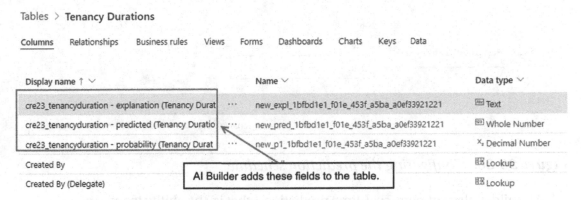

Tables > **Tenancy Durations**

Columns   Relationships   Business rules   Views   Forms   Dashboards   Charts   Keys   Data

Display name ↑ ∨	Name ∨	Data type ∨
cre23_tenancyduration - explanation (Tenancy Durat) ···	new_expl_1bfbd1e1_f01e_453f_a5ba_a0ef33921221	Text
cre23_tenancyduration - predicted (Tenancy Duratio) ···	new_pred_1bfbd1e1_f01e_453f_a5ba_a0ef33921221	Whole Number
cre23_tenancyduration - probability (Tenancy Durat) ···	new_p1_1bfbd1e1_f01e_453f_a5ba_a0ef33921221	Decimal Number
Created By		Lookup
Created By (Delegate)		Lookup

AI Builder adds these fields to the table.

Figure 20-35. *AI Builder adds fields to store the predicted values*

AI Builder runs the prediction model on a schedule. We can control this through the settings of the model, as shown in Figure 20-36. Using this setting, we can choose to run the prediction model daily, weekly, monthly, or never.

From the settings panel, we can also configure the model to retrain on a schedule. Retraining the model can help prevent the degradation of the model performance over time.

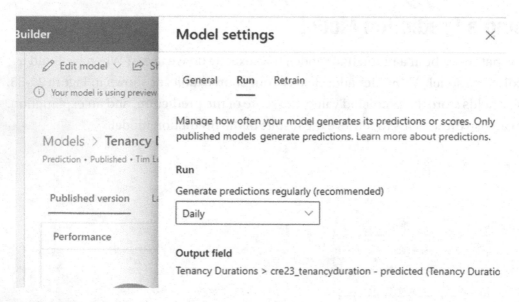

Figure 20-36. *Configuring the prediction schedule*

AI Builder also supports real-time prediction – that is, the ability to retrieve predictions at the time that we need it, rather than wait for a schedule. At the time of writing, real-time prediction works only from Power Automate. If we want to retrieve a real-time prediction from Power Apps, we would need to make a call to a Power Automate flow.

Summary

This chapter covered the topic of artificial intelligence (AI). AI-based systems mimic the cognitive behavior of humans, and a key characteristic is that they possess the ability to learn.

AI Builder is the tool that enables us to add AI capabilities to an app. In keeping with other products in the Power Platform, AI Builder is simple and intuitive to use. AI Builder offers features in three functional areas – vision processing, language processing, and prediction analysis.

In the field of vision processing, AI Builder offers business card scanning, text recognition, object recognition, and form processing capabilities. In a canvas app, we can add a business card reader or text recognizer control to a screen. At runtime, these controls allow the user to upload an image file. The business card reader control identifies fields on a business card and extracts the values. The text recognizer control extracts text from images. It can also recognize handwriting. With all the AI-based canvas controls, we can use formulas to retrieve the detected values.

To perform an AI task, we use a model. A model consists of two parts – a logical part that contains the AI logic and a part that contains what the model has learned. We can use a prebuilt model, or we can build a custom model. A prebuilt model is pretrained and ready for immediate use. The business card reader and text recognizer controls are examples of prebuilt models. For more complex scenarios, we can build a custom model.

In the vision category, we can build custom object detection and form processing models. An object detection model uses AI to recognize objects in images. A practical use for this is to recognize defects or foreign bodies in production line images. To train an object detection model, we need to provide a set of training images. When we build a model, we upload the training images, and we identify the objects that we want the model to detect. AI Builder provides an interface where we can highlight objects in training images by using the mouse. Once we train a model, users can access the object detection capabilities through an object detection control. This enables a user to upload an image and to see the objects that AI Builder detects.

Form processing is another area that requires a custom model. The benefit of automated form processing is that it can reduce the cost that is associated with data entry. We train this type of model by uploading PDF or image files with a common layout. Next, we identify the fields that we want AI Builder to detect. Once we train a model, users can upload forms and rely on the model to extract the data from the form.

In the language processing category, AI Builder can extract keywords or key phrases from input text. It can categorize text and detect the language of a piece of text, and it can also perform sentiment analysis.

Sentiment analysis measures how positive or negative a piece of text is. A use case for this feature is to monitor comments on social media. We can use this to manage brand reputations by identifying negative posts.

The key phrase model extracts phrases that correspond to the main talking points of a piece of text. A use case for this feature is to help build indexes or to identify key words in documents.

Sentiment analysis, language detection, and key phrase extraction all rely on prebuilt models. AI Builder enables us to access these models by writing formulas. It returns the results in table objects. This enables us to fully utilize the output in our canvas apps.

With text categorization and entity extraction features, we can use both prebuilt and custom models.

A text categorization model accepts an input value and returns matching categories. The prebuilt model matches input values against customer service categories that include issues, billing, and staff.

An entity extraction model extracts key and value pairs from unstructured input data. For example, given the input of a customer service message, an entity extraction model can identify and extract the name, address, telephone number, and other details from the input text.

To extend the text categorization and entity extraction features to use custom models, we need to provide training data through Dataverse tables. During the training process, we would identify the categories or the additional entities that we want our custom model to detect.

A powerful capability of AI Builder is prediction analysis. This uses historical data to predict the likelihood of a future outcome. There are many valuable ways in which we can take advantage of prediction analysis, including the ability to make smarter business decisions, predict sales, identify fraud, and more.

To build a prediction model, we provide a table that contains historical data. We specify the field that we want to predict, and we identify the fields that AI Builder should use to make the prediction. When we build a prediction model, AI Builder adds additional fields to the source table. These fields store the predicted value and the confidence rating of the prediction. We run prediction analysis models through a scheduled job. When the job completes, AI Builder stores the results in these additional fields.

PART VI

Reusability

CHAPTER 21

Building Reusable Canvas Components

Components enable us to work more efficiently by reducing duplication. With components, we can encapsulate canvas controls and logic in a single place and reuse those components multiple times in the same app or between different apps. For readers with some development experience, they behave like the user controls that exist in Microsoft products such as ASP.NET, Windows Forms, and WPF (Windows Presentation Foundation).

In this chapter, we'll learn how to build and to use components in a canvas app. The topics that we'll cover include

- The benefits of using components and the use case scenarios where components can be beneficial

- How to build a component that can interact and share data with the host screen

- How to reuse components between different apps and how to share components between users

What Can We Do with Canvas Components?

We'll start this chapter by exploring the benefits of components and the use case scenarios where they can help.

Components are particularly useful in cases where we find ourselves building the same set of features or rewriting the same formulas. By defining these common features once in a component, it reduces the duplication of work and helps us to work more efficiently. If we find ourselves copying and pasting the same group of controls multiple times, this is a good sign that we should be using components.

© Tim Leung 2021
T. Leung, *Beginning Power Apps*, https://doi.org/10.1007/978-1-4842-6683-0_21

A component behaves like a master control. When we make a change to a component, the change applies in all places where we use the component.

If we later discover a bug or if we need to modify our formula to reflect changes in business logic, we can make this change in a single place. Components can therefore reduce the effort to maintain and to update apps.

Another great use of components is to facilitate collaboration and to support multiple app builders. For larger projects where multiple app builders need to work on the same app, each app builder can carry out their work in a component. The final app will incorporate all the individual components.

A simple example of where we can use a component is to help build a common menu layout. Let's suppose we build an app with ten screens and we want the same menu to appear on each screen. Rather than duplicate this menu structure ten times, we would use a component to build the menu structure.

A great place to see some more sophisticated examples of components is the Power Apps blog:

```
https://powerapps.microsoft.com/en-us/blog/powerapps-ten-reusable-components/
```

In this post, Mehdi Andaloussi shares ten components that we can download and reuse in our apps (Figure 21-1). This includes a map component, a notification component, a numeric picker, a calendar control, a color picker component, and a wait/loading component.

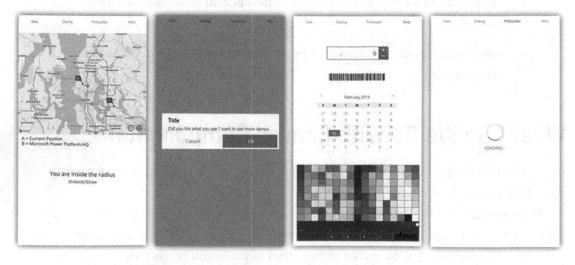

Figure 21-1. *Example components*

Are there any limitations or restrictions with components? The first limitation is that we cannot save data to a data source from a component. The second limitation is that we cannot insert components into galleries or forms.

Designing a Component

To demonstrate this topic, we'll build a text input component that accepts the input of an area in metric units. Our component will display the imperial value that corresponds to the metric input value.

Conceptually, a component behaves like a black box. From within a component, we cannot directly access controls on the host screen. Conversely, we cannot directly access controls that are internal to a component from the host app. It is also not possible to share variables or collections between the host app and component.

From within a component, we can define variables with the Set function, but we can only refer to these variables from within the component.

To share data and values between an app and the component, we define properties. We define input properties to pass values into a component, and we can expose data and values to the host app through output properties.

The component that we build will include a property called Value. This enables us to set the default area value of the component. We will also add two additional properties called AreaMetric and AreaImperial. These will enable us to retrieve the metric and imperial values the user enters. Figure 21-2 illustrates the high-level design of our component.

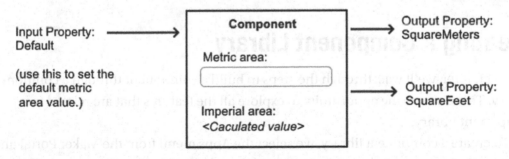

Figure 21-2. *The high-level view of our component*

Caution   We cannot directly access individual controls in a component through a host screen. Any access must occur through properties.

Where to Define Components

There are two places where we can define a component. We can build a component from within an app, or we can build a component from within a component library. If we define a component from within an app, the component will be usable from within the app only. In contrast, we can reuse components from a component library in multiple apps.

What are the pros and cons of each of these options? A component that we add to a component library acts as a master. Let's suppose we create a component and that we use it in ten apps. If we modify the component at a later stage, all ten apps that use this component can update to the latest version of the component. Component libraries make it easier to apply enhancements and bug fixes across multiple apps.

In circumstances where an instance of a component must deviate in some way from the master copy, component libraries do not work so well. For these use case scenarios, it can be easier to define the component from within an app.

A notable feature of components that we define in an app is that it is possible to export and import components between apps. Therefore, we can still take advantage of the benefits of defining logic in a single place, but in a way that is reusable between apps.

Another notable point is that it is currently not possible to export and import component libraries between environments. If, for example, we want to develop components in a development environment and to move them later to a production environment, this process can be easier to carry out with components that are defined within an app.

Creating a Component Library

In this chapter, we'll walk through the steps to build a component through a component library. This gives us the opportunity to explore all the features that are related to a component library.

To create a component library, we select the Apps menu from the Maker Portal and click the Component libraries tab (Figure 21-3).

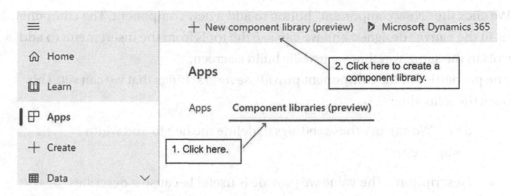

Figure 21-3. *Creating a component library*

The "New component library" button creates a new app, as shown in Figure 21-4. Although this app looks like a regular app, it exists for the sole purpose of creating components only. Although we can add screens through the screens area of the tree view, the screens we add are for testing purposes only.

From the tree view, we can switch to the Components tab. This section enables us to add and manage the components in our library.

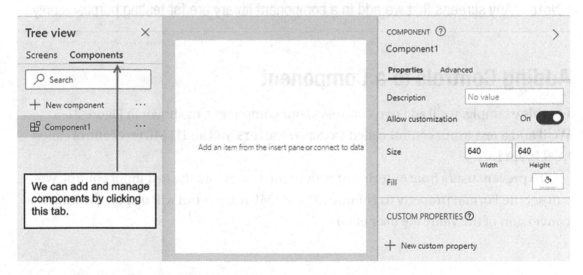

Figure 21-4. *Creating a component*

To define a component at an app level rather than within a component library, we use the Component tab from within the app.

We click the "New component" button to add a new component. The component opens in the canvas designer, and we can use the tools from the insert menu to add controls in the same way that we usually build a screen.

The properties of the component provide several settings that we can set. This includes the following:

- Size – We can use these settings to define the height and width components.

- Description – The value we provide is useful because it describes the component on the panel where we import a component from a component library into an app.

- OnReset – We use this to define the formula that runs when the component resets. On a host screen, we can reset a component by calling the Reset function and passing the name of the component.

To build our example, we'll create a component and name it "Area Input."

Note   Any screens that we add to a component library are for testing purposes only.

Adding Controls to a Component

For this example, we'll add two controls to our component, as shown in Figure 21-5. We'll add a text input control called txtSquareMeters and an HTML text control called htmlImperial.

To prevent users from entering non-numeric values into the text input control, we can set the Format property to Number. The HTML text control will display the imperial conversion of the value the user enters.

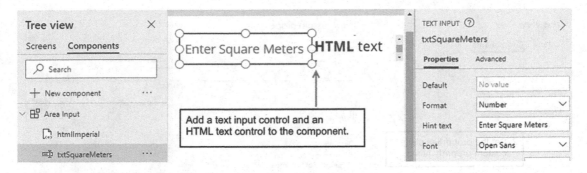

Figure 21-5. *Adding controls to a component*

Defining Properties

To define the input and output properties for our component, select the component and use the "custom properties" section of the properties pane, as shown in Figure 21-6. From this section, we can add properties to a component. When we add a component, a panel opens where we can enter the following settings:

- Name – This specifies the name that refers to the property in a formula. The name cannot include spaces.

- Display name – When we add a component to a host screen, this is the "friendly" name that appears in the properties pane.

- Description – This text appears in a tooltip when the user hovers the mouse over the display name.

- Property type – The available property type options are input and output.

- Data type – This defines the data type of the property. The available types include text, number, Boolean, date and time, screen, record, table, image, video or audio, color, and currency.

We can set the data type of the property to a wide range of data types. A notable type is the table data type. This is useful because it enables us to build components that can display lists of data.

An interesting setting is the "Raise OnReset when value changes" checkbox. With this checkbox checked, the formula in the OnReset property of the component will run when the value of the property changes. This feature is useful because it enables us to run a formula when the value of the property changes. For instance, we can reset internal variables that we've set with the Set function.

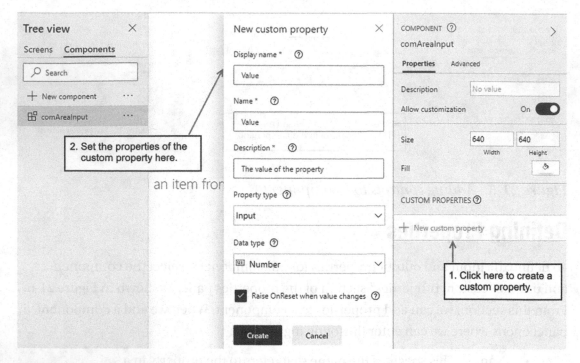

Figure 21-6. *Creating a custom property*

To build our example component, we'll use the custom properties section to add the following three properties:

- Default – Property type, input; data type, number

- SquareFeet – Property type, output; data type, number

- SquareMeters – Property type, output; data type, number

Setting Property Values

Let's now look at how to use input property values in our component and how to set the value of output properties.

To use an input property in a component, we can simply refer to the property in a formula by name. In our example, we want to set the default value of the text input control to the value of the Default input property. To do this, we set the Default property of our text input control to Parent.Default.

To display the imperial measurement of the value of the text input control, we can set the HTML property of our HTML control to the following formula:

```
"<b>m <sup>2</sup></b>   (" &
Text(Value(txtSquareMeters.Text) * 10.764, "[$-en-US]#.##") &
" ft <sup>2</sup>)"
```

The benefit of using an HTML control is that we can correctly display the superscript symbol to denote square feet and square meters. Figure 21-7 shows the layout of our screen.

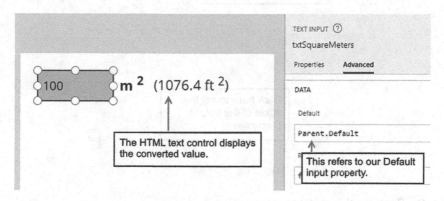

***Figure 21-7.** Using input properties*

To set the value of an output property, we click the "output property" link or select the output property name from the object drop-down. We can then provide a formula that defines the output value, as shown in Figure 21-8.

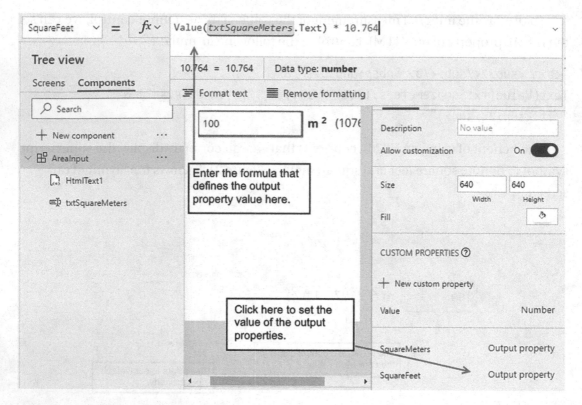

Figure 21-8. *Setting the output properties*

In our example, we set our output properties to the following values:

- SquareMeters – Value(txtSquareMeters.Text)

- SquareFeet – Value(txtSquareMeters.Text) * 10.764

This completes our component. The final step is to save and to publish our component library.

Adding Components to Apps

Let's now look at how to use our component in an app. When we create or edit an existing app, the bottom section of the insert panel includes a "Get more components" link. This opens the import components panel, as shown in Figure 21-9.

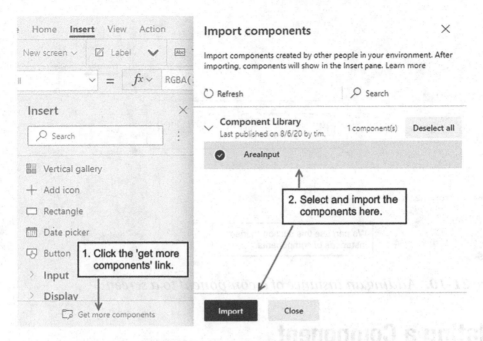

Figure 21-9. *Making components available in an app*

From here, we can import the component that we built in our component library. We can also import app-level components from other apps that are available to us.

When we import a component, it will appear as an item in the insert panel. This allows us to add instances of our component to our screen, as shown in Figure 21-10.

If we add an instance of our "Area Input" component to the screen, we can set the value of the Default property through the properties pane.

To retrieve the values of the output parameters, we can refer to the instance of the component by name. In this example, the name of the instance of this component is AreaInput_1. We can retrieve the output properties through a formula. To retrieve the value that the user enters in square feet, we use the syntax AreaInput_1.SquareFeet.

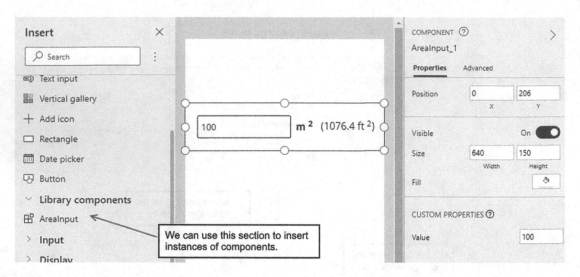

Figure 21-10. *Adding an instance of a component to a screen*

Updating a Component

With components in a component library, we can make modifications and choose to apply those changes to existing apps that use the component.

The first step is to make our amendments in the component library and to publish our changes. Next, we can edit an app that uses the component. When the app loads, the designer will show a notification that indicates the existence of an updated version of the component.

We can choose to update the component, or we can click the cancel button to continue using the older version. As Figure 21-11 shows, the notification includes the "version note" text that we can enter when we save our component library. Therefore, it's a good idea to provide a "version note" because it enables other app builders to see what's new in the updated component.

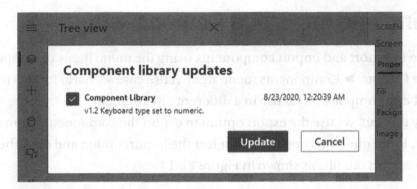

Figure 21-11. *Updating a component*

Editing a Component

Let's suppose we add a component from a component library to an app. We now want to modify this instance of the component, without affecting all other apps that use this component.

To cater for this situation, we can extract a copy of the original source component as a local component. We can then make our modifications in the local copy and modify our app so that it uses this copy.

To carry this out, we select the instance of the component from the tree view and select the "Edit component" menu item from the context menu. This opens the dialog that's shown in Figure 21-12. The "Create a copy" button makes a copy of the component, and it will appear beneath the Components tab of the tree view.

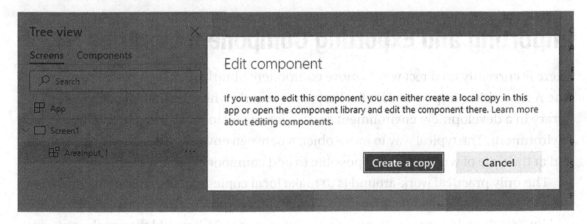

Figure 21-12. *Making a copy of a component*

Exporting and Importing Components

It is possible to export and import components using the menu items that appear beneath the Custom ➤ Components menu item. A use case scenario for this feature is to export local app components for use in a different environment.

To carry this out, we use the export option to export the components from our source app to a file. From our target app, we can select the import option and click the "Upload file" icon to import our file, as shown in Figure 21-13.

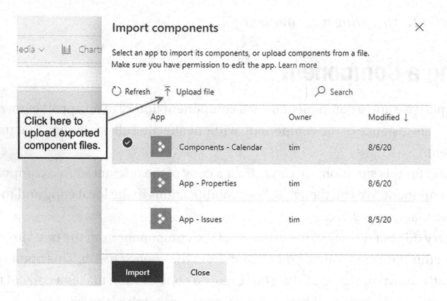

Figure 21-13. *Importing and exporting components*

Importing and Exporting Component Libraries

There is currently no direct way to move component libraries between environments. One reason this is important is to facilitate the scenario where we build a component library in a development environment and we later want to move it to a production environment. The typical way to move objects between environments is to use a solution, and at the time of writing, it is not possible to add component libraries to a solution.

The only practical work-around is to make local copies of the components that we want to move into a regular canvas app. We can then export the components into a file and import them into an app in our target environment. This would then make our components available in our target environment.

Summary

This chapter covered the topic of canvas components. Components enable us to define layouts and features in a single place. They help us work more efficiently by reducing duplication. They also help us build apps in a more maintainable way, because we can apply fixes and enhancements in a single place. A further benefit of components is that they enable multiple app builders to work toward building a single app. Each app builder can develop functionality within a component. The final app will bring together all the components that have been authored by each app builder.

Conceptually, a component behaves like a black box. From within a component, we cannot directly access controls on the host screen. Conversely, we cannot directly access controls that are internal to a component from the host app. It is not possible to share variables or collections between the host app and component. From within a component, we can define variables with the Set function, but we can refer to these variables only from within the component.

To share data and values between an app and the component, we define properties. Input properties allow us to pass values into a component, and we can expose data and values to the host app through output properties.

We can define components from within an app or from within a component library. Components that we add to a component library act as a master. When we change a component in a component library, all apps that use the component can update to the latest version. A feature that is currently missing is the ability to move component libraries between environments.

Components that we define in an app work well for features that we want to reuse within an app, such as menu controls. We can import and export local components between apps, so it is possible to take advantage of the reusable nature of local components.

To create a component library, we click the Component libraries tab from the Apps menu in the Maker Portal. When we add a new component library, the designer creates an app that appears like a regular canvas app.

The process to create a local app component and a component in the component library is the same. From the tree view, we select the Components tab. From here, we can add a new component. This will open the component in the designer. We can add controls to the component, in the same way as if we were building a screen. Through the properties pane of the component, we can create input and output properties. To create an input property, we provide a property name and data type. From within the component, we can use a formula to refer to input properties by name.

To define the value of an output property, we can select the output property link from the properties pane of the component, and we can enter a formula that defines the output value in the formula bar.

To use a component in an app, we use the insert panel. From here, we can add an instance of a local component to a screen. To use the component from a component library or to use a local component that we've defined in a different app, we click the "Get more components" link from the insert panel. From here, we can import the components we require. Following the import process, the components we select will appear in the insert panel.

To update a master component from a component library, we make our changes to the component, and we save and publish our component library. When we next edit an app that uses the component, the designer will offer the choice to update to the latest version of the component.

CHAPTER 22

Building Reusable Code Components

The most powerful way to extend Power Apps is to build custom controls using a framework called PCF (Power Apps Component Framework). PCF controls can display and edit single or tabular data items. Unlike canvas components, PCF controls are compatible with model-driven and canvas apps.

We build PCF controls using web-based languages that include HTML, CSS, TypeScript, and Node. Although this provides access to a wide range of features and capabilities, building a PCF control is not a simple task. However, the great news is that there are websites where we can download controls from other developers. This offers an easy way for us to incorporate PCF-based controls into our apps.

This chapter requires some basic web programming skills. Therefore, to keep things simple, we'll walk through the steps to build a simple control that validates user input. This control covers the most important ingredients of a PCF control, including how to define input and output properties, how to customize the control appearance with CSS, and how to call custom JavaScript.

The main topics that we'll cover in this chapter include

- How to set up a computer with the requisite development software.

- How to create a data-bound PCF control. This process will also equip us with the knowledge to use and modify components that other developers have created.

- How to build, package, and deploy a PCF control.

715

© Tim Leung 2021
T. Leung, *Beginning Power Apps*, https://doi.org/10.1007/978-1-4842-6683-0_22

What Can We Do?

In simple terms, a PCF control consists of HTML (Hypertext Markup Language) and associated logic. At runtime, model-driven and canvas apps can host and render the PCF control contents. There are many benefits to building a PCF control. Because PCF controls are based on HTML and web-based technologies, it's simple to reuse any skills that we've gained from building websites into building PCF controls. Through these web-based capabilities, we can build controls that can access the camera, location details, and microphone. Advanced developers can write code components that connect with external web services or incorporate code that's based on web frameworks such as React.

We can categorize PCF controls into two types – field components and dataset components. A field component displays a single value. For example, we can build a field control that replaces a textbox or a label on a screen. A dataset component binds to a list of data. An example of this could be a custom calendar control that displays multiple appointments.

Model-driven apps support both field and dataset components. However, canvas apps are more limited and support only field components.

The best way to understand the capabilities of code components is to examine some of the samples that are available.

Microsoft Samples

The Microsoft website provides the source code for several sample components. Table 22-1 summarizes these samples, including the compatible app types for each sample. We can download these samples from the following address:

```
https://docs.microsoft.com/en-us/powerapps/developer/component-framework/
use-sample-components
```

Table 22-1. *Microsoft PCF examples*

Name	Compatibility	Description
Angular flip	Model driven, canvas	The flip component can bind to a Dataverse "Yes/No" field and consists of a label and a button. A user can click the button to toggle between the two options. Technically, it provides an example of how to integrate with the JavaScript frameworks AngularJS and AngularUI.
Control state	Model driven, canvas	This component demonstrates how to persist user settings throughout multiple renderings of a control during a single user session.
Data set grid	Model driven, canvas	This sample displays a list of records in a tile format. It teaches how to build a component that binds to a list of records. There are model-driven and canvas versions of this sample; the canvas sample is less capable due to limitations in the dataset API.
Formatting	Model driven, canvas	There is a PCF formatting API that we can use to format currencies, numbers, and date/time values. This sample demonstrates the use of this API.
Iframe	Model driven, canvas	This sample demonstrates how to build a component that accepts longitude and latitude values as inputs and how to display the location through a Bing map that is embedded in an iframe.
Image upload	Model driven only	The image upload component enables a user to select and to upload an image in a model-driven app.
Increment	Model driven, canvas	The increment component contains a textbox and an "increment" button. A user can click this button to increment the value by 1. This sample demonstrates how to bind a numeric field to a control and how to implement error handling.
Linear input	Model driven, canvas	The linear input component enables users to enter numeric values through a slider control.
Localization	Model driven, canvas	The localization component extends the linear input component to show how to support multiple languages through the use of RESX (web resource) files.

(continued)

717

Table 22-1. (*continued*)

Name	Compatibility	Description
Map	Model driven, canvas	The map component displays Google Maps inside an iframe. It passes the value of an input property to Google Maps to enable the map to display a user-defined location.
Navigation	Model driven only	The navigation component demonstrates the navigation features that are available through the PCF navigation API. It demonstrates how to display alert dialogs, file open dialogs, and navigate the user to a different web address.
React Facepile	Model driven, Canvas	The React Facepile component displays profile pictures. It demonstrates how to interact with React (JavaScript UI library) and Office Fabric UI components.
Table	Model driven only	The table component displays the result of API calls in a two-column table. It demonstrates how to retrieve the current user and other user settings such as the language and formatting preferences.
Table grid	Model driven only	The table grid component demonstrates how to bind a grid that includes paging and column sorting capabilities.
Web API	Model-driven apps	The Web API component demonstrates how to use Web API calls to create, retrieve, and update records from the Dataverse Account table.

There are some very notable samples. The iframe control is very versatile because we can adapt it to build components that can incorporate web pages and other web content into our canvas apps.

The PCF API provides helper methods, and we can learn how these work through the formatting and table samples. For example, we can call API methods to format numbers in currencies according to user preferences, and we can also retrieve user details from a model-driven app such as the current username and settings such as the preferred language and time settings.

With PCF controls, there are methods to persist state during a user session. For example, if we build a control with a long scrollable list of data, we can remember the point that the user reaches when they navigate away from the list to view a specific record. When the user returns to the list, we can configure the list to resume at the point where they left.

For more advanced developers, there are samples that show how to integrate with common frameworks such as Angular, React, and Office Fabric UI components. These include the angular flip and React Facepile samples.

For clarification, the Office Fabric UI is a framework to build pages that mimic the look and feel of Microsoft Office. A facepile is a component that uses profile pictures to indicate interactions with a page or topic. We most often see facepile controls on pages that highlight the users that have liked or reacted to a page through Facebook.

Other Samples

Another valuable resource is the PCF Gallery website, as shown in Figure 22-1. The address for this site is `https://pcf.gallery/`.

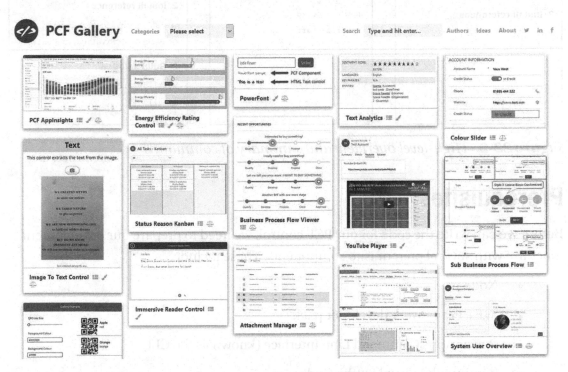

Figure 22-1. *Some of the code controls that are available*

Here, we can download a wide range of controls including barcode, chart, validation, and many other types of control. The samples on PCF Gallery can help us better understand how other developers take advantage of PCF controls. If we have a requirement to build a new control, we could save time by finding a similar control and adapting it to suit our needs.

Quick Guide: An Overview

Let's now look at the steps to create and to build a PCF control. There are several steps to follow which consist mostly of commands that we run through a command prompt.

Figure 22-2 shows a high-level overview and a summary of the commands to build a PCF control. As we develop a control, we can refer to this summary as an aide-memoire.

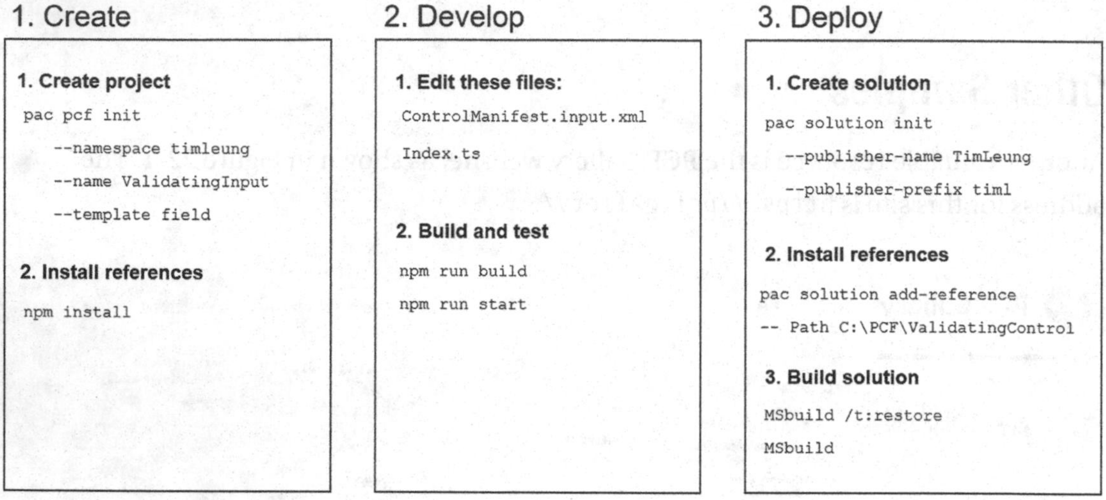

1. Create

1. Create project

```
pac pcf init
    --namespace timleung
    --name ValidatingInput
    --template field
```

2. Install references

```
npm install
```

2. Develop

1. Edit these files:

```
ControlManifest.input.xml
Index.ts
```

2. Build and test

```
npm run build
npm run start
```

3. Deploy

1. Create solution

```
pac solution init
    --publisher-name TimLeung
    --publisher-prefix timl
```

2. Install references

```
pac solution add-reference
-- Path C:\PCF\ValidatingControl
```

3. Build solution

```
MSbuild /t:restore
MSbuild
```

Figure 22-2.   High-level overview and summary of commands

Prerequisites

Before we can write the code for our PCF control, we need to prepare our development machine with several prerequisite components. These include

- Node.js

- .NET Framework developer pack

- Power Apps Command Line Interface (known as the CLI)

- (Optionally) Visual Studio Code

The key component is the CLI. This requires Windows 10, and therefore, it isn't possible to develop PCF controls on machines with earlier operating systems. To deploy a PCF control, there must be a Dataverse database in our target environment, and we must have System Administrator or System Customizer privileges in the environment.

The language that we use to write code components is called TypeScript. This is an open source language that was developed by Microsoft. The purpose of TypeScript is to overcome the limitations of using JavaScript to build large-scale, enterprise apps. TypeScript is a superscript of JavaScript. This means that any valid JavaScript code that we write is also valid TypeScript. Visual Studio Code is a popular TypeScript editor, but we can also use other compatible editors instead.

Installing NPM

Node.js is a JavaScript runtime that runs outside of a web browser. A key feature of Node.js is that it enables us to build JavaScript apps that can run on a server.

A PCF project requires us to download several software packages using the Node Package Manager (NPM). A simple way to install NPM is to download and install the full version of Node.js. We can download this from the following website:

https://nodejs.org/en/

The setup program will offer the option to install the "npm package manager," as shown in Figure 22-3. Beyond this initial screen, the installer will prompt us to install additional modules, including a package manager called Chocolatey. These components are optional and not required.

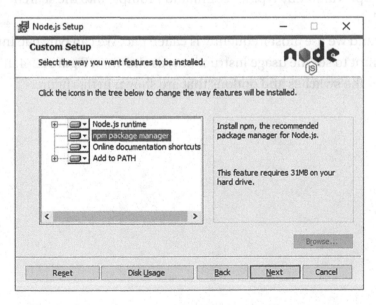

Figure 22-3. *Installing NPM through the Node.js setup*

Installing the .NET Framework Developer Pack

Another requirement is to install the Microsoft .NET 4.6.2 developer pack. We can download this from the following URL:

```
https://dotnet.microsoft.com/download/dotnet-framework/net462
```

The Microsoft .NET 4.6.2 developer pack provides the developer PowerShell environment and the MSBuild utility. These are needed to package and to deploy our component.

Installing the Command Line Interface (CLI)

The main tool that enables us to create code components is the CLI (Command Line Interface). We can download the CLI from the following URL:

```
https://docs.microsoft.com/en-us/powerapps/developer/component-framework/
get-powerapps-cli
```

The installation package contains a suite of command line tools that enable us to create, compile, and package our code components.

We access the tools in the CLI through a command prompt. We can open a command prompt window by typing "command prompt" into the search box in the Windows Taskbar.

The command we use most frequently is called pac. We can type pac into the command prompt to see the usage instructions, as shown in Figure 22-4. It's helpful to be familiar with the switches and options that are shown in this figure.

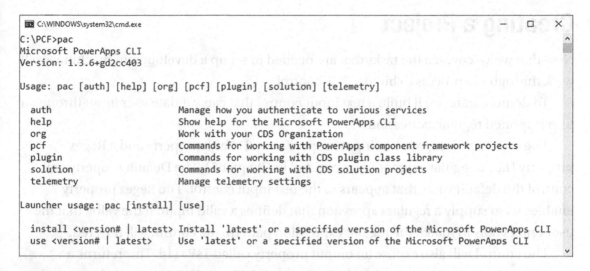

Figure 22-4. The pac command – usage instructions

Installing Visual Studio Code

To develop a PCF control, we need a code editor that can edit TypeScript and XML files. To build the example in this chapter, it's possible to use Notepad (the basic text editor built into Windows).

In practice, it's much better to use a dedicated code editor. Microsoft Visual Studio Code offers a great choice. It is free to use, and we can download it through the following address:

https://code.visualstudio.com/download

Visual Studio Code is lightweight and fast, especially in comparison with other commercial and professional IDEs (integrated development environments), such as the full version of Visual Studio.

The benefits of Visual Studio Code include IntelliSense, colored syntax highlighting, and the ability to enhance the editor through extensions – many of which are available for free.

Creating a Project

Now that we've covered the tasks that are needed to set up a development machine, we'll walk through the process to build a PCF control.

To demonstrate, we'll build a text input control that can validate user input through a user-supplied regular expression.

The control will expose two input properties – a Default property and a Regex property (i.e., a regular expression as covered in Chapter 5). The Default property will control the default value that appears in the text input control. The Regex property enables us to supply a regular expression that defines a valid input. If the value that the user enters fails to match the regular expression pattern, the control will turn red.

The control will also expose an output property called IsValid. This returns a Boolean value to indicate whether the input is valid. Figure 22-5 illustrates the control that we'll build.

Although this is a simple control, this example will highlight all the important steps that are related to building a PCF control. This includes how to retrieve values from the host screen through input properties and how to return values to the host screen through output properties. We'll also learn how to add custom JavaScript and CSS to a control.

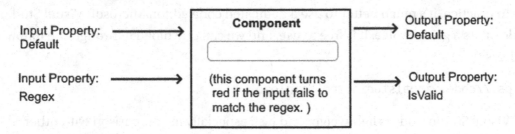

Figure 22-5. *The control that we'll create*

The high-level overview of the steps that are required to build a PCF control are as follows:

- Create a project and add references to code libraries.

- Build the control by writing TypeScript.

- Create a solution and package the component.

- Import the package into Dataverse.

We'll now look at each of these steps in detail.

Creating a PCF Project

The first step is to create a project. A project is a container that contains code files and references to necessary code libraries.

In our example, we'll store our project in the location C:\PCF\ValidatingControl. Therefore, the first step is to create this folder in Windows Explorer.

The next step is to open a command prompt window and to navigate to the project directory. We can use the cd command to change the working directory like so:

cd C:\PCF\ValidatingControl

Now run the following PCI command:

pac pcf init --namespace timleung --name ValidatingInput --template field

The pac pcf init command takes the following three arguments:

- namespace – This defines a unique identifier for the objects in our project.

- name – This defines the name of our project.

- template – The two acceptable values are field and dataset. To build a control that binds to a single value, we choose the field template. To build a control that binds to a table of data, we choose the dataset template.

Figure 22-6 illustrates the output from this command. As we can see, the output prompts us to run npm install, which we'll do later.

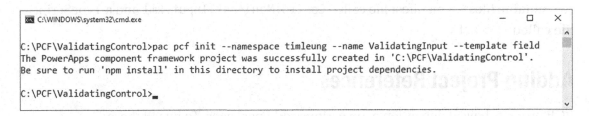

```
C:\WINDOWS\system32\cmd.exe                                                  —  □  ×

C:\PCF\ValidatingControl>pac pcf init --namespace timleung --name ValidatingInput --template field
The PowerApps component framework project was successfully created in 'C:\PCF\ValidatingControl'.
Be sure to run 'npm install' in this directory to install project dependencies.

C:\PCF\ValidatingControl>_
```

Figure 22-6. *Creating a project with pac pcf init*

Examining Our Project Layout

Let's now examine the files that have been added to our working folder by the `pac pcf init` command. Figure 22-7 illustrates the files that appear when we open our project folder in Windows Explorer.

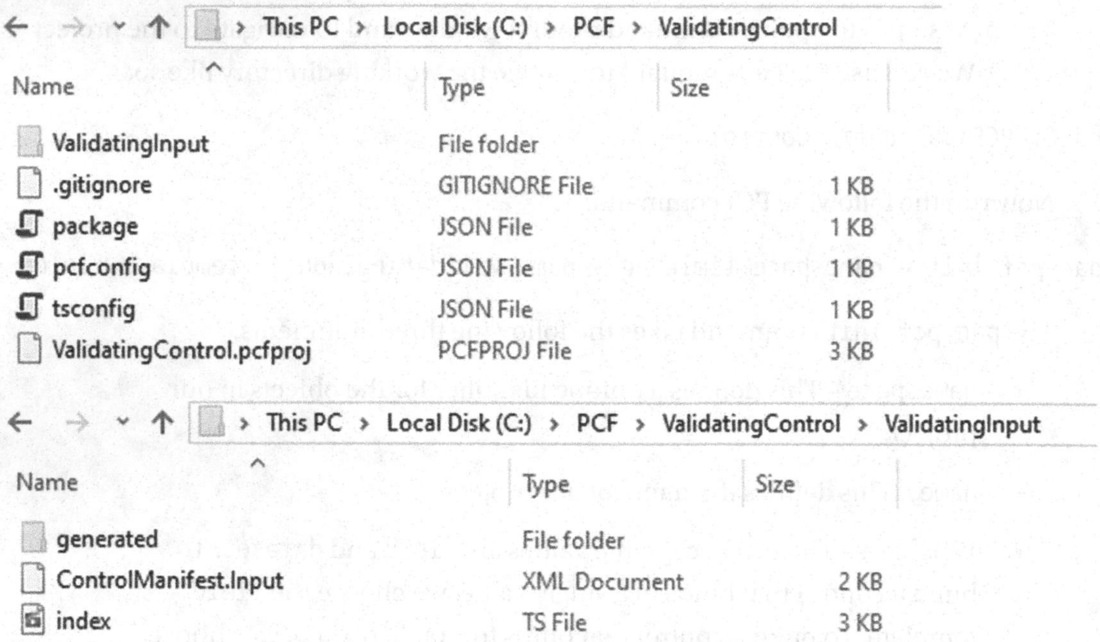

Name	Type	Size
← → ∨ ↑	> This PC > Local Disk (C:) > PCF > ValidatingControl	
ValidatingInput	File folder	
.gitignore	GITIGNORE File	1 KB
package	JSON File	1 KB
pcfconfig	JSON File	1 KB
tsconfig	JSON File	1 KB
ValidatingControl.pcfproj	PCFPROJ File	3 KB

Name	Type	Size
← → ∨ ↑	> This PC > Local Disk (C:) > PCF > ValidatingControl > ValidatingInput	
generated	File folder	
ControlManifest.Input	XML Document	2 KB
index	TS File	3 KB

Figure 22-7. *The files in our project*

The root folder contains a set of files, including a subfolder that matches the name of our control (`ValidatingInput`). This subfolder contains our working files, and there are two notable files – a manifest file called `ControlManifest.Input.xml` and a TypeScript file called `index.ts`.

Adding Project References

PCF projects have a dependency on various code packages. To install these packages, we return to the command prompt, navigate to the root folder (`C:\PCF\ValidatingControl`), and run the following command:

```
npm install
```

This command instructs the Node Package Manager to download the necessary files from the online repositories and to save the output into a subfolder called node_modules.

Figure 22-8 shows the appearance of this folder in Windows Explorer. As we see, the total size of these dependencies is around 180 MB. Due to this size, the download may take some time. Note that for any additional projects that we create, we can copy the node_modules folder from an existing project to save us from having to redownload the files with NPM.

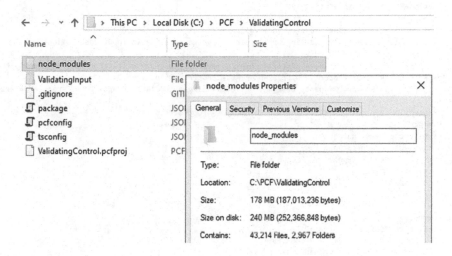

Figure 22-8. *The contents of the node_modules folder*

Developing a Control

Our project is now set up and we can now start to build our PCF control. This process consists of the following three parts, which we'll examine in further detail:

- Configure settings in the manifest file.

- Author the control by writing TypeScript.

- Style the control by writing CSS.

Defining the Control Manifest

The manifest file defines our control metadata. This includes details such as the name, description, and version number of a control. Most importantly, the manifest file is where we define the input and output properties of a control and the place where we define resources, such as CSS files.

Our example control will have three properties. A `Default` property that sets the initial value of the textbox, an input property called `Regex`, and an output property called `IsValid`.

To build the manifest file, open the file `ControlManifest.Input.xml` in Visual Studio Code or the text editor of your choice. Figure 22-9 illustrates the contents of this file.

```
C: > PCF > ValidatingControl > ValidatingInput > ⇖ ControlManifest.input.xml
 1   <?xml version="1.0" encoding="utf-8" ?>
 2   <manifest>
 3     <control namespace="timleung" constructor="ValidatingInput" version="0.0.1"
 4             display-name-key="ValidatingInput" description-key="ValidatingInput description"
 5             control-type="standard">
 6       <!-- property node identifies a specific, configurable piece of data that the control expects from CDS -->
 7       <property name="sampleProperty" display-name-key="Property_Display_Key"
 8             description-key="Property_Desc_Key" of-type="SingleLine.Text" usage="bound" required="true" />
 9       <!--
10         Property node's of-type attribute can be of-type-group attribute.
11         Example:
12         <type-group name="numbers">
13           <type>Whole.None</type>
14           <type>Currency</type>
15           <type>FP</type>
16           <type>Decimal</type>
17         </type-group>
18       -->
19       <resources>
20         <code path="index.ts" order="1"/>
21         <!-- UNCOMMENT TO ADD MORE RESOURCES
22         <css path="css/ValidatingInput.css" order="1" />
23         <resx path="strings/ValidatingInput.1033.resx" version="1.0.0" />
24         -->
25       </resources>
26       <!-- UNCOMMENT TO ENABLE THE SPECIFIED API
27       <feature-usage>
28         <uses-feature name="Device.captureAudio" required="true" />
29         <uses-feature name="Device.captureImage" required="true" />
30         <uses-feature name="Device.captureVideo" required="true" />
31         <uses-feature name="Device.getBarcodeValue" required="true" />
32         <uses-feature name="Device.getCurrentPosition" required="true" />
33         <uses-feature name="Device.pickFile" required="true" />
34         <uses-feature name="Utility" required="true" />
35         <uses-feature name="WebAPI" required="true" />
36       </feature-usage>
37       -->
38     </control>
39   </manifest>
```

Figure 22-9. *The contents of the manifest file*

As we can see, the manifest file is well documented with a series of comments. The attributes of the `Control` element enable us to specify details that include the control name, description, and control type.

Next, we can define properties by adding `Property` elements beneath the Control element. The `Resources` section enables us to add references to supporting files, such as CSS and RESX files (we use RESX files to help localize the content of our control).

The final part of this file includes parts that we can uncomment to enable access to app features, such as audio and video capture.

To build our example control, we modify the manifest file as shown in Listing 22-1. This simplified version here excludes the commented sections.

Listing 22-1. The contents of the manifest file

```xml
<?xml version="1.0" encoding="utf-8" ?>
<manifest>
  <control namespace="timleung" constructor="ValidatingInput" version="0.0.1"
          display-name-key="ValidatingInput"
          description-key="ValidatingInput description"
          control-type="standard">

    <property name="Default" display-name-key="Default"
            description-key="The default value of the control"
            of-type="SingleLine.Text"
            usage="bound" required="true" />

    <property name="Regex" display-name-key="Regular Expression"
            description-key="The Regex that defines a valid entry"
            of-type="SingleLine.Text"
            usage="input" required="false"
            default-value=".*"/>

    <property name="IsValid" display-name-key="IsValid"
            description-key="Returns true if the input is valid"
            of-type="TwoOptions"
            usage="output" required="false" />

    <resources>
      <code path="index.ts" order="1"/>
      <css path="css/ValidatingInput.css" order="1" />
    </resources>
  </control>
</manifest>
```

There are two main changes that we've made to this file. The first is that we've added three Property elements to define the properties of our control. The second change is that we've defined a CSS resource by uncommenting the CSS element within the Resources section.

The definition of each property warrants some extra description. For each property, there are several attributes we can set. These include

- name – This is what we use in our TypeScript code to refer to the property. This is also the name that appears in the canvas app designer.

- display-name-key – This is the name that appears in the app designer. In a model-driven app, this is the name that appears when we assign the control to a field in the form designer.

- description-key – This is the description that appears in the app designer.

- of-type – This specifies the data type of the property.

- usage – The valid options are bound, input, and output.

- required – We can set this to true to mandate the entry of a value.

- default-value – This specifies the default value of the property.

To provide a point of reference, Figure 22-10 shows how the property settings appear when we add our control to a screen in a canvas app.

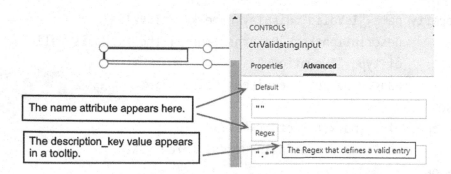

Figure 22-10. *How the property settings appear in the Power Apps designer*

The valid options for the usage attribute are bound, input, and output. A bound property can bind to a data field, and it acts like an input and output property. In contrast, we use an input property to receive read-only values into our control.

The of-type attribute specifies the data type of the property. The valid options include

```
Currency, DateAndTime.DateAndTime, DateAndTime.DateOnly, Decimal, Enum, FP,
Multiple, OptionSet, SingleLine.Email, SingleLine.Phone, SingleLine.Text,
SingleLine.TextArea, SingleLine.Ticker, SingleLine.URL, TwoOptions, Whole.None
```

These options correspond to Dataverse data types. Notice how we set the of-type attribute of our IsValid property to TwoOptions, which corresponds to the Dataverse "Yes/No" data type.

The Enum option enables us to define a property and to restrict the input choices in the designer. Here's an example of how we would use this option:

```
<property name="PropertyType"
    display-name-key="PropertyType" description-key="Property Type"
    of-type="Enum" usage="input" required="false">
        <value name="House"
                display-name-key="House">1</value>
        <value name="Apartment"
                display-name-key="Apartment">2</value>
</property>
```

Finally, instead of setting the IsValid attribute, we can set the type-group attribute to define a list of compatible data types. For a bound property in a model-driven app, this would allow us to define the data types that are compatible with the control. The built-in comment in the metadata file describes the usage of this syntax.

Writing the Code

The next step is to amend the TypeScript file. This is the central place where we define the functionality of our control, including the HTML markup and all the logic that runs.

TypeScript File Overview

Figure 22-11 illustrates the contents of this file in Visual Studio Code (excluding the comments in the file). This file consists of four methods which are init, updateView, getOutputs, and destroy. The process to build a control is to extend the code in these four methods.

```
C: > PCF > ValidatingControl > ValidatingInput > TS index.ts > ...
 1    import {IInputs, IOutputs} from "./generated/ManifestTypes";
 2
 3    export class ValidatingInput implements
 4          ComponentFramework.StandardControl<IInputs, IOutputs> {
 5
 6        constructor()
 7        {
 8        }
 9
10        public init(context: ComponentFramework.Context<IInputs>,
11                    notifyOutputChanged: () => void,
12                    state: ComponentFramework.Dictionary,
13                    container:HTMLDivElement)
14        {
15            // Add control initialization code
16        }
17
18        public updateView(context: ComponentFramework.Context<IInputs>): void
19        {
20            // Add code to update control view
21        }
22
23        public getOutputs(): IOutputs
24        {
25            return {};
26        }
27
28        public destroy(): void
29        {
30            // Add code to cleanup control if necessary
31        }
32    }
```

Figure 22-11. *The contents of the TypeScript file include four methods*

The purpose of these four methods is as follows:

- init – This method runs when the control initially loads. We can add code here to build the HTML of our control.

- updateView – This method runs when any of the properties of the control change. This includes field values and the properties that appear in the properties panel of the canvas designer, such as the height, width, and label text. This method also runs when the control loads.

- getOutputs – We can add code to this method to return values for bound or output properties.

- destroy – We can add code to this method to clean up the control and other resources. This method runs when Power Apps removes the control from the DOM (Document Object Model).

Defining Presentation/HTML

We use HTML and CSS to define the layout and presentation of a control. To build a control, we need to design the HTML that makes up the control.

Our example control is very simple – it consists of a text input control nested inside a DIV element. A DIV element defines a division or section, and we can use this as a container for child elements. The markup of our control will look like this:

```
<div>
    <input type="Text">
</div>
```

There isn't a place for us to add this literal markup. Instead, we build this HTML in code through the init method of our TypeScript file.

Initializing the Control

To build our HTML and to initialize other parts of our control, we add the code that is shown in Listing 22-2.

Listing 22-2. The init method of our control

```
//1 - Declare private variables
private _container: HTMLDivElement;
private _input: HTMLInputElement;
private _inputChanged:EventListenerOrEventListenerObject;
private _isValid:boolean;
private _regex:string;

//2 - The init method
public init(context: ComponentFramework.Context<IInputs>,
            notifyOutputChanged: () => void,
            state: ComponentFramework.Dictionary,
            container:HTMLDivElement)
{
    //2.1 - Build the HTML markup
    this._container = document.createElement("div");
```

```
this._input = document.createElement("input");
this._input.value = "" + context.parameters.Default.formatted;
this._input.className = "";

//2.2 - Add the event listener
this._inputChanged=this.inputChanged.bind(this);
this._input.addEventListener("change",this._inputChanged);

//2.3 - Add our HTML markup to the container
this._container.appendChild(this._input);
container.appendChild(this._container);

//2.4 - Store the Regex input property in a variable
this._regex = "" + context.parameters.Regex.formatted;
}

//3 This method runs when a user modifies the input value
//  (note - the default template does not include this method placeholder)
public inputChanged(evt:Event):void{

    var _regExp: RegExp;
    _regExp = new RegExp(this._regex);

    if (_regExp.test(this._input.value)){
                this._isValid = true;
                        this._input.className = "";

            }else
                {
                        this._isValid = false;
                        this._input.className = "notValid";

                }

}
```

In the first section of this code, we declare a set of local variables. We use these to store the value of the input properties and to store references to the HTML controls that we build.

The next block of code features our `init` method. The signature of this method includes the following four parameters:

- `context` – The context parameter provides access to all the property values that appear in the properties panel of the canvas designer. It is particularly useful because it enables us to retrieve the values of the input properties and other property values that the app builder enters through the properties pane, such as the height and width of the control.

- `notifyOutputChanged` – We can use this to specify a callback method that alerts the framework when the control has new outputs that are ready to be retrieved. Our example does not take advantage of this feature.

- `state` – We can use this to retrieve data that persists in one session for a single user.

- `container` – This represents an empty DIV element that Power Apps renders on the host screen. We add the HTML markup that we build to this container.

Although we do not use the state parameter, here's a brief description of how this works. It's possible to persist the state of a control across multiple instances and occurrences of the control in the same session. We call the `context.mode.setControlState` method to save a key/value pair of details, and we can then retrieve these details in a subsequent session through the `state` parameter. To give a practical example, let's suppose we build a control that shows a long list of data. By storing the point in the list that the user reaches when they navigate away from the list, we can add code to the `init` method to navigate the user to the point that they previously reached.

A great way to find out more about this feature is to study the Microsoft "control state API" sample that we covered earlier in this chapter.

The first section of code inside our `init` method builds an outer DIV element and an HTML input element. To configure this HTML input control so that it displays the value of the `Default` input property, we use the following line of code:

```
this._input.value = "" + context.parameters.Default.formatted;
```

We can access the value of the `Default` input property through the following syntax: `context.parameters.Default.formatted`. Notice how we concatenate this with an empty string to cater for situations where the input property is null.

Next, we add an event listener to the HTML input control. An event listener defines code that runs when an event happens, such as when a user clicks a button or presses a key or when an element loads. In this example, we configure our control to run the code in the `inputChanged` method when a user changes the text in the control.

We then add the text input control to our outer DIV, and we add this DIV to our control container. In the final part of the `init` method, we store the `Regex` input property into a variable. This enables us to access this value from other parts of our script.

The next section of this code contains the definition of our `inputChanged` method. When a user changes the value of the text input control, we use the built-in JavaScript `RegExp` class to test that the input value matches the regular expression. In the case of a mismatch, the code sets the CSS class name of the input control to **notValid**. We'll create this CSS class later and configure it to highlight the control in red.

Updating Control Values

An important step is to configure our control to update the textbox value when the value of the `Default` input property changes. To clarify why this is necessary, imagine that we add our PCF control to a screen in a canvas app and that we set the `Default` property to a variable. If we update this variable from other parts of the app, it would be necessary to update the value that appears in our PCF control.

To implement this functionality, we add the code that is shown in Listing 22-3. The `updateView` method runs whenever any of the property values change, and we can update any part of our PCF control as necessary. The `updateView` method also enables us to access all property values through the `context` parameter.

In this case, we can update the value of the textbox through the associated private variable that we defined (i.e., `_input`)

Listing 22-3. The `updateView` method of our control

```
public updateView(context: ComponentFramework.Context<IInputs>): void
{
    this._input.value = "" + context.parameters.Default.formatted;
    this._regex = ""+ context.parameters.Regex.formatted;
}
```

Setting Output Values

To set the value of output properties, we add code to the getOutputs method. Listing 22-4 shows the code that we add to set the value of the IsValid output property.

Here, we build an output object with attributes that match any properties that are defined as bound or output in our manifest.

Listing 22-4. The getOutputs method of our control

```
public getOutputs(): IOutputs
{
        return {Default:this._input.value,
           IsValid:this._isValid};
}
```

Cleaning Up the Control

Finally, it's important to carry out any necessary cleanup tasks when the host app finishes with our control. The destroy method runs when the framework removes the control from the DOM (Document Object Model). The DOM is the browser representation of the web page, and it provides access to web page elements through script.

Listing 22-5 shows the code that we need to add to the destroy method. Here, we remove the event listener that is associated with the text input control.

Listing 22-5. The destroy method of our control

```
public destroy(): void
{
    this._input.removeEventListener("change",this._inputChanged);
}
```

Style the Component with CSS

The final task is to create a CSS file and to define the CSS classes that we want to use in our control. In our manifest file, we defined a link to a CSS file called css/ValidatingInput.css.

This file does not exist, and therefore, it's necessary to create this file. From Visual Studio Code (or a text editor), we first create a blank file. Next, we can add the following class to the file, as shown in Figure 22-12.

```
.notValid{background-color:red}
```

This defines the notValid class that we reference in our inputChanged method. This CSS class specifies a red background color to indicate the presence of an error.

The final step is to save our file. The paths that we specify in the manifest file are relative to the TypeScript file. In this example, therefore, we would save our file to the following location:

```
C:\PCF\ValidatingControl\ValidatingInput\css\ValidatingInput.css
```

Figure 22-12. *Creating a CSS file*

Building a Control

Our PCF control is now complete. The next step is to build and to test our control. During this process, we can check that our control works as expected.

To build our control, we use the npm command. We open a command prompt and navigate to the root directory of our project. In our example, this would be the following directory:

```
C:\PCF\ValidatingControl\
```

Next, we run the following command:

```
npm run build
```

This will build our project. If there are any errors, the build process will fail and will alert us to what is wrong. For example, if our TypeScript contains syntax errors, the build output will display the precise error and indicate the file name and line number where the error occurs. If the build process succeeds, we'll see the output that is shown in Figure 22-13.

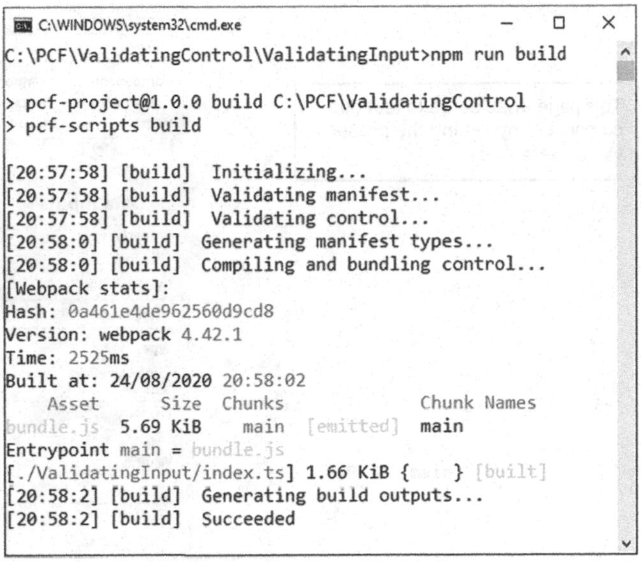

Figure 22-13. *Building our PCF control*

Testing a Control

To simplify the testing process, there is a test bed that enables us to test the behavior of a control. This is a great feature because it saves us from needing to deploy a control to test it.

To run the test bed, we open a command prompt, navigate to the root directory, and run the following command:

```
npm run start
```

The first time we run this command, Windows Defender will display a firewall alert. We can enable the option to allow the test environment to access the Internet. If all succeeds, we'll see the page that is shown in Figure 22-14.

The properties pane on this page enables us to set the values of the input properties for our control. Through the main part of this page, we can interact with our control and check that it works as expected.

To exit out of the npm process in the command prompt, we can press the Ctrl+K and Ctrl+C keystroke combination.

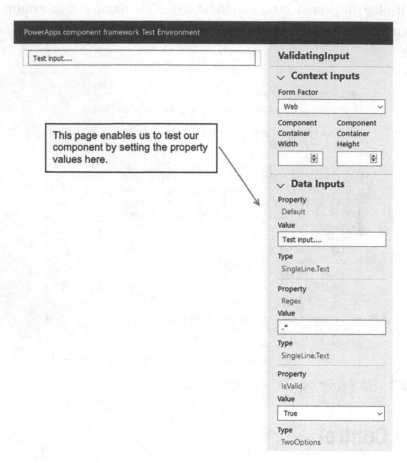

Figure 22-14. *Testing our PCF control*

Deploying a Control

Assuming that our control works as expected, we can move toward packaging and deploying our control in our target environment.

With Power Apps, we use solutions to deploy customizations or to move objects between environments. Therefore, to deploy our custom control to a target environment, there are two steps to carry out. First, we create a solution project. Next, we build and package this solution into a zip file, which we can then use to install our control into our target environment.

Creating a Solution

To create a solution, the first step is to create a folder to store our solution. For this example, we'll create the following folder:

```
C:\PCF\ValidatingControl\Solution
```

The next step is to open a command prompt. From here, we navigate to our solution and run the following command (as shown in Figure 22-15):

```
pac solution init --publisher-name TimLeung --publisher-prefix timl
```

This command creates a solution. It requires us to provide a publisher name and a publisher prefix. The publisher name can be a verbose description that identifies the publisher of the control. The publisher prefix defines the prefix that Dataverse adds to the items in the solution. For example, we've seen how Dataverse builds logical table names with a prefix (e.g., `cr8a9_property`). The publisher prefix refers to this same prefix.

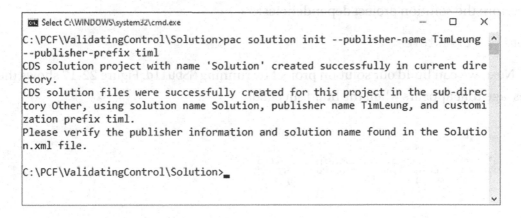

Figure 22-15. *Creating a solution project*

Once we create a solution, we need to add a reference to our control project. To do this, we call the `pac solution add-reference` command, and we pass the location of the root folder of our project like so:

```
pac solution add-reference --Path C:\PCF\ValidatingControl
```

Figure 22-16 shows a message that appears when this command succeeds.

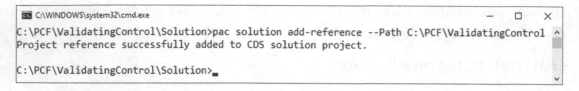

```
C:\WINDOWS\system32\cmd.exe                                      —    □    ×
C:\PCF\ValidatingControl\Solution>pac solution add-reference --Path C:\PCF\ValidatingControl
Project reference successfully added to CDS solution project.

C:\PCF\ValidatingControl\Solution>_
```

Figure 22-16. *Adding our control project to the solution*

Building a Solution Project

Our solution project is now complete, and the next task is to build our project. The tool that builds projects from the command line is called MSBuild. To build our project, we start the developer PowerShell prompt by searching for "Developer PowerShell for VS2019" from the Windows Taskbar.

When the developer PowerShell prompt opens, we navigate to the folder that contains our solution (C:\PCF\ValidatingControl), and we run the following command to restore the solution project dependencies:

MSbuild /t:restore

Next, we can build our solution project by running MSbuild. Figure 22-17 shows the message that appears when the build succeeds.

```
Windows PowerShell                                              —    □    ×

   Solution: bin\Debug\Solution.zip generated.
   Solution Package Type: Unmanaged generated.
   Solution Packager log path: bin\Debug\SolutionPackager.log.
   Solution Packager error level: Info.
CleanUpMetadata:
   Removing directory "obj\Debug\Metadata".
CleanUpIntermediateFiles:
   Completed intermiediate files clean up.
Done Building Project "C:\PCF\ValidatingControl\Solution\Solution.cdsproj" (defa
ult targets).


Build succeeded.
     0 Warning(s)
     0 Error(s)

Time Elapsed 00:00:45.14
PS C:\PCF\ValidatingControl\Solution>
```

Figure 22-17. *Building a solution project*

As we see from the output message, the build generates the output file bin\Debug\ Solution.zip. The output location is relative to the solution project, and in this example, we can retrieve the output by navigating to the following folder in Windows Explorer:

C:\PCF\ValidatingControl\Solution\bin\Debug

The Solution.zip file is what we use to install our component in our target environment.

Installing a Control

Now that we've built solution file, we can import it into our target environment. To do this, open the Maker Portal and click the Solutions menu item. From here, we can click the Import button, and we can upload our Solution.zip file. This opens the dialog that is shown in Figure 22-18.

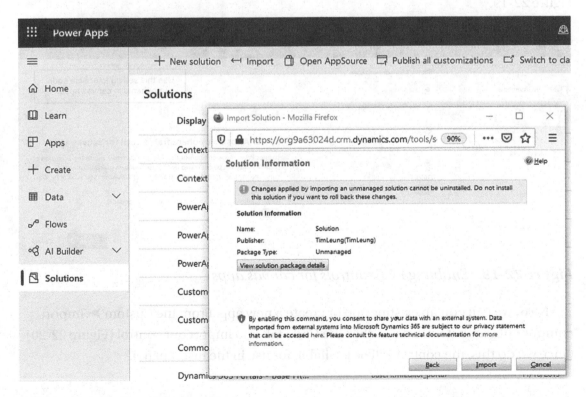

Figure 22-18. *Installing a solution*

This dialog warns that we are installing a managed solution which cannot be uninstalled. We can accept this warning and click the Import button to complete the installation of our control.

Using the Control

Now that we've installed our control into our target environment, we can use it in both canvas and model-driven apps.

Canvas App

To use a PCF control in a canvas app, there is an initial security step that we need to carry out. From the Power Platform admin center, open the settings for the target environment, and navigate to the Product ➤ Features section. From here, we need to enable the "Power Apps component framework for canvas apps" option, as shown in Figure 22-19.

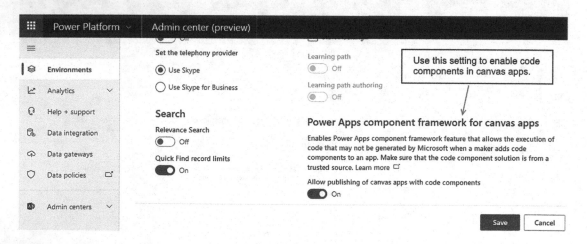

Figure 22-19. *Enabling PCF controls for canvas apps*

Next, we can edit an existing app or create a new app. From the Custom ➤ Import component menu item, we can click the Code tab and import our control (Figure 22-20). Once we do this, the control will be available for use in the insert panel.

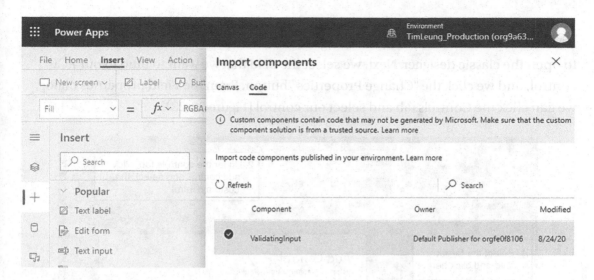

Figure 22-20. *Importing a component*

Figure 22-21 illustrates the use of our control on a screen and highlights how we can use the properties pane to set the regular expression that defines a valid entry.

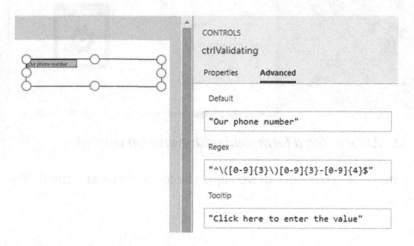

Figure 22-21. *Using a control on a screen*

Model-Driven App

To configure a form in a model-driven app to use a PCF control, we need to associate the control with a field.

We use the same process that we carried out when we associated a canvas app with a field (Chapter 13). From the form designer, we click the "Switch to Classic" button to open the classic designer. Next, we select the field that we want to bind to our PCF control, and we click the "Change Properties" button. From the Field properties dialog, we can click the Controls tab and select our control (Figure 22-22).

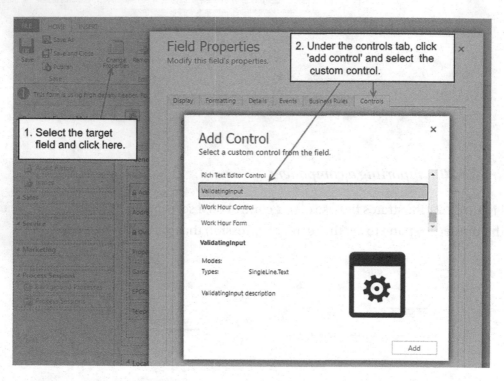

Figure 22-22. *Associating a form field with a custom control*

When we now run our model-driven app, the form will render the field with our custom control.

Summary

In this chapter, we learned how to build controls using the Power Apps Component Framework (PCF). This framework provides a powerful way for us to build custom controls that are compatible with model-driven and canvas apps.

We build PCF controls using web-based languages that include HTML, CSS, TypeScript, and Node. There are Microsoft samples that show how to interact with common JavaScript frameworks that include Angular and React. Through the PCF

Gallery website, we can download and examine the source code of many controls that other developers have built. These include controls for most imaginable scenarios, including charting, barcoding, and integrations with other platforms and APIs.

The first step of how to build a PCF control is to install the prerequisite software on our development computer. The next step is to create a PCF control project and to author our control with TypeScript. Next, we can build and test our control. There is a test bed that we can use to check that our control behaves as we expect. This test bed enables us to interact with the control and to set input property values.

To deploy our control to our target environment, we build a solution. A solution provides the means to deploy customizations or to move objects between environments.

The software that we need to install on our development machine includes the Node Package Manager (NPM), the Command Line Interface (CLI), the Microsoft .NET Framework developer pack, and a code editor such as Visual Studio Code.

The CLI enables us to create a PCF project. We use NPM to install the required project references, and we can also use it to build our project and to run the test bed.

A PCF project consists of two main files – a metadata file and a TypeScript file. The metadata file defines control details that include the name, description, and version number of the control. It also enables us to define other references, such as CSS files. Most importantly, the metadata file defines the input and output properties for a control.

The TypeScript file consists of four main methods. The `init` method initializes the control, and we can use this to construct the HTML for our control. The `updateView` method runs when any of the control properties change, and we can use this to update the display of our control. We add code to the `getOutputs` method to set the return values of output properties. Finally, we use the `destroy` method to perform cleanup tasks when the control unloads.

To deploy a control, we build a project solution and add a reference to our control project. The output from the build process is a zip file. In our target environment, we can import this zip file through the Solutions section of the Maker Portal. Next, it's necessary to configure the settings of the environment to allow PCF components.

To use our component in the canvas app, we import the component into the app. The component then appears in the insert panel, and we can use this to add the component to a screen. For a model-driven app, we modify the form that we want to use with the classic designer, and we associate the target field with our custom control.

PART VII

Offline and Integration

CHAPTER 23

Working Offline

Power Apps is designed to work well on mobile devices, but there are times when devices lose connectivity with the Internet. The ability for users to continue working during these times can be extremely useful. This is especially true for field service workers, users that work outside regularly, or users that travel often.

To cater for these scenarios, Power Apps offers the ability to cache data on the local device. We can use this feature to build apps that can work offline. Power Apps provides good support for offline model-driven apps. For canvas apps, however, building an app that works completely offline is a manual task; and it introduces a very difficult challenge – how to synchronize data and to resolve conflicts.

If an offline user modifies a record that another user modifies during an offline session, who wins? Can we merge changes from two users together? And how do we cope with situations where an online user deletes the record that an offline user modifies? In this chapter, we'll focus mainly on how to resolve these issues for canvas apps. The specific topics that we'll cover in this chapter will include

- What happens when a device becomes offline? We'll examine how standard canvas apps and model-driven apps behave when they become offline.

- How to view data offline. For canvas apps, we'll look at how to cache data to the local device and how to detect offline conditions. When an app becomes offline, we'll find out how to display the cached data.

- How to add and update records while offline. We'll develop a system to allow the offline update of data in a canvas app. We'll find out how to build a conflict resolution screen. When conflicts occur, users will be able to use this screen to keep the offline record or to revert to the most recent server version of the record.

© Tim Leung 2021
T. Leung, *Beginning Power Apps*, https://doi.org/10.1007/978-1-4842-6683-0_23

What Happens Offline?

To begin, let's examine what happens on the mobile player when a device becomes disconnected from the Internet. In the case of an auto-generated canvas app that becomes offline midway through a session, the app will continue to be mostly functional. The browse screen will continue to show the data that existed before the app became offline, and the search and sort buttons on this screen will continue to work. Individual records will still open in the display screen, and we can even open records in the edit screen to view the data.

As we would expect, the refresh button on the browse screen will not work. Also, the save button on the edit screen will not work because both these actions require an active Internet connection. In cases where Power Apps fails to carry out an action due to a lack of connectivity, it displays an error message like the one that's shown in Figure 23-1.

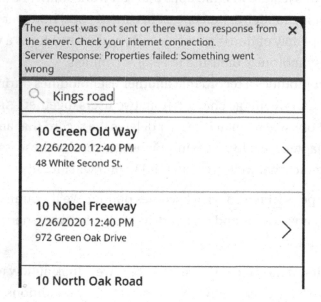

Figure 23-1. *The error that occurs when we attempt to search for a record while offline*

In cases where a user starts Power Apps while disconnected from the Internet, the user can only run apps that have previously run on the device. When an app loads while offline, it can't retrieve an initial set of data from the data source and therefore won't show any data.

How about model-driven apps – how do they behave while offline? Until recently, model-driven apps provided limited offline capabilities that extended to a range of standard Dynamics 365 entities only. The great news is that model-driven apps now work offline against custom tables. It is a built-in feature; and unlike canvas apps, we can provide offline support without needing to write any complex, custom formulas.

Note   A simple way to test how an app behaves offline is to run our app on a mobile device and to enable "airplane mode."

Canvas Formulas That Enable Offline Working

To build canvas apps that can work offline, there are two key features that can help us: the connection signal and the SaveData and LoadData functions.

We can use the connection signal to detect the connection status of an app. Table 23-1 highlights how to use this signal.

Table 23-1. *The connection signal*

Formula	Result
Connection.Connected	True when the device is connected to a network.
Connection.Metered	True when a device is connected to a metered network.

This signal can detect whether the active connection is a metered connection. The cellular connection is usually configured as a metered connection on smartphones. The ability to detect a metered connection is useful because we can adapt our app to use less data when the device is connected to a metered connection. For instance, we can write a formula to hide images in this scenario.

Saving and Retrieving Local Data

A key feature that enables us to build offline apps is the ability to store collections of data into a private area on the local device. The functions to save and retrieve local data are called SaveData and LoadData, respectively.

The SaveData function expects two parameters – a collection of data to save and a file name. Here's an example of how to store the data from a collection called colProperties into a file called OfflinePropertiesFile:

```
SaveData(colProperties, "OfflinePropertiesFile")
```

The SaveData function stores and encrypts the data in an area that is isolated from other users and other apps. If a file already exists with the same name, SaveData will overwrite the existing file. To retrieve the file data, we would call the LoadData function like so:

```
LoadData(colProperties, "OfflinePropertiesFile", true)
```

The first parameter specifies the target collection for the data, and the second parameter specifies the file name from which to retrieve the data. The third parameter configures the LoadData function to continue without error if the file doesn't exist.

We can only call LoadData to retrieve the data that we saved with SaveData from the same app. It's not possible to load data from other apps.

Note that the SaveData and LoadData functions do not work on apps that run in the browser and are also not available in the designer. Because of this, the designer indicates errors in the formula bar when we call these functions, but these are errors that we can ignore.

Making a Canvas App Available Offline

We'll now walk through the process to adapt an auto-generated app so that it works offline. Our app will be based on a Dataverse data source, but in practice, we can adapt the methodology so that it works against a different data source. The modification we'll apply will enable users to view, update, and add records while offline. We'll base this example on our property table. Figure 23-2 shows an overview of how this process will work.

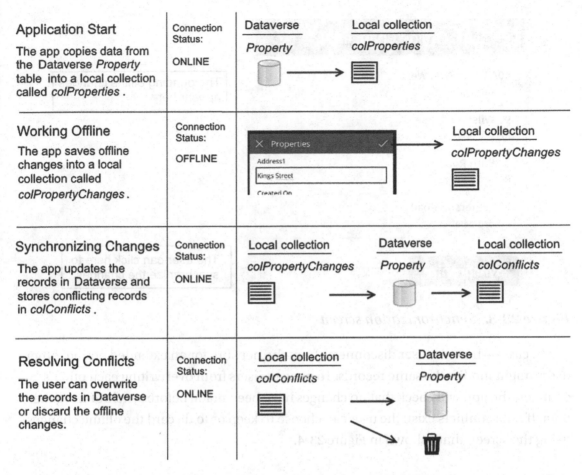

Figure 23-2. *Overview of how to adapt an app to work offline*

When the app starts, it loads data from Dataverse into a local collection. We'll adapt all the screens in the app to work against this local collection rather than directly against the property table. When a user edits or adds a new record, the app will save any changes to the underlying table if the device is online. If the device is offline, the app saves the changes to a holding collection (`colProperties`, in our example).

During any data refresh or update operation, the app will cache the changes to the local device by calling the `SaveData` method. If the device is offline when the app starts, it attempts to load the data from the local file rather than Dataverse.

The app will include a screen that shows the records in the holding collection, as shown in Figure 23-3. When the device becomes online, the user can use this screen to synchronize the changes to Dataverse.

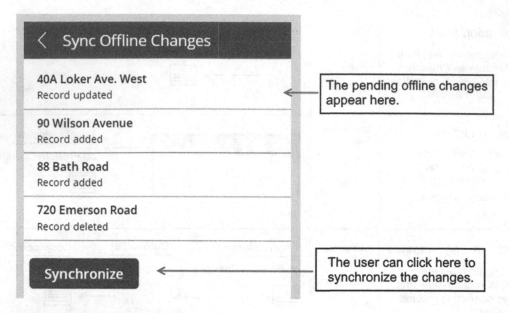

Figure 23-3. *Synchronization screen*

In cases where the user disconnects from the network for an extended period, other users might modify the same records. To prevent users from overwriting each other's changes, the app will check that no changes have been made before synchronizing the data. If data conflicts exist, the user can choose to keep or to discard the offline changes using the screen that's shown in Figure 23-4.

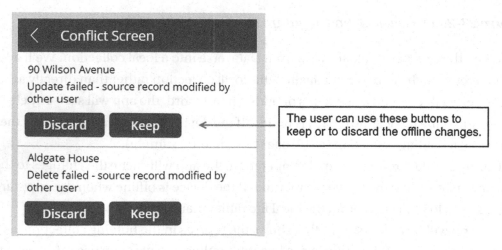

Figure 23-4. *The user can choose to keep or discard changes*

The prerequisite for this example is to build an auto-generated app that's based on the property table (Figure 23-5). The two important fields that our app relies on are the PropertyID and the 'Modified On' fields.

The PropertyID field is a custom autonumber field that uniquely identifies each record in the table. The 'Modified On' field is a standard field that Dataverse populates with the date and time of the last modification.

All Dataverse tables include a built-in ID field of data type "unique identifier" (otherwise known as GUID). A question we may therefore ask is – why not use this built-in GUID field, rather than create a custom autonumber field? The reason is because we cannot look up records in a delegable way based on GUID fields. By relying on a primary key field of data type GUID, we cannot reliably retrieve the source record in cases where we want to synchronize an offline change, if the Dataverse table were to exceed 2,000 rows.

Note that according to the documentation, calling the LookUp function with a condition that references a GUID field should resolve in a delegable query. In practice, however, this is not the case; and blue errors will appear in the formula bar when we attempt to use this syntax.

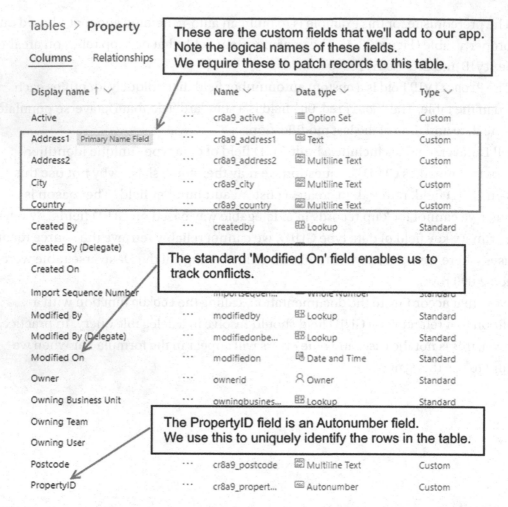

Figure 23-5. *The Dataverse property table*

To keep this example simple, we won't include any lookup data. To make lookup data available offline, we would need to extend our app to load the lookup data in a local collection.

Finally, it's important to appreciate that building an offline app is a highly customized process. Therefore, the main purpose of this example is to provide an insight into the challenges that exist and to provide the broad structure that we can apply to build offline apps.

Setting the Data Source to a Local Collection

When our app loads, the main task is to load the source data from the Dataverse table to a local collection, in addition to several other data initialization tasks. Listing 23-1 shows the code that we add to the OnStart property of our app.

Listing 23-1. Loading the data to a local collection

```
//1 Initialize collections that we use in the app
ClearCollect(colPropertyChanges,Blank());

//2 Main startup logic
If(Connection.Connected,
   ClearCollect(colProperties, Properties),
   LoadData(colProperties, " OfflinePropertiesFile", true)
);

UpdateIf(colProperties, IsBlank(Address1), {Address1:""});
UpdateIf(colProperties, IsBlank(Address2), {Address2:""});
UpdateIf(colProperties, IsBlank(City), {City:""});
UpdateIf(colProperties, IsBlank(Postcode), {Postcode:""});
UpdateIf(colProperties, IsBlank(Telephone), {Telephone:""});

SaveData(colProperties, "OfflinePropertiesFile");
LoadData(colPropertyChanges, "OfflinePropertyChangesFile", true)
```

In the initial part of this formula, we can optionally initialize the collections we use in our app. The first line in this formula initializes the colPropertyChanges collection and sets the value of this collection to blank. The purpose of this is to prime the designer so that it recognizes the collection and to prevent it from marking the collection with a red error when we refer to it later through the LoadData function.

The main part of this formula checks if the device is connected to the Internet. If so, it copies the data from the Dataverse table (called Properties) to the local collection, colProperties. If the device is offline, it retrieves the saved data from the file on the device and copies that data to the local collection.

The next section of code calls the UpdateIf function to replace with an empty string all null instances of the fields that we want to use in our app. The purpose of this is to fix a bug that affects edit forms that bind to local collections with null values. A card on a form will not update the value of a field in a local collection if the original value is null. Therefore, we work around this problem by initially replacing all null values with empty strings.

The next section in the formula caches the data to a local file by calling the SaveData function. This provides the app with data if a user subsequently starts the app later while offline. Next, the formula calls the LoadData function to load any unsynchronized data modifications that may have taken place during a previous offline session.

The next step is to reconfigure all the screens in the app to use the colProperties collection. On the basis that our source Dataverse table is called Properties, the step is to rename all references of the Properties data source to colProperties. The places in the app to modify are

- BrowseScreen1 ➤ BrowseGallery1 ➤ Items

- DetailsScreen1 ➤ DetailForm1 ➤ DataSource

- EditScreen1 ➤ EditForm1 ➤ DataSource

Finally, we need to modify the refresh icon on the browse screen so that it saves the data to the offline file after a refresh. Listing 23-2 shows the formula.

Listing 23-2. Refreshing the data

```
If(Connection.Connected,
   Refresh(Properties);
   UpdateIf(colProperties, IsBlank(Address1), {Address1:""});
   UpdateIf(colProperties, IsBlank(Address2), {Address2:""});
   UpdateIf(colProperties, IsBlank(City), {City:""});
   UpdateIf(colProperties, IsBlank(Postcode), {Postcode:""});
   UpdateIf(colProperties, IsBlank(Telephone), {Telephone:""});
   SaveData(colProperties, "OfflinePropertiesFile")
)
```

Caution   For forms that use a collection as a data source, a card will not update the field if the original field value is null. We must replace null values in the source collection with an empty string. Many app builders only discover this problem following hours of painful diagnosis into why a form isn't updating certain, random fields.

Handling Offline Deletions

For an app to be fully functional offline, it should handle the offline deletion of data. The display screen includes a delete icon, and Listing 23-3 shows how to adapt the formula in this icon to support the offline deletion of data.

Listing 23-3. Formula to delete records

```
RemoveIf(colProperties, BrowseGallery1.Selected.PropertyID = PropertyID);
If(Connection.Connected,
   RemoveIf(Properties,
            BrowseGallery1.Selected.PropertyID = PropertyID
   ),
   Collect(colPropertyChanges, {Record:BrowseGallery1.Selected, Status:"D",
   OfflineID:BrowseGallery1.Selected.PropertyID});
   SaveData(colPropertyChanges, "OfflinePropertyChangesFile")
);
Back()
```

The first line in this formula removes the record form the colProperties collection. If the device is connected to the Internet, it also removes the record from the main Properties data source.

If the device is offline, the formula stores the data in the colPropertyChanges collection. This collection keeps track of all offline changes, and Figure 23-6 shows the layout of this collection. The Status field indicates the type of modification that has taken place. The values we use are "D" for a deleted record, "A" for a new record, and "U" for an updated record. The OfflineID field stores the PropertyID of the record that is associated with the modification.

The next section in the formula calls the SaveData function to save the data to the offline file. This enables the app to retain the data modifications if a user quits an offline session and starts another offline session.

colPropertyChanges

Here's a preview of the first 5 items in this collection
Learn about working with collections

OfflineID	Record	Status
4		U
-1		A
-2		A
2		D

Figure 23-6. *The colPropertyChanges data collection stores offline changes*

Deleting Records from Local Collections

To clarify the syntax to remove an item from the collection, the most reliable way is to call the RemoveIf function to remove the item by a unique identifier. It's easy to think that we can perform this action with the Remove function using the following formula:

```
Remove(locProperties, BrowseGallery1.Selected)
```

Although the delete icon originally uses this syntax to delete the selected record from Dataverse, it's important to realize that this syntax works only with connected data sources.

With a local collection, the record that we pass to the Remove function must precisely match the record that we want to remove. The Selected property of a gallery also exposes the controls and values in the item template of the gallery. Therefore, this will not provide an exact match with the items in the collection, and the call to the Remove function will fail to remove the desired record.

Handling Offline Record Updates

To provide offline data edit and data entry capabilities, there are several changes that we need to make to the save icon on the edit screen. Figure 23-7 shows a flowchart of the high-level process that we'll build into our formula.

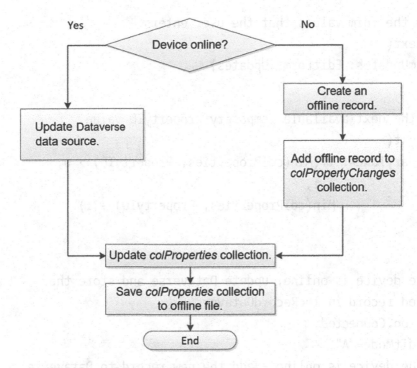

Figure 23-7. *Handling offline record updates*

A key modification is to adapt the edit form to avoid the use of the `SubmitForm` function to save the record to the `colProperties` collection. The reason is so that we can generate a temporary `PropertyID` value when the device is offline. Usually, Dataverse would generate this value, but this would not happen when a device is offline. We need to allocate a temporary `PropertyID` value to allow us to edit or delete records that were created offline. To avoid the possibility of generating duplicate `PropertyID` values, our formula will generate `PropertyID` values that are negative.

Listing 23-4 shows the formula to add to the `OnSelect` property of the save icon.

Listing 23-4. Formula to save a record

```
// 1. Collect values for use later in the formula.
UpdateContext(
    {locEditMode: If(EditForm1.Mode = FormMode.New, "A", "U")}
);
```

```
// 1.1 Get the form values that the user enters.
UpdateContext(
    {locFormUpdates: EditForm1.Updates}
);

//1.2 Get the next available temporary PropertyID value.
UpdateContext(
    {locPrimaryIdNew: If(Min(colProperties, PropertyID) > 0,
                    -1,
                 Min(colProperties, PropertyID) - 1)
    }
);

//2. If the device is online, update Dataverse and store the
//    updated record in locRecordDataverse.
If(Connection.Connected,
    If(locEditMode="A",
        // The device is online - add the new record to Dataverse
        UpdateContext(
            {locRecordDataverse:Patch(Properties,
                            Defaults(Properties),
                            locFormUpdates)
            }
        ),
        // The device is online - update the existing record in Dataverse
        UpdateContext(
            {locRecordDataverse:Patch(Properties,
                        LookUp(Properties,
                            PropertyID = BrowseGallery1.Selected.
                            PropertyID),
                        locFormUpdates)
            }
        )
    )
    ,
```

```
//2 The device is offline - we build a record that we can patch to
//    colProperties. The fields in this record match the logical field names
//    of the table. Note the use of the With function, to shortcut access
//    to the fields in the locFormUpdates variable.

With(locFormUpdates,
If(locEditMode="A",
    // The device is offline and the user is adding a new record
    // - build an offline record with a temporary negative PropertyID.
    // - note that Dataverse autonumber fields are text, so we need to covert
    // - locPrimaryIdNew to text

    UpdateContext(
        {locRecordOffline:{
                            cr8a9_propertyid: Text(locPrimaryIdNew),
                            cr8a9_address1: Address1,
                            cr8a9_address2: Address2,
                            cr8a9_city: City,
                            cr8a9_country: Country,
                            cr8a9_postcode: Postcode,
                            cr8a9_telephone: Telephone
                            }
        }
    ),
    // The device is offline and the user is editing an existing record
    // - build an offline record with the existing PropertyID and the
    //   existing modifiedon date/time value.
    UpdateContext(
        {locRecordOffline:{
                            cr8a9_propertyid: BrowseGallery1.Selected.PropertyID,
                            cr8a9_address1: locFormUpdates.Address1,
                            cr8a9_address2: locFormUpdates.Address2,
                            cr8a9_city: locFormUpdates.City,
                            cr8a9_country: locFormUpdates.Country,
```

```
                        cr8a9_postcode: locFormUpdates.Postcode,
                        cr8a9_telephone: locFormUpdates.Telephone,
                        modifiedon: BrowseGallery1.Selected.'Modified On'
                        }
            }
        )
    ))
);

//3. Synchronize the update with the colProperties collection.

If(Connection.Connected,
    //  The device is online - we update colProperties with locRecordDataverse.
    //  The locRecordDataverse record contains the server generated PropertyID
    //  and 'modified on' values.
    If(locEditMode="A",
        Patch(colProperties,
            Defaults(colProperties),
            locRecordDataverse
        ),
        Patch(colProperties,
            LookUp(colProperties,
                BrowseGallery1.Selected.PropertyID = PropertyID),
            locRecordDataverse
        )
    ),
    //  The device is offline - we update colProperties with
    //    locRecordOffline.
    If(locEditMode="A",
        Patch(colProperties,
            Defaults(colProperties),
            locRecordOffline
        ),
      Patch(colProperties,
            LookUp(colProperties,
                BrowseGallery1.Selected.PropertyID = PropertyID),
```

```
        locRecordOffline
    )
);

//4. The device is offline - store the modified offline record in
//  colPropertyChanges.

// Get the PropertyID of the updated record
UpdateContext(
    {locOfflineID: locRecordOffline.cr8a9_propertyid}
);

// If the user edits a record that was created offline,
// remove and re-add the record.
RemoveIf(colPropertyChanges, OfflineID = locOfflineID);

If(Value(PropertyRecordOffline.cr8a9_propertyid) < 0,
    // Add new offline record to colPropertyChanges.
    Collect(colPropertyChanges,
            {Record: locRecordOffline,Status:"A", OfflineID:locOfflineID})
    ,
    // Add updated offline record to colPropertyChanges.
    Collect(colPropertyChanges,
            {Record: locRecordOffline,Status:"U",
            OfflineID:locOfflineID})
    )
);
//5. Save the updated data to the offline file
SaveData(colPropertyChanges, "OfflinePropertyChangesFile");
Back()
```

The first section of the formula stores whether the user is adding or editing a record into a variable called locEditMode. Through the Updates property of the form, the next line retrieves the updated form values to a variable called locFormUpdates. The next line retrieves the next available negative PropertyID value and stores this in a variable called locPrimaryIdNew. This is required in the case where a user adds a new record while offline.

If the app is online, the next section of the formula calls the Patch function to create or to update the existing record in Dataverse. The Patch function returns the Dataverse record that was added or updated. In the case of a new record, the result from the Patch function will include the server-generated PropertyID value. We retain this record in a variable called locRecordDataverse so that we can update the local colProperties collection later.

If the device is offline, the code builds a record called locRecordOffline that we can patch into the colProperties collection. The field names in the locRecordOffline record match the logical field names in our property table. This enables us to patch the offline record back to the live data source at the synchronization stage, when the device comes online again.

The next section of the formula updates the colProperties collection with the locRecordDataverse or the locRecordOffline record.

If the device is offline, the next part of the formula adds the offline record to the colPropertyChanges collection. The final part of the formula calls the SaveData function to persist the changes to the offline file.

Merging Records

The formula that builds the locRecordOffline record (when the device is disconnected) effectively merges a source record with the updates that a user enters through the edit form. It might seem a good idea to call the Patch function to merge the two records using syntax like this:

```
Patch(BrowseGallery1.Selected, EditForm1.Updates)
```

In practice, this technique isn't reliable, and it's better to merge records with the more verbose syntax that we used. That is, to build the record with the UpdateContext function and to explicitly define the source values for each field. We can read more about the problems of merging records with the Patch function here:

```
https://powerusers.microsoft.com/t5/PowerApps-Forum/
Bug-report-Patch-function-not-working-as-expected-when-merging/m-p/29156
```

Using the With Function to Improve Code Readability

To improve the readability of formulas, we can utilize the function called With. This function accepts two arguments – an input record and a formula. From within the formula that we specify, we can access the fields of the record without needing to fully qualify field names with the name of the record. This provides a way to simplify formulas that refer to field values.

To demonstrate, the section of formula in the following illustrates an ideal place where we can apply this technique:

```
// The device is offline and the user is editing an existing record
// - build an offline record with the existing PropertyID and the
//   existing modifiedon date/time value.
UpdateContext(
    {locRecordOffline:{
                cr8a9_propertyid: BrowseGallery1.Selected.PropertyID,
                cr8a9_address1: locFormUpdates.Address1,
                cr8a9_address2: locFormUpdates.Address2,
                cr8a9_city: locFormUpdates.City,
                cr8a9_country: locFormUpdates.Country,
                cr8a9_postcode: locFormUpdates.Postcode,
                cr8a9_telephone: locFormUpdates.Telephone,
                modifiedon: BrowseGallery1.Selected.'Modified On'
                }
    }
)
```

Here, the formula refers to the variable locFormUpdates in multiple places. This variable stores the record that corresponds to the updates that the user made in EditForm1. We can express this same logic more simply by using the With statement as shown in the following:

```
With(locFormUpdates,
    UpdateContext(
        {locRecordOffline:{
                cr8a9_propertyid: BrowseGallery1.Selected.PropertyID,
                cr8a9_address1: Address1,
```

```
                    cr8a9_address2: Address2,
                    cr8a9_city: City,
                    cr8a9_country: Country,
                    cr8a9_postcode: Postcode,
                    cr8a9_telephone: Telephone,
                    modifiedon: BrowseGallery1.Selected.'Modified On'
                }
            }
        )
    )
```

Building the Synchronization Screen

The next stage is to build the synchronization screen. This screen shows a list of offline changes and includes a synchronization button. Figure 23-8 illustrates how the logic in this button handles the offline synchronization task.

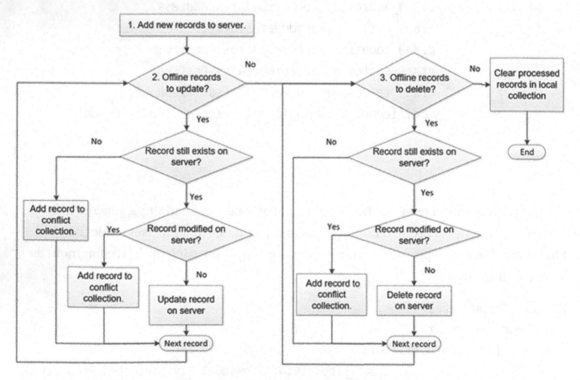

Figure 23-8. *Flowchart of the synchronization feature*

The first step to build this feature is to add a new screen. Next, add a gallery control and set the Items property to the colProperties collection. To display a field from the offline record, we can use the syntax ThisItem.Record.<Fieldname>, as shown in Figure 23-9.

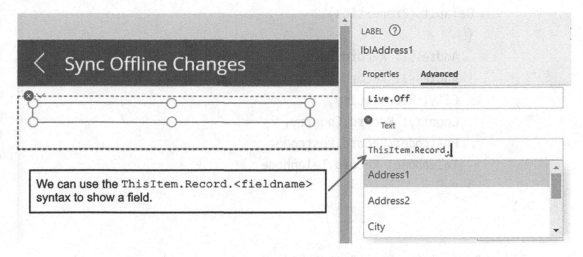

Figure 23-9. Appearance of the synchronization screen

From within a label in the gallery template, we can also provide a user-friendly description of the change status using the following syntax:

```
Switch(ThisItem.Status,
        "A","Record added",
        "U","Record updated",
        "D","Record deleted"
)
```

Beneath the gallery control, we can now add a button that synchronizes the data. Set the OnSelect property of the button to the formula that's shown in Listing 23-5. This formula carries out the process that's shown in the flowchart at the start of this section (Figure 23-7). There are three logical parts to this formula which consist of code to add the new records, code to synchronize the updated records, and code to synchronize the deleted records.

Listing 23-5. Synchronizing the records

```
//1. Save the records that were added
ForAll(Filter(colPropertyChanges, Status="A"),
      Patch(Properties,
            Defaults(Properties),
            {
                Address1: Record.Address1,
                Address2: Record.Address2,
                City: Record.City,
                Country: Record.Country,
                Postcode: Record.Postcode,
                Telephone: Record.Telephone
            }
      )
);

RemoveIf(colPropertyChanges, Status="A");

Clear(colChangeReview);
Clear(colConflicts);

//2. Refresh the Dataverse data source. For records updated offline, retrieve
//   the corresponding current record.
Refresh(Properties);
ForAll(Filter(colPropertyChanges, Status="U"),
      Collect(colChangeReview,
            {OfflineRecord:Record,
             CurrentRecord:LookUp(Properties, PropertyID = OfflineID)
            }
      )
);

//3. If the source record is not found, add the record to the
//   conflict collection.
If(CountRows(Filter(colChangeReview,IsEmpty(CurrentRecord))) > 0,
   Collect(colConflicts,
           AddColumns(Filter(colChangeReview,IsEmpty(CurrentRecord)),
```

```
                        "Status",
                        "Update failed - source record deleted"
            )
    )
);
RemoveIf(colChangeReview, IsEmpty(CurrentRecord));

//4. Process the records that have not been modified on the server
ForAll(Filter(colChangeReview,
            CurrentRecord.'Modified On'=
                        OfflineRecord.'Modified On'),
    Patch(Properties,
        CurrentRecord,
        {
                Address1: OfflineRecord.Address1,
                Address2: OfflineRecord.Address2,
                City: OfflineRecord.City,
                Country: OfflineRecord.Country,
                Postcode: OfflineRecord.Postcode,
                Telephone: OfflineRecord.Telephone

        }
    )
);
RemoveIf(
    colChangeReview,
    CurrentRecord.'Modified On'=OfflineRecord.'Modified On'
);
//5. The remaining rows in colChangeReview are conflicting records
If(CountRows(colChangeReview) > 0,
    Collect(colConflicts,
            AddColumns(colChangeReview,
                        "Status",
                        "Update failed - source record modified by other user"
            )
    )
);
```

773

```
//6. Collect the records that were deleted offline into colChangeReview
ForAll(Filter(colPropertyChanges, Status="D"),
       Collect(colChangeReview,
               {OfflineRecord:Record,
                CurrentRecord:LookUp(Properties, PropertyID = OfflineID)
               }
       )
);

//7. Remove records that have also been deleted on the server
RemoveIf(colChangeReview, IsEmpty(CurrentRecord));

//8. Process the records that were deleted offline
ForAll(Filter(colChangeReview,
              CurrentRecord.'Modified On'=
                   OfflineRecord.'Modified On'),
      Remove(Properties, CurrentRecord)
);
RemoveIf(colChangeReview,
           CurrentRecord.'Modified On'=
              OfflineRecord.'Modified On'
);

//9. The remaining rows in colChangeReview are conflicting records
If(CountRows(colChangeReview) > 0,
   Collect(colConflicts,
           AddColumns(colChangeReview,
                   "Status",
                   "Delete failed - source record modified by other user"
           )
   )
);

Clear(colPropertyChanges);

//9. Update the offline file
SaveData(colPropertyChanges, "OfflinePropertyChangesFile");
```

```
//10. Build a message that we can show to the user
If(CountRows(colConflicts) > 0,
   UpdateContext(
     {ConflictMessage:
        Text(CountRows(colConflicts)) & " conflicting record(s)"}
   ),
   UpdateContext(
     {ConflictMessage: ""}
   )
);
```

This formula works by processing the offline data modifications from the colPropertyChanges collection. When all the records have been processed, this collection will be empty.

As the formula processes the records, it stores working copies in a collection called colChangeReview. For each record that was modified offline, the process retrieves the up-to-date record and stores the result in the colChangeReview collection. Figure 23-10 shows the schema of this collection.

Figure 23-10.   *The colChangeReview collection*

If the process cannot locate an up-to-date record, this indicates that the source record was deleted. If the up-to-date record shows a different last modified datetime, this indicates that the source record was modified by another user. In both these cases, the formula stores the conflicting records in a collection called colConflicts. Figure 23-11 shows the schema of this collection

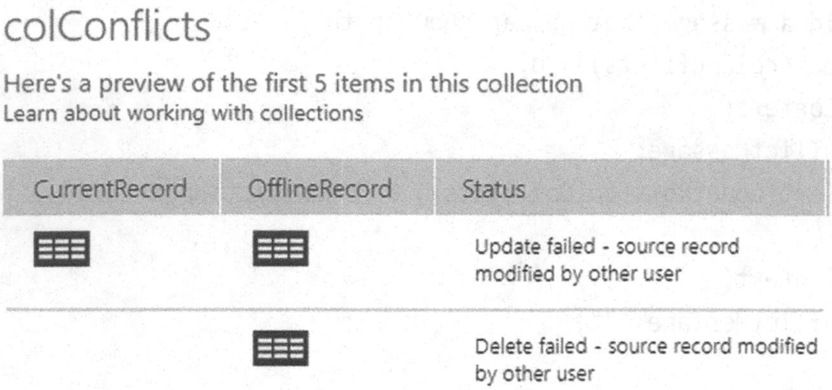

colConflicts

Here's a preview of the first 5 items in this collection
Learn about working with collections

CurrentRecord	OfflineRecord	Status
⊞	⊞	Update failed - source record modified by other user
	⊞	Delete failed - source record modified by other user

Figure 23-11. *The* `colConflicts` *collection*

During this process, the formula will add the new records to the data source and update the records that are not in a conflicting state. At the end of this process, we'll be left with only the records in the `colConflicts` collection.

To complete this feature, we can add an icon on the browse screen to navigate to our synchronization screen, as shown in Figure 23-12.

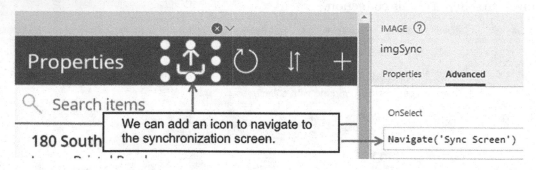

Figure 23-12. *Opening the synchronization screen*

Disabling Icons and Buttons

With all the controls that are associated with the synchronization process, we can disable a control based on the state of the app. As we saw earlier in this book, the `DisplayMode` property provides the means to disable a control. This can take one of three values: Disabled, Edit, or View. The main difference between the View and Disabled modes is that in View mode, the control will be disabled but visually appear as though it's not disabled.

In our example, we can use the following formula to disable the synchronization button when the device is offline:

```
If(Connection.Connected,
    DisplayMode.Edit,
    DisplayMode.Disabled
)
```

Figure 23-13 shows how this appears in the designer.

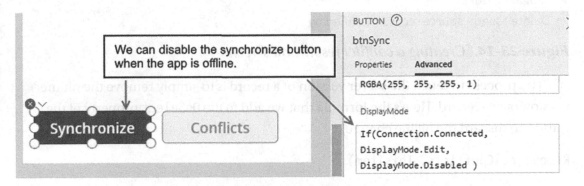

Figure 23-13. *The* DisplayMode *property of a control*

Building the Conflict Resolution Screen

If the synchronization process returns records that are in a conflicted state, we can provide a means for users to resolve these data conflicts. This will allow users to retain the offline change or to revert to the most recent server version of the record. To build this feature, the first step is to create a screen, add a gallery control, and set the Items property to colConflicts. We can configure the gallery control to show the fields that we desire using the syntax OfflineRecord.<Fieldname>.

The next step is to add the buttons that the users can click to retain or discard the offline changes. Add two buttons to item template of the gallery control, as shown in Figure 23-14.

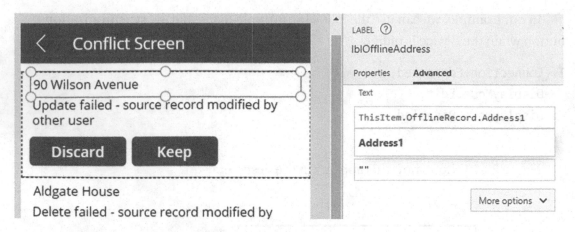

Figure 23-14. *Creating a conflict resolution screen*

The process to retain the server version of a record is to simply remove the offline version of the record. Here's the formula that we add to the OnSelect property of the button to discard the offline change:

```
Remove(colConflicts, ThisItem)
```

To retain the offline version of the record, we would patch the offline record to the data source. Here's the formula to add to the OnSelect property of the button to retain the offline version:

```
Patch(Properties,
    ThisItem.CurrentRecord,
    {
        Address1: ThisItem.OfflineRecord.Address1,
        Address2: ThisItem.OfflineRecord.Address2,
        City: ThisItem.OfflineRecord.City,
        Country: ThisItem.OfflineRecord.Country,
        Postcode: ThisItem.OfflineRecord.Postcode,
        Telephone: ThisItem.OfflineRecord.Telephone
    }
);
Remove(colConflicts, ThisItem)
```

Finally, to enable users to open the conflict resolution screen, we can provide a button on the synchronization screen as shown in Figure 23-15. As this screenshot shows, we can write a formula to disable or hide this button if there are no conflicting records.

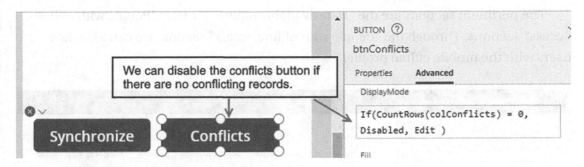

Figure 23-15.   Opening the conflict screen

Making Model-Driven Apps Available Offline

In the final part of this chapter, we'll walk through the steps to set up an offline-capable model-driven app. The great news is that compared to canvas apps, the process is much simpler and doesn't involve any complicated formulas.

To demonstrate, we'll walk through the process of how to make available offline a model-driven app that is based on our Dataverse property table.

Setting Up a Mobile Profile

To enable offline working, the key step is to create a mobile offline profile. A mobile offline profile applies to a set of users, and it defines the tables and the records that are available offline. We define these profiles at an environment level.

When a user runs an offline-capable app, Power Apps creates a local cache of data on the mobile device. It keeps this cache up to date by synchronizing the data on a schedule, which we can configure at a table level. If the device becomes disconnected from the Internet, the app continues to work against the cached data. When the network connection resumes, Power Apps synchronizes any changes that were made by the user while offline.

To configure an app for offline access, we must first enable all the tables that we want to make available offline. To do this, we open the settings of each table from the Maker Portal. From here, we check the "Enable for mobile offline" checkbox to enable offline access.

At this point, we can create a mobile offline profile. To do this, we open the settings for the target environment from the Power Platform admin center. From beneath the "Users + permissions" group, we select the Mobile Configuration menu item. From this page, we choose the option to create a new offline profile. In our example, we'll create an offline profile called "Property App Profile." Figure 23-16 shows the design view of our new profile.

The pertinent sections are the "Data available offline" and the "People with offline access" sections. Through the "People with offline access" section, we can associate users with the mobile offline profile.

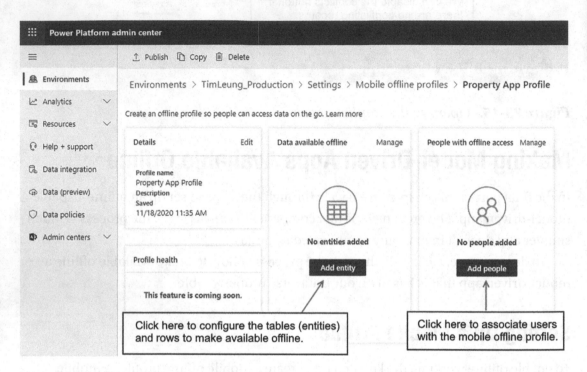

Figure 23-16. *Creating an offline profile*

From the "Data available offline" section, we select the tables and records that we want to make available offline. The "Add entity" button displays a list of all tables that are enabled for offline access. Once we select a table, we can select the records that we want to make available offline, as shown in Figure 23-17.

We can choose to make all records available offline. This works best on smaller tables with fewer rows. For best performance, it's best to only make a subset of records available offline.

The "Organization records" radio button reveals three checkboxes. We can use these to make available offline records that are owned by user, records that are owned by the user's team, or records that are owned by the user's business unit.

The custom radio button provides the most powerful way to configure the records that are available offline. This option presents a designer that enables us to build a filter based on the columns in the table. As an example, we could create a filter that makes available offline only those records that were created within a certain time period.

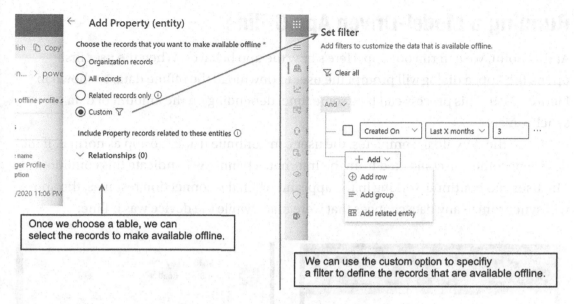

Figure 23-17. *Defining the records that are available offline*

The final step is to configure our app to work offline. To do this, we open the properties pane of our app, check the "Enable for mobile offline" checkbox, and choose the mobile offline profiles to associate with the app, as shown in Figure 23-18.

We would create and assign multiple mobile offline profiles if we want to amend the quantity of offline data that is available to different sets of users.

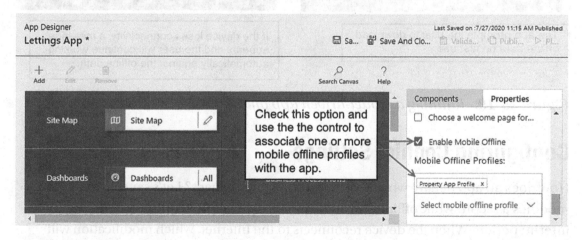

Figure 23-18. *Enabling a model-driven app for offline use*

Running a Model-Driven App Offline

At this point, we can run our app. Here's how the app behaves. When the user first opens the app, a dialog will prompt the user to download the offline data, as shown in Figure 23-19. This process can take some time, depending on the amount of data to synchronize.

Once the download completes, the user can continue using the app as normal. If the device becomes disconnected from the Internet, a banner will indicate this condition. The user can continue working in the app, and when the connection resumes, the app will synchronize any data changes that were made while the device was offline.

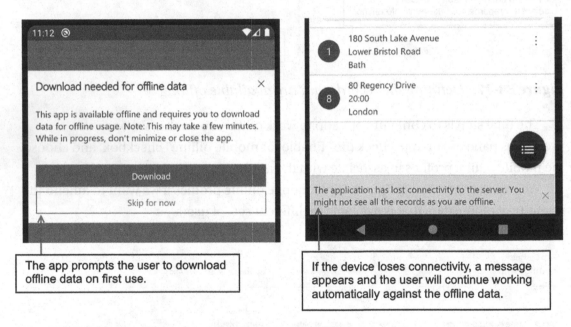

Figure 23-19. *Running a model-driven app offline*

Configuring Conflict Settings

How does an app behave when there are conflicting changes? Let's say that a user modifies a record while offline and another user changes the same record during this interim period. When the device reconnects to the Internet, which modification will apply?

By default, when an offline device reconnects, it will overwrite any changes that were made by other users during the offline period.

If we're not happy with this behavior, we can change this through the Dynamics 365 settings area. To reach this area, we open the settings for the target environment from the Power Platform admin center. Beneath the Resources group, we click the "All legacy settings" link to open the Dynamics 365 settings page. From the menu header, we click the Settings ➤ Mobile Offline item (this appears beneath the Business group). We then click the "Mobile Offline Settings" link to open the page that's shown in Figure 23-20.

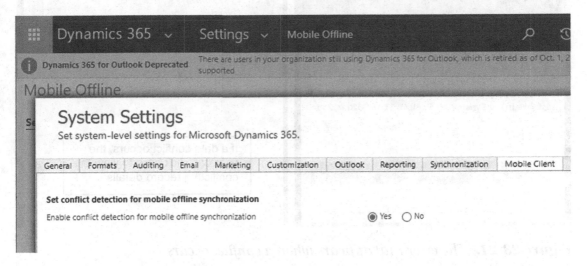

Figure 23-20. *Configuring conflict detection settings*

This offers a simple way to control conflict management. We can configure the mobile offline changes to always win or the server changes to always win. The "Enable conflict detection for mobile offline synchronization" setting controls this behavior through a yes/no radio button. Here's how an app would behave with these options:

- No – This is the default setting. When an offline device reconnects, it overwrites any changes that were made by other users.

- Yes – When set to yes, the mobile app rejects any conflicting changes when the device reconnects.

To illustrate what happens when "Enable conflict detection for mobile offline synchronization" is set to yes, Figure 23-21 highlights the error message that appears when an offline device reconnects and attempts to synchronize a conflicting change. The app rejects the offline change, and the user can drill into the details of the failure by clicking the "Show Details" button.

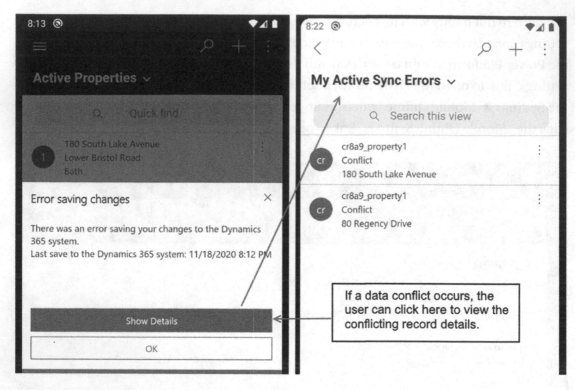

Figure 23-21. *The error that appears when a conflict occurs*

Summary

In this chapter, we examined what happens when an app becomes offline, and we walked through the steps to build a canvas app that works offline.

When an auto-generated canvas app becomes offline, the browse screen continues to show the data that existed before the app became offline. Not surprisingly, the refresh and save functions will not work. When disconnected from the Internet, users can start apps that they have run previously. However, an auto-generated app that starts offline will not show any data. Power Apps does not automatically retain app data for future offline sessions.

To cater for these offline scenarios, Power Apps provides two useful features that can help. First, it provides the ability to save and retrieve data from files on the local device. Second, it can detect whether the device is connected to the Internet, and it can also detect if the connection is a metered connection.

To build an app that can edit, create, and delete records while offline, the general technique is to call a function called SaveData to cache the data to a local file. If a user starts an app while offline, we can call a function called LoadData to load the contents of the local file into the app.

To support offline data modifications, we can save the offline data changes to a local collection and call the SaveData function to store the changes in a local file. When the app becomes online again, we can patch the offline changes to the data store.

Building offline editing capabilities in canvas apps is not a trivial task. The main difficulty is that other users can modify or delete source records during an offline session. During the data synchronization process, we need to check for conflicting records; and ideally, we provide some method for the user to resolve the conflict.

To convert an auto-generated app to work offline, we change the data source of all the data controls in the app to refer to a local collection. This includes the gallery control and the edit and display forms.

When the app starts, we populate the local collection with the data from the live data source. When a user modifies a record, we update both the live record and the record in the local collection. If the user is offline, we cannot update the live record, and we therefore save the update to a separate collection instead. This "change" collection stores all offline modifications. In the case where a user adds a record while offline, we allocate a negative primary key ID. This allows us to uniquely identify the record in the event that the user chooses to edit or to delete a record that was created offline. By allocating a negative ID, the value will not conflict with any existing primary key values.

When the app comes online again, the user can review and can synchronize the changes that were made offline. The synchronization process adds all new records that were created offline. With records that were modified offline, the process detects data conflicts by examining the last modified time of the source record. In the event of a data conflict, we can move the offending record to a conflict collection. At the end of the synchronization process, the user can review the conflicting records and choose whether to apply or to discard the offline changes.

The good news is that it's much easier to build offline-capable model-driven apps. Power Apps offers built-in support for this. To configure an app to work offline, the first step is to check the "Enable for mobile offline" checkbox through the settings of the source tables that we want to make available offline. The next step is to create a mobile offline profile. A mobile offline profile defines the tables and rows that are available to a given set of users while offline. This is important because it controls the amount of data that Power Apps copies onto the device. Performance would be slow if we were to configure a mobile offline profile to synchronize all records from a very large source table. We can limit the rows that are available offline by building a filter through a graphical designer. This enables us, for example, to limit the available offline records by the record owner or by date. The final step is to enable offline operation through the settings of the model-driven app and to specify the mobile device profiles that apply to the app.

When a user runs the model-driven app for the first time, it downloads the data for offline use. If the device becomes disconnected from the Internet, the app automatically continues to operate using the offline data. When the device reconnects, it synchronizes any changes that were made while offline. By default, the offline change would apply if another user were to modify the same record. We can change this behavior through the Dynamics 365 settings area.

CHAPTER 24

Creating Custom Data Connectors

With canvas apps, we can connect to a wide range of data sources through standard and premium data connectors. But what if we want to access data sources that are not natively supported – is this possible? The answer is yes. By building a custom data connector, we can connect to any data source that is accessible through a web service. And if our required data source doesn't include a web service interface, we can overcome this by building our own web service (although this falls outside the scope of this book).

For non-developers, however, this topic can be complex and involves plenty of jargon words such as RESTful services, JSON, and Swagger. To provide a simple example of this topic, we'll walk step-by-step through a practical example of how to call a postcode lookup service. The purpose of our exercise is to provide a method for users to enter data more quickly and easily. By the end of this chapter, we'll understand the process to call other web services and to add additional value to our apps. The key features that we'll cover in this chapter will include

- What we can accomplish with web services and how the Web works. We'll examine the technical terms that are related to this topic and look at how web requests and responses work. This will provide useful background knowledge for later parts of this chapter and beyond.

- How to build a custom connector. We'll walk through the steps to build a custom connector. This includes how to create a web service description file and how to register the service with Power Apps.

- How to use a custom connector. This chapter explains the most important task of all – how to call the web service from an app and how to display the results on a screen. We'll also find out how to save these results to a data source by adapting an auto-generated app.

© Tim Leung 2021
T. Leung, *Beginning Power Apps*, https://doi.org/10.1007/978-1-4842-6683-0_24

Overview of Web Services and Custom Connectors

To begin, let's look at what we can achieve through web services and explore what the pros and cons are.

There are thousands of web services that we can call. All modern social media sites provide access features through web services. These include sites such as Twitter, YouTube, Facebook, and many more.

For business purposes, practical uses can include the retrieval of stock prices, currency conversion rates, converting IP addresses to locations, or tracking brand sentiment through social networks. In fact, the list is almost endless. If we have some idea of what we want to achieve, we can probably find a service that fulfills our requirement by searching the Web. If no such service exists, we can write our own web service or find a developer to build a web service for us.

A powerful way to leverage this capability is to use a Microsoft Azure feature called Azure Functions. With Azure Functions, we can write code to carry out tasks using a wide range of languages. These include .NET (C# and F#) and non-Microsoft languages such as Node.js, Python, PHP, and Java. We host only the code function that we write in Microsoft Azure, and there is no need to perform any other infrastructure or server-related tasks. Because end users need not concern themselves with infrastructure tasks, this area of cloud computing is called "serverless computing."

The added benefit of using an Azure function is that the designer can generate an Open API definition for our function. As we find out later in this chapter, this is the most complex area, and the ability to more easily carry out this task is a big benefit. Once we create our Azure function, we can call it using a custom connector.

Another great feature with custom connectors is that we're not just limited to Internet-facing web services. Through the help of the on-premises gateway, we can use custom connectors to access web services that are hosted on servers in intranets or internal networks.

Are there any disadvantages or downsides to custom connectors? One issue to be aware of is that custom connectors fall into the premium connector category. This means that all users would require the more expensive per-user or per-app plans. Another issue is that diagnosing problems can be very difficult. For example, let's imagine the scenario where a custom connector fails to retrieve data. Tracing the cause of such problem can be difficult due to a lack of tools and logging at the custom connector level. Therefore, an alternative method we can consider is to call web services with a Power Automate flow and to use the HTTP connector. The benefit of this approach is that Power Automate maintains the run history that logs all calls, the arguments that the flow receives, and any errors that occur. We cover this topic in Chapter 25.

Overview of Steps

Here's an overview of the steps to call a web service from Power Apps. Once we build a custom connector, we can add it to our app and use it to access our data source, in the same way that we use the other built-in connectors such as SharePoint, Excel, and SQL Server. We can write a formula to call the web service methods and to retrieve data.

The main steps to build a custom connector are as follows:

- Identify or build a web service that we want to connect to.

- Document the web service and produce a contract.

- Define a custom connector through the Maker Portal.

- From within an app, add a data source that's based on the custom connector. .

- Write a formula to call the web service.

The most difficult part of this process is to document the web service and to produce a contract. This contract describes to the custom connector how the web service works and behaves, and it is therefore a crucial step.

To define this contract, there are two formats that we can use: The "Open API" (also known as Swagger) format or the Postman format. To create these files, we would use the Swagger and Postman programs. Both of these are fully fledged API documentation tools that provide a feature set way beyond what we require to create a custom connector.

Swagger is the de facto tool for documenting web services. With Swagger, we use a language called YAML (Yet Another Markup Language) to document a web service. Once this is complete, we save the output in JSON format because this is the format that Power Apps expects.

Because the target output format is JSON, we can avoid the use of Swagger and Postman and build the contract file by manually writing the JSON with a text editor. For beginners, this can be easier because it avoids the need to register for a Swagger account and to learn how to use an additional tool. Later in this chapter, we'll look at Swagger and Postman; but before that, we'll go through some basic web concepts such as HTTP requests, responses, and verbs. This is important because the configuration pages for a custom connector refer to these concepts.

Understanding How the Web Works

For non-developers, some of the terminology can be confusing. The documentation refers to REST, JSON, and other acronyms. Another term we frequently hear is "RESTful API." But what do all these terms mean?

REST stands for Representational State Transfer, and it describes a common characteristic of a modern web service. With REST, every call to a web service must provide all the data that the service needs to fulfill a request. We can provide this data through arguments in the web address or the body or headers of the request.

A purpose of REST is to avoid the storage of session data on a specific server, and in doing so, it avoids the need to restrict the communication between a client and a service to a specific web server. This enables infrastructure teams to more easily load, balance, replace, or scale up a service by adding more servers. When each request contains all the state data, it makes it possible to cache results on any intermediary device between the client and server, and this can help speed up performance.

We've seen the term API in previous chapters, which stands for application programming interface. Through an API, one system can call functionality or access data from another system with code. Therefore, a RESTful API describes something we can use to access a system through web calls that are REST based.

Another aim of a REST service is to provide addresses that are descriptive and understandable. For example, here's the format of a typical REST-based URL:

```
http://myserver.com/properties/item/1729
```

Due to the format of this URL, we can guess that the purpose of this request is to return a property record that matches the ID value 1729.

Making HTTP Web Requests

Web devices communicate with web servers through HTTP (Hypertext Transfer Protocol). With this protocol, the communication between a client device and a server consists of isolated requests and responses. When a client requires data from a web server, it makes a request to the server. The server replies with a response, and at this point, the communication finishes. A web session between a device and a server consists of a series of isolated requests and responses.

Every HTTP request includes a verb. This describes the type of request that the client makes, and it can be one of four types: GET, POST, PUT, and DELETE.

In all instances where a client wants to retrieve data from a server, it issues an HTTP request with the GET verb. The client can provide arguments through the path, like so. In this example, the URL specifies an ID of 1729:

```
http://myserver.com/properties/item/1729
```

HTTP requests can also specify arguments through query string parameters. Here's the format of a URL that uses a query string parameter. The parameter values appear after the ? symbol in the address and consist of name/value pairs that are separated with the = sign:

```
http://myserver.com/properties.aspx?id=1729
```

When a client calls a web service to add or submit data, it typically issues an HTTP request with the POST verb. The data that the client posts will be attached to the body of the request.

Understanding HTTP Responses

A web server replies to HTTP requests with responses that include a status code. Perhaps the most common status code that people are aware of is the 404 status code. A web server returns this status code when the user requests a page that doesn't exist. Another status code is 500, and this is the error code that a server returns when it encounters an error that the caller cannot resolve.

When we call a web service, the status code that we want to receive is 200. This is the status code that indicates success. Another success code is 201, and this is a code that indicates a successful POST or a PUT request.

The response from a web service method might include data which will usually be in XML or JSON format. Modern web services tend to return data in JSON format because this is the lighter-weight format. Listing 24-1 shows an example of a successful HTTP response with a JSON payload.

Listing 24-1. How a 200 response with JSON data looks like

```
200 OK
Content-Type: application/json
{
  "post code": "90210",
  "country": "United States",
  "country abbreviation": "US",
  "places": [
    {
      "place name": "Beverly Hills",
      "longitude": "-118.4065",
      "state": "California",
      "state abbreviation": "CA",
      "latitude": "34.0901"
    }
  ]
}
```

This structure will look familiar because we've seen this notation throughout this book. JSON encloses a data set in curly brackets and separates field items with commas. For each field item, JSON separates the field name from the field value with a colon.

In contrast, XML format wraps data items with start and end tags. In general, it takes more data to express the same thing with XML, and this is one reason why JSON is the format of choice for web services.

Documenting a Web Service

Now that we understand the relevant web protocols, let's walk through the process of how to build a custom connector that connects to a postal code lookup web service.

The first step is to find a web service that provides this functionality. The simplest way to find a service is to carry out a web search on the phrase "zip code api." This type of search returns numerous web services that we can use. This example uses a service called Zippopotam.us, but we can just as easily use any other web service.

Figure 24-1 shows the home page of this service. The description here provides simple instructions on how to call this service. For example, to search for the zip code "90210," we would use the following web address:

```
http://api.zippopotam.us/us/90210
```

Figure 24-1. *Zippopotam home page*

To test this service, Figure 24-2 shows the response when we enter this address into a web browser. As this screenshot shows, the service returns a result in JSON format.

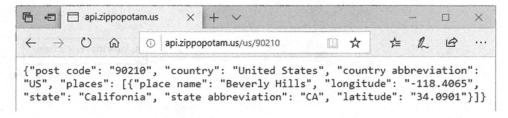

Figure 24-2. *The JSON result from the Zippopotam service*

Creating a Web Service Description

The next step is to build the contract that describes the Zippopotam web service. This is important because it enables Power Apps to understand the methods, parameters, and return values of the service.

For this example, we'll produce an "Open API" document in JSON format. We'll examine the two tools that can help us document Web APIs: Postman and Swagger.

Using Postman

Postman is a desktop program that runs on Windows and Mac. To use Postman, the first step is to download and to install the application. The website we can use to download Postman is

www.getpostman.com/

Figure 24-3 shows a screenshot of the app and provides a high-level overview of the areas in Postman that enable us to test a web service.

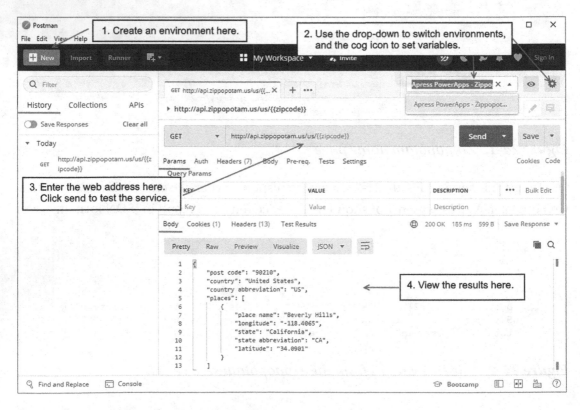

Figure 24-3. *Using the Postman app*

The best approach with Postman is to create an environment for our task. An environment provides a container where we can define variables. Variables enable us to provide parameter values for web requests, which we can quickly change through the UI.

We can then create a new "request" object and use the designer to call a web method and to see the response from the server. In this example, we set the GET request to the following value:

```
http://api.zippopotam.us/us/{{zipcode}}
```

Here, {{zipcode}} denotes a placeholder to a variable called zipcode. We can use the environment settings to define this variable and to assign a value.

After we confirm that our web service call works, we can click the save button. This feature saves a collection of files where each file represents a web request. Power Apps can create a custom connector based on this collection of Postman files.

Using Swagger

Unlike Postman, Swagger is a web-based tool. To use Swagger, the first step is to visit the Swagger website and to create an account. Swagger offers a range of subscription plans that include a free individual plan. This free plan provides enough functionality to document a web service for use with Power Apps. Here's the website for Swagger:

```
https://app.swaggerhub.com/
```

To use Swagger, create an account, log in, and select the option to "Start a new API project." Swagger provides the option to create a project based on a template. A helpful template is the PetStore API template. This template is designed for learning purposes and demonstrates lots of useful syntax.

For basic purposes, the easiest option is to build a project based on the blank or "Simple API" template. If we choose the Simple API template, the designer creates a project that includes the syntax that describes some simple web service calls. We can modify the YAML in the project to suit our web service call, as shown in Listing 24-2.

Listing 24-2. The YAML that describes a simple web service

```yaml
swagger: '2.0'
info:
  version: '1'
  title: PostCode API
  description: Call Zippopotam Lookup
schemes:
 - https
 - http
produces:
 - application/json
paths:
  /us/{zipcode}:
    get:
      summary: Get Postcode
      description: Enter the postcode to search
      responses:
       200:
         description: "JSON postcode result"
      parameters:
        - name: zipcode
          in: path
          description: US Zipcode
          required: true
          type: string
host: api.zippopotam.us
basePath: /
```

The code in this listing provides a template that we can use to describe simple web services. The first part specifies the title, description, and version number. The schemes section describes the acceptable protocols (https and http), and the produces section describes the output format of the web service.

The paths section can define one or more web methods. In this example, we define the web method that returns an address based on a zip code. Within a path definition, we can define parameter placeholders by enclosing the parameter names in curly brackets (e.g., /us/{zipcode})

The host and basePath settings are particularly important because they define the base URL for the service.

From the Swagger designer, the right-hand panel provides a button through which we execute the web methods that we define. This enables us to test our methods and to view the results from the server, as shown in Figure 24-4. Once we complete our task in Swagger, the final step is to click the export button and to choose the download API option. This offers the choice to export our document in JSON format.

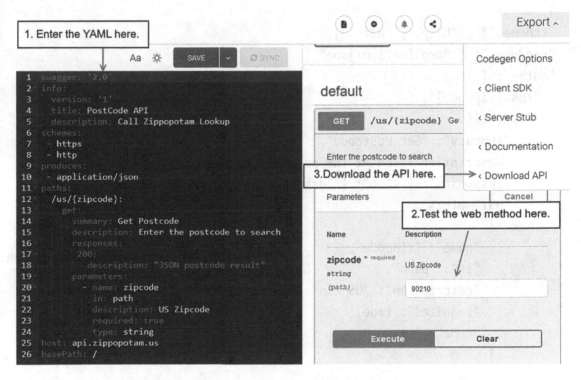

Figure 24-4. *The Swagger designer*

Examining an Open API Document

Listing 24-3 shows the ouput of our JSON export. The is an Open API document, and the structure looks similar to the source YAML that we entered into the Swagger designer.

This listing is useful because we can use it as a template to define other web services. As before, the crucial sections are the host and the paths settings. We can import this content directly into Power Apps when we create our custom connector. Therefore, this is the code that we would author manually if we choose not to use Swagger or Postman.

Listing 24-3. The Open API document

```
{
  "swagger": "2.0",
  "info": {
    "version": "1",
    "title": "PostCode API",
    "description": "Call Zippopotam Lookup"
  },
  "schemes": [ "https", "http" ],
  "produces": [ "application/json" ],
  "paths": {
    "/us/{zipcode}": {
      "get": {
        "summary": "Get Postcode",
        "description": "Enter the postcode to search",
        "responses": { "200": { "description": "JSON postcode result" } },
        "parameters": [
          {
            "name": "zipcode",
            "in": "path",
            "description": "US Zipcode",
            "required": true,
            "type": "string"
          }
        ]
      }
    }
  },
  "host": "api.zippopotam.us",
  "basePath": "/"
}
```

Creating a Custom Connector

Now that we've built an Open API document, the difficult part is over. The next step is to create a custom connector, and we can do this through the Data ➤ Custom Connectors section of the Maker Portal. Here, there is a "New custom connector" button that offers the choice to create a blank custom connector, to create a connector from an Azure service, or to import an Open API file or Postman collection. In this example, we choose to import an Open API file. This opens the dialog that is shown in Figure 24-5. Here, we can name our connector and click the button to import our Open API file.

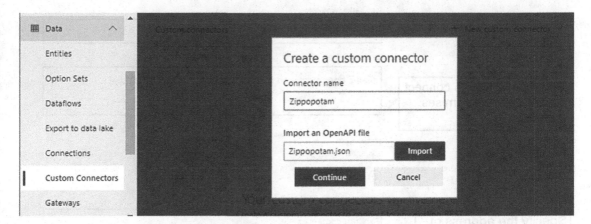

Figure 24-5. *Creating a custom connector*

The Continue button opens the page that is shown in Figure 24-6. The process to create a custom connector consists of four stages, and we can view these through the cookie trail menu that appears at the top of the page. These four stages are General, Security, Definition, and Test.

The General screen enables us to upload an icon and to provide a description. The most important step is to confirm that host and base URL settings resolve to the correct base web address of our target web service.

A useful feature is the ability to connect to a web service through an on-premises gateway. We can choose this option to connect to web services that are hosted within internal networks.

Another notable feature is the "Swagger Editor" option at the top of the page. If we enable this option, an editor appears that enables us to view and edit the YAML definition of the connector.

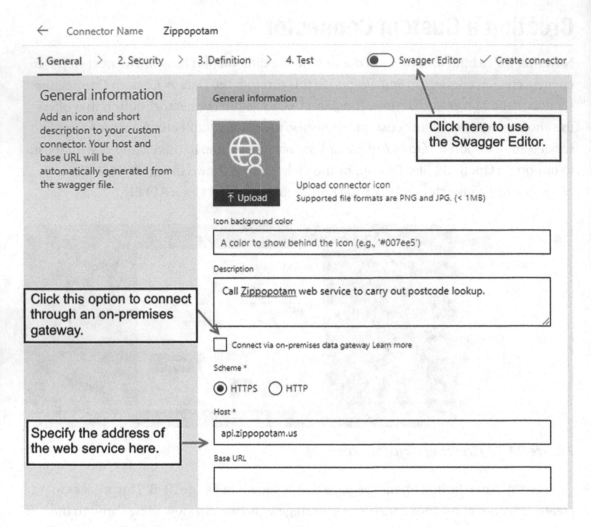

Figure 24-6. *Creating a custom connector*

The next screen enables us to configure the security of the web service. The Zippopotam web service does not require authentication, but many other web services do. To connect to a web service that requires authentication, we use the settings that are shown in Figure 24-7. There are three authentication types that we can choose, and here's a brief summary of each type:

- Basic authentication – This is a simple authentication type and relies on a username and password.

- API key – An API key identifies an app without referring to a user. We can specify the exact way in which the web service expects to receive the API key. This could be through the HTTP request header or through query string parameters.

- OAuth 2.0 – This method relies on a separate identity provider that performs the authentication. With this option, we can select a provider from a drop-down. This includes typical providers such as Google, Microsoft, and Facebook, as well as a generic OAuth provider that we can fully customize.

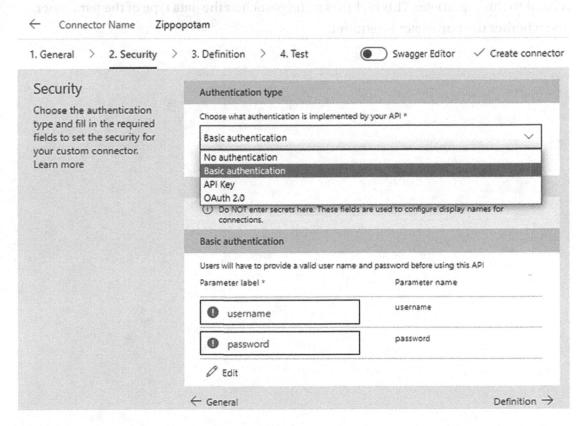

Figure 24-7. *Configuring authentication*

The next page enables us to define the web service methods or actions of our custom connector. The settings here derive their values from the contents of the Open API file that we imported.

Figure 24-8 shows the action that corresponds to our web service request. The general section defines the summary and description of the method.

The request settings appear lower down in the page. The URL setting defines the endpoint of the web service. This setting is not editable, but it's very important to make sure it is correct. The combined values of the host, root path, and URL settings should make up the correct web service address (in our example, `http://api.zippopotam.us/us/{{zipcode}}`).

The request parameters also appear in this section, and in this example, we see our zip code parameter. We can click this entry to view and to further configure settings related to this parameter. This includes settings such as the data type of the parameter and whether the parameter is required.

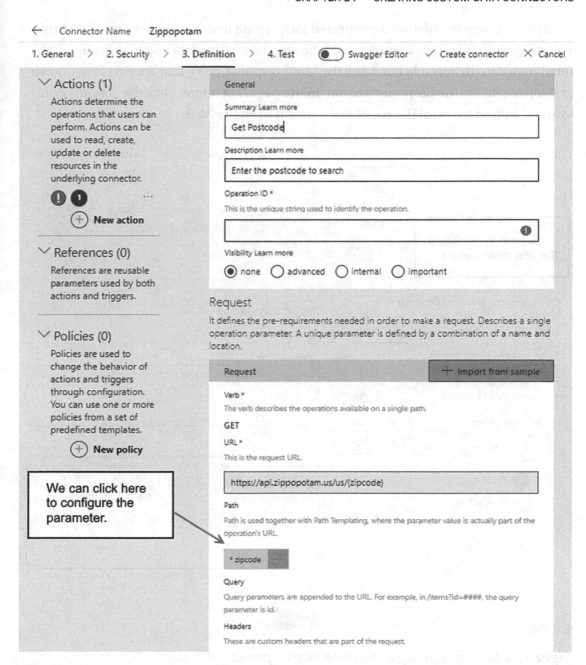

Figure 24-8. *Configuring the web service definition*

The next step is to define the expected JSON result that the web service will return. This enables Power Apps to understand the structure of the data and to provide suitable IntelliSence in the formula bar. Click the "200" response entry that appears lower down in the page inside the Response section. In the page that opens, click the "Import from sample" button to reveal the panel that's shown in Figure 24-9.

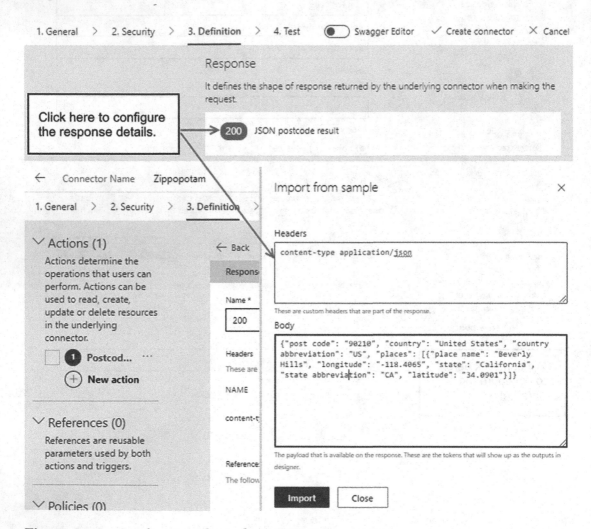

Figure 24-9. *Configuring the web service response*

Because our web service returns JSON, we enter "content-type application/json" into the Headers textbox. For the Body section, we enter JSON data that matches the data structure that the web service returns. We can call the web service from a browser (`http://api.zippopotam.us/us/90210`) and paste the response output into this box. When we click the import button, the output data fields from the web service will appear, as shown in Figure 24-10.

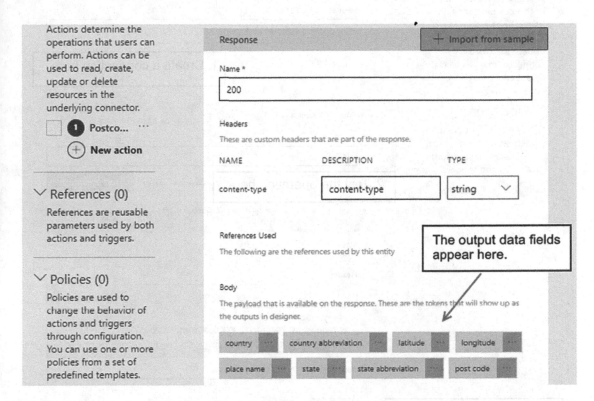

Figure 24-10. *Configuring the web service response body*

The next page enables us to test the connector. The first step is to create a new connection. We can then click the "Test operation" button to test our web service call. If the test succeeds, a success message appears, as shown in Figure 24-11. If the test fails, it can be difficult to diagnose the exact cause because the error message that comes back is not particularly helpful. In such cases, the first things to check are the host and URL values. Incorrect values here are a likely cause of error.

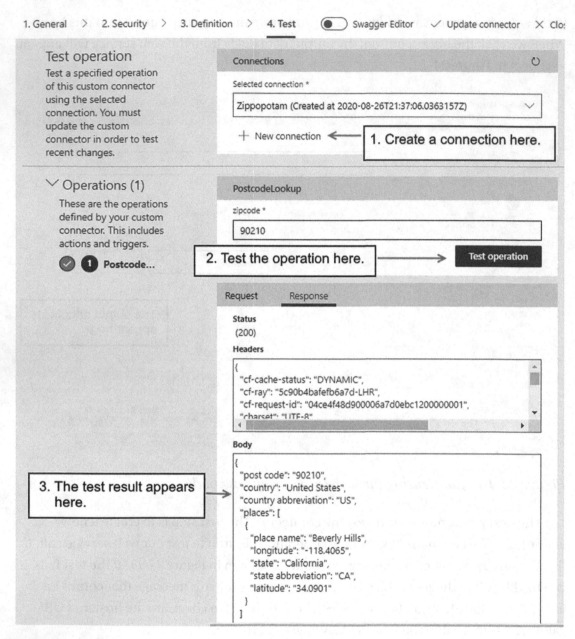

Figure 24-11. Testing the web service method

Using the Custom Connector

Now that we've created our custom connector, we can add a connection to our canvas app based on our custom connector.

To do this, we search for our custom connector by name (Zippopotam, in this example) though the data panel, as shown in Figure 24-12. The option to add a connection will create a connection with a default name that is based on the title setting that we define in the Open API file. In this example, the Open API file specifies the title "Postcode API"; and therefore, Power Apps creates a connection called `PostcodeAPI`. In a formula, we can refer to this connection using the keyword `PostcodeAPI`.

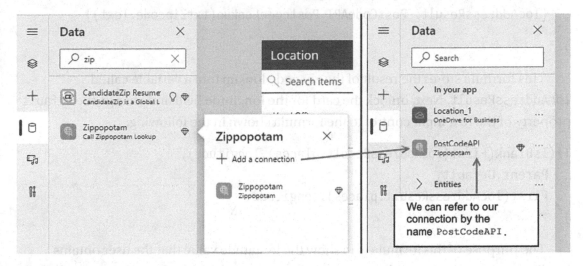

***Figure 24-12.** Adding a data source for a custom connector*

To show how to populate data controls on a screen with results from our web service, here's how to adapt the edit screen from an auto-generated app. We'll add a textbox for users to enter a zip code and a button that retrieves the associated data from the Zippopotam service.

In this demonstration, we'll use an app that's based on the location table from Chapter 18. The button will retrieve the longitude and latitude values for the zip code and populate the text input controls on the form. An important feature of this modification is that it retains the save feature of the form. As a reminder, Figure 24-13 shows the structure of the location table.

▲	A	B	C	D
1	Description ▼	Longitude ▼	Lattitude ▼	Heading ▼
2				

Figure 24-13. *Layout of the location table*

To create this example, the first step is to build an auto-generated app that's based on this data structure. On the edit screen, insert a text input control called txtZipcode. Next, add a button called btnGetLocation and set the OnSelect property of the button to the following formula:

```
UpdateContext(
    {locAddressResult: PostCodeAPI.PostcodeLookup(txtZipcode.Text)}
)
```

This formula stores the result of the zip code lookup into a variable called locAddressResult. Next, unlock the card for the longitude field and change the Default property of the text input control to the formula shown in the following:

```
If(IsBlank(First(locAddressResult.places).longitude),
    Parent.Default,
    First(locAddressResult.places).longitude
)
```

The purpose of this formula is to show the longitude value that the user obtains by clicking the btnGetLocation button. If this value is blank, the formula returns the existing longitude value for the record.

The next step is to repeat the same process for the latitude values. Set the Default property of the latitude text input control to the formula shown in the following:

```
If(IsBlank(First(locAddressResult.places).latitude),
    Parent.Default,
    First(locAddressResult.places).latitude
)
```

The final step is to clear the longitude and latitude values that are associated with the locAddressResult variable when the user leaves the screen. Here's the formula that we would add to the OnHidden property of the screen:

```
UpdateContext({locAddressResult: Blank()})
```

Figure 24-14 shows the layout of the screen in the designer. At this stage, we can run our app and save the updated location details to the data store.

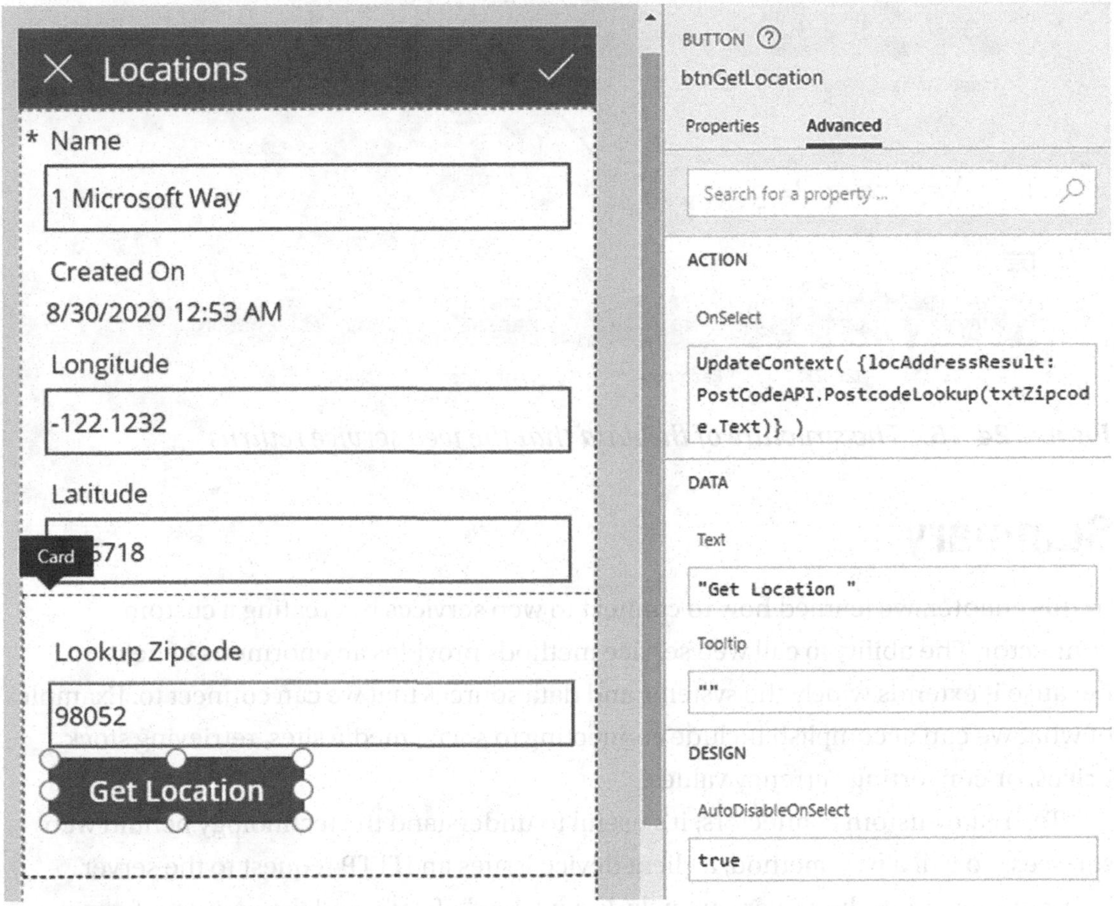

Figure 24-14. Layout of the sample screen

For completeness Figure 24-15 shows the view of the `locAddressResult` variable in the designer. This illustrates the structure of the data that our web service returns and highlights how the first record includes a child table called `places` that contains the latitude and longitude values of the result.

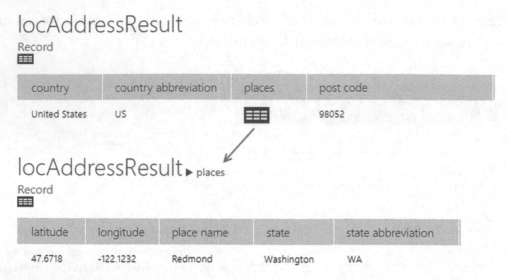

Figure 24-15. *The structure of the data that the web service returns*

Summary

In this chapter, we learned how to connect to web services by creating a custom connector. The ability to call web service methods provides an enormous benefit because it extends widely the systems and data sources that we can connect to. Examples of what we can accomplish include connecting to social media sites, retrieving stock prices, or converting currency values.

To create custom connectors, it's useful to understand the technology behind web services. To call a web method, a client device issues an HTTP request to the server. The response from the server can include a payload of data, and the common format for the return data is JSON. HTTP responses include a status code, and the code that we generally seek is 200 – this is the code that indicates success. It's important to understand these terms because they appear in the screens that we use the to create a custom connector.

After we build or identify a web service to use, the first step to create a custom connector is to document the web service and to produce a contract. The two tools that we can use to do this are Swagger and Postman. With Swagger, we can generate an Open API file in JSON format that describes the web service. The content of this file includes the address, expected parameters, and expected output of web methods.

Once we produce the contract, we can create a custom connector through the Maker Portal. The easiest way to create a custom connector is to import an Open API file or a Postman collection. There is also the option to begin with an empty custom connector. The process to create a custom connector consists of four steps. During the first step, we can set the web service address. The second step enables us to configure authentication and security settings, and the third step enables us to configure the parameters of the web methods and the data structures that the web methods return. The final step provides a test page to call our web methods and to confirm that we've set up the custom connector correctly.

After we create a custom connector, we can add a connection from the canvas app based on a custom connector. We can then write a formula to call the web method through the connection.

To demonstrate how to save the results from a web service, we adapted the edit screen from an auto-generated app. We saved the result of the web service to a local variable and modified the data entry controls on a form to refer to the variable values.

CHAPTER 25

Using Power Automate

Power Automate is a product in the Power Platform that facilitates the automation of tasks with flows. By building flows, we can connect to data and a wide range of systems. We can implement logic and workflow that includes looping constructs and approval processes. It is possible to run flows automatically and repeatedly on a schedule.

One reason why Power Automate is so useful is because it enables us to overcome the limitations and gaps in the feature set of Power Apps. It provides a glue that enables us to build more rounded and complete solutions. Importantly, it plays a key role in augmenting and adding additional value to apps and solutions that we build with the Power Platform.

Power Automate is a completely separate product, and there are complete books on this subject. Therefore, it is not possible to go into too much detail in any specific area. However, we will cover some very useful topics in this chapter which will include

- An introduction to Power Automate. We'll examine some of the use case scenarios of how we can use Power Automate to derive business benefit. We'll find out how to build flows and how to call them from Power Apps.

- How to develop flows. We'll find out how to connect to data and how to filter data using a query language called OData (Open Data Protocol). We'll cover how to accept input values into a flow and how to return output from a flow. We'll also learn how to program flows using a language called Workflow Definition Language.

- Examples of flow. To demonstrate the use of flow, the examples in chapter will include how to send emails, how to build approval processes, how to optimize the performance of calls to SQL Server using stored procedures, and how to connect to files on internal networks using the file system connector.

813

© Tim Leung 2021
T. Leung, *Beginning Power Apps*, https://doi.org/10.1007/978-1-4842-6683-0_25

What Is Power Automate?

To begin this chapter, we'll examine more closely the following question – what is Power Automate and how can it help us? Power Automate is a service that carries out tasks and workflows independently of Power Apps. Just like Power Apps, Power Automate is designed for non-developers, and it offers the ability to build automated processes without any coding skills. With Power Automate, we can design workflows through a simple graphical web-based designer. Because the designer is web based, there's no need to install any custom software.

A flow consists of a trigger and one or more actions. A trigger defines an event that starts a flow. We can trigger a flow from a button on a canvas app. Outside of an app, we can also trigger flows whenever changes occur in a data source, and we can also trigger flows from a schedule. We can add conditional and looping constructs to flows.

Flows use the same data connectors that we can access through Power Apps to access data. We can connect to all the popular data sources including SharePoint, Excel, SQL Server, and Dataverse. We can use the on-premises gateway to access internal company resources, including files and on-premise SharePoint and SQL Server servers. A benefit of using a flow is that we can access certain connectors that work only with Power Automate. An example of this is the Excel Online (Business) connector, which enables us to access Excel files that are stored in SharePoint document libraries.

To access other resources, we can utilize any custom connectors that we've built. We can also access web resources by making HTTP requests from inside a flow.

There is a separate licensing model that applies to Power Automate. A majority of Power Apps users will be licensed through Microsoft 365 subscriptions, and at the time of writing, Microsoft 365 users receive Power Automate usage rights. These rights include the use of standard connectors. This means, for example, that Microsoft 365 users can build flows to access SharePoint. To build a flow that uses premium connectors (e.g., a flow that accesses Dataverse or SQL Server), we can subscribe to a Power Automate plan. Alternatively, if a user subscribes to a Power Apps plan, this will also provide usage rights to access premium connectors through flows.

What Can We Do with Power Automate?

Power Automate can perform a wide variety of tasks. If there is something that we cannot accomplish directly in Power Apps, it is very possible that we can derive a solution through Power Automate. Here are some examples of what we can carry out with Power Automate:

- File handling – We can create, copy, and carry out file operations on OneDrive, Dropbox, and other supported cloud storage providers. We can transfer files through FTP. A great feature is the ability to access the files in internal networks through the on-premises gateway.

- SQL tasks – We can connect to on-premise and Azure databases and execute specific SQL queries. A very helpful feature is the ability to call stored procedures. This enables us to optimize the performance of our apps.

- Accessing web resources – We can make HTTP requests from a flow. For example, we can build a flow to create SharePoint lists by making HTTP POST requests to the SharePoint API. We can use this to help recreate SharePoint lists in new Microsoft 365 tenants.

- AI tasks – Flows can connect with AI Builder. We can use flows to analyze data with AI and to perform actions such as message routing.

- Looping – Power Apps doesn't include any looping constructs, besides the limited `ForAll` function. We can overcome this limitation by using a flow to carry out actions repeatedly until a condition becomes true.

- Scheduling – We can schedule flows to run at predetermined times. We can use this to carry out tasks such as data archiving, backup, or overnight reporting.

Power Automate provides the ability to build flows that include approval processes. This enables us, for example, to build purchase or vacation request systems.

We can easily build flows to copy, manipulate, and synchronize data. The practical application of this is that we can use flows to aggregate and to consolidate data in ways that overcome problems associated with query delegation limits. We can also use Power Automate to copy data between SQL Server or Dataverse and SharePoint. This strategy can help reduce licensing costs by minimizing the reliance on data sources that require premium connectors.

There is also a mobile app that provides the ability to manage and to start flows from a mobile device.

Finally, Power Automate can add great value to model-driven apps. Model-driven apps are tied predominantly to Dataverse. By integrating a model-driven app with Power Automate, we can carry out actions against data sources that are not natively available in a model-driven app.

Managing and Creating Flows

To create, edit, and manage flows, we can use the Flows section of the Maker Portal, as shown in Figure 25-1. Alternatively, we can access the same features directly through the Power Automate website:

```
https://flow.microsoft.com/
```

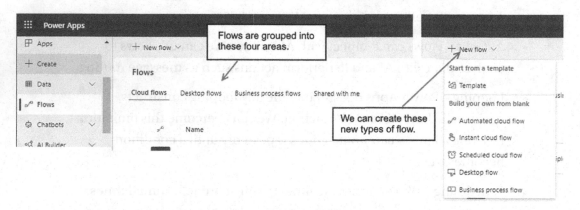

Figure 25-1. *The Flows section of the Maker Portal*

The Flows section in the Maker Portal organizes objects into four areas – Cloud flows, Desktop flows, Business process flows, and Shared with me.

"Cloud flows" describe those that we can trigger from Power Apps, a schedule, or whenever a change to a data source occurs. In contrast, "Desktop flows" provide the ability to record and to playback actions using a screen recorder. They can help simplify repetitive tasks and to automate data entry through older systems without API access.

The "business process flows" section shows business process flows that we covered in Chapter 13. A business process flow organizes data entry into sequential steps in model driven apps.

To create a new flow, the "New" button opens a drop-down that offers a range of options. We can create a flow from a template, create a scheduled flow, create an automated flow, and more.

Figure 25-2 shows the screen that appears when we choose the start from a template option. The benefit of using a template is that we can more quickly construct a flow by basing it on one of the available templates. We can also use templates as a learning tool by examining how a templated flow implements a specific task.

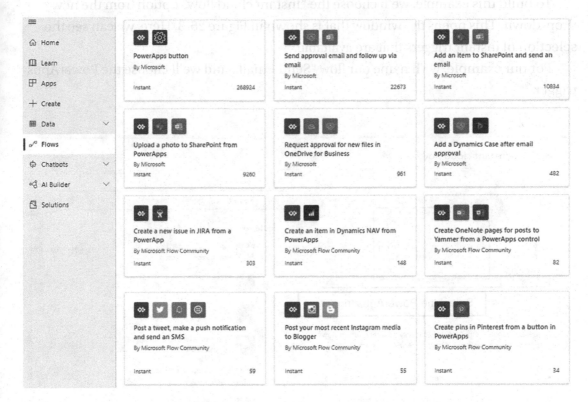

Figure 25-2. Creating a flow from a template

Defining Triggers

The execution of a flow begins with a trigger. The two main categories of triggers are automated triggers and instant triggers. Events that can raise an automated trigger include the insertion of a record in a database or a SharePoint list. The arrival of an email, the creation of a calendar event, or the creation of the file in OneDrive are other examples of automated triggers.

An instant trigger defines an event that occurs through manual intervention. Examples of instant triggers include buttons that we add to Power Apps or buttons that we add to the mobile app. Finally, we can schedule flows to run at specified times or to repeat flow runs at intervals.

In this first section, we'll demonstrate how to use Power Automate by building a simple flow that sends an email. We learn how to call this type of flow from canvas and model-driven apps.

To build this example, we'll choose the "Instant cloud flow" option from the new drop-down. This opens the window that is shown in Figure 25-3. Here, we can see the selection of instant triggers that are available.

For our example, we'll name our flow "Send Email," and we'll choose the PowerApps trigger.

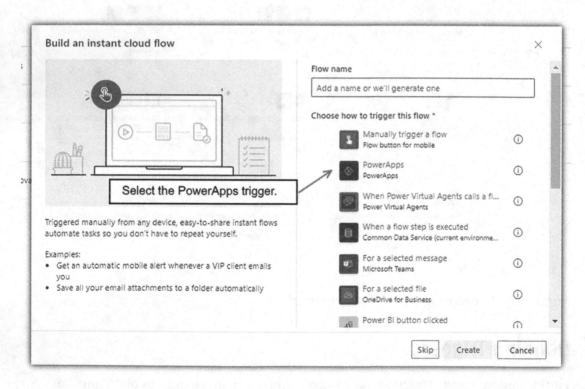

Figure 25-3. *Creating a new instant flow*

Adding Actions

When the designer opens, the trigger will appear at the top of the design canvas as shown in Figure 25-4. Beneath the Power Apps trigger, we can add actions that include data retrieval actions, conditions, switch cases, loops, and more. The "Choose an action" block presents a tabbed interface that groups the available actions into logical areas. The quickest way to find an action is to take advantage of the search textbox that appears in this block.

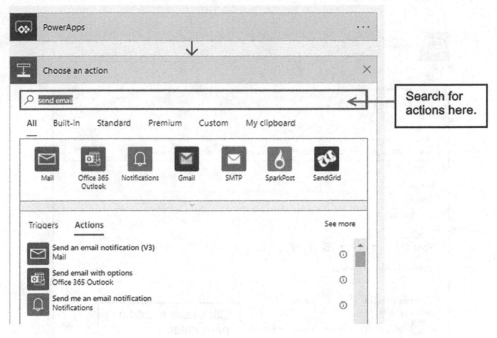

Figure 25-4. *Adding actions to a flow*

Once we add an action, we can use the designer to attach subsequent actions. A notable action is "condition." This enables us to define an if/else condition. We can also add other branching actions such as switch and "do until" loops.

For this example, we'll carry out a search on the key phrase "send email." This returns all actions that contain the key phrase "send email"; and in the list of results, we'll see the option to send emails through Gmail, Outlook 365, SMTP, and a range of many other providers. In this example, we'll choose the Outlook 365 option.

Accepting Input Values

When we connect a flow to Power Apps, a common requirement is to pass values from Power Apps into the flow. We accomplish this by first selecting a field or property where we want to accept input from Power Apps. We can then select the option to "Ask in Power Apps," as shown in Figure 25-5.

As an example, let's suppose that we want to pass the to address, subject, and email body of the message from Power Apps. To configure this, we would create an "Ask in Power Apps" input for each of these values in the step.

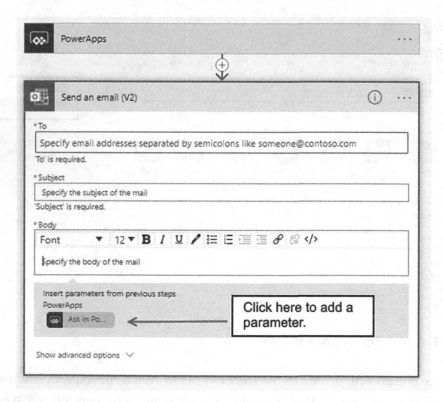

Figure 25-5. *Configuring an action to accept an input value*

Note that if the "Insert parameters from previous steps" panel doesn't appear, we make it visible by reducing the width of the browser.

At this stage, we can save our flow. There is a test button in the designer that enables us to check that our flow works as expected. The test page will prompt us to supply the required parameter values.

Calling Flows

Now that we've built our flow, let's see how to run it from our canvas and model-driven apps.

From Canvas Apps

From a canvas app, we can call a flow by selecting a button or control that we want to use to trigger the flow. Next, we click the Action ➤ Power Automate button to open the data panel (Figure 25-6). We can use this to choose our desired flow. In this example, we select our "Send Email" flow. This populates the OnSelect property of the button with a formula that calls the Run method of the flow. The IntelliSense in a formula bar indicates the parameter values that our flow requires. Here, we can pass the values from text input controls on our screen.

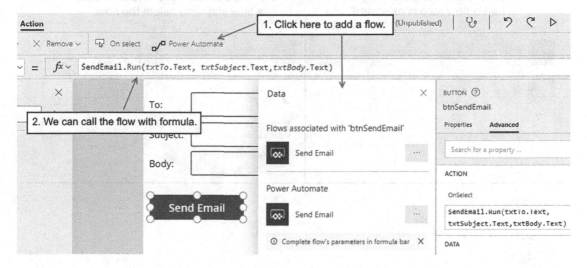

Figure 25-6. Calling a flow from a canvas app

Caution   When we update a flow and add additional "Ask Power Apps" parameters, an existing canvas app that uses the flow will not recognize the change unless we delete and re-add the flow to the app.

From Model-Driven Apps

Unlike a canvas app, we cannot add custom buttons to a model-driven app form. To trigger a flow from a model-driven app, there are three general approaches that we can adopt.

The first is to build an automated flow that runs when a Dataverse record is created, updated, or deleted. By using this trigger, we can run a flow whenever a user makes a change to a record.

The second method is to create a flow that uses the "When a flow step is executed" trigger. This enables the user to initiate a Power Automate flow from a step in a business process flow. With this type of trigger, we can access the fields from the step in the business process flow. At runtime, the user can click a button in the step to run the flow, as shown in Figure 25-7.

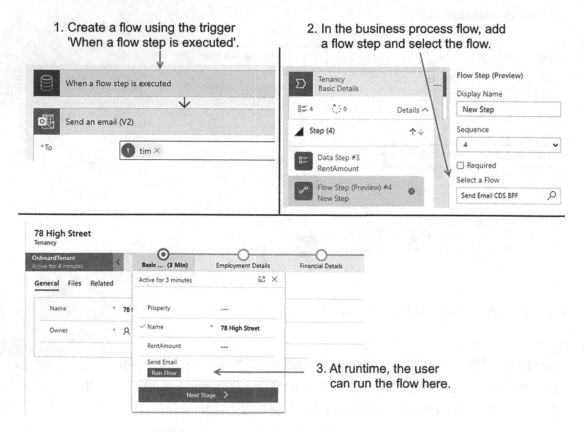

Figure 25-7. *Calling a flow from a business process flow*

Caution   For a flow to appear in the "Select a Flow" control in the business process flow designer, we must publish the flow to Dataverse. We can do this through a solution, and we'll cover this in Chapter 26.

The third option is to build a flow with the "When a record is selected" trigger. With this option, the user can navigate to a list of records and use the built-in flow button in the top menu to run the flow (Figure 25-8).

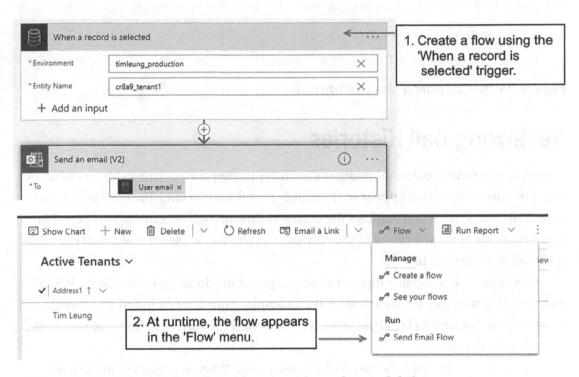

Figure 25-8. *Calling a flow from the menu bar of a model-driven app*

Unattended: From a Schedule

To build an unattended flow that runs on a schedule, we build a flow that is based on the recurrence trigger, as shown in Figure 25-9.

Here, we can define the interval and frequency of the flow. The available frequency options include second, minute, hour, day, week, and month. We can also define the time at which the task runs.

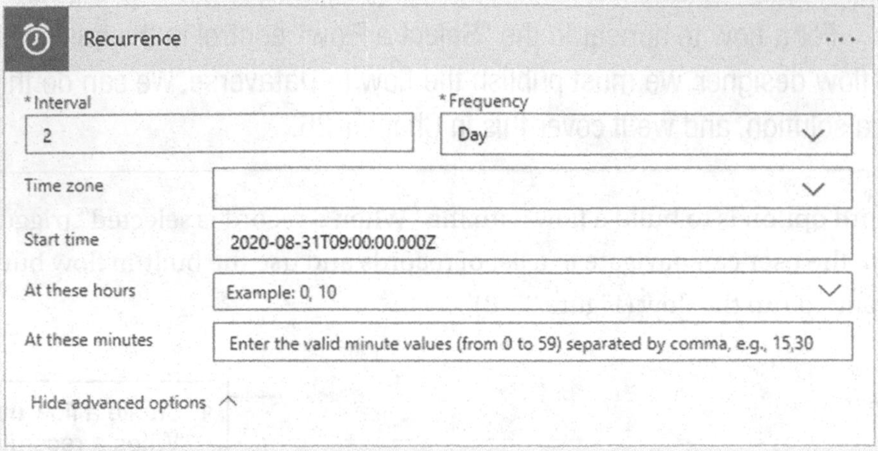

Figure 25-9. *Creating a reoccurring flow*

Reviewing Call Histories

A great feature with Power Automate is the ability to view the execution history of flows. From the list of flows that appear in the Maker Portal, we can click the run history menu item. This opens a list that displays the date and time of each execution, run duration, and run status. If we select one of the entries from this list, we see the detailed view that is shown in Figure 25-10.

This view shows the data inputs to each step and the duration of each step. We can also view the response from each step. For example, if our flow included an action to call a web server through an HTTP request, we could view the response from the server and any related error codes.

This feature makes it very easy to diagnose errors. When we connect to bespoke data sources using custom connectors, it's much easier to diagnose problems using this feature. From Power Apps alone, the ability to diagnose custom connector errors is more limited.

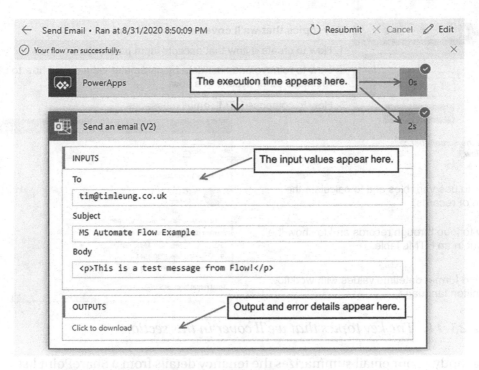

Figure 25-10. Viewing the run history of a flow

Working with Data

A key feature of Power Automate is the ability to connect to data. We can access all the familiar standard and premium connectors that are available through Power Apps. Data connectors expose actions that perform data operations. This includes the ability to retrieve rows, retrieve a single record, edit an existing record, and add a new record.

To provide a fuller example of how to work with data in a flow, we'll examine the individual parts to enable us to extend our example so that it displays a summary of records in the email body. This section will highlight several important and related topics. This includes how to filter the data based on arguments that we pass through Power Apps, how to process rows with calculations, and how to format data values that we retrieve from a data source. Figure 25-11 summarizes the topics that we'll cover in the form of a diagram.

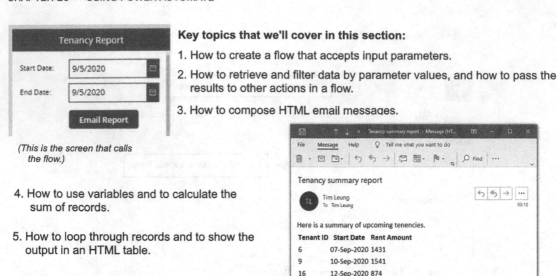

Key topics that we'll cover in this section:

1. How to create a flow that accepts input parameters.

2. How to retrieve and filter data by parameter values, and how to pass the results to other actions in a flow.

3. How to compose HTML email messages.

(This is the screen that calls the flow.)

4. How to use variables and to calculate the sum of records.

5. How to loop through records and to show the output in an HTML table.

6. How to format datetime values with workflow definition language.

Figure 25-11. *The key topics that we'll cover in this section*

The body of our email summarizes the tenancy details from a SharePoint list and displays the records with a tenancy start date that falls between values that a user supplies from Power Apps. The data structure of the SharePoint list is shown in Figure 25-12.

Tenancy

TenancyID ∨	TenantID ∨	StartDate ∨	RentFrequency ∨	RentAmount ∨
3	6	9/7/2020	Monthly	1,431
1	1	7/28/2012	Monthly	712
12	9	9/10/2020	Monthly	1,541
1	16	9/12/2020	Monthly	874
8	23	9/30/2019	Monthly	948
52	24	12/11/2012	Monthly	1,539

Figure 25-12. *The SharePoint data source that we'll use*

Connecting to Data

To introduce the topic of how to connect to data, here's how to carry out data operations against a SharePoint data source. First, we add an action and search for SharePoint. This displays the view shown in Figure 25-13, and as we can see, there are a range of actions that we can select.

The process to connect to other data sources is the same. We search for our target data source and select the action that we want to perform. If we connect to a SQL Server data source, the available actions would be slightly different. For example, there would be actions to execute a SQL query and to execute a stored procedure. We would also notice that the actions include a "premium" icon, to indicate that the end user requires a license plan with access to premium connectors.

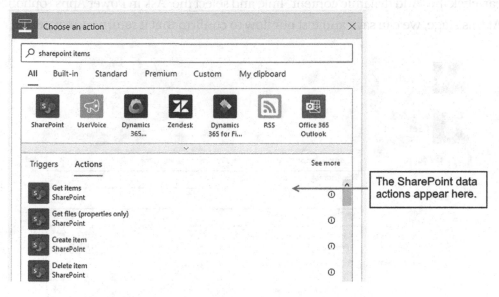

Figure 25-13. *Connecting to a SharePoint data source*

Filtering Data

In this example, our requirement is to connect to a SharePoint list and to retrieve the tenancy records that correspond to start and end dates that the user provides through Power Apps.

The first step is to add a new action and to select the "SharePoint – Get items" action. Figure 25-14 shows this action and highlights the settings that we can provide. The mandatory settings include the SharePoint site address and list name.

To filter this data, we provide an OData (Open Data Protocol) filter expression. OData defines a standard language to query data from web services. The benefit of OData is that we can learn a single query language and use it to filter data from a wide variety of data sources.

Let's suppose we want to return records with a start date between September 14, 2020, and September 20, 2020, inclusive. The OData expression to apply this filter condition looks like this:

```
StartDate ge '2020-09-14T00:00:00Z' and
StartDate le '2020-09-20T23:59:59Z'
```

To apply an OData expression that filters records by values that the user supplies through Power Apps, we start by composing an expression in the Filter Query textbox. Instead of entering hard-coded UTC date values, we select the location where the date value would appear, click the "Add dynamic content" link, and select the "Ask in Power Apps" option.

At this stage, we can save and test our flow to confirm that it returns our expected data.

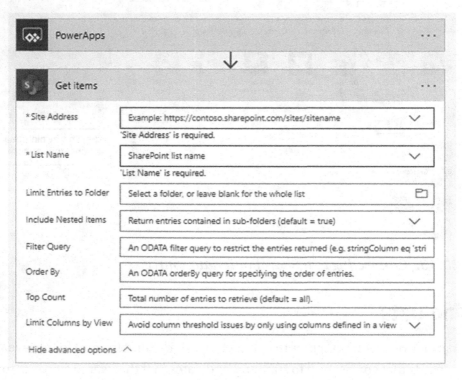

Figure 25-14. *The settings of a SharePoint "Get items" action*

There are a range of OData operators that we can use, which are summarized in Table 25-1.

Table 25-1. *OData operators*

Description	Operator	Example
Equal	eq	UserID eq 8
Not equal	ne	RentFrequency ne 'Monthly'
Greater than	gt	TenancyID gt 8
Greater than or equal	ge	TenancyID ge 10
Less than	lt	TenancyID lt 8
Less than or equal	le	TenancyID le 8
Logical and	and	TenancyID ge 10 and UserID eq 8
Logical or	or	UserID eq 8 or UserID eq 3
Logical negation	not	not UserID eq 8

For slightly more complex queries, we can combine these operators with OData functions. Table 25-2 highlights some of the more useful string and date functions that are available. As an example, we could use the month and year functions to return records with a start date in June 2020. The OData expression to apply this filter condition looks like this:

```
month(StartDate) eq 6 and year(StartDate) eq 2020
```

Table 25-2. *OData functions*

Description	Operator	Example
Starts with	startswith	startswith(Firstname, 'Tim') eq true
Ends with	endswith	endswith(Address1, 'Ave') eq true
Day	day	day(StartDate) eq 31
Hour	hour	hour(StartDate) eq 6
Minute	minute	minute(StartDate) eq 15
Month	month	month(StartDate) eq 6
Year	year	year(StartDate) eq 2020

Working with Variables

Power Automate provides support for variables and offers a range of looping constructs. To highlight these features, here's how to process our records from SharePoint and calculate the sum of the "rent amount" field. To calculate this sum, we initialize a variable, loop over the SharePoint rows, and increment the variable by the "rent amount" value for each row.

To declare a variable, we insert a step toward the start of our flow and select the "Variables – Initialize variable" action. This adds the action that is shown in Figure 25-15. Here, we can enter a name and define the data type and the initial value of the variable. In this example, we name our variable varTotalRent, set the data type to float, and set the initial value to 0.

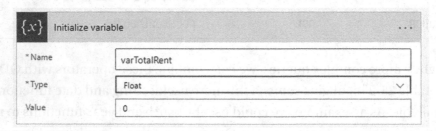

Figure 25-15. *Initializing a variable*

Next, we add an "Apply to each" step. To define the input for this step, we select the SharePoint "value" object in the "Select an output from the previous steps" textbox. This object defines a row from the SharePoint "Get items" action.

Inside the "Apply to each" step, we add an "Increment variable" action and select the option to increment the varTotalRent variable by the varTotalRent field. Figure 25-16 illustrates these settings and highlights how the designer simplifies the construction of an action by providing context-sensitive selections that correspond to current items in the loop.

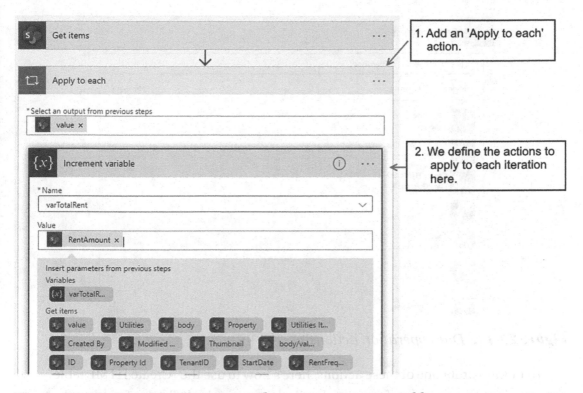

Figure 25-16. Looping over rows and incrementing a variable

Tip   We can move steps in a flow by dragging and dropping with the mouse. This is particularly useful when we define a step inside an "Apply to each" loop and want to move it outside at a later point in time.

Manipulating Data

To manipulate data, Power Automate offers a range of data operation actions and a programming language called Workflow Definition Language. We'll now examine these features in more detail in this section.

Constructing HTML Tables

When we add a step and search for "data operation," we see the seven data operations that are shown in Figure 25-17. Using these actions, we can create CSV and HTML tables, parse JSON, and manipulate the array values.

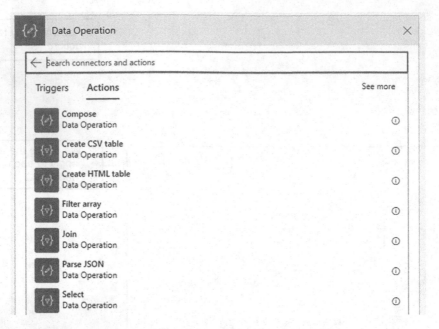

Figure 25-17. *Data operation actions*

To demonstrate one of these actions, here's how to use the "Create HTML table" action to build a summary of tenancy details that appear in the body of our email message.

The "Create HTML table" action accepts an input and builds an HTML table based on this input.

To build an HTML table that includes the tenancy ID and start date and rent amount, we would build an action as shown in Figure 25-18. In this example, we provide the input from our SharePoint "Get items" action. The "Create HTML table" action can automatically include all columns from the input data, or we can manually define the fields and column headings.

A slight limitation of the Header field is that it doesn't accept the entry of spaces. To overcome this limitation, we can define a variable and set the value to a space. This enables us to build a header text expression that includes a space.

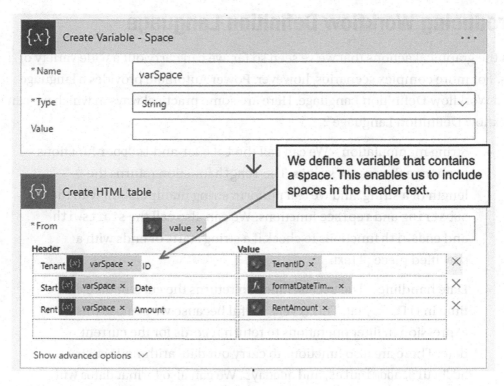

Figure 25-18. *Converting rows to HTML*

We can now insert the output the of "Create HTML table" into the body of our email message. At runtime, this action produces the HTML output that is shown in Figure 25-19.

Tenant ID	Start Date	Rent Amount
6	2020-09-07	1431
9	2020-09-10	1541
16	2020-09-12	874

Figure 25-19. *The HTML content that appears in the email*

Note that if we want to filter the rows that appear in the HTML table, we can process the input data beforehand by calling a "Filter array" action.

Introducing Workflow Definition Language

With the graphical actions that we've seen so far, we can carry out a wide variety of tasks. For more complex scenarios, however, Power Automate provides a language called Workflow Definition Language. Here are some practical ways in which we can use "Workflow Definition Language":

- String manipulation – We can call the toLower and toUpper functions to change the case of strings. The length function returns the length of a string, and we can perform string manipulation with the substring and replace functions. We can also call the startswith and endswith functions to check if a string starts or ends with a specified piece of text.

- Date handling – The utcnow function returns the current date and time in UTC format. This is very useful because we can use this expression in filter operations to return records for the current date. There are also functions to carry out date arithmetic such as addhours, addminutes, and adddays. We can also format dates with the formatDateTime function.

- Math – We can carry out addition, subtraction, multiplication, and division with the functions add, sub, mul, and div.

- Program control – The if function works like the if function in Power Apps. This is useful because it provides a way to test a condition and to return values depending on the result. We can utilize the if function directly in user-definable settings inside individual actions. The keywords of logical operators include and, or, not, greater, greaterOrEquals, and lessOrEquals.

Table 25-3 shows the example usage of some of the most useful functions.

Table 25-3. *Example Workflow Definition Language functions*

Description	Example Use	Result
Length of a string	length('tim')	3
Length of an array	length(['tim','tom'])	2
Concatenate strings	concat('hi ', 'world')	hi world
Get a substring	substring('hi world',3,5)	world
Replace text	replace('the dog', 'the', 'a')	a dog
Uppercase text	toUpper('Tim')	TIM
Lowercase text	toLower('tim')	tim
Math Functions		
Add two numbers	add(3,2)	5
Subtract two numbers	sub(10, 3)	7
Multiply two numbers	mul(4,2)	8
Divide two numbers	div(10/2)	5
Date Functions		
Get current UTC date/time	utcnow()	2017-07-14T13:30:00Z
Get current UTC date/time	utcnow('yyyy/MM/dd')	2017/07/14
Format a date/time	formatDateTime(utcnow, 'dd mmm yy')	14 Jul 2017
Add minutes	addminutes('2017-07-14T13:30:00Z', 35)	2017-07-14T14:05:00Z
Add days	adddays('2017-07-14T13:30:00Z', 10)	2017-07-24T13:30:00Z
Add months	addmonths('2017-07-14T13:30:00Z', -2)	2017-05-14T13:30:00Z
Logic Functions		
Equals	equals(1, 1)	True
Greater than	greater(15,20)	False
And	and(greaterOrEquals(5,5), equals(8,8))	True
If, and	if(equals(6, 6), 'yes', 'no')	Yes

This is just a small selection of useful string, number, date, and logic functions. Workflow Definition Language provides many extra functions, including functions to carry out XML operations, complex datetime calculations, data type conversions, and set operations such as unions and joins.

Power Automate is actually a service that's built on top of Azure Logic Apps. Azure Logic Apps is a workflow service that's very similar to Power Automate and shares the same graphical workflow designer. The main difference is that Azure Logic Apps contains additional developer features, such as security and support for source control and testing. Therefore, a good way to find additional help with Workflow Definition Language is to search for web resources that are targeted at Azure Logic Apps. For example, here's a useful page on the Microsoft Azure website that contains a list of all Workflow Definition Language commands:

```
https://docs.microsoft.com/en-us/azure/logic-apps/logic-apps-workflow-
definition-language
```

A caveat is that we must exercise some caution because subtle differences exist between Azure Logic Apps and Power Automate. Therefore, the syntax that we use with these two services is not always identical.

Applying Workflow Definition Language

Where exactly can we use Workflow Definition Language? The answer is that we can use Workflow Definition Language in almost all places where we can enter some text. However, one very versatile place is the "Data Operations – Compose" action. This action enables us to calculate output values for use in other parts of a flow.

To demonstrate this technique, here's how we could build a "Get items" action to return SharePoint tenancy records with a start date value of today.

The first part of the flow includes three compose actions to retrieve the day, month, and year of the current date. The compose actions call the utcnow function to retrieve the date components.

To compose a Workflow Definition Language expression, we click the Add dynamic content link. If this link is missing, we can make it visible by expanding the width of our browser window. This link opens a panel with two tabs – Dynamic content and Expression.

The Expression tab provides an expression builder with IntelliSense and context-sensitive help. We use this to compose our expressions (Figure 25-20). Once we complete our expressions, we click the update button to apply the expressions to our compose actions.

The expressions that we use to return the current day, month, and year are utcnow('dd'), utcnow('MM'), and utcnow('yyyy'), respectively.

Note that it's possible to rename actions. In this example, we rename our actions to CurrentDay, CurrentMonth, and CurrentYear. This makes our flows more readable, and it makes it easier to refer to the output of actions in later steps.

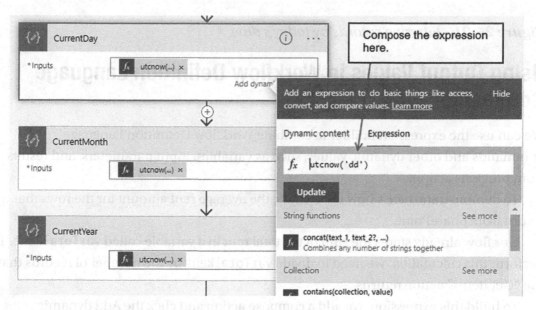

Figure 25-20. *Using compose actions to retrieve the current day, month, and year*

To complete this example, the final step is to incorporate the output of these actions into an OData query expression for the "Get items" action, as shown in Figure 25-21.

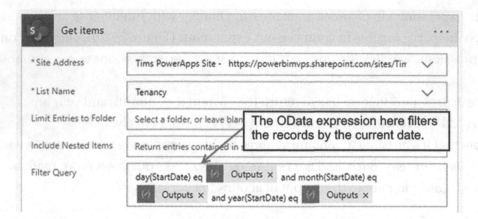

Figure 25-21. *Filtering records by today's date*

Using Output Values in Workflow Definition Language Commands

We can use the expression builder to combine Workflow Definition Language commands and other dynamic values, such as variables, input parameters, and results from previous actions.

To demonstrate, here's how to calculate the average rent amount for the rows that we return from SharePoint.

Our flow already stores the sum of the total rent in a variable called varTotalRent. To perform this calculation, we need to divide varTotalRent by the number of records that the "Get items" action returns.

To build this expression, we add a compose action and click the Add dynamic content link. From the Expression tab, we can start to compose an expression by entering the mathematical division function, div (Figure 25-22).

Figure 25-22. *Composing an expression*

The first argument we need to provide is the dividend. To specify the varTotalRent variable, we place the cursor at the desired insertion point and switch to the "Dynamic content" tab. Here, we can select the varTotalRent entry that appears in the list. When we select this variable, the designer adds the code that references this variable, in this case variables('varTotalRent').

We can continue to build our expression by composing the expression that defines the divisor. We can type length into the formula bar and use the list of objects to insert a reference to the output of the SharePoint "Get items" action. When we complete the composition of the expression, we can click the OK button to apply the expression.

The key point of this exercise is to show how we can switch constantly between the Expression and Dynamic content tabs to compose an expression that combines functions and dynamic values.

Figure 25-23 shows how the action appears when we complete the expression. A useful feature from here is the peak code feature. This enables us to view the Workflow Definition Language code.

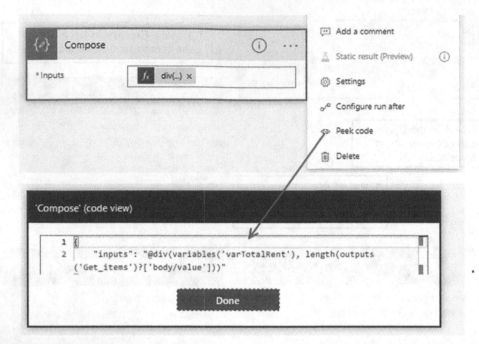

Figure 25-23. *Viewing the code for an action*

From here, we can determine that our Workflow Definition Language syntax looks like this:

```
"@div(variables('varTotalRent'),
    length(outputs('Get_items')?['body/value'])
)"
```

Some of the syntactical features of this expression include the following:

- All Workflow Definition Language expressions begin with an @ symbol. The purpose of this symbol is to differentiate an expression from a string literal.

- We use the `variables` accessor to access variables by name like so: `variables('varTotalRent')`.

- We can access outputs from previous actions using the `outputs` keyword like so:

  `outputs('Get_items')?['body/value']`

- In the preceding syntax, the purpose of the ? operator is to enable us to access null values without triggering a runtime error.

- The "Get items" action initiates a HTTP request to SharePoint. The response body will contain a value, which is a JSON array of records. The expression ['body/value'] returns this value.

Referring to Items in Loops

Within repeating actions (such as an "Apply to each" step), we can use the item keyword to refer to the current item in the iteration.

As an example, here's how to amend our "Create HTML table" action so that it formats the date values in day, month, and year format.

From the expression builder, we start to compose our expression by entering the formatDateTime function. If we now switch to the "Dynamic content" tab, we would discover a slight problem. The "Start Date" and other fields from the SharePoint list do not appear for selection.

To compose our expression, we remain in the Expression tab and enter the expression as follows: formatDateTime(item()['StartDate'],'dd-MMM-yyyy').

This technique highlights there are cases where the expected items don't appear correctly in the "Dynamic content" tab. In these circumstances, we can remain in the "Expression" tab, and we can use code to access the missing items (Figure 25-24).

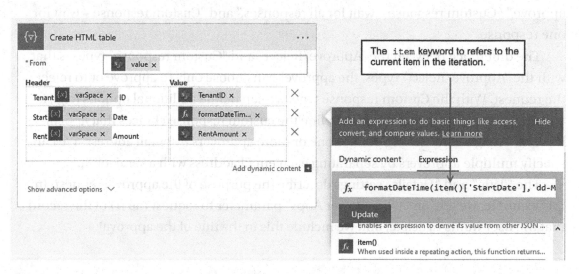

Figure 25-24. *Referring to items inside repeating actions*

> **Tip**   With "Create HTML table" actions, we can amend the presentation of the
> table by creating a subsequent compose action and calling the `replace` function
> to substitute the table and other elements to include styles or CSS classes. Here's
> an example expression:
>
> ```
> replace(body('Create_HTML_table'),'<table>',
> '<table border="1">')
> ```

Approving Actions

A feature of Power Automate is the ability to build workflow and processes with approval
phases. We can trigger actions that run following the approval of a single user, a set of
users, or a single user from a predefined list.

Some examples of how we can use this feature include building processes to approve
purchases, holiday requests, or updates to corporate website or social media accounts.

To demonstrate how to build an approval process, we'll build a flow to delete a user
record. The flow will only delete the record if a manager approves the action.

To build this flow, the first step is to add a "Start and wait for an approval" action
(Figure 25-25). This action type requires an approval type, and there are four types
we can choose: "Approve/Reject – everyone must approve," "Approve/Reject – first to
approve," "Custom response – wait for all responses," and "Custom response – wait for
one response."

The difference between the "Approve/Reject" and "Custom response" types is that
with the "Approve/Reject" types, the approver can choose only to approve or to reject
the request. With the Custom response type, we can define additional options (e.g., a
"pending" option), and we can also define the custom response choices that appear.

The "Assigned to" setting defines one or more approvers by email address. We can
specify multiple approvers by separating each email address with a semicolon.

The "Title" and "Details" settings describe the purpose of the approval request. In
this example, we add an "Ask in Power Apps" parameter to request the ID of the record
that the user wants to delete, and we include this in the title of the approval.

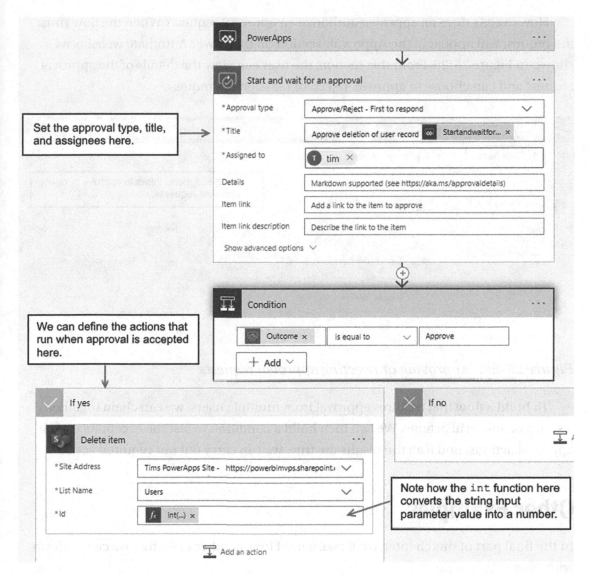

Set the approval type, title, and assignees here.

We can define the actions that run when approval is accepted here.

Note how the int function here converts the string input parameter value into a number.

Figure 25-25. *Starting an approval*

For the next step, we can create a condition to test the response of the approval request. Note that the acceptable response values are "Approve" and "Reject," and these are both case sensitive. If the response is equal to "Approve," we run a SharePoint "Delete Item' action" to delete the requested record. With the "Delete Item" action, it's necessary to supply a numeric ID value. Because the "Ask in Power Apps" parameter returns a string value, we can build an expression that wraps the "Ask in Power Apps" input value inside a call to the int function.

How exactly does an approver authorize an approval request? When the flow runs, the request will appear in the Approvals section on the Power Automate website, as shown in Figure 25-26. From this section, the user can view the details of the approval request and can choose to approve, reject, or reassign the request.

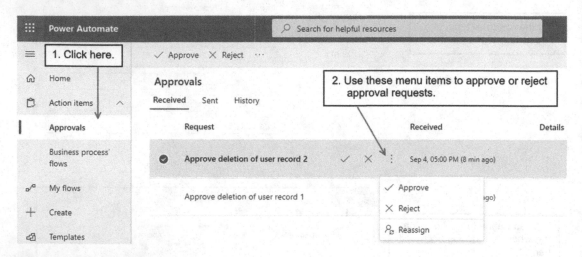

Figure 25-26. *Approving or rejecting approval requests*

To build a flow that requires approval from multiple users, we can chain together a series of approval actions. We can then build a condition to test the acceptance of all approval actions, and if all the results are true, we can carry out our required action.

Other Examples

In the final part of this chapter, we'll take a brief look at other tasks that we can perform with Power Automate.

Managing Files

Power Automate provides a great way to manage files. We can connect to cloud storage accounts, such as OneDrive, and we can perform all the common file operations that we would expect. This includes finding files, listing files in folders, and creating, copying, and deleting files.

A useful feature is the ability to access files and folders on local networks through the file system connector. The prerequisite to using the file system connector is to install the on-premises gateway. Figure 25-27 shows the start of a flow to copy a user-specified file from OneDrive. Through the file system connector, we can access file and folder locations using UNC (Universal Naming Convention) syntax (e.g., \\server\share\ filename.txt).

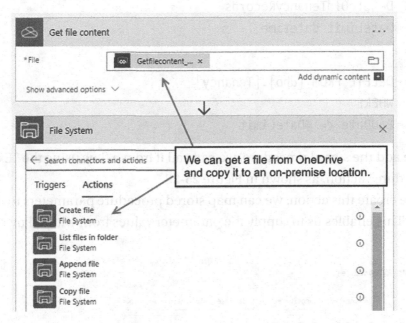

Figure 25-27. Examples of file operations with OneDrive and file system connectors

Calling SQL Stored Procedures

For app builders who work with SQL Server, we can use a flow to call SQL stored procedures. This capability opens many possibilities, and it provides a very effective tool to help improve performance.

To demonstrate this technique, here's how to delete all tenancy records with an end date older than a user-specified value.

Although we can perform this task in a canvas app by calling the RemoveIf function, there are two problems with this method. The first is that it performs very slowly, and the second is that because the function is non-delegable, it can delete only a maximum of 500 records. By deleting the records directly through a stored procedure, we can overcome these problems.

To demonstrate, Listing 25-1 shows the definition of a stored procedure to carry out our task. Writing stored procedures is a large topic and beyond the scope of this book. Therefore, the intention of this example is to simply create an awareness of this technique.

Listing 25-1. An example stored procedure to delete records

```
CREATE PROC DeleteOldTenancyRecords
        @DateLimit datetime

AS

        DELETE FROM [dbo].[Tenancy]
        WHERE
        EndDate <= @DateLimit
```

Once we add the stored procedure, we can call it from a flow using the "Execute stored procedure" action, as shown in Figure 25-28.

When we create this action, we can map stored procedure parameters to flow parameters. This enables us to supply the parameter values from within Power Apps.

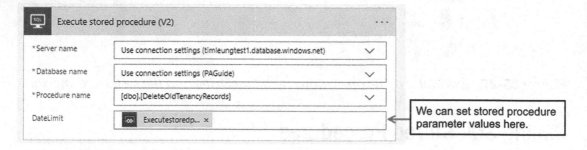

Figure 25-28. *Calling a stored procedure*

It's worth noting that for simple deletions and updates of records in SQL Server, an alternative is to use the "Delete" and "Update" actions.

Returning Results from a Flow

In the final example of this chapter, we'll find out how to return data from a flow to Power Apps. To demonstrate this technique, we'll cover another SQL Server–related performance enhancement. We'll create a flow to run a SQL query that returns a record count from our issue table. This provides a practical way to improve performance, because returning a record count from data sources can often be difficult, due to query delegation limits.

We'll create this example using the SQL query shown in Figure 25-29. This query returns a single row with a column heading of IssueCount.

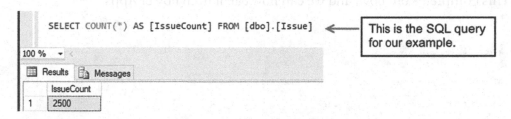

Figure 25-29. *An example of a SQL query and the result*

From our flow, we execute this query using an "Execute a SQL query" action. Figure 25-30 shows the result when we test this flow with just this single action. The notable feature is that this action returns an output called ResultsSets Table1. It is also apparent that the format of this output is in JSON.

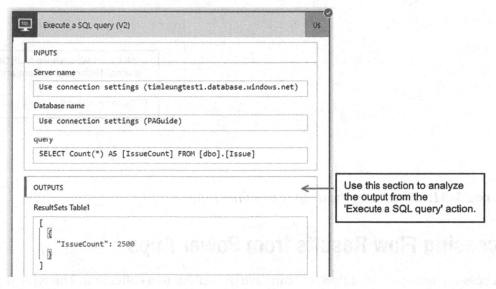

Figure 25-30. *Executing a SQL command that returns data*

Returning to our flow, we can now add the step to return this output. To do this, we add a response action. Here, there are two settings that we need to set.

The first is the body. This specifies the data that the flow returns, and for this example, we set the value to ResultsSets Table1.

The second setting is the "Response Body JSON Schema" setting. To set this, we click the "Generate from sample" button and enter the JSON output from the ResultsSets Table1 test output. This generates the schema that is shown in Figure 25-31.

This completes our flow, and we can now call it from Power Apps.

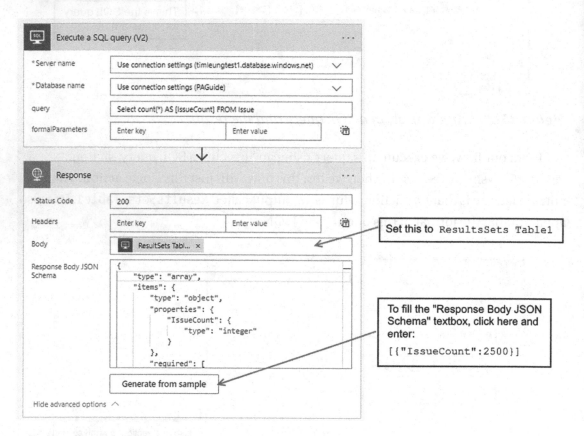

Figure 25-31. *Returning the output from the flow*

Accessing Flow Results from Power Apps

To access the output from a flow, we can save the output to a collection. The typical places where we can call a flow include a button, the OnVisible property of a screen, or the OnStart property of an app.

Assuming that we name our flow `GetIssueCount`, the formula to call the flow and to save it to a collection called `colIssueCount` looks like this:

```
ClearCollect(colIssueCount,GetIssueCount.Run())
```

Once we collect this output, we can then access the result through the collection. Figure 25-32 shows the structure of this collection in the designer.

Figure 25-32. *The schema of the collection that stores our result from a flow*

Summary

This chapter covered the topic of Power Automate, a product that carries out task automation through flows. The key benefit of Power Automate is that it offers the capability to perform tasks that are not possible with Power Apps. For example, we can optimize SQL Server performance by calling stored procedures, we can process data with AI Builder, and we can implement approval processes. It's possible to carry out file operations in internal networks by integrating flows with the on-premises gateway. We can even schedule tasks to run on a repeating basis. For model-driven apps, flows are particularly useful because they provide a way to perform tasks on data sources other than Dataverse.

Power Automate offers a browser-based graphical designer that caters for non-developers. The flows we build can include loops and conditions, they can accept input values from Power Apps, and they can also return data back to Power Apps.

A flow consists of a trigger and one or more actions. A trigger defines an event, for example, "when a new document is added to SharePoint." In response to a trigger, we can carry out an action, for example, "Send an email to a manager."

Flows use the same data connectors that are available in Power Apps. We can access SharePoint, Excel, SQL Server, and Dataverse data sources. We can access internal company resources through the on-premises gateway, and we can also connect to data sources using custom connectors and bespoke HTTP requests.

From within a flow, we can define variables and apply logic using a language called Workflow Definition Language. Workflow Definition Language includes functions that can carry out string manipulation, date formatting, and other programming tasks.

From the properties of any action, we can apply Workflow Definition Language commands in most places where we can enter text. We can build these commands using an expression builder. Through this designer, we can insert an "Ask in Power Apps" option in places where we want to accept an input value from Power Apps. The "Data Operations – Compose" action is particularly useful because it provides a place to execute and to return values from Workflow Definition Language commands.

To call a flow from a canvas app, we click the Power Automate button from the insert menu to add a flow to an app. From a formula, we can reference the flow by name, and we can call the Run method to execute the flow.

From a model-driven app, there are three ways to call a flow. First, we can use automated triggers to initiate a flow. This technique can execute a flow whenever a user makes a change to record. Second, we can attach a Power Automate flow to a business process flow. This adds a button to a model-driven form that enables the user to call a flow. Finally, we can configure flows so that they appear in the flow menu item in the header section of the model-driven app.

The approval framework in Power Automate enables us to build flows with actions that run only after the approval of one or more individuals. The approval requests will appear through the Approvals section on the Power Automate website.

We can configure a flow to return data to Power Apps. To do this, we configure the flow to return JSON data through a response action. To set up the response, we use the properties of the response action to define the output and the schema of the response data. To access this data from Power Apps, we collect the output of the flow into a collection.

PART VIII

Administration

CHAPTER 26

Transferring Apps and Data

Throughout the development of an app, there are stages where the ability to transfer apps and data is necessary.

Before the go live phase, there is often a requirement to perform data migrations from existing data sources. Additionally, there can also be ongoing requirements to perform regular synchronizations of data from other systems.

In larger organizations, we may choose to implement a structured development approach where we provision separate development, test, and production environments. There can also be scenarios where consultants need to build apps in a separate tenant and to deliver a complete solution when the project is complete. The common theme with these situations is the requirement to transfer apps, table definitions, and other related components.

This chapter will cover the themes that are related to transferring apps and data. Some of the specific areas that we'll cover in this chapter will include

- How to import related sets of data into Dataverse using dataflows. We'll also find out how to edit Dataverse data using the Excel add-in and look at strategies we can use to import data into SharePoint.

- We'll learn how to use the export and import controls in canvas apps. These controls provide the ability for end users to export and import data through an app.

- We'll find out how to transport apps and associated objects between environments by creating solutions. This includes how to prevent other users from changing the properties of our tables, how to reveal dependencies, and how to apply bug fixes by building patches.

853

T. Leung, *Beginning Power Apps*, https://doi.org/10.1007/978-1-4842-6683-0_26

Managing Data

In the first section of this chapter, we'll explore the data transfer capabilities that are available with two popular data sources – Dataverse and SharePoint.

Transferring Dataverse Data with Dataflows

We can easily transfer data into Dataverse from a wide range of data sources using a feature of the Power Platform called dataflows. Dataflows are based on a data transformation engine called Power Query. Dataflows offer a cloud-based service with a browser-based graphical interface. We can build dataflows to retrieve and transform data from a data source and to store the output in Dataverse or Azure Data Lake.

When we first deploy a system based on Dataverse, a common task is to carry out an initial migration of data from an existing data source. Dataflows are an ideal tool to carry out this task. We can also execute dataflows on a schedule, and we can use this to synchronize external data sources with Dataverse or to help create aggregated results for archiving or reporting purposes.

To demonstrate this feature, we'll walk through the process of migrating data from Excel into our property tables.

In keeping with a real-life scenario, we'll import a related set of data from two tables in a spreadsheet. The first Excel table contains a list of property types, and the second table contains a list of properties. Each property record includes a lookup to a property type record. The import process must retain this relationship. Figure 26-1 shows the data from these two Excel tables.

	A	B
1	PropertyTypeID	PropertyTypeDesc
2	1	House
3	2	Apartment
4	3	Bungalow
5	4	Villa

	A	B	C	D	E
1	PropertyID	PropertyTypeID	Address1	Address2	City
2	1	1	181 Hague St.	51 Green Firs	Sheffield
3	2	2	3 South Street	83 South Cla	Norwich
4	3	3	79 North Oak R	135 North G	Sunderlan
5	4	4	57 White Fabie	715 North Fa	Oxford
6	5	1	173 North Rock	23 East Fabie	Walsall
7	6	2	269 Clarendon	88 White Firs	Preston

Figure 26-1. *The layout of our source Excel data*

Let's review the schema of the Dataverse property type and property tables which will receive this data. The property type table includes a property type ID field and a property type description field.

The property table stores address details and includes a property type lookup field. Figure 26-2 illustrates the property table and highlights the relationship that defines the property type lookup field.

Tables > **Property**

| Columns | Relationships | Business rules | Views | Forms | Dashboards | Charts | Keys | Data |

Display name ↑ ∨		Name ∨	Data type ∨	Type ∨
Active	···	cr8a9_active	≡ Choice	Custom
Address1 Primary Name Column	···	cr8a9_address1	Abc Text	Custom
Address2	···	cr8a9_address2	Abc Multilin...	Custom

Tables > **Property**

| Columns | Relationships | Business rules | Views | Forms | Dashboards | Charts | Keys | Data |

Display name ↓ ∨		Relationship name ∨		Related table ∨	Relationshi... ∨
Regarding	···	cr8a9_property1_Pr	This relationship defines the Property Type lookup field.		o-many
Record	···	cr8a9_property1_Sy			o-many
PropertyType	···	cr8a9_PropertyType1_cr8a9_PropertyType_cr		PropertyType	Many-to-one

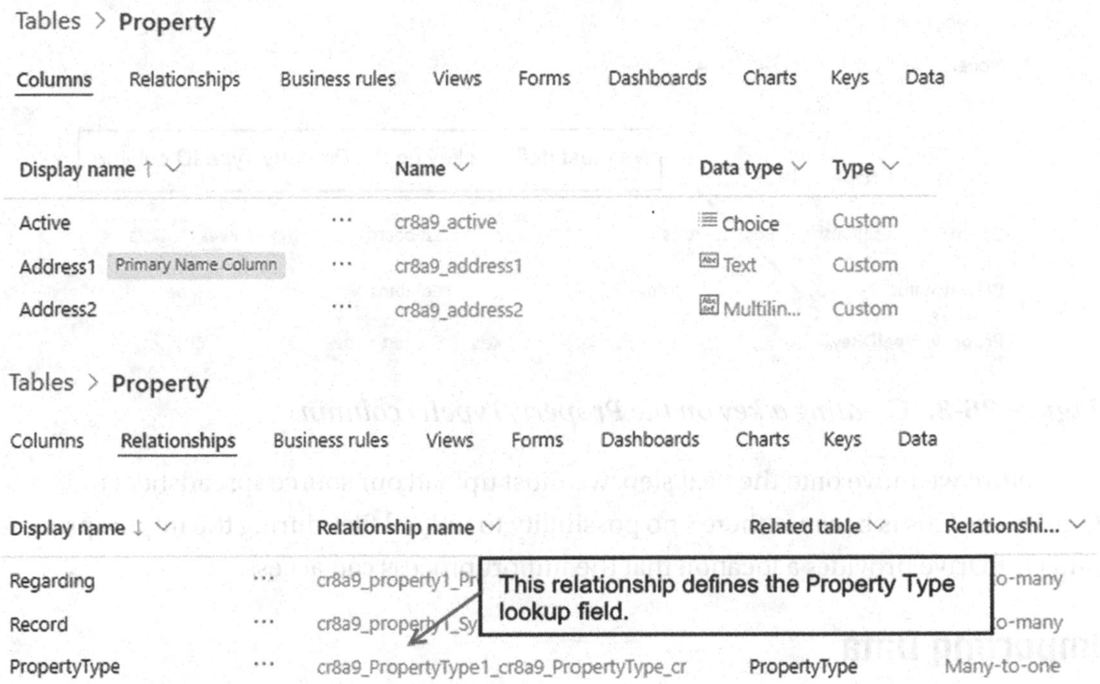

Figure 26-2. *The schema of the Dataverse property table*

To be able to set the lookup value that references the property type table when we import the property records, an important step is to define a key on the `PropertyTypeID` column, as shown in Figure 26-3.

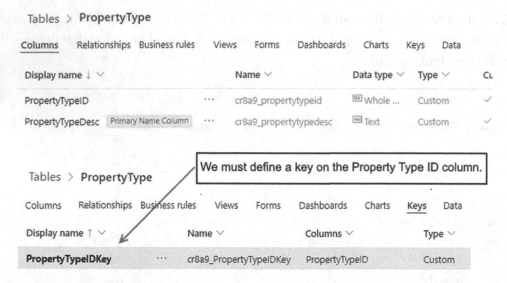

Figure 26-3. *Creating a key on the PropertyTypeID column*

Before we move onto the next step, we must upload our source spreadsheet to OneDrive. This is because there's no possibility to upload files during the import process, and OneDrive provides a location that the import process can access.

Importing Data

To build a dataflow, we select the Data ➤ Dataflows menu item from the Maker Portal. From here, we can create a new dataflow. The initial screen prompts us to enter a name and presents a screen that enables us to select our data source. If we choose the Excel option, the next screen enables us to provide the location of the source spreadsheet. From here, we can connect to OneDrive, or we can create a connection using the on-premises gateway (Figure 26-4).

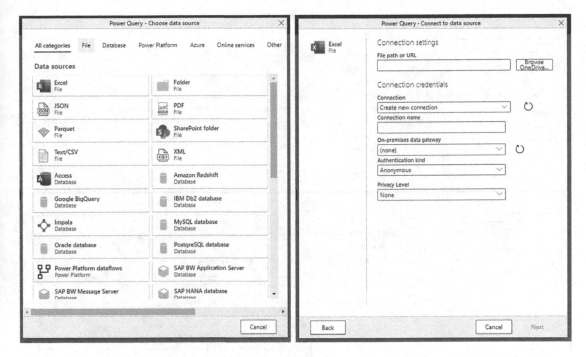

Figure 26-4. *Choosing and connecting to a data source*

The next screen displays a list of tables that are available in the selected Excel spreadsheet, and we can check one or more tables to import. In this example, we choose the property and property type tables.

The next screen enables us to review and to configure the source data (Figure 26-5).

We can use the left-hand panel to select the source Excel table to configure, and we can use the controls in the ribbon bar to filter and to transform the data.

Notable settings include the "Use first row as headers" option. We should select this if the first row in our Excel spreadsheet contains the column headings.

The other features we can find in the ribbon bar are powerful and intuitive to use. For example, we can use the Keep rows option to return a top number of rows.

From the transform menu, we can transpose and pivot columns and split source values into multiple columns. One reason why the transformation options are useful is because we can use the feature to populate reporting tables from a flattened data source. We can run these dataflows on a schedule, and this technique can help improve performance and overcome data retrieval limitations that may arise due a lack of query delegation support.

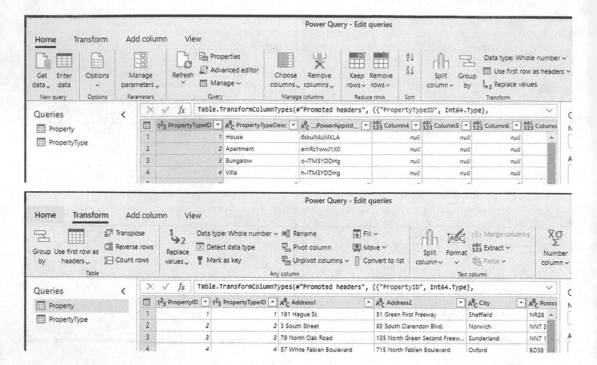

Figure 26-5. *Reviewing the input data*

The next screen in the dataflow process enables us to set the target table and column mappings. The left-hand pane enables us to select the source Excel table. From the "Load settings" section, we can choose to load the data into a new or existing table.

Figure 26-6 shows the setup for our property data. From the "Load settings" area, we choose to load the data to our existing property table. In the "Field mapping" section, we can define how to map the fields from the source Excel spreadsheet to our destination property table.

To correctly set the property type for the records that we import, notice that the property type lookup field appears as a destination field in the Field mapping section. This section identifies the field by logical name, so in this example, the field name that we see is cr8a9_PropertyType.cr8a9_PropertyTypeID.

We can map this lookup field to the source field PropertyTypeID. Because we earlier defined the "property type ID" field as a key in the property type table, the dataflow can set the lookup field based on the property type ID.

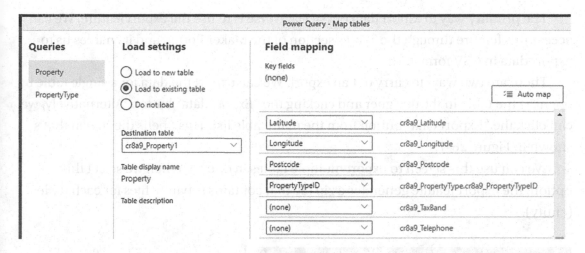

Figure 26-6. *Mapping tables and fields*

In the final screen, we can choose to schedule the job to reoccur. If we select the manual option, the job will rerun immediately. Assuming there are no errors, our data will import into our destination table.

In practice, it is likely that the source data will contain values that cause the import to fail. In these cases, we can diagnose the cause by viewing the refresh history of the dataflow through the Dataflows page in the Maker Portal. Here, we can download a spreadsheet that summarizes the result of a dataflow. This provides a count of the records that have been successfully imported. Where records have failed to import, the spreadsheet will describe the reason for the failure.

Tip   If we want to transform data to destinations other than Dataverse or Azure Data Lake, we can consider using Azure Data Factory. Although this is not a citizen developer tool, it supports a greater number of data destinations and works more effectively with source data that is very large.

Exporting Data

Although we can easily transform and transfer data into Dataverse, the ability to transfer data out to other systems is more limited.

The primary way to export data out of Dataverse is to use the export feature. We can access this feature through the Tables section of the Maker Portal, and it enables us to export data in CSV format.

There are two ways to carry out an export. We can export the data for a single table by opening the table in the designer and clicking the "Export data" button. Alternatively, we can click the "Export data" button from the main table list. This opens the screen that's shown in Figure 26-7.

We can use this screen to export multiple tables in one go. When we select this option, the export feature generates a zip file that contains separate files for each table (entity).

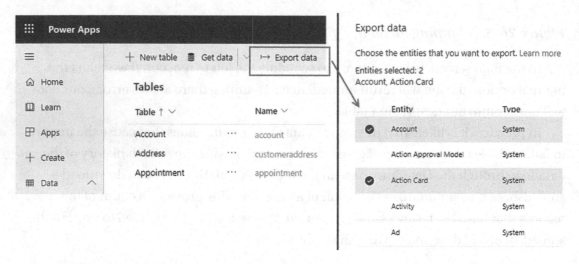

Figure 26-7.   *Exporting data to Excel*

Managing Dataverse Data with Excel

An effective way to work directly with Dataverse data is to use the Excel add-in. This works with up-to-date versions of Excel and Excel Online, and we can use it to view, edit, and delete rows from a table. A big benefit of the add-in is that we can take advantage of the copy and paste features in Excel. This enables us to quickly add, edit, and manipulate data.

To demonstrate how to use the add-in, here's how to edit our property table in Excel. The first step is to open the property table from the Maker Portal and to click the "Open in Excel" button. This initiates the download of an Excel file. When this file downloads, we can open it directly in Excel.

Excel opens this file in "protected view," and we need to click the "Enable editing" button that appears in the banner to enable the option to edit the file. At this stage, the add-in will appear as shown in Figure 26-8, and the initial view will prompt us to log in using our Microsoft login credentials.

Recent versions of Excel will install the add-in automatically, but if for some reason the add-in doesn't appear, we can download it manually though the details on the following site:

https://docs.microsoft.com/en-us/powerapps/maker/common-data-service/ data-platform-excel-addin

The icons in the lower part of the add-in enable us to add a new record to our table. We can edit existing rows directly in the spreadsheet, and we can use the add-in panel to set lookup values.

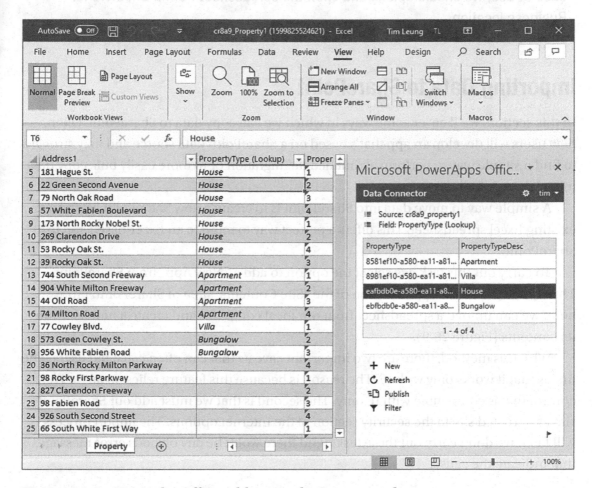

Figure 26-8. *Using the Office add-in to edit Dataverse data*

To access this feature through Excel Online, the best way is to upload the spreadsheet to OneDrive for Business. We choose OneDrive for Business because it uses Microsoft work accounts for authentication. The Power Apps add-in authenticates to Dataverse with a Microsoft work account, and by running Excel Online under the same security context as the add-in, we can avoid potential problems where the add-in fails to connect to Dataverse.

Once we upload the spreadsheet to OneDrive for Business, we can open the spreadsheet directly from the browser, and the add-in will appear in a panel, just like the desktop version of Excel.

Tip   Excel Online offers a simple way to edit Dataverse data. For the greatest ease of use, we should upload and open the spreadsheet from a OneDrive for Business location.

Importing Data to SharePoint

In this section, we'll cover some ways in which we can copy data to SharePoint. Often, new users will develop an app that's based on a SharePoint data source and may struggle to find a simple way to perform an initial data migration or to more easily bulk copy data into a SharePoint list.

A simple way to move data into SharePoint is to create a new SharePoint list from an existing Excel spreadsheet. This offers a perfect way to migrate an Excel-based app to SharePoint.

To carry out this task, we select the option to add a "New App" from SharePoint. This opens the "Your Apps" section of the "Site Contents" area of SharePoint. From here, we can upload a spreadsheet from our local computer and create a new list from its contents (Figure 26-9).

With this method, there are two important caveats that can often catch out users. The first is that it works only with IE. The reason is because this feature relies on an ActiveX control that is compatible with IE only. The second is that we must add our SharePoint site as a trusted site in the security section of the Internet options. The import process will fail if we don't carry out these tasks, and there won't be any obvious error messages that indicate the cause.

Figure 26-9. Importing Excel data into SharePoint

Working with SharePoint Data

An easy way to work with data in a SharePoint list is to use Microsoft Access. Microsoft Access is included with most Microsoft 365 subscription plans, and we can use it to link to SharePoint lists. We can then edit the data through a grid interface, and we can use copy and paste features of Microsoft Office to bulk insert or to edit records.

To link to a SharePoint list, we create a new Access database, and we use the New Data Source drop-down from the External Data section of the ribbon menu. From here, we can access a dialog to enter our SharePoint details and to select the lists that we want to link (Figure 26-10).

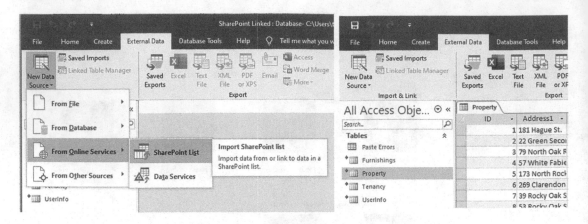

Figure 26-10. Linking to SharePoint lists from Microsoft Access

Transferring Data from Canvas Apps

In this section, we'll examine a way to allow end users to export and import data from a canvas app. To carry out this task, we can add export and import controls to a screen through the Insert ➤ Media menu item, as shown in Figure 26-11.

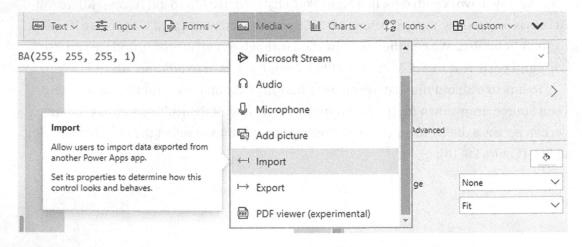

Figure 26-11. Adding the import and export controls to a screen

To demonstrate this feature, we'll build a screen that enables the user to export and to import records from our SharePoint furnishings list.

A practical use case scenario of this could be to enable users to initialize a table of data for first-time use or to build a process that resets a set of records in a table to a predetermined state.

Here's how these controls work. The export control displays a button. The user clicks this button to download and to save an export file to the local file system. The export control produces a compressed zip file that contains data in XML format. We can specify the data that we want the control to export. This could include all records from a data source or a filtered subset of data.

The import control also displays a button. When a user clicks this button, the control prompts the user to select an export file. From within an app, we can write a formula to process the data that the user uploads. We can patch this data to a data source, or we can carry out other custom tasks.

Exporting Data

To build our example, the first step is to create an app and to add a connection to our SharePoint data source. Next, we create a new screen and insert an export control. We use the Data property to specify the data to export, as shown in Figure 26-12. We can set the value of this to a table; or we can call functions like Filter, Search, or Lookup to limit the export data. In this example, we call the Filter function to return items from our SharePoint Furnishings list with a GroupID of 1.

Figure 26-12. *Adding an export control*

At this point, we can run our app and examine what happens. When we click the export button, the browser will download the export file. We can use this later with the import control.

The export file that Power Apps produces is a compressed zip file that contains three separate files, as shown in Figure 26-13. The main file that contains the data is called data.xml. It's possible to modify the contents of this file in a text editor. If we were to modify the contents manually, we would need to recompress the file with the header and schema files before importing it into Power Apps.

Name	^	Date modified	Type	Size
📄 data		19/06/2017 23:10	XML Document	2 KB
🗍 header		19/06/2017 23:10	JSON File	1 KB
🗍 schema		19/06/2017 23:10	JSON File	5 KB

Figure 26-13. *The extracted contents of the export file*

In this example, we export a single table. If we want to export multiple tables, we can build a collection that contains the multiple child tables. We would then set the Data of the export control to the collection. This provides a method that we can use to export sets of related data.

As an example, here's the formula to build a collection that contains a single row with two child tables – a child table with records from the SharePoint Furnishings list and a child table with records from the Inventory list:

```
ClearCollect(colData,
            {FurnishingsTable: Furnishings, InventoryTable: Inventory}
)
```

Note   At the time of writing, the browsers that provide best support for the export feature are Chrome and the newest (Chromium-based) version of Edge.

Importing Data

To build the feature that enables users to import the exported data, we add an import control to our screen. The default name of the control will be Import1, as shown in Figure 26-14.

At runtime, a user clicks this control and uploads an export file. We add a formula to the OnSelect property of the control to store the results to a collection. At this stage, we can add additional formula to process this data. For example, we could use the collection as a data source to add new records to a data source.

Alternatively, we could synchronize the collection with the existing live data source using the same technique that we used to synchronize offline records from Chapter 23.

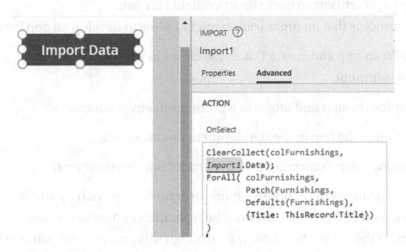

Figure 26-14. *The import control*

To complete this feature, here's how to add each record from the import operation as a new record in the SharePoint furnishings list. We would add the following formula to the OnSelect property of the import control:

```
ClearCollect(colFurnishings, Import1.Data);
ForAll( colFurnishings,
        Patch(Furnishings,
        Defaults(Furnishings), {Title: ThisRecord.Title})
)
```

Transporting Apps with Solutions

Solutions enable us to move apps and components from one environment to another. Following an initial deployment, they provide a means to apply updates to apps and components that we've already deployed.

Solutions also help us to organize our work. Each environment can only contain a single Dataverse database, and once we develop a few apps, the list of tables and apps in the Maker Portal can be overwhelming. A solution keeps related apps and objects together and can help us stay more focused and organized while we work.

Another practical use of solutions is to publish objects to Dataverse during the development phase. As we saw in previous chapters, it's necessary to publish various model-driven app artifacts to make them available for use.

A simple process that an organization might follow to develop an app looks like this:

- Build an app and create Dataverse tables in a development environment.

- Deploy the app and tables to a production environment.

- Enhance the app in the development environment.

- Deploy the enhancements to the production environment.

Some organizations may choose a more structured approach by adding additional phases such as test and pre-production. The principles of how to use solutions would however remain the same. We'll now walk through this process and examine how solutions can help us at each stage.

Note   We can think of a solution as a project or a container for items that we create in Power Apps.

Managing Solutions

The Solutions section of the Maker Portal enables us to create and manage solutions, as shown in Figure 26-15.

The notable items in the toolbar include menu items to create a new solution and to import an existing solution.

The main body of the page shows a list of existing solutions. Here, we see solutions that correspond to features that we've added to our Dataverse database. This could include portal and AI Builder features.

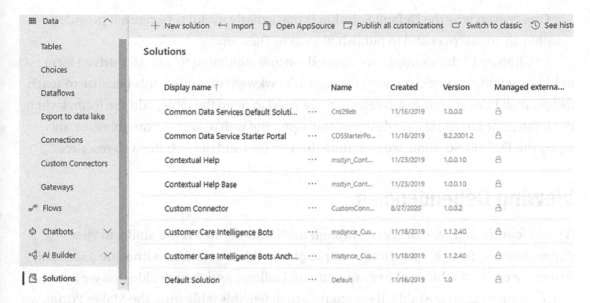

Figure 26-15. *The Solutions section of the Maker Portal*

Using the Default Solution

A special solution that appears in the list is the Default Solution. This solution is special because it automatically contains every Dataverse object and customization in an environment.

Figure 26-16 shows the view when we open the Default Solution. Here, we can see a list of everything that we've added to Dataverse, including tables, site maps, option sets, forms, and a whole range of other object types.

Display name ∨	Name	Type ∨	Managed...	Modified	Owner	Status
Application Ribbons	-	Application ribt		-		
Site Map	-	Site map		4 d ago		-
Account	account	Table		-	-	-
Account Manager	Account Manager	Connection role		4 d ago	-	Off
Account Reconnect	Account Reconnect	Email Template		4 d ago	SYSTEM	-
Account Summary	Account Summary	Report		4 d ago	SYSTEM	-

Solutions > Default Solution ← The default solution contains all items in an environment.

Figure 26-16. *The Default Solution*

One reason why the Default Solution is particularly useful is because it provides a simple way to discover and to publish objects to Dataverse.

In Chapter 13, for example, we applied custom validation to a model-driven form field by creating a JavaScript web resource. It's awkward to publish this because to reach the publish button on the web resource, we need to open the table, edit the form, switch the form editor to the classic designer, and open the web resource from this area. By using the Default Solution, we can more directly find and publish the web resource.

Viewing Dependencies

A great feature that we can access through the Solutions area is the ability to view dependencies. To give a practical example of why this is useful, let's imagine a scenario where we create a table, make various customizations, and then decide that we no longer want to keep the table. If we attempt to delete this table from the Maker Portal, we can encounter situations where the designer prevents the deletion of the object due to dependencies (Figure 26-17).

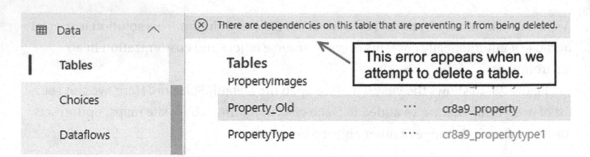

Figure 26-17. *Deleting a table*

It can be difficult to trace where these dependencies exist, especially if we've created objects such as business process flows where Power Apps creates supporting dependencies for us.

By using the "Show dependencies" option (Figure 26-18), we can discover the dependent objects and remove them through the Default Solution before we delete the target object.

Figure 26-18. *Finding dependent objects*

An equally important use of the "Show dependencies" option is to help us understand the dependencies of an object so that we can make sure to include all dependent items in a solution.

Creating a Solution

To create a solution, we click the "New solution" button from the Solutions section of the Maker Portal, as shown in Figure 26-19. This opens a panel where we can provide the basic solution settings. This includes the display name, name, and publisher values. The display name is the friendly descriptive name that appears in the user interface. The name defines the unique identifier for the solution, and this value cannot include any spaces.

Each solution is associated with a publisher, and we can use the publisher drop-down to set this value or create a new publisher. For solutions that we use internally within our organization, we can use the drop-down to select the default publisher for our organization.

A benefit of creating a bespoke publisher record is that we can use it to define the default prefix for the items that we add to the solution. In cases where we want to distribute our solution widely, it makes sense to associate our solution with a custom publisher and to apply a prefix that more clearly identifies the objects in our solution.

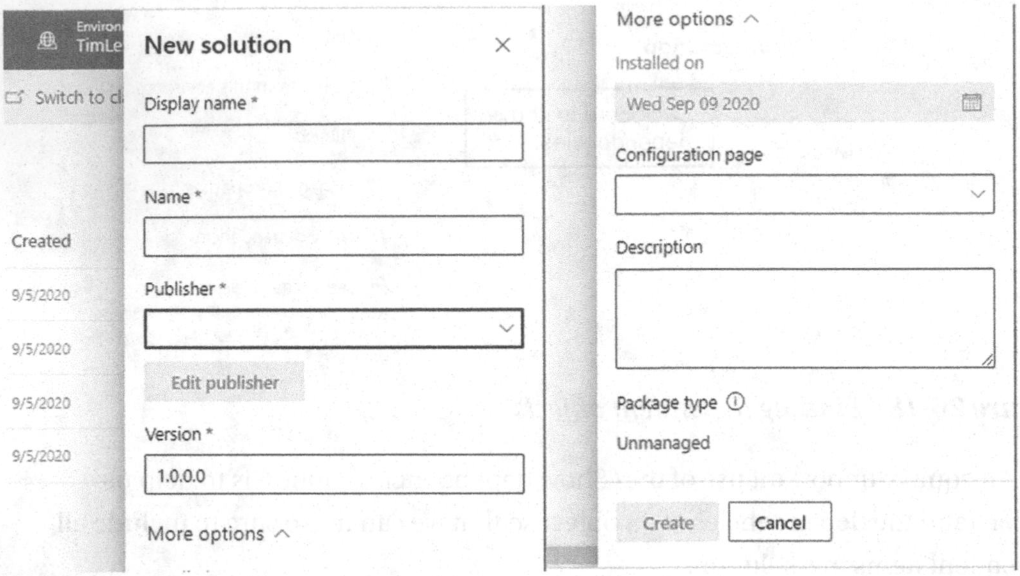

Figure 26-19. *Creating a new solution*

The configuration page drop-down enables us to select a web resource. A typical use of this setting is to define an HTML page that provides usage instructions or notes that pertain to the solution.

The most notable detail on this panel is the label that indicates the package type. Solutions are categorized into two types – unmanaged and managed.

The designated process is to develop our apps in unmanaged solutions. We use unmanaged solutions for the sole purpose of development and for moving apps and resources between development environments. During development, we can also utilize a Microsoft tool called Solution Packager. This decomposes a solution into XML files, which we can then add to a source control system.

To deploy a solution, we export our unmanaged solution as a managed solution and import this into our target environment. We then publish the managed solution to install all the components into the target environment.

The key characteristic of a managed solution is that we can uninstall the solution. That is, we can uninstall the solution and remove all the components that were installed as part of the solution.

In contrast, if we were to install an unmanaged solution into an environment, uninstalling the solution would delete just the solution. Any components that were installed as part of the solution will remain.

Furthermore, if we import an unmanaged solution that contains components that we have already modified, the solution items will overwrite the existing items.

In summary, therefore, we use unmanaged solutions to develop our work and to transfer work between development environments. We deploy and distribute our work using managed solutions.

Adding Objects to a Solution

Once we create a solution, we can add components to the solution using the buttons in the menu bar, as shown in Figure 26-20. We can use the new drop-down to create new items, or we can use the "Add existing" button to add existing items to our solution.

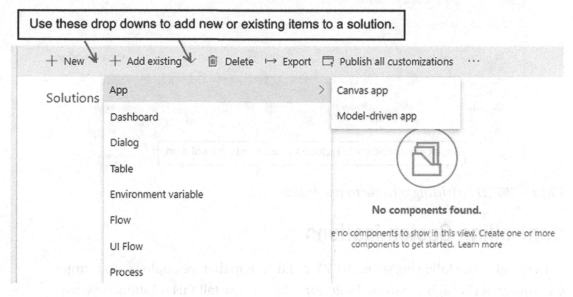

Figure 26-20. *Adding components to a solution*

Working on the basis that we've already created a canvas app based on a table, we can add the app and table through the "Add existing" menu item.

To add existing tables, the "Add existing" ➤ Table menu item displays a panel that we can use to choose the tables to add to our solution. The next page enables us to select for each table whether to include all components. If we select this option, the solution will include all child components that are associated with the table. This includes all properties, relationships, business rules, views, forms, dashboards, charts, and keys. If we choose not to select this option, we can select precisely the components that we want to include (Figure 26-21).

873

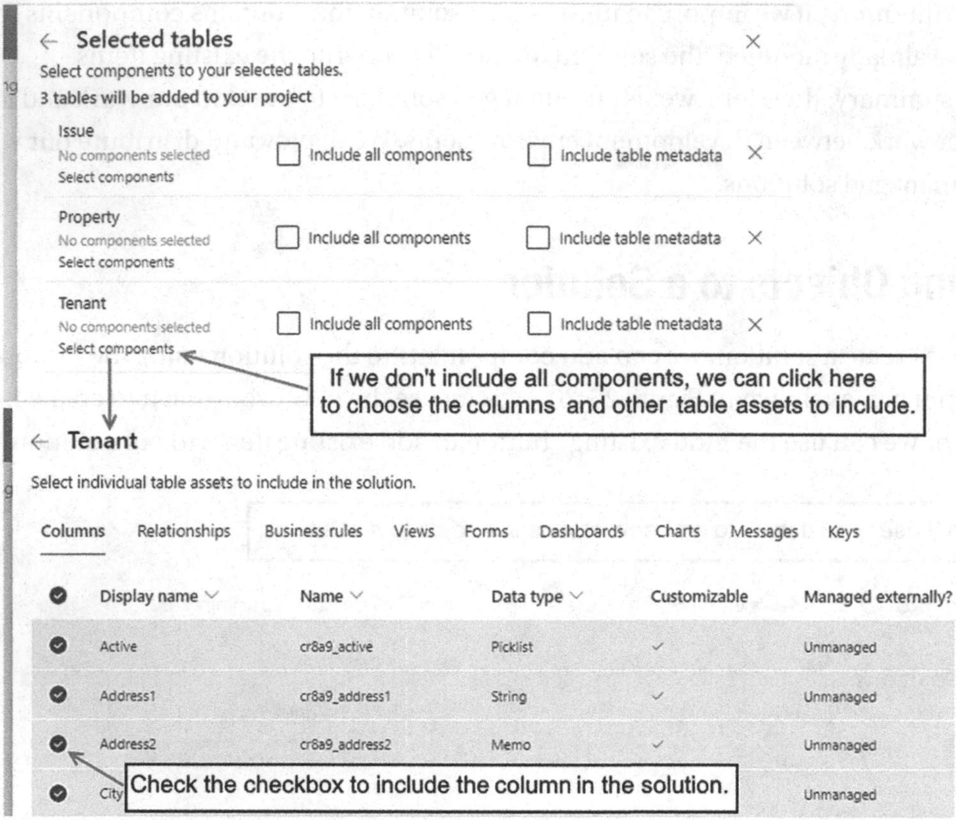

Figure 26-21. Adding a table to a solution

Controlling Customizations

Let's imagine the following scenario. We build an app that we deploy onto a target environment through a managed solution. Once we install this solution, we want to prevent further changes to our tables. A typical reason to do this is to reduce the possibility of other users breaking our apps by modifying tables that our apps rely on.

From our unmanaged solution, we can use the Managed Properties panel to control the customizations that are permissible when we export the unmanaged solution as a managed solution.

As we can see from Figure 26-22, we can control the ability for users to customize the display name and the ability to change additional properties and to add new forms, views, and more.

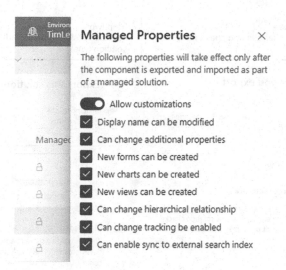

Figure 26-22. *Managing properties*

Exporting a Solution

To export a solution, we open the solution and click the export button from the toolbar. This opens the panel that's shown in Figure 26-23.

There are two buttons in this initial panel. The first button publishes the changes in our solution. The reason this is important is because the export operation exports the latest published version of the components. If there are unpublished changes, the export operation will not reflect the latest changes.

The second button enables us to run the solution checker. This validates our solution and produces a report that indicates any problems.

The next step enables us to choose whether to export the solution as a managed solution or an unmanaged solution. We can also set a version number. In terms of ongoing developments, a typical practice is to continue development in our unmanaged solution and to increase the version number each time we release a change by building a managed solution.

For this example, we'll choose to export our solution as a managed solution. The export button will initiate the download of our exported solution file.

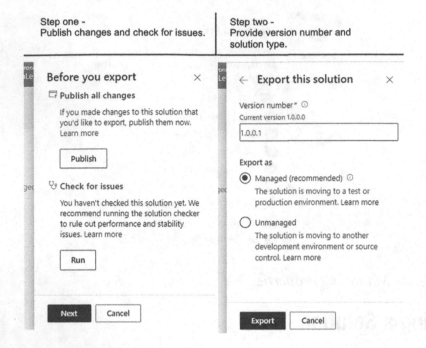

Figure 26-23. Exporting a solution

Importing a Solution

Now that we've exported our solution, we can import it into our target production environment.

From our target environment, we go to the Solutions section of the Maker Portal and click the import button from the top menu. This opens a panel that enables us to select our solution file. When the import process completes, we can open the solution, as shown in Figure 26-24. With a managed solution, the import process will publish the components in the solution. With an unmanaged solution, we can click the "Publish all customizations" button to manually publish the items in the solution.

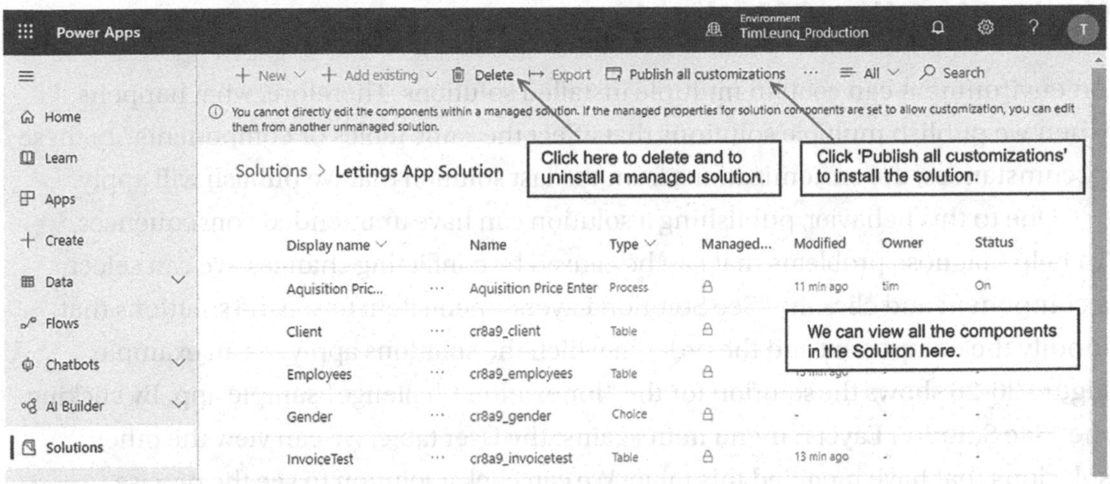

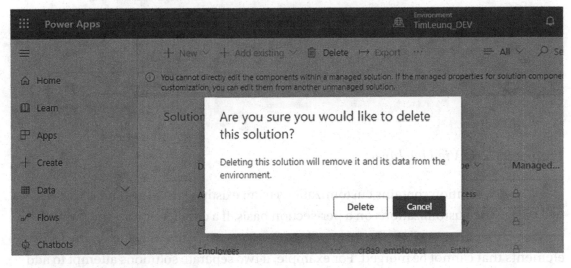

Figure 26-24. Viewing an imported managed solution

After we publish our customizations, it's possible to undo this action because our solution type is a managed solution. We would click the delete button to uninstall all the customizations and to delete the solution. As Figure 26-25 shows, the designer shows a warning that describes this behavior when we click the delete button.

Figure 26-25. Deleting a managed solution

Understanding Solution Layers

An environment can contain multiple installed solutions. Therefore, what happens when we publish multiple solutions that affect the same tables or components? In these circumstances, the customizations from the last solution that we publish will apply.

Due to this behavior, publishing a solution can have unintended consequences. To help diagnose problems that can be caused by conflicting changes, we can select a component and click the "See Solution Layers" menu item to see the solutions that modify the component and the order in which the solutions apply. As an example, Figure 26-26 shows the solution for the "Innovation Challenge" sample app. By clicking the "See Solution Layers" menu item against the User table, we can view the other solutions that have modified this table. We can click a solution to see the precise properties that were modified by the solution.

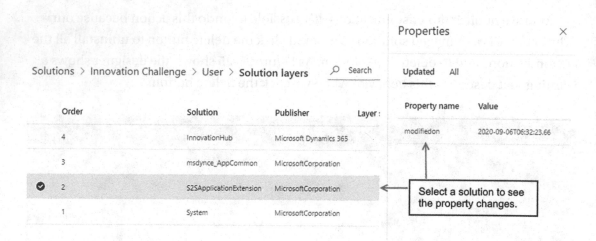

Figure 26-26.   *Viewing layers*

Where a solution contains customizations to an existing form, the publish process will merge the customizations on a per-section basis. If a conflict occurs, the publish process creates a new tab in the form called "Conflicts tab." This will contain the form elements that cannot be merged. For example, if two separate solutions attempt to add a new tab with the same name, the new tab elements from the second tab will appear in the "Conflicts tab."

Creating a Patch

Let's suppose we deploy our solution into our production environment, and soon after, we discover a bug in our app. To deliver a minor fix, we can build a patch. To do this, we locate our source unmanaged solution and click the Clone ➤ "Clone a patch" menu item (Figure 26-27).

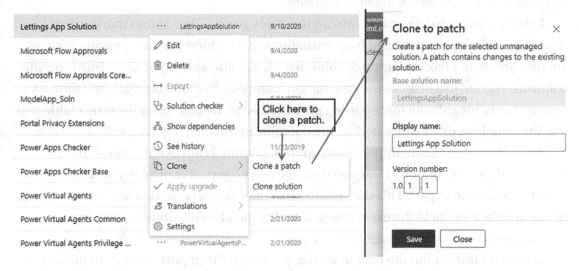

***Figure 26-27.** Cloning a patch*

After we clone a patch, it will appear in the solutions list. We can open this patch solution and add our updated components. Next, we can export the solution as a managed solution. As with any other solution, we can import and publish the solution in our target environment to install the changes.

Summary

This chapter covered the topic of how to import and export data and apps. In the first section, we covered data transfer features that relate to Dataverse and SharePoint. Next, we looked at how to build a feature to enable users to import and export data from canvas apps. In the final section, we looked at how to use solutions to transfer apps and components between environments.

Dataflows are a feature that facilitates the transformation and transfer of data into Dataverse. We can use dataflows to carry out one-time transfers of data (e.g., during an initial data migration), or we can execute dataflows on a schedule. This can help synchronize external data sources with Dataverse, or we can run scheduled jobs to create aggregated results for archiving or reporting purposes.

We can build a dataflow using a wide range of data sources (around 50 in total). This includes Excel, SQL Server, flat files, and more.

Once we select a data source, we can use a designer to filter and to transform our data. We can carry out powerful transformations that include the transposition of data and the ability to pivot and unpivot columns. We can also split input fields into multiple columns. A great use of these transformation features is to shape our data into formats that are more meaningful for reporting purposes. Next, we can select the target table and run the dataflow, or we can schedule the dataflow to run on a regular basis.

To enable end users to import and export data from a canvas app, we can use the import and export controls. To export data, we add an export control to a screen and specify the data to export. This data could be a collection, a table, or a filtered set of data. At runtime, a user clicks the export control to download an export file. This file contains a compressed copy of the data in XML format.

Users can import this file data into an app through the import control. To utilize this control, we add the control to a screen and attach a formula to the OnSelect property to define the actions to carry out. Typically, we first add the data to a collection, and we can then cleanse, validate, and transform the data prior to saving it to a data source.

To export and import sets of related data, we can export a collection that contains a nested set of tables. We can then import these records and patch the parent records, followed by the child records.

A useful tool is the Power Apps Office add-in. This enables us to add, edit, and delete Dataverse records from Microsoft Excel. The reason this is very useful is because it enables us to work with multiple rows, and we can take advantage of productivity features in Microsoft Office, such as copy and paste. To use this feature, we download an Excel file from the table designer. When we open the file, the add-in will appear in a panel from within Excel.

Solutions enable us to move apps and components between environments. They support the development process of using separate environments to build and to deliver an app. Solutions also help organize our work by providing a container that contains all the components that pertain to a project.

We use the Solutions area of the Maker Portal to add and to manage solutions. A special solution is the Default Solution. This solution contains every object and component in our Dataverse environment. We can use this to quickly locate components, and we can also use it to publish individual components.

From within a solution, a useful feature is the ability to view all the dependencies. This can be very helpful when the designer prevents the deletion of an object due to dependencies.

There are two solution types – unmanaged and managed solutions. We use an unmanaged solution to develop an app. To deploy and distribute a solution to a production environment, we export our unmanaged solution as a managed solution and import this into the target production environment.

The key characteristic of a managed solution is that it is possible to uninstall the solution and to delete all the components that were installed as part of the solution. We can also control the ability to customize components that are installed as part of a managed solution.

From within a solution, we can add new or existing items. When we add a table to a solution, we can include all components (e.g., fields, relationships, forms, and views), or we can select individual components.

From within an environment, many solutions can target the same component. If we select a component from a solution, we can use the "See Solution Layers" menu item to view the solutions that modify the component and the order in which these modifications take place.

If we release a solution and discover a bug that we need to fix, we can distribute minor changes by building a patch. To do this, we clone the source unmanaged solution as a patch, add the updated components to the patch solution, and then export the patch as a managed solution. We can then import this managed solution into the target environment and install the patch.

CHAPTER 27

Administering Security

This chapter focuses on security-related features and covers the tasks that an administrator would typically perform. We'll cover how to strengthen the authentication process, how to control access to Dataverse and SharePoint data sources, and how to protect sensitive corporate data with data loss prevention policies.

We'll learn how to manage apps and settings using the command line scripting language PowerShell. This can be particularly helpful in cases where we need to carry out identical actions across multiple environments or tenants.

We'll also find out how to trace user activity through the auditing and analytic features of the Power Platform. Some of the key topics that we'll cover in this chapter will include

- How we can configure multifactor authentication to strengthen the authentication process.

- How the Dataverse security model works. We'll find out how to control access to tables, including how to configure row access security. We'll also find out how to better protect SharePoint and techniques that we can use to hide lists from users.

- How we can use the analytic features to review the geographic locations of app launches, the devices and platforms that users are using, and summaries of performance and errors.

Securing Data Sources

We'll begin this chapter by looking at how to strengthen the authentication process and how we can better protect data in Dataverse and SharePoint data sources.

© Tim Leung 2021
T. Leung, *Beginning Power Apps*, https://doi.org/10.1007/978-1-4842-6683-0_27

Configuring Authentication Settings

To protect against hackers and unauthorized logins, we can configure settings to strengthen the authentication process.

Users authenticate using AAD (Azure Active Directory) accounts. Through AAD settings, we can enable multifactor authentication, and we can also configure conditional access policies.

With multifactor authentication enabled, users log on by entering a username and password. To complete the authentication process, the user must verify the login through a mobile device. It's possible to configure AAD to call or to send an SMS code to the user's mobile device. The default method is to verify the authentication attempt using the "Microsoft Authenticator" app. This is a mobile app that is available on Android or iOS devices. A user links the "Microsoft Authenticator" app with their user account during the first login attempt. During this first login attempt, the login screen displays a QR code. The user scans this code with the "Microsoft Authenticator" app to associate the mobile device with the user account.

By configuring conditional access policies, we can further tighten the authentication process. A conditional access policy relies on if-then statements. As an example, if the user is an administrator, multifactor authentication is required.

A conditional access policy can apply rules based on account group membership, IP addresses, and the device profile, and it can also assess the risk level in an automated way. Depending on the condition, the policy can block the login attempt, it can require multifactor authentication, or it can impose other security requirements.

To configure authentication settings, we log onto the Azure Portal (`https://portal.azure.com/`) and navigate to the "Azure Active Directory" section by using the search.

When we provision a new tenant, AAD imposes tight security defaults and requires all users to log in using multifactor authentication. The setting that controls this is the "Enable Security defaults," beneath the properties section (Figure 27-1).

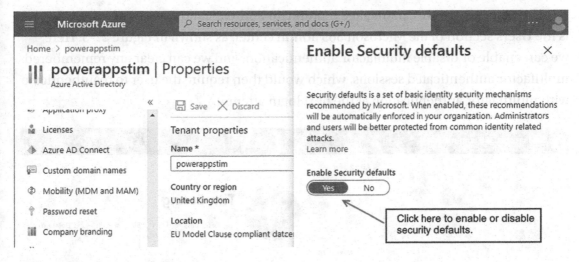

Figure 27-1. *Enabling security defaults*

Through the security section, we can navigate to the conditional access policy section. Here, we can create and manage conditional access policies as shown in Figure 27-2.

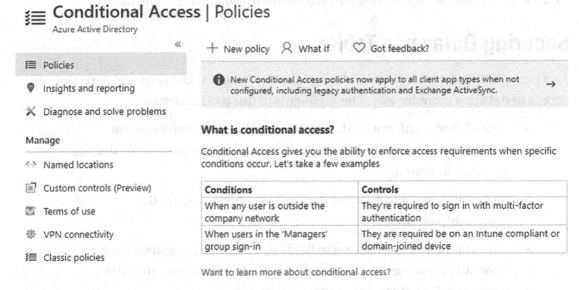

Figure 27-2. *Managing conditional access policies*

The place where we can manage multifactor authentication settings for specific users is the Users section of the Microsoft 365 admin center, as shown in Figure 27-3. Here, we can enable or disable multifactor authentication, and we can clear any remembered multifactor authenticated sessions, which would then require the user to reauthenticate with multifactor authentication at the next login attempt.

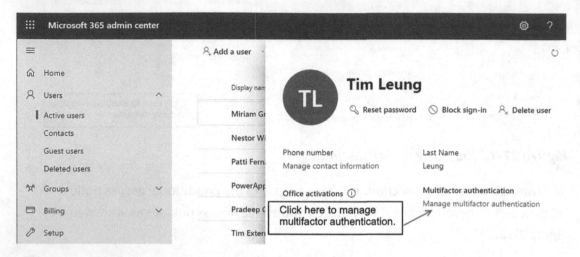

Figure 27-3.   Setting up multifactor authentication for a specific user

Securing Dataverse Tables

As a premium data source, Dataverse provides a powerful security model that controls access to data in a granular way. The highlights of this model include

- The ability to enforce read, edit, create, and delete privileges on tables. We can also apply additional permissions that apply to sharing and collaboration.

- The ability to control access to rows in a table, based on the ownership of rows.

- The ability to restrict access to fields in a table. For example, if we have an employee table that includes a salary field, we can restrict access to this field to only certain users.

We'll introduce this topic by walking through a simple example. Let's imagine that we've built a canvas app that's based on the tenancy table. There are three active users in our system – Tim, Jenifer, and Jill. The requirement is to grant Tim and Jenifer full access to the data and to restrict Jill to read-only access only.

Introducing Security Roles

The Dataverse security model is based largely around security roles. When we configure security, this is the area where we typically spend most time.

From within a security role, we specify tables and the associated privileges. For example, we can create a security role called "Manager"; and we can assign read, edit, create, and delete privileges to the tenancy table for all records in the organization.

Once we create a security role, we can assign the role to a specific user or a team. Figure 27-4 illustrates this setup.

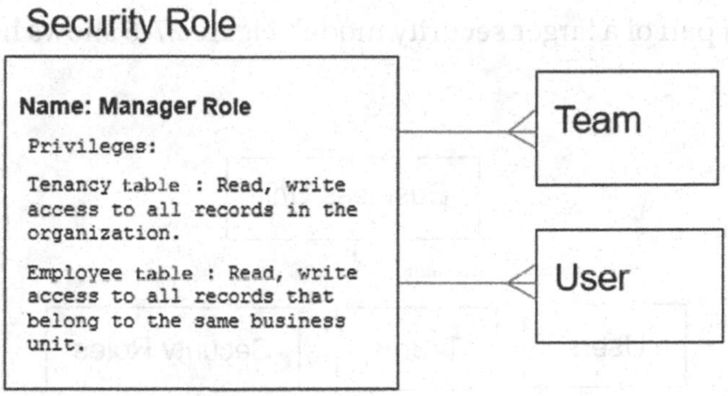

Figure 27-4. *Security roles*

Dataverse provides several built-in roles. Two notable roles are the "System Administrator" and "System Customizer" roles. The "System Administrator" role is the most powerful and effectively allows any user in that role the ability to perform everything in Dataverse.

The "System Customizer" role is a lighter version of the "System Administrator" role. The main purpose of this role is to provide permissions to edit table views and forms.

There are also a number of predefined security roles that we can use. These include Sales Manager, Salesperson, Support User, and more.

Multiple security roles can apply to the same user. Where there are overlapping privileges, the most permissive privilege will apply.

> **Note**   A privilege (or permission) defines the right to perform an operation (or action) on a table. Read, write, and create privileges are the most common. The access level defines the scope of the privilege. For example, the access level of a read privilege can extend only to records that the user creates. Where there are overlapping privileges, the most permissive privilege will apply.

Business Units and Teams

Security roles form part of a larger security model. Figure 27-5 shows how security roles fit into this model.

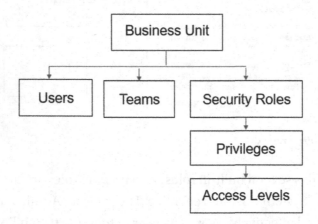

Figure 27-5.   *The parts that make up Dataverse security*

The top-level object in the security model is the business unit. A business unit owns teams, users, and security roles. By default, each Dataverse instance contains a single root business unit. We can create child business units beneath the root business unit.

A primary purpose of a business unit is to help organize users. Each user in Dataverse can belong to a single business unit only.

Business units provide a boundary for record access security. We can configure privileges to enable users in the same business unit to access records that are owned by users in this same business unit. Due to the hierarchical nature of business units, we can also apply these rules to descendant business units. For example, we can permit users in parent business units to access records that belong to child business units.

It may seem natural to build a business unit hierarchy that models the organizational chart or the departments in an organization (i.e., to create a business unit for each department). In practice, this structure can be difficult to manage, especially in cases where we want to encourage the sharing of data.

A security structure based on business units can be inflexible because it isn't possible to move security groups between business units. Also, moving users between business units can be awkward because users lose all assignments to existing security groups following a move. Therefore, it can be much simpler to maintain a single or simple business unit structure and to rely mostly on security roles to implement security roles.

Separate business units work best in scenarios where there is a clear segregation of data. An example could be a government project where all active users require a certain level of security clearance. A separate business unit can assist the separation of data for this use case scenario.

Teams provide a key way to group together sets of users. The benefit of using a team is that members can span multiple business units. Therefore, team membership provides a good way to share records between users from different business units. Unlike business units, a user can belong to more than one team.

Another useful feature is that each business unit includes a built-in team. This team automatically includes all users in the business unit, and it provides a simple way to share data with all current users in a business unit.

Understanding Record Ownership

An important topic is record ownership. This is important because row-level access relies on record ownership. For example, we can restrict a user to only being able to access records that are owned by the user.

For each table, we can specify one of two ownership types at the time of creation. These two types are organization or "user or team." It is not possible to change the ownership type after we create a table.

A table that is owned by an organization works well in situations where we want to store reference data that is visible to everyone in the organization.

With the "user or team" ownership type, each record will be owned by a user or team. This enables us to restrict access to records on a more granular basis.

Creating a Security Role

We configure security settings at an environment level through the Power Platform admin center. First, we choose an environment and navigate to the Settings ➤ "Users + permissions" section, as shown in Figure 27-6. From this area, we can also manage teams, users, business units, and hierarchical security settings.

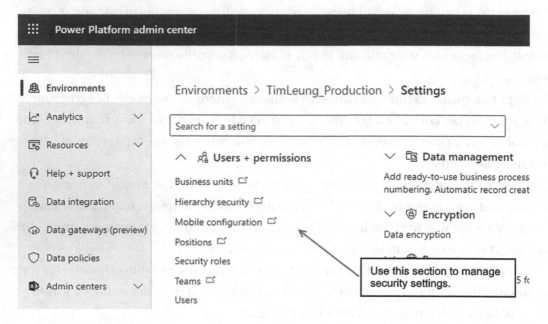

Figure 27-6. *Managing security roles settings*

To create a security role, we click the security roles link. This opens a page that displays the available security roles in the environment. From this page, we can edit or create new security roles. The new role button opens the dialog shown in Figure 27-7. This dialog organizes the objects that we can secure in separate tabs. From the details tab, we can provide a name for the security role.

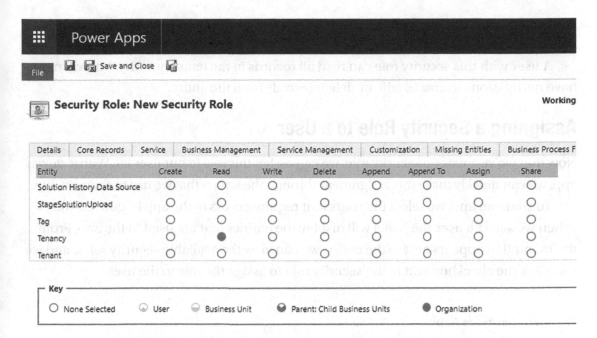

Figure 27-7. *Creating a security role*

In this example, we'll create a security role called "Lettings Viewer." The purpose of this security role is to grant read-only access to the tenancy table (from this point on, I'll refer to tables as entities because at the time of writing, the labels in the designer have not yet been updated to use the updated terminology).

We can find our tenancy entity beneath the "custom entities" tab. Here, we can configure the privileges through a grid of radio buttons. For each entity, we can set eight privileges. These are the create, read, write, delete, append, append to, assign, and share privileges.

The create, read, write, and delete privileges are self-explanatory. The append privilege defines the right to attach the entity to another entity (e.g., to use the record in a lookup field). The append to privilege defines the right to attach other entities to this entity. The assign privilege defines the right to make other users or teams the owner of a record.

We can grant a privilege by clicking the radio button that corresponds to the privilege. When we click the radio button, the color and appearance of the radio button change to indicate the access level. We can click the radio button again to toggle through the available choices and to set one of five available access levels. These access levels are none, user, business unit, parent-child business units, and organization.

Let's say that for our tenancy entity, we click the "read" radio button and set the access level to user. If a user were assigned this security role, the user would have read privileges only on the records that the user owns.

For this example, we'll set the "read" access level to "organization," and we'll leave the remaining privileges set to none.

A user with this security role can read all records in the tenancy entity, but will not have permissions to create, edit, or delete records from the entity.

Assigning a Security Role to a User

Now that we've created a security role, we can assign this role to our user Jill. With a canvas app, we can quickly make this assignment through the screen that we use to share an app.

To share an app, we select the users that require access to the app (Figure 27-8). When we select a user, the panel will display the entities that are used in the app. From the menu that appears next to the entity, we can view the available security roles, and we can click the checkbox next to the security role to assign the role to the user.

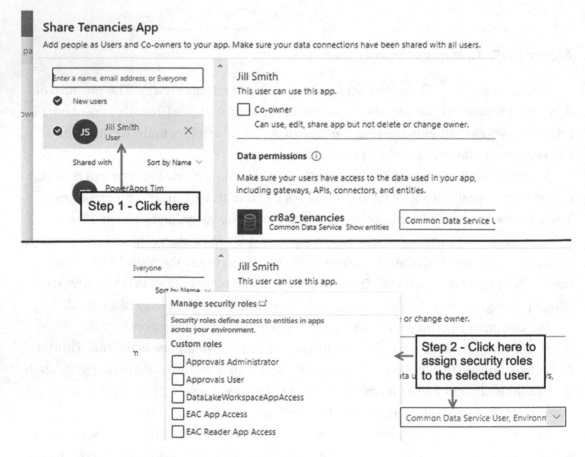

Figure 27-8. *Assigning a security role to a user*

For the other users of our app (Tim and Jenifer), we can assign a security role that grants full permissions to the tenancy entity. This completes our example, and our app will work as expected.

Testing Our App

For completeness, let's examine what happens if we did not assign the "Lettings Viewer" security role to Jill. At runtime, any control that attempts to read data from the tenancy entity will fail. Figure 27-9 shows the error that appears in the browse screen.

The error message in the banner contains the following error:

```
Missing prvReadcr8a9_Tenancy
```

To help decipher this error, prv stands for privilege, Read denotes the read privilege, and cr8a9_Tenancy describes the logical name of the entity. Errors that relate to permissions will follow this format, and we can use it to determine the exact cause.

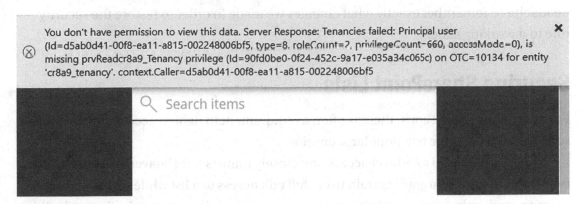

Figure 27-9. *The error that appears due to insufficient read privileges*

Concluding Notes

This section covered the basics of how to set up table/entity-level permissions. The Dataverse security model is very powerful, and we can configure permissions from many directions, including hierarchical settings. The record sharing feature enables users to share records beyond the scope of the security roles that we define, and there are management and performance challenges that are related to this.

The Power Apps share screen guides us toward assigning security groups directly to users, but it can be more manageable to assign security groups to teams. Specifically, it can be preferable to prevent users from owning records and to enforce record ownership by teams. This prevents the situation where records can end up without an owner when the owner leaves an organization.

To apply this rule, the typical setup is not to grant create privileges to individual users, but to grant create privileges to a team and to assign users to the team. As this example highlights, there are often complex patterns that we use to enforce common security use cases.

There are a couple of tips that can help when we work with Dataverse security. First, it can be very difficult to work out the effective permissions for a user because the effective rights can derive from so many places. A great tool that can provide specific details is the "User Security Manager" plug-in from XrmToolBox.

A second tip is to copy a security role before we make modifications. We can easily make mistakes when we edit a security role, and without a backup copy, it can be a headache to remember exactly what changes we made in order to restore the security role to a working state.

Securing SharePoint Lists

For SharePoint-based apps, there is often a requirement to tighten access to data. In this section, we'll examine two popular scenarios.

The first relates to role-level access and closely mimics our Dataverse example. The requirement here is to grant certain users full edit access to a list while restricting other users to read-only access. A related requirement is to restrict users to viewing and editing only the records that they own.

A second popular requirement is to hide SharePoint lists and to prevent users from directly editing records from SharePoint. We'll examine some techniques that can help with this requirement.

Implementing Role-Level Access

We'll first look at how to implement role-level access for a SharePoint list. We'll mimic our Dataverse example and find out how to grant a set of users full edit access to a list while restricting other users to read-only access.

SharePoint provides groups that we define at a site level. Groups are containers for users. Against each group, we can assign a permission level. The permission level defines the actions that are permitted, and we can use this to grant read, edit, or delete permissions on list items.

In this example, we can set up SharePoint groups for "Company Managers" and "Company Viewers," just like our Dataverse example.

To create a group, we click the cog icon from our SharePoint list. This reveals a settings panel with a "Site Permissions" menu item. We click this and click the "Advanced permissions settings" link. This opens the page that's shown in Figure 27-10. From here, we can click the "Create Group" button in the ribbon bar to create our new groups.

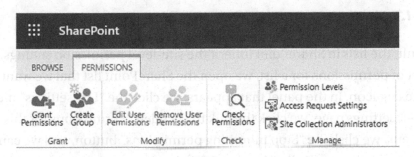

Figure 27-10. *Creating a new SharePoint group*

When we create a new group, we can associate a permission level with the group. In the case of our "Company Managers" group, we can set the permission level to Edit, as shown in Figure 27-11. This permission level provides members with the ability to add, update, and delete list items. We can set the permission level of our "Company Viewers" group to Read, to provide read-only access to list items.

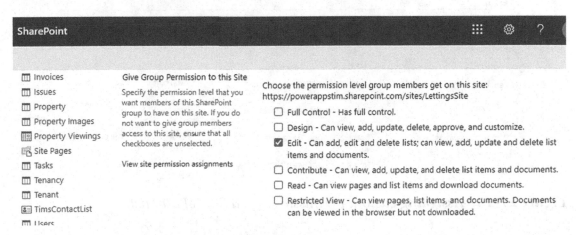

Figure 27-11. *Specifying group permissions*

After we create the "Company Managers" and "Company Viewers" groups, we can open them and add members, as shown in Figure 27-12.

Figure 27-12. *Adding users to the "Company Managers" group*

By default, the lists in SharePoint inherit the site-level permission settings. To apply a custom set of permissions for a list, we open the SharePoint list that we want to protect and click the cog icon. In the panel that appears, we click the "List settings" menu item. From this List settings page, we click the link that's titled "Permissions for this list." When this page opens, we click the "Stop inheriting permissions" button, and we can then manually assign groups to the list (Figure 27-13).

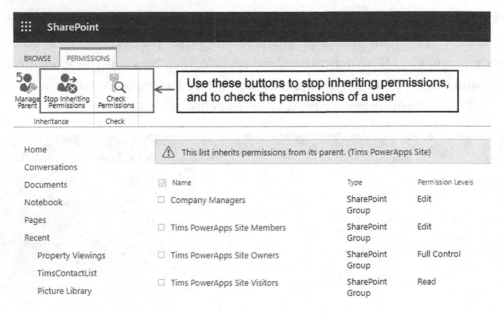

Figure 27-13. *Assigning custom permissions for a SharePoint list*

A very useful feature on this screen is the Check Permissions button. Because a user can belong to multiple groups, it can be difficult to determine the exact permissions of a user. The Check Permissions button allows us to easily see the effective permissions of a user.

The built-in permission levels are adequate for most scenarios. For more granular control, we can create custom permission levels. For example, the built-in Edit permission level enables members to add, update, and delete list items. If we want to allow members to add and update but not delete list items, we would need to create a custom permission level. As we'll see shortly, a custom permission level can also prevent users from creating custom SharePoint views.

The place to create a custom permission level is through the "Advanced permissions settings" page that we used to create our security groups.

Restricting Access to SharePoint Lists

In cases where we build apps with validation routines and formulas to implement business rules, a natural requirement is to prevent users from accessing the underlying SharePoint list directly. Unfortunately, there is no robust way to prevent users from directly accessing a list, but there are measures that we can apply to make it more difficult.

A first line of defense is to define our SharePoint lists in a separate SharePoint site. We keep the address of this site secret, and this can provide a simple way to protect our lists from curious users.

Next, we can use SharePoint settings to disable the list controls. Figure 27-14 illustrates a SharePoint list and describes where in the SharePoint settings we can disable the functionality.

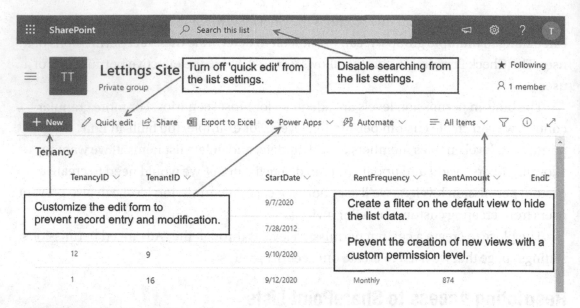

Figure 27-14. *Disabling a SharePoint item*

We can hide all records that appear in the list by editing the default view. When we click "All Items" ➤ Edit current view, we can define a filter condition. If we define a filter condition that never returns any rows (e.g., an ID value less than 0), the list will always appear empty.

To prevent users from interacting with the "New" and "Edit" menu items, we can define a custom form by clicking the "Power Apps" ➤ Customize forms menu item. We can create a custom form that is completely empty. This means that if a user were to click the new button, the data entry panel would contain nothing.

The "Quick edit" button provides in-line editing of the list. To disable this feature, we click the cog icon and select the "List settings" ➤ "Advanced Settings" menu item. From this page, we disable the "Quick property editing" option.

In this "Advanced Settings" page, we can also disable the search option. This prevents users from finding specific records through the search box.

Finally, we can hide a list from the Site Contents area of a SharePoint site. This setting can make it more difficult for a user to discover the address of a list. We can accomplish this using a PowerShell command, and we'll find out how to do this later in this chapter.

> **Caution**   Although these settings can go a long way toward preventing users from directly accessing SharePoint data, it can't prevent determined users. There is a saying "Security through obscurity is not security at all." If the SharePoint address is known, a user could connect to the data through a new Power App, Microsoft Access, or some other client.

Restricting Access to Records

Another common requirement is to restrict users to viewing and editing only the records that they own. We can easily apply this rule through the Advanced Settings of a SharePoint list.

As Figure 27-15 shows, we can use the "Item-level permissions" area to secure a SharePoint list to restrict users to only being able to read and to edit the records that they originally created.

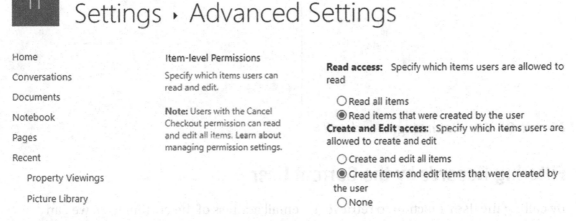

Figure 27-15. *Controlling access to records*

Canvas App Formulas

From a canvas app, we can use formulas to retrieve the details of the current user or to verify data source permissions. In this section, we'll see some examples of how to use these functions.

899

Retrieving the Current User

The User function retrieves the full name, email address, and profile image for the current user.

We can retrieve additional details about the logged-on user or other users by using the Office 365 connector. This connector enables us to retrieve and to update Office 365 profiles. We can access details that include the manager of the user and contact details such as names and telephone numbers.

Once we add a data source with the Office 365 Users connector, we can access a range of methods. The MyProfileV2 method returns a record with the profile details of the current user, as shown in Figure 27-16.

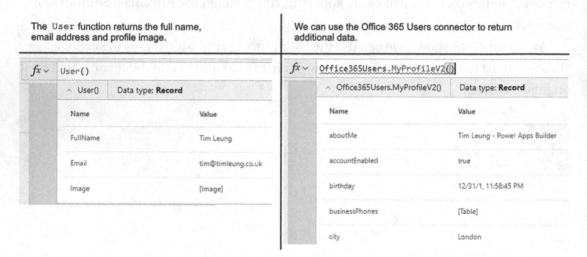

Figure 27-16. *Returning user details*

Filtering Records by the Current User

By calling the User function to retrieve the email address of the current user, we can modify gallery controls in our apps to show only the data that relates to the logged-in user. We can use this technique to show only records that were created or modified by a specific user.

Let's suppose we want to filter the records in the gallery control to only show the records that were modified by the current user. As an example, we'll take a gallery control that uses our SharePoint tenancy list as the data source.

In the OnStart property of our app, we store the email address of the current user in a variable using this formula:

```
Set(varCurrentEmail, User().Email)
```

We can then set the Items property of our gallery control to filter the source SharePoint list using the following formula:

```
Filter(Tenancies, 'Modified By'.Email=varCurrentEmail)
```

A key learning point of this exercise is that when we filter a SharePoint list by the email address of the "created by" or "modified by" user, we should filter the list against a copy of the email address from a variable. If we filter directly against User().Email, this results in a non-delegable query as shown in Figure 27-17.

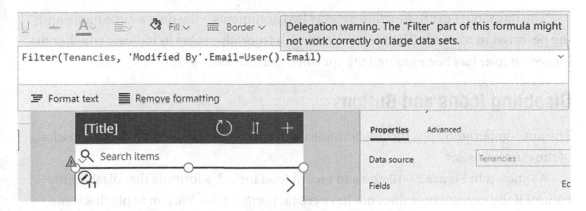

Figure 27-17. Filtering against User.Email results in a non-delegable query

Verifying Permissions Within an App

In cases where we apply SharePoint role-level security or where we use the Dataverse security model to control access to records, we can use formulas to determine whether the current user can read, edit, create, or delete records from a data source. Table 27-1 summarizes the formulas we can use.

Table 27-1. *DataSourceInfo methods*

Example Call	Description
DataSourceInfo(Tenancy, DataSourceInfo.ReadPermission)	Returns whether the logged-in user can read tenancy records.
DataSourceInfo(Tenancy, DataSourceInfo.EditPermission)	Returns whether the logged-in user can edit tenancy records.
DataSourceInfo(Tenancy, DataSourceInfo.CreatePermission)	Returns whether the logged-in user can create tenancy records.
DataSourceInfo(Tenancy, DataSourceInfo.DeletePermission)	Returns whether the logged-in user can delete tenancy records.

The DataSourceInfo function expects two arguments – the data source name and the permission to verify. The function returns a true/false value to indicate whether the logged-in user has been granted the specified permission.

Disabling Icons and Buttons

The auto-generated apps include formulas to restrict actions based on the permissions of the current user.

As shown in Figure 27-18, the add record icon includes formula that disables the control if the current user does not have create permissions. We can apply this same method to the custom buttons or features that we add to an app.

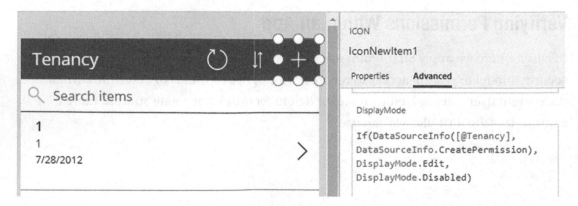

Figure 27-18. *The new record icon refers to the create permission*

To clarify the behavior of the DisplayMode property of a control, this can take one of three values: Disabled, Edit, or View. What exactly is the difference between these three settings – specifically, the difference between Disabled and View?

The View setting disables a control and will not run the formula that is attached to the OnSelect property. However, the control will not look disabled to the user – it will appear like a working control. In contrast, the Disabled setting configures a control to look disabled, and it will also not run any formula attached to the OnSelect property. The Edit setting configures a control to be fully functional.

Controlling Record Amendments

We can combine the methods that we've covered so far to more tightly control the actions that the current user can carry out.

For example, we can apply a formula to enforce the rule that only the user that creates a record can delete the record. We would amend the Display mode property of the delete icon as follows:

```
If(!IsBlank(BrowseGallery1.Selected) &&
    DataSourceInfo([@Tenancy], DataSourceInfo.DeletePermission) &&
    BrowseGallery1.Selected.'Created By'.Email=varCurrentEmail,
  DisplayMode.Edit,
  DisplayMode.Disabled
)
```

This formula disables the icon if the create user of the record does not match the current user that we stored in the variable varCurrentEmail (Figure 27-19).

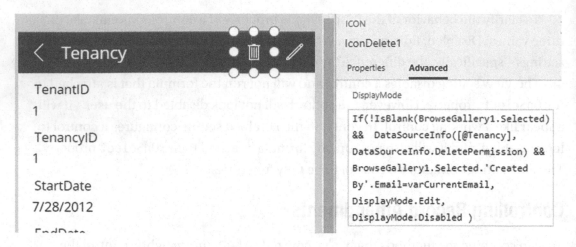

Figure 27-19. *Disabling the delete button*

We could extend this methodology to secure data in a more granular way by creating a list or table to store the users that are permitted to view, update, or delete individual records.

The caveat of using this formula to control permissions is that there is possibility that users can circumvent the rules in our app by accessing the data source outside of Power Apps. Where possible, it is always preferable to secure our data at the SharePoint, Dataverse, or data source level.

Signing Out Users

Finally, a notable function is the Exit function. This function accepts an optional argument. If we set this to true (as shown in the following), the function quits the running app and signs out the user:

Exit(true)

This technique is particularly useful in cases where multiple users share the same device and we want to provide a method to make sure that users completely sign out.

If we omit the optional sign-out argument or pass a value of false, the function quits the running app and returns the user to the list of apps. The user will remain signed in.

Creating Data Loss Prevention Policies

In this section, we'll explore one of the bigger security features in the Power Platform – data loss prevention polices (usually abbreviated as DLP policies). A DLP policy prohibits users from copying sensitive company data to unintended destinations. As an example, a company can prevent users from copying on-premise SQL Server data to a spreadsheet that's hosted in OneDrive. DLP policies can also completely block access to connectors.

DLP policies protect data by grouping data sources into two groups: business data and non-business data. Policies prevent app builders from mixing data sources from different groups in the same app. Typically, we place the data sources that we want to protect into the business group, and we place other permissible data sources into the non-business group.

To demonstrate, here's how to build a DLP policy to isolate SQL Server and SharePoint data sources. To create a DLP policy, we select the Data Policies menu item from the admin center and click the New policy button. This opens a screen that contains a series of steps. The first step is to provide a name for our policy. The next step enables us to assign connectors to our policy.

This page allows us to allocate each connector to one of three groups – business, non-business, and blocked. By default, all connectors appear beneath the "non-business" group. We can select a connector and use the items in the context menu to move the connector to the business group or to block the connector, as shown in Figure 27-20. For this example, we'll move the SQL Server connector to the business group.

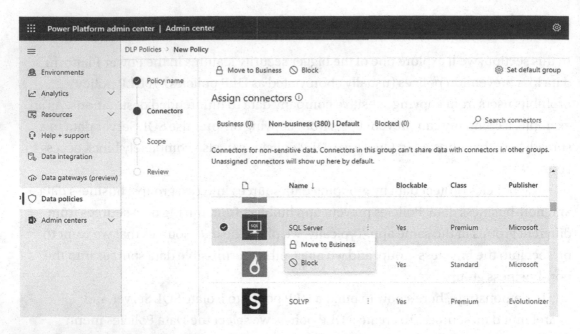

Figure 27-20. *Creating a data loss prevention policy*

The next step enables us to define the scope of our policy. We can apply the policy to all environments or specified environments, as shown in Figure 27-21. Once we define the scope, we can complete the creation of the policy from the review screen.

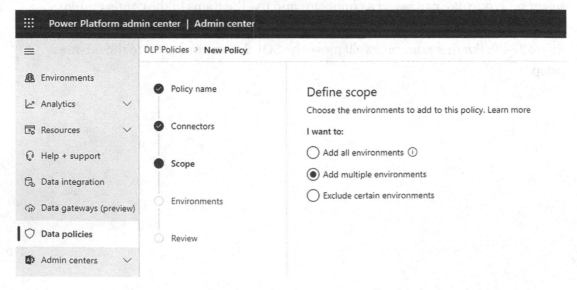

Figure 27-21. *Adding connectors to the business data only group*

Testing a DLP Policy

Now that we've created a DLP policy, let's see what happens when we attempt to build an app that includes both SQL Server and OneDrive data sources.

To test our policy, we'll create an auto-generated app based on a SQL Server data source. When we try to add an Excel spreadsheet from OneDrive as a data source, the designer shows a warning that prevents the addition of the data source, as shown in Figure 27-22. This confirms that our DLP policy works.

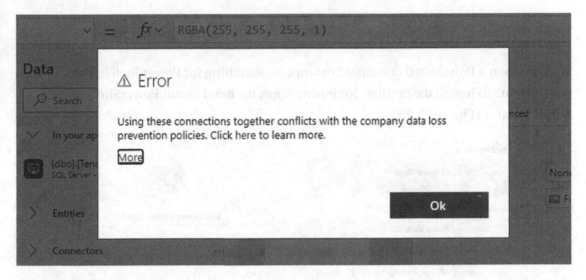

Figure 27-22. *Data loss prevention policy warning*

An interesting question is, does Power Apps apply policies retrospectively? For instance, if we have an existing app that contains both SQL Server and OneDrive data sources, would any new policy that we create apply to the existing app?

At the time of the first edition of this book, DLP policies did not apply retrospectively. Following a change in 2020, any DLP policy that we create will now apply to all apps, which is more in keeping with the expected behavior.

Using PowerShell

PowerShell is a command line scripting environment. It supports operating systems from Windows 7 onward, and it is included as part of Windows 10. By writing script, we can more easily carry out repetitive tasks and actions.

There are groups of PowerShell cmdlets that cater for app builders and administrators. A cmdlet (pronounced "command-let") is a lightweight script that performs a single function. We can use PowerShell to carry out almost all actions that we can perform through the Maker Portal. This includes the ability to list environments, to return a list of apps and owners, and more.

PowerShell is useful because there are some tasks that we can only carry out with PowerShell. In this section, we'll find out how to install the required components, and we'll focus on some of the actions that are exclusive to PowerShell.

Installing Components

We can open a PowerShell command prompt by searching for PowerShell in the Start menu. To install the cmdlets for Power Apps, we need to run PowerShell as an administrator (Figure 27-23).

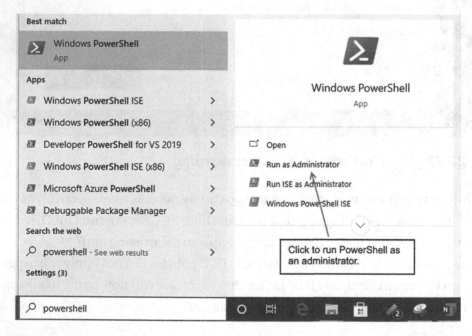

Figure 27-23. *Opening PowerShell as an administrator*

When the PowerShell command prompt opens, we install the Power App–related modules by running the following commands:

```
Install-Module -Name Microsoft.PowerApps.Administration.PowerShell
Install-Module -Name Microsoft.PowerApps.PowerShell -AllowClobber
```

To use the Power Apps–related cmdlets, the first step is to log in using our AAD username and password. We can issue the following command to open a login prompt in a separate window: `Add-PowerAppsAccount`

To log in without opening a separate login prompt, we can use the following command:

```
$pass = ConvertTo-SecureString "password" -AsPlainText -Force
Add-PowerAppsAccount -Username user@yourDomain.com -Password $pass
```

By scripting our credentials, we can execute scripts through unattended, scheduled jobs. If we save scripts with passwords, we should take care to protect those files in order to prevent any exposure of security credentials.

Hiding the Data Source Consent Screens

As an example of a task that we can carry out through PowerShell only, we can configure an app to not show the data source consent screen when a user runs an app for the first time. This is a popular request from administrators and users. Figure 27-24 illustrates the consent screen that we want to hide.

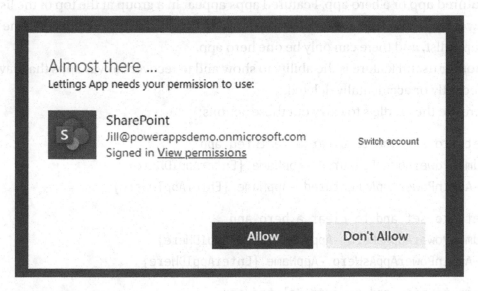

Figure 27-24. *The consent screen to remove*

To hide this screen for a specific app, we issue the following command:

```
Set-AdminPowerAppApisToBypassConsent
    -AppName ad3c5ff5-cf2e-4db7-a27a-7eb77f9448a7
```

The `Set-AdminPowerAppApisToBypassConsent` cmdlet requires us to pass the app ID (i.e., the GUID identifier for the app) which we can find through the app details in the Maker Portal.

To undo this action and to revert the behavior of the app so that it shows the consent screen, we run the corresponding "Clear" command:

```
Clear-AdminPowerAppApisToBypassConsent
    -AppName ad3c5ff5-cf2e-4db7-a27a-7eb77f9448a7
```

Although this technique can be very helpful, it's useful to note that custom connectors will not honor the command to bypass consent.

Other Useful Commands

Other unique actions we can carry out with PowerShell include the ability to set an app as a featured app or a hero app. Featured apps appear in a group at the top of the list in the Power Apps mobile player. A hero app is a single app that always appears at the top of the apps list, and there can only be one hero app.

Another useful feature is the ability to show and to recover canvas apps that have been recently or accidentally deleted.

Here are the cmdlets to carry out these actions:

```
#Cmdlets to set and to clear a featured app
Set-AdminPowerAppAsFeatured -AppName {EnterAppIDHere}
Clear-AdminPowerAppAsFeatured -AppName {EnterAppIDHere}

#Cmdlets to set and to clear a hero app
Set-AdminPowerAppAsHero -AppName {EnterAppIDHere}
Clear-AdminPowerAppAsHero -AppName {EnterAppIDHere}

#Cmdlets to view and recover deleted apps
Get-AdminDeletedPowerAppsList
Get-AdminRecoverDeletedPowerApp -AppName {EnterAppIDHere}
```

Hiding SharePoint Lists

Earlier in this chapter, we looked at ways to more tightly control access to SharePoint. We can use PowerShell to hide a SharePoint list from the Site Contents area of SharePoint, which helps to make it more difficult for a user to discover the address of a SharePoint list.

To carry out this task, the first step is to install the SharePoint Management Shell and the SharePoint Patterns and Practices (usually abbreviated to PnP) librares of cmdlets. Here are the commands to carry out the installation:

```
Install-Module -Name Microsoft.Online.SharePoint.PowerShell
Install-Module SharePointPnPPowerShellOnline -Force
```

During the installation, we'll see a message that warns that the source comes from an untrusted repository. We can enter "yes" to acknowledge this warning and to continue.

Once we install these components, we can log in to our SharePoint site using the following command:

```
Connect-PnPOnline -Url https://yourDomain.sharepoint.com/sites/YourSite/
```

Finally, we can hide or unhide a SharePoint list with the following commands:

```
Set-PnpList -Identity NameOfListToHide -Hidden $true
Set-PnpList -Identity NameOfListToHide -Hidden $false
```

Auditing and Analytics

In this section, we'll explore the logging and auditing features that are available. These can help us diagnose errors and identify performance problems and can highlight the actions that users have carried out.

Auditing App Activity

A primary way to track user activity is to use the Audit Log feature that we can access through the Microsoft 365 Security & Compliance Center.

This provides a centralized way to track activity across a range of Microsoft services, including Dynamics 365, Exchange, Power BI, Azure AD, as well as Power Apps.

To use this feature, the first step is to log onto the Microsoft 365 Security & Compliance Center using an account with tenant administration privileges. The address for this site is as follows:

```
https://protection.office.com/unifiedauditlog
```

Once we log in, we click the Search ➤ "Audit log search" menu item. When we visit this page for the first time, a banner message prompts us to turn on auditing. Once we enable auditing and allow time for some activity to take place, we can use the controls on this page to review the activity, as shown in Figure 27-25.

We can use the Activities drop-down to filter the results. The audit events include the launch, creation, modification, deletion, and restoration of an app. Other events include the publication of an app and changes to user permissions.

The audit log list shows the date and time of the event, the IP address, and the email address of the user. We can click an item to show additional details. For example, if we click a log entry that relates to the launch of an app, we can view the app ID, the environment ID, and other object details.

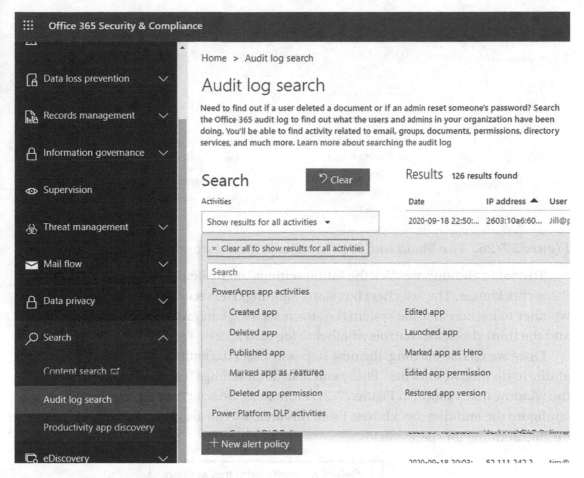

Figure 27-25. *Security auditing*

Auditing Dataverse Record Activity

A great feature of Dataverse is the ability to audit data changes. We can find out who updated a record and when. When a record changes, we can review the previous and new values.

To enable data auditing, the first step is to enable this feature from the Power Platform admin center. We select our environment and expand the "Audit and logs" section in the settings, as shown in Figure 27-26.

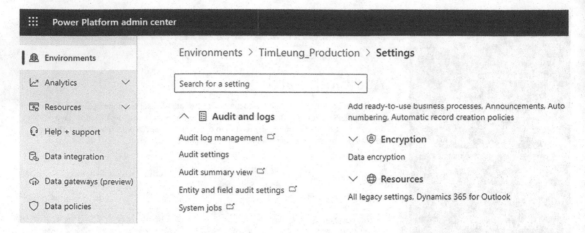

Figure 27-26. *The "Audit and logs" section in the environment settings*

To enable auditing, we click the "Audit settings" menu item. This opens a page with three checkboxes. The first checkbox starts auditing. The second checkbox controls whether to log access to the system (i.e., to create a log entry whenever a user logs on), and the third checkbox controls whether to log read access.

Once we enable auditing, the next step is to select the entities that we want to audit. To do this, we click the "Entity and field audit settings" menu item. This opens the window that's shown in Figure 27-27. From here, we select our desired entities and configure the auditing checkboxes. From this area, we can also choose to enable or disable auditing for specific fields.

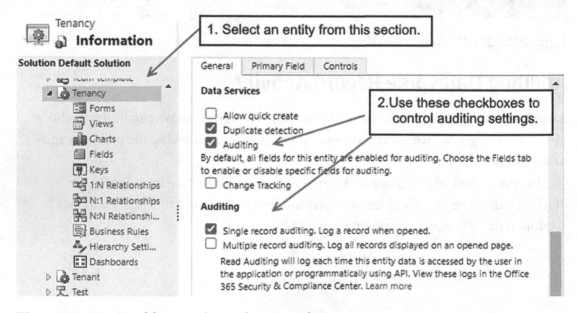

Figure 27-27. *Enabling auditing for an entity*

After we enable auditing for an entity, we can view the log entries by clicking the "Audit summary view" menu item from the environment settings page in the Power Platform admin center. This opens the page that's shown in Figure 27-28. As this illustration shows, we can click an event to open a window with additional details. This example highlights the update of a record. Here, we can see the field that was modified, along with the old and new values.

Figure 27-28. *Reviewing record changes*

Viewing Analytic Data

Through the Power Platform admin center, we can access analytic data. This powerful feature can provide some very interesting insights into the way that users use our apps.

We can find out who exactly uses our apps and from where. We can see the devices that users are using, review the errors that users encounter, and also assess the overall performance of the Power Platform.

To access this feature, we select the Analytics ➤ Power Apps menu item from the Power Platform admin center. This opens the page that's shown in Figure 27-29. This page includes the following five tabs: Usage, Location, Toast Errors, Service Performance, and Connectors.

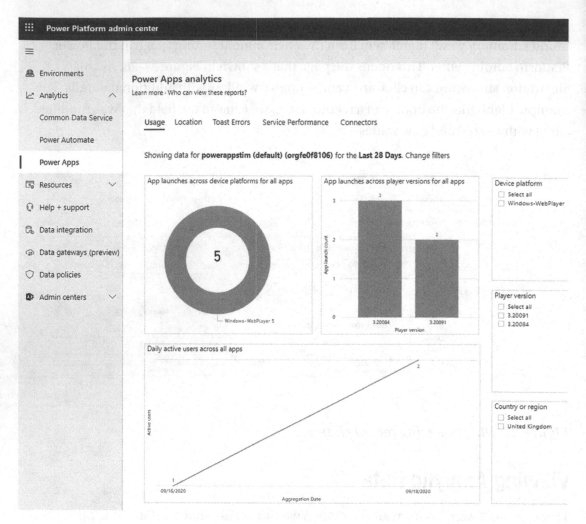

Figure 27-29. *Viewing analytics*

Here's a summary of what each tab contains:

- Usage – This tab displays charts that summarize the number of app launches. We can review the daily activity, the device platforms, and the player versions that are used.

- Location – This tab shows a Bing map that pinpoints the geographic locations of app launches. It includes a table that provides a count of app launches by country/region and by app name.

- Toast Errors – Toast errors are errors that are displayed to users in an app. This tab summarizes the number of toast errors by app name and displays a chart that summarizes error counts by date.

- Service Performance – This tab displays connectors (e.g., SharePoint) and summarizes the response times and the HTTP success rates. It includes a chart that shows the percentage of requests that result in HTTP 500 error by date.

- Connectors – This tab displays a table that shows the number of connectors per app and a summary of the number of times that an app has been shared, the number of app sessions, and the last access time.

Summary

This chapter covered a range of security-related topics including authentication, access control, user-related formulas, data loss prevention policies, PowerShell, and auditing.

Starting with authentication, we can configure multifactor authentication and conditional access policies. The place where we configure these settings is through the Azure Active Directory section of the Microsoft Azure Portal. With multifactor authentication enabled, users must verify any login attempt through a mobile device for the login to succeed. With conditional access policies, we can apply rules to more tightly control the authentication process. For example, we can mandate multifactor authentication for administrators only.

Dataverse enables us to implement role-based security using a powerful model that can secure tables on a row and field basis.

We create security roles to define sets of privileges and access levels for tables. Common privileges we can set include read, create, write, and delete privileges. Access levels define the scope of a privilege. We can define a privilege to apply to the current user only, users in the same or related business units, or the organization as a whole. Once we create a security group, we can assign it to individual users or teams.

With SharePoint, we can apply permissions by creating groups. We can assign a permission level to a group, and we can then assign users to the group. A common requirement is to prevent users from directly accessing a SharePoint list. A good way to hide lists is to create a separate SharePoint site to host lists that we use in our apps and to keep the address of this site secret. Additionally, we can run PowerShell script to hide a list from the Site Contents area of SharePoint. Through the SharePoint settings, we can also configure a range of settings to prevent users from interacting with the SharePoint list.

From a canvas app, we can call the User function to determine the email address and details of the current user. We can access additional profile details through the "Office 365 Users" connector. We can use these functions to filter lists of data by the current user. To implement record security for data sources without a native role-based security model, we can create a security list or table to store the users that are permitted to view, update, or delete individual records. We can then use formulas to disable controls based on the current user and the content from our security table.

A data loss prevention (DLP) policy prevents users from copying data between data sources. As an example, we can use a DLP policy to prevent users from copying SQL Server data into spreadsheets on OneDrive. We can also use DLP policies to block the use of connectors. A DLP policy groups data sources into business and non-business groups and prevents app builders from creating apps that mix data sources from both groups.

We can use the command line scripting language PowerShell to carry out a range of Power Apps–related tasks. This can be particularly useful for repetitive tasks that we want to apply across multiple environments or tenants. We looked at how to use PowerShell to hide the data source consent screen.

Finally, there are a range of auditing and analytic features that can help us track user activity and analyze the ways that users are using our apps. The Microsoft 365 Security & Compliance Center provides a place where we can track user activity across a range of Microsoft services, including Dynamics 365 and Exchange.

Through the Power Platform admin center, we can enable auditing for Dataverse tables. This enables us to track data changes. We can find out which user edited a record, and we can see the previous and new values for each update. From the Power Platform admin center, we can also access analytic data. We can use this to review the geographic locations of app launches, the devices and platforms that users are using, and summaries of performance and errors.

Sadly, we now reach the end of this chapter and the end of this book. I hope you have found the content useful, and I wish you every success with the apps and solutions that you build with Power Apps and the Power Platform.

APPENDIX A

Sample App Data Structure

This appendix summarizes the data model for the examples in this book. The data diagrams show the tables and relationships that support an app that can manage the operations of a property or real estate company.

In this book, we covered all the popular data sources including Excel, SharePoint, SQL Server, and Dataverse. Although the diagrams in this appendix are aimed at SQL Server, the SharePoint and Dataverse implementations of this model will be very close variations. For example, we can directly define relationships in a Dataverse table rather than define primary and foreign key columns as we would in SQL Server.

The tables in this data model include the following:

- **User tables (Figure A-1)** – the user table stores details that include the user name and address. A separate user image table stores multiple images per user.

- **Property tables (Figure A-2)** – the property table stores property details such as the address, number of rooms and floor area. The property type table describes the property type (eg, house, apartment). Each record in the property table references the property type table. We can store multiple documents and images for each property through related tables.

- **Tenancy tables (Figure A-3)** – the tenant table stores details that include the name and address. The tenancy table stores the contractual dates, and rental amounts for each tenancy. This table references the property and tenant tables.

919

© Tim Leung 2021
T. Leung, *Beginning Power Apps*, https://doi.org/10.1007/978-1-4842-6683-0

- **Issue tables (Figure A-4)** – the issue table stores problem details that are associated with a property. It is possible to store multiple documents and replies/responses that are associated with each issue record through related tables.

- **Inventory tables (Figure A-5)** – the inventory table stores inventory items that are associated with each property.

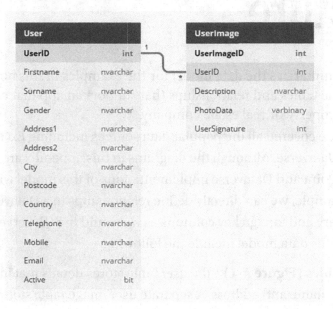

Figure A-1. *User tables*

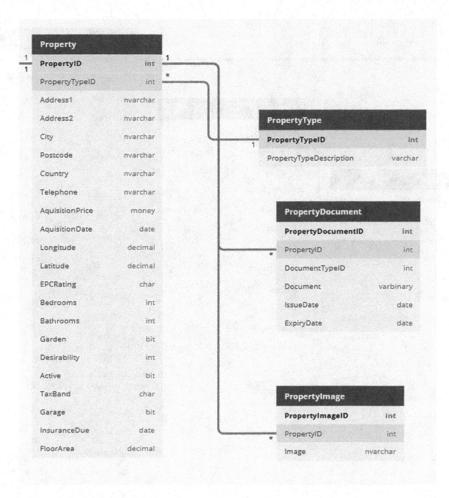

Figure A-2. *Property tables*

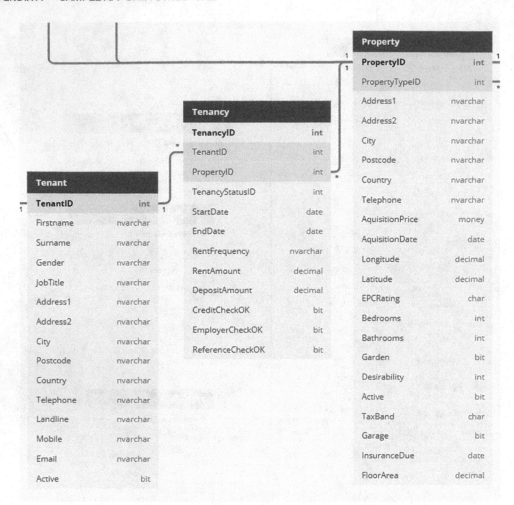

Figure A-3. *Tenancy tables*

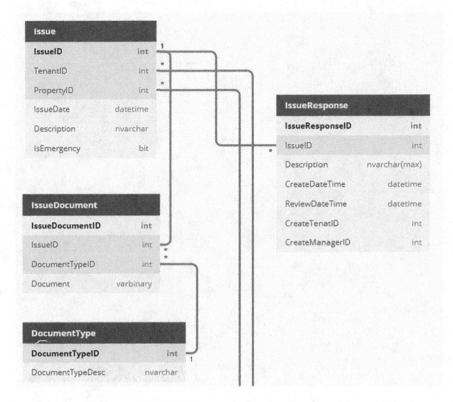

Figure A-4. *Issue tables*

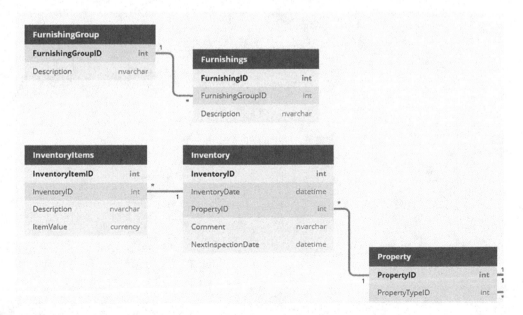

Figure A-5. *Inventory tables*

Index

A

© Tim Leung 2021
T. Leung, *Beginning Power Apps*, https://doi.org/10.1007/978-1-4842-6683-0